URBAN GROWTH AND DEVELOPMENT IN ASIA

Urban Growth and Development in Asia

Volume II: Living in the Cities

Edited by
GRAHAM P. CHAPMAN
Department of Geography, Lancaster University, United Kingdom
ASHOK K. DUTT
Department of Geography, University of Akron, Ohio, USA
ROBERT W. BRADNOCK
Department of Geography, School of Oriental and African Studies, London, United Kingdom

Ashgate

Aldershot • Brookfield USA • Singapore • Sydney

Published by
Ashgate Publishing Ltd
Gower House
Croft Road
Aldershot
Hants GU11 3HR
England

Ashgate Publishing Company
Old Post Road
Brookfield
Vermont 05036
USA

Ashgate website: http://www.ashgate.com

British Library Cataloguing in Publication Data
Urban growth and development in Asia
    Vol. II: Living in the cities. - (SOAS studies in development
    geography)
    1.Cities and towns - Growth - Social aspects - Asia
    I.Chapman, Graham P. , 1944- II.Dutt, Ashok K. , 1955-
    III.Bradnock, Robert W.
    307.1'4'16'095

Library of Congress Catalog Card Number: 99-73699

ISBN 0 7546 1039 X

Printed and bound by Athenaeum Press, Ltd.,
Gateshead, Tyne & Wear.

Contents

PART II
GENDER, ACCESS AND ENVIRONMENT

PART V
OBSERVING THE CITY

List of Figures

List of Tables

List of Maps

List of Contributors

Takafumi Arima	Department of Architectural Engineering, Oita University, Japan
J.V. Bentinck	Faculty of Spatial Sciences, University of Groningen, The Netherlands
Robert Bradnock	Department of Geography, School of Oriental and African Studies, UK
Natalie Cavasin	Department of Economics, Keio University, Tokyo, Japan
Graham Chapman	Department of Geography, Lancaster University, UK
Vincent F. Costello	Faculty of the Built Environment, University of the West of England, UK
Satish K. Davgun	Department of Geography, Bemidji State University, Bemidji, USA
Vandana Desai	Department of Geography, Royal Holloway University of London, UK
Ashok K. Dutt	Department of Geography, University of Akron, Ohio, USA
C. Cindy Fan	Department of Geography, University of California, Los Angeles, USA
Satoshi Hagishima	Department of Architectural Engineering, Kyushu University, Fukuoka, Japan
Tanja Haque	Department of Geography, University College London, UK
Therese Gladys Hingco	Division of Geography, Staffordshire University, UK
Naishen Hsiao	Department of Architectural Engineering, Oita University, Japan
Kao-Chiao Hsieh	Department of Sociology, National Chengchi University, Taiwan
Youqin Huang	Department of Geography, University of California, Los Angeles, USA
K. Jayashree	Department of Geography, Queen Mary's College, Chennai, India
Hitomi M. Kato	Department of Architecture, Kyushu University, Fukuoka, Japan
Kyunghee Kim	Department of Architectural Engineering, Oita University, Japan
Sungkon Kim	Department of Architectural Engineering, Dong-A University, Korea
Kuntala Lahiri-Dutt	Department of Geography, The University of Burdwan, India

Jae-Won Lee	*Kyonggi Development Institute, Kyonggi-Do, Korea*
Man-Hyung Lee	*Department of Urban Engineering, Chungbuk National University, Korea*
Chun-Ju Li	*Institute of Building and Planning, National Taiwan University, Taiwan*
Laurence J.C. Ma	*Department of Geography, University of Akron, Ohio, USA*
Hamish Main	*Division of Geography, Staffordshire University, UK*
Shii Okuno	*Department of Economics, Tokuyama University, Tokuyama City, Yamaguchi, Japan*
Anindita Parai	*Department of Geography, University of Akron, Ohio, USA*
Clifton W. Pannell	*College of Arts and Sciences, University of Georgia, Athens, USA*
Pushpa Pathak	*National Insitute of Urban Affairs, New Delhi, India*
George Pomeroy	*Department of Geography and Earth Science, Shippensburg University, Pennsylvania, USA*
Wilke Ruiter	*Department of Infrastructure Planning, Faculty of Civil Engineering, Delft University of Technology, The Netherlands*
F.M. Sanders	*Faculty of Civil Engineering, Delft University of Technology, The Netherlands*
Seiji Sato	*Department of Architectural Engineering, Oita University, Japan*
Helmut Schneider	*Institute of Geography, Heinrich-Heine-University, Düsseldorf, Germany*
R.K. Sharma	*Centre for the Study of Regional Development, School of Social Sciences, Jawaharlal Nehru University, New Delhi, India*
B.R.K. Sinha	*Department of Geography, Visva-Bharati University, Santiniketan, India*
J. Skornsek	*Faculty of Spatial Sciences, University of Groningen, The Netherlands*
Jan Turkstra	*ITC, Enschede, The Netherlands*
R.J. Verhaeghe	*Faculty of Civil Engineering, Delft University of Technology, The Netherlands*
Jan Veenstra	*ITC, Enschede, The Netherlands*
A.C. de Vries	*Department of Physical Geography, University of Gröningen, The Netherlands*
Vandana Wadhwa	*Department of Geography, University of Akron, Ohio, USA*
Hung-Kai Wang	*Institute of Building and Planning, National Taiwan University, Taiwan*
Anita M. Weiss	*International Studies, University of Oregon, USA*
Jack F. Williams	*Asian Studies Center, Michigan State University, USA*
B. Zondag	*Faculty of Civil Engineering, Delft University of Technology, The Netherlands*

Editors' Preface

This is the second of two volumes deriving from the 5th Asian Urbanisation Conference, held at the School of Oriental and African Studies in London in August 1997. We believe that together the two volumes give a wide-ranging review not just of the massive changes that Asia is undergoing as it urbanises, but also of the many contrasting insights into this phenomenon provided by such a wide range of disciplinary approaches and analytical styles. But this is of course an ongoing dialogue – and we look forward to the 6th conference to be held in Chennai (Madras) in January 2000, to help fill in the gaps. Further conferences are planned - the 7th Conference in Athens, Georgia, USA in 2002, and the 8th Conference in Japan in 2004.

Why have a conference, let alone a series of conferences, on Asian Urbanisation? The developed OECD countries and most of the Former Soviet Union are highly urbanised, and Latin America is more 50% urbanised. The less urbanised areas of the world include sub-Saharan Africa – with a small part of the total world population – and most of Asia – with urbanisation (apart from in Japan and the Tiger Economies), averaging less than 25%. This Asia includes more than half the world's population. In the last decade or so urbanisation has begun to take off, and the shift of population to the cities represents one of the greatest population movements the planet has ever seen. Projections are by definition untestable at the time they are made, so there is no point in quibbling about the detail too much. But if we accept, as most current projections do, that by 2030 more than 50% of Asia's population will be urban, then over the next three decades more than 500 million people in Asia will have moved - looking for jobs, housing, food and water. They will be both part of a problem and most of the solution – building around them the cities they will live in. Whether this is for better or worse will partly depend on how local and national government and the city dwellers interact with each other, and partly on much broader issues such as environmental stress and the evolution of the global economy and the relationship of those with urbanisation. Simple considerations like these are enough to explain why we should hold such conference(s).

The fifty seven chapters of the two volumes answer questions about how culture affects urban planning, how China attempted industrialisation without urbanisation, about how Bangalore has emerged as the silicon champion of India, about how Korea's urban and rural administrative system has been reformed, about how different programmes attack poverty in Indian slums, about the contrasts between women's lives in the old city of Lahore

1

and the new suburbs, about the experience of migration in the Philippines and Thailand, about the use of Geographical Information Systems in analysing growth or providing services, and so on and so forth. It is of course impossible to find a single way to divide this material between two volumes. In what we believe to be the best compromise, we have sub-titled Volume I 'Making the Cities' and this Volume II ' Living in the cities.' Thus in Volume I we have grouped chapters under the headings of:- 'The Urban Base' – meaning the economic activities and economic foundations which underpin urbanisation; 'The Urban Land Market' – which shows how land is allocated to new functions in the urban area; 'Urban Land Use and Architecture' – which concentrates on the construction of the physical forms; and 'Transport and Infrastructure' – which allow the cities to function. Volume I is therefore angled towards an examination of urban structures.

This volume is more orientated towards the activities that take place in those structures – somewhat along the lines of the distinction between 'backcloth' and 'traffic' in some social analyses. But no division can be perfect: the living streams of migrating people and the flows of goods are influenced by the structures, but the structures also adapt over time to the flows – sometimes through ephemeral forms such as some of the shanty towns, sometimes through more permanent developments like new deep-water ports or permanent slums or shiny new business centres. This overlap is perhaps most obvious in the Part I of this Volume, where we consider patterns of activity which define Urban Systems. Part II Gender, Access and Environment is more obviously about the different experiences of men and women, rich and poor, in the new urban areas. Part III is on Migration, and Part IV on Government and Institutions, taking a sympathetic view of the problems of governing these massive concentrations of population and employment. Part V Observing the City has a more technical feel about it - we can talk and we can speculate, but if we need good data, how can we know what is happening in the cities?

The two volumes together comprise something of an impressionist painting – by the end of reading them any reader must have some sense of the whole panorama and drama. Each chapter is like one of the flecks of paint in an impressionist painter's picture, contributing to the whole. However, as with the painting, so much more of 'reality' is left out than is included, that it is necessary to stress that the 'whole picture' created is still a limited and partial picture of all that could be written or said. Some Asian countries are not represented, some topics not dealt with (for example air pollution only gets passing reference.) We hope we stimulate scholars and students to research into these gaps.

There can inevitably be no simple overall conclusion to these 57 chapters, but we, the Editors, do end with a few summary thoughts.

Acknowledgements

The conference would not have happened and the volumes would not have been produced but for the support of many institutions and people. We thank the School of Oriental and African Studies (SOAS) for hosting the event, Farah Ahmed and Alison Henley of SOAS for being girl Fridays and running excellent field trips, the University of Akron for logistic and material support, Dr. Charles Clift, the Department for International Development (UK) and the Developing Areas Research Group of the Institute of British Geographers, for subsidising the air fares of some delegates, the India Development Group (UK) for similar support, and the University of Lancaster - really in the guise of Siobhan Waring - for the conference secretarial and subsequent editorial support. We thank Chris Beacock of Lancaster Geography Department for keeping his equanimity as the flood of illustrations and maps inundated his office – with the excellent results evident in these volumes – and for his skills at DTP. We also thank George Pomeroy for extensive help with the editing.

Graham Chapman, Department of Geography, Lancaster University, UK
Ashok Dutt, Department of Geography, University of Akron, Ohio, USA
Bob Bradnock, Department of Geography, School of Oriental and African Studies, UK

PART I
URBAN SYSTEMS

Editors' notes to Part I
These chapters reflect on a range of problems and issues in dynamic
urbanising societies. As a rural country becomes urban, and as urban
centres increasingly dominate the spatial organisation of society, so
local government jurisdiction has to change perhaps to keep the two
sectors apart, perhaps to reflect more accurately new distributions of
power. These issues are looked a critically by Jae-Won Lee and Mau-
Hyung Lee in the case of South Korea. Jack Williams looks at a whole
range of issues thrown up by Taiwan's transition – now in one sense
'over' – because it is now urban and industrial and almost fully 'de-
veloped'. And yet the 'development' has been so compressed in time,
that there are plenty of 'rough edges' and the country is still to work
out how to make its transport infrastructure adequate to meet the de-
mands placed on it. Kao-Chiao Hseieh also looks at Taiwan – to see
how the patterns of commuting have or have not developed between
central cities and satellites - patterns which both reflect available trans-
port and which will demand transport changes. Sanders, Verhaeghe
and Zondag develop a quantitative model to show how the population
structure of Jabotabek – Indonesia's vast metropolitan conurbation –
may develop. The interested reader may also like to look back to Vol-
ume I to Haryo Winarso's Chapter 15 on land agents in Jakarta. Natalie
Cavasin introduces the Japanese approach to using Science Cities and
Technopoles to stimulate innovation – perhaps the ultimate illustration
of cities as 'thought' centres. Finally Dutt reflects on the differences
between those areas of India where city systems are developing tenta-
cles of urban corridors in contrast to the remaining areas where cities
are still individual and alone in their rural hinterlands.

1 Urban-Rural Conflicts in the Provision of Public Services in Korea

Man-Hyung Lee and Jae-Won Lee

1.1 Introduction

For more than four decades after the Second World War, the majority of Korean politicians and administrators have supported the upgrading of rural counties to city status, regardless of the geographical characteristics of any region. With the advent of a new local autonomy system, however, the normal means of making provision for public services has changed. From early 1994, about a year ahead of the general election in which local autonomy was a major issue, the form of local jurisdictional arrangements became a 'hot potato' in Korea. Advocates of reform disliked what they saw as the historical pattern of fragmentation. They strongly supported the policy of urban-rural consolidation as the most feasible method to tackle conflict deriving from urban-rural segregation. The protagonists of consolidation policy insisted that the integration of two different entities could more easily handle or at least ameliorate regional sectionalism, manifested by NIMBY (Not In My Back Yard) syndromes in which necessary but undesirable functions are always pushed onto someone else's territory.

The consolidationists won, and as a result, the jurisdictional rearrangements were carried out on a large scale. With a series of opinion surveys and policy directives, altogether 45 Consolidated, or urban-rural Complex Cities were reorganised in no more than fifteen months. In fact, these major institutional rearrangements are regarded as a once-in-a-hundred years event in the history of Korean local administration.

Juxtaposing the two antithetical points of view between fragmentation and consolidation, this paper critically reinterprets explicit and implicit meanings in the organisational restructuring of the Korean local governmental system. Furthermore, it analyses major issues that have occurred after the 1994 administrative reshuffle and suggests policy recommendations stemming from the relative performances of the remaining fragmented regions and the new consolidated city complexes.

1.2   Local Jurisdictional Reforms in Korea: From Fragmentation to Consolidation

1.2.1 Lessons from the Past History

In 1948, the newly born Republic of Korea started with three basic tiers of government – provincial , regional and local: 9 Provinces, 134 Counties, and 1,448 Myeon. In addition there was 1 Special City, and there were 18 Cities, 9 Gu, and 75 Ub. During the initial period of urbanisation up to the late 1960s, the central government initiated the organisational adjustment only on a small scale. For example, after the advent of the Third Republic, Pusan was the only city which was upgraded into Direct Jurisdictional City in 1963. The Direct Jurisdictional Cities are independent of the government of the Province within which the city lies (see Figure 1.2). By contrast, the government of the smaller Ub falls under the County. In other cases, with the adjustment of provincial and city boundaries, the jurisdictions of Taegu and Kwangju had also been enlarged.

Starting from the 1970s, as the industrialisation and urbanisation of Korea accelerated, the structural adjustment of local units also speeded up. Seoul began to suffer from an over-concentration of development, and jurisdictional reform around Seoul metropolitan area became inevitable. In the middle of 1970s, as a basic means to alleviate these metropolitan problems, parts of Goyang County in Kyonggi were incorporated into Seoul and the large satellite Ubs like Anyang, Seongnam, and Bucheon located in the outskirts of Seoul were given City status.

These trends were furthermore strengthened in the 1980s lower down the settlement hierarchy. The carving out of new or promoted urban jurisdictions resulted in the increased fragmentation of local administration. In 1981 Taegu and Incheon upgraded their legal status to Direct Jurisdictional Cities, and 10 Cities including Kwangmyeong, Namwon, and Seogwipo were born. The same trend was repeated again in the late 1980s: Kwangju and Daejeon became Direct Jurisdictional Cities and 15 other Cities from Ubs were created.

In short, the usual means of revising local jurisdictions before the 1990s have focused on rearrangement of boundaries. Firstly, as major cities have the right to enforce their urban planning administration into partial areas of neighbouring counties, they repeatedly tried to annex these areas by the expansion of their administrative boundaries. Secondly, upgrading and separation based on legal standards was another common change. Whenever the first level city reaches over 1 million, the law permits that it may separate from the Provincial Government and acquire the status of an independent

Direct Jurisdictional City. In contrast, the upgrading of the Ub within county has been usually carried out in rural areas: an Ub is endowed with city status when its population reaches 50,000 or more.

It is well known that fragmentation was also heavily dependent on political interests, regardless of geographical characteristics and/or residential boundaries of the region. As a specific example, every candidate at any sort of election pledged the voters to upgrade their hometown Ub into a City. No consideration was given to the negative impacts resulting from ill thought-out fragmentation. In some cases, even if the Ub was not eligible for city status, mainly because the population was less than the legal limit, leaders of the Ub mobilised every possible means to annex neighbouring rural areas, enlarging their territory and population enough to fulfil city status. As a result, the former centrally-planned administrative arrangement segregated the cities and their hinterlands. They split the yellow (central city) from the white (rump county) of an egg: the popularist patterns of local institutional changes made doughnuts with a big hole in Korean society.

1.2.2 The 1994 Reshuffle: The Politics of Urban-Rural Consolidation

Advocates of reform blamed this fragmentation for aggravated social problems of inefficiency and inequity, especially in terms of provisions of local public services.[1] In their view under the fragmented administration system, the supply and management of major public service facilities would be undertaken by independent local governments without co-ordination.

In Korea, the pros and cons between fragmentation and consolidation were dichotomised in terms of prescriptions for problems originating from the rapid urbanisation. The dominant motto within the pro-consolidation group is summarised as 'the bigger the better.' According to their judgement, metropolitan reforms have to rely on centralisation because urban areas continue to be characterised by unnecessary duplication, and overlapping jurisdictions. The pro-consolidation group usually concludes that fragmentation leads to confusion in responsibility for service provision, reductions in political scrutiny and control, duplication of effort, inefficiencies leading to less than effective methods of providing services, higher per-unit costs, larger government outlays, and units of government concerned only about their own problems (Stein, 1990: 3).

---

1 *The main contents of consolidation group are summarized as follows : first, diseconomies of scale and geographical externalities in public service provisions; second, overlapping of financial investment for public utilities like main stadium, public library, and third, the existence of wide fiscal disparities and beneficial inequalities between city and her hinterland(county).*

At last, in 1994, the central government, which had been active in promoting fragmentation for more than four decades, decided to change tack and face the challenge of urban-rural consolidation. In fact, the initiatives for policy revolution were taken under ruling political party. While the Ministry of Home Affairs started to seriously examine the reform agenda in January 1994, the ruling party which presided over party-government coalition meetings established a new policy.[2] On February 15, the task force team to deal with the urban-rural consolidation was set up within the Ministry of Home Affairs.

Since then, most Koreans have supported the new stream for consolidation. For instance, even though several conferences or seminars were prepared by political parties, conclusions in every meeting were "induced" to assent for consolidation. According to the governmental documents, the Ministry of Home Affairs at first designed a small scale reform on 10 trial regions, fearing that consolidation might give rise to dissent by residents at the local level. In addition, the reforms were encumbered with the tricky adjustments of electoral districts.

However, after weighing the merits and demerits of consolidation, the central government and ruling party decided to include a much larger number of target regions at their own discretion: in fact they dared to carry out a total reshuffle of Korean local organisation, for their political gain. Consequently, the Ministry of Home Affairs published the governmental resolution that 50 Cities out of the existing 68 should prepare for consolidation between each City and its neighbouring County, which would create about 30 urban-rural Consolidated Cities, or Complex Cities.

Because the policy authorities were anxious about the dissent by local councils, they decided that the final decision for consolidation should take into account the result of a "residential opinion survey" (one vote per household). They insisted that the survey was no more than referential, not legally binding, even when the local council passed a resolution against the decision of the central government or the will of constituency. In the event that the local council did not agree to consolidation but the result of the opinion survey showed that residents did, then the governor of the province could make the final decision.

On March 24 1994, the Ministry of Home Affairs made the final lists under consideration, which included 47 Cities and 43 Counties out of the existing 68 Cities and 136 Counties. The central government and ruling party altogether expected that this reform would increase public efficiency as well as their political gain. According to governmental estimation, the amount of

---

2 *There were also dissent among several localities with rich financial sources. They were anxious about the possibilities of losing their financial benefits.*

Table 1.1 Spatial Characteristics of Korean Cities after 1994 Reform

Province (No. of Cities)	Urban-rural Complex Cities	Cities without Rural Area	Cities Segmented from Their Rural Counties
Kyonggi (21)	Pyeongteak/Icheon* Namyangju/Yongin* Paju*	Bucheon/Gwacheon Euiwang/Anyang Gwangmyeong/Goyang Gunpo/Siheung Seongnam/Ansan Hanam	Suwon/Dongducheon Guri/Osan Euijeongbu
Kangwon (7)	Chuncheon/Wonju Gangreung/Samcheok		Donghae/Sokcho Taebaek
Chungbuk (3)	Chungju/Jecheon		Cheongju
Chungnam (6)	Cheonan/Gongju Asan/Boryeong Soesan/Nonsan*		
Jeonbuk (6)	Gunsan/Iksan Jeongeub/Namwon, Gimje		Jeongju
Jeounnam (6)	Suncheon/Naju Kwangyang		Mokpo/Yeosu Yeocheon
Keongbuk (10)	Pohang/Gimcheon Andong/Kyungju Mungyeong/Yeongju Sangju/Yeongcheon Gumi/Gyeongsan		
Keongnam (11)	Changwon/Ulsan Masan/Jinju Tongyeong/Sacheon Gimhae/Milyang Geoje/Yangsan*		Jinhae
Jeju (2)			Jeju/Seogwipo
Total (72)	45	11	16

Note: * After 1994 reform, five counties including Icheon, Yongin, Paju, Nonsan, and Yangsan were upgraded to urban-rural complex cities.

reduction would reach to 15 billion Won per consolidated city local civil servants would become redundant.

Map 1.1 Geography of Urban-Rural Complex Cities in Korea

1.2.3 The Implementation of Reform

The first residential opinion survey was held between Milyang city and Milyang county on April 15 1994, and other regions were asked to complete theirs by May 3. This first attempt went far beyond the expectation of the central government. The option of consolidation was almost unilaterally adopted: 33 Cities and 32 Counties came out in favour of consolidation. Based on survey results, 33 Cities were reincarnated as urban-rural Complex Cities. In fact, no more than four months after the new policy agenda had been made public, this major jurisdictional reform was accomplished on a nationwide scale. This was an administrative accomplishment.

As the next legal steps following consolidation, the Ministry of Home Affairs initiated a special bill for urban-rural Complex Cities, which passed the National Assembly in late 1994 and early 1995[3]. Again, owing to the second round of opinion surveys, another 7 cities including Ulsan and Kwangyang were added to Complex City in the late 1994 and the early 1995.[4] At the same time, the central government approved 5 Counties the status of Complex City on March 1 1996. Altogether 45 Consolidated Cities were established in Korea during less than fifteen months. After the organisational reshuffle of local units, the central government did not hesitate to implement other types of reform. It turned next to the adjustment of the Direct Jurisdictional Cities (Jik-Hal-Si) and the Metropolitan Cities (Kwang-Yeok-Si) by merging them with their neighbouring counties. After a series of administrative reshuffles, as of January 1997, while the number of Counties decreased from 136 to 93, the number of cities increased from 68 to 72. (see Table 1 and Figure 1).

1.2.4 Organisational Problems

As shown in Figure 1.1, the Korean local governmental system is composed of three tiers of national-regional-local. Before the 1994 Jurisdictional Reform, there were three types of government at the national level: Seoul Special City, 5 Direct Jurisdictional Cities (Jik-Hal-Si), and 9 Provinces (Do). While Seoul Special City and Direct Jurisdictional Cities had Autonomous

---

3 *As a legal standard, the central government initiated 'A Special Administrative Act for Establishing Urban-Rural Complex City,' through which the consolidated localities would continue without any further changes in the next five years (1996-2000).*
1994.

4 *Cities like Pyeongtaek, Cheonan, Iksan, Sacheon, and Gimhae had a hard time to accept consolidation alternative, because Counties took a stand against consolidation with their central Cities. It was estimated that their county possessed sufficient ability and financial resources as a self-sufficient autonomous unit. county residents.*

Districts, Provincial Governments had City and County bodies under their direction. After the 1994 Reshuffle based on urban-rural consolidation, it became almost impossible to distinguish rural areas from cities except by the title of local government. Confusion mainly comes from the breakdown of the traditional urban-rural dichotomy. For example, the shaded segment in Figure 1.2 shows that Ub and Myeon have dual characters. If Ub and Myeon are located within Complex City, they are regarded as urbanised areas. In contrast, Ub and Myeon under the existing County are still calculated as rural areas. Therefore, even for the so-called 'urban specialist', it is not an easy job to figure out the urban statistics. Both policy-makers and scholars in Korea are now confronted with new challenges and responses.

1.2.5 Unresolved Questions

The issue of local government fragmentation and its effects have been debated for decades, with arguments often based only on impressionistic view and little gained in the way of resolution of the question of whether fragmentation creates harmful side effects (Dolan, 1990: 28-29). Roughly speaking, in a dozen of western societies, local public sector organisation has been dominated by the principle of "the bigger the better." Policy-makers and scholars concerned with metropolitan reforms have sought centralisation, as a means to minimise unnecessary duplication and overlapping jurisdictions which characterise the recent relationship between city and county.

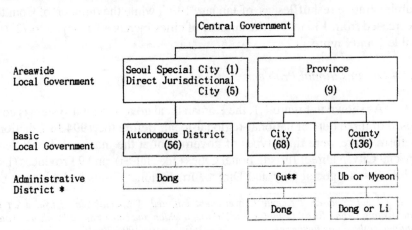

Notes: • Non-autonomous legal status
•• If the urban population is over 500,000, the city can establish non-autonomous administrative district called Gu.

Figure 1.1 Local Government System before the 1994 Reform

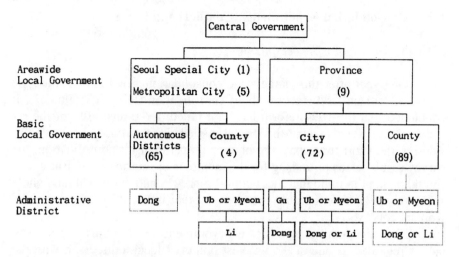

Figure 1.2 Local Government System after the 1994 Reform

The 1994 Reshuffle in Korea partially shows this tendency, but it also contains the distinctive characteristics of Korean local policy, particularly attached to a top-down approach. In Korea, the central government which sets up basic policy guideline and direction repeatedly guides adjustments, regardless of local preferences. To acquire political legitimacy, however, the central government sometimes needs to wrap its policy in the guise of bottom-up methods. In case of the 1994 Reshuffle, residential opinion surveys and public forums prepared by either political party or the central government were the typical tools for policy rationalisation. In reality, the policy authorities would not seriously consider why some localities had taken a stand against governmental recommendation, dismissing what would be the major effects of consolidation on local autonomy.

Even though data collection and analysis to evaluate Korean experiences is still under way, some critics dare to point out intrinsic or extrinsic limitations of the policy of consolidation. As systematic evidence that supports the reform view has not been collected, it is still difficult to judge whether fragmentation was inferior to the consolidation option. At the same time, despite several opportunities to adopt metropolitan reforms with the consent of citizens, performance based on consolidation is not always satisfactory. Considering conflicting empirical evidences gathered in the early years of the debate, the argument over the adverse effects of fragmentation has been still intuitive, rather than empirically driven. Presently, it may be more imperative for Korean local government to devise proper co-ordination mechanism between neighbouring local units.

1.3   Consolidation Experiments: Conflicts and Issues

1.3.1 Was the Reform Successful?

One year after this large scale consolidation, KRILA examined the degree of citizen's satisfaction about consolidation (KRILA, 1996: 27). It concluded that the 1994 reform had not failed: more than 40% of the respondents answered that they had been satisfied with the consolidation.[5] Considering the short time-span and clumsy preparation for consolidation, the survey result seems promising for the members of reform group. But it also should be kept in mind that the opinion survey could not reveal the whole spectrum of opinion because there exist other inherent limitations in the Korean contexts.

First, the poor ability of local government for providing public services is regarded as one of the weakest points of local units. Even with the advent of local autonomy system, most localities with poor political and financial powers have played meagre or passive roles in providing local services. Their legal status still remains just that of an agency of the central government, and their jurisdiction merely delineates an administrative unit for management. As a result, it is not easy or almost impossible for residents to realise the true meaning of local "autonomous" government and its "governance" area.

1.3.2 Conflicting Examples after Consolidation

1.3.2a Political Conflicts at Pyeongtaek

The Pyeongtaek Complex City (PCC)[6] had been composed of three local jurisdictions of Songtan City, Pyeongtaek City, and Pyeongtaek County, as shown in Map 1.2. Among them, Songtan Ub was upgraded into a City in 1981 and Pyeongtaek in 1986, both of which were separated from the Pyeongtaek County. Before the consolidation, these three local jurisdictions functioned as independent local bodies and prepared individual development plans. Even though residents within these areas opposed consolidation in the first residential opinion survey and the local council also rejected consolida-

---

5 *Respondents are composed of residents(42.2%), local councilors(48.3%), and local civil servants(39.7%). In addition, as the government carried out consolidation policy between city and county, it was inevitable there would be a reduction in the number of governmental officers and positions. Reflecting this circumstance, the percent of dissatisfaction among the local civil   servants was more than 30%, while the percent of satisfaction was 39.7%, the lowest rate among the groups that joined the survey.*
6 *After the consolidation, jurisdictional area covers 437.02 and the population is more than 300,000.*

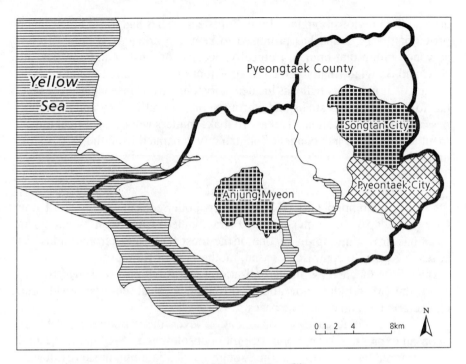

Map 1.2 Geography of Pyeongtaek Complex City

tion, they decided to merge their regions by a narrow margin in the second round in 1995.

. Still, the leftover problems of hasty consolidation remain unresolved. Political or economic hegemony is regarded as the hottest issue between Pyeongtaek and Songtan. For example, as all the local social organisations in the private sector[7] must be consolidated according to the jurisdictional consolidation, the local political movement and pride related with the selection of the head of the merged social organisation has become extremely sensitive. Even though the PCC authority has tried to induce equal distribution of the head positions among the three areas, the consolidation has made the whole situation more complicated. Furthermore, all kinds of regional events, including conferences, meetings, and festivals, have to be evenly distributed within three areas. Especially, as Songtan has strongly defended its own resources and interests, the PCC authority has not dared to

---

7 *For example, Local Association for Saemaul, Local Woman Association, Local Association for Food, Local Association for Natural Preservation are the typical examples, whose numbers are more than 70 in each locality. It is customary for the local government to allocate a little subsidy supporting their operational expenses.*

abolish the previous Songtan city hall. Instead, it has had to set up a branch office of the PCC and has promised to keep the previous volume of civil servants within that branch. Ironically, because of tension and conflict, the PCC and Songtan finally agreed to construct PCC council at Songtan, even though their main city hall was located at Pyeongtaek. Consequently, the PCC has to devise various sticks and carrots to increase efficiency and effectiveness among the consolidated areas. To make matters worse, a political movement to restore an independent Songtan city separated from the PCC seems under way.

1.3.2b Regional Disparities at Kumi

Kumi Complex City (KCC)[8] covers both Seonsan County and Kumi City (see Map 1.3). Kumi, separated (fragmented) from Seonsan county in 1978 has grown up rapidly as one of the most famous electronic industrial bases in Korea. In contrast, Seonsan, motherland of Kumi, stagnated and remained little touched by industrialisation fever for almost three decades. In short, the two regions show totally different physical, cultural, residential characteristics, and economic bases.[9]

In the initial stage of consolidation, even though some residents in Seonsan expressed strong opposition to consolidation, Seonsan and Kumi were merged by a narrow margin through residential opinion survey, just as in the case in the PCC. The consolidation of the two heterogeneous regions, however, was problematic from the beginning.

As the name for the complex city was titled Kumi, stressing the new complex's economic rationale, the local historic meaning and identity of Seonsan has disappeared. At the same time, the regional economy of Seonsan Ub, the previous centre of Seonsan County, was exacerbated after the abolishment of Seonsan county hall. In return, the regional disparity between urban Kumi and rural Seonsan has left the KCC a heavier policy burden. Especially, as the regional main centre, Kumi, is located at the periphery of the KCC area, it seems less sympathetic to the northern rural areas than the previous government structure.

1.3.2c Incongruence at Namyangju

Both Miguem City and Namyangju County are local units which were incorporated in Namyangju Complex City (NCC) under the consolidation policy, in 1995 (Map 1.4). While urban Miguem has experienced rapid

---

8 *With population of 284,775, the area of the newly born KCC is 617, almost the same size as Seoul(606).*

9 *As a major electronic base, Kumi has experienced unprecedented urbanization during the last three decades, importing so many immigrants from outside.*

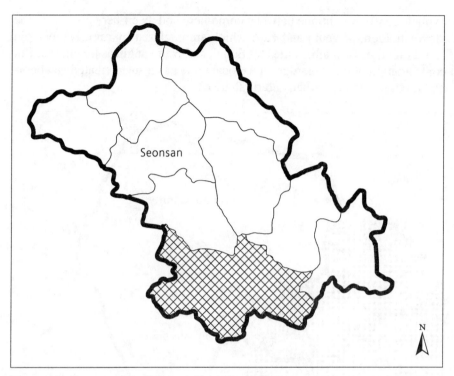

Map 1.3 Geography of Kumi Complex City

growth in the hinterland of Seoul,[10] Namyangju developed as a typical rural area with several famous leisure places along the North-Han river. Even though they were separated from each other in 1989, they were reunited again only six years later. Although their time apart was short, the policy guidelines of these two areas have been based on quite different socio-physical landscapes. Although no severe conflicts associated with consolidation have been reported, the NCC has to deal with managerial problems merging the two distinctive areas.

Unlike other cases, the initiatives for consolidation came from Namyangju county. On the one hand, most of the urban residents within the NCC have migrated from Seoul Metropolitan areas and seem indifferent about their locality. Their main concern is whether the NCC would provide them high quality of public services just like Seoul. On the other hand, along with many residents at Namyangju, both the local government and local council are more rural-oriented. Therefore, under the current consolidated system,

10 *Recently, more than 10,000 people per year have migrated from Seoul, searching for low rent housing or enjoying the pleasure of nice residential environment.*

explicit conflicts continue between come-here and been-here groups. In the ideal situation, Migeum and Kuri which are enclosed by rural Namyangju could function as satellite cities for Seoul, and Namyangju as hinterland. But consolidation of two heterogeneous local units has instead created an abnormal mixture between urban and rural areas.

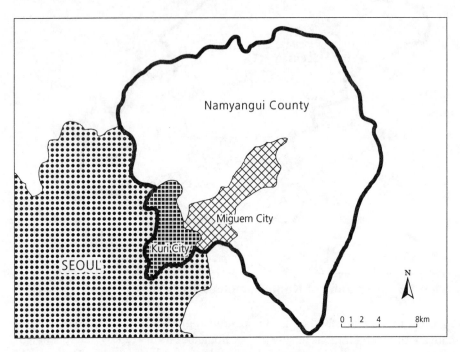

Map 1.4 Geography of Namyangju Complex City

1.3.2.d Co-ordination Issues in Cheongju Metropolitan Areas

Cheongju Metropolitan Areas (CMA) which includes mother city Cheongju and her neighbouring rural county Cheongwon is one of only three exceptional examples in which the urban-rural consolidation alternative was completely opposed by one group in the residential survey of 1995. In fact, the pros and cons were categorised according to the geographical characteristics: the majority of constituents from mother city Cheongju supported the consolidation, but those from the neighbouring rural county Cheongwon rejected it. The objection might indicate that the majority of residents within Cheongwon County were worried about the adverse side effects of consolidation in view of local autonomy and political responsibilities.

From the analyses of the present management and operation of public service facilities within the CMA(Man-Hyung Lee & Jaw Won Lee, 1995), it was confirmed that service provision remained unequal. That is, there is no proper co-ordination mechanism between Cheongju and Cheongwon in service provision. As the CMA can obtain economies of scale from the unified management and operation of those facilities, it is imperative that future plans for public service facilities has to cover total demand of the whole CMA, not being confined to each jurisdiction. Again, as externalities cannot be properly internalised or controlled under the current situation, CMA has to devise new policy alternative(s) on the basis of a unified supply or production system.

1.4   Conclusions: Policy Recommendations

The above four tales tell us that the recent administrative reshuffle in Korea presents diverse characteristics. First of all, the central government's

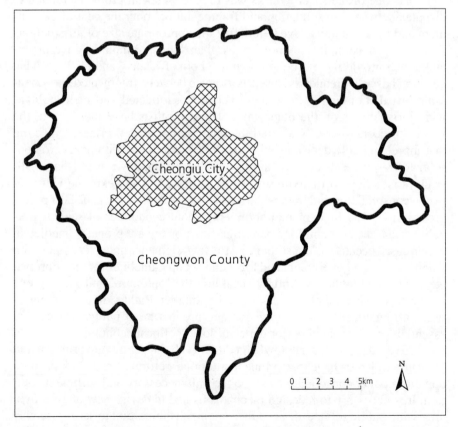

Map 1.5 Geography of Cheongju Metropolitan Area

sudden and rapid imposition of consolidation on a large scale has occurred without concrete plans. In this context, it is regrettable that policy has been based on political gains. Even though the central government has intended to eliminate or at least ameliorate problems with the previous overly fragmented structure, it seems that the tentative results are not satisfactory. Issues of duplication and overlapping of public service provisions remain unresolved even within the consolidated cities. Furthermore, it has rather strengthened local conflicts and complaints in the consolidated cities as well as in the existing areas like the CMA. For the time being, it would be extremely difficult for the local units to resolve these problems, because most Korean local governments are not self-sufficient in terms of financial and administrative resources. Instead, they must devise other plans to integrate the two heterogeneous areas. Here, it should be kept in mind that mergers should be social and organic rather than just physical or jurisdictional.

As one of the specific tasks was to resolve social problems related to disputes between consolidation and fragmentation, both the central government and the local units have to redefine the appropriate size of jurisdictions in service provision. It is no more or less than "how big should a governmental service-providing unit be to maximise both efficiency and equity?" That question has been frequently raised as a choice between fragmented and small-scale jurisdictions on the one hand versus consolidated and metropolitan-wide jurisdictions on the other hand. The centralists have indulged in the virtues of economies of scale and the increased options it brings, expecting that more equitable decisions will emerge from a polity with access to consolidated resources. In contrast, the decentralists commonly contend that small-scale jurisdiction will maximise responsiveness. But any extreme view between consolidation and fragmentation can easily deviate from the best policy prescription. The fundamental arguments about economies of scale, externalities, and the best unit for a particular function are not properly handled in either case, because it constitutes just a few elements under consideration when the central government and local unit set up guidelines for the appropriate size of any authority. Simply speaking, the 'optimum' unit for any one public service is unlikely to be optimal for another. Rather, diverse organisational arrangements for the provision and production of public services are essential for the optimal performance of local political economies.

Even though it is acknowledged that both the central government and local unit in Korea have to continue institutional reforms, we do not propose that city-county consolidation can be the only necessary and sufficient solution. It is necessary to redesign mechanisms and to devise new ones to treat area-wide public service affairs. Once again, it is important to scrutinise why the service consolidation issues should be reoriented and what the appropriate implementation tools should be in either the central government or local unit. In addition, it should be checked whether jurisdictional rearrangements are in harmony with the fragile local autonomy.

As the existing vertical and horizontal mechanisms cannot properly handle intergovernmental issues, new standards for the provisions of public service have to be established. The current norms which mainly depend on the ownership (supply-side) of public service facilities have to be replaced by the new models which pay attention to the actual users and geographical impacts (demand side) of these facilities.

References

Advisory Commission on Intergovernmental Relation (ACIR) (1987) *The Organisation of Local Public Economies*, Washington, DC.

Cowing, T. G. & A.G. Holtmann (1976) *The Economics of Local Public Service Consolidation* Lexington: Lexington Books.

Dolan, D.A. (1990) "Local Government Fragmentation: Does It Drive Up the Cost of Government," *Urban Affairs Quarterly* 26(1).

Gustely, Richard D. (1977) "The Allocational and Distributional Impacts of Governmental Consolidation: The Dade County Experience," *Urban Affairs Quarterly* 12(3).

Hirsch, Werner Z. (1968) "The Supply of Urban Public Services," in Harry, Perloff and Lowden Wingo Jr. (eds.) *Issues in Urban Economics* Baltimore: Johns Hopkins Press.

Keating, Michael (1991) *Comparative Urban Politics: Power and the City in the United States, Canada, Britain and France* Hants: Edward Elgar Publishing Limited.

Korea Research Institute for Local Administration (KRILA) (1996) *Performance Analysis of Urban-Rural Complex City* Seoul (in Korean).

Lee, Jae-Won (1995) *A Fiscal Analysis on Regionalizing the Local Pubic Service Provision: The Case Study on Regional Public Service in Cheongju Metropolitan Area* Unpublished Ph.D Dissertation, Seoul National University (in Korean).

Lee, Jae-Won, Man-Hyung Lee, and Byung-Ho Park (1996) "Local Institution Reforms for the Public Service Provision in Korea," Reshaping Urban Vision and Development Towards 21st Century, Paper Presented at *International Symposium on City Planning 1996*, Chinese Institute of Urban Planning.

Lee, Man-Hyung & Jae-Won Lee (1995) "Management and Operation Systems of Public Service Facilities within Metropolitan Area", *Journal of Korean Planners Association* 31(1) (in Korean).

Ostrom, V., C.M. Tiebout, & R. Warren (1961) "The Organisation of Government in Metropolitan Areas: A Theoretical Inquiry," *American Political Science Review* 55(4).

Stein, Robert M. (1990) *Urban Alternatives: Public and Private Markets in the Provision of Local Services* Pittsburgh: University of Pittsburgh Press.

2   Taiwan's Urban System in Transition
Jack F. Williams

2.1   Introduction

As Taiwan nears the millennium, roughly half a century has passed since Japanese colonial rule ended and Taiwan embarked on a new era of development as a de facto independent state. Properly speaking, Taiwan has moved beyond the "newly industrialised economy" (NIE) label that has been attached to it for some three decades or more.   Taiwan's industrialisation is no longer new, nor is its urbanisation process.   Taiwan's urban system and urban development process reflect the island's transition from "developing" to "developed" status (at least as defined by the OECD). Taiwan is now in the latter (or terminal) phase of the urbanisation curve, in which the rate of urban population growth decreases, reflecting in part a similar slowing of the island's overall population growth (currently hovering at just under one per cent per year).

Thus, some fifty years into Taiwan's modern transformation from former Japanese agricultural colony to quasi-independent industrial powerhouse, this is an appropriate time to examine Taiwan's urban system from a variety of perspectives, to see where its urban development process stands in terms of both positive and negative characteristics, and to attempt to discern future directions and options.   This topic is also timely given the fact that very few Western geographers or others concerned with urban issues outside of Taiwan have studied Taiwan's urban development, especially in an ongoing basis. Although Taiwan admittedly is a relatively small island and discrete geographical region of just 24,000 sq. km., the entire industrialisation and urbanisation process experienced by much larger Western countries, such as the United States, has been condensed in Taiwan both spatially, in a very small area (about the size of Massachusetts, Connecticut and Rhode Island combined, or slightly larger than China's Hainan Island and about half the area of the island of Sri Lanka), and temporally, in the space of a few decades. Thus, Taiwan's urban development experience is not only interesting in and of itself, but also for what it can tell us in a comparative sense with other Asian countries and with Western countries.

2.2   Taiwan's Urban Development, 1945-1995[1]

By 1940, just before the impact of World War II began to be felt in Taiwan, the island's urban population was about 10-12 percent of an islandwide population of just under six million, concentrated in a few modest-sized towns and cities (only four over 100,000, led by the capital of Taipei at about 160,000) (Speare, Liu and Tsay, 1988.) By 1950, after a decade of military and political turmoil, with the Republic of China government now in exile on Taiwan, the island's urban population had swelled to about 25 percent, fuelled largely by the huge influx of mainland refugees and Nationalist government forces that fled to the island in the late 1940s. Taiwan was on the threshold of its modern industrial transformation. By 1995, Taiwan's total population was 21.3 million, of which more than 80 percent lived in urban places. The largely agrarian, rural-based economy and population had been transformed into an overwhelmingly urban/industrial nature. The story of Taiwan's "economic miracle", and the political transformation that came along later in the 1980s and 90s, has been well documented in innumerable studies (for example, Jacobs, Hagger and Sedgley, 1984). Here I briefly summarise the key developments that relate directly to Taiwan's urban and regional development through the five decade period.

In the 1950s the ROC government embarked on a development strategy that focused first on agriculture and food processing, accompanied by textiles and import-substitution manufacturing. Although farmers started to prosper, because of land reform and other measures, urban migration began in response to job creation in the cities, especially in the Taipei region, secondarily the Kaohsiung area. Urban population growth soared at three times the rate of the total population. By 1960, Taipei had 1.8 million in its metro region, while Kaohsiung had less than half that.

During the 1960s Taiwan passed the 50% urban population mark as the economy took off under an export-promotion strategy that saw formal U.S. economic assistance end in 1965. Export processing zones in Kaohsiung and Taichung, among the first in the world, heralded a new approach to industrialisation in Third World countries. Taiwan's economy moved into more sophisticated products, including electronics, plastics, and optical equipment. Taipei was the focal point of industrial development still, with its total population reaching 2.8 million by 1970, a 67% increase over 1960. Kaohsiung, the second ranking city, reached 1.1 million in 1970, a growth rate equal to that of Taipei. Taipei's growth in this decade was in part a response to an expansion of its municipal boundaries. In 1966, Taipei was elevated to the

---

1 *For an earlier study by the author, see: Jack F. Williams, 1988.*

status of a special municipality and its boundaries were pushed outward in 1968 to annex six townships surrounding the older central city. Taipei's exceptional growth in this period can also be attributed in part to its unusual political status, as the 'provisional national capital' of China. The ROC government maintained large operations in various ministries, employing thousands of people, to fulfil this role. Many of these bodies, and the buildings they occupy, are really larger than would be required to serve just the island of Taiwan. Moreover, the government built a new planned city for the provincial government, headquartered in Chung Hsing New Town just south of Taichung in central Taiwan. This city served the province of Taiwan, while ostensibly Taipei served the larger national interests, even though Taiwan had no effective control of the vast mainland.

In the 1970s Taiwan underwent further industrial transformation, with special emphasis on heavy industry (chemicals, petrochemicals, iron and steel, automobiles, and other basic goods). Kaohsiung received major government (and private) investment, but Taipei outdistanced Kaohsiung's population growth rate, increasing from 2.8 million to 4.3 million by 1980, while Kaohsiung grew only to 1.67 million. Total population growth for the island had slowed, but was still at a high 2.1%, while urban population grew by 5% or more a year. The urbanisation rate reached 66% by 1980.

Taiwan's urban system was dominated then by the four major metropolitan regions of Taipei, Kaohsiung, Taichung, and Tainan, in that order (Taichung surpassed Tainan in the 1970s) (see Map 2.1). The Taipei metro region contained 25% of Taiwan's total population, while Kaohsiung had 9%. Taichung had just over 7% and Tainan about 4%. The four metro centres collectively accounted for over 8 million people, or some 45% of the island's population. By the mid-1990s, the Taipei metro region had a total population of about 5.6 million, of which some 2.6 million were within Taipei Municipality itself, but a majority of just under 3 million were located in the urban areas of the surrounding Taipei basin (calculated from Urban and Regional Development Statistics, ROC, 1996). This meant that Taipei had about 26% of Taiwan's total population in its metro region.[2]

This leads us directly to some needed commentary about the issues of urban primacy, rank-size distribution, and balanced regional development. The few Western authors who have examined Taiwan's urban system over the decades have generally agreed that Taiwan has been able to avoid true urban primacy, at least the extreme situation such as that found in the Philip-

---

2 *This is admittedly a broad interpretation of the metro region for Taipei, in that it includes Tanshui, the coastal port town that has now become effectively a bedroom suburb and recreation site for Greater Taipei, with the completion of the MRT to Tanshui, and Keelung, the northern port that has served the Taipei region since the Japanese era.*

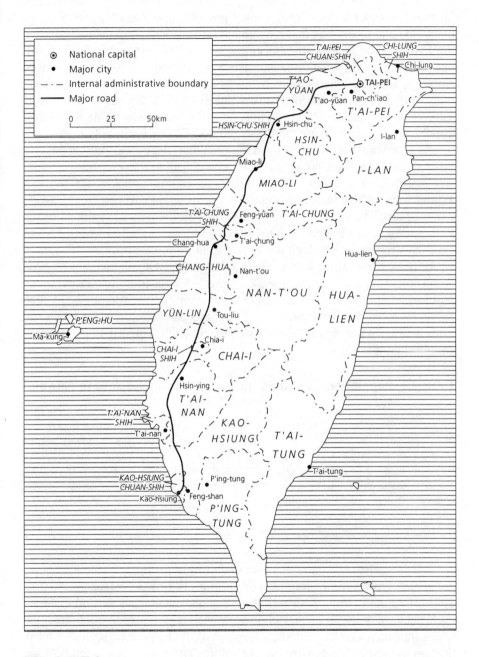

Map 2.1 Taiwan

pines with Manila, or in Thailand with Bangkok. Pannell (1974) argued that
Taiwan has never had an "exaggerated primate condition of urban development" in spite of the fact that it exhibited (at least still so in the early 1970s)
the five conditions typically associated with urban primacy in underdeveloped countries: (1) small area and dense population; (2) low per capita income; (3) export or agriculturally based economies; (3) high population growth
rates; and (5) a history of colonialism. Speare et al. (1988) came to much the
same conclusion in their study completed in the mid-1980s. Nonetheless, it is
important to note that these, and other, authors focused primarily upon a statistical determination of primacy, and noted that Taipei was only about two
times the size of Kaohsiung, and that Taiwan had a relatively normal rank-
size distribution of cities. While that is all true, nonetheless, Taipei does
exhibit some characteristics of functional primacy, in part because of its peculiar or artificial role as the so-called "provisional national capital" of the
ROC and the distorted pull that role has exerted on migration within Taiwan
over the decades. Although the government no longer peddles this line in
public (since admitting several years ago that the ROC, in fact, has no governmental control of the mainland), there is no question that Taipei is the
political, cultural, educational, and business centre of the island, and as such
continues to be the prime attractor of migrants, as it has since the 1950s. In
some ways, Taipei is the "New York" of Taiwan. Thus, it is incorrect to
simply state that Taiwan has no urban primacy.

**Table 2.1 Population Growth of the Four Planning Regions in Taiwan,
1956-82**

Region	1956		1971		1982		1995		Growth Rate (%)		
	A	B	A	B	A	B	A	B	1956-71	1971-82	1982-95
Northern	2.84	30.2	5.23	34.9	7.35	39.8	9.04	42.4	84.2	40.5	23.0
Southern	3.20	34.1	4.95	33.0	5.70	30.9	6.24	29.3	54.7	15.2	9.5
Central	2.96	31.5	4.18	27.9	4.76	25.8	5.41	25.4	41.2	13.9	13.7
Eastern	0.39	4.2	0.63	4.2	0.64	3.5	0.61	2.9	61.5	1.6	-4.7

A = Population in millions
B = Percentage share of total population

The statistical data reveal some interesting patterns. Table 2.1 shows
population growth for the four planning regions in Taiwan, for the years 1956,
1971, 1982, and 1995. Although these regions encompass several counties
each, because of the small size of Taiwan each region is focused around one
of the four metro areas, with the exception of the Eastern region (which has
the two modest towns of Hualien and Taitung anchoring the two ends of the

elongated region). Thus, the North is centred around the Taipei metro region, the Centre is focused on the Taichung metro region, while the South is primarily centred on the Kaohsiung metro region, with Tainan as a nearby secondary urban focal point. As of 1995, the North had 42% of Taiwan's total population, the South had 29%, the Centre 25%, and the East less than 3%. Note the contrast with 1956, when there was actually much greater balance between the three major regions and the South was the largest. While population growth rates for all four regions have slowed since 1956, the North has slowed the least, resulting in its increasing dominance in terms of population, although not necessarily in economic importance, as Table 2.2 reveals. The North's share of Taiwan's GDP barely changed between 1976 and 1992, as was true for all four regions. On a per capita income basis, however, there was a significant improvement between 1976 and 1992 in terms of lessening the inequality, even though the North was still well ahead of the other three regions.

Table 2.2 Measures of Regional Inequality in Taiwan

Region	Shares of GDP (%)		Per Capita Increase By Region (Index)	
	1976	*1992*	*1976*	*1992*
Taiwan	*100.0*	*100.0*	*100.0*	*100.0*
N	49.8	50.4	140.3	118.3
S	27.9	28.0	82.6	94.5
C	19.8	19.4	71.2	78.0
E	2.5	2.2	61.2	76.2

Source: Urban and Regional Development Statistics (CEPD, Urban and Housing Development Department, 1996): 168, 169.

Comparing just the Taipei metro region and the Kaohsiung metro region for 1995, the data show Kaohsiung slipping further behind Taipei in population. Taipei municipality, as already noted, had 2.64 million people in 1995, while Kaohsiung municipality registered 1.4 million. Kaohsiung has long suffered from an inferiority complex. Even though it is the centre of Taiwan's heavy industrial base and the second city of the island, it remains basically a blue collar, rough-hewn town, in contrast to Taipei's cosmopolitanism and sophistication, a Cleveland or Pittsburgh next to New York. People in Taiwan who can do so prefer to live in the Taipei area (Hwang, 1996). What holds Kaohsiung back? The mayor, Wu Den-yih, can name many reasons: insufficient central government investment, lack of administrative control over the harbour (the Kaohsiung Harbour Bureau is under the provincial government[3]), insufficient cultural resources, serious pollution problems (unlike Taipei, Kaohsiung's problems stem primarily from industry, not automobiles (FCR, 1996b). The Taiwan government's ambitious APROC plan, intended to make the island an Asia-Pacific Regional Operations Centre, could have beneficial implications for Kaohsiung, which would have to be one of the principal players in that plan, particularly because of its port, the largest and most important in Taiwan. The opening of the door to direct shipping with the mainland, by allowing third parties to sail directly from Xiamen to Kaohsiung (with certain restrictions), is a step toward that APROC goal.

One might conclude, thus, that urban primacy, in some respects, is increasing in Taiwan, although to be sure the degree of primacy is still relatively small compared to many developing countries. How has Taiwan managed to slow, if not altogether stop, the development of urban primacy, in spite of having the key indicators, as already noted, for primacy? The answer lies, I believe, in the development policies Taiwan followed from the 1950s onward, and the rapid success of the government in promoting industrialisation, rural and urban prosperity, and slowed population growth (Todd and Hsueh, 1988). If Taiwan had not successfully done these things, it is quite likely that Taipei would have become a bloated, but economically underdeveloped primate city filled with hundreds of thousands of squatter migrants forced out of overcrowded rural areas, in a pattern all too familiar in the Third World today. Actually, the more likely scenario is that the ROC would not have survived militarily and politically and would have been absorbed by the PRC. In that situation, Taipei probably would have remained a relatively secondary provincial city, something like Xiamen in Fujian province, at least until China's opening up under the New Open Door Policy that started in the late 1970s.

More specifically, Taiwan was quite successful in promoting rural industrialisation, which brought job opportunities to the farmers rather than waiting for the farmers to move to the cities. This policy was part of the government's efforts at balanced regional development, a planning approach that began to take off in the 1970s. Industrial estates developed by the government for private investors to locate in were built primarily in rural counties, not the major metro regions. The positive effect was to transform the majority of farmers into part-time farmers, thus lowering the gap between rural and urban incomes and keeping excessive migration away from the big cities. Simultaneously, the government embarked on a long series of mas-

---

3 *The recent decision by Taiwan's government to gradually phase out the provincial government has not only created a storm of controversy in Taiwan but could have major implications for the two 'national' level municipalities, Taipei and Kaohsiung.*

sive, expensive infrastructure improvement programs aimed particularly at improving the transportation systems of the island, so that urban centres would not have excessively attractive advantages in transportation access and thus pull too much industrial investment toward the cities. These projects included such things as the North-South Freeway, electrification and other improvements of the main west coast railway, rail and road links to the Eastern part of Taiwan that ended the physical isolation of that area (although this enhanced access did not significantly increase the attractiveness of the East for industrialisation), major improvements in secondary and local roads, port improvements, new airports, and so on.

Policy failures occurred, nonetheless. Two significant examples include the new port at Taichung, and the new town movement. The Taichung Harbour project was started in 1973 as a system bringing port and industries together in a regional development centre that would not only give Taiwan a third major port (to take some of the pressure off Kaohsiung, especially) but also help promote the growth of the Taichung metro region growth (Todd and Hsueh, 1990). Unfortunately, the port has failed to live up to expectations, for a complex mix of reasons, including not paying enough attention to detail in growth-centre planning, failure to commit enough resources to bring the project to fruition, and improper co-ordination among the parties involved in the project.

In the case of new towns, Taiwan first attempted new town planning and development in the late 1970s (Liu, 1991). Also as part of the push for more balanced regional development, the government decided to try to introduce the new town concept as originated in Britain and widely used there, especially after World War II in the Greater London area. Taichung Harbour New Town, part of the harbour project discussed above, was one of these new towns, along with Linkou (near Taipei), Chengching (near Kaohsiung), and Nankan (also near Taipei). The results of these new towns have not been impressive, for many of the same reasons found in the relative failure of new towns elsewhere in the world (including the U.S.), especially the failure to develop true economic self-sufficiency in the new towns and hence their remaining at the level of bedroom suburbs at best (Linkou is the most successful of the lot, but even it falls far short of original goals). In spite of their relative failure, the government had plans to build 19 more new towns during the Sixth Five-Year Plan (1991-96), including Tanshui New Town, which has a target of 200,000 people by 2014.

Within the metro regions, a pattern familiar to Western cities has also occurred in Taiwan over the decades, in terms of migration patterns (Speare et al, 1988). In the 1950s and 1960s the migratory flow was a net movement from rural areas to the large central cities, especially Taipei. By the 1970s, however, migration had shifted to a net movement from rural areas and large central cities to intermediate cities, particularly those cities adjacent to Taipei and Kaohsiung. That pattern has basically continued to this day, albeit at a slower rate. Thus, in the case of Taipei, satellite cities such as Panchiao, Yungho, Sanchung, Chungho, and Hsinchuang, have all experienced explosive growth, increasing their individual populations several times over during the past 20-30 years. For example, Panchiao is the largest satellite city of Taipei today, with a population over 530,000; in 1951 Panchiao had a mere 30,000 people, but by 1983 the figure had jumped to 454,000. Chungho and Sanchung are vying for second place, each with over 380,000 population; Chungho had only 24,000 in 1951, but 304,000 in 1983, while Sanchung was at 39,000 in 1951 and 343,000 in 1983. While these growth rates are indeed significant, it should be remembered that the growth almost certainly would have been even larger without the various measures aimed at balanced regional development. This suburban growth was the consequence of cheaper land in the suburbs, congestion in the central city, improved transport (especially highways), mass ownership of motorised transport (initially motorcycles, then later automobiles), and rising incomes encouraging families to seek better quality and larger housing. The only difference from the U.S., at least, was the absence of racial conflict as a push factor encouraging the middle and upper classes to migrate to the suburbs.

2.3 Key Urban Issues Facing Taiwan: The Next Half Century

What then are the key urban issues facing Taiwan as it approaches the new century? There are obviously a great many issues, but space limitations require me to focus on just a few key ones.

2.3.1 Urban Planning

The overarching problem is how to institute real urban planning. Taiwan actually has been in the planning business since the 1950s, when development plans were initiated for Taipei and the other three major metro regions. Larger regional plans began to evolve from the 1960s onward. Those plans have been modified and updated numerous times since then, but the plans themselves have been implemented only partially and often unsuccessfully. One of the root causes of this limited degree of success lies in the high cost of land and the difficulties of land acquisition, which tend to stymie the best of government plans and efforts (FCR 1991a and 1996a). This is very observable in the contrast between Taipei and its suburbs. As one editorial put it, "Panchiao today is Taipei of the 1970s" (FCR 1992). This refers to the fact that Panchiao, and other satellite cities, tend to exhibit the random street patterns, poor architecture, lack of order or planning, dirt, and general ugliness that was once the case for much of Taipei (not to suggest that such defects are close to elimination in the bigger central cities of Taiwan). Urban redevelopment has brought some order, modernity, and even pockets of beauty to parts of Taipei, when it was easier and cheaper to acquire land. An example is New Taipei, the eastern district that has developed largely in the last 20 years, focused around Tunhua Road and Hsinyi Road with the International Trade Centre. In any event, the suburbs have yet to catch up with the core city. The task gets harder, but it is not hopeless when there is the political will.

2.3.2 Transportation

Nowhere are the difficulties of planning more evident than in the case of transportation, both interurban and intraurban. Taiwan's dramatic success in economic development over the past decades was due in substantial part to vast improvements in the island's transportation systems, greatly increasing the ease and efficiency of moving people and goods between and within cities (Shaw and Williams 1991). Good transportation is essential for success in any developing country. No wonder thus that Taiwan continues to put great emphasis on further infrastructure improvement. As already noted above, Taiwan has had a series of major infrastructure improvement projects underway since the 1970s. Some of these have succeeded, some have not. In general, however, over the years the projects increasingly have been plagued with management chaos, scandalous delays, and massive cost overruns (Baum 1987). For this reason, the government recently has been pushing increasingly for linkups with private participation in these projects. The scope of the current construction roster is staggering - some 634 projects estimated to cost US$233 billion, even after being sharply pared back from original plans. The list includes as the centrepiece the high-speed rail line linking Taipei and Kaohsiung, a rail line linking Taipei's international and domestic airports, industrial parks to be built on government land, incinerators, recycling plants, private power plants, and a new urban rapid-transit system for Kaohsiung.

Transportation is what concerns us here, however, and one of the troubled major projects currently is the high-speed 345 km rail link between Taipei and Kaohsiung. This largest-ever public works venture in Taiwan's history is now scheduled to be completed by 2003; private investment (out of an estimated total cost of $18 billion) has been targeted at a minimum of 40%, in a collaborative approach known as "build-operate-transfer" (BOT). Based on the experience of both the Taipei and Kaohsiung mass rapid transit systems (MRTS), however, critics are sceptical about the prospects for smooth public/private collaboration on the high-speed railway. For one thing, high-speed railways are notoriously unprofitable in almost all countries where they have been built. That fact, plus the dismal experience in Taipei and Kaohsiung (see below), contribute to the worry that the government will be unable to attract sufficient foreign investors to meet the government's minimum capital needs, and even if they do the relationship will bog down into acrimony and construction delays (Harmsen 1996).

The Taipei MRTS has become perhaps the most infamous public works project in Taiwan's modern history. The idea for a MRTS goes back at least to 1972, but unfortunately Taiwan did not get serious about the matter until the 1980s. In 1987, the Department of Rapid Transit Systems (DORTS) was established under Taipei's city government to take full charge of planning and building of the MRTS. A multinational consortium of American, French, and German companies got the contract to build the system (Yeung 1991). The initial MRTS network is designed to meet the transportation needs of eight major corridors in metro Taipei and strengthen the links between downtown and suburbs in a system covering a total of 88 km. Within that system there are to be eight lines (to Tanshui, Hsintien, Mucha, Nankang, Panchiao, and Chungho, plus a short maintenance line in the centre) (Dept. of Rapid Transit Systems n.d.). Beyond this initial system, originally supposed to be completed by 1997-98, an expanded system with lines to all the other suburban centres, including CKS International Airport, was to be completed by 2021.

From the beginning, however, DORTS suffered a string of problems because of difficulties in acquiring land, shortages of skilled labour, and horrendous troubles with the foreign contractors. Especially troublesome has been the relationship with Matra Transport, the French builder of the Mucha line (Chiu 1996). Construction began in 1989 and the opening date was supposed to be 1993; the Mucha line did not open until March, 1996. Railcar fires, tire blowouts, and fissures in the elevated platform's support pillars were among the technical problems the government complained about. On the management level, the two sides' relationship completely broke down, and the Taipei city government still owes Matra nearly $84 million.

The Tanshui line finally opened on March 28, 1997 (and is expected to give a strong boost to development of the Tamsui area, which has a population already over 90,000).   The Hsintien and Chungho lines are now scheduled to open in 2000; the Nankang and Panchiao lines in 2001. The Tucheng line will begin in 2004; no target date has been set yet for the Neihu line (Liu 1997).

Not only has the MRTS system take far longer to complete than originally planned, and cost far more than predicted, but all sorts of other concerns have been raised as well. First, the cost of riding the system is not cheap; the highest charge on the Tamsui line is $2.91 per ride. Officials claim the fares are being kept to the lowest possible level, but the fares are even higher than what one pays in some U.S. MRT systems, hardly a way to entice people to give up their motorcycles and cars for the MRTS. Undoubtedly, the huge cost overruns in building the system have been a contributing factor to the high fares. A second problem is public concern about the safety of the system, after the widely publicized technical problems with the Mucha line. A third concern is whether the MRTS will actually do the job it is designed for, that is, reduce reliance on private transportation within Taipei. DORTS claims that the system initially will absorb 36% of the daily commuter load of metro Taipei, and will expand to absorb 51% by 2021; American consulting companies put the figure closer to 20% (Yeung 1991). If the Americans are right, Taipei will be in big trouble in the next century, with a white elephant MRTS not fulfilling its purpose.

Kaoshiung, unfortunately, has not fared any better so far in its efforts to develop a MRTS (Baum 1996). For Kaohsiung MRTS estimated to cost $7 billion, an international consortium known as International Transit Consultants (ITC) won the consultancy contract to design the system. In a repetition of Taipei's experience, however, the two sides got bogged down in mutual mud slinging, acrimony, and complete breakdown of trust. One would think officials there would have learned from Taipei's experience, but Kaohsiung's situation suggests that Taiwan's problems with MRTS (and perhaps other public works projects) is culture-based, rather than scientific or technical in nature (Connolly 1996). The result was cancellation of the contract with ITC in 1995 and a year or more of delays and legal manoeuvring by both sides. Planning of the MRTS has yet to be done, let alone the start of construction. Kaohsiung's experience, like that of Taipei, highlights the fact that Taiwan is not yet a truly developed country, in terms of adhering to internationally accepted practices in awarding and implementation of contracts. Taiwan officials and the foreign companies were operating from quite different cultural bases and with very different ideas about regulatory, contractual and procedural practices.

Even if the MRTS works in Taipei, Kaohsiung, and elsewhere eventually, dealing with road traffic problems is likely to continue to be a big headache for Taipei and other cities, and for Taiwan as a whole. To solve the problems of inter-urban road traffic, the government has already begun the second North-South Freeway, paralleling the older freeway, sections of which first opened in 1974 (Liu 1991). That freeway greatly improved north-south movement along the west coast, but as in the experience of the U.S. and other countries, the better the roads the more traffic generated. In other words, the freeway became clogged to capacity within a decade, contributing to the high death rate on Taiwan highways (19.23 traffic-related deaths per 100,000 people each year, compared with just 6.1 in Japan) (Tseng 1991). Thus, in 1985 Taiwan decided to build a second northern freeway, starting in Taipei and running south to connect with the existing freeway near the Hsinchu Science-based Industrial Park (108 km.). As with other recent public works projects, because of difficulties in land acquisition and shortages of labor, the second freeway proceeded much more slowly than the first. Because of land acquisition problems, the highway also had to be routed through mountainous country to the east, extending along the periphery of urban areas. This added to the construction cost, with many tunnels and bridges, not to mention concerns raised about slopeland erosion problems (a long standing issue in Taiwan, particularly associated with agricultural practices (Williams, Chang and Wang 1983)). The remainder of the second freeway, from Keelung all the way to Linpien in Pingtung county at the southern tip of the island, was originally targeted for completion by the end of 1998 (at a total accumulated investment of nearly $17 billion, about nine times the cost of the first freeway) (Liu 1991). That target date has now been pushed back at least to the year 2000 just for the section from Chunan to Nantou in central west Taiwan (ROC Yearbook 1996). No mention is made of the extension further southward, which probably will not be built until sometime in the next century. Even with the second freeway, Taiwan is likely always to experience severe congestion on its freeways and lesser highways, simply because of the high population density and nature of the urban/industrial system.

Within the major cities, especially Taipei, the intra-urban traffic problems are the stuff of legend. Traffic chaos is virtually endemic to most modern Asian cities today; hence, there is no need to go into great detail about this. Taipei simply exhibits the problems to an extraordinary degree. Taipei also demonstrates a remarkable inability to resolve the problems (Hwang 1991). As of 1994, Taipei had over 638,000 automobiles, over one million motorcycles, not to mention some 3500 buses and at least 36,000 taxis; each month an additional 10,000 vehicles join the fleets (ROC Yearbook 1996). To make matters worse, the number of parking spaces available in the city is far below the number of vehicles (Chang 1991). The MRTS construction makes the already congested streets even worse. One result has been rampant disregard for traffic laws and courtesy. Cars and motorcycles are parked anywhere a space can be found. Every conceivable violation of traffic rules can be observed just standing on a street corner for a short time (assuming one can find space to stand, since many sidewalks are nearly completely used up as motorcycle parking lots, with itinerant vendors occupying what little space might remain).

The MRTS, even if underutilized, certainly will take some of the strain off the surface roads. But the MRTS is not a panacea for traffic woes. Among the widely discussed cures for the mess: better co-ordination among the government bodies involved with transportation planning and traffic regulation; much stricter enforcement of traffic laws (the Singapore model is much admired); improved bus service simultaneously with measures to discourage automobile and motorcycle ownership (or at least usage within the central city), i.e., making such ownership and usage punitively expensive (FRC 1991c). Experts seem to share the opinion that building more and better roads, or more parking spaces, is not the answer: rather, planners should seek to keep as many cars and motorcycles out of the city as possible (FRC 1996a). It sounds fine in theory, but in Taiwan's case the highly liberalized and contentious political atmosphere today does not bode well for such authoritarian methods.

2.3.3 Environmental Protection

Environmental protection is one of the most pressing problems for Taiwan's urban areas, and a topic I have addressed in detail in other publications (Williams 1996). Although Taiwan appears to be on the comeback in terms of certain types of pollution or environmental degradation a decade after creating the Environmental Protection Administration, the process of restoring a quality environment has just begun. Air pollution is one of the most serious problems, especially in the cities, because of heavy traffic and high concentration of industrial plants. In Taipei, 95% of the air pollution is from vehicular exhaust. As of December, 1994, there were 16.5 million vehicles registered in Taiwan, and between 1983 and 1993 the number of passenger cars increased 2.75 times, while the number of motorcycles rose 50%.[4] Equally serious problems exist with water pollution, land subsidence, solid waste disposal, and hazardous waste disposal. Space does not permit going into detail on these. The government has adopted a large-scale program of studying and measuring these problems, developing programs and policies for dealing with them, and begun to institute specific measures to clean up problems and prevent future occurrences. All things considered, I am cautiously optimistic about Taiwan's long-term prospects for resolving its environmental problems. I base this optimism on a number of factors: (1) the high educational and technological levels of the people of Taiwan; (2) the

---

4 *'Environmental Protection,' (...cchome.com/info/yearbook/nf_html/chl3_l.html)*

rapid slowing of Taiwan's population growth; (3) the relatively small size of Taiwan and hence manageable dimensions of the problems; (4) the relatively moderate size of Taiwan's cities, and absence of a huge mega city (with all the problems implied) on the scale of a Manila, Bangkok or Jakarta; (5) the large amounts of surplus capital that Taiwan has, plus a high, and rapidly rising, standard of living; (6) the growing environmental consciousness of the Taiwanese people; (7) the profitability of environmental cleanup, and hence opportunities for natural Taiwanese entrepreneurship (Williams 1996).

2.3.4 Historical Preservation

Unfortunately, in the rush to develop countries tend to pay little attention to the record of the past. As a result, historical preservation is seldom seen as one of the major issues facing urban planners. It should be, however. After all, cities are the repositories of culture. People live in cities not just to work but to enjoy life. Reminders of one's cultural heritage are essential to a whole life. Taiwan's experience in this regard is no different from most other countries, of course. Only after development was well underway, and much of the past already obliterated, has historical preservation finally begun to find an audience in Taiwan.

Historical preservation started in the 1970s with an effort in academic and cultural circles to preserve the Lin An-tai homestead, dating back to 1783, in Taipei. Since then, the movement has been slowly gaining supporters and projects. Currently, the ROC Ministry of the Interior has designated 280 sites in Taiwan as national relics, of which 24 are in the "first class", 48 in the second, and 208 in the third class. Among the more important structures, besides a large number of temples, are several major buildings in downtown Taipei built by the Japanese; the landmark structure is the former Governor-General's Headquarters, and still used by the ROC government as its headquarters. Fortunately, it is still possible to see remnants of the Japanese era in Taipei and other places on the island, but the sites are diminishing. One of the more controversial sites has been Minchuan Street, in Sanhsia, a suburb of Taipei. The 200-metre long street is considered historically valuable for its 102 family houses built in 1916 during the Japanese colonial era and classified as a third class site. Government policy is to exempt owners of designated historic sites from paying taxes on them and the land they occupy, as a compensation for maintaining the cultural heritage, but this tax exemption is not always enough to satisfy the people who occupy such sites. Local residents of Minchuan Street ended up pitted against each other, some arguing for preservation, others for modernization.

One is reminded of the experience of Beijing, a far larger and grander city, which has seen so much of its cultural heritage destroyed in the past, and now increasing numbers of people there lament the irreplaceable losses, most notably, of course, the great city wall of Beijing that was dismantled under Mao's orders starting in the late 1950s. Can Taiwan learn from the mainland's mistakes? Is it really too late anyway?

Many problems stand in the way of historical preservation:

(1) Money is always in short supply. Government appropriations are insufficient to cover all the sites, and there is not much private sector support.

(2) Second and third class relics are the responsibility of the cities or counties where they are located, but local governments would rather spend money on more practical public works.

(3) Public indifference is still pervasive, even though the number of enthusiasts for preservation has increased.

(4) Skilled craftsmen capable of restoring old structures are in short supply, and few young people want to learn such trades nowadays.

(5) Irresponsible domestic tourists obstruct the work of preservation, by looting, littering, or defacing historic sites; it is ironic that foreign visitors are often more interested in protecting and enjoying local historic sites than the residents, who tend to be preoccupied with making money and the stresses of daily life.

Taiwan's experience in this regard seems to repeat a pattern one can note in many other developing countries. In the typical development model, it appears that a country has to give full attention to development and significant raising of material living standards before there is time and interest by government and public in the non-material quality of life, including environmental protection, historical preservation, and other qualitative aspects of contemporary life. When interest is finally aroused, however, it typically is grassroots, that is, from the bottom up, not the top down. Hard core activists publicise a cause or issue, arouse larger public opinion, often followed by demonstrations and petitions to the government, which then responds with policies and action to correct the problems and meet public demands. This is exactly what happened in Taiwan with environmental cleanup and historical preservation, and, to some extent, with transportation and other aspects of urban and regional development.

2.4   Conclusion

The issues for Taiwan's future urban development might be summarised by making reference to a provocative, and subjective, recent article in

Asiaweek (October 25 1996) that supposedly measured and compared Asia's "Best Cities", using 22 statistical indicators that carried different weightings. Several Japanese cities made the list, including Tokyo which was named the best Asian city of all. Two cities in Taiwan were picked, with Taipei ranked 11th, and Kaohsiung 14th among the 40 cities in the list, which included every Asian capital east of Kabul, with minor exceptions (e.g. Pyongyang was not measured). In larger nations, the ranking included another major metro area besides the capital While one can argue about the criteria used to measure a city's "livability", and how to quantify some of those measures for purposes of comparability, nonetheless, Taiwan's two key cities probably ended up with higher rankings than some people who have lived in Taipei or Kaohsiung would be willing to grant them.

An editorial published in Taiwan, by the Taiwan government itself, may have described the reality best by referring to Taiwan's cities as "cities with rough edges" (FRC 1991c). The comparison was with U.S. cities, such as Chicago and St. Louis just after the completion of the railways, and the excitement, disregard for official restraints, and frenetic entrepreneurship that characterised those cities long ago, similar to what one sees in Taiwan's cities today. This is an apt description of Taiwan's urban places in the 1990s, as the island hovers on the brink of "developed" status and major structural changes are occurring or planned for the economy, at the same time that the political system continues to evolve at a dramatic pace. In a manner of speaking, the Republic of China on Taiwan is having to reinvent itself, to reflect changing political and economic realities, and thus it is hardly surprising that the cities have rough edges indeed. The challenge facing Taiwan now - its government, planners, and citizenry - is how to take the rough edges off the cities and truly bring Taiwan up to international standards. Look at the dramatic improvements in Japan's cities today, compared with the 1960s and even 1970s. Taiwan should be able to do at least as well in the years ahead.

References

Asiaweek (1996) "Asia's Best Cities" October 25.
Baum, Julian (1987) "Private Property" *Far Eastern Economic Review* March pp. 42-44.
Baum, Julian (1996) "Off the Rails: Disputes Stall Taiwan's Second Mass-Transit System" *Far Eastern Economic Review* July p. 73.
Chang, Winne (1991) "Taipei Parking Blues" *Free China Review* March pp. 26-28.
Chiu, Ken (1996) "Matra Withdraws Officials Amid Rail Closure Dispute" *Free China Journal* June p.4.
Connolly, Janis (1996) "Double Trouble: Taiwan's Second Mass Rapid Transit Project Is On The Rails" *Topics* (Taipei American Chamber of Commerce) September pp. 27-31.
Department of Rapid Transit Systems (.n.d) *An Introduction to the Rapid Transit Systems of*

the Taipei Metropolitan Area Taipei: TMG.

Environmental Protection (...cchome.com/info/yearbook/nf_html/chl3_l.html).

FCR (1991a) "Growth Outruns Policies" *Free China Review* August pp. 12-18.

FCR (1991b) "Cities with Rough Edges" *Free China Review* August..

FCR (1991c) "Transportation Tensions" *Free China Review* March pp. 14-18.

FCR (1992) "Edge Cities" *Free China Review* February.

FCR (1996a) "City Life" *Free China Review* June pp. 30-33.

FCR (1996b) "Heart Trouble: Kaohsiung City Profile," *Free China Review* September.

Harmsen, Peter (1996) "Railway Slowdown" *Far Eastern Economic Review* July pp. 50-52.

Hwang, Jim (1991) "Sliding toward Gridlock" *Free China Review* March pp. 4-13.

Hwang, Jim (1996) "Boomtown or Bust: Kaohsiung City Profile," *Free China Review* September.

Jacobs, J. Bruce; Jean Hagger, and Ann Sedgley (1984) *Taiwan: A Comprehensive Bibliography of English-Language Publications* LaTrobe University, Australia, and Columbia University.

Liu, Philip (1991a) "Stuck On The Freeway," *Free China Review* March pp. 30-35.

Liu, Philip (1991b) "New Towns, Old Problems, Bigger Plans," *Free China Review* August pp 26-31.

Liu, Weiling (1997) "Tamsui Mass-Rapid-Transit Line Opens" *Free China Journal* April p. 4.

Pannell, Clifton W. (1974) "Development and the Middle City in Taiwan," *Growth and Change* Vol. 5 pp. 21-29.

Republic of China Yearbook (1996) (Government Information Office), p. 230.

Shaw, Shih-lung and Jack F. Williams (1991) "Role of Transportation in Taiwan's Regional Development" *Transportation Quarterly* Vol. 45, No. 2, April pp. 271-296.

Speare, Alden, and Paul K. C. Liu, Ching-lung Tsay (1988) Urbanisation and Development: The Rural-Urban Transition in Taiwan , Westview Press.

Todd, Daniel; and Yi-chung Hsueh (1988) "Taiwan: Some Spatial Implications of Rapid Economic Growth," *Geoforum* Vol. 19, No. 2 pp. 133-145.

Todd, Daniel; and Yi-chung Hsueh (1990) "New Port Developments and Balanced Regional Growth: A Taiwan Example," *Geoforum* Vol. 21, No. 4: 421-433.

Tseng, Osman (1991) "Auto Insurers in a Crunch" *Free China Review* August pp. 49-53.

Urban and Regional Development Statistics, Republic of China (1996) Executive Yuan: Council for Economic Planning and Development, Urban and Housing Development Department.

Williams, Jack F. (1988) "Urban and Regional Planning in Taiwan: The Quest for Balanced Regional Development," *Tijdschrift voor Economische en Sociale Geografie* Vol.79, No. 3, pp. 175-187.

Williams, Jack F. (1996) "The Quality of Life in Taiwan: An Environmental Assessment," The *American Asian Review* Vol. 14, No. 3 pp. 79-105.

Williams, Jack F.; and C.Y. Chang, and C.Y. Wang (1983) "Land Settlement and Development: A Case Study From Taiwan" *Journal of Developing Areas* Vol. 18, No. 1 pp. 35-52.

Yeung, Irene (1991) "A Slow Start to Rapid Transit" *Free China Review* March pp. 20-25.

3   Central City and Satellite Towns: A Study of Metropolitan Structure in Taiwan

Kao-Chiao Hsieh

3.1   Introduction

In Taiwan the metropolitan city has become the dominant form of Taiwanese settlement. Between 1956 and 1995 the number of urban places increased from 11 to 35, increasing their share of the national population from 25% to 56%. During this period the number of cities with populations exceeding 500,000 increased from 1 (0.3% of the total population) to 5 (29% of the total population), and the number between 100,000 and 500,000 from 5 (25%) to 22 (24%).

In this urbanisation process, differences exist among the cities, towns and smaller communities not only in size but also in function (Hsieh 1992). These different sized places are interrelated: they exchange different sorts of goods and services and are connected by communications lines. Industrialisation and economic development produces a system of city sizes. The larger the place, the wider the range of market functions it performs, serving large hinterlands as well as other communities. Small places serve very general market functions for small hinterlands. Small places serve fewer functions, while large places serve more and provide for increasingly specialized needs. All the places, large and small, perform such functions as residence, employment, consumer activity, and administration but have different emphases. Metropolitan development not only represents a decentralization of the residential population, but also includes a redistribution of many industrial, commercial, and cultural activities over an ever-expanding land area surrounding the central cities. Metropolitan growth generally has consisted of the movements of people and activities from the centre of urban concentrations outward toward the periphery over an ever-expanding radius of land. There are functional interdependence and linkages between central city and its surrounding areas. But what is the relationship of a central city to its surrounding areas and what is the linkage among them? This question has fascinated urban sociologists and geographers for generations (Choldin 1985).

The traditional ecological theory of metropolitan organisation considers the central city as integrating and supporting a resident population and the population of the surrounding area. Nearby communities are oriented toward

42

this dominant centre and provide labor and consumer for the central city economy. Thus, the metropolitan area is dominated by a single centre that coordinates and integrates a dependent periphery.

However, with the deconcentration of manufacturing and retailing, the suburbs gain significant autonomy (Hunter 1974; Muller 1981), and in many cases compete with the core (Stanback 1991). Many research findings show that suburbia is a dynamic setting, its social, institutional, and demographic structure becoming more diverse, complex, and urban than previously realized (Berry and Kasarda 1977; Gold 1982). New perspectives recognize the growing influence of suburbs and other off-centre activities (Dunn 1983). As Hughes (1993) reviewed, the researchers agree that significant reorganization of the metropolitan community has occurred over the past 20 years, but they agree less on the structure of the evolving system, the role of suburbs in the metropolitan hierarchy, or the causes of metropolitan restructuring.

This chapter asks, what is the relationship of central city in Taiwan metropolis to its surrounding areas? Can the pattern of western metropolitan structure adequately apply to the case of Taiwan?

3.2   Growth of Metropolitan Structure

I review here briefly some of the main structural themes concerning metropolitan growth.

3.2.1 Urban Expansion

Cities grew to be quite large before they began to interact routinely with their outlying settlement units to form a single interdependent system (Berry and Kasarda 1977). In the early 19th century, the introduction of the railroads and barge canal systems, both adapted for long-haul movement, released cities from a previous dependency on their immediate hinterland and the natural waterways for the provision of agricultural commodities. With the importation of food surplus and other raw materials from distant inland territories, cities grew rapidly in size. Their growth, however, occurred to a large extent through increases in population density; the scope of community interdependence remained essentially constant. Outlying towns and villages continued to function as semi-independent entities, each providing its own specialized services and community facilities.

Efficient transportation signalled the beginnings of widespread population deconcentration and functional specialization of local land areas. No longer was it necessary to reside in an area close to the workplace. Places of employment and places of residence became increasingly separated. Similarly, the differentiation of local areas was made possible, so that professional, administrative, clerical, financial, and other specialized activities could each be efficiently concentrated in certain location rather than distributed throughout the community. The urban centre area developed as an organisational hub, and as population dispersed outward along the rail lines, the entire community or metropolis began to acquire a new structure.

3.2.2 Spatial differentiation of social and function

According to Hawley (1950), improvements in transportation and communication reduce the friction of space and permit a wider scatter of an interrelated population without loss of contact. When the cost of travel is high, differentiation of function is limited, but, when the friction of space is overcome by improved systems of transportation and communications then and then only can an area develop fully its various use potentialities (1950:238).

Zoning is another factor of spatial differentiation. It is a municipal legal process that divides the land area into zoning districts, each having specific conditions under which land and buildings may be legally developed and used (Choldin 1985). Zoning has tended to reinforce the ecological process producing differentiation among sub-areas in urban area.

3.2.3 Division of Residence and Work

In the modern metropolis few people live and work in the same place, and this separation, multiplied by large numbers of individuals, contributes strongly to the spatial differentiation of the metropolis (Choldin 1985). In the West there is an increase in tele-working from home – so perhaps the differentiation has passed its peak.

3.2.4 Central Business District

The central business district is the centre of the central city, and is the focus of commercial, social, and civic life, and transportation. The CBD itself is differentiated into two parts, the core and the surrounding frame. The core has the highest intensity of land use, with its multistoried buildings, and has the densest daytime population. It accommodates the functions of finance, department stores, and the headquarters and main-office of corporation (Berry and Kasarda 1977). Typical activities in the frame are wholesaling with stocks, light manufacturing, service industries, and transportation facilities. A great deal of functional change has taken place since Berry and Kasarda made the above observations.

3.2.5 Satellites and Suburbs

The mature industrial city has at least a few suburbs and is likely to have one or more satellite cities. Satellites differ from suburbs in that they are separated from the central city by many miles and in general have little daily commuting to or from the central cities, although economic activities of the satellite are closely geared to those of the central city (Harris and Ullman 1945). The satellite is basically subordinated to the larger city, but it retains a high degree of independence stemming from its importance as a production and employment centre (Schnore 1968). The satellite has one or two major factories and offers employment to its own residents and, in some cases, to commuters as well, unlike the suburban "bedroom community." (Choldin 1985) However, suburbs recently have evolved into much more highly differentiated areas: there are business suburbs and residential ones, new and old, large and small.

These characteristics imply a pattern of metropolitan structure. The central city plays a dominant role in the relationship with its surrounding areas, but suburbs or satellites retain certain degrees of self-sufficiency, even creating employment opportunities for attracting people. The relationship between central city and suburbs or satellites is not linear but reciprocal with strongly toward the central city.

3.3   Data and Method

3.3.1 Data Source

The data used in this study were adopted from 1990 Taiwan-Fukien Census' data files, and based on the observation units of the district of city and the urban township or the village township of county.

3.3.2 Variables and Definitions

Commuting patterns are the indicator of function and dominance. They are recognized as a principle indicator of economic and social integration in early theories of intra-metropolitan relationships (McKenzie 1933), and they have been used to define metropolitan cities (Filina 1987). Commuting patterns are a more tangible indicator of intra-metropolitan relationships (Hughes 1993). Thus, the commuting patterns are an important factor in forming metropolitan structure, and their variations between central city and satellite town are used to observe their relationships or the metropolitan structure.

The question "Where is your workplace?" is included in 1990 Census. This question is used to measure commuting patterns. It has four responses: present address, different place in same district or township, different district or township in the same city or county and different cities or counties. According to the question, the employed population who are 15 years old and over are our subjects, and they are classified into two categories: workers at home and commuting workers. The former are those who work at home; the latter includes workers working outside home but in the same district or township, different district or township in the same city or county and different cities or counties. They all are defined as commuting workers.

The Metropolitan area is defined using the criteria described in *Statistical Areas of Republic of China*. The criteria are described as follows:

A metropolitan area refers to one central city (or two central cities) and its (their) satellite towns which are socially and economically integrated to the central city.

(1) Central city: the central city of a metropolitan area has a population of 200,000 and over, 70% of the residents living in the urbanised area, and 70% of the employed residents working in the city and the townships.

(2) Satellite town: lies outside the central city limit and also has one of the following conditions:

At least 10% of the residents commuting to central city for work; less than 10% and over 5% of the employed residents commuting to central city for work.

If the commuting rate of employed residents of a city, an urban or rural township can be included in two different metropolitan areas, then the satellite is assigned to the city with which it has the greater flows, or if the flows are the same, then to the nearer one.

A large metropolis has a population over one million, and a sub-metropolis has a population under one million and over 300,000.

According to these criteria, eight metropolitan areas are identified in Taiwan, as follows (see also Map 2.1):

I. Large metropolis
Taipei-Keelung
Kaohsiung
Taichung-Changhwa Tainan
Chungli-Taoyuan

II. Sub-metropolis
Hsinchu
Chiayi (on Map 2.1 spelt Chia-i)

According to the criteria of population size, manufacturing, commerce, financing and transport, these eight metropolitan areas can be ranked in order. Taipei-Keelung is the largest one, Kaohsiung next, and Taichung-Changhwa third, the others are Tainan, Chungli-Taoyuan, Hsinchu, and Chiayi in order (Hsieh 1997).

3.3.3 Measurement of Metropolitan Structure

We defined the following indices to measure the metropolitan fields:
(1) Functional activity index: daytime population/ the employed population. If the value is over one, the functional activity of area is toward employment; if the value is less than one, the functional activity of area is toward residence.
(2) Employment self-sufficiency: (workers at home + workers outside home but in the same town)/employed population. The higher the value of index, the higher the employment sufficiency.
(3) Commuting index: (workers coming to work from other districts or towns + workers going to work in other districts or towns)/ employed population. It indicates the level of commuting activity.
(4) Influence index: this index divides into three parts: the influence of central city on satellite towns (ICCS), the influence of central city on the areas outside the metropolitan area (ICCM), and the influence of satellite town on the areas outside the metropolitan area (ISTM).

ICCS = (workers from satellites coming to work in central city – workers from central city going to work in satellites)/ employed population.

ICCM = (workers from coming non-metropolitan areas to work in central city – workers from central city to work in non-metropolitan areas)/ employed population.

ISTM = (workers from non-metropolitan areas coming to work in satellites – workers from satellites going to work in non-metropolitan areas)/ employed population.

High positive values indicate the city is a dominant employer for the subordinate area. High negative values show the reverse.

3.4   Analysis and Results

The results of computation for all the study areas is given in Tables 3.1 to 3.7. Here commentary is restricted to Taipei Metropolitan area and Table 3.1, but the reader will be able to make similar diagnoses of the other areas.

Table 3.1 Analysis of Relationship between Central City and Satellite Towns in Taipei-Keelung Metropolitan Area

	Functional Activity Index	Employment Self-Sufficieny Index	Commuting Index	Influence Index		
				Central city to Satellite towns	Central city to non-metropolitan	Satellite towns to non-metropolitan
Taipei Metropolitan Area	1.00	0.59	0.82	-	-	-
Central City	1.17	0.60	0.98	0.17	0.01	-
Sungshan	1.89	0.67	1.54	0.38	0.09	-
Ta-An	1.24	0.60	1.04	0.21	0.01	-
Chungchen	2.30	0.74	1.82	0.63	0.05	-
Wanhwa	0.95	0.63	0.69	0.11	-0.01	-
Tatung	1.27	0.67	0.94	0.20	0.02	-
Chungshan	1.99	0.74	1.51	0.40	0.06	-
Wenshan	0.63	0.42	0.79	-0.02	-0.02	-
Nankang	1.03	0.57	0.89	0.09	0.03	-
Neihu	0.59	0.43	0.74	-0.01	-0.02	-
Shihlin	0.82	0.58	0.67	0.02	-0.01	-
Peitou	0.71	0.58	0.56	-0.02	-0.02	-
Hsin-I	0.77	0.56	0.64	0.02	-0.02	-
Satellite Towns	0.82	0.59	0.65	-0.16	-	-0.01
Panchiao	0.79	0.61	0.58	-0.16	-	-0.01
Sanchung	0.91	0.68	0.56	-0.12	-	0.00
Yungho	0.47	0.35	0.77	-0.43	-	-0.03
Chungho	0.67	0.49	0.69	-0.26	-	-0.03
Hsintien	0.76	0.50	0.77	-0.24	-	-0.02
Hsinchuang	0.94	0.67	0.60	-0.07	-	-0.01
Shunlin	1.10	0.70	0.69	-0.04	-	0.01
Sanhsia	0.95	0.73	0.49	-0.02	-	0.00
Tanshui	0.98	0.71	0.57	-0.06	-	0.00
Hsichuh	0.74	0.49	0.76	-0.28	-	0.06

Tucheng	0.90	0.63	0.63	-0.08	-	-0.01
Luchou	0.79	0.60	0.58	-0.12	-	0.00
Wuku	1.22	0.68	0.86	-0.01	-	0.00
Taishan	0.93	0.61	0.71	-0.05	-	-0.01
Linkou	1.56	0.72	1.11	0.12	-	0.08
Shenkeng	1.00	0.59	0.83	-0.07	-	0.00
Shihting	0.69	0.50	0.68	-0.15	-	0.00
Pinglin	1.23	0.79	0.66	0.14	-	0.07
Sanchih	0.83	0.66	0.51	-0.05	-	0.02
Shihmen	1.03	0.72	0.60	-0.02	-	0.03
Pali	1.00	0.72	0.56	-0.03	-	0.03
Pingchi	0.58	0.45	0.68	-0.15	-	-0.01
Shuangchi	1.42	0.44	1.54	0.13	-	0.16
Kungliao	0.71	0.61	0.48	-0.09	-	-0.04
Chinshan	0.87	0.66	0.55	-0.07	-	0.03
Wulai	0.81	0.63	0.58	-0.12	-	-0.04
Keelung						
Metropolitan Area	0.81	0.53	0.76	-	-	-
Central city	0.83	0.52	0.79	0.01	-0.02	-
Chungchen	1.17	0.64	0.90	0.02	0.12	-
Chitu	0.89	0.57	0.75	0.01	-0.03	-
Nuannuan	0.52	0.37	0.78	-0.02	-0.06	-
Jen-Ai	1.06	0.62	0.83	0.01	-0.03	-
Chungshan	0.78	0.53	0.71	0.01	-0.06	-
Anlu	0.51	0.38	0.76	0.00	-0.07	-
Hsin-I	0.59	0.39	0.80	0.00	-0.05	-
Satellite towns	0.73	0.57	0.59	-0.04	-	-0.07
Juifan	0.73	0.57	0.59	-0.02	-	-0.08
Wanli	0.75	0.57	0.61	-0.07	-	-0.04

Notes: 1. The influence of central city on satellite towns(central city)=(workers from satellites to central city-workers from central city to satellites)/employ population(satellites)=(Workers from central city to satellites-workers from satellites to central city) / employed population.
2. The influence of central city on non-metropolitan area=(workers from non-metropolitan area to central city-workers from central city to non-metropolitan area) / employed population.
3. The influence of satellites on non-metropolitan area=(workers from non-metropolitan area to satellites-workers from satellites to non-metropolitan area) / employed population.

Table 3.2 Analysis of Relationship between Central City and Satellite Towns in Kaohsiung Metropolitan Area

	Functional Activity Index	Employment Self-Sufficiency Index	Commuting Index	Influence Index: Central city to Satellite towns	Central city to non-metropolitan	Satellite towns to non-metropolitan
Kaohsiung Metropolitan Area	0.99	0.15	0.69			
Central City	1.11	0.12	0.79	0.10	0.01	-
Yenchen	1.47	0.21	1.24	0.19	0.10	-
Kushan	0.90	0.12	0.72	0.03	-0.01	-
Tsoying	0.83	0.11	0.70	0.02	-0.01	-
Nantzu	1.31	0.08	0.93	0.17	0.02	-
Sanmin	1.00	0.14	0.59	0.03	0.02	-
Hsinsing	1.42	0.19	1.28	0.21	0.04	-
Chienchin	1.61	0.17	1.48	0.22	0.07	-
Linya	0.91	0.11	0.67	0.03	-0.01	-
Chienchen	1.21	0.10	0.79	0.15	0.01	-
Chiching	0.97	0.09	0.55	0.06	-0.01	-
Hsiaokang	1.43	0.08	0.88	0.23	0.05	-
Satellite Towns	0.85	0.18	0.58	-0.12	-	-0.02
Fengshan	0.69	0.15	0.66	-0.27	-	-0.02
Kangshan	0.99	0.20	0.61	-0.04	-	-0.01
Chishan	0.85	0.18	0.40	-0.09	-	-0.07
Mwinung	0.73	0.33	0.32	-0.10	-	-0.11
Linyuan	0.92	0.13	0.62	-0.10	-	0.05
Taliao	1.04	0.25	0.67	-0.06	-	0.00
Tashu	0.84	0.16	0.45	-0.08	-	-0.03
Jenwu	1.43	0.17	1.12	0.19	-	-0.08
Tashe	0.98	0.11	0.70	-0.01	-	-0.02
Niaosung	0.96	0.14	0.91	-0.08	-	0.00
Chiaotou	0.77	0.22	0.74	-0.18	-	-0.02
Yenchao	0.90	0.18	0.45	-0.05	-	-0.05
Mito	0.67	0.12	0.50	-0.11	-	-0.12
Tzukuan	0.34	0.11	0.48	-0.17	-	-0.05
Shanlin	1.07	0.33	0.37	-0.10	-	-0.16
Pingtung	0.95	0.14	0.44	-0.05	-	0.02
Linlo	0.70	0.41	0.64	-0.08	-	-0.03

Note: 1. The influence of central city on satellite towns(central city)=(workers from satellites to central city - workers from central city to satellites) / employed population (satellites)=(Workers from central city to satellites - workers from satellites to central city) / employed population.

2 . The influence of central city on non-metropolitan area=(workers from non-metropolitan area to central city - workers from central city to non-metropolitan area) / employed population.
3. The influence of satellites on non-metropolitan area=(workers from non-metropolitan area to satellites - workers from satellites to non-metropolitan area) / employed population.

Table 3.3   Analysis of Relationship between Central City and Satellite Towns in Taichung-Changhwa Metropolitan Area

| | Functional Activity Index | Employment Self-Sufficieny Index | Commuting Index | Influence Index | | |
				Central city to Satellite towns	Central city to non-metropolitan	Satellite towns to non-metropolitan
Taichung Metropolitan Area	0.50	0.70	0.62	-	- -	
Central City	0.52	0.71	0.69	0.05	0.06	-
Central	0.49	0.77	3.08	0.70	1.18	-
East	0.47	0.70	0.61	0.05	0.02	-
West	0.48	0.66	0.75	0.04	0.04	-
South	0.48	0.69	0.78	0.10	0.07	-
North	0.57	0.73	0.55	0.01	0.02	-
Hsitun	0.61	0.79	0.59	0.07	0.04	-
Nantun	0.54	0.71	0.59	0.04	0.02	-
Peitun	0.49	0.67	0.48	-0.04	-0.03	-
Satellite Towns	0.48	0.69	0.53	-0.08	-	-0.03
Tantzu	0.54	0.74	0.71	0.04	-	-0.07
Taya	0.43	0.75	0.50	-0.03	-	-0.07
Wujih	0.47	0.66	0.60	-0.09	-	0.03
Tatu	0.49	0.69	0.47	-0.10	-	-0.03
Lungchin	0.44	0.66	0.48	-0.08	-	-0.15
Wufeng	0.53	0.70	0.49	-0.07	-	0.00
Taiping	0.48	0.71	0.48	-0.10	-	-0.02
Tali	0.45	0.66	0.55	-0.12	-	0.00
Changhwa Metropolitan Area	0.62	0.81	0.40	-	-	-
Central City	0.65	0.84	0.41	0.01	0.08	-
Satellite Towns	0.55	0.77	0.37	-0.05	-	-0.01
Homei	0.57	0.81	0.32	-0.05	-	0.02
Huatan	0.53	0.71	0.45	-0.05	-	-0.05

Table 3.4 Analysis of Relationship between Central City and Satellite Towns in Chungli-Taoyuan Metropolitan Area

	Functional Activity Index	Employment Self-Sufficieny Index	Commuting Index	Influence Index		
				Central city to Satellite towns	Central city to non-metropolitan	Satellite towns to non-metropolitan
Chungli Metropolitan Area	0.51	0.69	0.59	-	-	-
Central City	0.63	0.78	0.63	0.16	0.03	-
Satellite Towns	0.43	0.63	0.57	-0.10	-	-0.04
Yangmei	0.53	0.70	0.56	-0.05	-	-0.02
Lungtan	0.49	0.65	0.68	-0.03	-	0.07
Pingchen	0.40	0.54	0.57	-0.18	-	-0.10
Hsinwu	0.33	0.68	0.48	-0.08	-	-0.06
Kuanyin	0.32	0.70	0.46	-0.10	-	-0.01
Taoyuan Metropolitan Area	0.54	0.70	0.60	-	-	-
Central City	0.60	0.74	0.66	0.06	0.07	0.10
Satellite Towns	0.51	0.68	0.57	-0.04	-	0.01
Yingko	0.57	0.71	0.49	-0.06	-	-0.01
Tachi	0.52	0.72	0.49	-0.05	-	0.02
Luchu	0.55	0.78	0.58	0.03	-	0.09
Kueishan	0.49	0.65	0.70	-0.03	-	0.01
Pate	0.48	0.62	0.57	-0.08	-	-0.03

Table 3.5   Analysis of Relationship between Central City and Satellite Towns in Tainan Metropolitan Area

	Functional Activity Index	Employment Self-Sufficieny Index	Commuting Index	Influence Index		
				Central city to Satellite towns	*Central city to non-metropolitan*	*Satellite towns to non-metropolitan*
Tainan Metropolitan Area	1.01	0.70	0.61	-	-	-
Central City	1.03	0.72	0.59	0.02	0.01	-
East	0.98	0.67	0.64	-0.01	0.01	-
South	1.03	0.77	0.49	0.04	-0.01	-
West	0.97	0.63	0.71	0.02	0.04	-
North	0.89	0.67	0.55	-0.03	-0.04	-
Central	1.54	0.66	1.22	0.15	0.12	-
An-Nan	0.98	0.82	0.34	0.00	0.01	-
Anping	1.33	0.64	1.05	0.11	0.12	-
Satellite Towns	0.99	0.68	0.62	-0.02	-	0.02
Chiku	0.75	0.65	0.44	-0.09	-	-0.14
Anting	0.80	0.69	0.41	-0.09	-	-0.07
Jente	1.41	0.75	0.90	0.12	-	0.14
Kueijen	0.89	0.68	0.52	-0.03	-	-0.01
Kuanmiao	0.81	0.68	0.44	-0.06	-	-0.03
Yungkang	1.11	0.69	0.73	0.02	-	0.08
Hu-Nei	0.88	0.67	0.54	-0.05	-	0.03
Chiehting	0.63	0.57	0.49	-0.25	-	-0.06

Table 3.6   Analysis of Relationship between Central City and Satellite Towns in Hsinchu Metropolitan Area

	Functional Activity Index	Employment Self-Sufficieny Index	Commuting Index	Influence Index Central city to Satellite towns	Influence Index Central city to non-metropolitan	Influence Index Satellite towns to non-metropolitan
Hsinchu Metropolitan Area	0.93	0.75	0.44	-	-	-
Central City	1.04	0.87	0.30	0.07	-0.03	-
Satellite Towns	0.79	0.59	0.61	-0.08	-	-0.14
Hsinpu	0.79	0.61	0.58	-0.05	-	-0.15
Chutung	0.78	0.59	0.59	-0.12	-	-0.09
Hengshan	0.62	0.50	0.62	-0.10	-	-0.29
Hsiunglin	0.63	0.52	0.58	-0.10	-	-0.20
Paoshan	0.67	0.56	0.55	-0.21	-	-0.09
Peipu	0.66	0.54	0.58	-0.11	-	-0.10
Chupei	0.94	0.63	0.68	0.00	-	-0.16

Table 3.7   Analysis of Relationship between Central City and Satellite Towns in Chiayi Metropolitan Area

	Functional Activity Index	Employment Self-Sufficieny Index	Commuting Index	Influence Index Central city to Satellite towns	Influence Index Central city to non-metropolitan	Influence Index Satellite towns to non-metropolitan
Chiayi Metropolitan Area	0.94	0.76	0.39	-	-	-
Central City	1.00	0.80	0.40	0.02	-0.03	-
Satellite Towns	0.80	0.72	0.37	-0.09	-	-0.11
Shuishang	0.81	0.71	0.39	-0.08	-	-0.11
Chungpu	0.78	0.72	0.35	-0.09	-	-0.12

3.4.1 Differentiation of Taipei-Keelung Metropolitan Area Functional Activities

The central city has a functional activity index over 1 – the day-time population exceeds the resident employed population. Some districts within the central city show high values (like Chungchen and Chungshan) - but others are below 1 showing that there are areas which are more residential. A few of the satellite towns (Linkou, Shunlin, Pinglin) are employment centres, but quite a number are more residential like Yungho, Chungho, Shihting and Hsintien with much lower values.

As for Keelung metropolis, the index of functional activity is 0.83, because Keelung metropolis is adjacent to Taipei metropolitan area, and it has gradually fallen under Taipei's social and economic influence. Taipei and Keelung have merged into one large metropolitan area.

To summarise from these and the other cases in Tables 3.2 to 3.7, according to the functional activities index, it seems that employment and residence are not so much differentiated, but areas are more mixed. Both central city and satellite perform both functions, the only difference between them is that the employment activity is more developed in the central cities and the residential function is more developed in the satellites.

However, functional variations do exist among the sub-areas of central city and satellites. Some industrial centres have developed in the satellite towns.

3.4.2 Taipei-Keelung Metropolitan Area and Commuting Patterns

The commuting index is defined as the ratio of those commuting in and out to the employed population. In Taipei city only 10% of the employed population are home workers and 50% outside-home workers in same district. The indexes of employment self-sufficiency and commuting in the central city of Taipei are respectively 0.60 and 0.98, meaning that it has lower employment self-sufficiency and higher commuting movement. As for the sub-areas of central city, the outer districts like Neihu, Wenshan, Peitou and Shihlin have lower employment self-sufficiency; the inner districts like Chungchen, Sungshan and Chungshan have higher commuting movement; and the older districts like Tatung, Wanhwa, Chungshan and Shihlin have higher home workers. It clearly shows that the age and ecological location can account for the difference of employment self-sufficiency and commuting movement among the sub-areas of central city.

The indexes of employment self-sufficiency and commuting in the satellites of Taipei metropolis are respectively 0.59 and 0.65. Based on the proportion of home workers, the satellites also have lower employment self-sufficiency, but their commuting index is not so high, because they have a higher proportion of outside-home workers remaining in their own towns. Among the satellite towns, Yungho, Chungho, Hsintien, Hsichuh, Pingchi and Shuangchi have lower employment self-sufficiency; Linkou, Shuangchi, Shenkeng and Wuku have higher commuting movement. It is found that the towns adjacent to central city have lower employment self-sufficiency, the towns that developed the institutional and industrial activities have more commuting workers, and the outer towns have more home workers.

As for Keelung metropolis, the indexes of employment self-sufficiency and commuting in the central city are respectively 0.52 and 0.79. As the figures show, both central city and the satellites have the same employment self-sufficiency, particularly in home workers, but the central city has more commuting workers. In comparison with Taipei, Keelung not only has lower employment self-sufficiency but also has lower commuting movement, because it has great outflow of workers.

From the employment self-sufficiency and commuting movement described above, it is found that the scale of metropolitan areas and the ecological location of the sub-areas are mainly related to the division of work and residence. (1) The larger the metropolitan scale, the lower the employment self-sufficiency and the higher the commuting movement. In other words, the larger the metropolitan size, the larger the separation of work and residence. In the early period of metropolitan growth, e.g., Hsinchu, Chiayi and Changhwa, the separation of work and residence is lower and mostly limited in the local area. Then, with the increasing of metropolitan growth, e.g., Tainan, Taichung, Chungli and Taoyuan, commuters increase and home workers decrease, it results in the widening of the separation between work and residence.

The separation of work and residence varies with the central cities and the satellites. The central cities have fewer home-workers and more outside-home workers in the local area or the other areas, the satellites have more home-workers and less the outside-home workers. With more metropolitan growth, more and more the satellite workers commute to work in the central city.

3.4.3 Dominance and Self-sufficiency

For understanding the relationship between central city, satellites and non-metropolitan areas, three 'influence' indices were established. These are: the influence of central city on satellites or non-metropolitan areas, and the influence of satellites on non-metropolitan areas. If the value of index is positive, it is dominance; if negative, it is dominated. The larger the value, the greater the dominance; the more the value comes to close zero, the more the self-sufficiency.

Taipei-Keelung Metropolitan Area

The influence index of central city on satellites is 0.17 and that of satellites on central city is –0.16. (Table 1) Generally speaking, Taipei city has dominated its satellites by the force of employment. However, the dominance varies with sub-areas. The core places of the central city, e.g., Chungchen, Chungshan, Sungshan and Tatung, have greater dominance over the satellites; and the outer areas of Wenshan, Neihu and Peitou are less dominant over the satellites. On the other hand, the satellite towns adjacent to the central city like Yungho, Chungho, Hsintien and Hsichuh were much dominated; the towns of Wuku, Shihmen, Pali, Sanhsia and Shunlin retain a relatively self-sufficient position; and the towns like Linkou and Shuangchi are dominant.

The influence index of central city on non-metropolitan area is weak - 0.01. In fact, the satellite towns like Hsichuh, Pali, Shihmen, Shuangchi and Chinshan have greater dominance in the non-metropolitan area. This may appear logical in that the satellites are 'nearer' the non-metropolitan areas.

In Keelung metropolis, the influence index of central city on satellites is 0.01 and that of satellites on central city is -0.04. It shows that all the sub-areas of Keelung metropolis are dominated by non-metropolitan areas, meaning in this case Taipei.

In sum, the central city does provide employment for the workers of satellites. With the metropolitan growth the dominance increases, but its intensity varies with the development of central cities. For example, Chungli recently developed rapidly and has a greater influence, but the limited development of Keelung and the slow development of Tainan only have a light influence. Generally speaking, the influence of central city on the satellites in the metropolitan area is not strong and the satellite towns retain certain degree of self-sufficiency. Moreover, the influence of central city and satellites on the non-metropolitan area varied with the scales and developments of central cities. For example, such larger central cities as Taipei, Kaohsiung, Taichung and Tainan, or the rapidly developing central cities like Chungli, Taoyuan and Changhwa exercised greater influence on the non-metropolitan area. On the contrary, the small scale of central city, or slowly developed central cities, tend to be influenced by the non-metropolitan area, particularly industrial areas.

3.5   Summary and Conclusion

Based on the commuting data in the 1990 Taiwan Census, this chapter uses three dimensions of structure: functional activity, division of work and residence, and dominance to analyse the metropolitan structure in Taiwan.

Employment and residential activities are mixed together in both the central cities and the satellites, but, the employment is more developed in the central cities, and the residential functions are more developed in the satellites.

The separation between work and residence has different developments in both the central cities and the satellites. Generally speaking, the central cities have a lower proportion of home workers and a higher proportion of commuting workers than the satellites do, but both places have a moderate proportion of outside-home workers working in the local area.

The movement of workers in the central cities and the satellites is not unilateral but multidirectional. The central cities or the satellites and their sub-areas have simultaneously experienced the inflow and outflow of workers: how much the workers flow in or out an area will depend on which functions developed more significantly in the area.

However, the commuting of the metropolitan workers is not limited to the mobility between the central city and the satellites, there is a higher mobility among their sub-areas or between the sub-areas and non-metropolitan area. Therefore, commuting between areas is not unilateral mobility or reciprocal mobility but multidirectional and cyclical mobility. However, if the satellite towns developed more significantly, the central city mobility may change, and the satellite town may become a centre for mobility and have an inflow. This occurred in the satellites of Chiayi, Changhwa, Keelung, Chungli, and Taoyuan.

Generally speaking, the workers who live in the central cities mostly engage in short-distance movement, and the workers in the satellites made more long-distance movement. The relative absence of short-distance commuting in Taiwan metropolitan areas may reflect the poor links between central cities and satellites, so that commuters cannot adequately play their role and promote the complex development of industrialised Taiwanese society.

Finally, regardless of the central city's dominance the satellite towns remained moderately self-sufficient in the metropolitan area. From the observation of the satellites which retained a higher proportion of their own workers, and even attracted workers from other places, the satellites in Taiwan have not lost their self-sufficiency in response to the dominance of central city, conversely, they have created employment opportunities for workers.

In fact, the satellite towns are not newly created residential areas, rather they are trade or commercial townships which had existed independently in the surrounding areas. With the industrialisation and economic development of Taiwan, they gradually became socially and economically involved in the network of large cities. They came to be the parts of a large metropolitan area, attracting the relocation of manufacturing industry and population from the central cities. The satellites of metropolitan areas in Taiwan are neither typical residential nor typical industrial towns, and their functions of residence and employment go together and make it possible to maintain a relatively self-sufficiency.

So far, metropolitan growth has not produced a high level of integration and co-ordination between the central city and the satellites in Taiwan.

References

Baldassare, Mark. 1992. "Suburban Communities." *Annual Review of Sociology* 18: 475-494.

Berry, Brian J.L. and John D. Kasarda. 1977. *Contemporary Urban Ecology*. NewYork: Macmillan.

Bogue, Donald J. 1949. *The Structure of the Metropolitan Community*. Ann Arbor: University of Michigan.

Castells, Manuel. 1985. "High Technology, Economic Restructuring, and the Urban-Regional Process in the United States." Pp.11-40 in *High Tecnology, Space and Society, edited* by M. Castells. Beverly Hills, CA: Sage Publications.

Choldin, Harvey M. 1985. *Cities and Suburbs: An Introduction to Urban Sociology*. New York: McGraw-Hill.

Clark, C. 1951. "Urban Population Density." *Journal of the Royal Statistical Society*, Series A, 114: 490-496.

Dunn, Edgar S. 1983. *The Development of the U.S. Urban System: Industrial Shifts, Implications*. Vol.2 Baltimore, MD: Johns Hopkins University.

Filina, V. N. 1987. "The Influence of Local Commuting Patterns on Urban Settlement Systems." *Soviet Geographer* 28: 728-741.

Gold, Harvey. 1982. *The Sociology of Urban Life*. Englewood Cliffs. N. J.: Prentice-Hall.

Gottdiener, Mark. 1985. *The Social Production of Urban Space*. Austin Tx: University of Texas Press.

Greene, David L. 1980. "Urban Subcentres: Recent Trends in Urban Spatial Structure." *Growth and Change* 11: 29-40.

Harris, Chauncey and Edward L. Ullman. 1945. "The Nature of Cities." *Annals of the American Academy of Political and Social Science* 242: 7-17.

Hawley, Amos H. 1950. *Human Ecology: A Theory of Community Structure*. New York: The Ronald Press.

Hawley, Amos H. 1971. *Urban Society: An Ecological Approach*. New York: Ronald Press.

Hsieh, Kao-Chiao. 1990. *Urban Structure Pattern: A Case Study of Kaohsiung City*. Taipei: Chiu-Liu Publisher.

Hsieh, Kao-Chiao. 1992. "The Differential Distribution of Demographic and Socio-Economic Characteristics Between Metropolitan Area and Non-Metropolitan Area." *Journal of National Chengchi University*. 65: 133-162.

Hsieh, Kao-Chiao. 1997. The Metropolitan Structure of Taiwan-An Analysis of Daytime Population and Night-time Population. *Research Report* (NSC 84-2412-H-004-008 K6) National Scientific Commission of Executive Yuan. ROC.

Hughes, Holly L. 1993. "Metropolitan Structure and the Suburban Hierarchy." *American Sociological Review* 58: 417-433.

Hunter, Albert. 1974. "Suburban Autonomy / Dependency: Elite Perception." *Social Science Quarterly* 65: 181-189.

James, Franklin J. 1974. *Models of Employment and Residential Location*. New Jersey: Rutgers University Press.

Logan, John R. 1976. "Industrialization and the Stratification of Cities in Suburban Regions." *American Journal of Sociology* 82: 333-348.

Marshall, Harvey and John Stahura. 1986. "The Theory of Ecological Expansion: The Relationship Between Dominance and Suburban Differentiation." *Social Forces* 65: 352-370.

Mckenzie, R.D. 1933. "Industrial Expansion and the Interrelations of Peoples." In E.B. Reuter (ed.), *Race and Cultural Contacts*: 19-33. New York: McGraw-Hill.

Mckenzie, R.D. 1951. "The Rise of Metropolitan Communities." In Paul K. Hatt and Albert J. Reiss, Jr. (eds) *Cities and Society* pp 201-213 New York: The Free Press.

Ministry of The Interior, ROC. 1996. *Taiwan-Fukien Demographic Fact Book*. TAIPEI.

Moses, Leon N. and Harold Williamson, Jr. 1974. "The Location of Economic Activity in Cities." In Franklin James (ed.), *Models of Employment and Residential Location*: 99-110 New Jersey: Rutgers University Press.

Muller, Peter O. 1981. *Contemporary Suburban America*. Englewood Cliffs, New Jersey: Prentice-Hall.

Schnore, Leo. 1968. "Commutation" in *International Encyclopedia of the Social Sciences* 16: 140-144. New York: Macmillan.

Stahura, John M. 1982. "Determinants of Suburban Job Change in Retailing, Wholesaling, Service and Manufacturing Industries." *Sociological Focus* 15: 347-357.

Stanback, Thomas M. 1991. *The New Suburbanisation: Challenge to the Central City*. Boulder, CO: Westview Press.

Wheaton, William C. 1979. "Monocentric Models of Urban Land Use: Contributions and Criticisms." Pp. 107-129 in *Current Issues in Urban Economics*, edited by P. Mieszkowski and M. Straszheim. Baltimore, MD: Johns Hopkins University Press.

Wilson, A.G. et al.(eds) 1977. *Models of Cities and Regions: Theoretical and Empirical Developments*. New York: John Wiley & Sons.

Wolforth, John. 1971. "The Journey to Work." In Larry S. Bourne (ed.), *Internal Structure of the City*. Pp.240-247. New York: Oxford University Press.

4 Projection of the Urbanisation Pattern for the Jabotabek Region

F.M. Sanders, R.J. Verhaeghe and B. Zondag

4.1 Introduction

The region around Jakarta, including the districts JAKarta, BOgor, TAngerang and BEKasi (JABOTABEK) experiences strong demographic/ economic development. Population projections for this region and fringe areas indicate an increase from the present 20 million to 50 million over the next 25 years. A very large development of infrastructure involving housing, transportation, energy and water supply will be required to support this development. In turn, the provision of such infrastructure will strongly shape the region. Projection of population and associated activities and its location in the region over a longer time period, determines the demand for future facilities and allows the prediction of environmental impacts for the region. Such projection forms the primary basis for the planning of facilities, as well as derivation of appropriate remedial measures (zoning, regulation) to counteract for example predicted adverse environmental conditions for the region. Preparation of such projections form a particular challenge for this fast developing region: an integrated projection which allows the capture of the driving processes in the region is required; this requires in particular appropriate links between demographic and socio-economic changes and the spatial plan for the region. Modelling of spatial allocation of functions forms a basic instrument to project the location of future activities. Such modelling effort and its application to the Jabotabek region is presented below.

4.2 Major Processes Shaping the Region- Development Vision

The current settlement pattern for the Jabotabek region is presented in Map 4.1 based on the 1990 census. A differentiation can be made between the core DKI Jakarta and the surrounding districts Bogor, Tangerang and Bekasi (Botabek). Over the past decades expansion has taken place according to a T shape with a dramatic acceleration of growth along the East-West axis expanding into Bekasi and Tangerang. In fact population growth has shifted away from the densely populated core toward the urban fringe areas.

Based on an interpretation of present trends, two major spatial forces

61

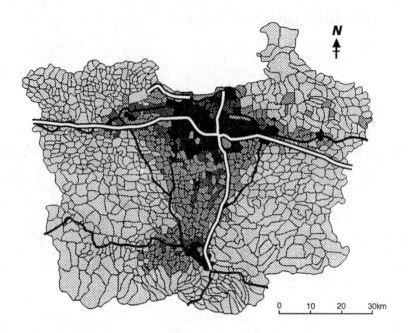

Map 4.1 Relative Population Density in Jabotabek 1990

can be identified, which will place significant limits on the amount of future growth in DKI Jakarta but which will support sustained growth in Botabek. First is the accelerated shift in land use, particularly in central parts of the city from residential to non-residential use. Second is the clear trend toward residential dispersal within the region, spurred in large by the formal housing sector and by changes in transport infrastructure which have permitted increased spatial separation of residence and work. Available data demonstrate urban expansion as opposed to densification. Within DKI Jakarta, the average population density (of all areas with densities of over 50 persons per ha) declined from 175 persons per ha in 1971 to 167 in 1980 and 151 per ha in 1990, indicating out-migration from the central core urban area. It can be concluded that current growth patterns suggests a development in urban spatial development away from concentration toward the urban core and toward increased dispersion in relatively open areas on the urban fringe. The result of these growth processes has been a strong expansion of urbanised area in the Jabotabek region. From the present stage of urbanisation the development of the Jabotabek region could follow several alternative patterns which have advantages and disadvantages. Three visions on urban form have been put forward in earlier studies: those are:

- the new town concept in which the region will further develop into a set of self-sustaining new town centres spread out as satellites around the present core urban area (DKI Jakarta),
- the finger city concept in which the further urbanisation will take place along some elongated urbanised stretches radiating from the DKI, and
- the linear city concept in which the new urban areas will consist of expansions to the current urban areas with a pronounced East-West axis and a further expansion of the Bogor Jakarta axis to the south (T-shape).

Nine criteria were used in a multi-criteria assessment to determine an overall attractiveness measure for each of the above concepts. These were: concurrence with the environmental zoning model which in particular favours concentration of urban development in the triangle Bekasi-Tangerang-Bogor; flexibility (sufficient capacity for further growth without initiating internal conflicts); need for additional infrastructure; risk of urban sprawl; efficiency of public transportation and utility infrastructure; protection of agricultural areas; open areas/greenbelts; traffic pressure on the urban core area; and enforcement potential. The new town concept scores negatively on a majority of the nine criteria although most of the new town sites are in the development area, favoured by the environmental zoning model and the potential to implement greenbelts is good. A main expected negative effect associated with the required new infrastructure would be the strong pressure to create further urbanisation in between the new town centres and that sprawl-type growth would take over, filling the buffer zones between the new towns. The score for the finger city concept was roughly similar to the new town concept. The urban form is more concentrated, it therefore runs a lower risk of urban sprawl and has a somewhat higher level of infrastructure efficiency. This concept provides also good opportunities to develop a creative interplay between urban- and greenbelt functions. The traffic implications for Jakarta would however be more serious than in the new towns option, as flows would be channelled into the city along the radial fingers. The linear city concept scores better than the above two options on most criteria and therefore received the best overall score. There will be, for example, less negative pressure on major agricultural areas. There is also less need for additional major infrastructure. There would also be less traffic on the urban core area as a ladder type road structure (based on parallel arterial routes interspersed with cross-links) would be suggested, thus potentially dispersing congestion among a larger number of nodes. The concept shows however a negative score for the accessibility of open space as the built-up area could be as wide as 20 km.

While the linear city concept is favoured from an overall viewpoint, the Government is not in a position to completely control the development of urbanisation. Government can only promote and encourage the favoured "option" by stimulating growth through infrastructure provision, co-development initiatives and negotiation of benefits with the major developers. Negative controls have in most cases been ineffective.

The selection of the basic paradigm for urban development has consequences for the type of part of the modelling that is required to project the urbanisation pattern for the region. With respect to the type of processes a differentiation is also necessary between the core urban area DKI and the surrounding area. The developments in DKI, with a shift from residential to commercial, are much more dependent on price developments and will be particularly sensitive to the economic situation.

A criterion for urban development, which has not yet received sufficient (quantitative) attention concerns the current and rapidly worsening environmental impact which is for example most strongly illustrated by water quality. The pattern of further development will have considerable effects on the environmental impact and different growth patterns may be explicitly tested for their ability to cope with environmental aspects.

4.3   Modelling Concept

The general modelling concept is presented in Figure 4.1 : two main parts are differentiated, viz. projection of the total need for space in the particular region over a selected time period, based on its internal socio-economic characteristics and in relation to the surrounding region(s), and a simulation of the allocation of this total requirement to different parts within the region. The modelling of the total projection has followed a fairly standard approach, relating to other regions and containing three sectors, population, housing and business, linked to each other through various (feedback) relationships. The population sector as well as the housing sector differentiates a low and upper income group. The business sector differentiates between industry and commerce. The dynamic allocation within the region is based on an inventory of available space (land-use) and a determination of overall attractiveness for the different land parcels or cells of the region. This attractiveness is based on the specific characteristics of the site and the position (spatial relations) of each individual part with respect to the other parts. The attractiveness is (re-) computed for each time interval in the simulation and used to allocate the increment in total space required for the region. The scores on a set of individual parameters are combined into a single attractiveness potential by means of a Multi-Criteria Analysis (MCA). The weights on the different parameters reflect the importance of those aspects in determining the attractiveness for settlement. Those weights are of particular interest for the calibration of the model. The total increment in space requirement for a particular simulation interval is allocated proportional to the attractiveness potential.

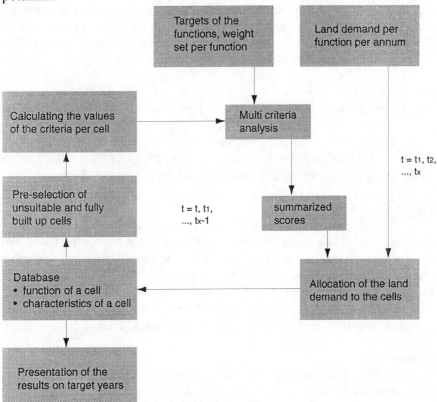

Figure 4.1 Main Components of the Population Model

Often in the application of spatial modelling a limited number of parameters appear to have a dominant influence in the allocation process. There are however a considerable number of "candidates", for the present analysis accessibility, groundwater availability and environmental impact were considered in the analysis. The individual cells covering the region have been characterised by 4 types of space viz., urban, industrial, agricultural, and special. Several processes have an influence on shaping the settlement in a region. They have a different span of spatial influence and an appropriate schematisation should be applied for modelling. For this purpose two levels of spatial schematisation have been considered in the modelling, viz. a set of larger cells to represent spatial relationships, determine and compare attractiveness and allocate the share of growth, and a set of smaller cells to address urban densification. For each (larger) cell the stock of different types of space is updated throughout the simulation. The urban expansion in the Jabotabek region has up to now been largely at the expense of agricultural area and such transfer is expected to continue into the future. In the model such encroachment on agricultural area has also been allowed if no free space was available for expansion in an otherwise attractive cell.

4.4 Specification of Criteria and Calculation

The *criteria* in the model represent the characteristics of the cells that are the major influences on the allocation of functions. In the second version of the allocation model the following criteria are programmed:-

Physical Condition
The physical condition of an area determines the preparation costs of the construction site. Cells with high land preparation costs are unattractive for the allocation of urban functions. The value of this criterion consists of the state of various physical conditions. Examples of physical conditions are the soil type, percentage of the cell with slopes and the steepness of the slopes. The availability of data and the characteristics of a region determine which physical conditions will be included in the physical criteria.

Accessibility
In almost all spatial models the accessibility plays an important role in the allocation of functions. Good accessible areas are attractive as location for residential and industrial land use. The accessibility criterion gives a value for how far it is from the centroid of a cell to the closest main road. The position of a cell in the network, e.g. central or fringe, will be evaluated in the next criterion. It is common to integrate these two criteria. The division has been made because for some functions it is more important to be close to a main road than to be close to other main urban or economical centres (e.g. distribution centres).

Position Cell in Network (Gravity Criterion)
This criterion is a parameter for the distance of a cell to urban and economic activities. This criterion refers to spatial regularities as movement-minimization and the tendency to agglomerate. The idea behind this criterion

is that a cell close to urban or economical centres is more attractive than an isolated cell. Variables included in this criterion are the distances between cells, the number of inhabitants of the cell's population and the number of jobs of the cells. The value for this criterion is calculated with the formula.

$$Gf_i = (aP_i+bE_i)/I + \sum_j (aP_j+bE_j)/D_{ij}^n$$

Gf$_i$	= *Gravity factor, value for criterion for cell i*
P	= *Population*
E	= *Economic indicator, e.g. number of jobs*
I	= *Internal distance factor*
D	= *distance between two cells*
a,b,n	= *calibration parameters*

The population and economic parameter will indicate the urban and economic importance of a cell. The influence of one cell on another will diminish with the distance. Distance can be expressed in geographical distance or in distance between cells following the main road network. It is also possible to express this parameter in travel time or costs. The internal distance factor is an indicator of the distance inside a cell to urban or economic activities. The need to involve the internal distance factor depends on the size of the cell. The value of the internal distance factor is normally calculated from the area of a cell. The calibration parameters can differ from situation to situation. Parameter n gives the model user the possibility to describe non-linear relationship between the influence of a centre and the distance.

Water Supply Criterion

This criterion gives a value for the water supply conditions in a region. In the Jabotabek region over 70% of the water demand is supplied by groundwater. Based on the condition of the ground water resources in the cells a division can be made into different ground water classes. Indicators of the suitability of the ground water resources for water supply use are the pollution, salination and depth of the ground water.

Pollution Criterion

As an indicator for the surface water pollution the biological oxygen demand load per cell has been calculated. A high BOD load in a cell will cause bad surface water conditions, this will give annoyance e.g. smell. A high score on this criterion makes a cell less attractive for settlement.

Planning Zones, Governmental Influence
Planning zones are spatial zones defined by the government where specific land-use plans or restrictions exist. The knowledge of which cell is in which planning zone can be obtained with an overlay analysis. The importance of a planning zone for a land demanding function can be managed in the weight set. For example a cell within the zone where industrial development is allowed, will have a positive value for this criterion in the allocation of new industries .

Land Prices
The price of the land depends on the present function, the distance from urban centres and the type of development allowed by the government. Within a cell it means that the land containing the function with lowest cost of purchase will be developed. This criterion is not operational in the second version of the allocation model. There was inadequate land price and land use data available in the Jabotabek study to study this criterion.
The criteria are standardized before they are used in the multi criteria evaluation. They are standardized between 0 and 1 with the formula:

standardized score $Yx = (Y_x-MinY)/(MaxY-MinY)$

Y_x = score of cell X on criterion Y
$MinY$ = score of cell with minimum score of all cells on criterion Y
$MaxY$ = score of cell with maximum score of all cells on criterion Y

The *targets* of the different land demanding functions are expressed in the weight set. The weights should reflect the importance of the criteria in determining their attractiveness for settlement. Insight in the targets of the functions and an accurate estimation of the weights is an essential factor for the validity of the model. In the Jabotabek study the weights were obtained by calibrating the model.

A *Multi-Criteria-Analysis* (mca) is used to evaluate the attractiveness of the different cells. The multi criteria analysis serves to investigate a number of choice possibilities in the light of multiple criteria and confliction priorities (Voogd, 1983). The mca is used to determine the attractiveness of the cells. For each function an independent mca should be executed. The score of the attractiveness potential of one cell for a specific function is:

$$A_x = Y_{1x} * W_{y1} + Y_{2x} * W_{y2} + \text{etc.}$$

A_x = attractiveness potential of cell x
Y_{1x} = standardized score of cell x for criterion y_1
W_{y1} = weight for criterion y_1 (for specific function)

In the *allocation phase* the new functions will be allocated to land in the cells. This allocation is based on the attractiveness potential of the cells. The needed additional land for a function for one time step is allocated to the cells proportional to the attractiveness potential. This method was used in the Jabotabek case, an other method is to allocate all the land demand to the cell with the best score. The land demand will be allocated to this cell until the cell is full and excluded from the allocation process. The formula of the allocation proportional to the attractiveness potential is, for population, for example:

$$P_{i,t} = (A_i / \Sigma_j A_j) * P_{\text{tot, }t}$$

$P_{i,t}$ = allocated population to cell i at time t
A_i = attractiveness potential of cell i
$\Sigma_j A_j$ = attractiveness potential of all cells
$P_{\text{tot, }t}$ = total additional population at time t

4.5   Schematisation of the Jabotabek Region

Administrative units have been used in the schematisation because the bulk of information is available in this format. The smallest unit is the "desa" level; the Jabotabek region covering a total area of 5100 km2 is covered by 1409 desa's. The next larger administrative unit is the "kecematan" level of which there are 77 in the Jabotabek region. The kecamatan level has been used as the basic schematisation for the comparison of attractiveness and allocation of growth share while the desa level has been used to consider density differences. Map 4.2 illustrates the schematisation using the 77 kecamatans. The centre point for each kecematan is used as a node in a regional network to evaluate spatial relations such as e.g. accessibility.

The further development of the present core urban area (DKI Jakarta) will be governed by different processes and in particular by the transformation from residential to commercial which will be strongly determined by land prices. This area has therefore been considered separate and was not assumed to participate in the allocation of growth. However it is considered

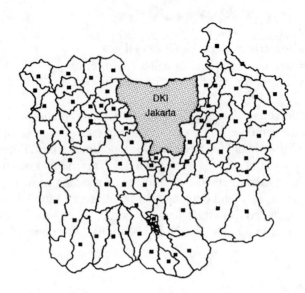

Map 4.2 Schematisation of the Jabotabek Region

as a node with constant population and functions as a node of urban gravity attracting further urbanisation to its fringe areas.

4.6   Model Calibration- Projection Results

The capacity of any model to represent a particular system and deal with the changes in this system depends largely on the level of conceptual modelling of the processes in contrast with black box type of modelling that relies on statistical relationships. The objective is to be able to apply the model to a particular case with a minimum of parameters. This holds in particular for simulation of spatial development which is (potentially) influenced by a large number of aspects. Fortunately in most cases only a limited number of aspects are dominant and the calibration focuses on identifying the most relevant processes. A statistical calibration of the spatial allocation model (e.g. through a minimization of the squares of the deviations), would be difficult in view of the large spatial dimension, incorporating non-linear relationships in combination with a development over time which very likely has been non-stationary over the period of observation (e.g. different preferences determining the attractiveness of individual cells at different times). For the Jabotabek region there is no doubt that accessibility has gained in importance over the last decade due to the rapid urbanisation in the area, rapidly increasing mobility, and a limited provision of infrastructure that could not keep up with demand. Similar to the difficulty with non-stationarities in the calibration one has to be aware of the occurrence of non-stationarities in the future affecting the accuracy of the projection: the actual future situation will likely be influenced by changing preferences, economic conditions, etc. Such situation puts emphasis on having a good conceptual model, that represents the most relevant processes, and a prudent use of the predicted development pattern in planning. Of particular interest in the growth allocation process are the weights used in the MCA to reflect the influence of different site specific and spatial characteristics in the determination of the total attractiveness of each cell. The weights comprise a limited number of parameters and estimating them forms part of the calibration process. A heuristic approach combining visual inspection and judgment to adjust the weights in a trial and adjustment process has been used to produce a "practical" minimization of deviations of predicted versus measured. The growth allocation model has been calibrated to the Jabotabek region using the population census for 1980 and 1990 using the MCA weights as parameters to steer the calibration. A proper introduction and timing of the major transport links as they materialized during the calibration period had an anticipated strong influence on the calibration results. An average deviation of 16 % between the actual measured and predicted situation for the different cells was obtained. Map 4.3 presents a projection of the urbanisation pattern of the Jabotabek region for the year 2020 starting on base year 1990. This simulation is based on a continuation of the present preferences and no particular measures to steer development in any particular direction. A further development of the urbanised area along the east-west axis and expansion to the south can be observed. Present observations (1997) on the region strongly confirm this direction of development. Although a reasonable calibration could be obtained with a schematisation that is considered sufficient to contain the spatial developments in the past, it is felt that due to the expected scale of future development an enlarged schematisation may be necessary, to represent fully the trade-offs within the region.

4.7   Observations, Conclusions and Further Developments

Calibration of the model gives confidence that the model concept is suitable for simulation of the type of development that is occurring in the Jabotabek region. It is felt that the use of several levels of cell representation adds considerable flexibility to include different processes at the appropriate level of detail.

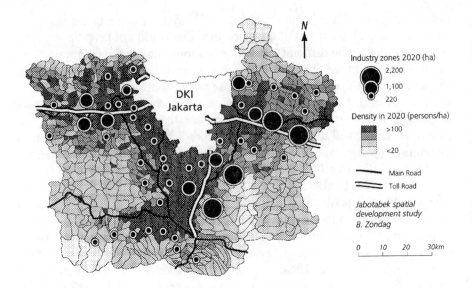

N

DKI
Jakarta

Industry zones 2020 (ha)

2,200

1,100

220

Density in 2020 (persons/ha)

>100

<20

———— Main Road

Toll Road

*Jabotabek spatial
development study
B. Zondag*

0   10   20   30km

Map 4.3 Population Projection Jabotabek 2020

The price of land will become increasingly important as a parameter in the allocation of space and in the determination of the type of settlement and transfer from one function to another. A module covering the influence of the price of land is considered for a future expansion of the modelling. A separate determination of attractiveness for residential and industrial settlement is also being considered.

A particular challenge in growth allocation modelling forms the evaluation of a particular spatial pattern in the format of some characteristic parameters which can be used to compare alternative patterns. In particular for evaluation of the environmental impact associated with a particular pattern it would be very useful to develop such indicators. As indicated above such assessment would help plan the urban development of the Jabotabek region. Further research will be undertaken to develop such assessment method.

References

Sanders, F.M., *Allocation modelling using cellular grids*. Urban planning conference in Spa, advanced studies in systems research, 1996.

Kribbe, W. and F.M. Sanders, *Growth of spatial network construction*. Urban planning conference Spa, 1996.

Verhaeghe, R.J. and W.N.M. van der Krogt, *Decision support system for river basin planning*. Hydro informatics 1996.

Lambregts, B.W. and F.M. Sanders, *Sustainable development in the Gaza strip, a system dynamics approach*. Delft University of Technology, 1996.

Verhaeghe, R.J. and P. Schrijnen, *Multi-sectorale planning en infrastructuurontwikkeling voor het Jabotabekgebied*. Planologische discussiebijdragen ,1996.

Engelen, G., *The theory of self-organisation and modelling complex urban systems*. European journal of operational research 37 page 42-57, 1988.

Engelen, G., 1. Uljee and R. White, *The use of constrained cellular automata for high-resolution modelling of urban land use dynamics*. European colloquium on theoretical and quantitative geography, Budapest 1993.

Jabotabek metropolitan development plan review, second planning report. Government of the Republic of Indonesia, Ministry of Public Works, Directorate General of Human Settlement, Jakarta 1993.

Jabotabek metropolitan development plan review, third planning report. Government of the Republic of Indonesia, Ministry of Public Works, Directorate General of Human Settlement, Jakarta 1993.

5   Science Cities and Technopolis in Japan: Innovative Networks and Regional Planning

Natalie Cavasin

5.1   Introduction

The new economic trends for the construction of a system which efficiently produces technological innovation requires the organisation of new spaces, territories and also urban mechanisms. Innovation will take place by creating specific spatial forms distinct from the traditional industrial concentration. The different phases of the Japanese's innovation process have taken place in the classic metropolitan areas. The Japanese methods of production have been continuously innovative, nevertheless no specific areas of innovation were identified until the 1980s. The technological revolution had already broken out before the start of the Japanese Technopolis voluntarist form, the R&D complex.

Spatial economic theory has come to be associated with the notions of territory, milieu, local production system and network.

The spatial approach concerning innovation milieu is based on three considerations:

> 1. Innovation is considered as a collective process which implies enterprises and institutions as being a functional/sector-based phenomenon;
> 2. Innovation is the result of interactions and the synergies of processes and not the result of individual factors;
> 3. The spatial proximity of actors is considered as a preliminary condition for interaction and cooperation and as a factor to further innovative activities.

Stöhr (1987) insisted on the notion of synergy resulting from the interaction of functions relating to innovation (training program, collection of information, consulting, finance, etc.) at the regional level.

We can find different kinds of networks around the world. The most well known are the networks of SME (Small and Medium Enterprise) in the Third Italy, represented by flexible vertical disintegration (Camagni, 1991), the network formed by the spatial concentration of branches functionally integrated like Sophia Antipolis in the South of France (Burnier and Lacroix, 1996), the network resulting from using incubation as a new model of spatioindustrial organisation as in Silicon Valley (Scott, 1993).

The Japanese government was led to modify its own practice in the field of territorial intervention. Land planning policies have been directed toward the diffusion of high technology industry as a means for a balanced regional development. In Japan, the whole idea of science cities and Technopolis was built on an inherent concept of creating a special environment for the scientific and engineering population. This paper, firstly explores the major lines of Japanese regional planning within the context of a broader appreciation of the logic of territorial innovation, and secondly attempts to contribute to the understanding of a strategic network inside high technology nodes with a particular focus on spatio-economic linkages.

5.2 Convergence of Land Planning and Technological Innovation in Japan

The Japanese policy of land planning was perceived as a priority after the Second World War. During the past 30 years, national land planning in Japan has focused on the simultaneous solution of two problems: the over-concentration of population and industry in metropolitan areas and the unbalanced development of national land. The industrial location policy after the post-war period can be classified into five different periods, all closely related to the economic growth of the country. The first period is that of the post-war recovery followed by the period of introducing new technologies and innovations from the mid-1950s to mid-1960s, the third period is characterised by high economic growth until the first oil shock, the fourth is the period of stable growth, and the fifth is the period from 1986 when Japan entered the era of industrial, structural adjustment.

5.2.1 Industrial Location Policy

Period of Rapid Growth
A very precise policy for the location of industries was generated during the period of high economic growth between 1960 and 1970. The objectives of regional development are: reinforcement of the industry in comparison to the competition with western countries and the construction of industrial complexes under the direction of the national government. One of the major problems confronting modern Japan is the regional imbalance of economic development (Takahashi and Sugiura, 1996). Since the period of high level economic growth during the 1960s, there has been a marked emigration of people from rural areas in Hokkaido, Tohoku, Shikoku, Kyushu and an

excessive concentration of the population in the metropolitan districts of To-kyo, Osaka and Nagoya.

Investments in private industrial equipment has increased because of the development of technical innovations and the emergence of new industrials sites. Many local governments have attempted to attract firms into their areas by giving them special privileges including tax exemptions and land for industrial development.

According to the national income doubling plan of 1960 approved by the Cabinet, Ikeda was to double the GNP (Growth National Product) in ten years (Tachi, 1993). This plan also advocated the role of government in social infrastructure like public works, housing and urban planning. It is essential to correct the regional disparities and to solve the problem of congestion in over-populated cities.

The Vision for the Pacific Belt policy illustrated the policies used in Yamaguchi and Fukuoka prefectures. The conclusion was that this region should assume the role of a base for the development of other regions. In fact, this vision linked economic and regional development, with the priority on industrial development. From this period onward, there was much concern regarding the balance of the national economy as a necessity. At the same time it was also important to consider social policy. Japan entered a new area of regional development with the creation of the Comprehensive National Development Plan (CNDP) which is the starting point of the policy toward industrial decentralisation (Yada, 1982).

On the October 5th, 1962, the first CNDP was approved by the Cabinet Council. This plan considered regional problems under two objectives: first, the prevention of excessive growth in the main urban areas and second, the reduction of regional disparities with an appropriate regional distribution of capital, labor and technologies. It was most important to increase economic growth in regions outside of Tokyo-Osaka-Nagoya. The idea was to develop a strategic growth pole for encouraging the dispersion of industries and the development of depressed areas (Chill Hill and Fujita, 1993). This plan consisted, in part, of a law related to the construction of NIC (New Industrial Cities) (Map 5.1). The goal was to restrain population growth and industries in the concentrated metropolitan region, to advance the level of local industries, to correct regional disparities and to build new industrial cities as centres for development. One problem was the government's choice of the number of regions to be designated. By designating too many places it had accentuated problems related to the distribution of industry. During the second period of economic growth new problems have emerged like the acceleration of urbanisation in the metropolitan area and industrial pollution which started during the period of rapid economic growth and became a major social prob-

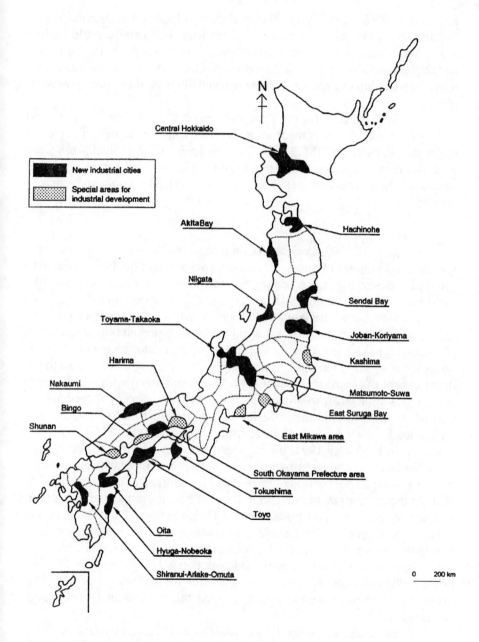

Map 5.1 New Industrial Areas in Japan

lem in the 1960s. Local governments started to focus on preserving nature and the living environment rather than industry. Industrial complexes like Sakai, Mizushima and Fuyama were completed rapidly along the Pacific Coast, and the last one was Kashiwa in Ibaraki Prefecture. Nevertheless some industrial plants in Mutsu Ogawara, Tomakomai and Shibushi Bay were never completed.

In 1964, the Law for the Development of Special Zones was enacted for the industrial reinforcement in the regions which were more developed under the previous law (Map 5.1). The four major metropolitan areas were excluded from the program: Keihin, Chukyo, Hanshin and Kitakyushu. The program of new cities and special zones for industrial development were successful.

First Step toward Decentralization

On May 30, 1969, the Second Comprehensive National Plan (shinzenso) was enacted in order to create an economy with a high quality of life, help protect the environment, create a transportation network with technology like the shinkansen bullet train, and to encourage industrial decentralization. This second CNDP led to the law of 1972 on industrial redeployment with the reduction of industrial growth rates in the Kanto region and the distribution of industrial resources. After these considerations related to regional development, Japan started to think about the possibilities of growth related to the development of innovative technology. The slogan of 'the high tech archipelago' was coined (Morris-Suzuki, 1994). This new concept of regional development has involved the diffusion of innovations from the Pacific Belt area to the less developed regions or from big companies to SME.

From 1965 until 1975, the Japanese economy was in a period of high growth with the economy growing at an annual rate of more than ten percent, ushering in the longest period of prosperity since the end of the Second World War. At the same time, the neighbourhood protest movement against pollution and environmental destruction intensified as industrial pollution became a major social problem. This made it necessary for the Japanese government to establish new policies for the location of industry. In 1968, while trying to solve the problems of urbanisation and pollution MITI (Ministry of International Trade and Industry) announced a scheme for the future location of industries geared to economic growth, called the "Industrial Development Scheme".

Tanaka Kakuei, elected Prime Minister in 1972, announced in his vision for national land reform a new plan for infrastructure policy. It was very ambitious. For example, it proposed the development of industrial modern cities across the nation with more than 250,000 inhabitants and decentralizing the functions of the major conurbations. His project called "rebuild Archipelago" created a rise in land prices nationwide. He also came up with a policy of public investment in order to stimulate growth, but his law on industrial decentralization gradually failed and the tax project met too much opposition to be successfully implemented. The 1973 petroleum crisis came and obviously highlighted the failure of Tanaka politics. Thus the Japanese economy was then plunged into a long recession which did not end until the mid-1980s.

The national regional policies tried to control the urban concentration of the population and industries and promote regional development. But the results show that the inflow of population into the major metropolitan areas of Tokyo, Osaka and Nagoya slackened while the growth in the major regional cities did not slow down.

5.2.2 Creation of Tsukuba Science City

In 1963, the Japanese technological policy gave a fresh boost to regional development with the creation of a science city: Tsukuba academic new town (Tsukuba kenkyu gakuen toshi) located in the southwestern part of Ibaraki Prefecture, approximately 50 km north-east of Tokyo. Tsukuba was establish in order to reduce the over-crowded conditions in Tokyo. Most national research laboratories were relocated from the capital Tokyo to Tsukuba, and in order to develop Tsukuba as a national centre for promoting higher education a university was established. The University of Tsukuba was the former Tokyo University of Education and was transferred to Tsukuba for promoting science and technology and to improve the ties with other laboratories. In 1985, when Tsukuba international Expo under the theme of science and technology was held, the city became widely known as the greatest centre of research for science and technology. Many corporations decided to locate and relocated laboratories into Tsukuba. This time research collaboration between private and public research laboratories began on a small scale. Tsukuba has now 46 national institutes (half of all national institutes in Japan), several academic organisations, nearly 200 high tech companies and a total researcher population of about 13000, with a total population of about 180 000 (with around 6000 foreign residents). Tsukuba became a model science city for the world. This new wave of urban planning that was not seen in other places in Japan at that time makes more sense for good living conditions, and also for the territorial agglomeration of science and technology.

In the context of creating a science city, MITI organized a certain number of national projects in the field of robotics, new materials, opto-electronics, biotechnology, semiconductors...

5.3   Urban Planning after 1973 and the Strategy for Developing High Technology Industries

High economic growth came to an end with the two oil shocks. For this reason, the industrial relocation policy had to be strengthened (Gonda, 1994). Measures were taken to support economically depressed regions. In 1977, MITI adopted the "Industrial Relocation Plan" based on "the Industrial Promotion Law " (1972). The same year the cabinet created the "Third Comprehensive National Plan". Moreover, the oil crisis brought considerable qualitative change to Japanese industries. Key industries such as steel and petrochemicals that led the rapid economic growth prior to the oil crisis, relinquished their position to "high tech" industries such as computers, robots and biotechnology.

5.3.1 The Need for Industrial Development in Local Areas: Technopolis

In 1983, the Technopolis Law was enacted to create a new urban society where these advanced technologies producing higher value-added products were expected to serve as the nucleus for regional revitalization (Glasmeier, 1988; Masser, 1990; Nishioka, 1985; Tatsuno, 1986). MITI first announced the "Technopolis" concept in 1980. The content of the concept itself was defined by the Japanese to mean a high technology industrial complex. The Technopolis Plan is a new strategy for the development of relatively backward regions in Japan, with the objective of creating attractive towns in which industry, academic institutions and residential areas are closely interrelated. At the end of 1989, 26 areas had been authorized by the government as "Technopolis Development Regions", and specific activities have been undertaken in each region. For example, in all areas new research institutions, universities and college have been established and old ones expanded. The essence of Japanese Technopolis is the imagination of a new city composed of: industry (factories, centres of industrial distribution and services), research (university and research laboratories) and a zone of habitation with a pleasant environment. The goals of Japanese Technopolis according to the MITI are as follows:

· set up a strategic policy for regional economic revitalization by developing and transmitting new technologies;

· support the whole country by creating an environment favourable to the development of R&D activities and production;

· promotion of regional development by taking advantage of private sector vitality.

The Technopolis concept is the largest industrialisation plan since the program of New Industrial Cities was established in 1962 for the development for growth poles. The Technopolis aims at building industrial complexes in which a local university must act as a core research centre. Consequently, local government is trying to promote linkages between local colleges and small-and medium sized enterprises in each region.

Technopoles are territorial concentrations of "technological innovations with a potential to generate scientific synergy and economic productivity" (Castells and Hall, 1994). These areas with economic activity focused on advanced products can be distinguished by their culture of innovative scientific developments and the inter-firm linkages which also include cooperative reciprocity in terms of sharing technical and technological information.

5.3.2 Other Concepts for Promoting Regional Development: New Trends of Science Parks in Japan

The research core concept has the following main objectives: to raise the level of research and development being done at the regional level, to provide training opportunities for the work-force requiring creative thinking, and the realization of advanced industrial structures in the regions. The objective is to establish an advanced industrial support function in the region (leasing businesses, industrial machines and instrument rental businesses, office machine and instrument rental businesses, information processing services, information consulting services, display businesses, designing and engineering businesses, management consulting). As of 1997, there are 12 of these research parks. In 1988 the Brain Accumulation Act was established by MITI as its regional economic policy, ("Act for promoting the Accumulation of the specific works contributing to the upgrading of regional industry") and 26 areas were nominated.

All theses recent projects show that Japanese science parks have a short history of around 10 years. Even if new laws have been developed, science parks have been planned and developed based on the model of American and European projects, although they have some peculiar features in their designs and functions.

5.3.3 Future Prospects for Regional Planning and Innovative Territory

In 1987, the fourth CNDP aimed at the formation of the "Multi-polar pattern of National Land Use" through the development of polar regions which have diverse functions, such as industrial technology, international business, and academic research. In June 1994, the CNDP had been reviewed to emphasize the importance of reinforcing the basics for R&D and research information networks. It also indicated that science cities will play a much more important role in regional development. Moreover, in 1994, a new law called "Industrial Brain Act" was enacted to encourage the accumulation of laboratories, institutes, R&D firms, and the software industries in specific districts. Also the Act for the formation of Multi-Polar Pattern of National Land Use in 1988, provided a new system for regional development in which specific areas called "Strategic Development Areas" were selected to bring together outstanding industries and cultural functions.

These acts are more or less based on the same idea as science parks or science cities. They will play a key role in regional development. The Kansai Science city Development Act of 1987 symbolizes the advent of a new epoch in the construction of science cities.

5.4   Innovation, Networks and Regional Development

The Japanese governmental policy for the development of techno-poles and science cities is based on a logic of cooperation between different kinds of actors. Technological linkages are mainly developed through the supply of specific materials and technological contracts, and more importantly, through human knowledge and communication. It is interesting to think of these as the concepts of "proximity" and "propinquity". "Geographical proximity" and "social propinquity" could generate some economic processes related to technological creations or the development of specific advantages allowing regional growth. The condition required for the formation of this network is the spatial propinquity of actors. According to Camagni (1991), this propinquity is necessary because human capital is less mobile between regions than within regions. This author suggested that relations between the actors are generally made on the basis of personal contacts.

5.4.1 Constitution of Networks

These places where institutions are highly concentrated as in science cities and Technopolis are at the starting point for the functioning of synergy's networks which depend on the propinquity "necessary for collective learning" (Perrin, 1991) and the competence of the actors. In this case, the circulation of scientific and technological information is the key for contributing to innovation and setting up relations and networks between different actors. On a national level, the STA (Science and Technology Agency) started in 1988 a research information network in regional areas. Research exchange and information exchange is promoted and takes place within regions, and between regions and Tsukuba Science City. Some information networks have been constructed in the prefectures of Oita, Shizuoka, Toyama and Ishikawa, and in the regions of Tohoku, Keihanna, Chugoku and Shikoku. Another is the information network set up by JICST (Japan Information Centre of Science and Technology) which provides an on-line service which accesses international and domestic information and uses a science and technology data base. Also the Patent On-Line Information System (PATOLIS) provided by the Japan Patent Information Organisation started twenty years ago. Japan Technomart Foundation distributes technical information and has branch offices in ten regions. The existence of these electronic communication networks inside the city and between the different areas is a condition needed for the system of partnership and human networks to function.

5.4.2 *The Relations and Networks among Public, Academic and Private Sectors*

The constitution of relations between different milieu such as business, research, and education does not result exclusively from the effect of geographical juxtaposition, but by a complex working of social networks. These networks are not only intense relations between types of structures, they are also organized on a territorial bases to favour innovation. Innovation is perceived as a collective phenomenon which is developed inside an interface between the actors (industry, research) which have functional and sector-based know-how different and complementary in a territorial environment. The creation of a specific environment is realized by the alliance or strategic relations. In this context lasting spatial proximity is a key element for the synergy between multiple partners. The synergy at the local level plays an important role toward innovation. The effect of spatial element is not limited only to the proximity and propinquity that account for traditional regional science. The territorial system and its organisation allow us to appreciate the synergetic capacity.

In order to characterise various processes of intercommunication that generate technological innovation, it is necessary to isolate the actors, to analyse their contents, form and structure, and also to take into consideration the organisational system. These operators of communication are the first institutions established in the Technopolis areas, called Foundations. They are in charge of the promotion of creative communication by bringing together the different scientists or business people inside the Technopolis area. The aim is spin-off and the promotion of development of human resources. These foundations also provide incubation services to entrepreneurs.

5.4.3 *Cooperation Between the Actors: a Type of Network*

It is at Tsukuba Science city that the links between research and industry have been increasing during the last ten years: the scientists are at the origin of these new relations. Different kinds of systems for the circulation of data banks through computer networks have been implemented for the development of technological transfer toward the industrial sector. The circulation of information is related to the result of the scientific community's work. Some national laboratories in Tsukuba work in closed relation with the industry like the AIST (Agency of Industrial Science and Technology), and MITI laboratories. About 92 percent of private companies and 71 percent of national laboratories in Tsukuba have experienced R&D cooperation during the past six years[1] . Companies which do not have any experience of cooperation mentioned the uselessness of cooperation and the difficulty to find partners motivated for this kind of relation. In the case of the internationalisation of the R&D, companies and public laboratories agreed on the importance of establishing contacts with research organisations from foreign countries, of inviting foreign scientists to Japan and to collaborate with foreign universities and laboratories.

In the Technopolis synergy are expecting with companies of different industrial sectors and with public research institutes. These laboratories do not establish the same connection or relationships as private companies. In the case of basic and applied research the companies answer most of the time to the objective of reinforcement of technology or the obtaining of new technologies. In the case of research development only the reduction of expenses is observed. The cooperative research in the R&D tends to head towards basic research. In Tsukuba science city or Hamamatsu Technopolis the percentage of basic research in R&D cooperatives represented about 20 percent of contracts. On the contrary, for product development, contacts exceed more than 50 percent.

In comparison with American or Europeans companies, the relations in Japanese companies between different divisions like production and marketing are very closed. The Japanese divisions do not produce results independently. They exchange information very often in order to reach objectives in an effective way. The Japanese firms invest in the R&D, and their contribution to innovation is significant.

---

1 *The survey of Hamamatsu (Miyakoda Technopark) and Tsukuba R&D laboratories were conducted in 1994.*

5.4.4 *Various Kinds of Partnerships*

Relations between Private Research Institutes

More than 52 percent of private R&D companies of the Miyakoda science park in the Hamamatsu Technopolis are concerned with scientific cooperation with other private research institutes. In the case of Tsukuba Science City 75 percent of R&D private companies are involved in this scientific cooperation. Most of them deal with common contract research, and the exchange of information, methods and infrastructures.

Relation between University and Industrial Sector

More and more MITI tries to develop cooperation between university laboratories and private laboratories for the same project. Since the beginning of 1980, MITI promoted policies for cooperation between university-industry in order to help technological innovation and economic competitiveness. Financial aid for cooperation comes from the government. The promotion of links between universities and industrial sectors is realised by local government which creates support centres for cooperative research and technology assistance inside the Technopolis park. Generally, contract research between industry and university laboratories is extremely limited. A consideration of the relationship between university research and the growth of innovation in Japan shows that even if a more open attitude from university toward industry is desired, the mentalities concerning the status of university professors and researchers are not easy to change. Civil servants are not allowed to have other posts, and professors at national universities are also government employees. They may not at the same time serve as consultants to private companies. This restriction limits cooperation between universities and industry.

The subsidiaries of head offices in Tsukuba have created cooperative research with the university. In the Hamamatsu Technopolis for this type of cooperation a university has been created in the Miyakoda Park. This is to promote contracts with local SME. The role of the university within the region has been changed the five past years concerning the regional innovation for the cooperation with the industrial sectors. The Technopolis project has changed the situation by promoting science and technology inside the regions. In 1997, thirty four centres of research cooperation between university and industry have been created by the Ministry of Education.

5.5   The Innovation Network in Tsukuba Science City: Toward a Creative Environment

Several requirements take part in the preparation of an environment adapted to the promotion of innovation like: high level researchers and scientists, financing, organizing of research meetings. According to Tetzuo Kawamoto[2] , it is possible in Tsukuba science city to plan meeting with scientists from different fields because of their motivations, and technological fusion is realised more rapidly.

5.5.1 Circulation of Scientific and Technological Information in Tsukuba

The network between the scientists in Tsukuba had promoted circulation of information because of the unity of a considerable number of researchers (more than 10 000), multiple specialization, and the geographic proximity of the R&D laboratories. The synergetic effects of Tsukuba have been focused on the creation of new research areas and innovative measures to solve global problems.

Tsukuba Science City represents a special environment having a distinct culture. In this regard three very important points need to be take in consideration :
- the accumulation within a relatively small area of a large numbers of researchers and scientists particularly those belonging to the national laboratories with very high qualification;
- a scientific population living close to their work places;
- the proportion of research-related population in Tsukuba being much larger than non-researchers.

All these points contribute to the synergetic effects of the science city. The networks among researchers are easy to create or are created naturally by meeting each other in everyday life (e.g. shopping).

With this environment of scientific culture, intensive exchanges of information are being promoted by private organisations. One example is the TCR (Tsukuba Research Consortium) located in the Tokodai research park in the west part of Tsukuba which organizes different kinds of programs for the promotion of networks. This centre was born of an idea that it would be important to create an interdisciplinary environment to foster innovative research and the growth of new researchers, engineers, technical leaders. The result of this idea was a private sector initiative to create a campus-like setting in 1980

---

2 *He was at the origin of planning of synergies between different organizations and for this reason he was a pioneer of construction of networks in Tsukuba Science City.*

that became home to laboratories of the seven core companies that founded Tsukuba Research Consortium. To increase the flexibility and stimulation of the "campus", a satellite group of rental laboratories and offices was created to allow other companies to start their own business. TCR sponsors a wide variety of meetings, seminars, workshops, informal meetings aimed at improving the interaction between the researchers who are interested in this kind of human network. For cooperative research TCR organized seminars:

- cooperative research groups: around one hundred are represented in Tsukuba in the high technology field;
- networks between researchers: they opened by informal meetings inside TRC;
- meetings of motivation: cooperative research by the motivation of public sector. National research laboratories stimulate cooperative research when private companies cannot take a risk in new activities because of unsteady market conditions. Private companies tend to join public laboratories as a member in a group of cooperative research with government funds or as a technological subcontractor.

5.5.2 *National Research Laboratories and the Creation of Networks in Tsukuba*

The coexistence of a vertical system, formed by the nine ministries and the horizontal system created by the activities of circulation of information and meetings between the scientists, is the characteristic of the research system in Tsukuba.

When the research activities in Tsukuba started in the seventies, very few researchers were working together. In 1978, the Tsukuba Centre for the STA and in 1980 the Council of Liaison composed of directors of more than one hundred private or public research laboratories started mutual cooperation among research institutions in Tsukuba Science City (Map 5.2). Thus, increasingly the forms of circulation of information imply specialized groups. Informal scientific groups have been created between the researchers of different national institutes working on a similar field, but when the private companies went to Tsukuba, they also entered in this kind of social network.

5.5.3 *Constitution of a Social Network*

It seems that George Simmel was the first to use the concept of social network. The social anthropologist Barnes was therefore a pioneer to show the existence of social networks and their importance for communication,

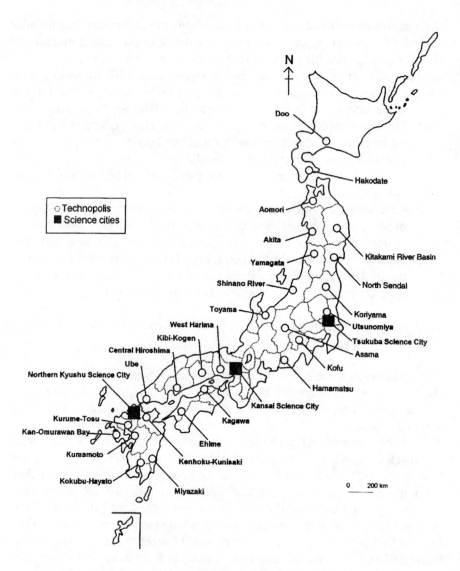

Map 5.2 The Science Cities of Japan

transmission of custom, method, and behaviour (Johnson, 1994). The theoreticians of the Chicago School in the United States who have developed empirical research and theoretical ideas on the subject. In 1977, Claude Fisher from the department of sociology at U.C. Berkeley gave more operational definitions of the social network. According to him social networks are a particular system of ties linking social actors. His definition is broad but permits the development of studies on the social networks.

In western science cities and techno-poles, some social networks are woven naturally and have not been planned or instituted. We can observe cross fertilization passed by informal relations, or friendship relations. Japan has a socially and culturally different context for social networks. In general, personal relationship are based on the same-group experiences. Common interests and common professions often do not count. The engineer who works for one company does not develop a relation or network with an engineer who works for another firm. The longer the time-span between company experience of a junior (kohai) and a senior (senpai), the more significant the relationship becomes. There are some government agencies or private companies in which it is virtually impossible to reach the highest executive levels if one is not a member of the same school group that presently monopolises these positions. Many university professors emphasise to their students that the most important thing is the membership in the exclusive network of graduates who preceded them.

When the transfer of national research institute was over in Tsukuba, the cooperation with the private companies was able to take shape, and more than 700 researchers from the private sector started cooperation with those of the government for periods of six months to one year. In 1993 more than 90 researchers from national research institutes were visiting researchers from university of Tsukuba. The numbers are increasing, since in 1992, the university adopted a new system which allow Ph.D. students in the field of science to research in national laboratories as a trainee under the supervision of a professor. In 1993, around 1000 students were covered by this system. This kind of formal exchange reinforces strong ties between universities and national laboratories and creates long established networks rooted in informal partnership among individual researchers and professors.

In Tsukuba Science City information exchange circles have been created from 1979 in different themes: environment, earth science, the electron microscope, insects, genetic breeding, structural engineering (Kawamoto, 1994). More than one hundred circles are counted today which represent the participation of researchers from public and private research R&D laboratories. These circles are dealing with a diversity of research fields, high level research abilities, freedom to join study teams and strong motivations for participation.

In the Technopolis areas we cannot observe yet the same characteristics of social network as in Tsukuba. The concentration of R&D companies inside the park and the dispersion of industries inside the city or the prefecture cannot create yet a special technopolitan environment. Nevertheless some foundations inside the park have created some meetings open to industrialists, academics professors and researchers. For example, the Akita Technopolis Foundation has created a business group where everybody can exchange ideas, some of which may be realized as venture business.

In Japan, the research institutions private or public are bureaucratic and hierarchical, and the promotion of the circulation of information and communication is essential to develop creative research. Moreover it is important to remark that the scientists from the private sectors are under the strict control of their organisations and are very hesitant to disclose their true opinions.

The technological innovation cannot result only from the production factors of high technology industry. Synergy depends on specific forms of social organisation and different institutional supports. The social network within the context of information exchange of technology are essential component for the formation of autonomous innovative milieus. In fact, we can distinguish two dimensions in the processes involved in the structuring of the territory. The first one is cognitive: it is a matter of circulation of information and scientific knowledge. The second one is institutional: it takes in consideration the local government actions for the energising of local industry (Perrin, 1991).

5.6 Conclusion

While a number of problems have to be resolved in the local Japanese high tech areas, Tsukuba Science City represents the most successful effort concerning the stimulation of scientific research and production of innovations. In the Technopolis areas, local social networks are not really woven yet. The continuous concentration of high technology industries and R&D activities inside the metropolitan areas do not help the development of the Technopolis. We have to consider that the Japanese experience of technopole phenomena is still in an experimental state. The Technopolis are confronted to the difficulties of promoting exchange and the conception of new infrastructure in an urban environment. Finally, if we refer to the major approaches of technopoles analysts:-

the economists' innovation process: Aydalot, Perrin (1991);

synergetic effect between the actors: Stöhr (1987);

technological districts: Marshall and others;

proximity: Camagni (1991),

the Japanese model only partially corresponds to these theories: the place and the role of the state, little mentioned in the above, remains fundamental in Japan.

References

(J.) indicates references in Japanese

Burnier M., Lacroix G. (1996), Les technopoles, Paris, Presses Universitaire de France.

Camagni R. (1991) Innovation Networks: Spatial Perspectives, London, Belhaven Press.

Castells M. (1996) The Rise of the Network Society, Oxford, Blackwell.

Cheung C. W. (1991) "Regional innovation strategies and information society: a review of government initiatives in Japan", Asian Geographer, Hong Kong, 39-61.

Conti S. Malecki E., Paevi O. (1995) (eds) The Industrial Enterprise and its Environment: Spatial Perspectives, The Organisation of Industrial Space, Sydney, Avebury.

Dearing J. W. (1995) Growing a Japanese Science City, Communication in Scientific Research, New York, Routledge.

Dore R. (1986) Flexible Rigidities: Industrial Policy and Structural Adjustment in the Japanese Economy 1970-1980, London, The Athlone Press.

Glasmeier A. (1988) "The Japanese Technopolis Programme: high tech development strategy or industrial policy in disguise", International Journal of Urban and Industrial Research, Great Britain, 268-284.

Eto H. (1993) R&D Strategies in Japan: The National Regional And Corporate Approach, Tokyo, Elsevier.

Fujita K. and Child Hill R. (1993) (eds) Japanese Cities and the World Economy, Philadelphia, Temple University Press.

Gonda K. (1994) "Framework of Industrial Location Policy and Roles of Regional Science and Technology Policy In Japan", in Okamura S. Sakauchi F. Nomaka I. (1994) (eds), Science and technology policy research , new perspectives on global science and technology policy, Tokyo, Mita Press, 133-147.

Japan Industrial Location Centre (1991), Technopolis suishin chosa kenkyu hokokusho. (J)

Japan Industrial Location Centre (1996), Technopolis suishin chosa kenkyu hokokusho. (J.)

Japan Industrial Location Centre (1997), Present circumstances of regional development in Japan. Keirin.

Japan Regional Development Corporation (1996), Overview of Japan's Regional Development Policies.

Johnson J.C. (1994) "Anthropological contributions to the study of social networks: a review" In: Wasserman S., Galaskiewics J. (1994) (eds) Advances in Social Network Analysis: Research in the Social and Behavioral Sciences, California, A Sage Focus Edition.

Kawamoto T. (Oct. 1993) "Towards innovative regions, from the experience of scientific communication in Tsukuba Science City", Paper presented to the international meeting: "innovative on innovation: tomorrow's Technopolis" in Seville.

Kawamoto T. (1994) "Research environment in Tsukuba Science City", Tsukuba, Tsukuba Research Consortium.

Kawashima T. Stohr W. (1988) "Decentralized technology policy: the case of Japan" Environment and Planning C: Government and Policy, 6, 427-439.

Komiya K. Okuno M, Suzumura K. (1988) (eds) Industrial Policies of Japan, Tokyo, Academic Press Japan Inc.

Masser I. (1990) "Technology and regional development policy: a review of Japan's Technopolis Programme", Town Planning Review, 351-364.

Morris-Suzuki T. (1994) The Technological Transformation of Japan: from the seventeenth to the twenty-first century, Cambridge, Cambridge University Press.

Nishioka H. (1985) "High technology industry: location, regional development and international trade fictions", The Aoyama Journal of Economics, Tokyo, 295-341.

Normille D. (1993) "Breaching Industry-University barriers: Japan," Science, USA, 1585.

Perrin J. Cl. (1991) "Réseaux d'innovation - milieux innovateurs, développement territorial", Revue d'Economie régionale et urbaine, Paris, n°3/4.
Sassen S. (1991) The Global City: New York-London-Tokyo, Princeton, Princeton University Press.
Saxenian A. (1994) Regional advantage, culture and competition in Silicon Valley and Route 128, Massachusetts, Harvard University Press.
Scott A. J. (1993) Technopolis, High Technology Industry and Regional Development in Southern California, Berkeley, University of California Press.
Smilor R.W., Kozmetsky (G.), Gibson D.W. (eds) (1988) Creating the Technopolis, Linking Technology commercialization and economic development, Cambridge, Ballinger
Sternberg R. (1995) "Supporting peripheral economies or industrial policy in favour of national growth? An empirically based analysis of goal achievement of the Japanese Technopolis Program," Environment and Planning C: Government and Policy, 13, 425-439.
Sternberg R. (1996) "Regional growth theories and high tech regions", International Journal of Urban and Regional Research, 3, 518-537.
Stohr W. (1987) "Territorial Innovation Complexes", Papers of the Regional Science Association, Germany, 29-44.
Tachi R. (1993) The Contemporary Japanese Economy: an Overview, Tokyo, University of Tokyo Press.
Takahashi J., Sugiura N. (1996) "The Japanese urban system and the growing centrality of Tokyo in the global economy", In: Lo F. Yeung Y-M. (eds), Emerging World Cities in Pacific Asia, Tokyo, United Nations University Press.
Tanaka, T. (1996), Technopolis Chiiki keizai, Koyoshobo, Tokyo. (J.)
Tatsuno Sh. (1986) The Technopolis Strategy. Japan, High Technology, and the Control of the 21st Century, New York, Prentice Hall.
Vidal Fl. (1994) L'entreprise et la cité partenaires ou adversaires, Paris, InterEditions.
Yada T. (1982) "On the economic geographic", Keizai Shirin, University of Hosei, Tokyo, 375-410.
Yamazaki, A. (1992)nettowaku gata haichi to bunsan seisaku, Taimeido, Tokyo. (J.)

6 Defining Urban Corridors: Case Studies of Four Mega Cities of India

Ashok K. Dutt and Anindita Parai

6.1 Introduction

Throughout the world, urbanisation patterns are changing. Change exists not only in the levels of urbanisation, but also in the spatial distribution of cities. A city of a million inhabitants today does not have the same characteristics as a city of the same size in 1800. Jones and Sheperd (1987) in their analysis of the urban agglomerations of the world noted that in 1800 the world's largest city, Peking, had only 1.10 million people. By 1950 three major urban agglomerations developed - New York, London, and Shanghai all with more than 10 million inhabitants. By 2000, projections estimate there will be 25 urban agglomerations of more than 10 million, with Mexico City the largest with about 26 million inhabitants (United Nations, 1990).

Although there are cases where much of the pressure for urbanisation results in the growth of a primate city like Bangkok, it is also possible for urban population to be diffused within a network of closely linked urban centres. Thus the prime variables that have been of interest to town planners have been numbers and locations. The growth of London led even in the depths of World War II to the formulation of a plan to constrict its growth (the Green Belt) and to diffuse new growth (to the satellite New Towns) (Greater London Plan, 1945). Another vision was that of Doxiadis (1966). Noting that the city, hemmed in by built-up area, found tremendous resistance from its surrounding areas and could not expand, he suggested that if the city was to grow it should break through in "one direction and one direction only." He supported the idea of unidirectional growth by arguing the fact that:

> expansion in several directions means that the city's centre of gravity remains in the same place, where it is subjected to all the pressures and must break into pieces if the growth of the urban area exceeds the limits which the centre can serve. (Doxiadis, 1966, p. 55).

To induce change in these prime variables of population and location, the functioning of the space economy has to be understood. An urban system is comprised of three major elements: functional units in space (factories, offices, homes), links between them (transport and communication), and the environment (economy, society) (Johnston, 1982). Change in any of these three will induce changes in the others. Improved transport and communication has resulted in increased urbanisation and metropolitan dispersion, leading to new spatial specialization and exchange. Continued urban growth in this fashion has reduced the disadvantages of urbanisation and resulted in interlinked networks of different urban nodes. One pattern to emerge on strategic transport links is that of the "urban corridor." These "corridors" are strongly interacting linear urban development with a highly developed transport and communication axis (Whebel, 1969).

Doxiadis identified the growth of three major megalopolises. A megalopolis in Great Britain linking settled areas from London to Birmingham, Manchester, and Liverpool was one of them (Doxiadis, 1966). He foresaw the growth of a megalopolis in the United States stretching along the northeastern seaboard of the country, which had first been suggested by Gottman (1961). Doxiadis also identified the growing megalopolis in the continent of Europe connecting the Netherlands and the Ruhr. He forecast that with increasing economic stability this megalopolis would extend towards Czechoslovakia, Poland, northern Italy, and other parts of Europe. With the expansion of the transportation network, he envisaged the connection of continents over the whole world resulting ultimately in a Universal City - the Ecumenopolis (Doxiadis, 1966).

The urban agglomeration of Paris, like London, is a single-city-centred metropolis. Consisting of ten central arrondissements, the major built up area of Paris forms an oval conveniently bounded by the big terminal railway stations of St. Lazare in the northwest, Nord and Est in the northeast, Lyon and Austerlitz in the southeast, and Montparnasse in the southwest (Hall, 1984). However, too much attention was devoted to the development of the centre. Thus, suburban areas lacked basic necessities like proper housing and transport facilities and there was very little communication between the centre and its suburbs. To overcome the problem of Paris sucking the life blood of France, the master regional plan of 1960 aimed to reduce congestion in the centre by decentralization. This would be achieved by improving transportation facilities radiating outward from the centre and also by creating new nodes in the suburbs away from the centre. Thus, the aim was to transform this urban complex from a single historic centre to a new type of polycentric region. However, the development of Paris, in contrast to Abercrombie's green belt and new towns planned around London (Greater London Plan 1945), was based on an axial pattern of growth along which new communities were incorporated. These new urban nodes like Abercrombie's new towns, would be centres of new communities and providers of service to a wide zone and they would be linked with each other and with the centre by highways and rail lines (Hall, 1966; Hall, 1984; Eldridge, 1975).

In Holland the cities of Rotterdam, The Hague, Haarlem, Amsterdam, and Utrecht have expanded rapidly , especially since World War II. Together they have emerged as one of the leading urban agglomerations of the European continent. Popularly known as the "Randstad" or "ring city" the rapid growth of this horseshoe shaped urban agglomeration has been checked through utilizing the concepts of the London plan. Planning intervention in the form of green belts and buffer zones between the cities was carried out by the National Physical Planning Service (Dutt, 1970; Dutt, 1968). The agricultural heart of the Randstad is protected with the aid of preservation policies. However, growth had to occur in some direction. Thus, expansion was encouraged along the main transport routes in radial lines extending outward from the Randstad (Hall, 1984). The spread of urban settlements outwards along corridors was being promoted with the aim of "concentrated decentralization" (Physical Planning, 1966). Besides, new industrial sites were encouraged to be developed in the less developed areas. These areas, commonly known as "stimulus areas" would relieve maximum pressure away from the Randstad (Dutt, 1970).

6.2   Formation of Urban Agglomerations: India

Compared to the megalopolitan pattern of urban growth that Western countries have reached, urbanisation patterns in Asia show a very sharp urban-rural dichotomy, and the frequent existence of primate cities. The primate city pattern is largely the influence of the colonial past, reinforced in the present by inadequate development in the economic sector. Population growth in these settlements is rapidly outgrowing developments in transportation and communication systems. Core areas of the primate metropolises in the low income Asian countries stand out as "enclaves" of development with sharp distance decay effects.

India's urban patterns have illustrated a highly polarised and spatially imbalanced urban system with a "sharp urban-rural and core-periphery dichotomy" (Rao, 1983). Urban demographic and socio-economic characteristics reflected a core-periphery exploitative relationship (Raza et. al., 1979), between city and rural hinterland. However, recent trends show that with improved mobility, Indian urban patterns are forming urban-industrial corridors, linking cities together as much as linking each city to its rural locality. Thus with the growth of transportation and communication networks, the million-plus cities are slowly integrating their hinterlands and emerging "into a national metropolitan system with greater national links" (Rao, 1983). For example, Bombay and Calcutta have served as regional primate cities since colonial times. By 1990 they were amongst the world's largest agglomerations. With a population size of 12.6 and 11.2 million respectively, they both ranked in the global top ten (United Nations, 1991).

The growth of the Calcutta Conurbation stretching along a few miles of the Hooghly River is an example of the emerging trend of linear growth and diffusion of cities. In an earlier study, Dutt and Chakraborty (1963) identified the extent and characteristics of the Calcutta conurbation. They traced the historical growth of urbanisation in the city and tried to relate the growth of the city to its waterways, roadways, and later on, the railways. They concluded that urbanisation in the Calcutta conurbation took place in three stages, with each one having its own unique characteristics. The first phase of the growth of the Calcutta conurbation (1757-1850) set the stage for later urbanisation. This period laid out the initial structures of Calcutta, which was still on the threshold of being converted into a metropolis. The second phase of urban development (1850-1920) witnessed the establishment of factories, construction of roadways and railways, and the development of means of communication. Coalescence of urban areas along the two sides of the Hooghly river with Calcutta as its primary centre, and Howrah the secondary centre, started to occur during these years. The last phase of urban growth in this region since 1920 has witnessed large-scale development all along the conurbation, in industries, communication, and urban population, in a un-broken north-south built-up area with spurs developing in different directions along the radially diverging rail and road network.

6.3   Delineation of Urban Corridors: Case Studies and Methodology

India's urban growth has been very rapid in the last four decades. Urban growth has accelerated not only in the major cities, but has also stimulated satellite towns. The growth is showing a tendency to spread out from the major centres in a linear fashion, as suggested by the 'urban corridor' concept. Aided by industrial growth, the spread of these emerging cities is occurring along major transportation routes. This section looks at four case studies: - the four metropolises of India – Bombay (Mumbai) , Delhi, Calcutta, and Madras (Chennai). It uses the prime variables noted above, population and location, to define the corridors.

6.3.1 The Case Study of Delhi Region

Delhi, the capital of India, occupies a pivotal position in a relatively flat water divide between the two most agriculturally productive areas of South Asia, the Indus plains in the west and the Ganges plains in the east. North of the metropolis lies the insurmountable Himalaya ranges and to the southwest lies the inhospitable Thar desert in the state of Rajasthan in the northern region of the country. The strategic significance of the site on the banks of the Yamuna for defending the Ganges valley from invaders from the northwest is witnessed by the number of ancient cities that have been built and re-built here. It became one of the centres of the Moghul Empire, and in 1911 the British adopted it as the capital of India. After independence in 1947, Delhi continued as the national capital. Delhi witnessed excessive growth just after independence due to a flood of new refugees from Pakistan and the expansion of the government leading to growth in the commercial and industrial sectors of the economy. As the capital city of the nation, Delhi received prime attention for its infrastructural growth related to housing, drainage, and sewers. Expansion was so rapid that for the first time a master plan was

Map 6.1   Class I Cities in Delhi Region

developed for the city. Growth was promoted in secondary urban centres surrounding the metropolis like Noida, Meerut, Faridabad, and Sonipat. In recent years the Delhi metropolis has extended both to the north and south. Its activities include not only administration, but also trade and commerce, manufacturing, and many service sectors

With a population of 8.4 million in 1991 Delhi is not only the third largest metropolis of the country, but also ranks 20th among the world's largest metropolises. With a growth rate of 46.10 percent in the 1981-91 decade,

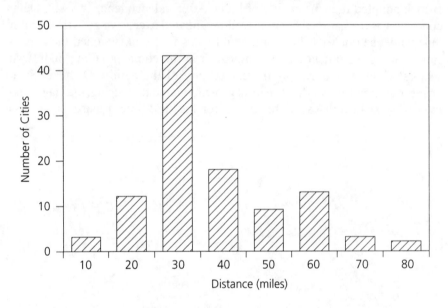

Figure 6.1   Nearest Neighbour Distances of Cities in Delhi Region

Delhi is the most rapidly growing metropolitan area of India.

The Delhi Corridor
The analysis is divided into the following steps:
1) In the first step the geographic hinterland around the metropolis is defined. Identification is based on the influences of the main metropolis and physical barriers.
2) Within each region, Class I cities (having a population over 100,000) are plotted on a map. There are 76 cities plotted within the Delhi region (Map 6.1).
3) The nearest-neighbour distances for all cities are plotted in a histogram. For the Delhi region a plot of the nearest neighbour distance

(Figure 6.1) reveals a break at 50 miles.

4) Taking the main city (Delhi in this case) as the starting point, all the cities located within 50 miles are selected, and in turn those within 50 miles of them etc. This step results in the identification of 56 cities (Map 6.2) .

5) For these 56 cities a map is produced showing both road and rail connections (Map 6.3). Cities that do not have both major road (National and State highways) and major rail (broad and metre gauge) connections are then eliminated.

6) Thus, only 37 cities within the Delhi region (Map 6.4) are within 50 miles of each other, and are connected both by railway lines and roadways.

The pattern suggests a corridor extending from Pathankot in the north to Gwalior in the south. From Delhi the northern extension of the corridor has taken two paths with both of them merging at Ambala. It has a secondary corridor extending in the northeast and southwest due to physical barriers (as explained in the above section).

The inclusion of 37 cities also suggests the exclusion of 39 cities – those which are less linked, and which remain independent nodes within their

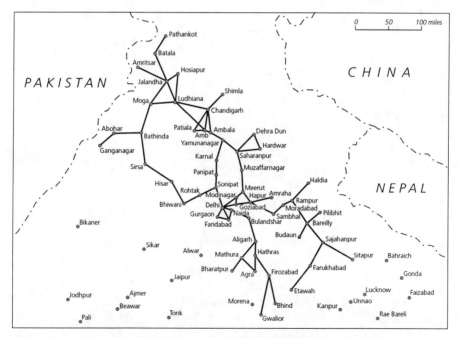

Map 6.2 Network of Neighbouring Cities in Delhi Region

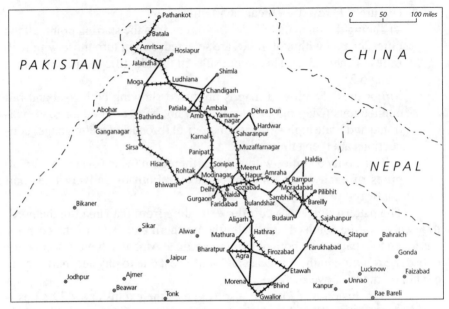

Map 6.3   Road and Rail Connections between Cities, Delhi Region

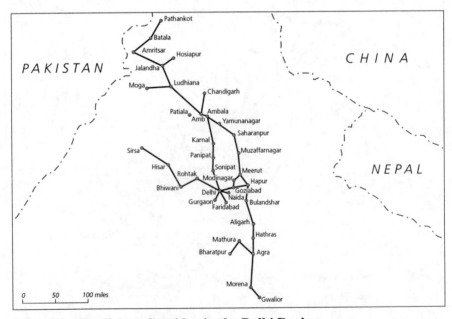

Map 6.4   The Urban Corridor in the Delhi Region

own rural regions. They are the other side of the coin of India's urbanisation.

6.3.2 The Case Study of Calcutta Region

Calcutta is located eighty miles from the open sea on the Hooghly river, a major distributary in the Ganges delta. It is a nodal city within a rich agricultural region. Calcutta, with its easily accessible location and its resource-based hinterland provided the ideal site for early British traders who made it their capital from 1772 to 1911. The seaport facilitated import of machines to develop its jute industries (raw jute being produced along the fertile Hooghly river). Calcutta attracted all modern activities - export and import, finance, administration and industry. The partition of Bengal between India and East Pakistan at independence in 1947 stripped Calcutta of commercial exchange with much of its hinterland, while leading to an influx of millions of refugees. One unique feature of the metropolis, compared to Delhi, Bombay, and Madras is that Calcutta's regional location has no other major centres within hundreds of miles. The rest of the cities located in the eastern region are provincial centres with comparatively small population and limited economic activities and employment opportunities. The small urban growth centres of Asansol-Durgapur, Bokaro, Ranchi, Jamshedpur, and Rourkela cannot counter the overwhelming attraction of Calcutta in the eastern region. Thus, although Calcutta is going through a period of stagnation, it still attracts thousands of migrants and is still the second largest metropolis of the country, with 11 million people in 1991.

The Calcutta Corridor

The same method is used again. Within Calcutta's region there are 18 Class I cities. A plot of the minimum distances for the cities revealed a distinct natural break at 30 miles. All cities within 30 miles of another are identified, and then a further selection is based on the existence of major road and rail links between them. The resultant Map 6.5 delineates the urban corridor of the Calcutta region. In the delineation of the Calcutta corridor, one important point was taken into consideration. The boundary of Calcutta city extends 30 miles to the north and 12 miles to the south. Thus, while calculating the distance between the selected cities, in step 3, the distance from the edge of the city boundary, and not from the location of the city itself, was considered. For example, Barddhaman's actual distance from Calcutta is 59 miles. But when the distance is calculated from the edge of the northwest border of the city the distance is reduced to 29 miles. Thus, Barddhaman is selected as one of the cities within the corridor. The same consideration was applied in the calculation of distances between Calcutta-Santipur, and Calcutta-Ranaghat.

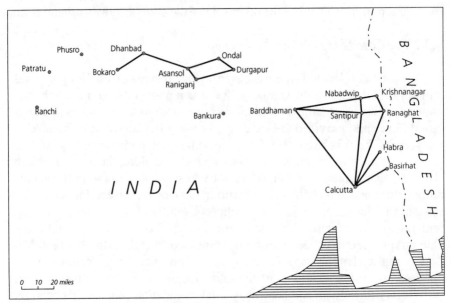

Map 6.5 The Fragmented Urban Corridor of West Bengal

The histogram drawn to identify the natural break was therefore the distance of each city from the edge of the Calcutta city boundary.

The Calcutta corridor, including only 8 cities, extends its wings only in the north and northwest. It has not yet been linked to any city in the south. It extends in the northeast up to Krishnanagar, in the north till Nabadwip, and in the northwest up to Barddhaman. There is another well developed corridor including the cities of Durgapur-Raniganj-Asansol-Dhanbad-Bokaro. However, the two cities Durgapur and Barddhaman, 100 miles apart, do not meet the distance criterion. They are also not linked strongly.

Again, if 8 out of 18 cities are included in the prime network, 10 are excluded. These represent that other independent kind of urbanisation, although 6 of them have a little regional system to themselves, but without a central metropolis.

6.3.3 The Case Study of Chennai (Madras) Region

Covering an area of 174 square km, Madras lies on low lying flat terrain, intersected by two creeks, the Cooum and Adyar. Like Calcutta, Madras and its hinterland are covered by an extensive network of rivers, most of the rivers emptying themselves in the Bay of Bengal. However, unlike Calcutta, the rivers draining the region are not navigable the year round. The rivers dry up during the winter and summer season, limiting their use of the rainy season. This factor has significantly retarded the growth of Madras. Like Calcutta, Madras was founded as a trading post by the British but the hinterland of Madras was not as well developed with potential resources as in Bengal. It was connected early by the railways, and it had significant government functions. With a population of 5.4 million in 1991, it is the fourth largest metropolis of India. Located on the Coromandel coast, Madras is still the major port of Southern India and capital of the state of Tamil Nadu.

Delineation of The Urban Corridor

There are 33 cities in the region with a population over 100,000. Analysis of nearest neighbours suggested a distance cut-off function of 50 miles. Using this and the overlay of rail and road routes produces the resultant (Map 6.6.)

This final delineation of the Madras corridor reveals only 13 selected cities. The corridor extends both towards north and south from Madras. In the north it is connected up to Tirupati. However, there is no direct connection between Madras and Tirupati. It connects via Kanchipuram-Arcot-Vellore. The same applies in the southern extension of the corridor. However, Map 6.6 shows the connection between Madras and Pondicherry. The two cities

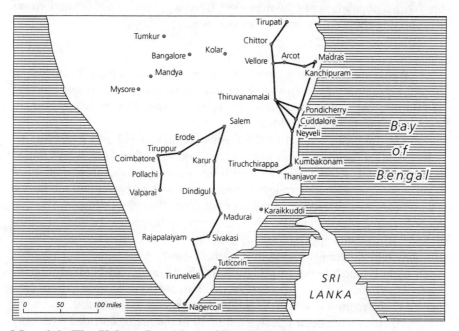

Map 6.6 The Urban Corridors of Tamil Nadu

are connected by rail and roadways, but the distance criterion of 50 miles is exceeded in this case. In order to show that there is a connection between the two cities, the cities have been directly linked in the Map 6.6. In the south the corridor extends to Tiruchchirappali.

Like the Calcutta corridor, a secondary corridor has developed in the region. This corridor extends from Salem in the north to Nagercoil in the south.

Note that 20 cities lie outside the major corridor..

6.3.4 The Case Study of the Bombay Region

Bombay, sometimes referred to as the "Gateway to India," is located on the western coastal plains along the commercially active Konkan littoral. Bombay, unlike Madras, has a superb natural harbour, and the city is located on an island, limiting its development to a north-south axis. There are no natural waterways connecting the metropolis to its hinterland. Although acquired early by the British as a trading post, its true rise to prominence awaited the building of the railways and the expansion of cotton growing in the hinterland from the 1860s. It is now capital to India's most industrialised state, Maharashtra, it is the centre of India's industry, and the centre of its financial life. With a population of 12.6 m in 1991 Bombay ranks first in the nation and sixth among the world's largest metropolises.

Delineation of the Urban Corridor

Applying the same methods as before, 39 Class I cities are noted in Bombay's region. The nearest neighbour analysis suggests a cut-off function of 60 miles. Applying then the major road and rail network leaves 10 selected cities in growth corridors.

The final delineation of the Bombay Corridor (Map 6.7) reveals 10 selected cities. Starting from Bombay, the corridor extends its wings inland up to Khandwa. All the cities along this line are within a distance of 60 miles from each other and are strongly connected by both railways and roadways. There is another extension of the corridor from Bombay to Pune. The distance between the two cities is 64 miles, outside the distance criterion established. But in this special case we take into account the city boundary of Bombay which extends for about 20 miles inland. A secondary corridor has been established connecting Gandhinagar-Ahmedabad-Nadiad-Anand-Vadodara-Bharuch-Surat-Navsari-Valsad. This corridor, however, is not connected to the main one under the established criteria in this study.

10 cities have been selected out of 39 in the major corridor – i.e. only about one quarter. Given the dispersed nature of the population of Maharashtra

and the known concentration of industrial activity in the west, this suggests that many urban nodes are isolated (they are) and as yet unable to participate in the benefits of urban-urban exchange in an urban regional economy, as opposed to an urban-rural economy operating in an isolated state.

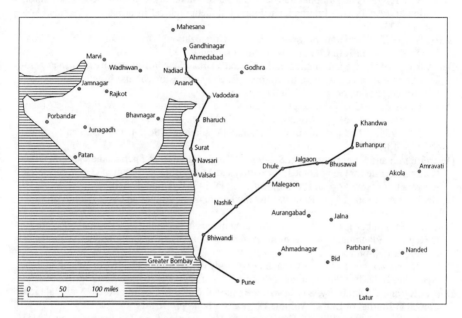

Map 6.7 The Urban Corridors of Maharashtra and Gujarat

6.4 Conclusions

Taking this simple approach to the location and size of the urban population around the four largest metropoli of India, we have shown that there are dispersed urban populations in connected urban systems. This simple fact should encourage government and planners: there are alternatives to the suffocating growth of primate cities. On the other hand these systems do not extend very far yet. In fact, using our criteria, many of the Class I cities of India still lie outside such systems. This is not surprising, given the level of development of the country. Recent analyses by the government have identified crippling capacity shortages in infrastructure such as transport and power – and in consequence invited joint ventures with foreign capital. Part of this development task is to foster growth in the gaps in the system so that they too can become part of the linked metropolises, India's version tomorrow of the Randstadt of today.

References

Abercrombie, P. 1945. Greater London Plan 1944. His Majesty's Stationary Office. London. pp.220.

Abler, R.F. 1987. "The National Science Foundation National Centre for Geographic Information and Analysis." International Journal of Geographical Information Systems. Volume 1: 303-326.

Berry, B.J. 1973. The Human Consequences of Urbanization: Divergent Paths in the Urban Experience of the 20th Century. Metheun, London.

Berry, B.J.L. 1977. Transformation of the Nation's Urban System; small city growth as zero-sum growth in small cities in transition." The Dynamics of Urban Growth and Decline. H.J. Bryce. Ballinger. pp. 283-300.

Davis, Kingsley. 1955. "The Origin and Growth of Urbanization in the World." The American Journal of Sociology. Volume LX, No. 5. March. pp. 429-437.

Davis, K. 1965. "The Urbanization of Human Population." Scientific American. Volume 213. pp. 40-53.

Ding, Yuemin and Fotheringham, A.S. 1991. "The Integration of Spatial Analysis and GIS." National Centre for Geographic Information and Analysis, Department of Geography, State University of New York at Buffalo, Buffalo, NY 14261. Unpublished.

Doxiadis, C.A. 1966. Urban Renewal and the Future of the American City. Public Administration Service, Chicago. pp. 173.

Dutt, A.K. December 1968. "Levels of Planning in the Netherlands, with Particular Reference to Regional Planning."" Annals of the Association of American Geographers. Volume 58, No. 4. pp. 670-685.

Dutt A.K. November 1970. "A Comparative Study of Regional Planning in Britain and the Netherlands." The Ohio Journal of Science. Volume 70, No. 6. pp. 321-335.

Dutt, A.K. and Chakraborty, S.C. 1963. "Reality of Calcutta Conurbation." National Geographical Journal of India.. Volume IX, Parts 3 & 4. pp. 161-175.

Eldridge, Hope Tisdale; 1975. "The Process of Urbanization." in J. J. Spengler and O. D. Duncan (eds.). Demographic Analysis. Glencoe, Ill. Free Press. pp. 338-343.

Fotheringham, A.S. and Wong, D.W.S. 1991. "The Modifiable Areal Unit Problem in Multivariate Statistical Analysis." Environment and Planning A, Volume 23: 1025-1044.

Friedmann, J. and Miller, J. 1965. "The Urban Field." Journal of the American Institute of Planners. Volume 31. pp. 312-319.

Geddes, P. 1915. Cities in Evolution: An Introduction to Town Planning Movement and to the Study of Civics. London: Williams and Norgate.

Gottmann, Jean. 1961. Megalopolis: The Urbanized Northeastern Seaboard of the United States. The M.I.T. Press. p. 810.

Hall, Peter. 1966. The World Cities. McGraw Hill Book Co., New York, Toronto. p. 256.

Hall, Peter. 1984. The World Cities. St. Martin's Press, New York. Third Edition. p. 276.

Horn, M. et al. 1988. "Design of Integrated Systems for Spatial Planning Tasks." Proceedings of the Third International Symposium on Spatial Data Handling. August 17-19, Sydney, Australia.

Howard, E. 1966. Garden Cities of Tomorrow. Preface by F.J. Osborn and introductory essay by L. Mumford. Massachusetts Institute of Technology Press. p. 159.

Jones, Barclay and Sheperd, William. 1987. "Cities of the Future: Implications and Relative Decline of the Cities of the West." Journal of Planning Education and Research. Vol. 6, No. 3: 162-166.

Johnston, R.J. 1982 The American Urban System. St. Martin's Press, New York.

Klosterman, R.E. and Xie, Yichun. "Planning Analysis in a GIS Environment: A Low-cost Alternative." (unpublished).

McGee, T.G. 1969. The Southeast Asian City: A Social Geography of the Primate Cities of Southeast Asia. Frederick A. Praeger Publishers, New York. pp. 204.

McGee, T.G. 1971. The Urbanization Process in the Third World: Explorations in Search of a Theory. Bell and Sons Ltd., London. pp. 179.

Papaioannou, J. November 1969. "Comment on the Corridor Concept." Ekistics. Volume 28, No. 168: 354-55.

Physical Planning in Netherlands. Second Report. The Hague. 1966.

Rao, Prakasa VLS. 1983. "Urbanization Process, Patterns and Correlates." Urbanization in India: Spatial Dimensions. Concept Publishing Co., New Delhi. pp. 13-67.

Raza, Moonis et al. 1979. "Spatial Organization and Urbanization in India: A Case Study of Underdevelopment." Rural Area Development Perspectives and Approaches. R.P. Misra and K.V. Sundaram (eds.) Sterling. pp. 333-377.

Smailes, A.E. 1971. "Urban Systems: Presidential Address." Institute of British Geographers. University of Sussex.

United Nations. 1991. World Urbanization Prospects 1990. Estimates and Projections of Urban and Rural Populations and of Urban Agglomerations. New York 1991.

Weber, A.F. 1899. The Growth of Cities in the Nineteenth Century. The Macmillan Co., New York.

Whebell, C.F.J. March 1969. "Corridors: A Theory of Urban Systems." Annals of the Association of American Geographers. Volume 59, No. 1: 1-26.

PART II
GENDER, ACCESS AND ENVIRONMENT

Editors' notes to Part II

This is the largest Part of Volume II – with 13 chapters. It seemed a priori that we ought to be able to break these into obviously different sections – for example on environment, and on gender. However, except at the domestic scale, men and women cohabit urban space, and it is not easy to concentrate on one sex without reflecting on the relationships between both and their urban areas. Nor is it easy to think of the environment, without realising that it can impact differently on rich and poor, on women and men. So we have kept these chapters together. Hitomi Kato starts by discussing the social differences between town and country, and the social complexities of the marginal area where the two interdigitate. The chapter has some innovative approaches to interpreting spatial perception and mental maps. Vincent Costello looks at public space in Tehran as an amenity that can help maintain mental and physical health for the city's citizens and draws a north (rich) and poor (south) divide of the city, with the north having a much greater amount of open space. K. Jayashree notes that even in a low income country, local tourism can be substantial, and 'distort' urban structure from higher social priorities. Tanja Haque looks at how women in Bangladesh can gain in self-esteem through learning new skills and finding financial independence – a process not unlike changes taking place in the West – except that these women start from a far more disadvantaged background – particularly with regard to education and world-awareness. Lahiri-Dutt shows how the casualisation of the work-force on India's coal-mines affects the two sexes differen-tially, and Sharma takes up a similar theme. Anita Weiss compares how the twin structures of the urban built form and Islamic social norms combine to affect women differently in the old town and the new sub-urbs of Lahore. Thinking of the social norms without thinking of the architecture, or vice versa, is pointless. Wilke Ruiter, Helmut Schneider and Pushpa Pathak all look at aspects of poverty, and in particular at programmes designed to alleviate urban poverty – an aim which is increasingly seen as central to the work of aid agencies and govern-ment aid departments. Ruiter and Pathak concentrate on formal pro-grammes. Schneider looks more at networks – those that are often referred to as 'social capital'. Gladys Hingco and B. R.K.Sinha look at environmental and health aspects of the urban population – in Sinha's case by contrasting urban and rural areas and different social classes. George Pomeroy's chapter is a necessary reminder of a theme touched on in Nigel Harris' opening chapter in Volume I – that urban societies do not work within social norms all the time. Fast growing urban ar-eas, creating new wealth in new ways, employing new migrants who live in not-yet stable neighbourhoods, also provide the opportunities for many forms of crime to flourish – having both social and economic impacts.

7 Structure of Urbanisation and Environmental Planning in the Marginal Area of Town and Country

Hitomi M. Kato

7.1 Introduction

Urbanisation has been spreading rapidly even in to local metropolitan areas in Japan. Therefore drastic changes have been occurring in urban fringe environments, associated with friction between locals and newcomers in the communities. In this study we call this urban fringe area "the marginal area" of town and country (Kato, 1995). "The marginal area" is a concept of the region which is derived from "the marginal man" that George Simmel (1908) and Robert Park (1928) theorized in sociology. We regard the rurban (a word coined by compounding rural and urban) community area as the marginal area and also regard town and country as two equal worlds not as a core and its fringe (Fig. 7.1). Utilising the concept of "marginal area" as a method to analyse the region provides a new way to grasp and solve the problems of these regions. Therefore we should pay attention not only to the negative side but also to the positive side of the marginal area where inhabitants overcome the problems of their settlements through the dynamic relationship of social and cultural contradiction and coexistence.

Today, due to the dominance of urbanisation, it seems that urban life styles and cultures have spread all over society, but still cultural conflicts arise in individual communities. Therefore, to utilise the concept of "mar-

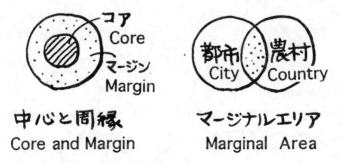

Figure 7.1 Concept of 'Marginal Area'

ginal area" as a method to analyse the region provides a new way to grasp and
solve the problems of these regions.

The main purpose of this study is to find out how to make comfortable dwellings and sustainable agricultural environments, as well as lively
rurban communities consisting of locals and newcomers in the marginal area
of town and country as in the case of Koga town in the eastern part of Fukuoka
metropolitan area in Kyushu, Japan.

7.2   Methods of study

Many natural environments of Japan have been colonised by agricultural communities. But environmental quality in marginal areas has been in
danger due to the retreat of agriculture and the increase of newcomers. We

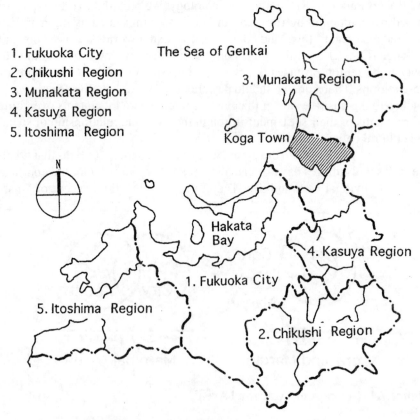

1. Fukuoka City

2. Chikushi Region

3. Munakata Region

4. Kasuya Region

5. Itoshima Region

The Sea of Genkai

3. Munakata Region

Koga Town

N

Hakata Bay

4. Kasuya Region

1. Fukuoka City

5. Itoshima Region

2. Chikushi Region

Map 7.1 Fukuoka Metropolitan Area

believe it is important to restore these environments and to educate subjects in their maintenance.

To begin with we investigate the management of communities and the maintenance of environments by means of communal work. Secondly we try to grasp inhabitants' common images of environments by utilizing a spatial consciousness map to sketch the region.

The results of our investigations are used as materials to ameliorate the environmental planning and to improve "ecological" towns.

7.3   Structure of Urbanisation: the Case of Fukuoka

Fukuoka is the largest city in Kyushu, and the centre of commercial and information activities. Fukuoka city has sprawled in three directions in a Y pattern dictated by Hakata Bay and coast of the Sea of Genkai to the north. Each axis is located as follows in the master plan of Fukuoka city. The southern part of Chikushi is information city axis, the eastern part and the northeastern parts of Kasuya and Munakata are production and circulation axes, and the western part of Itoshima is the green-housing axis.

The growth of population of Fukuoka metropolitan area from 1960 to 1990 is shown in Table 7.1, and illustrated in Fig. 7.2. The population of Fukuoka city has doubled in last 30 years as large numbers of people have flowed to the mother city from rural areas during the period of high economic growth in 1960s. The Chikushi region, whose population began to increase first, has the highest 5-year rate of increase of population, peaking at 38 % in 1970-75. The Munakata region and the Kasuya region came next and the Itoshima region started its growth last in the 1970s (Fig. 7.2).

7.4   Zoning of the Urbanisation Promotion Zone and the Urbanisation Control Zone

A new zoning act of 1968 came into force in 1970 in many local governments in the Fukuoka metropolitan area, to control the disordered urban sprawl. The city planning area was divided into two parts; a zone which promotes urbanisation and another zone which controls urbanisation. The urbanisation promotion zone was revised to include more areas than expected because many landowners wished to register their lands as part of it. But high land prices have deterred urban development in the approved zone. Furthermore farmlands in the city areas have been classed as green areas by the system of reserved agricultural zones.

Table 7.1 Population Change of Fukuoka Metropolitan Area (1960-1990)

	1960	1965	1970	1975	1980	1985	1990
Fukuoka city	682365	769176	871717	1002201	1088588	1160440	1237062
(Change Rate %)		*12.7*	*13.3*	*15*	*8.6*	*6.6*	*7.6*
Munakata region	57148	60337	71332	92386	109116	118893	127770
(%)		*5.6*	*18.2*	*29.5*	*18.1*	*9*	*7.5*
Kasuya region	113893	115516	129506	151816	178307	197412	212824
(%)		*1.4*	*12.1*	*17.2*	*17.4*	*10.7*	*7.8*
Chikushi region	91486	117660	151693	209269	263026	296838	333194
(%)		*28.6*	*28.9*	*38*	*25.7*	*12.9*	*12.2*
Itoshima region	59549	56863	56204	59697	66220	73649	77610
(%)		*-4.5*	*-1.2*	*6.2*	*10.9*	*11.2*	*5.3*
Fukuoka metropolitan area	1004441	1119552	1280452	1515369	1705257	1847232	1988460
		11.5	*14.4*		*12.5*	*8.3*	*7.6*

7.4.1 Zoning and Characteristic of Urbanisation in the Eastern Part of Metropolitan Area

The characteristics of urban development are influenced by, for example, accessibility, traffic, convenience, natural and living environments, water resources, price of land, the character of communities and so on. They also however depend on zoning and on agriculture promotion areas.

There are 5 patterns of zoning in Kasuya region (Fig. 7.3). These are also related to increases of population. In cases of type 1- type 3 all the areas are designated city planning area, and divided into two zones. The differences between each type rely on the relative size of the two zones and on population growth. The urban development zone of type 3 is very small, so growth of population is limited. Type 4 has three zones including on beyond the city planning area. The population has consistently grown. Type 5 so far has no designated zoning.

We selected Koga town (type 4) to investigate the situation and the problems of each the three zones. The following settlements were investigated carefully: Kazurugaoka and Chidori new towns in the urban development zone, Aoyagi and Mushirouchi agricultural communities in the urban control zone, Odake and Taniyama as rurban communities beyond the zone of city planning (Map 7.2).

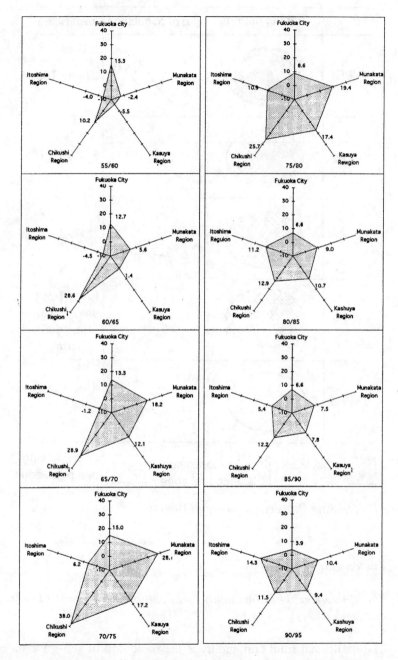

Figure 7.2 Population Changes in Fukuoka Metropolitan Area

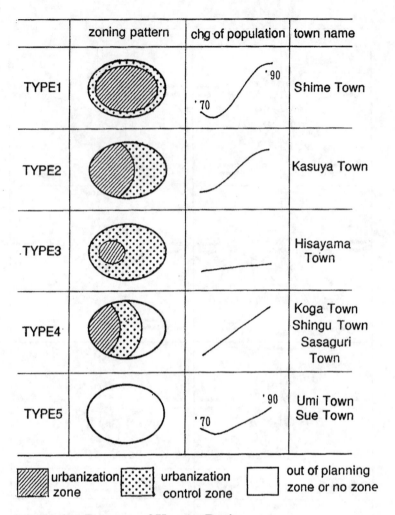

	zoning pattern	chg of population	town name
TYPE1		'70 ↗ '90	Shime Town
TYPE2			Kasuya Town
TYPE3			Hisayama Town
TYPE4			Koga Town Shingu Town Sasaguri Town
TYPE5		'70 ↗ '90	Umi Town Sue Town

urbanization zone   urbanization control zone   out of planning zone or no zone

Figure 7.3 Zoning Patterns of Kasuya Region

7.5   Locals and Newcomers

7.5.1 *The Management of Community and Relationships between Locals and Newcomers*

The traditional rural community is the basic unit of self-government whose three functions are the administration of the district, the management of agricultural affairs and the management of common property. So when

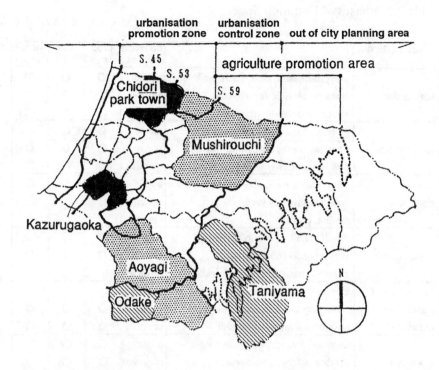

Map 7.2 Zoning and Settlements of Koga Town

newcomers increase, this system is sometimes divided into administration and management. About two thirds of communities in and near Koga town divide the system of administration this way. The system is divided in Mushirouchi, but not yet in rurban Odake and Taniyana, despite the fact that their populations have increased 20 times and 5 times respectively during these 30 years.

7.5.2 Festivals and Events of Community

Various annual events are held in the agricultural community all year around. Various traditional festivals take place at main shrines and at lesser shrines on important agricultural periods. Other rites of passage may take place too. Community activities help to build common feelings and a community spirit. However, there are fewer activities today than in the past. Sports events and cultural activities are more popular among newcomers and in rurban communities.

Table 7.2 Phases of Common Space

spatial item	object	common aspect	property	use	maintenance
way space	way, road, lane, pass, path, walk	public	◎	◎	○
	track, approach, farm road,	common	○	◎	○
	footpath between rice field	private	○	○	○
water space	river, stream, brook, waterway	public	◎	○	○
	channel, creek, lake, pond, marsh	common	○	◎	◎
	well, water gate	private		○	○
open space	open space, park, play lot, garden	public	◎	◎	◎
	ground, gate ball yard,	common	○	○	○
	square, plaza	private		○	
living facilities	meeting hall, community center	public	◎	○	○
	youth center, coop shop,	common	◎	◎	◎
	common bath, fire fighting facility	private		○	
farmland and agricultural facilities	common rice field, common meadow	public			
	collecting and forwarding place	common	◎	◎	◎
	country elevator, water mill	private	◎	◎	◎
wood space	common forest, windbreak forest	public	○	○	○
	tidebreak forest, homestead forest	common	○	○	○
	hill at the back of home and village	private	○	○	○
beach		public	◎	○	○
	beach, wharf, sand, fishing port	common	○	◎	◎
		private		○	
religious space	shrine, small shrine, forest of shrine	public			
	holy place, stage, temple, cemetery	common	◎	◎	◎
	common charnel, monument	private	○	○	○
common image of space	spatial image, landscape, boundary	public			
	sign, symbol, landmark, area	common	◎	◎	◎
	place name, language of space	private			

7.5.3 Use and Maintenance of Common Space

In the past all the space of a rural settlements was shared. It could be said that all the space of a rural settlement was common. But much of what was common has now been differentiated into public and private spheres because of modernization, so that what remains common has gradually declined. What is common is regarded to have three aspects: common property, common use and common maintenance. These aspects also tend to divide. We classify various common spaces into following eight groups: ways, water spaces, open spaces, living facilities, agricultural facilities, wood spaces, beach, religious spaces and lastly common images. The common spaces imply not only physical spaces but also concepts such as common images, common feelings and common norms of rural community.

Table 7.2 elucidates aspects of common spaces by a matrix on the vertical axis of "public, common and private" and the horizontal axis of "property, use and maintenance" (Shigemura and Kato, 1989). Only religious spaces have remained completely common. These common spaces are important for the following reasons: some of them are the economic bases of self-government; social bonds that have been intensified through use; and they define elements of spatial structures of the settlements.

It is one of main themes how newcomers participate in the use and maintenance of these common spaces in the marginal areas.

7.6   Inhabitants' Common Image

"The spatial consciousness map", that we devised to investigate the common image of settlements, is a map which is marked with signs by inhabitants in answer to questions on the settlement map. This investigation was carried out in six settlements (at two different dates in four of them) by using a questionnaire (Table 7.3).

7.6.1 Analysis of Spatial Consciousness Map by Overlay

The questionnaire elicited responses drawn directly on maps about three spatial groups; recognition of spatial elements, the structure of space, and the evaluation of space. The responses for each spatial group is summed up by overlay and indicated on a map.

Maps 7.3 – 7.6 are the examples of results of Kazurugaoka in the urbanisation promotion zone. The newcomers in Kazurugaoka have a weak sense of the boundary of their district (Fig. 7.8). The difference of common images between locals and newcomers was well revealed in the case of Odake.

7.6.2 Distribution of Recognised Spatial Elements

For any one spatial point, responses by individuals asked to plot its location will be marked with a degree of error. A small variation in collective errors will show that it is commonly recognised, whereas a large collec-

Table 7.3 Population of Investigated Settlements and Data of Questionnaire

Population

Zone	Settlement	Population 1970	1990	Household 1970	1990	Farm household 1970	1990
Urbanisation Promotion zone	Kazurugaoka		4661		1481		
	Chidori Park		1347		350		
Urbanisation Control zone	Aoyagi	872	1018	182	312	123	97
	Musirouchi	1316	1516	299	429	133	83
Outside of city Planning zone	Odake	212	2101	30	565	30	26
	Taniyama	344	1136	67	316	50	42
Koga town Total/Total		25194	45178	6295	14373	1012	649

Questionnaire

Zone	Settlement	Distribution New	Local	Collection New	Local	Answer New	Local	Total
Urbanisation Promotion zone	Kazurugaoka	53		48		48		36
	Chidori Park	50		46		46		35
Urbanisation Control zone	Aoyagi		46	43			31	31
	Musirouchi	12	38	12	34	12	21	33
Outside of city Planning zone	Odake	36	23	27	18	27	18	34
	Taniyama	37	26	23	19	23	19	33
Koga town Total/Total		188	133	156	114	156	114	202

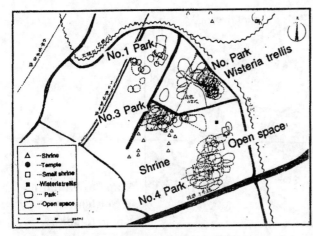

Map 7.3 Recognition of Religious Space: Kazurugaoka

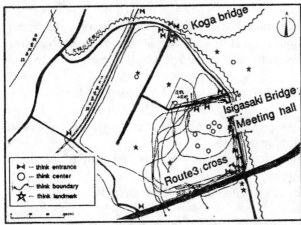

Map 7.4 Perceived Boundaries and Entrances: Kazurugaoka

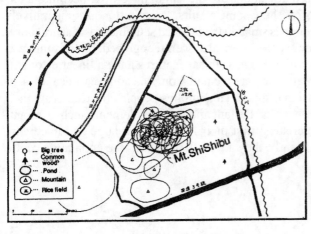

Map 7.5 Natural Spaces: Kazurugaoka

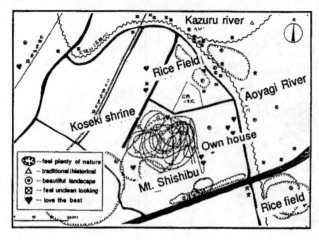

Map 7.6 Valuation of Settlement: Kazurugaoka

tive error will indicate common disagreement or unfamiliarity. The errors can be summarised by plotting an ellipse whose parameters are derived from a regression analysis of the individual plotted points. The regression analysis gives:

A central point - which may be displaced from the true location of the object

An angle of slope – representing the major axis along which most variation of spatial estimate occurs

A standard deviation along that axis – giving a measure of the size of error on the main axis

And a standard deviation orthogonal to the main axis.

If the two standard deviations are the same, the ellipse becomes a circle. Table 7.4 and Map 7.7 show some results. Recognition is comparatively accurate and the distribution is small in the planned settlement as Kazurugaoka. Elements along roads or at corners are also well recognized, but it is interesting to note that places which are near linear features have a linear error pattern, showing that mentally they are located along the adjacent linear dimension, not in two-dimensional space. This implies people are structuring their image around network features. Distant and general elements such as mountains show two characteristics: first their locations are large and uncertain, but, secondly and importantly, they are shifted towards the population centre and access points.

Table 7.4 Indices of Recognised Spatial Elements in Aoyagi

spatial element	entry ratio %	coordinate of real position (X,Y)	centre of distribution (x,y)	inclination of regression line θ	major axis of ellipse x_θ	minor axis of ellipse y_θ	gap from center point
Gosho hachiman shrine	77.4	(17.1, 8.0)	(17.3, 10.5)	-38.8	1.7	0.8	2.5
Tori of Gosho shrine	19.4	(20.0, 12.0)	(19.0, 12.2)	-18.4	1.1	0.6	1.0
Chosenji temple	71.0	(16.0 17.0)	(16.1, 16.7)	-19.7	0.6	0.4	0.3
The old Mr. K's monument	38.7	(10.0, 20.0)	(10.1, 20.5)	-24.6	1.5	0.4	0.5
The old Mr. U's monument	22.6	(12.0, 18.0)	(13.1, 17.6)	-27.9	1.0	0.2	1.2
Open space of hall	61.3	(16.0, 15.0)	(16.0, 14.5)	0.0	0.6	0.0	0.5
Wisteria trellis	16.1	(11.0, 21.0)	(12.2, 20.4)	-22.0	2.1	0.6	1.3
Mt. Takegoshi	77.4	(18.0, 22.0)	(18.8, 19.7)	-18.2	2.6	1.7	2.4
Mt. Oto	45.2	(8.0, 8.0)	(9.2, 11.4)	-7.8	3.0	1.9	3.6
Oura pond	12.9	(22.5, 20.0)		28.6	2.0	1.1	
Big camphor trees	19.4	(17.0, 8.0)	(17.0, 9.0)	-7.1	1.2	0.9	1.2

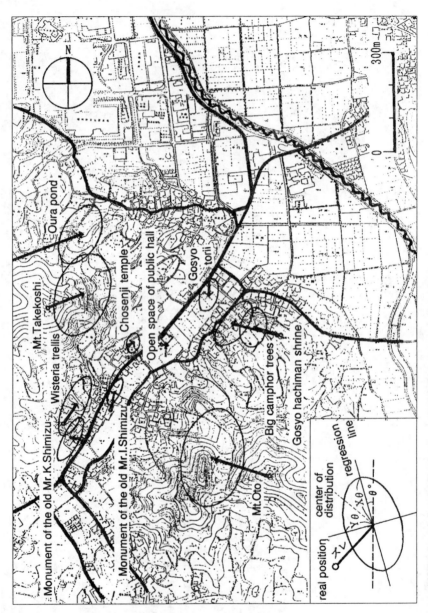

Map 7.7 Recognised Landscape Elements in Aoyagi

7.6.3 Common Images of Inhabitants Concerning Environments by Using "The Spatial Consciousness Map"

Not all places are known by all respondents. We can simply calculate the percentage recognition rate (even if the location is inaccurate) to find which elements are common – to find the images similar to the "public images" of Kevin Lynch (1960). It is roads, parks and open spaces that are commonly recognised in Kazurugaoka planned new town (Map 7.8). Mountains and shrines have high recognition and valuation in spite of being outside of the district. This suggests that natural, historical and religious places are also required despite the fact that this is a new town. In contrast to this, in Aoyagi there is no park but many other spatial elements are recognised, for example shrines, small shrines, temples, open spaces, mountains, waterways and so on (Map 7.10). A strong common image is evidence that common norms for the maintenance and improvement of environments are retained in traditional communities. Only shrines and open grounds are recognized by both of locals and newcomers in Odake rurban community (Maps 7.9 and 7.11). Other features are recognised by only one of both, so differences of the images appear clearly. Images of newcomers are diversified and become individualised, and spread beyond the boundary of the settlement. This means that newcomers have no clear idea of settlement boundary and have not yet matured as subjects of local environmental maintenance.

Spatial elements recognized by many inhabitants can be regarded as important elements to establish a context of space and an identity of the set-

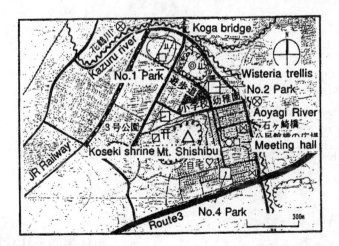

Map 7.8 Kazurugaoka New Town

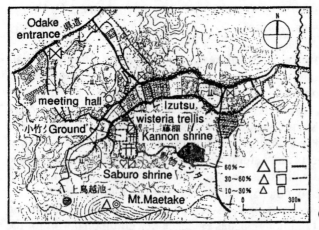

**Map 7.9
Odake Community**

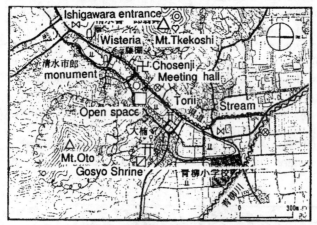

**Map 7.10 Aoyagi
New Town**

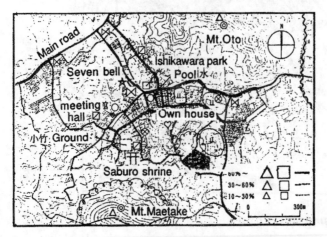

**Map 7.11 Odake
Community**

tlement. In the group relating to spatial structure, junctions, bridges and cross roads mark entrances at the boundary of the settlement, and the meeting hall marks the centre. Locals agreed on the real boundary, newcomers did not. In the group relating to valuation of the environment, spatial items were identified as: mountains (ponds or fields) as places abounding in natural and beautiful landscapes, shrines as historical and traditional places, rivers as places which looked unclean. Thus 'green' environments were highly valued, but river environments were poorly regarded because of actual or suspected pollution.

7.7 Environmental Planning and Ecological Towns in the Marginal Area - Conclusion

In this study we regard the urbanizing urban fringes as "the marginal areas" where town and country are regarded as two equal worlds. Zoning affects the way settlements develop, but the legal force of the zoning has weakened because of the recent farmland reservation act which prevents development in many parts of zones otherwise designated for building development, and the rural settlement improvement which does the opposite – promotes development in the zones designated for control of urban development. As a result, a mosaic of urbanisation has been spreading again. Therefore more and more areas are marginal (in our sense) and we believe that fine-grained environmental planning is required in these marginal areas. So we have considered the management of communities and community activities such as festivals and events. In the former rationalisation is occurring so that the management system is divided into administration of district and into management of agricultural affairs according to urbanisation. In the latter various community activities are useful to integrate locals and newcomers. It is necessary to investigate further the relationship between them in other spheres, such as the allotment of gardens. One of main themes is how to educate new subjects to maintain and to establish environments in the marginal area.

Common images were investigated to find out how inhabitants recognized and evaluated their environment. We have researched a planning method to evaluate environmental stock and to make the most of it on the basis of local participation. Maps of common images are useful in part because they inform the researcher of community attitudes, but also because they are understood by local people, and can motivate joint discussion on their environment and its value and conservation.

Our results suggest that there are common images of natural environments in the marginal areas. We need to study further green areas and water bodies not only from the viewpoint of amenity but also from the viewpoint of ecology to realise the plan of creating the sustainable towns in marginal areas.

Acknowledgments

This research was supported in part by grant from Japanese housing centre. I am indebted to a number of my students at Kyushu university and inhabitants in the study area. I wish to express my gratitude to all of them.

References

Kato, Hitomi (1995) "Structure of Urbanisation and Environmental Planning in the Marginal Area of Town and Country: Part 1" Journal of Architectural Institute of Japan.
Kato, Hitomi (1996) "Structure of Urbanisation and Environmental Planning in the Marginal Area of Town and Country: Part 2", Journal of Architectural Institute of Japan.
Kato, Hitomi (1997) "Structure of Urbanisation and Environmental Planning in the Marginal Area of Town and Country: Part 3" Journal of Architectural Institute of Japan.
Simmel, Georg (1908) *Sociology* Stranger.
Park, Robert E. (1928) "Human Migration and Marginal Man" *The American Journal of Sociology.*
Shigemura, Tsutomu; Kato, Hitomi, et al. (1989) "Settlement - space and planning", *Toshibunkasya.*
Lynch, Kevin (1960) *The Image of the City* MIT and Harvard University Press.

8   Open Space in Tehran

Vincent F. Costello

8.1   Introduction

Adequate provision for open space, whether public or private, may be seen as one of the touchstones for a healthy city. This paper looks at the provision of open space in Tehran, one of Asia's largest and fastest growing cities and in particular it critically examines the quality of open space in relation to variations in socio-economic status between different parts of the built up area and to a number of health indicators. Tehran has grown from a population of just more than half a million in 1940 to 5.4 million in 1980 and is currently at about 9 or 10 million, growing at about 2 percent per annum, though there are problems of statistical definition here.

The city's physical expansion has also been rapid. Urban growth out from the core has been much influenced by the environmental contrasts between north and south. The modern commercial sector together with many of the suburbs where the wealthier sections of the population live, have developed northward from the old core, while the poorer suburbs have developed south towards the desert.

Growth has been on a site where the physical environment imposes a number of limitations. Tehran is built at an average altitude of about 1200 meters on a slope running south from the Alburz mountains. There are broadly four different environmental zones in the city and most of the 20 census districts fall completely into one of the zones (Map 8.1):

- the far southern parts towards the edge of the desert with low slopes of silt and clay sediments - Districts 15, 16, 18, 19 and 20
- the middle parts where the slope increases - Districts 17, 9, 10, 11, 12, 13 and 14
- the dissected hills formed from glacial outwash fans - Districts 2, 3, 6 and 7
- the mountain foothills and the mountains themselves - District 1.

The climate has marked seasonal contrasts, with a short spring and autumn separating a long and cold winter with daytime maxima rarely over 10^0C and minima below 0^0C and a lengthy hot, dry summer with daily maxima over 35⁰C. Summer temperatures in the north close to the mountains are up to seven degrees cooler than those in the south.

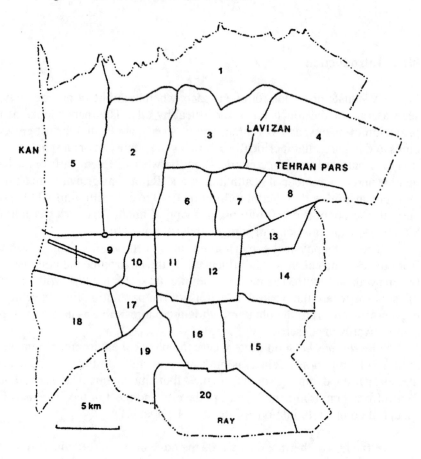

Map 8.1 Census Districts of Tehran

8.2   The Environmental Context

The old core of Tehran is some twenty kilometres from the foot of the mountains, some distance from either of the two principal rivers of the region - the Karaj and the Jajrud - and far enough from the mountains to be beyond the reach of perennial streams. Tehran has always had to rely on artificial water supplies, initially through the use of gravity-fed underground canals called *qanats*, which tap ground water sources. These increased in number in the

19th Century. The inadequacy of the water supply has been a continuing feature of Tehran's history, and there are still problems with the provision of domestic water and with sewage disposal. The demand for water has consistently far outstripped supply. Potable water is available throughout the city, but the quality of ground and surface water varies very greatly between the north and the south.

In the northernmost suburbs and in the mountains surface water runs off in well contained waterways - either storm drains or through *jubes* - open gutters - which serve to water trees lining the boulevards and incidentally to carry garbage dumped in them by householders and shopkeepers. Ground water is available through *qanats* or can be pumped up from deeper down. However nearly all households in Tehran discharge sewage directly into the ground. The solids are at intervals dug up from cesspits and the liquid soaks into the ground. This gradually seeps downhill under the force of gravity and the slope is down to the south. It has proved to be a major problem in the excavations for the Tehran metro. The city has only just begun to have an integrated sewage system. Down the slope in central and southern Tehran groundwater may be heavily polluted, but nonetheless it is pumped up to irrigate parks and open spaces. The far southern fringe of the city suffers from flows of polluted surface and underground water (Leghaii, 1990).

Urban growth has also led to acute problems of atmospheric pollution. The transport network has become progressively less capable of dealing with the volumes of traffic created by increasing population and rising car ownership rates. In central Tehran, despite a variety of traffic management measures, the accumulation of exhaust gases from the vehicles that crowd the streets - vehicles uncontrolled by emission regulations - produces severe air pollution. Analysis of lead levels in plane tree leaves has shown that they are up to three times higher in central Tehran than in the north, and also that they are much lower in the interior than on the edge of parks in the city (Ekhbatar, 1991).

As may be imagined, there are contrasts in public health between the north and the south and central districts. The incidence of reported lung diseases and eye infections in children are two and a half times higher in District 12 - in the centre - than in District 1 in the far north.

In this context, open space could have a major role in providing opportunities to improve people's lives, whether through the ameliorative effect it may have on the environment, particularly on local climates and air quality, or on providing possibilities for outdoor recreation. Open spaces in Tehran have fulfilled these roles in the past and are intended to so in the future.

8.3   The Preindustrial City

Before the middle of the last century Tehran had most of the features common to large Middle Eastern Islamic cities. The physical form of the city partly reflected its social structure (Costello, 1977). Preindustrial technology and adaptations to the local climate were significant, but the all-pervading cultural values were those of Islam. These directly influenced the details of urban form, such as house design, and the overall plan. Tehran was not blessed with great open spaces like those laid out in Isfahan by the Safavid shahs, and it had no overall plan. The public places comprised the twisting streets, the bazaar and the occasional open square used as a temporary market, a recreation ground for children, or as the scene of public events, such as funerals, or the mourning processions associated with the month of Moharram. The courtyards of the larger mosques, with their pools and trees were available to all for prayer, but there were no public gardens.

Private gardens however had much meaning for those who could afford them. The garden has great cultural significance in Iran and in the rest of the Middle East (Sackville-West, 1953). In Islamic Iran its role was tied intimately to the role of the house and the family. The family was the holder and transmitter of property. It had a right to live enclosed within its house once the basic necessity of water had been secured from the community. The individual secured complete privacy from the city within the family home.

The basic residential unit for the wealthy was a house built around a central courtyard, often with a pond. It faced inward, away from the hurly-burly of public life. The form of the house resulted from the demands of climate, of family life and of Islamic ideology. Temperatures in Tehran in the summer months are high during the daytime, but the nights are cool. High desiccating winds are common. These climatic conditions were solved in the traditional house by a number of adaptations. Various parts of the house suited different times of the day and year. Rooms opened into the courtyard and windows on the exterior walls of houses were lacking or of a minimal size, and the high narrow shape of the courtyard restricted insolation. During summer nights when everyone slept on the roof, cool air sank into the courtyard; during the day radiation from the protected courtyard surface helped cool the house (Dunham, 1960). The emphasis on family privacy meant that if possible visitors were segregated. Male friends and callers were received in the public rooms, while the private rooms remained a family sanctuary. A large family might live in several conjoined courtyards.

Only the wealthy could afford a garden. The layout was nearly always the same:

the long avenues, the straight walks, the summer house or pavilion at the end of the walk, the narrow canals running like ribbons over blue tiles, widening out into pools which oddly enough were seldom circular   (Sackville-West, p.269).

There was a great variety of trees to be found in these gardens, and above all the ever present plane tree. Tehran was known as the 'city of plane trees' (Soltani, 1990). These deciduous trees need plenty of water. Water was most readily available where the qanats entered the city mostly at the northern end. Here were the most desirable districts with more gardens, while downhill to the south were the poorer districts. The royal palace complex was in the north.

The city expanded in the second half of the nineteenth century and in the early 1870s an earthen rampart and a fosse on the model of Thiers' Paris fortifications were added, encompassing much open space. This new secure space became available for development and many of the wealthiest families acquired substantial plots, built houses and laid out gardens.

S. Farman Farmaian grew up in such a family in 1930s Tehran:

The subcompounds where we and our mothers lived were known collectively as the *andurun*, the 'inner' quarter, or harem; everything else, including the central garden and the other buildings surrounding it, was the *biruni*. This was the 'outer,' or public, quarter where my father lived, and was the realm of men. It reflected the greater world beyond, which was also a realm of men. (Farman Farmaian, 1993, p.18).

Foreign embassies also acquired land to the north and laid out extensive grounds. The largest were the Russian and British compounds, with the Americans acquiring one later outside the line of the 1870s walls. It was desirable and fashionable to own also a summer house and grounds in the foothills, and the villages of Shemiran, Tajrish and Golhak all had numerous private walled estates.

8.4   Twentieth Century Changes

In the middle decades of the twentieth century the Pahlavi regime dismembered the preindustrial city by clearances for broad new avenues. Thousands of plane trees were planted along them and the trees were watered by open *jubes*, channels which were supplied from groundwater. Open squares with fountains, flower beds and monuments to the regime and its heroes appeared at the main intersections. The authorities cleared houses and burial grounds from a 25 hectare area to the west of the old palace citadel complex and laid out a public park. The City Park became, and remains, the only large public garden space in the centre of Tehran.

8.5   The Period of Rapid Expansion

In the 1950s and 1960s the city expanded rapidly. The market in land was practically free, with few planning controls. There was relatively little outward expansion to the south of Tehran's old core, where continued immigration increased pressure on the housing stock. In the older neighbourhoods north of the bazaar available open space became exhausted. In Districts 10, 8, 13 and 7 rows of two- and three-storey houses were built to the east and west of the downtown area. At first most of these had some associated private open space - a courtyard or a small garden with an ornamental pool and some shade. While to the north, uphill towards the mountains more spacious and expensive houses were built with their own gardens. Development in District 6 was partly blocked by government land ownership and long term plans to move the capital functions of Tehran to a new purpose-built centre in Districts 6 and 3. The resort towns of Tajrish and Niaveran, in District 1, in the foothills gradually became commuter towns as rising car ownership among the wealthier classes freed them from living close to their work.

After the 1969 Master Plan the authorities tried to check the outward sprawl of the city by forbidding development outside lines which were moved outward every five years. The incidental result is that population densities per hectare and per room continued to rise, with greater pressure to build additional storeys on existing buildings and to fill in private gardens with housing development. Cultivated land on the edge of the city had always provided open space for recreation, for outings and picnics. However these places were now developed or no longer had a water supply. Without water the land reverts to inhospitable scrub and camel thorn.

The secularisation of parts of Iranian society led to a clear division between the westernised cosmopolitan classes that ran the country and the intensely Islamic poorer classes with traditional merchant and clerical groups. The social geography of Tehran reflected this gap. In the north the lifestyle was modern and the demand for public open space high. Parks and recreation areas were laid out and lavishly irrigated. In 1977 Bahrambeygui (1977, p. 172) wrote:

Apart from being limited in number, parks in Tehran are not very evenly distributed. In fact the Park-e-Shahr (City Park) with a central location is the only one reasonably accessible to the general public. The northern parks are relatively inaccessible to the majority of Tehranis. In the whole of the Central Area of Tehran which is almost 30 sq. km there are only two parks and some very small children's playgrounds. In the densely populated areas to the west of the city the situation is even worse, as there are no more than two small parks. The same applies to eastern Tehran with the exception of the small park of Khayyam. The southern part of the city is, to some extent better provided with open space than the eastern and western districts. It contains 5 parks and 4 children's playgrounds although because of the high population density and proximity of industrial area more are urgently needed."

8.6   Planning for Open Space

The Master Plan of 1969 projected a future image of Tehran that had great bands of open space around Tehran and much greenery within it. In fact the total of green space was calculated as 1.5 sq.m per head in 1969, though this was, as we have seen, very unevenly distributed. Planning for new public green spaces and the renovation of old ones is done by Tehran Municipality. Responsibility for planting and maintaining the forest parks which should form green belt on the edge of the city is borne by the Municipality and by the Forest and Range organisation of central government. After the Islamic Revolution of 1979 the Municipality produced five year development plans for green spaces within the city and for the Green Belt (Municipality of Tehran, 1981 and 1982)

There is a range of types of open space, which have varying degrees of utility for public recreation or for environmental amelioration.

- Urban parks created and maintained by the authorities, usually with some landscaping, fountains and pools, and with mixed deciduous and coniferous planting
- Squares at traffic intersections, usually with artificial soil and some flower beds
- Green strips along highways - the most attractive of these are along the boulevards laid out in the middle of the century
- Private green spaces maintained by corporations, such as universities, or the military, to which the public do not have access
- Private gardens - these may range from small household plots to the vast enclosed parks of the major embassies, some of which probably contain the only examples of the pre twentieth century soil cover to be found in Tehran. These large gardens are well planted and maintained and are inaccessible to the public
- Forest parks - in the city and on the fringes, which do ameliorate the environment but are planted largely with conifers and are not used by the general public.

Taken overall the distribution of the public open spaces is not based on any plan. Most are created wherever there is empty undeveloped land which comes into the hands of the Municipality. It is "space left over after planning has ended". How much open space there *should* be is a matter of some contention. The Municipality has announced that their goal is 9 square metres of green space per person, the Ministry of Parks has chosen 15 Square metres, and the Ministry of Housing and Urban Development has selected 12 square metres (Soltani, 1990). How much is really available and how does this vary from one part of the city to another? The next section of this paper attempts partly to answer this question. It should be remembered that availability of open space comes not just from proximity of the space to people's residence or workplace but also from personal mobility. The poorest sections of the population are also the least mobile, so proximity to open space is more critical for them, if they choose to use it.

8.7   Open Space in the Districts of Tehran

In this section unpublished empirical data from the Municipality and from the 1986 and 1991 censes are used to give a broad picture of where the space is and how it may relate to differences in the social geography of the city. The data are summarised in Table 8.1. The columns relate to the 20 Districts of Tehran, and the data relate to population totals, population density per hectare and per room, average age, and the amount of 'green' space per person.

It will help to interpret these data if reference is made to the four broad environmental zones of the city, since these correlate quite well to aspects of the social geography of the city.

• Districts 15, 16, 18, 19 and 20 are in the southernmost zone. The average age of the population is below 20 years, and in each district the percentage of the total economically active population who are females is below 8 percent. They are also the districts with the highest densities of population per room. Although the amount of 'green space' per person is quite high for Tehran most of this is composed of edge of town Forest Parks which for the most part the public do not use for recreation.

• Districts 8 to 14 and 17 are the old core and its east and west fringes - corresponding largely to the second zone. Average ages are in the mid to lower twenties. They have the highest population densities per hectare, and females are most between 8 and 16 percent percentage of the economically active population, with the exception of District 17 which

Table 8.1 Selected Characteristics of the Population of Tehran, by District; 1991 Unless Otherwise Stated

	Population ('000)	Persons Per hectare		Hectares of Public 'Green' Open Space	Sq.m. of Public 'Green' Open Space per Person	Average Age 1991	Persons per Room 1986
		1980	*1991*				
1	264	23.6	29.4	36.8	1.4	24.2	1.2
2	369	43.9	73.5	88.7	2.4	26.0	1.1
3	228	69.4	71.3	122.1	5.4	27.5	1.1
4	574	55.8	101.1	68.9	1.2	21.2	1.5
5	398	12.9	76.6	23.8	0.6	21.7	1.3
6	252	116.4	126.6	59.1	2.4	28.1	1.0
7	284	220.0	185.1	15.1	0.5	26.7	1.2
8	372	294.8	299.2	15.4	0.4	24.6	1.4
9	249	108.5	132.4	34.3	1.4	20.9	1.6
10	315	477.2	342.4	11.7	0.4	24.4	1.5
11	243	249.3	218.9	N/A	N/A	24.7	1.3
12	263	230.5	174.1	37.9	1.4	23.7	1.5
13	197	144.6	135.9	11.4	0.6	24.9	1.3
14	407	193.2	196.6	78.5	1.9	22.3	1.5
15	579	90.7	139.6	199.6	3.5	18.7	1.9
16	324	198.7	178.0	107.2	3.3	20.8	2.1
17	348	504.9	435.0	19.9	0.6	19.7	2.1
18	345	218.2	387.6	43.7	1.3	16.9	2.3
19	255	341.7	708.3	64.2	2.5	16.6	2.4
20	345	76.5	103.3	62.3	1.8	19.1	2.0
	6620				1.6		

See Map 8.1 for location of sectors

has only 5.3 percent. They are poorly off for local 'green' space and people in the inner districts are furthest from any form of open space.
• Districts in the alluvial fan can by divided into two types. Directly north of the older part of the city is wealthy Tehran, that is Districts 2, 3, 6 and 7. The average age of the population is in the higher twenties, and females comprise between 18 and 23 percent of the total economi-

cally active population. The figure is highest in District 6. Population densities are low and, apart from District 7, there is a relatively favourable proportion of 'green' space per person. The superhighway network of Tehran criss-crosses this zone and the inhabitants who have cars have easy access to the mountains to the north or even further afield to the Caspian coast. Districts 4 and 5 are on the fringe of all this, and in District 5 provision of 'green' space has lagged behind the rapid expansion at the edge of the city.
• Finally District 1 in the foothills is a mixture of wealthy established suburbs, assimilated villages and new fringe development.

8.8 Conclusion

The house design of the traditional city did allow for open air activity but preserved the privacy of the family. Most of modern Tehran, particularly in the less well-off areas is being developed as high rise. This does not, in Tehran or anywhere else, allow for easy outdoor activity. The open spaces of Tehran do not provide alternative and easy access to the outdoors for the vast majority of Tehranis. The total amount of open 'green' space is well below the expectations of those charged with providing it and the spaces are unevenly distributed about the city, favouring the already well-off districts. The role which is expected of them for climate amelioration and recreation probably cannot be fulfilled, and this has consequences for the present and future health of Tehran's citizens. There is no real prospect of planners' ideals being met. The distribution patterns were in place in some respects well before this century and will surely continue well into the next.

References

Bahrambeygui, H. 1977. *Tehran: an Urban Analysis.* Tehran: Sahab Books Institute.
Costello, V. 1973. Iran: the Urban System and Social Patterns in Cities, (with B.D. Clark), *Trans. Inst. Br. Geogr.*, July.
Costello, V. 1977. *Urbanisation in the Middle East* Cambridge: Cambridge University Press.
Costello,V. 1993. Planning Problems and Policies in Tehran, in Amirahmadi,H. and El-Shakhs,S.(eds) *Urban Development in the Muslim World* New Jersey: Rutgers University.
Dunham, D. 1960. The Courtyard House as a Temperature Regulator. *The New Scientist*, 663-6.4
Ekhbatar, T. 1991. *Air Pollution in Tehran* (in Persian). Tehran.
Farman Farmaian, S. 1993. *Daughter of Persia.* London: Corgi Books.
Gita Shenassi, 1993. *Atlas of Tehran*,pp 5-9, (in Persian), Tehran: Gita Shenassi.
Leghaii, H. 1990. The Need to Create Mountain Parks in Tehran (in Persian). *Journal of Environmental Studies*, 16, no.15. Tehran: Institute of Environmental Studies, University of Tehran.

Municipality of Tehran. 1981. *Green Belt Plan for the City of Tehran* (in Persian). Report no. 89. Tehran.

Municipality of Tehran. 1982. *Five Year Development Plan for Green Spaces in the City of Tehran* (in Persian). Report no. 136. Tehran: Tehran Planning Organisation.

Sackville-West, V. 1953. Persian Gardens, in Arberry, A.J., ed. *The Legacy of Persia.* Oxford: the Clarendon Press.

Soltani, K. B.. 1990. The Green Spaces of Tehran (in Persian). *Scientific Magazine of Architecture and Urban Development,* No. 8, July/August.

9 The Impact of Tourism on Chennai (Madras), India

K. Jayashree

9.1 Introduction

The growth of tourist traffic in any area demands more hospitality services, more airport capacity, and more ground transport. Tourist facilities also place extra demands on services such as water supply and power supply. Tourism can bring new wealth to an area, but it can also bring ecological pressure and cultural shock. Many studies of tourism and its impact concentrate on resort areas: but by being most frequented by the tourists, metropolitan cities deserve greater attention in terms of tourism development.

In recent times, there has been a realisation in Chennai (Madras) metropolis that tourism is indeed a powerful tool to aid regional development. This chapter begins with a review of two general frameworks, one of which is aimed at structuring a wide variety of impacts which tourism may generate in general, and the other which deals exclusively with an impact assessment of Chennai city.

With the emergence of environmental impact assessment / auditing procedures in the 1970s, in the United States and New Zealand, for example, the focus has been given to this issue everywhere in the last two decades. In order to understand the full implications of the environmental issues emerging from any new development project, aspects such as the physical environment, society and economy of the area where it is to be implemented should be assessed 'before the fact'. There are also instances where such an assessment has been made 'after the fact', mostly in response to problems developing. The present study is one such, where 'after the fact' analysis and assessment has been done.

9.2 Chennai

Chennai metropolis is located on the eastern coast of Tamil Nadu and has played a significant historical and economic role not only in the home state but also in the entire South India. In fact, it is referred to as the 'Gateway of South India', and has all the qualities of a cosmopolitan and metropolitan city. Being on the eastern coast and at the southeastern part of the subcontinent India, it gets rainfall during the months of October-November from the cyclonic activities in the Bay of Bengal. Its hot, humid climate is pleasant only during the rainy and 'cold' weather season, while the summer months of April-June are too hot. The southern seat of the British Raj for long and one of the four major metropolises of India now, the city has several historical monuments such as Amir Mahal, Museum, and Temples, and Beach Resorts like Mahabalipuram, VGP Golden Beach and Memorials. Two wildlife sanctuaries are at Guindy and Vandalur, one within the city limits and the other in the Chennai Metropolitan Development Area (CMDA). Besides these, several entertainment parks, theme parks and water parks have been added to the list of tourists' attractions of Chennai city.

Chennai has 5.3 million people residing within the city limits. The population includes many ethnic groups, religions, nationalities, and many cultural groups as well. The cultural diversity of the population is very impressive, because representatives of almost all important cultural groups of the world have found a home in Chennai city.

The city is the major port of South India. Many major industrial and commercial establishments are located there, and since liberalisation multinational corporations have been establishing industrial units, particularly the car companies, with local industrial tie ups. Services are stretched: in particular the water supply is erratic and inadequate: in summer months tanker trains bring water to the city as the municipal system runs out of water. The State is in a sometimes violent dispute over water with neighbouring Karnataka, particularly over allocations from the River Cauvery (Kaveri). The city also has extensive slums and squatter settlements, and inadequate sanitation and waste disposal, in common with other major metropoli. Sometimes it is tempting to write that the city 'suffers' from them.

9.3   Scale of Tourism Development in Chennai City

The scale of the problem can be illustrated quite simply. There are nearly 4 million visitors per year – that is almost one tourist for every inhabitant. (Though the average length of stay is not known.). The speed with which tourism is increasing (the majority of it domestic) reflects growing incomes in India – especially in the urban middle classes – the growth of vehicle ownership, the multiplication of public buses (long distance as well as short), and a shift in cultural attitudes favouring more mobility and more 'visiting'.

The metropolis significantly suffers from 'mass tourism' which usually happens during international events like the 'one-day cricket matches', national games, annual exhibitions, cultural fairs and religious activities. There

Table 9.1 Chennai City: Tourist Arrivals 1991-95

Year	Domestic	Foreign	Total
1991	2,480,408	160,151	2,640,559
1992	2,604,347	172,610	3,217,150
1993	3,026,905	180,245	2,776,957
1994	3,269,550	197,835	3,467,385
1995	3,531,586	250,938	3,782,524

Source: Tamil Nadu Tourism Development Corporation.

are annual religious features such as the Ayyappa worship and pilgrimage to Sabarimalai in Kerala from the city, religious processions during Vinayaka Chaturthi (the celebrations connected with the elephant-headed god) and yatras (walks) to Melmaruvathur, a nearby town, and political meetings. During the period attracting mass tourism, the city reels under the pressures of over congestion, garbage (per capita waste production is 50% higher during the height of the season) traffic jams and even the non-availability of public transport because of crowding. The Marina beach is especially crowded during the evenings of the peak seasons. It is the only tourist spot without an entry fee, and so it attracts teeming crowds: tourists, besides congesting the beach, also cause serious damage to the beach sand: the sea shells are removed, and people use it as open urinal and defecation spot.

9.4   Tourism and Inflation

The development of tourism requires funds. The superior buying power of the wealthy tourists causes prices to rise, in those cities and towns of tourist attractions, beyond the ability of the local people to pay. Tourist development could also cause shock waves of inflation. Tourism is a seasonal activity and little of it continues throughout the year. To mention a few, Chennai city has an annual exhibition called the Pongal Fair (in celebration of the harvest festival) every year and it is a fair open for at least four months. During these four months, January to April, there is a huge influx of tourists who put demands on the city amenities and services, causing regular upsets and also detectable inflation.

9.5   Tourism is Not Very Productive for the City People

Tourism ties up scarce capital. It wastefully uses land and other natural resources in the construction of luxury hotels and resorts for the enjoyment of the rich, and for ostentatious foreigners. For example, the latest addition to Chennai city's tourist attractions are Kishkinda Theme Park, MGM Water World, Little Folks and these together with the VGP Golden Beach have absorbed more than 1,000 acres of land approximately, which otherwise could be given to construction of schools, hospitals, and low cost housing facilities for the city people. Though tourism is productive in terms of foreign exchange, it is not directly productive for many city people.

9.6   Tourism Depresses Growth in Other Industries

It has already been observed that tourism and its enticements draw scarce educated, skilled manpower and capital resources away from manufacturing or agriculture, with the result the growth of other industries is hampered. This may be an acceptable way to specialise according to comparative advantage, but the long term future of the city may depend as much on basic industries and services.

9.7   Tourism and Increase in Land Prices

The demand for more hotels and tourist facilities (such as 3- or 5-star hotels and sea front water recreation facility) bring huge income to real estate owners and builders and also land owners. So, local residents are made to pay more for their homes and large duties, due to increases in land prices. The disproportionate use of land results in the high prices and an associated alienation of land occurs for many city people.

Tourism frequently clashes with the demand of agricultural land. Most tourist areas coincide with low lying coastal areas which are primarily devoted to arable farming, thus causing strain and damage to farm property and hazards to farm stock.

9.8   Tourism and Morality

Tourists seek entertainment. In certain cases, the undesirable demand on the child sex workers is also a claim tourists make. In Chennai alone it is said there are 60,000 child sex workers who cater to the immoral needs of the tourists. There can be no economic or other justification for such an horrific trade – but to stamp it out will require more than just police-work and prosecution so long as there is not enough paid work for poor families.

9.9 Spoilt Cityscape

Here the problem is not so much the tourist as the city authorities and public. Indeed tourist pressure may be beneficial. The most significant problem of Chennai city at present is the restoration or renovation of the historical monuments, which has long been neglected because of lack of funds and commitment and lack of management and pride. The tourists feel disappointed to see the sorry state of the historical monuments and the vandalism they are subjected to. Their reactions prompt the realisation that there are assets worth saving.

9.10 Local Transport

More important than most of the above is the lack of parking facilities for the tourist buses and vans and cabs at different touristic spots in the city and beyond. There is often a chain of parked vehicles which occupy half the roads and they overspill the main highways into the lanes. The parked vehicles and the pavement markets and little encroachments on the roads, in places such as Egmore, Central Railway Station, T. Nagar and other busy places, impede passing traffic and cause extensive jams as well as endangering pedestrians.

9.11 Waste Disposal

The primary negative impact of tourism development is the generation of new or increased waste residuals. The lack of waste collection leads to the dumping of the wastes in the sea, lakes and rivers. This habit over the years has led to the eutrophication of the water bodies; the examples are the lake near Adambakkam and Nungambakkam, Buckingham Canal, Cooum and Adyar rivers.

9.12 Cultural Impact

It is hard to ascribe changing cultural attitudes towards any one source – be it the press, magazines, radio, TV , satellite TV, films or indeed tourism. But tourism is undoubtedly one means of demonstrating other values, material acquisitiveness, and new styles, often liberal rather than conservative (because tourists want to unwind and relax from normal restrictions). It frequently represents a 'corrupting' impact on local culture.

9.13   Conclusion

This brief chapter is not written to decry tourism – which can bring wealth to a region. Nor does it blame all the evils of development - slums, garbage, polluted water bodies , impossible traffic - manifest in a metropolis such as Chennai, on tourism. But it does show that the scale of tourism can exacerbate all these problems, even in a city as large as Chennai, and that it can contribute to problem-making as much as problem solving. In such a case, the proper management of tourism and its impact is essential.

References

Bhatia, A.K. (1997) Tourism Management and Marketing, New Delhi, Sterling Publishers.
Bull, A. (1993) The Economics of Travel and Tourism, New York, John Wiley and Sons.
Chaturvedi, A.N. (1984) A Grave Ecological Threat, The Hindustan Times, April 6 Issue.
Dhar, P. (1997) Development of Tourism and Travel Industry, New Delhi, Kanishka Publishers.
Mill, R.C. and A.M. Morrison (1984) The Tourism System, Englewood Cliffs, NJ Prentice Hall.
Nagi, J. (1995) Tourism Development and Resources Conservation, New Delhi, Metropolitan Publishers.
Robinson, H. (1976) A Geography of Tourism, London, MacDonald and Evans.

10 Redefining Gender Roles and Identities in Urbanising Bangladesh

Tanja Haque

10.1 Introduction

Research on the status of South Asian women has been carried out from different angles. According to Sharma (1990), Western studies (e.g. Jacobson 1970, Mandelbaum 1988) have overemphasized the 'purdah-complex' i.e. the effects of seclusion on women, whereas South Asian researchers (e.g. Agarwal 1984, Gulati 1981) and some Marxist western scholars (Mies 1982, Omvedt 1980, Arens and van Beurden 1977) are more concerned with the organisation of women's work. With regard to Bangladeshi women, White (1992) presents a challenge to the existing literature on women's work and status. She contests notions of a strict division between 'inside' and 'outside', arguing against the common image of Bangladeshi women being totally isolated in the home. Women have to go out of the house in order to perform their daily household chores. On these occasions they engage in 'informal cooperation networks' with other women in the village. White also argues that the fact of leaving the home in order to participate in wage work is not necessarily an empowering force in women's lives.

In this chapter I discuss how women from low-income groups in Bangladesh experience new situations and identities when entering waged work and how this is negotiated with their families and communities, principally through a study of the non-governmental organisation Gonoshasthaya Kendra (GK), which is located in a rapidly urbanising area, and which provides this new 'away from home' work environment.

10.2 The Situation of Women in Bangladesh

Bangladesh has a population of approximately 118 million people. It is ranked amongst one of the poorest countries in the world, with a per capita income of not much more than US $ 210. Every year $2-2.5 billions of aid disbursements are channelled into Bangladesh , accounting for 85-100 per cent of the country's development budget . (Jansen 1992). According to Sobhan (1990) the benefits of this aid are distributed very unevenly. It has mostly benefited a small urban élite consisting of bureaucrats, commission agents,

146

contractors, indentors and consultants. Similar to the pattern of other aid recipient countries structural adjustment policies were carried out at the expense of the poor.

Growing pauperisation in rural areas and unequal land distribution drives many landless or land-poor households to migrate to urban centres, finding shelter in squatter settlements (in 1973 35 per cent of the urban population in Dhaka were living in slums - Pryer and Crook 1988). These trends have particularly exposed women to severe economic pressure. Rahman and Hossain (1992) describe the burden of poverty as falling disproportionately on the female half of the population.

In Bangladesh, as in several other South Asian countries, the life expectancy for women is lower than for men. The World Bank (1990) records a sex ratio of 94 females for 100 males in 1985. One of the reasons for the masculine sex ratio in Bangladesh is the high rate of maternal mortality (800 per 100,000 births - World Bank 1990). An early start to childbearing and the frequent pregnancies are among the main factors responsible for this. Female malnutrition resulting from biased food allocation must also be taken into account (Chen et al. 1981). Women are supposed to eat last and least, and their nutritional intake is only eighty-eight per cent of men's (Rahman and Hossain 1992, Kabeer 1989). There is strong gender discrimination in access to health care, education and training. When they fall ill, men and boys are more likely to receive medical attention than women and girls (Pryer and Crook 1988, Kabeer 1989, World Bank 1990). Literacy rates for men and women are 49 per cent compared to 29 per cent respectively (Rahman and Hossain 1992). According to Bangladesh's First Five Year Plan (1973-1978) women's education was seen merely as a means of training them for their roles as 'mothers of the nation's future leaders' (Islam 1979). As a matter of fact only about five per cent women are enrolled in technical and professional education (Mohila Parishad Commission Report, 1993).

In addition, women's seclusion, sanctioned by traditional practices and beliefs, reduces mobility and limits women's employment opportunities (Kabeer 1989). Those women that do participate in the paid labour force are usually employed in low paid sectors of the highly gender segregated labour market due to their insufficient educational qualifications.

Recently, however, an increased percentage of women entering the labour market has been noted. This trend has been related to the push of rural poverty and the pull of urbanisation and industrialisation. Savar where GK is located, close to Dhaka, has been booming over the last ten years transforming from a rural background into a semi-urban industrial zone. The peaktime of industrialisation and urbanisation was during the 80s (Hossain et al., 1990) when many new industries sprung up such as pharmaceuticals, garment, glass, brick, ceramic and shoe factories, textile mills, leather, dying, printing and construction industries. The setting up of an export processing zone in 1993 in Dhamsona Union, which is very close to GK, had a huge impact on the surrounding villages. Its 'proximity to rural areas has made room for drawing upon abundant low-cost labour' (BIDS, 1994).

10.3   The Case Study Organisation Gonoshasthaya Kendra

Currently 1600 NGOs are registered under the Women's and Children's Affairs Department and 850 under the Bureau of NGO Affairs (Ministry of Women and Children Affairs, 1995). In recent years 'gender-sensitive' policies have become quite popular and certainly lucrative amongst the NGO community. The majority of these organisations, however, concentrate on generating income for women through standard handicrafts programmes (Afsar, 1990). GK, in contrast, was one of the pioneers in offering women training in non-traditional skilled manual and technical trades with the aim of achieving equality for women. This approach has the potential for leading eventually to the construction of alternative gender roles and identities.

GK began as a field hospital on the Indian border for the freedom fighters and refugees fleeing Bangladesh during the liberation war in 1971. After the war, in 1972, it transferred to Savar, 40 km north of the capital Dhaka. Initially it provided preventive and primary health care service for the surrounding villages. Over the years GK developed into a complex integrated rural development project. GK now has about 2000 staff and operates in twelve locations. It receives sixty per cent of its funding from international and national donors and generates the remaining forty per cent from its own resources.

The vocational training centre for rural landless women was set up in 1973. The reasons for starting the vocational training centre were related to women's vulnerable position in society which was hindering their access to health services. In addition GK was confronted by several attempted suicide cases of married women who could no longer cope with oppressive marriage situations. Without alternative options it is difficult for women to walk out of oppressive marriages. Those women who do leave their husbands or who are abandoned by them are treated by society as outcasts. In general women are blamed for marital failure and these situations therefore bring disgrace to the family. The woman's parents and siblings are often pressurized and stigmatized by the community and therefore regard them as a burden. The reasoning behind GK's vocational training centre was that if the health programme was to achieve any lasting impact it would first have to assure women access to income and education. GK's idea was to change the general attitude towards women being regarded as liabilities to their families (GK Report, 1990).

Training in traditional handicrafts did not offer women alternative roles and simply reproduced gendered stereotyped images of women and home-making. GK therefore broke with 'tradition' and expanded into new areas of work from 1976 onwards. Various gendered vocational skills were introduced in the following years, for example, metalwork (welding, lathe operation and sheet bending) in 1976, carpentry and shoe-making in 1978, bakery and catering in 1979, fibre glass fabrication in 1982, blockprinting in 1984, professional driving in 1986, construction work in 1987, letter composition and printing in 1988 and irrigation pump operation, repair and maintenance in 1989.

The specific aims of the vocational training programme as stated by the programme personnel are:

1. to offer women skills in non-traditional professions
2. to increase women's confidence and self-respect
3. to improve their position in family and society
4. to make women economically independent
5. to demonstrate that given the opportunity and right environment, women can contribute to the country's development
6. to make women literate
7. to make women conscious.

(GK Evaluation Report, 1994)

The next sections describe women's process of leaving their home villages and adapting to a new 'urbanised' lifestyle at GK.

10.4 Leaving Village Identities and Family Roles Behind

Before discussing the dichotomies women drew between village and urban lifestyles one has to keep in mind that when referring to the 'home village' women are speaking about different local spaces and times. In this collection of perceptions and/or memories of village life women's perspectives are influenced in different ways by factors such as class, life cycle phase, region and marital status. Although there are differences in terms of where GK women come from and which places they identify as 'home', common grounds still emerge from the interviews in women's stereotyped images of village lifestyle.

10.5   Village and Isolation at 'Home'

Women at GK often described their former lifestyle in the villages in terms of having 'no freedom', 'no mobility', 'no chance to mix with people', 'fewer friends' and 'no social life'. Mimoza, who has been in GK for the last ten years, recalls the time she lived in the village and refers to her former lifestyle as 'being surrounded by four walls'. But compared to her mother she did not stay isolated all her life:

> *My mother stayed at home all her life, but I left. I didn't spend all of my life in the corner of my house like her. (Mimoza[1])*

Mothers who were stuck at home were described as not having any idea of the 'world outside', of places other than home, since they could not see and move within this world beyond the home.

> *My mother didn't go anywhere, but I have been roaming around at home (bari) and abroad (bidesh). My mother was always in the village, she doesn't know East and West, she doesn't know anything. (Mazeera)*

The assumption is that mothers/'typical village women' do not know how to move around by themselves and would get lost immediately without the necessary 'road knowledge' one acquires when going out to work. Mothers/village women would not be able to 'roam around'. GK women on the other hand do precisely that nowadays, but in their past they remember being afraid to 'walk on the roads alone'. They also remember the early days at GK and how they were afraid of being approached by men on their way to work.

> *We were afraid of walking on the roads alone, we were afraid that some man might make a bad comment or come up and ask us something. (Hurga)*

> *Before I worked only at home, I didn't know anything. I didn't know that women work outside. It is by going to GK that I learned something - the roads, how to catch a bus, all this. (Nargis)*

> *The poor lass [her mother] hasn't even boarded a bus yet [hi, hi, hi]. (Nasmun)*

In her detailed ethnographic study on 'cultural constructions of womanhood' in a Bangladeshi village, Kotalova (1996) describes the following social units as most influential in women's lives. The smallest unit is the

---

1 *All the names I have used are pseudonyms*

household, followed by the wider homestead unit 'bari' which usually comprises co-resident households in a courtyard. 'Para', the neighbourhood, is a 'territorial-cum-moral boundary surrounding a community'.

Though, for a visiting outsider and local children, the beginning and the end of a para are hardly noticeable, for village women a para boundary divides the world into home (bari) and abroad (bidesh). For the unmarried it surrounds the home (of their fathers); for the imported wives it encircles one of their homes (shashur bari). For both latter categories it is a boundary of their self-control, as their transgressions have implications for community's reputation '(Kotalova 1996:41).

Village women's mobility therefore remains well defined within the village or 'para' boundaries. Their spaces remained limited and uncontested. Everything beyond the clearly defined home and village boundaries is 'bidesh' i.e. abroad, foreign, unknown and slightly intimidating. Villagers whether women or men are not that keen on leaving the familiar home behind.

Separation from one's land, water sources and rice yielded from the fields that surround it, is always experienced as an immense discomfort...To make use of food, water, women and medical services abroad (bidesh), is believed to have detrimental consequences for a man's wellbeing. Young men may be instructed before embarking on a journey to avoid touching unknown people (Kotalova 1996:60).

GK women on the other hand are bound to have an extended mobility space through the simple fact of being forced to transgress home and village boundaries to get to work. They do not move only within their own 'paras' or to make the occasional visit to their parents home. They enter 'bidesh' territory which also involves using public transport that carries them away to spaces further away from the 'bari'. Road knowledge is necessary as well as communication with foreigners (bideshi) i.e. the need to behave in a different way.

10.6 Village and Illiteracy

Majilla, one of the older GK women, portrays her village in negative terms. She associates 'typical village' life with poverty and illiteracy. People in her village appear ignorant of family planning issues and unaware of the significance of education for progress in life. Conventional roles for women and girls remain unchallenged and unquestioned.

I come from a typical village. There is no environment of education. Young children catch fish, collect paddy grains, but God put sense in my mind, so I left my village and came here. I don't even feel like going back to my village. There is too much poverty. People are so typical. In every home there are five or six children...They can't feed the children properly, can't give them proper clothing...(Majilla)

Majilla could not see any future for herself and her family in the village and decided to leave, hoping to give her two children better prospects.

I have two children and I never want to have more. Two are enough if we can take care of them properly. My parents did not think about that...they thought giving birth is the major thing. But to feed them, clothe them, send them to school...they didn't think of all that. (Hurga)

The parental generation is described as having failed to map out a future for their children, in particular for their daughters, whereas most GK women have very clear cut visions and aspirations for their daughters. They want them to be educated, have an 'established life like a man' and eventually get married - ideally to an educated man - but not without having the security of a decent job.

10.7   Adapting to Alternative Lifestyles

GK women believe themselves to be considered as 'smart' in their families and communities because of 'mixing' and working with 'people from outside'. 'Outsiders' are defined as educated people from outside the village (bidesh). Women argued once you leave the 'illiterate village/home (bari) atmosphere' and mix with the 'educated society' from 'outside' (bidesh) you adapt to the lifestyle and behaviour of the outsiders i.e. the educated.

In the village the lifestyle is different. Here [in GK] is an educated atmosphere [shikito pori besh i.e. educated society] and I pretend to be educated also in my behaviour. I act like them and talk like them [bhodro bhasha i.e. the language of the bhodrolok[2]] that is how I am learning...How much can you learn from staying indoors? (Kodeza)

Tamina explains the difference between her own situation and that of

2 *Bhodrolok are the upper class educated town people, whereas rural people are usually defined by their occupation, which is often family tradition eg farmers or weavers etc. Therefore villagers can be classified more easily. In towns nobody knows what people do, so town people are simply referred to as bodrolok i.e. gentlemen. Village and urban language and lifestyles are quite different.*

village couples. She and her husband both live and work in GK. At GK they have the opportunity to meet people from various areas and therefore have a wider scope for conversation. They believe the atmosphere and interaction with others at GK has broadened their horizon.

> *Village couples talk about village people. We move around very much, are on the streets, can watch many people and have social communication. That's why we discuss more things. (Tamina)*

Village women were described as being afraid of people - especially outsiders (bideshi) and tending to behave in ways that would not risk social disapproval.

> *My mother walks in the streets covering her face with a veil. She doesn't look at people's face properly. She prays regularly. But I can't do that at present. I pray only Fridays.*

Majilla wants a different life from her mothers:

> *...because time is changing. People don't lead their lives the way people of the past did. I want my life to be like that of modern people. You know how people live in the villages! (Majilla)*

It was also interesting how GK women perceive women from very conservative areas such as Cox's Bazar after having been sent to do rehabilitation work there and hence being confronted with them. They depict women from these "traditional spaces" as 'purdasin' i.e. women following extremely strict versions of purdah.

> *They always wear veils. The veil is a must during daytime and they bring umbrellas too. Most of the time they came out at night...We told them 'come with us, we will give you work'. But they don't like jobs. Women from there don't go out, they always stay in the house. (Mazeera)*

One GK woman, whose original home is in Noakhali, another very conservative corner in Bangladesh, follows the expected behavioral norms when in her village, but when she is away she leads the 'free' lifestyle she now prefers.

> *Dhaka's life is good. I can mix with anyone here. [But] if I go outside without a veil in the village everyone will say 'that girl is bad'. (Tarunessa)*

GK women also differentiate themselves from 'typical village women' by making them look as if they were either not interested in working too far away from home or not capable of performing the kind of work requested in GK. Comments suggest village women are not prepared or flexible enough to do men's work i.e. 'hard' tough work.

Majilla, who used to work at GK in the carpentry section and is now working in the export processing zone thinks village women couldn't perform efficiently in outdoor jobs.

> *GK makes women strong...A village woman will not be able to start at raptani (garment factories at the EPZ). That's what I think.*
> Q: Why?
> *Our village women are very scared of foreign people. (Majilla)*

Shongita feels that, with her GK background, she can now help the women in her village to look for jobs by correcting their 'unsociable' behaviour:

> *I help them. If they are illiterate I tell them how their behaviour should be, because I know that the girls of my village are not so sociable. (Shongita)*

'Typical' village behaviour can get traded in for 'educated' behaviour.

> Q: Were you very shy before [coming to GK] ?
> *I didn't know what to talk about then. And there were also those inhibitions that a woman should not talk much to other people. People would think badly of it. Or if I went to some place with somebody people would give it a bad name. So I abstained from doing those things.*
> Q: What made you feel more open to people?
> *When a person can mix with many people at one place the atmosphere becomes different. By mixing with 'educated people' the whole behaviour of a person changes. (Hassina)*

> *I couldn't mix with anybody in the village; now I mingle with many people from home (bari) and abroad (bidesh)...I have learned the language, manners and conversation...I have become more intelligent than before. I have learned how to mix with others. (Monju)*

GK women refer to having gained identities beyond the mere family identity of the 'devoted wife' or 'nurturing mother' type. They realise they now have an identity as an individual, which does not automatically entail being linked to a male family member. The women are not simply referred to as wife of X or daughter of Z, but instead - at least within GK - they are now treated as a separate person, as individuals in their own right and are called by their own names and even have their own address (tikana). They are discovering a new side of themselves and a new feeling of independence, which neither they nor their mothers had experienced before.

My mother and aunts were indoors and listened to whatever their husbands said, but we have gone out, are earning our own living, moving around on our own...They stayed in the house, because they had to give love and care to those at home and rear the children. (Kodeza)

10.8 GK's Impact on Changes in Women's Lives

10.8.1 GK the Work Place

The type of non-conventional work women perform at GK and GK as a workplace itself offer women an insight into new horizons and experiences. With a few exceptions most women's conceptions of work and perceptions of their own potentials have changed. They have considered leaving their homes for pragmatic reasons i.e. survival. Many women started their working lives with negative attitudes towards formal work outside the home and were afraid and slightly intimidated by the demands of this new situation. After having overcome an initial phase of dislike and discomfort, however, they began to give formal work other meanings besides that of covering their essential needs.

People go out only for money, hardship, but then they learn and understand. (Kodeza)

The survival background has not disappeared from the agenda, but women have redefined their attitude to formal work and furthermore defined new values for themselves since joining GK.

I never thought that women could do all these kind of jobs. You never see female carpenters anywhere, but I myself am doing it here. (Mimoza)

GK proved that if an illiterate girl gets training she can do everything. (Firoza)

Besides having gained economic independence most women at GK developed a sense of self-worth. This reflects GK's objective of building up women's confidence by making them aware of their dormant potentials and challenging the myth that women are incapable of performing roles other than the ones society has ascribed for them. Obviously the women at GK were changing according to their own pace and one could find women in various stages of change within GK. There was also a handful of women who could not see any particular change in their lives, and maybe they never will. Most women, however, expressed their increased confidence by pointing out that they were now capable of doing things they would never have dreamed of doing before. They were capable of teaching others (e.g. other trainees in GK, other women in the villages). They understood that they could pass on their knowledge to others (e.g. children, husband, their own parents and siblings, villagers). They were able to support others even though they were 'their father's daughters' (e.g. They should support family members, contribute to family income, pay for siblings education etc.). Furthermore they could help others in need (e.g. women being sent to do relief work in flood hit areas). Most women realized that they could do a job just as well as a man, contrary to the beliefs they have been brought up with.

All the men working over here (GK), none of them is more capable than I am. Anything a man can do, I can do as well. (Hassina)

Slowly slowly I learned how to do my work. Nobody is born an expert out of the mother's belly, but you can do anything if you try. (Mimoza)

This self-realization was expressed in confidence and assertiveness. The women experienced a feeling of being an autonomous person and having acquired a new identity that was purely related to themselves and their capacities.

10.8.2 GK the Gender-Sensitive Organization

Adult education is a compulsory part of GK's vocational training programme. GK's target was to keep people in school for at least five years in order to avoid them lapsing back into illiteracy. Literacy classes used to run parallel to vocational training. Now trainees who are illiterate have to go through a preliminary training period of four to six months during which they receive basic literacy and numeracy classes. Trainees with some education still have to attend the adult education course for at least one month in order to learn GK specific subjects such as history especially regarding the language and the liberation movement, women's situation in Bangladesh and basics in health and nutrition. Women's participation in the monthly group meetings and the national women's movement adds to their awareness of gender and class related issues. The meetings would deal with various subjects: production issues, wage rises, specific topics such as new canteen committee, the introduction of a new project, preparation for the women's marches and discussion of specific gender topics. It could take the form of a lecture on a particular informative subject or be a discussion round amongst the participants.

They talk about how women are oppressed, why they are oppressed, how we should take initiatives against it... They also say 'go to the villages and spread your knowledge'. (Bina)

GK women build up strong intellectual debates on equal rights issues and often react very emotionally on the topic.

Is only a man's life of value and not mine! (Razina)

I am a human being and a man is a human being, so if they get freedom why shouldn't we get it too! (Hassina)

Whatever they do, we can do too, but wherever they go, we can't go. (Monju)

GK and the women's marches are associated with equality. They are perceived as 'places of equality', places where one talks about equality, where one sees equality, where equality is practised and lived. The success of the women's movement is taken as an indicator of change.

Men and women are equal, though not in all places, but in cities...in Dhaka...I went on the women's day march. I saw there that men and women had become equal...Outside GK women still cannot do the same jobs men do, but gradually the differences will be removed. It is obvious. (Majilla)

GK women are obviously well aware of the various ways cultural and patriarchal structures or hierarchies oppress women. This is not to say that other women, such as village women, are not aware of oppressive structures and therefore ignorant, but what strikes me in the GK women is their eloquence and passion when talking about equal rights. They are far more prepared to challenge dominant hierarchies in their thoughts and in some cases in their actions than the village women with whom I spoke.

To summarise: GK's training consists of following three key elements. The first is making *knowledge* available and meaningful to people through the adult education programme, skills training and participation in GK meetings and the national women's movement. The second element is having people, in particular women gain their own *experience* while they are learning, observing, working, living and communicating with others within the GK boundaries. The third element is building up women's *confidence* and making them believe in their own potential.

10.9 Negotiating New Roles and Identities in Households and Communities

10.9.1 The Households

As stated above, most of the women came to GK for economic survival reasons. It was therefore not surprising that the majority had not faced any particular objections from their families. Those who did had been told that women should not work, as working women would neglect children and housework. Furthermore, their security and chastity would be in danger. Unmarried women were told they should get married. In the case of married women only a few husbands had objected initially: in general, as a result of their extreme poverty husbands could not really afford to object to their wives working. One third of the currently married women's husbands did not have regular jobs, reflecting the stagnant rural labour market. This suggests a situation where men are losing the opportunity to be adequate breadwinners, whereas women are entering a market which presents new work opportunities for them. This may well lead to circumstances where women find themselves performing new roles. The vast literature on the internalization of labour suggests on the one hand possibilities of new roles for women, but on the other hand old roles may also be reinforced (Young, Wolkowitz, McCullagh 1981; Fuentes, Ehrenreich 1983; Mackintosh 1990; Hossain, Jahan, Sobhan 1990; Stichter, Parpart 1990, Wolf 1992)

Changes in power relations within the household, however, are far more subtle than the past literature on women's work and status has suggested. Access to income alone does not automatically lead to increased decision-making in the household. Instead of following standard decision-making models, which tend to measure women's status by the type and amount of decisions they make in the household after engaging in paid work, I focused on women's redefinitions of their roles and identities within the household. Kabeer suggests to widen the approach 'from decisions concerning intra-household allocational issues to the broader aspects of women's lives...[e.g.] their capacity to form, survive and prosper in alternative arrangements, including living on their own' (Kabeer, 1995:28).

For example, work is now considered by many women as a viable alternative to oppressive marriages and has the potential to undermine patriarchy. Women find themselves in better intra-household bargaining positions than before. Married women can walk out of oppressive marriages or are prepared for the future in case marriages break up. Abandoned women have a means of survival and are no longer a liability to others. They can also escape remarriage and unmarried women can delay marriage. If one recalls GK's objective of changing women's status as a liability to their families the outcome of my interviews can clearly confirm that GK has succeeded in this point for most women. Women state that they don't need to ask others for help anymore, depend on the mercy of relatives, they don't need to burden anybody in times of crisis. Now they no longer feel as if they are a liability to others. One of my respondents mentioned she would not have left her husband if she had not been sure of the job at GK as she knew her parents would not have been able to take on an extra financial burden. In general women in Bangladesh tend to avoid living alone, but having a job can now enable them to walk out on the husband if they really want to, which would not have been possible before. They are more prepared for the future and consider their earning skills as a valuable asset in case of abandonment (Kabeer, 1995).

In our society many women must live with their husbands no matter how badly they are treated by them. They have no other option. But now men see that women can earn their own living. So they [the men] think that if the women become independent they will not have their superiority over them anymore. (Hassina)

Men are afraid [of women's increased participation in the labour market]. For this reason they say remove Khaleda[3]. Industries are now taking women workers and dismissing men. Men's salary would be 3000, but you can hire a woman for 1200 for the same work, there is a good supply of women. The production rate of women and men is equal, so employers are interested to hire women. (Alea)

Most women at GK have also established alternative support networks to traditional family and kinship networks. At GK women exchange ideas, learn from each other, help each other out, console each other and give each other advice. Hassina, for example, has a lot of experience at GK. She is often approached by younger women for her advice.

When someone comes up with a problem I give my advice as best as I can...I feel good about that, because everybody is fond of me. If someone shares a problem or secret with me I remain discrete about it, that's why people trust me.
Q: Do you talk about women's problems?
Certainly, when girls sit together they talk about all sorts of things. For instance this one girl. Her husband does not give her any of his money. She often

---

3 *Kaleda Zia was the president of Bangladesh during the period I conducted my fieldwork.*

mentions that to us. He is supposed to go abroad, so I told her if you send him abroad, he will never come back to you. (Hassina)

For some women the organisation has become a proxy family. Fatema is a widow whose children are now grown up. She has been in GK for a long time and has developed a feeling of belonging. Her attitude to GK has changed over the years. In her case it goes as far as feeling bored if she is at home and not at work. GK and the friendships she has developed over years have become a surrogate for her family.

Now I can't sit back at home because I get bored with that. Before when I had to come to work and leave my children at home it felt really bad, but now I can't stay at home...As I told you, if I stay home for a whole day I get bored because there is no one to chat with. (Fatema)

Some women think they did not have the same kind of friendship, the same opportunities to be comforted when necessary back home in their villages. Establishing these kind of friendships in GK i.e. making their *own* friends is very significant, especially for young women, as they often have to leave their childhood friends behind once they get married and move to the husband's village. Within this new work environment women are making friends of their own, other than family-related friends such as sister-in-laws or husband's friends. These new friends are women (and men) who share the same or similar work identities with them.

I have friends everywhere, only in my village I had fewer. Here at GK I have made most friends...I used to have friends in my village, but they are all married now. (Majilla)

I tend to visit my husband's house only for a short period. The family is good, but I see very little of the people there. I mix more with GK people. (Nasmun)

GK's overall philosophy is geared towards building up a collective, hence the stress on the 'togetherness' factor. Institutions such as the family, the kin, the 'para' are replaced by a new institution, where emphasis is placed on relationships between non-blood related members. GK can almost be pictured as a new 'home' away from the old 'home'. This new home can give women a feeling of liberation from old bonds and old lifestyles, a feeling of belonging, a feeling of loyalty to the new home, and a sense of solidarity with the new family members.

10.9.2 The Communities

In general the GK women seem to find that objections from the villagers to their new roles are not as strong as they used to be. According to White (1992) poor women tend to be criticized less because exceptions are made for them on the grounds of their poverty. This must surely apply to the GK women. In addition, however, GK women's comments suggest that the lower level of objections women face nowadays are on the one hand a response to the women's individual behaviour and influence on the community and on the other hand a sign of changing times, in the sense that people's general attitude towards women going to work has changed. The latter point is supported by the BIDS Poverty Report 1994, which indicates no major change in women's economic position, but a dramatic change in people's attitude to women working. The literature on women and work suggests that 10-15 years ago women were just not as visible in the public sphere as they are now. According to Rahman[4], it was impossible to imagine women working outside then, for instance in road construction activities. Early studies (e.g. Cain et al. 1979, Greeley 1983) speak of heavy resistance towards women violating norms of purdah. In Khan's (1985) study only women of a certain age and in a certain position within the household were allowed to work outside. The older generation women at GK, who started working at GK as pioneers of their villages, remember how villagers used to pressurize their families, 'talk bad' about them and other women at GK. In some cases women were ostracised by the community: villagers would not invite them into their homes anymore, they cut off relations with them and denied them support in times of crisis.

People's resistance towards women engaged in formal work began to slowly break down during the industrialisation and urbanisation process and due to the impact the growing emergence of NGOs had on the villages. The forces linking villagers' changing attitudes towards working women to various global trends are also reflected in most of the GK women's remarks. This suggests quite a remarkable understanding of the world beyond the immediate family/household context. For example, the reason for the changed atmosphere in the villages was explained by the increasing literacy rates, which were related to the impact of the NGOs.

Since our villagers are educated [now] they don't make bad remarks regarding our going out, rather they say it is good. Had they remained illiterate, they surely would have spoken ill of us. (Kodeza)

---

4 *Rahman, personal communication, Dhaka, 1993.*

Many people have known through those who have gone to the villages and opened up organisations that education is something valuable...Many village girls have learned to read and write thereafter. (Majilla)

One woman specifically mentions the urbanisation process she has been witnessing in the last years:

The whole atmosphere has changed. Before people were mainly uneducated. Now they are becoming educated and more industries and work places have come. Many women are working now. People are getting used to seeing women work... My village was very rural, but now electricity is there, roads are there. It has changed completely. Before girls hardly used to go up to class 6, but now we have a college in the village and many girls are studying. (Mazeera)

Besides demonstrating economic benefits to their communities, GK women earned respect from villagers through the knowledge they had gained at GK. They are now being looked upon as more 'intelligent' than before and being identified as a member of an organisation i.e. 'the GK woman'. In some cases women are specifically identified with GK as a health organisation and therefore labelled 'the medical woman[5]. GK women can serve as a link between the organisation and the community.

When someone is sick they ask me what should be done. I give advice and if someone is very sick I advise them to take the patient to the hospital... They say I work at the medical [hospital], so I know many things about medicines. I tell everyone about many things so everyone thinks good of me. (Alea)

As mentioned above, many GK women had been pioneers of formal work in their villages. They therefore see themselves as role models for the village women, breaking a path for others to follow.

I was the first to work outside the village... I started and later other women became crazy for work - so many women asked me for work[6] (Kamrun)

It is not only women's income earning capacity that had this effect; it is also their changed personal appearance. Most women are presenting themselves to their communities in a very confident way. They get attention due to their own new identity and have hence managed to redefine their roles within

---

5 *The GK hospital is well known in the surrounding villages. People usually refer to it as 'medical'. Therefore people seen going in and out of GK are automatically associated with the term 'medical'. Women, who work at GK are expected to have some medical knowledge.*
6 *She estimates that in one out of five households in her village a woman is working outside the home.*

the community. Most of them feel they are now capable of speaking up, complaining, criticizing and protesting when the need arises.

Q: If someone in the village did or said something bad to you would you be afraid?

Now I am not afraid anymore. I have the power to protest. They are not saying anything anymore. They will not say anything, they don't have the guts. I am not like that anymore. (Alea)

10.10 Conclusion

In this chapter women's individual experiences of urbanisation were outlined, emphasizing the process they underwent when transgressing village boundaries in their search for waged work in urbanizing areas. Gonoshasthaya Kendra (GK), in its dual role as an employer as well as a gender-sensitive organisation, provided the framework for the analysis of women's process of change. This paper focused on women's voices and perspectives, explaining their strategies of adapting to new lifestyles and situations.

Obviously women's experiences vary and not every woman at GK necessarily acquired new roles and identities after becoming involved with GK. The potential for change, however, is there, even if at times this ongoing process of change is contradictory. One can easily imagine these women constantly experiencing new situations that involve enormous struggles with their new identities. For most women, their old values and beliefs have not been completely replaced with new ones, and it is clear that most women find themselves in a situation where they are forced to find a way of reconciling their new roles and values with their old value system and social surroundings. Women negotiate their work identity with traditional religious and cultural values, for example, by differentiating themselves from 'typical village women' or by adjusting their religious behaviour to the new situation (*I pray only on Fridays*). Women had to go through a process of negotiation with their families and communities before these eventually began to recognize them in their new roles and identities.

What has been argued in this chapter is that most GK women have managed to redefine their roles and identities. Beyond their traditional family roles (such as mothers, sisters, daughters) women have adopted new roles in the GK collective. By interacting daily with non-family related women and men and making new friends in GK, many women have built up collective relationships i.e. alternative networks to family and kinship support. Some women identify so much with the organisation that they have substituted the family with the collective entirely.

Many women have also negotiated new roles within their communities through their identification as 'medical women' or role models for the village women. Through their participation in the women's marches, women identify with an even wider community i.e. the national women's movement. When marching in the streets of Dhaka they feel a sense of togetherness with many women from various other organisations, who unite on a broader political basis.

Women cannot move freely, they don't get their proper rights - to obtain those rights... I go for those reasons. I go every year. I never miss it. I like going...Without such an initiative things won't change. We are doing it for a better future. (Alea)

References

Adnan, S. (1989) 'Birds in a Cage: Institutional Change and Women's Position in Bangladesh', in *The Journal of Social Studies*, 46(October), 1-34.

Afsar, R. (1990) 'Employment and Occupational Diversification for Women in Bangladesh', *ILO Asian Regional Programme for Employment Promotion (ARTEP) Resource Paper n.II*, ARTEP, New Delhi.

Agarwal, B. (1984) 'Rural Women and High Yielding Variety Rice Technology', in *Economic and Political Weekly 19(13)*, 39-51.

Akhter, F. (1995) 'Joutuk: Devaluation of Women in an Era of Globalisation and Developmental Interventions, mimeo.

Arens, J. and van Beurden, J.(1977) *Jhagrapur. Poor Peasants in a Village in Bangladesh*, Third World Publications, Birmingham.

Bangladesh Institute of Development Studies (1994) *An Evaluation of the Export Processing Zones in Bangladesh*, Final Report, Dhaka.

Bangladesh National Report to the Fourth World Conference on Women Beijing 1995, Women in Bangladesh: Equality, Development and Peace, Ministry of Women and Children Affairs, Government of the People's Republic of Bangladesh, 1995.

Cain, M., Khanam, S., Nahar, S. (1979) 'Class, Patriarchy and the Structure of Women's Work in Bangladesh', in *Population and Development Review* 5(3), 405-438.

Chen, L., Huq, E. and D'Souza, S. (1981) 'Sex Bias in the Family Allocation of Food and Health Care in Rural Bangladesh,' *Population and Development Review*, 7,1.

Elson, D. and Pearson, R. (1981) 'Nimble Fingers Make Cheap Workers: An Analysis of Women's Employment in Third World Export Manufacturing', in *Feminist Review* 7.

Fuentes, A. and Ehrenreich, B. (1983) *Women in the Global Factory*, The Institute for New Communications, New York.

Goetz, A.M. (1996) 'Dis/organizing Gender: Women Development Agents in State and NGO Poverty-Reduction Programmes in Bangladesh, in Rai, S. and Skinner, G. (eds) *Women and the State: International Perspectives*, Taylor and Fraces, London.

Goetz, A.M. and Sen Gupta, R. (1996) 'Who Takes the Credit? Gender, Power, and Control over Loan Use in Rural Credit Programmes in Bangladesh', *World Development 27(1)*.

Gonoshasthaya Kendra (1990) *Development of Nari Kendra: Vocational Training Centre for Women*, Savar, Bangladesh.

Gonoshasthaya Kendra (1994) *Evaluation Report* Savar, Bangladesh.
Greeley, M. (1983) 'Patriarchy and Poverty: A Bangladesh Case Study' in *South Asia Research 3(1)*, 35-55.
Gulati, L. (1981) *Profiles in Female Poverty*, Hindustan, Delhi.
Hossain, H., Jahan, R. and Sobhan, S. (1990) *No better Option? Industrial Women Workers in Bangladesh*, University Press Ltd., Dhaka.
Islam, M. (1979) 'Social Norms, Institutions and Status of Women', in *Women for Women*, (ed.), Dhaka.
Jacobson,D. (1970) 'Hidden Faces: Hindu and Muslim Purdah in a Central Indian Village', PhD dissertation for the University of Columbia.
Jansen, E.G. (1992) *Interest Groups and Development Assistance - The Case of Bangladesh*, Paper presented at the European Network of Bangladesh Studies Conference, Denmark, August 27-29, 1992.
Kabeer, N, (1985) 'Do women gain from high fertility?', in Afshar, H. (ed.) Women, *Work, and Ideology in the Third World*, Tavistock Publications, London.
Kabeer, N. (1989) *Monitoring Poverty as if Gender Mattered: A Methodology for Rural Bangladesh*, IDS Discussion Paper 255, University of Sussex, Brighton.
Kabeer, N. (1994) *Reversed Realities, Gender Hierarchies in Development Thought*, Verso, London.
Kabeer, N. (1995) 'Targeting Women or Transforming Institutions? Policy Lessons from NGO Anti-poverty Efforts, in *Development Practice 5(2)*.
Kabeer, N. (1995) 'Necessary, Sufficient or Irrelevant? Women, Wages and Intra-Household Power Relations in Urban Bangladesh', *Institute of Development Studies Working Paper 25*, Brighton.
Khan, Z.R. (1985) 'Women's Economic Role: Insights from a Village in Bangladesh', in the *Journal of Social Studies 30*, Dhaka, Bangladesh, 13-26.
Kotalova, J. (1996) *Belonging to Others. Cultural Construction of Womenhood in a Village in Bangladesh*, University Press Ltd., Dhaka.
Mackintosh, M. (1990) 'Abstract Markets and Real Needs', in Bernstein et al. (eds), *The Food Question: Profits Versus People?*, Earthscan, London, 43-45.
Mandelbaum, D. (1988) *Women's Seclusion and Men's Honour. Sex Roles in North India, Bangladesh and Pakistan*, University of Arizona Press, Tucson.
McCarthy, F.E. and Feldman, S.(1983) 'Rural Women Discovered: New Sources of Capital and Labour in Bangladesh', in *Development and Change* 14(2), Sage, London, 211-236.
Mies, M. (1982) *The Lacemakers of Narsapur. Indian Housewives Produce for the World Market*, ZED Books, London.
Mies, M. (1886) Patriarchy and Accumulation on a World Scale. Women in the International Division of Labour, ZED Books, London.
Mohila Parishad Commission Report 1993, Dhaka, Bangladesh.
Nash, J. and Fernandez-Kelly, M.P. (eds) (1983) *Women, Men and the International Division of Labour*, State University of New York Press, Albany, New York.
Omvedt, G. (1980) *We Will Smash this Prison*, ZED Press, London.
Pryer, J. and Crook, N. (1988) *Cities of Hunger: Urban Malnutrition in Developing Countries*, Oxfam, Oxford.
Rahman, H.Z. and Hossain, M. (1992) *Rethinking Rural Poverty: The Case for Bangladesh*, Bangladesh Institute of Development Studies, Dhaka.
Rogers, B. (1980) *The Domestication of Women. Discrimination in Developing Societies*, Kogan Page, London.
Sharma, U. (1990) 'Public Employment and Private Relations: Women and Work in India' in Stichter, S. and Parpart, J. L. (eds) *Women, Employment and the Family in the International Division of Labour*, Macmillan Press, London.

Sobhan, R. (1990) *From Aid Dependence to Self-Reliance - Development Options for Bangladesh*, University Press, Dhaka.

Standing, H. (1991) *Dependence and Autonomy. Women's Employment and the Family in Calcutta*, Routledge, London.

Stichter, S. and Parpart, J.L. (eds) (1990) *Women, Employment and the Family in the International Division of Labour*, Macmillan Press, London.

Westergaard, K. (1983) *Pauperisataion and Rural Women in Bangladesh. A Case Study*, BARD, Comilla.

White, S.C. (1991) 'Evaluating the Impact of NGOs in Rural Poverty Alleviation. Bangladesh Country Study', *ODI Working Paper 50*, Overseas Development Institute, London.

White, S.C. (1992) *Arguing with the Crocodile. Gender and Class in Bangladesh*, Zed Books Ltd, London and New Jersey.

Wolf, D.L. (1992) *Factory Daughters: Gender, Household Dynamics and Rural Industrialisation in Java*, University of California Press, Berkeley.

World Bank (1990) *Bangladesh: Strategies for Enhancing the Role of Women in Economic Development*, World Bank Country Study, Washington D.C.

World Bank (1992) *World Development Report 1992*, World Bank, Washington D.C.

Young, K., Wolkowitz, C. and McCullagh, R. (1981) (eds) *Of Marriage and the Market. Women's Subordination in International Perspective*, CSE Books, London.

11 Gender Inequalities in the Mining-Industrial-Urban Economy of the Raniganj Coalbelt of West Bengal, India

Kuntala Lahiri-Dutt

11.1 Introduction

One of the impacts of technology, urbanisation and growth of market economies in India has been an increase in poverty and marginalisation among women. This is partly because of the very nature of the 'development path' avidly followed in post-independence India. This path is based on a model of improved well-being through the universalization of needs, productivity and growth. It is actually an extension of the modern capitalist patriarchy's economic vision based on the exclusion of women from the productive process (Shiva, 1991). Another reason is that modernization and technology have by and large been introduced in India without changing the rural social structure (Kalpagam, 1994). Many planning measures land reforms, extension services and access to modern inputs and credit - have been explicitly class and male-biased, thereby widening the gender gap.

This chapter presents a case study of the Raniganj coalbelt where mining-industrial-urban growth has led to gender inequalities and marginalisation of the poorer women.

11.2 The Region

The Raniganj coalbelt of Bharddhaman (Bharddhaman) district, West Bengal, comprises a total area of nearly 2,000 sq. km. and is located about 250 kms. northwest of the Calcutta metropolis. The Barakar river marks its western margin and the Ajoy and Damodar make up the northern and southern boundaries respectively. The initial development of coal mining in Raniganj was intended to meet the colonial needs of the British government - for their mint, arsenals, steamboats and later, largely for the railways (Munsi, 1980) and the newly developing jute and tea industries (Murty and Panda, 1988). Rothermund (1978) described it as an 'enclave industry' which was imposed within this forested and agricultural tract.

There was a considerable participation of women in the labour force

workers from the beginning till the 1930s (Roy Chaudhury, 1996). From Independence in 1947 women's role in the mining industry declined gradually
(Akhauri, 1969), but during the last two and half decades under state-owner-
ship it has decreased at an alarming rate. With the development of modern
technology, women have been assigned mostly unskilled tasks, whereas there
has been no attempt to impart training and skills so as to enable them to adjust
to the re-organisation of work. Women now occupy a marginal position in the
Indian coal mining industry because they were made redundant in the capitalist labour process (Ghosh, 1984).

On the one hand, large-scale government investments in mining and
industrial sectors in this resource-rich region have given rise to a corridor-
type (Roy, 1993) urban growth along the main transport arteries - the Grand
Trunk road and the Eastern Railways - joining the Calcutta metropolis with
the Dhanbad-Bokaro-Sindri mining-industrial belt of Bihar (NIUA, 1988).
This is probably the most spectacular feature of the urban scenario to have
emerged in the recent decades in West Bengal (Dasgupta, 1988).

On the other hand, exclusion of women from the productive process
combined with a rapid rate of ecological destruction is now threatening the
livelihood of women in the Raniganj coalbelt. Mining and industrial development and consequent urban growth has superimposed the scientific and economic paradigms created by capitalist, gender-based ideology on the subsistence farming and forestry economy, and in the process has damaged the life-
support systems of local people, particularly women.

In the Raniganj region, urban growth, environmental degradation and
the marginalisation of women have been the results of state-controlled mining development of the last 25 years, turning women into what has been described as 'special victims of the environmental crisis' (Shiva, 1988).

11.3 Mining and Urban Growth

The extent and pace of urban growth in the region have been phenomenal. An extensive built up area, running in an east-west direction for nearly
75 kilometres along the main transport corridor, has emerged during the last
two and a half decades. The narrow interfluve of the Damodar-Ajay is now a
rapidly merging conurbation. The level of urbanisation in Raniganj coalbelt
is higher than the national average, and also the state average. In the 1991
census Bharddhaman emerges as one of the most ubranised sitricts (Roy,
1992).

The region contains 9.09 per cent of the urban population of West Bengal, a notable fact for a state with a primate city like Calcutta having over 10

million inhabitants in its metropolitan district. The region also has the largest number of new census towns in 1991 - as many as 19 of the total 105 'new-born' towns shown in the 1991 census, and 13 of the total 48 urban outgrowths of West Bengal.

Not all the new towns meet the recommended minimum population to be classed as urban. However, their occupational structures are sufficiently urban to justify their inclusion in the list of census towns.

Whereas in 1971, there were only 3 mining towns, namely Dishergarh, Jamuria and Ukhra, a distinct group of mining towns have emerged in 1991. These towns are characterised by an above average proportion of their respective workforce engaged in mining and quarrying, but a negligible representation of female workers in mining.

Table 11.1   Levels of Urbanisation in the Raniganj Coalbelt, 1991

Name of Country/ State/Region	Per cent Urban to Total Population
India	25.51
West Bengal	27.48
Maharashtra	38.69
Bharddhaman	35.09
Raniganj Coalbelt	67.27

Table 11.2   Urban Growth in the Raniganj Coalbelt, 1951-91

Year	Total Population	% increase in pop.	Urban Population	Level of Urbanisation	% Increase in Urban pop
1951	663,140	-	204,712	30.87	-
1961	817,747	18.91	316,360	38.69	64.71
1971	941,452	13.14	465,996	49.50	67.89
1981	1,178,566	20.12	738,709	62.68	63.25
1991	1,765,171	33.23	1,222,660	69.27	60.42

Table 11.3   Size-Class Distribution of New Urban Units in the Raniganj Coalbelt, 1991

Size-Class	Population	New Census Towns	Outgrowths
VI	<5,000	2	12
V	5,000 – 9,999	14	1
IV	10,000 – 19,999	3	-

Table 11.4 Employment Pattern in Mining Towns in the Raniganj Coalbelt, 1991

Rank	Name	% in Mining	%Female to Total Population	%Female Mining Workers	%Female to total workers
1	Mukundapur	86.13	38.89	1.78	2.00
2	Madhusudan	86.12	40.03	0.50	0.60
3	Paraskhol	85.34	43.55	4.45	4.10
4	Chapui	84.67	41.34	3.34	3.20
5	Konardihi	84.63	41.56	2.11	2.18
6	Amkula	84.45	39.25	1.44	1.58
7	Murgathaul	81.51	41.47	6.29	6.20
8	Parasia	80.78	39.98	5.92	5.70
9	Chak Bankola	77.84	42.56	1.72	2.00
10	Satgram	76.24	43.11	5.63	5.33
11	Mandarbani	75.07	41.08	3.03	2.90
12	Kenda	74.87	42.57	1.97	3.46
13	Bagra	74.65	42.59	5.24	4.60
14	Ratibati	74.54	41.73	4.33	5.56
15	Sankarpur	73.19	45.34	4.65	4.50
16	Ninga	72.76	41.46	4.20	4.56
17	Bahula	72.19	42.60	2.88	2.97
18	Siduli	71.83	44.47	3.28	5.15
19	Gaidhoba	71.78	36.22	2.49	2.74
20	Nimcha	69.37	45.77	6.60	6.34
21	Chelad	68.48	42.60	5.33	6.53
22	Khandra	65.14	43.87	4.58	5.22
23	Haripur	64.81	39.16	3.11	4.36
24	Kajora	64.76	43.25	3.75	6.19
25	Dalurband	63.70	42.27	3.73	4.92
26	Sripur	62.81	43.10	3.46	3.81
27	Bhanora	62.67	43.51	5.73	5.37
28	Siarsol	62.66	43.50	5.23	6.81
29	Kankhaya	61.67	43.52	3.01	3.96
30	Chhora	61.26	44.21	5.40	9.20
31	Dishergarh	55.23	45.26	5.13	7 93
32	Sarpi	52.63	43.68	2.41	3.57
33	Kaithi	51.55	46.88	4.10	3.24
34	Dakshinkh	51.02	44.95	3.93	4.64
35	Banagram	47.83	44.92	5.42	6.86
36	Banli	45.35	46.95	7.23	16.44
37	Jemari (J.K. Nagar)	43.17	42.98	14.25	7.53
38	Pariharpur	42.43	45.79	3.72	3.70

*Note : Outgrowths have been taken as individual urban units for analysis.

Table 11.5 Size Distribution of Mining Towns

Population Size range	Number of mining towns
50,000- 99,999	1
20,000-49,999	1
10,000-19,999	11
5,000 – 9,999	18
< 5,000	7

In general, these mining towns are small in size.

Table 11.6 Second and Third Ranking Occupations in Mining Towns of Raniganj Coalbelt, 1991

Occupational Category	Towns where 2nd Rank	Towns where 3rd Rank
Cultivators	Madhusudanpur, Nimcha Dakshinkhanda, Khandra	Parasia, Pariharpur
Agricultural Labourers	Kenda, Pariharpurm Haripur, Bhanora, Gaidhoba, Mukundapur, Banli, Chhora, Kajora, Mandarbani, Chelad, Paraskhol, Sarpi, Murgathaul, Banagram	Ratibati, Chapui, Siduli, Siarsol, Satgram, Dalurbandh, Dakshinkhada
Livestock, Forestry & Fishing	-	-
Manufacturing I	-	Nimcha, Chhora
Manufacturing II	Kaithi, Jemari	Dishergarh
Construction	-	-
Trade & Commerce	Chapui, Siarsol, Dalurbandh, Sripur, Kankhaya, Konardihi, Siludi, Shankarpur, Parasia, Bagra, Bahula, Ninga, ChakBankoka	Mukundapur, Amkula, Banagram, Chelad, Bhanora, Jemari, Kenda, Paraskhol, Gaidhoba, Murgathaul, Haripur, Madhusudanpur, Sarpi, mandarbani, Kajora,
Other Services	Dishergarh, Satgram, Ratibati, Amkula	Kankhaya, Konardihi, ChakBankola, Bahula, Ninga, Sirpur, Kaithi, Bagra, Banli, Khandra, Shankarpur

The two larger mining towns - Dishergarh and Siarsol have lonqer histories than the smaller mining towns and well -developed tertiary sectors, whereas the smaller and newer mining towns in most cases have 'agricultural labourer' or 'cultivators' as the second or third ranking occupations in terms of the share of workers. The second and third ranking occupations, therefore, not only reveal the functional composition of the mining towns but also throw light on the nature of the process of urbanisation in the region. Table 11.6 clearly brings out the fact that the mining towns had been in near past agriculture-based villages, where a decay has set in the agricultural sector consequent to mining expansion.

11.4 Gender Inequalities

In the Raniganj coalbelt there are an average of 839 females per thousand males. The figure is much below the national average (929), state average (917), and district average (899). Again, there are intra-regional variations; on a tehsilwise basis, Barabani has the highest FMR (910) while Pandaveswar has the lowest (786) within the study area.

The Census divides the population of the region into three categories - the tribals, the scheduled castes and the rest of the population (normally referred to as the 'general' category). The differences in their participation levels in the mainstream mining-industrial urban economy is implied by the data on the FMR. The tribal groups are the indigenous people of the region. In India they are characterised mainly by a subsistence economy, with a high female labour participation, primitive cultivation techniques and a low level of monetisation of the economy (Boserup, 1976; Agnihotri, 1995). The scheduled castes on the other hand are the major supplies of casual labour both in agricultural and non-agricultural sectors and are the 'unprotected' class (described by Mies, 1987). The general castes are comparatively the more privileged ones, enjoying a higher position both in the economic and social ladder, with the ability to acquire and develop special skills for well paid jobs both in the formal and informal sector.

Among the subgroups of the population, the FMR of scheduled tribes population is better (949) than in the other two groups. The mean FMR of scheduled castes population in the region is 868, which is above the region's average of 839. The general population has a very poor FMR (813), much below the average. This clearly indicates there has been immigration of males, mostly from the general castes but not from the scheduled castes and definitely not from the tribal populations.

There is an inverse and significant correlation between the level of

Table 11.7 Urbanisation and Gender Inequalities Administrative Units of the Raniganj Coalbelt, 1991

Name of Tehsils/P.S.	Level of Urbanisation	FMR Total Pop	FMR General pop.	FMR Scheduled Caste pop.	FMR Scheduled Tribe pop.
Salanpur	9	880	847	906	1009
Kulti	100	843	823	878	959
Hirapur	100	838	822	874	981
Asansol (North)	87	835	827	866	956
Asansol (South)	0	861	804	856	968
Barabani	13	910	884	908	1026
Jamuria	54	832	804	873	913
Raniganj	79	804	776	852	939
Pandaveswar	401	786	755	832	885
Ondal	82	797	775	837	863
Faridpur	21	847	825	871	943
Average	67	839	813	867	949
Correlation 'r ' with level of urbanisation	1.00	-0.66	-0.62	-0.60	-0.54

urbanisation and all four FMR measures, though the strength of the relationship is less strong for the Scheduled Tribes FMR. This implies their FMR ratios have been disturbed less by mining, but in any event their FMR is much higher – because they are in their home territory. The figures for the other groups reflect the inmigration of males. They imply the greatest level of inmigration for males from the general caste groups.

In the initial phase of mining development in the Raniganj coalbelt, local people along with their families were employed in large numbers. Paterson (1910) reported in the *Gazetteer of Burdwan* (now Bharddhaman) that two-thirds of the total workforce in the mining industry was locally born. The Bauris were the first to bring their womenfolk into the collieries and their contribution in the early development of Indian coal mining industry was quite significant. The Santhals, Kols, Koras and Bhuiyas also joined the mining industry with their womenfolk. As long as the family was the unit of production in mining, women had a more direct contribution to the economy. In the transition from a traditional to an industrial mode of production, the family unit was broken up into individual units. The lack of opportunities to develop new skills in the new system of production using a different technology mean that women were unwanted in the new.

Women in collieries were initially employed as 'gin girls' (from the term 'engine'), but switched to various other kinds of surface and underground work when the mechanical system of lifting coal from shallow shafts was phased out. The main role performed by women in the early decades of the present century was, however, that of a loader of coal cut by their male partners - father, brother or husband (Roy Chaudhuri, 1996). The system operated well for several reasons - the tribal sentiments of family attachment, unwillingness of women to carry coal for men of another caste, and above all, for providing uninterrupted maintenance of work rhythm. Changes in the technology of coal production in India led to the replacement of open cast mines by deep shafts which were considered 'unsuitable' for women. The technological shift produced in its wake a ban on women labour for underground mine work. Since independence, the numbers of women mine workers have gradually been falling in the Raniganj coalbelt. The public sector company, Eastern Coalfields Limited (ECL), responsible for mining in the region since the nationalization of the coal industry in 1972, now actively discourages women in collieries without opening any alternative employment opportunity for them.

The recent thrust in India on the modernization of coal mines (Bengara, 1996) will bring another wave of technological change and the alienation of women from the mining industry will be complete. In the process of switching over to still higher technology, women are being considered as dispensable; the resultant modern urban economy is by-passing the women who have contributed so much to the growth of the coal mining industry itself. The following table gives an overview of the declining role of women in the coal mining industry of the Raniganj region.

Table 11.8   Proportion of Women Workers in ECL 1901-96

Year	Female	Male	% of Female to Total
1901	26520	55682	47.62
1921	70831	115982	61.07
1981	15451	172705	8.21
1991	12804	165085	7.20
1996	9879	151855	6.11

Source : Compiled from B . R. Seth (1940) Labour in the Indian
Coal Industry, Bombay; and ECL Reports.

The figures also include those women who are employed in white-collar jobs in the various offices of ECL. The overwhelming majority of the women, however, are employed as sweepers, office bearers or, if it has to be a mining-related job, as mud pellet-makers at best.

11.5 Conclusions and a Question: WHERE DID ALL THE WOMEN GO ?

Clearly, the Raniganj coalbelt has become an overwhelmingly male domain. The case of the coal industry exemplifies how changes in the technology and economic organisation of pre-independence India and post-nationalization times have interacted to produce a rigidly hierarchical and patriarchal urban society. Such a gender based segregation of lives was also noted in the colliery settlements of Durham, England, by McDowell and Massey (1984). They showed how men viewed themselves as the industrial proletariat but enjoyed the ownership of the home. In Raniganj too, women's banishment from the male world of work has, in several ways, excluded them entirely from the power to determine their own lives. The modern urban sector has absorbed the women at the lowest strata of the society as rag pickers, casual labourers in various factories, brick kilns and stone crushing units, domestic help, sex workers, and participants in the flourishing illegal mining business. As decay in agriculture sets in, and the urban growth process gains momentum, then gender relations radically change (Thorbeck, 1994). The family no longer remains a valid unit of production; the family and the factory are of no concern to each other, and may even have contradictory interests. The result is a lowered, powerless status for women who continue to get drawn to the mainstream mining-urban-industrial economy at the lowest level as unskilled, low-paid, high-risk, illegal workers, while taking the full brunt of environmental degradation.

References

Agnihotri S.B. (1995) 'Missing Females : A Disaggregated Analysis ' *in Economic and Political Weekly*, Vol . XXX, No . 33, August 19, 1995; pp.2074-84.

Akhauri, R.K. (1969) *Labour in Coal Industry in India*. Sterling Publishers Pvt. Ltd., New Delhi.

Banerjee, N. (1991) *Indian women in a Changing Industrial Scenario*, Sage, New Delhi.

Bengara, Ratnakar (1996) 'Coal Mining displacement', *Economic and Political Weekly*, Vol. XXXI, No. II: 647-649.

Boserup, E. (1970) *Women's Role in Economic Development*, Allen and Unwin, London.

Dasgupta, Biplab (ed) (1988) *Urbanisation, Migration and Rural Change : A Study of West Bengal*, A Mukherjee and Co. Pvt. Ltd., Calcutta.

Kalpagam, U, (1994) *Labour and Gender*: Survival in Urban India, Sage, New Delhi.

McDowell, Linda and Doreen Massey (1984) 'Coal Mining and Place of Women : A Case of Nineteenth Century Britain' in Doreen Massey and John Allen (eds.) *Geography Matters ! A Reader*, The Open University, Cambridge.

Mies, Maria (1987) *Indian women in Subsistence and Agricultural Labour*, Sage, New Delhi.

Munsi, Sunil Kumar (1980) *Geography of Transportation in Eastern India Under the British Raj*, CSSSC Monograph I, K.P. Bagchi and Co., Calcutta.

NIUA (1988) *State of India's Urbanisation*, National Institute of Urban Affairs; New Delhi.

Paterson, J.C.K.(1910) *Bengal District Gazetteer.~: : Bharddhaman* , Bengal Secretariat Book Depot, Calcutta.

Roy Chaudhury, Rakhi (1996) *Gender and Labour in India : The Kamins of Eastern Coalmines*, Minerva, Calcutta.

Roy, B.K. (1993) 'Urban Corridors in India' in Bidyut Mohanty (ed) *Urbanisation in Developing Countries : Basic Services and Community Participation*: 125-135, ISS and Concept, New Delhi.

Shiva, Vandana (l991) *Staying Alive : Ecology and Development in India*, Kali for Women, New Delhi.

Thorbeck, Susane *(1994) Gender and Slum Culture in Urban Asia*, Vistaar Publication, New Delhi.

Wignarja, Ponna (1990) *Women, Poverty and Resources*, Sage, New Delhi.

Erratum

Chapter 12 Female Labour Force Participation in Urban India: Some Socio-Economic Correlates (facing page)

is authored by

R.K. Sharma and Rajeev Sharma

Rajeev Sharma is
Consultant, Institute for Human Development, New Delhi; Visiting Faculty, V.V.G. National Labour Institute

12 Female Labour Force Participation in Urban India: Some Socio-Economic Correlates

R.K. Sharma

12.1 Introduction

Female employment has been regarded as a critical variable for the improvement of women's status. In India, in all the successive Five Year Plans, there has been a significant shift in the approach towards the well-being of women, from 'Welfare during Fifties' to 'Development during Seventies' and to 'Empowering during Nineties' (GOI, 1997). Empowerment of women is one of the major objectives of the Ninth Plan. Due emphasis on women's participation in economic activities and the decision making process at all levels would help in realising this goal.

The relationship of women to the economy has been a widely discussed and debated issue. It has been argued that the nature, scope and intensity of women's work has either been ignored or wrongly measured. One cannot deny that much of women's work largely remains invisible in the national statistics and it continues to remain unquantified. As a category of workers, women need special attention, and the factors hindering their participation in economic activities need to be properly analysed.

The Indian economy is predominantly an agricultural economy with a small but a fairly well-developed urban sector. Agriculture has traditionally many, though poorly paid, female labourers. In towns the participation of women has been and continues to be abysmally low. This may be attributed mainly to the invisibility of women's work in the prevailing measures of labour force participation and the prevalent sociocultural constraints that limit women's participation in economic activities outside the family domain. In India, the position of women has been subordinate to men for centuries. Earlier women faced lot of resistance from their families to work outside their home for wages. They were confined to the home, which was considered to be the rightful place for them. However, this resistance is now fast disappearing, mainly due to the economic burden imposed by high cost of living in the urban areas.

In India it has been observed that participation in economic activities, especially for females, remains tied to class and caste and religious affiliations. Society embraces religious tenets that glorify the economic role of men and accord dependent status to women. Today, economic independence is considered to be the prime basis for improving the status of women in India. It is generally agreed that women's participation in economic activities would result in reducing their dependency, and enhancing their social and economic status as well as empower her more in household decisions.

The present study uses the data from the National Sample Survey Organisation to capture a better picture of the female labour force in India.

12.2 Objectives of the Study

The main objective of this chapter is to explore the socio-economic correlates and urban and regional variation of female labour force participation rates (hereinafter referred to as FLPR). The major socio-economic variables included in the analysis are: poverty ratio, per capita income, dependency ratio, proportion of Scheduled castes population, proportion of Muslim population, male labour force participation rate, crude birth rate, sex-ratio, literacy rate of female, level of female education (graduates & above), crimes committed against women (incidence of dowry deaths and rapes), etc. This analyses attempts to identify the factors that suppress or enhance the urban FLPR in the Indian context.

12.3 Conceptual Biases and Data Sources

Women's work has been particularly sensitive to biases in methods of enumerating workers. The statistics pertaining to their participation in the labour force have come under heavy criticism in the recent years. A World Bank study on India, terms them "statistical purdah" (World Bank, 1991) because the measurement of labour renders invisible much of the work performed by women. The kind of work they do, where, how, under what terms - all these are determined by women's position in the society. Thus, women workers form a special category, therefore they need special attention and analysis because the problem and issues that face them are different from men.

Women perform a much greater variety of tasks than do men. Nearly all women spend a major portion of their time in activities that would be regarded as work, if they were performed by a person unrelated to the household or a hired helper. For an adult male, the role of a worker or an earner is the standard stereotype and there is hardly any reservation about reporting him as a worker even when he works on the family farm or in the family enterprise (Visaria, 1996). On the contrary, there are always attempts to conceal the facts about women's participation in work as it is not approved by caste ridden religious society. It is also thought to be a mark of higher status that women do not work outside the home.

In India, the major data sources on work participation are the Decennial Population Censuses and the quinquennial surveys of the National Sample Survey Organisation (NSSO). Among other sources, the Employment Market Information (EMI) programme of the Ministry of Labour provides data on levels of employment of women in the organised sector of the economy. As women are mainly concentrated in the unorganised (informal) sector, women's work participation even in urban areas is grossly under-estimated. Though the decennial population Census has a more complete enumeration however, it has been conducted at a point of time using a single concept. The categorization of workers has also varied, especially with regard to the 1971 Census. The 1981 and 1991 Census had no such definitional problems, but an extra emphasis was put on capturing the female work participation through various means, including gender sensitisation among the enumerators and the respondents. The results have turned out to be quite revealing.

It has been observed that the National Sample Survey Organisation (NSSO) has been more sensitive in its attempts to capture women's contribution to work by adopting multiple approaches to define economic activities (Premi and Raju, 1994). The National Sample Survey (NSS) is undertaken periodically and its results are compiled at the All-India and state level. The NSS has been continuing with the same conceptual framework under a quinquennial work programme since launching the first survey in October, 1972, in the 27th round. The NSS data is based on a scientifically drawn representative sample with an exhaustive questionnaire, captures a better picture of females in the labour force along with some of the social and economic variables. Keeping this in mind, the present paper has utilised the National Sample Survey (NSS) data to analyse the female labour force participation in the urban areas.

The chapter focuses on the previous NSS rounds with a special emphasis on the latest 50th round (July 1993 - June 1994). The 50th round is the fifth quinquennial survey on employment and unemployment. The previous four quinquennial surveys were conducted between October 1972 - September 1973 and July 1987 - June 1988. The basic approach in all these surveys have been the collection of data to generate the estimates of employment and unemployment according to the 'usual status' based on a reference period of one year, the 'current weekly status (cws)', and the 'current daily status (cds)'.

The current daily status approach, in fact, measures person-days and not persons.

12.4 Trend and Pattern of Women's Employment in India

In the context of gender empowerment, a major concern is of increasing the female labour force participation rates. There has been consensus amongst scholars that increasing work force participation for women will raise not only their economic status, but social status as well. The capacity of the State to create jobs for women and other vulnerable groups of the population is limited. Besides, direct involvement of international agencies, there have been many governmental and non governmental agencies (NGOs) working towards furthering the cause of women in general and enhancing employment opportunities for them in particular. It can also be achieved by attaining high growth rates of the economy, though with the recent liberalisation proc-

Table 12.1a Percentage of Workers by Usual Status to Total Population in India (National Sample Survey)

Round (Year)	Employed (All Workers)					
	Rural			Urban		
	Male	Female	Total	Male	Female	Total
50th (1993-94)	55.3	32.8	44.4	52.0	15.4	34.7
43rd (1987-88)	53.9	32.3	43.4	50.6	15.2	33.7
38th (1983)	54.7	34.0	44.5	51.2	15.1	34.0
32nd (1977-78)	55.2	33.1	44.4	50.8	15.6	34.1
27th (1972-73)	54.5	31.8	*	50.1	13.4	*

* Proportions could not be derived for the 27th Round of NSS.

Table 12.1b Percentage of Workers to Total Population in India (Census)

		Rural			Urban		
		Male	Female	Total	Male	Female	Total
1981	Total	53.70	23.06	38.79	49.06	8.31	29.99
	Main	52.61	16.09	34.80	48.53	7.30	29.23
	Marginal	1.16	6.97	3.99	0.53	1.01	0.76
1991	Total	52.43	27.06	40.13	48.96	9.73	30.45
	Main	51.29	19.07	35.67	48.43	8.62	29.64
	Marginal	1.14	7.99	4.46	0.54	1.11	0.81

ess in the country, this route has become questionable. In this section, an attempt is made to analyse the trend and pattern in employment growth for urban females vis-a-vis urban males.

Table 12.1a depicts the percentage of workers by usual status to total population in the various NSS rounds. Table 12.1b depicts data from the 1981 and the 1991 Census. The under-enumeration of women workers in the Census is clearly brought out in the above tables, with female urban employment being below 10% in the Census, but nearer 15% in the NSS. Compared to the male rates, the reported female participation rates are low in India and this is substantiated both by Census and NSS data. Age specific participation rates for males and females in different age-groups for the years 1987-88 and 1993-94 are presented in the following table.

Table 12.2   Age Specific Rates of Labour Force Participation (percentages)

Age	Rural				Urban			
	Male		Female		Male		Female	
	43rd	50th	43rd	50th	43rd	50th	43rd	50th
5-9	2.3	1.1	2.4	1.4	0.5	0.4	0.3	0.4
10-14	19.3	13.9	18.3	14.2	9.2	7.1	6.6	4.7
15-19	63.0	59.8	41.5	37.1	42.9	40.4	16.9	14.2
20-24	91.8	90.2	48.4	47.0	79.2	77.2	22.5	23.0
25-29	98.1	98.0	53.9	52.8	96.7	95.8	24.4	24.8
30-34	99.0	98.8	58.8	58.7	98.5	98.3	28.2	28.3
35-39	99.1	99.2	60.8	61.0	98.9	99.0	31.3	30.4
40-44	98.4	98.9	62.0	60.7	98.6	98.4	31.1	32.0
45-49	98.2	98.4	59.0	59.4	97.7	97.6	30.7	31.7
50-54	96.2	97.0	53.0	54.3	94.4	94.5	26.9	28.7
55-59	92.9	94.1	46.3	46.8	84.9	85.6	23.5	22.5
60+	67.0	69.9	22.0	24.1	48.2	44.3	12.3	11.4
All	54.9	56.1	33.1	33.1	53.4	54.2	16.2	16.4

Source: National Sample Survey Organisation: Fifth
Quinquennial Survey NSS Fiftieth Round (July 1993 - June 1994).

Interestingly labour force participation rates have gone up for the 'All' category, except for rural females, which remained unchanged. It also suggests an increase in the male labour participation rates for the rural as well as urban areas. In the case of urban females there is positive change in the participation rate. A significant revelation of this table is the decline in child participation rates (5-14 years) for both male and female in the rural as well as urban areas. The possible reason for this sudden fall could be because of increased attendance in schools, or because of the social awareness against child labour, or possibly because of the 'social clause' incorporated in the GATT agreement which prohibits the export of goods manufactured by children. There is also the possibility that age is mis-reported.

Table 12.3 Industrial Distribution of Workers (in Terms of Usual Status) in Urban India by Sex

	32nd 1977-78		38th 1983		43rd 1987-88		50th 1993-94	
	M	F	M	F	M	F	M	F
1.Agriculture	10.6	31.9	10.3	32.0	9.1	30.5	9.0	24.8
2.Mining&Quarrying	0.9	0.5	1.3	0.8	1.3	0.7	1.3	0.6
3.Manufacturing	27.5	29.6	27.0	27.1	25.9	26.9	23.6	24.3
4.Electricity,Gas&Water	1.1	0.1	1.1	-	1.2	0.2	1.2	0.3
5.Construction	4.2	2.2	5.2	3.3	5.9	3.5	7.0	4.1
6.Trade	21.6	8.7	20.2	9.0	21.7	9.9	22.0	10.1
7.Transport&Storage	9.8	1.0	9.9	1.0	9.6	0.7	9.8	1.3
8.Services	24.3	26.0	25.0	26.2	25.3	27.6	26.1	34.5
	100.0	100.0	100.0	100.0	100.0	100.0	100.0	100.0

Table 12.4 Status Distribution of Workers (in terms of Usual Status) in Urban India by Sex

Year	Round	Self-Employment		Regular Employees		Casual Labour	
		M	F	M	F	M	F
1993-94	50th	41.1	36.4	42.7	35.5	16.2	28.1
1987-88	43rd	41.0	39.3	44.4	34.2	14.6	26.5
1983	38th	40.2	37.3	44.5	31.8	15.3	30.9
1977-78	32nd	39.9	42.2	47.2	30.8	12.9	27.0

Source: NSSO.

Tables 12.3 and 12.4 presents data by sector and by type of employment. There have been noticeable changes during eighties and early nineties. It is clear that the share of casual workers amongst the employed workers is higher in case of women than men, and that over a period, it has significantly increased. The increase in casualisation has been higher among the males, around 3.2 per cent points in urban areas as compared to 1.1 per cent points for females. In case of urban males there is a decline in the regularly employed, whereas amongst females there is an increase. Another important finding from the table is that the share of self employment has declined for urban females. Nevertheless there has been rise in the self employed category for the urban males. The decline in share in case of urban females may be due to poorer access to credit by females. It has been argued that the system of subcontracting of jobs in the urban economy is adversely affecting females, though they are getting poorly paid work of a more regular basis. This reflects a significant change in the organisation of work and subcontracting system in the urban informal sector (Kundu, 1996). However, this can not be substantiated by the data on Industrial Distribution of workers in terms of usual status by sex, 1977-78 to 1993-94 presented in Table 12.4 where contrary to expectations, a decline is also seen in the case of manufacturing sector. It has declined from 29.6 per cent in 1977-78 to 24.3 per cent. However the major activities which have become more prominent are the services sector where the share has increased from 26.0 per cent in 1977-78 to 34.5 per cent in 1993-94 and construction where share has increased from 2.7 per cent to 4.1 per cent in the same period.

12.5 Interstate Differences in FLPR and some Socio-Economic Correlates

In this section, the variations observed in FLPR across states are analysed, and an attempt has been made to bring out some socio-economic correlates of FLPR.

One of the striking structural characteristics of female labour in India is the regional differences. Broadly speaking, the Southern states are the regions where women's work participation is high while Northern states by contrast have low participation. In the north, the patriarchal traditions are severe and this inhibits women from working outside the home. This can also be explained in terms of socio-cultural factors that restrict entry of women in the labour market. Further, the work participation rates, both for males and females, as discussed earlier, are lower in urban areas as compared to rural areas. This is because the agrarian economy has the capacity to carry a large number of disguised persons or absorb people at low level of productivity, by subdividing a job into many.

Table 12.6 presents the correlation coefficients between the FLPR rates and different socio-economic indicators. One very important factor which has surprisingly received little attention is the child bearing responsibilities of the women. There is no dearth of studies working out the impact of the female work participation upon the fertility behaviour of the women: how-

Table 12.5 Labour Force Participation Rates according to Usual (Principal) Status by Sex for Major States in Urban India

	Male	Female	Total
Andhra Pradesh	554	176	369
Bihar	466	63	283
Gujarat	546	104	335
Haryana	527	76	322
Karnataka	549	154	356
Kerala	587	201	389
Madhya Pradesh	493	126	321
Maharashtra	545	146	356
Orissa	542	125	346
Punjab	570	63	330
Rajasthan	493	110	312
Tamil Nadu	596	220	408
Uttar Pradesh	493	70	296
West Bengal	583	129	374
INDIA	538	132	345

Source: 50th round (July 1993 - June 1994), NSSO.

Table 12.6 Some Socio-Economic Correlates of Female Labour Force Participation Rates: 1993-94

CRUDE BIRTH RATE	-.66	*
MALE PARTICIPATION (USUAL PRINCIPAL STATUS)	.64	*
SEX RATIO	.82	**
URBANISATION	.43	
SC POPULATION(%)	.21	
PROP'N OF MUSLIM POP.	.17	
FEMALE GRAD.& ABOVE	-.65	*
FEMALE LITERACY	.46	
DEPENDENCY RATIO	-.74	*
POVERTY RATIO	.41	
PER CAPITA INCOME	-.06	
INCIDENCE OF RAPE (PER 100,000 WOMEN)	-.16	
INCIDENCE OF DOWRY DEATHS (PER 100,000 WOMEN)	-.52	

N of cases: 14   1-tailed Signif: * - .01 ** - .001

Notes: (i) FLPR rates are according to Usual (Principal Status) 50th Round NSS (July 1993 - June 1994).

(ii) All the variables except the crime variables relate to urban areas only.

ever, there are not many studies to measure the impact of fertility on the female participation rate. The results as presented in table show a significant negative correlation between crude birth rate and FLPR. It suggests that increased employment opportunities for the women will have reduce their fertility rates, and help in slowing down the population growth.

The sex ratio measured as the number of females per thousand males, is considered to be a possible indicator of women's status. The sex composition of India's population shows a shortage of females per 1,000 males. Although the country as a whole is marked by an unbalanced sex-ratio, regional variations are quite significant. The North-South divide in sex ratio in India is startling. If we assume as Census does, that a sex ratio of 950 or above indicates a position of relative equality, every single state in the northern region is below this ideal and every single southern state is above it (Basu, 1991). The Sex ratio in a population is a surrogate for the value placed by the society on the sexes. Here the sex ratio positively and significantly correlated with the FLPR suggesting there is more female employment where females are also better valued.

The efforts to promote women's participation in the labour force are sometimes opposed on a false notion that it will have a depressing effect on male employment. This stems from the belief that males are the bread winners of the families, and their unemployment or underemployment will result in suffering for the family, so their needs should be met first. However, the present analysis shows a positive significant correlation between female employment and male employment rates. It indicates that female employment is higher in those areas where male employment is higher. This is can be attributed to higher economic activity in the urban areas where male and female participate in different activities. Basically the argument over employment for women or for men reflects a misunderstanding of the origins of unemployment and the nature of development.

The disparity between rural and urban incomes encourages constant rural-urban migration and makes it worthwhile for the educated unemployed to wait for suitable employment (Ware, 1981). There are many studies showing that incidence of female participation is higher in the informal sector and male participation is higher in the formal sector. In fact, one finds that most of the labour intensive activities like garment manufacturing are carried out by women. Regular workers would generally be male and more costly. It may also be mentioned that women are ready to work at minimum wages as their incomes are supplementary to the household income, mainly generated by males. Women generally accept lower wages or minimal piece rate contracts as their opportunity cost is zero as envisaged by them.

The importance of education for bringing about social change and for reducing the inequality is well accepted. Educational level is considered to be one of the most important indicators of women's status. Despite the fact that the percentage of female literates as compared to the total population has increased, it continues to be low, and as such it is unsatisfactory. There are striking variations in the state-wise literacy rates in India. The proportion of women educated at higher levels is also very small. In the present analysis, the FLPR is positively (but not significantly) related with female literacy.

The share of women in overall employment has increased mostly in sectors offering only low paid, insecure and unstable employment. The lack of requisite skills and education do limit women's employment opportunities in the urban areas. This is very much substantiated by the negative and significant correlation between graduates and the female participation. It is widely recognised that the rapid expansion of education, particularly of higher education, has also contributed to the mismatch in the labour market. While shortages of middle level technical and supervisory skills are often experienced, graduates and postgraduates in arts, commerce and science constitute a large proportion of job seekers (Planning Commission, GOI, 1992). This can also be because women even after getting educated are not willing to work or because social conditions prevailing in the society do not permit them to do so or they are discriminated against in the urban labour market where they compete with their male counterparts.

The correlation between poverty ratio and FLPR exhibits a positive relationship. The poverty of the household forces women to work for a living and supplement the family income. Many studies have found that female participation rates decline sharply in prosperous states, which are characterised by high male earnings (Sinha; Sawant and Dewan; Parthasarthy and Ramarao). However, the estimates for Punjab reveals a low FLPR, mainly due to the increased prosperity of the region consequent on the success of the Green Revolution. The World Bank report on Gender and Poverty in India observes that the most prosperous northern states like Haryana and Punjab share low female participation in labour force with the eastern states of Bihar and West Bengal where the incidence of poverty is extremely high (World Bank, 1991). The analyses presented in this paper at the state-level, have to be viewed more as suggestive than conclusive and as mentioned earlier, there have been studies indicating an association between income and FLPR.

The dependency ratio indicates the proportion of economically inactive population per 1000 economically active population. It is calculated as the number of persons in the age-group 0-14 and 60 & above per 1000 persons in the age-group 15-59. The correlation result between dependency ratio and FLPR shows a significant negative correlation, as it ought, since as the FLPR goes up, women are transferring from the inactive to active population.

This relationship highlights women's role in easing the economic burden of the family.

The alarming rise in the crimes committed against women in India during the nineties and its bearing on the FLFP cannot be ignored. In India, crimes against women show an upward trend. In the country, on an average, every day 32 women are raped and 16 killed for dowry. In all about 7000 cases of crimes against women were registered in India every month throughout 1993. To examine the impact of the crime against women on the FLPR, rapes and dowry variables were included. These are based on the data compiled by National Crime Records Bureau (NCRB) on the basis of reported cases. The actual figures may still be much higher. Nevertheless, they reflect the level of violence in Indian society vis-a-vis women. In India, there is gross under-reporting of the crimes against women due to secrecy, insufficient evidence, social and legal barriers. The crime studies in India are further hampered by the deficient crime statistics. Besides under-reporting of crimes, data are presented as aggregated values not separated by urban and rural areas, sex and age. The result suggests that in states where participation of women in the labour force is higher, the incidence of dowry deaths is lower. This presumably shows that women have a value whilst alive where they have a chance of working. The relationship between crimes against women and FLPR, as revealed in this analysis, calls for further research in this largely neglected area.

12.6 Conclusions

Urbanisation is usually represented as a modernising force, which may be expected inter alia to increase female participation rates in the economy. In the case of India, this is not the case. Participation rates for women remain higher in rural areas, though in poorly paid labouring jobs. Urban India is both old and new - there are both traditional and modern urban centres. In traditional urban centres there has been class and caste prejudice against women working. In the new squatter settlements the same prejudice may not prevail, but participation rates are still not detectably as high as one might have expected.

This study focuses mainly on the National Sample Survey (NSS) data. A comparative picture of the women workers in the Population Census and NSS is also presented. Though female employment in urban India has increased during the last two decades, it still lags far behind the male labour force participation. The increase in female participation has been seen by many scholars as a process of feminisation of workforce, specifically in urban areas. This has been generally attributed to the growth of informal sector, which has also resulted in casualisation of workforce. Informal sector workers, women in particular, are generally not organised, have greater job turnover and often accept inferior working condition and lower paid job. The age-specific labour force participation rates exhibit a clear decline in the child labour (5-14 years) in the rural and urban areas for males as well as females during the period 1983-93.

Tradition and traditional values again raise their heads at the regional scale. The difference between northern and southern urban India is not related to urbanisation per se, but to the differences between northern and southern culture, both urban and rural. In other words, the cities grow in their local context, and though they may be agents of change, they also show as agents of continuity.

Note

The NSS classifies workers according to 'usual status'. This means the activity in which they spent most of their time in the previous year. A person is categorised as 'worker' or 'employed' on the basis of the principal employment, and is included within 'principal status -worker' or 'principal status -employed'. A person is considered as 'seeking or available' for work or 'unemployed' if the person was not working but was either seeking or was available for work for the majority of the previous year. Persons who spent most of their time in a non-economic activity are considered 'out of labour force'. A person categorised as a non-worker who pursued some economic activity in a subsidiary capacity is called a 'subsidiary status worker' or 'subsidiary status employed'. These two groups viz. principal status workers and subsidiary status workers together constitute 'all workers' according to the usual status classification.

References

Basu, Alka Malwade (1991) 'The North-South contrast',(*The Economic Times*, New Delhi) 18 April.

Government of India (1997) *Approach Paper to Ninth Plan* (Planning Commission, New Delhi).

Government of India (1992) *Report of the NDC Committee on Employment* (Planning Commission, New Delhi).

Government of India (1997) *Approach Paper to Ninth Plan* (Planning Commission, New Delhi).

Jain, D. and Bannerji, N. (ed) (1985) *Tyranny of the Household: Investigative Essays on Women's Work*, (Shakti Books, Delhi).

Kundu, Amitabh (1996) 'Women Employment and Casualisation of Work in India', Paper presented in the seminar *Gender and Employment in India: Recent Trends, Patterns and Policy Options*, (Institute of Economic Growth, New Delhi) December 18-20.

Kundu, A. and Premi, M.K. (1992) 'Work and non-work in the official statistical system: issues concerning data base and research on women in India' in A. Bose and M.K.Premi (eds) *Population Transition in South Asia*, (B.R. Publishing Corporation, Delhi).

Nayyar, Rohini (1987) 'Female Participation Rates in Rural India'*(Economic and Political Weekly*, Bombay), December 19.

Parthasarthy, G. and Ramarao, G.D. (1974) *Employment and Unemployment of Rural Labour and the Crash Programme*, (Andhra University Press, Waltaire).

Visaria, Pravin (1996) 'Level of Pattern of Female Employment in India, 1911-1994' paper presented in the seminar *Gender and Employment in India Recent Trends, Patterns and Policy Options* (IEG, New Delhi) December 18-20.

Premi, M.K. and Raju, Saraswati (1994) *Gender Issues in Workforce Participation in the 1991 Census in India* (IASP, New Delhi).

Raju, Saraswati and Bagchi, Deipica (eds.) (1993) *Women and Work in South Asia: Regional Patterns and Perspectives* (Routledge, London).

Sawant, S.D. and Dewan, R. (1979)'Rural female labour and economic development',*(Economic and Political Weekly*, Bombay) 24 (26): 1091-9.

Ware, Helen (1981) *Women, Demography and Development* (Australian National University, Canberra).

World Bank Country Study (1991) *Gender and Poverty in India* (The World Bank, Washington, D.C.).

13 The Gendered Division of Space and Access in Working Class Areas of Lahore

Anita M. Weiss

13.1 Introduction

This chapter is about the gendered space of Pakistan's most important city, Lahore in the province of Punjab. Although founded earlier, Lahore became the archetypal Mughal city, the "grand resort of people of all nations and a centre of extensive commerce" (Abdul Fazl, as quoted in Research Society of Pakistan , 1976:325). The first Mughal Emperor, Babur, invaded Lahore in 1524. His famous grandson, Akbar, made a significant architectural change by enclosing that part of the city housing the bulk of its residents within "a brick wall of considerable height and strength" sometime during his residence there between 1584-1598 (Latif, 1892: 85). Akbar's son, Jehangir, is said to have loved living there as it was near his favourite hunting grounds, just past Sheikhupura. Jehangir is credited with creating the city's legacy as a cultural centre by encouraging music, art and drama to flourish during his tenure. He fixed his court there in 1622, and was later buried just on the other side of the Ravi river. His son, Shah Jehan, built some of Lahore's greatest architectural treasures including Shalimar Gardens and the Badshahi Mosque, which is within the Walled City.

During the forty years of the Sikh Raja Ranjit Singh's rule, Lahore regained some of its prosperity and population~ and the Walled City was physically enhanced by the construction of some more spectacular havelis (mansions) (Mumtaz, 1987:15). After the British annexation of the Punjab in 1849, Lahore's political importance increased while Amritsar's decreased. The indigenous population of Lahore remained largely restricted to the interior of the Walled City. In 1855 the first official British census of Lahore showed it had a population of 94,143. In 1859, the British filled in the moat which encircled the Walled City and had gardens planted there instead. They totally destroyed the outer defensive wall, and reduced the inner wall by half. However, while the British governed it, they themselves rarely lived within the Walled City. Instead, they built up a colonial city around it and only went within the walls when necessary, thereby enabling the Walled City to retain its indigenous sociocultural essence. The few Europeans who did live within the walls usually resided in important historic structures (Goulding, 1924).

Pakistan's independence on August 14, 1947 occurred in tandem with the partition of the subcontinent. Many parts of the Walled City erupted in flames, especially those *kuchas* historically identified with Hindus and Sikhs. Popular lore estimates that about half of the old city's residents abandoned their homes and fled to India during Partition; new Muslim occupants replaced them. It is assumed that many of the *muhajirs* (Moslem migrants from India) who settled in the Walled City were poor as it was here that the "evacuee property" was in the least demand (PEPAC, 1987: 19). Some *muhajirs* came with kin, others had to create 'kin', and a renewed culture comprising over a quarter of a million people was built upon the rubble of the old. Fictive kinship relationships developed, based on a common region of origin, the shared experience of a refugee camp, or residential proximity in a common *kucha*. These have then often become real, cemented through marriages.

Lahore now has a population of over 7 million. The city's expansion has had an impact on all aspects of its economic and social spaces. The Walled City is witnessing its demise as a residential warren. Azim Cloth Market - the regional wholesale centre - has substantially extended its reach as developers demolished ancient neighbourhoods and old *havelis*[1] to make way for new shops. No figures exist on the numbers of people who have been dislocated in this process. However, through talking to people in neighbourhoods from Akbari Gate to Taksali Gate, it becomes obvious that the sociocultural breakdown is considerable. Poor residents are increasingly anxious about where they will move: the fictive kinship ties which they had enjoyed with long-term neighbours are breaking down as neighbourhoods are physically razed. The rapid expansion and suburbanisation that has occurred has brought about an unprecedented plethora of new middle and working class communities in locales physically distant from the cultural centre in the Walled City. Waves of long-term residents and migrants from rural areas have been settling in less crowded living areas, ultimately causing the very notion of a 'centre' in Lahore to break down.

Gendered space in Lahore has not undergone as substantial a reconfiguration as has class-based space. Allocation and use of gendered space is still derived largely from one's family's class norms, although degree of piety within a given family is also an important consideration. Conditions under which women live in the Walled City, where there is both a symbolic and practical divide in the way space is used by men and women, frame perceptions and expectations of the allocation of gendered space in many working class areas of Lahore. In most instances, prevailing gendered norms and values remain an integral part of life as families move into less crowded housing in the new communities.

---

1 *Havelis were once large residences housing generations of extended family members. Since the turn of the century, it is more common to find them divided up into separate living quarters, housing either biological kin or fictive kin.*

This chapter seeks to understand the gendered division of space in Lahore's quintessential working class enclave, the Walled City, and looks at the ways in which the allocation and use of physical space translates into differential gendered access in newer working class neighbourhoods of Lahore.

13.2 The Walled City

We think of the Walled City as the quintessential working class quarter in Lahore, given its sociocultural and historical significance. Its spatial organisation, laid out hundreds of years ago, is marked by high buildings providing cooling relief to the thin streets and *galis* (alleyways) below while ostensibly hiding the pavements in shadows. Minimum space exists for movement along the narrow walkways. Buildings are occupied usually by a store or workshop on the ground level, with two or three levels of family living quarters above, and topped with a latrine and a flat roof, all accessible through a common stairwell. It is difficult to recognize people in the darkness of the alleyways, in the inner sanctum of some *kucha*s, the Walled City term for neighbourhoods. Social exchanges are often carried out on rooftops, where people sleep in the summer, wash dishes and clothes year-round, and from which they greet each other whenever possible.

The Walled City is divided up into large residential groupings, each identified by the name of the Gate in its proximity. There are certain associations made with each gate (darvaza) and many *kucha*s which to most residents demarcates both a spatial and a conceptual image of fictive extended family. Though most of the wall no longer exists, continuous waves of buildings have virtually recreated the wall, enabling the maintenance of a symbolic demarcation of identity between the Walled City and the outside. Contributing to this notion is the extremely high density found in most parts of the Walled City, seven times greater than that found in metropolitan Lahore as a whole. Such high densities, however, are not a new feature in the Walled City. An early twentieth century account describes the city as being overcrowded and already in a decrepit shape and that "the streets of the Old City are narrow and tortuous, and are best seen from the back of an elephant." (*Encyclopaedia Britannica*, 1929).

Most of the Walled City is framed by the Circular Road which is about three miles in circumference. Until recently, the Walled City had retained its essential character as a pedestrian enclave (Johnson 1979:197). Except for the entrance at Shah Alami Gate leading to the wholesale bazaar at Rang Mahal and the cloth bazaar at Azim Market, there is no true two-way thoroughfare. Increasingly, motorised vehicles trying to transit Kashmiri Bazaar have carved out two-way routes via Delhi, Kashmiri and Taksali Gates. Trucks, cars and motorised rickshaws at best can navigate with difficulty in only limited areas near most entrance gates, necessitating horse-drawn or hand-pulled carts to transport people and goods within the city walls.

Most of the buildings are either physically decaying, shoddily built, constructed with inappropriate materials, or are in highly congested areas. Services remain limited; for example, most of the Walled City is still not connected to natural gas lines necessary for cooking and heating. The environmental and sanitary conditions are poor, to say the least. Given the arduous living conditions, it is not surprising that residents accept offers of hard cash to give up their homes within the Walled City and shift outside of it to the many *katchi abadis* and other new settlements which have been springing up throughout Lahore. While abundant social amenities greet many of the new residents, whether or not these settlements suit the needs of gendered space is largely left unconsidered.

13.3 Gendered Space in the Walled City

When we ponder the way in which space is used differently by men and women living within these walls, we are reminded of Fatima Mernissi's writing on Moroccan women. Mernissi (1987:148) argues that the design of sexual space in Muslim society projects "a specific vision of female sexuality." This vision in the Walled City is one of being protected from the outside world where a woman - and therefore her family's respectability - is at risk. Women here live under the traditional constraints associated with *purdah*, which necessitate the separation of women from the activities of men, both physically and symbolically, thereby creating very differentiated male and female spheres. Most women spend the bulk of their lives physically within their homes; they go outside only when there is a substantive purpose. The culture outside the home, now as in the past, revolves around the actions of men; now, as in the past, it is considered shameful (*be-sharam*) when it becomes known that a woman leaves her house to work and help support her family, especially since the conditions of high density enables everyone in the neighbourhood to witness the exodus.

Life here appears to the outsider to exist in the public space of the male world. We see men active in all spheres of activities: they hawk fruits, vegetables and samosas from small carts; run sewing machines in their tailoring shops; sell dry goods to a largely male clientele; work by hand fabricating tools in workshops and seem to endlessly congregate around tea stalls. The noise, the crowds, the tumult~ the cramped alleyways, the *halwa/puri* and *nihari* food stalls, the blaring *filmi* music, are all a part of this accessible public sphere of life. But what is not, what is conspicuously absent to an outsider, is the presence of women.

Women indeed engage in vibrant social interactions within the Walled City, but either within homes or in what Janet Abu-Lughod (1993) refers to as "semi-private space." Staircases and *jharokas* [windows] provide for gender-specific meeting places, as do the ends of alleyways. It is in such "spillover space" where fictive kinship becomes established between neighbours. Abu Lughod (1993 :27) could have been writing about social networks in the Walled City of Lahore when she wrote, about the Islamic city in general:

It is clear that when densities are high and houses too small to contain the manifold activities women are supposed to do in them, the spillover space becomes appropriate as semiprivate space and co-residents who might inadvertently have visual access are appropriated into a fictive kinship relationship to neutralize danger.

Restrictions on most women's mobility within a *kucha*, which contains fictive kin, are relatively relaxed and women often meet with female neighbours. Restrictions on a woman's mobility are strictest when she considers leaving her neighbourhood (Weiss, 1992).

Women's social activities are generally constrained within the walls of the old city. Perceptions of great distances are relative as most tasks are performed in a very concentrated parcel of space: food, spices, fresh milk, cloth and household goods are found within a short walk of every *kucha*. People attend weddings nearby as relatives often live within walking distance of each other. Girls generally attend schools usually if they are in their own neighbourhoods, though as female higher education is gaining greater acceptance in the whole of Pakistan, we see more girls from the Walled City studying at the Cooper Road campus of Islamid College.

Social constraints confine women to home-based piecework, often at the behest of a middleman and under discriminatory and highly exploitative circumstances (Weiss,1992). For example, a widow living in Muhalla Namd Garan, behind Masjid Wazir Khan, has been stringing flowers at home, everyday, for the last twenty-five years. She is provided with all the necessary materials she needs — the needles, thread, flowers, cardboard, foil paper for the centre of earrings, etc. — and is paid ten rupees for each kilo of flowers she and her daughter strings, which is usually 2-3 per day. The man who gives them the work is a neighbour whose family owns gardens outside of the Walled City and a shop behind a shrine near Masjid Wazir Khan where they sell the flowers. Five women in her *kucha* string flowers for this man, though many others string flowers for other shopkeepers. She feels that stringing flowers is a pleasant social activity; they give off a wonderful fragrance and she can talk with her friends and relatives while she works. To earn extra money, she also occasionally shells almonds, which she doesn't enjoy as much. All decisions regarding this widow's children - their education, their marriages, her son's career - are made by her late husband's older brother. She observes strict purdah and is fearful of upsetting her brother-in-law. As she is not his wife, she doesn't have the opportunity to wait for 'the right time' to discuss things with him; instead, she has no recourse but to listen to him.

People think badly if a woman works at all. Whether she works as a lady doctor, or a teacher, people still say that her mother and father eat from her labour. The point is that whatever kind of work a girl does, if she has to walk outside to do it, it doesn't look good for the family. A girl can work inside of her home, and no one knows.... (Weiss 1992:105)

Prevailing norms and values associated with the gendered division of space in the Walled City are under severe strain in poor households, compelling women to work surreptitiously. Such labour, limited to one's home, characterises many women's lives in the Walled City as additional economic opportunities are not easily available.

Importantly, these living conditions also contain significant advantages for women. It enables frequent interaction with one another, thereby facilitating informal communication networks regarding health-care delivery systems, schools, local news and events, income-earning prospects and how to access government programs (e.g., *zakat* funds and land allocation schemes). Meeting with each other provides psychological outlets, a chance to find support among one's own gender away from the power-based interactions that define most marital relationships. It also contributes to a lower incidence of domestic violence, as residents reserve the right - based on perceptions of fictive kinship - to intervene when a family dispute turns physical, similar to how extended family members would intervene in a village setting.

But what happens when these same people move away from their high density, traditionally-oriented neighbourhoods?

13.4 Gendered Space in Working Class Areas outside of The Walled City

As 'traditional' working class families from the Walled City shift to new locales in such areas as Karim Park, Wahdat Road, Shalimar Bagh, and

Township, their physical and social environments change radically. These new settlements are of three types: planned communities; *katchi abadis* [2] which the Lahore Development Authority (LDA) recognised (and hence regularised) in the *Punjab Katchi Abadis Act of 1992*; and newer unplanned settlements ('rogue' *katchi abadis*) which despite being essentially illegal settlements, continue to grow but without civic amenities. These working class areas have an entirely distinct atmosphere from the older bungalow communities of the suburbs. They are far more congested than most housing outside of the Walled City had been, though appear far more open than the Walled City. A status hierarchy of sorts exists in the three types of communities, with houses in the planned communities being in the greatest demand, those in 'rogue' *katchi abadis* considered the most run-down and unsafe, and *recognised katchi abadis* falling somewhere in-between. Housing conditions in the planned communities and the recognized katchi abadis are overseen by the state. Hence, people living in these locales are entitled to such facilities as electricity, water, sewerage, and trash cleanup, unlike residents of 'rogue' *katchi abadis* (those built after March 1985) who often must bribe officials and service workers for such luxuries. Important though both kinds of katchi abadis are as residential areas for the poor of Lahore, as the goal of this paper is to provide suggestions for shifting the gendered division of space in new working class zones to empower women and enhance their access, the focus here will be on planned communities, for it is within these that state-community cooperation has the greatest potential to succeed.

The planned community of Anguri Bagh and the regularised katchi abadi of Sukhnagar are illustrative of the two types, and make for an interesting contrast. Located in the eastern part of Lahore north of Mall Road, the two settlements are a short distance from the commercially important Grand Trunk (G.T.) Road and the Mughal remains at Shalimar Gardens. The entire area is said to have once been a part of the extended Mughal gardens; Anguri Bagh is assumed to have been Dara Shikoh's garden, built near the shrine of the saint Mian Mir.

Some sort of housing settlement had existed in Anguri Bagh for over a century. The LDA held a competition in the early 1970s to select an architect who could construct a planned community on the site. Karachi-native Yasmin Lari won with her design for 900 housing units to be constructed in two plot sizes of 21/2 or 33/4 *marlas* (1 marla = 1/400 of an acre) to house an average of 7-8 persons. While making for cramped living space, the housing was to

---

2 *The term katchi abadi implies impermanence, and is generally considered to apply to informally organised housing settlements. These were often illegally occupied or illegally sold, and civic amenities were poor. In Punjab, the Punjab Katchi Abadis Act of 1992 regularised all such unauthorized settlements that existed prior to March 23, 1985.*

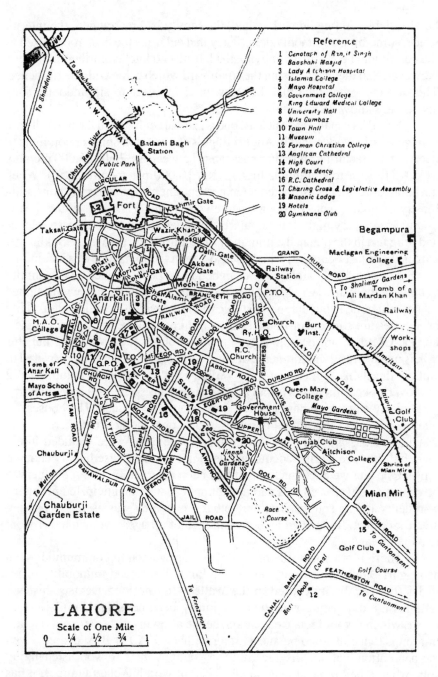

Reference
1. Cenotaph of Ranjit Singh
2. Baoshahi Masjid
3. Lady Atchison Hospital
4. Islamia College
5. Mayo Hospital
6. Government College
7. King Edward Medical College
8. University Hall
9. Nila Gumbaz
10. Town Hall
11. Museum
12. Forman Christian College
13. Anglican Cathedral
14. High Court
15. Old Residency
16. R.C. Cathedral
17. Charing Cross & Legislative Assembly
18. Masonic Lodge
19. Hotels
20. Gymkhana Club

LAHORE

Scale of One Mile

0   ¼   ½   ¾   1

Map 13.1 Lahore

be affordable. In one home I visited, the family had rearranged the interior space, something commonly done. They had enlarged the back room, used as the communal bedroom, by moving the latrine and kitchen further to the rear. However, that meant enclosing the small yard which came with the residence. The women complained that they now have no place to sit outdoors. They also do not know their neighbours.

Families usually have at least one wage-earner living in the home. These men generally work either in Anguri Bagh's commercial spine or commute to nearby manufacturing areas. Incomes range between Rs. 2,500 - 5,000 monthly ($75 - $125); a few climb as high as Rs. 10,000 per month ($250). When questioned, residents estimated a ten percent unemployment rate, consisting mostly of young men. Residents perceive that the crime rate in the area is tolerable, not very high. It is popularly considered that there is less violence and drug use in the planned community of Anguri Bagh than in the Sukhnagar katchi abadi just behind it, which is also perceived to have lower incomes.

The residential areas were designed to be pedestrian enclaves, similar to those in the Walled City. The perimeter of the residential area was designed as a commercial spine though its usage did not develop as anticipated. Daily necessities are sold either in the smaller commercial area or out of people's homes. Children are occasionally sent to purchase food products, but this task is usually reserved for men as a considerable distance must be covered to walk to the shops. But unlike in the Walled City, an important cultural detail was overlooked: there is virtually no semi-private space in the community, particularly any which has been reserved for use by women. The houses are interconnected in that they physically touch one another, but there are no conduits of passage between them. Open space areas were included in the plan, but they are neither adequately used nor equitably used, in a gendered sense. One site we encountered that had been reserved by urban planners to be open space was used as a garbage dump, causing unanticipated problems of rodents and mosquitos. The only other one nearby was used as a playing area for cricket, frequented by boys and men of all ages. Women never went to either area.

There is a distinct dilemma confronting women in communities such as Anguri Bagh. In many instances, the kind of enforced immobility of females that familiarity caused in the Walled City no longer exists. Instead, families are embracing what had previously been considered middle class norms which favour female education, hence allowing girls to travel together in groups to a college to pursue an Intermediate (F.A.) or B.A. degree. Even the perception that it is disgraceful for a young woman to work is changing somewhat, albeit more slowly. In a handful of working-class families, it has become a mark of pride that a well-educated daughter is working in a government office or a bank, even living in one of the new government-built working women's hostels.

Based on research I conducted among working class students at various girls' colleges in Lahore, I found that many educated women expect to work *shana bashana* - shoulder to shoulder - with men, but this expectation is not usually reciprocated by men in regards to working alongside women. There is a noted increase of girls pursuing higher education from neighbourhoods previously unrepresented in girls' colleges. They are expected not only to attend classes but also to participate in extramural sports and civic activities. The latter often includes fund-raising to assist the 'freedom fighters' in Kashmir or gathering food and clothes for flood victims. Indeed, such experiences reinforce a sentiment among these girls that there is a place for them in the larger Pakistani civil society, an environment clearly beyond the confines of their homes. While girls from the Walled City return from college in their *burqas* (fitted body veils) to quell any intrusive questions from neighbours, girls in other working class neighbourhoods such as Anguri Bagh increasingly walk home from their college with simply a *dupatta* (long scarf) over their heads. While many still do not expect to have to find employment, a significant and growing proportion fully expect to have a career whether they need to or not. The allegorical walls which once prevented access to the outside world - as in their physical migration moving outside of the Walled City - are perceptibly shattering.

The girls I interviewed have retained a degree of compliancy which, when pressed, transforms into strong resilience. Islamic norms of female modesty remain important, but these girls are also demanding rights which exist within Islam which they feel local culture, including the built environment, has denied them. The challenge is to find some way of accommodating such educated, qualified women while enabling them to retain their *izzat* and public integrity.

However, what is not changing is the negative perception of women using or congregating in public space within the locale where they live. Working class women's occupations now, for most families, remain similar to those of women in the Walled City. Women mostly remain at home doing piece-work, but for reasons other than preserving their *izzat* in the neighbourhood. It is important to note that the industrial infrastructure in Lahore has not changed as dramatically as that of Karachi. Men still dominate the service industry in most parts of the city. While the number of women working within offices has conspicuously increased, this has only occurred in concentrated locales. Transportation to get to those areas is a problem for many women. The mass transit system in Lahore has markedly deteriorated in the last two decades, leaving only a few hundred buses plying the roads of the city. Working women invariably must travel by way of private minivans which either force men and women to have to sit huddled together in the rear or for women to sit very cramped in the front seat next to the driver. Additionally, commuters must often change once or twice to reach their destinations, making journeys excessively long.

The anonymity in new high-density residential areas is redefining where the barriers between 'insiders' and 'outsiders' once stood. Virtually no formal sector employment exists for women in these places. The lack of semi-private or spillover space severely limits the prospects of women even meeting each other in these locales. As such, there is little to link neighbours with one another.

13.5 Conclusions: Development Interventions to Empower Women

Most studies of physical and social problems associated with urbanisation in the Third World look at such issues as increasing access to a clean water supply and sanitation, health services, education, housing, transportation, and economic growth. They include little mention of how to reconcile perceptions of gendered space with spatial organisation within planned communities. Gilbert & Gugler (1992:104) do recognize that cultural norms affect the roles women can play outside the home, and that while "the Islamic rule of seclusion is the most striking example, [but] in fact there is considerable variation in its application across Muslim countries." Richard Stren et. al. (1992:51-55) point out that there are many lingering stereotypes about issues confronting poor women in cities that are no longer accurate and which have to be replaced by recognition of the new realities such women are experiencing. They make note of five facts which must be considered to incorporate gender awareness in urban assistance and design: (i) the predominance of female-headed households; (ii) the predominance of women in the informal sector; (iii) that women earn significantly lower wages in comparison to men; (iv) such urban women must play 'triple roles' (domestic, economically productive, and community maintenance); and (v) women still have limited access to land and wealth.

The UNDP has identified five urban challenges for the 1990s: alleviate poverty; provide the poor with infrastructure, shelter and services; improve the urban environment; promote the private sector; and promote NGOs (Harris 1992:215). National studies of urban problems in Pakistan have hardly taken working class areas into consideration, and when they have, no attention has been paid to the kinds of spatial layouts that would facilitate improving women's access to goods, employment, services and each other as support networks. Instead the centre, as Kenneth Watts (Harris 1992:132) argues, has often tried to second-guess local governments as to how to open up potentials in urban areas. While such studies may be useful in revealing general urban trends, they give us little insight into how urban residents are trying to transform their locales themselves, or provide answers to the UNDP's five challenges in the Pakistan context.

Jan van der Linden (1989:91) has noted that urban social movements in slum areas, similar to those popular in Latin America, have been uncommon in Pakistan. The most well-known is the Orangi Pilot Project (OPP) in Karachi, founded by Akhtar Hameed Khan. Having a solid track record in starting a Community Based Organisation (CBO) earlier in East Pakistan, he and a number of social activists began to organise residents in the sprawling slum of Orangi in Karachi. Families were mobilised to dig trenches so lines could be laid for clean water and sewer systems. Area residents were also taught simple maintenance techniques. Women's components of the project concerned food acquisition, income generation, health, and basic literacy. Limited attempts have been made in Pakistan to replicate OPP's successes. Importantly, OPP's experiences lay out a model for potential CBOs in planned communities in Lahore to consider, to recognise the most pressing problems in the locale, and actively to include residents in brainstorming efforts to devise solutions for them. Community members must be brought into planning, problem identification and decision-making at the outset. While this principle applies wherever people may become organized into self-help communities, it is particularly true when considering including women in places like Lahore. A family's *izzat* - its respectability and place in society - is at risk anytime women leave the home. All the more reason for facilitating this kind of organisation in locales where women live under conditions not physically dissimilar to house arrest.

We must remember, however, that distrust of formal institutions and state actions currently plagues Pakistan. In popular opinion, the state is no benevolent actor which will work to serve its citizens well. Instead, the state is seen largely as its component parts, especially those offices to which one has access through kin and friends. This scepticism provides further incentive for the state, urban planners, and development professionals to share responsibility and decision-making power with area residents.

A good example of why poor urban dwellers may mistrust the state is apparent when we look at the way Anguri Bagh's sewer system was laid out. A caring state would never have let the planners get away with putting lines *beneath* homes, especially in such a way that to clear a blockage one must literally dig up a neighbour's floor. What needs to be done, therefore, is something more than self-help housing. Rather, community members must meet together, identify common needs, challenges and goals, and finally reach an understanding of the effects that spatial organisation has on these issues. Attention must be paid to including women's voices in this process. While this should be easy to implement, little work has been conducted to support such efforts, especially in including women in Lahore.

Therefore, a viable way to enhance women's access and develop a sense of community would be to facilitate the creation of a CBO in a locale such as Anguri Bagh. Initially, it could focus on organizing local clean-up efforts that include *all* residents. This enables women - especially the relatively new recipients of higher education who are the ones more likely to participate - to play constructive roles within their community as well as meet one another. From this experience, the group could then meet to identify important common problems together. Particular issues confronting women include lack of access to semi-private space, limited access to local employment, limited access to public transport (which could convey them to jobs elsewhere), and hardly any access to the local bazaar. The opportunity exists in the new settlements and regularised *katchi abadis* to create new social institutions and structures, such as a neighbourhood itself setting aside space for women. This could be used for a range of purposes, including health education programs, legal literacy, or to find employment. A micro-enterprise component (a current priority among development planners) could be built into this, especially incorporating training in record keeping, ordering, marketing and quality control.

I am arguing that by focusing on organising women into a CBO to increase their access to goods, employment, services and to each other, in effect a larger crucial transformation will occur: people taking pride in and responsibility for public space around them. Frans Schuurman and Ton van Naerssen (1989:2) have argued, after reviewing an array of urban social movements, that one feature stands out:

> territorial organisations of the urban poor do not act within a political vacuum and have to reckon with the limits set by the social and political structure of society.

These limits are being pushed throughout Pakistan as more and more people are participating in a new phenomenon on the rise: the creation of a civil society. In unprecedented ways, ordinary people are taking it upon themselves to commit to a cause, which in Pakistan's history has been fairly rare outside of kinship circles. There is a marked proliferation of NGOs and CBOs in the past decade dedicated to various social concerns such as promoting democratisation, human rights, community organizing, and low income housing. Independent groups are trying to make a difference on the social landscape irrespective of the fleeting idiosyncrasies of the national government. This emergent civil society is neither engineered by the state nor by elite groups, but is emanating from the enthusiasm, commitment and perseverance of individuals agreeing to work together to achieve envisioned goals. It is their actions, promoting the rise of a civil society, which hold the greatest promise for Pakistan's collective future.

References

Abu-Lughod, Janet L. 1993. "The Islamic City: Historic Myths, Islamic Essence and Contemporary Relevance" in Amirahmadi and El-Shakhs: 11-36.

Amirahmadi, Hooshang and Salah S. El-Shakhs (eds.) 1993. *Urban Development in the Muslim World* New Brunswick: Centre for Urban Policy Research, Rutgers University.

Amnesty International. 1995. *Women in Pakistan. Disadvantaged and Denied their Rights* New York: Amnesty International.

Baqir, Muhammad. 1985. *Lahore Past and Present* Lahore: Punjabi Adabi Academy.

Beneria, Lourdes and Shelley Feldman (eds.) 1992. *Unequal Burden: Economic Crises, Persistent Poverty, and Women's Work* Westview Press.

Drakakis-Smith, David W. 1987. *The Third World City* London & New York: Methuen.

Encyclopaedia Britannica 1929, "Lahore" ,Volume 13, 1 4th Edition, London

Gilbert, Alan and Josef Gugler. 1992. *Cities, Poverty and Development. Urbanisation in the Third World* Oxford University Press.

Goulding, H.R. 1924. *Old Lahore: Reminiscences of a Resident Lahore*: Universal Books.

Government of the Punjab. 1992. "Punjab Katchi Abadis Act, 1992" Lahore: Directorate General Katchi Abadis, Local Government & Rural Development Department.

Gugler, Josef (ed.) 1988. *The Urbanisation of the Third World* Oxford University Press.

Harris, Nigel (ed.) 1992 . *Cities in the 1990s. the Challenge for Developing Countries* New York: St. Martin's Press.

Herbert, John D. 1979. *Urban Development in the Third World: Policy Guidelines* Praeger.

Johnson, B.L.C. 1979. *Pakistan* London: Heinemann Educational Books.

Kahne, Hilda A. & Janet Z. Giele (eds.) 1992. *Women's Work and Women's Lives: the Continuing Struggle Worldwide* Westview Press.

Kazi, Shahnaz. 1992. "Women, Development Planning and Government Policies in Pakistan" *Pakistan Development Review*, vol. 31, No. 4, Part 2, Winter: 609-620.

Latif, Syed Muhammad. 1892. Lahore: *Architectural Remains* Lahore: New Imperial Press (reprinted in Lahore by Sandhu Printers, 1981).

Mernissi, Fatima. 1987. *Beyond the Veil: Male-Female Dynamics in a Modern Muslim Society* revised edition. Bloomington: Indiana University Press.

Moser, Caroline O.N. 1993. *Gender Planning and Development: Theory, Practice and Training* Routledge.

Mumtaz, Kamil Khan. 1987. "Appendix II: Preliminary Notes on Political, Social and Physical Evolution of Lahore" prepared for the Walled City Study Team for the Lahore Development Authority.

PEPAC (Pakistan Environmental Planning and Architectural Consultants, Ltd.). 1987. *Conservation Issues and Intervention Alternatives: a Strategic Framework* prepared for the Lahore Development Authority, Conservation Plan for the Walled City of Lahore, April.

Population Census Organisation, Government of Pakistan. 1984. 1981 *District Census Report of Lahore* District Census Report No. 54. Islamabad: Statistics Division, February.

Research Society of Pakistan. 1976. *Extracts from the District and States Gazeteers of the Punjab (Pakistan)* Vol. I. Lahore: Punjab Educational Press.

Roberts, Bryan R. 1978. *Cities of Peasants. The Political Economy of Urbanisation in the Third World* Sage.

Schuurnan, Frans and Ton van Naerssen (eds.) 1989. *Urban Social Movement in the Third World* London and New York: Routledge.

Shaheed, Farida and Khawar Mumtaz. 1992. *Women's Economic Participation in Pakistan: A Status Report* Lahore: Shirkat Gah for UNICEF Pakistan.

Smith, David A. 1996. *Third World Cities in Global Perspective the Political Economy of Uneven Urbanisation* Boulder: Westview Press.

Stren, Richard et. al. 1992. *An Urban Problematique the Challenge of Urbanisation for Development Assistance* Prepared for CIDA, Toronto: Centre for Urban and Community Studies, University of Toronto.

United Nations Development Programme (UNDP). 1996. *Human Development Report, 1996* Oxford University Press.

van der Linden, Jan. 1989. "The Limits of Territorial Social Movements: the case of housing in Karachi" in Frans Schuurnan and Ton van Naerssen (eds.) *Urban Social Movement in the Third World* London and New York: Routledge: 91-104.

Ward, Kathryn (ed.) 1990. *Women Workers and Global Restructuring* ILR Press.

Weiss, Anita M. 1992. *Walls within Walls: Life Histories of Working Women in the Old City of Lahore* Boulder: Westview Press and Lahore: Pak Books.

World Bank. 1996. From *Plan to Market: World Development Report*, 1996 Oxford University Press.

World Bank/Lahore Development Authority. 1980. *Walled City Upgrading Study* Final Report, IV, Lahore, August.

14 Equity and Slum Redevelopment in Mumbai (Bombay)

Wilke Ruiter

14.1 Introduction

Throughout the world within a few years there will be more people living in cities than in rural areas. This trend towards more urbanisation is inevitable - no matter what policy is implemented to prevent it. Moreover, it is considered to be logical, since most of the added-value in financial terms is produced in urban areas . Nevertheless, it is a trend which includes a lot of negative consequences. Worldwide around 600 million urban dwellers live in poor-quality homes or neighbourhoods that lack the basic infrastructure and services that are essential for good health (Hardoy, 1990). Tens of millions are homeless, while most of them live in shacks, rent a small room for the whole family, or build their own dwellings on illegally occupied or subdivided land. Since the 1980s the situation in most countries in the South even deteriorated due to lower economic growth rates and structural adjustment policies which resulted in moves towards privatization, cuts in public spending - including the housing sector, and an increasing gap between the rich and the poor. Besides higher mortality rates and all kinds of "diseases of poverty" it can be stated that the consequences include very bad housing conditions of the urban poor. It is a remarkable fact though that this is not because the urban poor lack the capacity to pay for housing with basic services but that such housing is unnecessarily expensive or not available (UNCHS, 1996 p. 115). Because this is hardly recognized, most of the solutions related to housing have so far failed. That is because most housing 'policies' do not offer (i) a solution, (ii) an affordable solution, and/or (iii) a solution at urban scale. Slum clearance policies and relocations only ignore and postpone the problems of the urban poor. The supply of flats, turn-key housing programmes, and even Sites- & Services programmes are not affordable by the poor. Successful slum upgrading programmes are implemented at project level leaving the majority of the urban poor empty-handed. To tackle inequity and the shortage of affordable housing properly, the concept of "enablement" is proposed. Within this policy government intervention focuses on managing the legal, regulatory and economic framework so that the poor themselves are able to produce housing and related services more effectively. This solution is interpreted in many different ways, however. Especially where it coincides with a policy favouring more privatization certain contradictory features are to be expected. If the private sector only is given the framework to produce houses the urban poor will probably not benefit after all. If enablement is elaborated so that the urban poor themselves have direct influence in both the policy framework and the implementation of the construction of houses there is a bigger chance of success. In Mumbai particular programmes have been set up which illustrate these tendencies.

14.2 Mumbai

The Mumbai Metropolitan Region, now covering an area of 4.275 sq. km., is an outstanding example of the contemporary urbanising world. From 3.1 million in 1951, approximately 8.5 million in 1980 to more than 15 million people right now the metropolitan area is facing problems which are characteristic for most urban areas - which include traffic congestion and pollution, a lack of employment facilities, lack of infrastructure, and most of all: a lack of affordable land for housing the poor. 50% of the city's population lives in slums without proper sanitation, water supply and other services.

The identified need for 60,000 new housing units a year far exceeds the number constructed in the formal sector, which is reported to be about 20,000 units a year (Sivaramakrishnan, 1986). The pressure for urban growth is confronted by Mumbai's constrained physical shape: a narrow strip of land surrounded by water. The shortage of land results in a very high land price. In Nariman Point, the commercial centre at the southern tip of the old Bombay peninsula, this was up to Rs. 30,000/sq.ft in 1995 (appr. US$ 8,000/sq.m.). To the north, near the new Bandra Kurla complex along Mahim Bay, Dharavi, the biggest slum in Asia, was founded in 1890. Land in the new Bandra Kurla complex at that time was around one third of the price at Nariman Point (Accommodation Times, December 1995), but this is becoming higher every day. Considering an average income per family of around Rs. 2,000 a month it is clear that land in Bombay is not affordable for the poor. On the other hand this Economic Weaker Section of the population (EWS - maximum income per household: Rs. 2,650; HUDCO, 1994)) pays a lot for daily services. The 250,000 pavement dwellers, for instance, pay twenty times more for water per litre than the municipal rate charged to other residents of the city (Environment & Urbanization, vol. 7, no.1, 1995). In other words, even pavement dwellers have money to spend, but that money can be used much more efficiently. Besides the existence of pavement dwellers the consequence of the high land price is a rapid decline in the number of people living in the central areas of Bombay due to redevelopment of central locations for offices or other uses which yield higher returns (UNCHS, p. 246). This creates pressure on land and affordable housing even in the outskirts, again leaving a lot of the EWS homeless or in slum areas. Today, the city is comprised of two different worlds, a rich and a poor one, that have different social as well as physical manifestations, but which are also united by their sheer presence in a single space.

The policy of the government to tackle this land and housing problem, and hence to promote equity among her citizens, is ambivalent. On the one hand it seems that the city authorities - following the market forces - want to get rid of the informal world, the illegal pavement dwellers and the slum areas. Solutions for city improvement are aimed at the removal of the (home-less) poor to the city peripheries. Similarly, the logic underlying spatial zoning by function results in segregation - especially segregation between work- and residential places. This hinders the establishment of small scale local activities and services which need a close-knit and integrated environment. These can be, among others, supplied through high density slum areas.

However, instead of keeping the (poor) residents where they are - which is supposed to be the best solution in the long term – government policy, which involves forced evictions because of requests for new housing and infrastructure projects in the outer areas, "... involve(s) the transfer of high value land from the inhabitants of the settlements who are evicted to middle- or upper-income groups or to free land for the construction of houses, com-mercial developments, roads and other forms of infrastructure that primarily benefit wealthier groups" (UNCHS, 1996 p. 244). Note that certain re-devel-opments are always needed and hence evictions cannot always be avoided, but experience has shown that it should not be adopted as the main policy. The same city authorities who are making evictions know this, and they have instituted programmes of slum improvement as well.

14.3 Urban Redevelopment Solutions

The central government's Slum Clearance Plan was the first one. It started in 1956, while the Slum Areas (Improvement, Clearance and Rede-velopment) Act was enacted in 1971, which enabled the State (of Maharashtra) government to coordinate and ensure speedier execution of this programme. Although more residents were protected more or less from eviction and more slums got improved it was still a programme at minor scale. Other programmes followed, however, of which six are briefly described (see Table 14.1).

**Table 14.1 Overview of the Low-Income Housing Solutions - Covered
by This Study**

Sort of slum development	Government as controller	Government as provider	Government as facilitator/enabler
Land control	ULCRA 14.3.1		
Slum improvement		SIP 14.3.2	
Slum upgrading (+ land tenure)		SUP (under BUDP) PMGP 14.3.3	
Sites & Services		LISP (under BUDP) 14.3.4	
Reconstruction/ Redevelopment		PMGP 14.3.5	SRD I (DC-rules) SRD II 14.3.6

14.3.1 The Urban Land Ceiling and Regulation Act (ULCRA, 1976)

This act imposed a ceiling on vacant land ownership, set at 500m^2. in
Bombay. The state governments would take over the surplus of vacant land at
the low rate of Rs. 10 per sq.m. The act provides a lot of possibilities for
exemptions, however, which are open for wide interpretation. If, for instance:
-the land is going to be used for housing the EWS;
-the land use is within public interest;
-acquisition would cause undue hardship to the landowner; the land
owner can keep his land.
Aiming at reducing land speculation and redistributing the land to the
poor it "...froze the urban land market as property owners took advantage of
its slow appeal process" (World Bank, 1993). As a result the land price increased enormously due to a lack of land supply "... since public authorities
have been unable to continue acquiring surplus land under existing land-ac-
quisition statutes..." (UNCHS, 1996 p 258). Besides, the results for the EWS
were negligible. Although 4,836 ha. excessive land was notified, in 1992 only
243 ha. or 5% of this land was actually acquired and handed over to various

agencies (BMRDA, 1992). But even if the exemption clause for land used for housing the EWS (Section 21) is used, the poor cannot afford to buy a house, because of the high construction costs. Cheaper land does not necessarily mean a cheaper house. Since there is no ceiling on the cost of constructing a flat under the section 21 scheme, even the smallest price of Rs. 100,000 is way beyond the affordability of most of he population.

14.3.2 The Slum Improvement Programme (SIP)

The Slum Improvement Programme (SIP) also started in 1976. According to the 1976 census, the slum population of Bombay was 3.5 million people, around 650,000 families. Within SIP a minimum of basic amenities were supposed to be provided: water taps, 1 tap per 30 households; drainage; toilets, 1 seat per 50 persons, roads, and street lighting. It was provided for free until 1985, by MHADA, the Maharasthra Housing & Area Development Authority.

SIP was poorly managed and funded though. The responsibility for maintenance was not covered and there was a lack of people's participation. As a result the hygienic situation did not become as good as planned. But the main drawback was the lack of land tenure arrangements. So shelter security did not exist, evictions took place anyway, and in many areas SIP appeared to be a waste of investments. Besides, because no investments came from the people themselves this programme would inevitably dry up.

14.3.3 The Slum Upgradation Programme (SUP)

In 1985 the Slum Upgradation Program (SUP) was launched, as an important part of the World Bank sponsored Bombay Urban Development Project (BUDP). The total costs of this BUDP were about Rs. 282 crore - of which the World Bank paid Rs. 151 crores, and the remaining Rs 131 crore was funded by the State government and the implementing agencies' (MHADA, BMC, BMRDA) own resources. The SUP component (Rs. 53 crores) of the project involved the lease of the land of the slums to the housing societies and loan assistance to slum dwellers for environmental- and home improvement (1 tap for 10 households). The land tenure was given in the form of 30-year renewable landlease to housing societies on a nominal rate of Rs. 1 per annum. Loan assistance to slum dwellers consisted of Rs. 2000 per household for environmental improvement and Rs. 5,000 to Rs. 14,250 per household for house improvement. The loan is repayable in 20 years and carries interest rate of 12% (BUDP) or 5% (PGMP; see 5). Downpayment is Rs. 251, whereas the slum dwellers have to pay maintenance-costs of Rs. 10-15 per month to the society. The BUDP was officially wound up in March 1994.

The objective was upgrading 100,000 slum households in Greater Bombay. By September 1993, about 15,475 households in some 140 housing societies had received collective tenurial rights (Panwalkar), around 1,500 sites per year average. According to MHADA (1994) only 24% of the available budget was spent (482 out of the 1982 crores - until March 1993).

Apparently the implementation of the program was the hardest. It was hard to convince the slum dwellers to co-operate. Some preferred SIP, where no payment for basic amenities was needed, while others could not pay the interest. 12% interest over a Rs. 10,000 loan means Rs. 1,200 repayment a month, which is about the salary of one person within the EWS group. It was hard to convince the local politicians, because they considered the housing societies would become too powerful. It was hard to negotiate with the landowner. And finally a lot of problems coordinating government agencies were encountered as well.

14.3.4 *The Land Infrastructure Servicing Programme (LISP)*

The other part under the BUDP was the Land Infrastructure Servicing Programme (LISP). This is a Sites & Services Scheme. Creeks and marshy open lands in suburban areas of Bombay were reclaimed. Of this area 60% was divided into small serviced sites up to 40 sq.m. Subsidies were ranging from Rs. 10,000 to 25,000 per plot. This money was obtained through the profit of the remaining 40% of the land which was sold to the Middle and Higher Income Groups at a much higher price. The poor could build their own house on their serviced plot by collective participation. LISP provided about 40,000 sites out of the World Bank's total target of 80,000 sites (1985 - 1994). The sites, however, were located far away, and the programme still proved to be too expensive for the EWS.

14.3.5 *The Prime Minister's Grant Project (PMGP)*

After visiting Bombay in December 1985, Prime Minister Rajiv Gandhi declared a grant of Rs. 100 crores, to ameliorate the housing conditions of around 60,000 poor families in the old island city of Bombay. This project was called the Prime Minister's Grant Project (PMGP). Rs. 37 crores were allocated to slum redevelopment projects in Dharavi. Slum dwellers were rehabilitated on-site in regular multi-storied and high density buildings. The housing society gets land tenure and the slum dwellers can get a loan through MHADA. After withdrawing money for main infrastructure around 17 crores were left to reconstruct 2,600 tenements, to relocate 1,000 households, to build 1292 transit tenements and provide the benefits of environmental improvements along with the lease of land to 15,000 households. These quantitative goals are more or less achieved.

The costs per unit (200 sq.ft.) was estimated to be Rs. 37,500 in 1987. Downpayment was Rs. 5,000 per family. Subsidy per tenement was Rs. 5,400, while Rs. 20,000 was given as a loan from HUDCO. The remaining Rs. 7.100 was an interest free loan from the PMGP.

Many slum dwellers eventually sold their units, however, specially after the 1988 Gulf War, when prices of building materials went up. After the Gulf War the construction costs went up to Rs. 50,000, and there was no subsidy left to fill this extra gap of Rs. 12,500. Moreover, the 4-storey high apartments had much higher maintenance costs than the low buildings, which all had to be covered by the residents themselves. Many others sold their unit, because they could get Rs 2.5 - 4 lakh (1 lakh = Rs. 100,000) or they could not practice their home-based professions anymore.

14.3.6 The Slum Redevelopment Scheme (SRS)

In 1991 the State Government realised that since it had neither the money nor the land to rehouse Bombay's 5.5 million slum dwellers it had to come up with a feasible and self-sustainable policy. So it brought out the Slum Redevelopment Scheme (I) under the Development Control-Rules (Section 33 - 10), the latest national policy for rehabilitation of slum dwellers in general.

It allows an additional Floor-Space Index up to 2.5 (normally: 1.3 on the island of Bombay) in case of a land-sharing project on land which is occupied by slums. A landowner, builder, even a housing society is allowed to execute a project, consisting of offering 180 sq.ft. (16.75 sq.m.) plot - excluding common areas - in multi-storied tenements *on-site*, whereas the commercial tenements will have the same size as prior to the redevelopment of the property to a maximum of 180 sq.ft. as well. At least 70% of the original slum dwellers have to approve this landsharing idea. They have to pay Rs. 10,000 (against the normal costs of about Rs. 65,000; 1991 PGMP-rates), plus an initial down-payment of Rs. 5,000. The loan has to be repaid in 15 years.

The profit margin is only 25%, however, which led to a disappointing response of builders and housing societies. Besides, in very densely populated areas the programme is not feasible, because the remaining land, after rehabilitating the slum dwellers, is not enough to cross-subsidize the rehabilitation itself.

Under the SRDI only 144 homes were built from 1991 - 1995 (Sunday Observer, June 11, 1995). Of the 160 schemes submitted to the government, only 69 involving 17,600 units were cleared, and just four are under actual implementation (Rego, 1995).

So, whereas the BMRDA in 1992 still "... considered slums to be a nuisance which were to be provided services till finally they were removed and the people rehoused" (BMRDA, 1992) a lot of effort has been put into redeveloping these slums. Four major conclusions can be drawn so far:

1- Co-operation and participation of land-owners, the private (construction) sector, local politicians, and the majority of the slum dwellers is essential;

2- It is crucial to calculate properly the monthly instalments per family, which include maintenance costs, taxes, and other expenses;

3- Fast processing, management and coordination from government agencies is an important prerequisite for the implementation of any programme.

4- Whereas the role as controller is doomed to fail and the role of provider is too expensive the role of facilitator/enabler turns out to be the only feasible one for the government.

The Second Slum Redevelopment Scheme (SRD II)

The Shiv Sena's (the local majority and right wing Hindu political party) progressive SRD II scheme aims to provide free houses for 50 Lakh slum dwellers within 5 years. The Studygroup, assigned to recommend improvements of the SRDI stated that everybody should have the right to be rehabilitated since rehabilitation is the *only* way to deal with the problem of informal settlements. If there is no other option than displacement this would be up to a maximum distance of 5 km from the old site to protect employment opportunities. The basis of the programme is to use the market, the private sector, to generate the necessary funds for reconstruction. The programme has the basic characteristics of the SRD I (FSI of 2.5; 70% of slum dwellers have to agree on the project, etc.), but it has at least five main differences:

1)   the beneficiaries do not have to pay Rs. 15,000;
2)   225 sq.ft. instead of 180 sq.ft. per tenement;
3)   reduced municipal tax for the first 15 years
4)   transit camp is arranged!
5)   more profit than 25% is allowed for the builder.

An additional incentive is created for developers in the Dharavi area. Since Dharavi is predominantly a depressed area with depressed prices for free-sale tenements it is hard for a private developer to get his money back as a cross-subsidy. Given the constraint of 500 tenements per ha. in case of redevelopment of part of Dharavi it is allowed to convert unutilised FSI into another area outside Dharavi, where he can get a higher sale-price. In Dharavi this Transfer of Development Rights (TDR) 13.33 sq.ft. is permitted for open market sale in return for redeveloping 10 sq.ft. in Dharavi itself. In other words, if you redevelop 3ha. in Dharavi you are allowed to develop 4ha. outside Dharavi to make profit! The only limitation is the minimum density which is 500 tenements per ha. in Dharavi. Because of this TDR the density in Dharavi itself is not becoming higher than it already is.

The organisation who will take the initiative for rehabilitation has to pay an amount of Rs. 20,000 per family as a deposit to cover the monthly expenses. Plus the monthly running costs it means a monthly amortization of around Rs. 450 per month, which include a maintenance charge of Rs. 40, and only Rs. 70 muncipal taxes per month for the first 10 years. Compared to the average income per household per month of Rs. 2,000 a month this is pretty good.

To check whether this programme is feasible to all parties involved, a pilot area has been selected in Dharavi.

14.4   Dharavi/Sanjay and SRD II

Dharavi is slum-settlement with a size of 2.2 sq.km. and a present population of around 500,000 people. It is bound on the north by the Mahim creek, on the east by the central Railway. The southern boundary is the Harbour Railway and on the west the Western Railway (see Map 14.1). Since the settlement is so old most employment is generated by activities in the area itself, such as raw leather processing, leather goods manufacturing, pottery making, recycling old plastic materials and tallow manufacturers. Hence, Dharavi is characterised by an organically knit built form with narrow winding streets on a pedestrian scale and a high degree of functional mix. The texture of Dharavi is a result of the high population density and an intensive utilisation of land, whereby the homes, work places and trade centres are closely integrated. Organisationally Dharavi is divided in 50 co-operative Housing societies, which are all members of PROUD (People's Responsible Organisation of United Dharavi).

North of Dharavi, on the other side of the Mahim creek, a new commercial centre, the Bandra-Kurla complex, is being developed. The entire Bandra-Kurla compex is envisioned as a complete '21st century' city in itself according to plans of the BMRDA. Land prices in the Bandra-Kurla area have risen to very high levels, putting an increasing over-spill pressure on

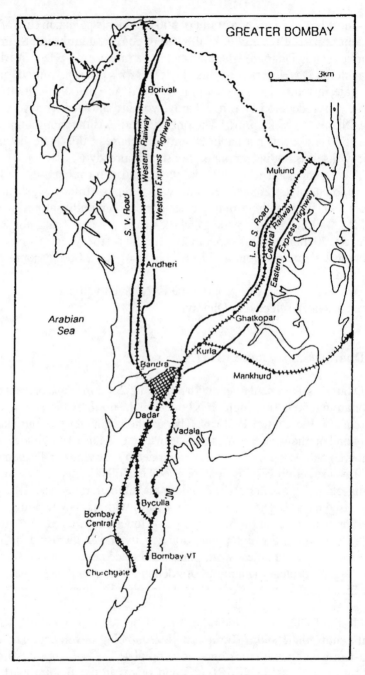

Map 14.1 Mumbai and the Location of Dharavi Slum

land in Dharavi.

Within Dharavi five possible pilot areas have been described and checked of which Sanjay has been selected as a representative area for testing the feasibility of SRDII. With a surface of 2,180 sq.m. and 168 households Sanjay has a density of 770 households/ha. Note that 48 of the 168 dwellings are commercial units. The residential land price is around Rs. 1,500 per sq.ft. and for commercial up to Rs. 3,000 (late 1995). The landowner is the BMC, the Bombay Municipal Corporation. The average income level is around Rs 1,500 - 2,000 per household per month.

14.4.1 Public-private-partnerships

The National Housing Policy (1994) states that "...the private developers and the organized sector will be encouraged to invest in various forms of housing and land development by access to finance, speedier approval of schemes and other forms of support, removal of constraints to assembly and development of land, while they will be induced to devote a significant proportion of the investment in housing for lower and middle-income groups at affordable prices and conform to non-exploitative practices" ['assembly' means consolidating plots of land]. This means that the government admits it does not own land in the city, it has limited resources for housing and that it has not succeeded in improving the housing situation, whereas the private sector has both vacant land and capital to invest, so it is given the responsibility for building more houses (Das, 1995).

The government therefore accepts the premise of the United Nations Commission for Human Settlements, which mentions in its Global Strategy for Shelter for the year 2000 that Public Private Partnerships are the key for a successful enabling approach.

For a proper PPP certain basic prerequisites should be fulfilled:

1)   Relational conditions should be good; mutual trust among parties is important, and so are good and clear decision-making proce-

Table 14.2   The Four PPCP-Options

	Option 1	*Option 2*	*Option 3*	*Option 4*
Initiative for Redevelopment	Builder	*Housing society*	*Housing society*	*Housing society*
Management of project	Builder	Builder	*Housing society*	*Housing society*
Management of construction	Builder/ contractor	Builder/ contractor	Contractor	*Housing society*

dures;

2) Political conditions should be good: local politicians should agree + sufficient safeguards for all parties involved should be built-in;

3) Legal conditions should be clearly written down, including rights + obligations;

4) Organisational conditions should be perfect: no bureaucracy, good planning, co-ordination and management, transparency of papers, and no corruption;

5) Financial and economical conditions should be well worked out beforehand: the ways spreading the risks, distribution the profit for various financing options + the organisation and control of finance!

Many different types of PPP which conform to these principles can be distinguished, mainly based on the extent in which the different partners are involved and financially responsible. As under SRDI a landowner, a builder, and a housing society is allowed to execute a project as long as at least 70% of the citizens concerned agree. Based on this starting point four options have been defined, related to three stages of a SRDII project (see table 2). In option 1 the private builder and/or developer totally controls the redevelopment project, whereas in option 4 the housing society takes all responsibilities. The options 2 and 3 are transitional options in a way the different responsibilities are defined during the management phases of a project.

The management of the project consists of planning the project, defining the final plan and specification of building materials, procurement of building materials, hiring a contractor, selling the houses and/or FSI, providing transit accommodation, etc. The manager of the project takes the financial risks, but also obtains the profits. Management of the construction consists of procurement of building materials, provision of construction skills and planning and execution of the construction itself. Sometimes the builder hires a

Table 14.3 Comparison of the Four PPP Options

	Option 1	Option 2	Option 3	Option 4
Financial risk	++	+	-	--
Profit (money for repair, maintenance, etc.)	--	--	+	++
Organisational activities (skills, knowledge, time-energy)	++	+	-	--
People's participation	--	+/-	+	++
Decision power	--	-	+	++
Speed of redevelopment	++	+	-	--
Dependency	--	+/-	+	++

contractor to manage and execute the construction.

Note that the (enabling) role of the government is defined in the SRDII programme and hence is the same in all four options.

To decide what is the optimum PPP-option within the SRDII program for the Sanjay community these four options have been tested against the consequences for all parties involved, varying from the government, the builder, the architect, and financial institutions to the NGOs, CBOs, Housing society and slum dwellers themselves. This has been done along eleven criteria: initiating activities, and input and activities related to land, finance, planning & design, construction skills and -implementation, infrastructure, selling the houses and FSI/TDR, transit camps and maintenance on the long term.

Note that it is extremely important to check all these different aspects of a theoretically perfect PPP. It is necessary to think especially through the eyes of the housing society of all phases and aspects of a redevelopment programme. The following matrix has been filled in through the eyes of the Sanjay housing society.

Option 3 has been selected under the condition that the financial risks of the whole project - the possible burden on the housing society - are small.

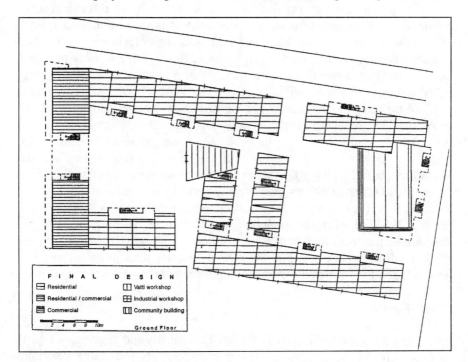

Figure 14.1 Planned Resettlement

Profit can be made through a lot of self-help. This takes some time, because a lot of organisational activities should be taken care of by a rather inexperienced group, but the people are definitely involved and will probably be so until the maintenance phase. It also fits perfectly with the goal of the SRDII programme, stating that "the co-operative societies of slum-dwellers need to be placed on a higher pedestal and given support so that they are in a position to execute the project themselves".

14.4.2 Feasibility

To calculate realistically the feasibility of the SRDII programme - based on PPP-option 3 -a spatial design has been made for Sanjay area in co-operation with a group of 25 representatives (Fig 14.1). It consists of the following functions:
- 120 residential units of 27 sq.m. each (second, third, and fourth floor);
- 32 residential-cum-commercial units of 27 sq.m. each;
- 6 commercial units (total 83.6 sq.m)
- 10 separate commercial (polluting) units of 27 sq.m. each.

Using the building regulations 15% of the area is used for recreation, while the set-back area from the plot boundary to the road is at least 1.5m.

The permissible saleable area for the landowner/developer is (10:13.33 for Dharavi!) 5,941.9 sq.m. Since the area is already very densely built it is not recommended to use saleable area within Sanjay. The housing society (PPP-option no.3!) commercially sells extra TDR to make profit. Because 10% of the redeveloped Sanjay is designed to be commercially sold (273.8 m^2), the TDR recovery for the developer is 5,668 m^2. Assuming a price of Rs. 10,000 per m^2 this means proceeds amounting to about 56 million Rupees. The costs of the redevelopment project in Sanjay is estimated at about 38 million, based on Rs. 100,000 construction costs per tenement, plus infrastructure, management costs, transit camps, and 18% interest during 1 year of construction. These costs were calculated in co-operation with local developers late 1995. In short, the implementation of the SRDII program is highly feasible with a profit margin of Rs 18 million (47%), based on a very modest (TDR) selling price per m^2. If the housing society manages the project as suggested in PPP option 3 this profit might go to them.

14.4.3 Equity

Equity is needed. Equity is needed theoretically and practically. Equity is needed for whatever reason, varying from fears for social unrest, crimes and epidemics to the simple fact that every government admits that it cannot take care of all drop-outs of the society. Equity is needed for the accessibility to adequate housing, employment, and infrastructural facilities, but equity has to be defended, because the market forces naturally take care of the survival of the fittest, the urban rich, who can afford a piece of land, a house, and the travel expenses. Equity is also profitable. It relieves part of the burden of the government to provide houses and facilities itself and it is efficiently utilizing the resources of the poor people themselves.

If the slum dwellers are taken seriously, if participation is really considered to be crucial, if affordability is essential and the slum dwellers themselves are the best decision-makers - then it is highly advisable to support housing societies. Equity is not guaranteed by theoretical statements in the SRDII programme - not even when the underlying ideas are both rational and (politically) sincere.

The urban practice is different. The private, commercial sector is better organised and always ready to take the initiative when profits are expected. The housing societies should take initiative themselves, otherwise individual members will be sold out and factions in the community organisations will be the result. In fact, this has already taken place in and around Dharavi, leaving many people behind disillusioned.

These housing societies need support in the following fields:
- community organising: how to prevent quarrels and factions;
- negotiating: with landowners, financial institutions, developers, and builders;
- legal issues: to make a contract, supervise the construction, etc.
- financial matters: to check the calculations related to all ins and outs of the SRDII project alternatives,
- scout for saleable land elsewhere in Bombay;
- take care of a proper plan, hire a good architect, so that everybody is satisfied...

It is only the professional housing society which is a serious competitor to the private developer. Partnerships are definitely needed, with the government to get practical support, and with the private sector to take care of the construction, the sub-contractors, etc. The Public-Private-Community-Partnerships are best, since the interest of the community should be the key in solving the problems in Dharavi.

14.5 Conclusions

1 - On-site development, including employment facilities and workshops, is the only solution for improving slum areas, because all other poli-

cies have failed so far in Bombay. The second Slum Redevelopment scheme is a promising programme for the citizens of Dharavi - theoretically, and a big step towards equal treatment of interest groups.

2 - The SRDII programme is based on cost recovery by input of market forces, whereas the government plays an enabling role. While SRDI was very much builder driven with restricted profit margins the SRDII seems to be more community driven. It is even the housing societies which have the possibilities for transferring Floor Space Index numbers and development rights to cross-subsidize redevelopment projects.

3 -The SRDII creates a legal framework for the application of Public Private Partnerships. It is advocated to introduce Public Private Community Partnerships as an important elaboration of this principle, since:

a - the participation of slum dwellers needs to be high (theoretically at least 70% according to the regulations, but also for real participatory reasons);

b -the decision-making power of slum dwellers needs to be high, because they know the affordability, the detailed desires for spatial design, employment facilities, etc.

c - the profit which is most likely to be made is definitely needed by the slum dwellers to take care of maintenance, running costs, taxes, and other community expenses.

Note that for every successful PPCP certain basic conditions are essential: mutual trust, support from local politicians, no bureaucracy, no corruption, and transparency of all (financial) papers,

4 -The SRDII might be very successful, because it becomes highly profitable to build in slums and it is hard to build somewhere else in Bombay because of the lack of (vacant) land. On the other hand it is unlikely to expect developers/builders to spend part of their profit in a cross-subsidizing system whatsoever.

This argument leaves the housing society as a potential initiator, but is doubtful whether they will get involved at a large scale, since they do not have the experience in this kind of (high-rise) building project and it still seems to be hard for them to get access to finances. It is therefore absolutely needed to support housing societies.

5 -Moreover it is doubtful at all if builders, who normally borrow from public and semi-public financial institutions such as HUDCO, can get hold of the Rs 16,000 - 40,000 crores of money to implement the whole scheme as planned: 16,5 lakh houses: around 10 for the EWS and another 6.5 for 3 other categories - in 5 years!

Even more: *if* this scheme will be fully implemented as planned a crash in the real estate market is to be expected. Because of the TDR there will be too much supply of land and houses, through which the prices will go down. Hence, in the end there will be no incentives to implement SRD II anymore. For this reason the consequences of the SRDII should be evaluated annually.

References

BMRDA - *Shelter needs and strategies for BMR*; BMRDA, Bombay, 1992.

Das, P.K. - *Manifesto of a housing activitest. In: Bombay, Metaphor for modern India*. Bombay, 1995.

Delissen, W. and others - *Dharavi in its own movement; Public Private Community Partnership as survival strategy under the Slum Redevelopment Scheme;* Delft University of Technology, 1996.

Dwivedi, S. and R. Mehrotra; in: *The cities within;* Bombay, 1995.

Hardoy, Jorge E., Sandy Cairncross & David Satterthwaite - *The poor die young*; Earthscan, 1990.

HUDCO, *Financing Pattern*; internal report; 1995

Panwalkar, P. - *Upgradation of slums. In: Bombay, Metaphor for modern India*. Bombay, 1995.

Rego, S. - *Courting a roof or a disaster?* In: The Metropolis, Bombay, July 22, 1995.

Sivaramakrishnan, K.C. and Leslie Green - *Metropolitan Management, The Asian Experience*, EDI, Oxford, 1986.

SPARC, *"Waiting for water: the experience of poor communities in Bombay"*... cited in Swaminathan, Madhura, 'Aspects of urban poverty in Bombay'; Environment & Urbanization, vol. 7, no.1, 1995.

UNCHS - *An urbanizing world; Global report on human settlements*; OUP, 1996.

World Bank - *Enabling markets to work*, Washington, 1993.

15 Livelihood Strategies of Urban Households in Secondary Cities in Thailand and the Philippines - a Comparison

Helmut Schneider

15.1 Introduction

Southeast Asia, especially from a European point of view, has been seen until recently as a successful boom region. The everyday efforts of millions of people trying to make a living under rapidly changing socioeconomic and cultural conditions are, however, in comparison rarely taken into account. In this context and especially in the course of accelerated urbanisation, growing numbers of persons coming from rural areas are confronted with the need to adjust to urban living conditions and urban life styles. The degree of urbanisation in Southeast Asia - with an average of 34% of the population living in urban areas - still is very low, markedly below the figures for Europe, North and South America. Thailand, with an urban population of only 20%, belongs - in demographic terms - to the least urbanised countries in the world. With 54% of its population living in urban places the Philippines, on the other hand is already one of the more urbanised nations. But presently, the towns and cities of Southeast Asia are among the fastest growing urban areas in the world, only surpassed by those in Africa, especially in East Africa. The average rate of annual urban population growth (1995-2000) for the Philippines is estimated at 3.7%, well above the global average and as high as the regional average. The respective figure for Thailand (2.8%) is also above the global average, although below the regional average (UN 1996).

The settlement patterns in the Philippines and especially in Thailand are marked by the formation of large metropolitan areas with high demographic and functional primacy and a less developed middle segment of secondary or intermediate cities. Although the primacy of metropolitan areas like Bangkok or Manila still increased during the last two decades, small and secondary urban centres had already started growing at an even faster pace. This may be illustrated with a regression model of the rank-size distribution of urban places. Although in both cases the primacy ratios have increased between 1970 and 1990, the distribution of urban settlements *below* the primate city level is now described better by the respective regression line.

222

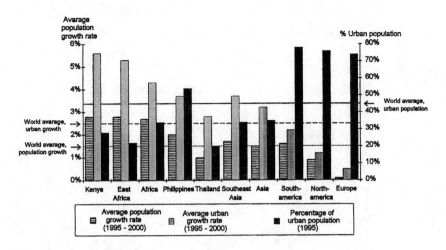

Figure 15.1 Population Growth and Urbanisation
Source: United Nations, World Population Report 1996.

In some cases, secondary cities have already become the target areas of urban-urban-migration, attracting overspill because of negative agglomeration effects in large metropolitan areas . The Northern Thai city of Chiang Mai, which is dealt with in more detail below, serves as an example, where already a considerable number of migrants from Bangkok has been recorded.

In the following, I will focus on two secondary cities in Thailand and the Philippines: Chiang Mai and Baguio City, both located at a considerable distance from the capital metropolitan areas in their respective countries. Both cities were part of an extended research project on secondary city urbanisation in cross-cultural perspective funded by the German VW-Foundation, all together including six secondary cities in Thailand, the Philippines and Kenya. In each of the selected cities a total of 1,000 household surveys were conducted and subsequently complimented by in-depth interviews.

15.2 Socio-Spatial Networks and Urbanisation

During the last decade, a growing interest in social networks research can be noted. Until then the leading and competing paradigms in development research, which, when over-simplified, could be labelled as modernisation and dependency theories, focused either on the positive effects of self regulating liberal markets or on the rational planning competence of state intervention. This might explain why social networks, which are located *be-*

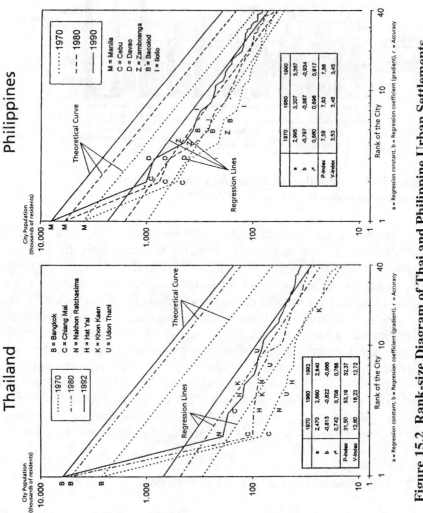

Figure 15.2 Rank-size Diagram of Thai and Philippine Urban Settlements

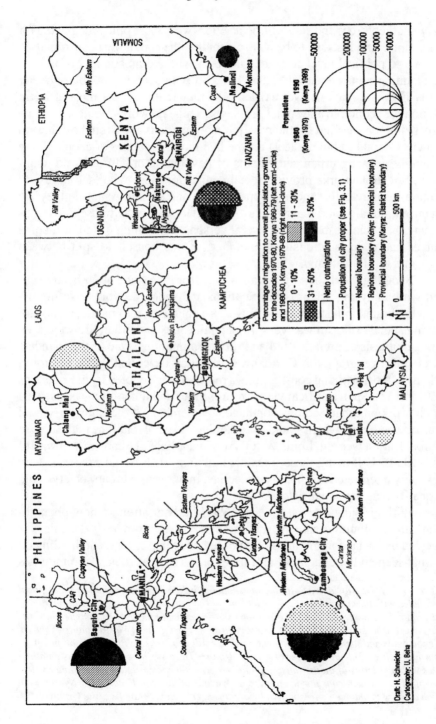

Map 15.1 The Survey Cities in Thailand and Philippines

tween market forces and state political action, were more or less neglected for a long time. And it seems to be no accident that the end of bloc confrontation on a world political level coincided not only with a dramatic loss of trust in the planning competence of states, but also with growing doubts whether totally liberated markets ever existed or if they really are the most efficient solution for economic and social problems. Social networks are now increasingly being seen as vital for the functioning of markets and even the cohesion of society - and last but not least for the livelihood strategies of people living in rapidly growing urban settlements of developing or Third World countries[1]. Social networks provide social capital for those who lack access to essential resources like income opportunities and shelter. As a rule they are organised, bundled and managed not by individuals but by households, thus pooling the social resources of several persons, combining different income sources and even locations (e.g. members of one household split between urban and rural locations).

Sociology and social geography has, from the start, often been occupied with analysing urban social relations and social networks. Noting the impacts of rapid industrialisation in western countries, a romantic, backward looking social criticism was very influential. Cities and urban life were seen as the antithesis of preindustrial and rural communities. One of the founders of scientific geography in Germany, Carl Ritter, described the large city in 1817 as a 'most artificial construction, a real monster' (quoted from Friedrichs 1995, p. 153). Such a critical view towards cities and urban life was also true for the work on urban ecology conducted by members of the Chicago School of urban sociology, which stated a weakening of social relations in the course of urbanisation (see e.g. Louis Wirth's seminal article, 'Urbanism as a way of life', 1938). Following these lines of thinking, urban social relations were inevitably interpreted as a history of decline. In this sense, urban society could be qualified as *'community lost'*.

With growing interest in Third World urbanisation , a new phenomenon called 'ethnic urbanism' was discovered (see Bruner 1961): this was revealed by social communities often based on ethnic criteria and holding on to what seemed to be their cultural traditions. These were not 'communities

---

1 *The term 'Third World' was already questionable before bloc confrontation on a global level ended with the crumbling of the Soviet Union. The 'Third World' never was that political and economic homogeneous union of nations sharing common interest as it sometimes was imagined. But in spite of a growing heterogenization among Third World countries due to different paths and speeds of development, there are still good reasons not to fully abandon the term. Following Nohlen/Nuscheler (1992, p. 30), the 'Third World' consists of those nation-states which in terms of industrialisation and per capita income are to be classified as 'less developed' and which consider themselves as 'victims of the world economy' (Nyerere) but which also try to change their situation by organised collective action (e.g. the Group of 77).*

lost' in the sense which Wirth, Park and others in the urban ecology tradition had conceptualised them, rather they looked more like *'communities saved'*: These were social communities which had changed their location from rural to urban contexts while keeping or saving their social networks and cultural traditions.

As early as 1908 German sociologist Georg Simmel stressed - in an article titled 'The crossing of social circles' (*'Kreuzung sozialer Kreise'*) - the emergence in urban areas of new forms of social relations, of new chances and opportunities (Simmel 1908). This article is nowadays seen as the starting point of social network analysis. The empirical results of urban studies conducted in the years after World War II have, however, disproved both views, the more pessimistic one of 'communities lost' and the more optimistic and romantic version of 'communities saved'. Concerning the latter, geographical, ethnological and sociological research has shown that socio-cultural forms like ethnicity - at first sight seeming to be a traditional relic - in most cases are modern inventions and adaptations to urban life (e.g. Hobsbawm 1984, Lentz 1994). Based on the results of urban research in different disciplines, a more realistic view of urban social relations and social networks has developed that could be described with the label *'communities liberated'* (for this typology see Wellman/ Carrington/ Hall 1988). Following this view, new social relations and networks are created when persons or groups of persons move from rural to urban places and traditional, social forms may change their meaning or vanish all together. The loss of social ties is compensated by gaining access to new chances and opportunities in an urban context. This *ambivalent* situation may be seen as typical for rapidly growing urban centres in the Third World with a high share of migrant population.

Social networks are fabrics of social relations which as a whole affect the behaviour of individuals. They are made up of very diverse contacts and links and are formed for various reasons, such as gathering of information, support or emotional security. For the most part, social networks reach far beyond the boundaries of families, social groups or organisations. Furthermore, they are not limited to one spatial level, they may be confined to a street or urban quarter but they may also reach into the surrounding area or even the global level. But as a rule, the density of social networks declines with growing distance[2] (for network analysis see e.g. Boissevain/Mitchell

---

2 *Although the revolution of information and transportation technologies has led to a dramatic time-space-compression (Harvey), places of densely interwoven social interaction have not lost their meaning as, e.g. the agglomeration of high ranking financial and service industries and complex decision making in a few leading global cities shows (e.g. Sassen 1994). Amin/Thrift (1995) have tried to explain this new logic of agglomeration with the development of time, place and culture specific 'institutional thickness' including social networks of individual actors and institutions and face-to-face contacts.*

1973, Mitchell 1974, Schweizer 1989, Wegmann (1995, Friedrichs 1995: 153 ff.). Due to limited time and resources, it is normally impossible for empirical research to analyse complete or total networks. That would mean to include *all* kinds of relations of *all* persons belonging to a specified group of people. Most studies - as also conducted in the following - confine themselves to the analysis of *partial, ego-centred social networks or relations.* In doing so, not all kinds of social relations are considered, but only selected ones: for this purpose only relations concerning central aspects of livelihood strategies like access to employment, income and accommodation are included. And not all relations between all persons are considered, but only those of one person (ego) - in this case the respondents of the questionnaires - to other persons (alter).

15.3 Demographic Growth and Migration

The two cities selected here have very different historical and cultural backgrounds. Chiang Mai is the product of an authochtonous urbanisation process reaching as far back as the 13th century; in the course of early state formation in Indianized Southeast Asia performing the functions of a 'sacred city' or, more general, an 'orthogenetic city' (Swearer 1986, Redfeld/Singer 1954). Baguio City on the other hand was only founded in 1900 as a colonial

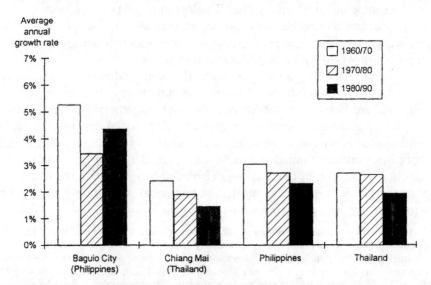

Figure 15.3 Average Annual Population Growth Rates 1960-90
Source: NSO/P 192, NSO/T 1994.

hill station, the summer capital for the American 'Philippine Commission'. It soon became a rest and recreation centre for the colonial, but also for the indigenous, élites (Reed 1976). Due to their central place functions and their demographic size (inhabitants in 1990: Chiang Mai 166,883, Baguio 183,146) both cities can be ranked as secondary centres, on a hierarchical level next to the primate city of the respective country.

The demographic development of the last three decades already reveals some differences between the two selected cities. The variations of population increase in the decades under consideration indicate, at least for Baguio City, that the inflow of migrants was not a linear process. Relatively low growth rates in the decade 1970-80 in Baguio reflect the political and economic crisis during the martial law regime of President Marcos. Otherwise, the figures show that population growth for Baguio was well above the national level, indicating high levels of in-migration compared to overall population growth.

For Chiang Mai, the annual population growth rates for the whole period in consideration were always slightly below the national average, suggesting a negative migration balance. Unfortunately, no reliable migration data on a municipal level are available. Therefore, the following estimate was calculated (see Table 15.1). It is based on a comparison of actual population growth with a *theoretical expected* growth (see Bähr et al. 1992: 468 ff.). The average population growth rate on the national level is used as an indicator for overall natural population increase. Due to several assumptions, which had to be made, the estimate should only be interpreted with great caution[3].

For Chiang Mai, the above estimate seems to indicate a negative migration balance since 1960, or at least a very slow population growth. An explanation for the negative migration balance might be, that accelerated economic growth in Thailand, which in the eighties made the country a candidate for the club of 'tiger economies' in eastern Asia (Muscat 1994), to a large extent took place in and around the Bangkok Metropolitan Area. The

---

3 *National population increase may be seen as a useable indicator for natural population increase because the absolute numbers of international migration are negligible and in- and out-migration are almost balanced for all three countries. But the figures based on the national average probably underestimate in-migration and overestimate out-migration in the three cities because natural population increase in all three countries is higher in rural areas. Furthermore, the administrative boundaries of Chiang Mai were expanded considerably since 1960: The expansion of the administrative urban area from 17.5 km² to 40 km², which was undertaken in 1983, at once increased the urban population by about 44.000 inhabitants. For this reason, only the years from 1983 to 1990 were included in the estimate. A second estimate for the same period was based on an assumed natural population growth rate of only 0.7 per cent per annum in Chiang Mai, given in the report of an international consulting agency (Louis Berger International 1991), which would be well below the national average. This would lead to a slightly positive migration balance for the years 1983-1990.*

Table 15.1 Estimate of the Share of Net Migration of Population Growth in Chiang Mai and Baguio City, 1960-90

	absolute population increase	estimated share of migration	inhabitants
Baguio City/Philippines			
1960 - 1970	34,102	47.6%	84,538 (1970)
1970 - 1980	34,471	23.7%	111,009 (1980)
1980 - 1990	64,133	51.4%	183,143 (1990)
Chiang Mai/Thailand			
1960 - 1970	17,993	-11.7%	83,729 (1970)
1970 - 1980	17,865	-29.6%	101,594 (1980)
(1983 - 1990)(1)	16,384	-26.0%	166,883 (1990)
(1983 - 1990)(2)	16,384	5.3%	

Sources: NSO/P 1992, NSO/T 1994.
(1) based on the rate of 1.98 per cent for population growth at the national level
(2) based on an assumed rate of 0.7 per cent for natural population growth in Chiang Mai

highly centralized political and economic structure and the extreme primacy of Bangkok (with a population 35 times larger than that of Chiang Mai) are a legacy of the Siamese élite's strong export trade orientation from the beginning of the Bangkok period, and of the country's struggle to defend its independence against the colonial aspirations of Great Britain and France during the peak of European imperialism in the nineteenth and the beginning of the twentieth century (see e.g. Evers a.o. 1987, Keyes 1987). These processes led to the present dominance of Bangkok - at least in terms of job opportunities and income generation. Despite its expanding economic base, especially in the tourist sector, Chiang Mai's chances to attract Bangkok -bound migrants from the surrounding rural areas seem to be not very favourable. However, due to a good road network and the complementarity of farm work and work in the booming construction sector, some persons living in nearby rural areas participate in the labour market without settling in Chiang Mai. For many workers, commuting provides a viable alternative to migration (Rüland 1992, p. 97 ff.; Singhanetra-Renard 1982).

Population growth in the secondary centres under consideration is, to a large but varying extent, due to in-migration. This is even true for Chiang Mai, where there is a migration deficit. Without in-migration, the population growth rate would be even lower. This situation is reflected in the results of the surveys undertaken in each city in 1991 and 1992. The share of migrants among the respondents (i.e. persons who were not born in the respective city) was highest in Baguio City with around 76%, followed by Chiang Mai with a clearly lower but still respectable share of 47% (Source: VW-project 1991/ 92).

15.4 Migration and Social Networks

For most persons, the transition from one living place to another, especially from rural to urban life spaces, implies the enlargement of those parts of their everyday lives which are regulated by market forces, mainly in the areas of income generation and housing. In view of a weak state - at least in terms of ensuring social security - and the potentially destructive effects of self-regulating markets on the livelihood basis of urban dwellers (for a critical analysis of the effects of liberated markets see Polanyi (1990)) the maintenance of existing or the development of new social networks is essential. They may complement existing subsistence production of households and intra family relations based on reciprocity and redistribution. Social networks in this sense are of special importance to migrants, helping them to survive and settle down in a new, culturally strange environment. They may ease the difficulties of adaptation to an urban environment. But they may also work as a hindrance to integration and adaptation to the urban situation by reinforcing the ties with the own social group. 'Too often the role of social networks is seen as ideally supportive, while the other side of the coin, their restrictive nature, is overlooked.' (Pohjola 1991, p. 440). It is not possible to deal with this argument in detail here, but the results of the VW-project show, that - although on different levels - in both cities, links with the home areas decrease and social integration in the urban context increases in the course of time. The decision to temporarily or permanently change the place of residence in most cases may be seen as a part of livelihood strategies of individuals, but more often of families and households.

In Baguio City, the persons included in our sample had mostly migrated directly from a rural area (74%). In Chiang Mai, however, more than half of the migrants named urban places of origin, many of them small urban settlements. This might indicate more developed forms of step-wise-migration, but as mentioned above for the rural population in nearby areas, commuting seems to be an alternative to migration, possibly explaining the lower figure for rural-urban migration.

The reasons people gave for migrating are shown in Figure 15.5. Overwhelmingly, the respondents named economic motives, like the hope to get access to jobs and income sources, the hope to improve one's livelihood, as

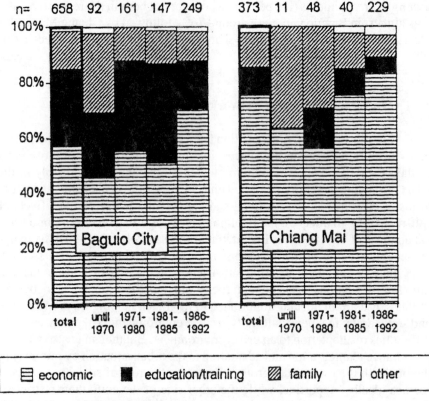

Figure 15.4 Reasons for Migration
Source: VW-Project 1991/92.

the decisive factors for their move. This was true for around 76% (valid answers) in Chiang Mai and nearly 60% in Baguio City. Family reasons - e.g. children following their parents, spouses following each other, held almost the same share (12-13%) in both towns, ranging second in Chiang Mai, but only third in Baguio City. Migration for educational reasons contrasts Baguio 27% with Chiang Mai at 10%. The former figure reflects the functional role of Baguio City as an educational centre not only for the surrounding province of Benguet but for the whole of Northern Luzon. Educational reasons to migrate may also be seen as part of livelihood strategies, an investment in the future, to improve one's chances on the labour market. Other reasons for migration were almost irrelevant in both cases.[4]

---

4 *'Other reasons' for migration were named slightly more often in Chiang Mai. This might already be a reflection of the fact that due to its better living conditions the city has meanwhile become an attractive retirement place for Bangkok citizens.*

15.5 Migration Partners and Entry into the Urban Society

In the following only a few indicators are selected to illustrate possible connections between social networks and access to employment and housing. One central hypothesis concerning social networks in the process of development and social change is that with economic growth and the modernisation of society - urbanisation is seen as part of this process - social relations based on kinship ties will be reduced in favour of more purpose-oriented social relations with non kin. Whether migrants come alone, together with family members or relatives, with friends or other persons (e.g. the employer) may give a first impression of how the migratory move itself is embedded in social relations. In Baguio City and in Chiang Mai, more than 50% of the migrants were accompanied by other persons (58.4 and 57.5%).

Among the migration partners, persons with kinship ties (parents, children, spouses, relatives) are the majority in both cases. And out of the different types of migration partners, 'friends' vary the most. They are of little importance in Baguio with 7.5%, but in Chiang Mai nearly 20% of the migrants were accompanied by friends. An explanation might be found when looking at the distribution of females and males: In Chiang Mai a majority of migrants (52.4%) in our sample were women (compared to 45% in Baguio City). But among those migrants who came with a friend in Chiang Mai, more than 72% were female. In Baguio City females were under-represented in this respect. In the Thai context migrating with a friend seems to be a pattern applying especially to young women. Among single migrants, women are underrepresented in both cases, but also hold a high share in Chiang Mai with 46% (compared to 45% in Baguio City). If these results are taken together, then Thai society seems to be more 'modern' than the Philippines', a conclusion that would be in accordance with low population growth and good economic performance. To get a rough impression of the differences in economic performance between the two countries, but also between developing and developed countries, the per capita gross domestic products (GDP) of Thailand and the Philippines are calculated as shares of the same figure for Germany (25,580 US$ in 1994): With 9.4 % Thailand holds the highest share, followed by the Philippines with only 3.7% (World Bank 1996).

Comparing how the pattern of migration partners developed over time, one interesting result stands out. The share of the *closest kin* (parents, children, spouses) is declining in both cities, but most rapidly in Chiang Mai. In both cities *'intermediate groups'* (other relatives, friends, other persons) increased considerably. The growth of those 'intermediate groups' may be interpreted as an indication of the aforementioned process of social change, especially when non-relative persons like 'friends' and 'other persons' al-

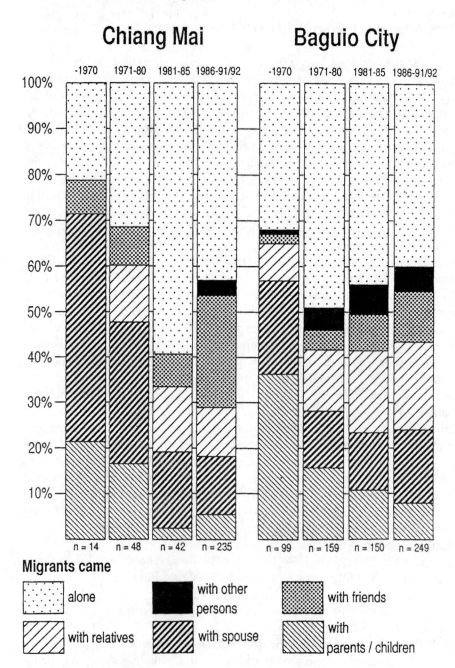

Figure 15.5 Migration Partners and Migration Periods
Source: VW-Project 1991/92.

ready hold high shares.

15.6 Social context of migrant's first accommodation

The fact whether migration is undertaken alone or in company does not, however, give a clear picture of existing social ties and networks at the urban destination. Through existing social contacts, potential migrants try to secure sufficient information about their planned destination and, if possible, try to make the first arrangements for housing and jobs. Possible indicators for these arrangements are whether one has the chance to share the first accommodation or whether one gets help finding the first job.

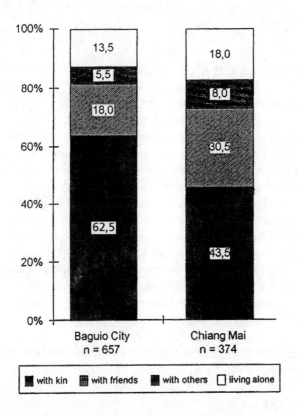

Figure 15.6 Social Context of Migrant's First Accommodation
Source: VW-Project 1991/92.

The observable pattern is similar to the one just described for the migration partners but with one important difference: the share of migrant persons living alone is considerably lower than the share of single migrants. In Baguio City and Chiang Mai, only a minority of the migrants who arrived alone also lived alone in their first accommodation (31% and 36% respectively), the majority found accommodation with relatives and friends, friends again being of greater importance in Chiang Mai.

Having the chance to find accommodation with kin, friends or other persons (i.e. mostly the employers) when first arriving at the migration destination, normally implies that the social networks of migrants already included persons living in the respective town *before* they had made their move. Such *migration bridgeheads* may be a great advantage when the newcomers to town try to get access to urban jobs and income sources. Persons already living in town can give important hints and information or they might even be able to mediate the first employment.

15.7 Social Networks and Access to Employment

If this hypothesis is valid, then for those migrants already having social contacts in town the time span before getting the first job should be shorter. Looking only at the group of single migrants - for whom economic migration motives were most pronounced - those who were able to share accommodation with persons already living in town should also have better chances on the labour market. But the results of the survey do not show *significant* correlations. No correlation at all is observable in Chiang Mai, where the job situation is relatively good and migrants entering the labour market do not have too many difficulties getting access to income sources, although not necessarily to the job they wish. In Baguio City, however, migrants who came alone but shared accommodation with others, more often than those living alone, were able to get a job immediately after arrival or within a few days.

An explanation might be the overall labour market situation. The time period necessary for migrants to find their first job is used here as an indicator for the labour market situation (Fig. 15.7).

In Chiang Mai (n=321) and Baguio City (n=420) more than half of the respective respondents (55%) were able to find a job within a few days, but around 17% had to look for their first employment for from several months up to one year. On tight labour markets, it is extremely difficult for migrants to find employment immediately, irrespective of the social contacts they might have in advance. If they cannot find a job during the first few days, they often must wait for a longer time to be successful. Social networks, however, still

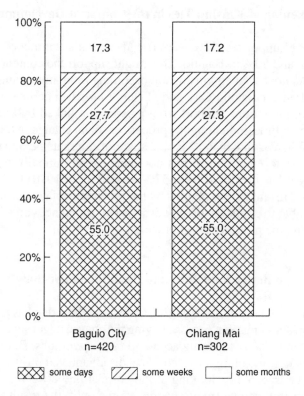

Figure 15.7 Duration until Migrants Found Their First Employment
Source: VW-Project 1991/92.

can reduce the time span by weeks, months or even years until the first employment is secured. In Baguio City, where, compared with Chiang Mai, getting access to employment is more difficult, having social contacts in town is clearly a help in finding a job quickly. On the other hand, in a situation like in Chiang Mai, where labour market chances for newcomers are better, social networks seem to offer no special advantage in securing the first job when arriving in town.

In both cases, however, the chances for migrants getting help in finding the first job were better when they shared accommodation on arrival in town. Relatives and friends already living in town proved to be especially helpful in this respect. In Chiang Mai and Baguio City ca. 60% of the migrants in our sample could count on the help of other persons in getting their first job.

15.8   Weakening of Kinship Ties in the Course of Development?

Among supporters, 57% were friends and other unrelated persons in Chiang Mai, and 50% in Baguio. This might support the contention that social networks *not* based on kinship are becoming more important. This trend can be verified for Baguio City and Chiang Mai when comparing different periods of in-migration: Support from persons not linked by kinship ties is increasing over time, indicating the process of social change in the respective societies. Whereas in Chiang Mai the share of migrants being supported in gaining access to employment has not changed substantially over time, in Baguio City it has increased from 57% (period up to 1970) to 67% (period 1981/1992). This may be explained by the fact that the latest in-migrants are more often able to count on already established social networks which were formed during the past migration process.

15.9   Access to Better Paid Jobs and the Informal Sector

If personal mediation for getting a job has to be judged as an advantage on the urban labour market, persons having the chance to get such help should also have better chances gaining access to *better paid* jobs. But if such help rather is a makeshift solution for those in a disadvantaged position, the opposite should be true. When looking at the correlation between personal help finding a job and income (main income source only) the result is strikingly uniform for both cities: persons who got their present job without help from other persons are more likely to be in the above average income bracket. Personal mediation for getting a job seems to be more an indication of disadvantage than of advantage.

These findings have to be differentiated when the informal sector alone is taken into account. The informal sector is defined here as consisting of all employed persons working in enterprises with five and less employees and all self-employed persons without having their businesses formally licensed. Based on the work force, as it is represented in the sample survey, the share of the informal sector is similar in both cities: 17% in Baguio City and 23% in Chiang Mai.

As a rule, incomes in the informal sector are on the average lower than those in the formal sector in both cities (Table 15.2). Income disparities between both sectors are most expressed in Baguio and least in Chiang Mai: in Baguio City the average income (main income source only) per month in the informal sector is 70% of the average formal sector income – and about 90% in Chiang Mai. On the other hand income polarisation in each sector seems to

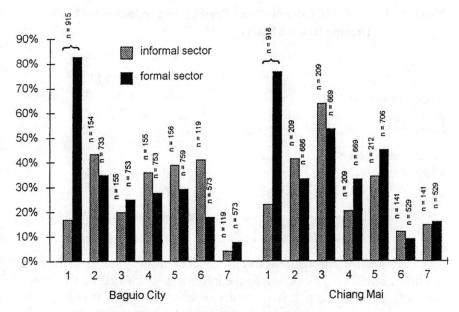

1: Informal/formal workers (percentage of working population)
2: Persons getting help to find their present job (percentage for each sector)
3: Urban born persons (percentage for each sector)
4: Migrants arriving since 1986 (percentage for each sector)
5: Persons up to 25 years (percentage for each sector)
6: Persons in the lowest income group (percentage for each sector)
7: Persons in the highest income group (percentage for each sector)

**Figure 15.8 Informal and Formal Sector Employment in Baguio City
and Chiang Mai (selected variables)**
Source: VW-Project 1991/92.

grow in the course of economic development as the figures for the standard
deviation show.

This supports the hypothesis that for a majority working in the informal sector is a function of lacking access to better paid formal sector jobs.
One would then assume that new entrants on the urban labour market - young
persons and migrants who just arrived in town - should be well represented
among the informal sector workers. This is true only for Baguio City, where
young persons up to 25 years and migrants who arrived since 1986 are clearly
overrepresented among the informal sector workers. In Chiang Mai, however, the situation is somewhat different: here, persons 36 years and older,
urban born persons and migrants already living for several years in town are
the majority (Fig. 15.9).

Looking finally at the pattern of support for getting the present job, in

Table 15.2   Monthly Informal and Formal Sector Incomes (Main Income Source Only) (1991-92)

	average income	median	standard deviation
Baguio City (Peso)*			
informal jobs	2,763	2,100	2,244
formal jobs	3,974	3,000	3,936
Chiang Mai (Bath)*			
informal jobs	5,364	3,200	7,072
formal jobs	5,886	3,200	9,606

* In 1991/92 the equivalents to one German Mark (DM) were 14.9 Peso and 15.2 Bath
Source: VW-Project 1991/92.

both cases and for informal and formal jobs, the majority relied on their own activities. But nevertheless, among the informal sector workers, the share of those who received support from family members, relatives, friends etc. was considerably higher compared to formal sector workers in both cities. Access to informal sector jobs seems to be generally more dependent on personal mediation, but as the case of Chiang Mai shows, the *kind* of social networks which are helpful in getting access not only to jobs but to jobs with relatively higher incomes are, in both sectors, to a high degree a function of time (duration of stay in town, age).

This argument can further be strengthened when the membership in urban organizations is taken into account. In general, the probability of being a member in such an organization increases with age and the duration of stay in town. If membership in an urban based organization is taken as an indicator of integration in urban social networks, the different frequencies again reflect the different economic situations of both countries and cities: it is lowest in Chiang Mai (approx. 21% of all respondents, n=707); for Baguio City the share of members is around 36% (n=711). This result would indicate that the necessity and/or the will to organize decreases with progressing economic development. This might be true when the two countries are compared (although a closer look would have to take into consideration the specific social and cultural situation in each country and city). But if each city is looked at individually, then it becomes apparent that in both cases there is a positive correlation between membership in an organization and a position in the higher income brackets, and that this positive correlation is even more distinct when only those organizations are considered whose purpose is dominantly economic (e.g. business unions, trade unions).

15.10 Conclusion

Demographic growth in both selected secondary cities is caused in strong but varying degree by in-migration, mainly in the form of rural-urban migration - with the important exception of a relatively large group of migrants to Chiang Mai coming from Bangkok. For the majority, migration is part of a livelihood strategy. Economic motives dominate, but educational motives, which can be interpreted as investments in one's *future* livelihood, are also important: due to the city's history, this is the case especially in Baguio City. Whether migrants move alone or in company should not be interpreted as an indicator for the strength or weakness of social ties. The share of kin among the migration partners is, however, decreasing in both cities, indicating a process of social change or 'modernization', although on different levels.

Another fact enforces the argument that the status of single migrants should not be seen as an indication of lack of social ties: the majority of single migrants in both cities was able to share accommodation with others, which may be seen as a sign for already existing social networks between urban destination and areas of origin of the migrants. Whereas sharing accommodation with others seems to be an advantage for migrants for also getting support finding the first job, the chance for gaining quick access to employment seems to be more a function of the respective labour market conditions than of social relations. High shares of migrants getting their first job through personal mediation in Chiang Mai and Baguio City can be interpreted as an expression of more established social networks between urban destination and source areas of migration due to a longer migration history. And again, high shares of unrelated persons among the supporters correlate positively with the level of economic development and tend to increase in the course of time.

Urban-born job seekers are in a better position compared to migrants in terms of labour market information, and they less often need to ask others for help finding a job. Persons who found their present job without help of others are, in both cities, clearly mostly in the higher income brackets. Access to informal jobs on the other hand is more dependent on personal mediation than access to formal jobs. The kind of social networks which are useful for that purpose differ from those which are helpful for just getting a job. Forging social links with the right persons clearly is a function of time, i.e. age and duration of stay in town. This also applies to the membership in explicitly urban organisations: membership in urban based organisations, especially those with a dominating economic purpose like saving clubs, trade unions and business organisations seems to be an advantage for gaining access to *better paid* jobs.

The analysis of social networks has shown that the urban population in Third World secondary cities cannot be defined as a 'community lost' with little or weak social ties. But according to economic development, a change of social networks is observable: kinship ties are reduced in importance, while other, more purpose oriented social links are developing. This seems to confirm the more optimistic picture of an urban 'community liberated' as described above. But in any case, culture, as an *intervening variable* modifying urbanisation and urban livelihood strategies, must be taken into account.

References

Amin, A. and Thrift, N. (1995) 'Globalisation, Institutional Thickness and the Local Economy'. In: Healey, P. et al. (Eds): Managing Cities. The New Urban Context. Chichester: 91-108.

Bähr, J. et al. (1992) Bevölkerungsgeographie. Lehrbuch der Allgemeinen Geographie, Band 9, Walter de Gruyter, Berlin and New York.

Boissevain, J. and Mitchell, J.C. (Eds) ( ): Network Analysis. Studies in Human Interaction. Monographs under the auspices of the Afrika-Studiecentrum-Leiden, Mouton, The Hague, Paris.

Bruner, E.M. (1961) 'Urbanization and Ethnic Identity in North Sumatra'. The American Anthropologist, (63): 508-521.

Evers, H.-D. a.o. (1987) 'Trade and State Formation: Siam in the Early Bangkok Period'. Modern Asian Studies, 21: 751-771.

Friedrichs; J. (1995) Stadt-Soziologie. Leske & Budrich, Opladen.

Hobsbawm, E. (1984) 'Inventing Traditions'. Hobsbawm, E.and Ranger, T.O. (Eds) The Invention of Tradition. Cambridge: 1-14.

Kammeier, H.D. (1986) 'Thailand´s Small Towns: Exploring Facts and Figures Beyond the Population Statistics' Husa, K. et al. (Eds.) Beiträge zur Bevölkerungsforschung. Ferdinand Hirt, Wien: 299-320.

Keyes, C.F. (1987) Buddhist Kingdom as Modern Nation State. Westview Press, Boulder and London.

Lentz, C. (1994) 'Tribalismus und Ethnizität in Afrika: eion Forschugsüberblick'. FU-Berlin, Institute of Ethnology, Sozialanthropologische Arbeitspapiere, 57, Berlin.

Louis Berger International (in association with Chiang Mai University) (1991) 'Initial Study Findings' Report for Chiang Mai Planning Project. Chiang Mai.

Mitchell,, J.C. (1974) 'Social Networks'. Annual Review of Anthropology, (3): 279-299.

Muscat, R.J. (1994) The Fifth Tiger. A Study of Thai Development Policy. M.E. Sharpe/ United Nations University Press, Armonk/N.J.

National Statistics Office, Philippines (NSO/P)(1992) 1990 Census of Population and Housing. Manila.

National Statistics Office, Thailand (NSO/T)(1994) 1990 Population and Housing Census. Bangkok.

Nohlen, D. and Nuscheler, F. (1992), 'Ende der Dritten Welt?' dies. (Hrsg.): Handbuch der Dritten Welt. Band 1: Grundprobleme, Theorien, Strategien. J.H.W. Dietz Nachf., Bonn: 14-30.

Pohjola, A. (1991) 'Social networks - Help or Hindrance for the Migrant?' International Migration, (24)3: 435-443.

Polanyi, K. (1990): The Great Transformation. Politische und ökonomische Ursprünge von Gesellschaften und Wirtschaftssystemen. Suhrkamp, Frankfurt am Main. (Orig. 1944).

Reed, R.R. (1976) City of Pines. The Origins of Baguio City as a Colonial Hill Station and Regional Capital. Berkley.

Redfield, R. and Singer, M.S. (1954) 'The Cultural Role of Cities'. Economic Development and Cultural Change, 3: 53-73.

Rüland, J. (1992) Urban Development in Southeast Asia. Regional Cities and Local Government. Westview Press, Boulder.

Sassen, S, (1994) *Cities in a World Economy.* Pine Forge Press, Thousand Oaks/ Ca.

Schweizer, T. (1989): 'Netzwerkanalyse als moderne Strukturanalyse'. ders. (Hrsg.) *Netzwerkanalyse - ethnologische Perspektiven.* Dietrich Reimer, Berlin. pp 1-34.

Simmel, G. (1908) 'Die Kreuzung sozialer Kreise'. Rammstedt, O. (Hrsg.): Georg Simmel - *Gesamtausgabe, Bd. 11: Soziologie* - Untersuchungen über die Formen der Vergesellschaftung. Suhrkamp, Frankfurt am Main: 456-511.

Singhanetra-Renard, A. (1982) *Commuting and the Fertility of Construction Workers in Chiang Mai City.* Institute of Southeast Asian Studies, Singapore.

Swearer, D.K. (1986) 'The Northern Thai City as a Sacred Centre'. *Journal of Developing Countries,* (2)2: 251-261.

United Nations (Ed.)(1996) *World Population Report.* New York.

Wegmann, J. (1995)'Soziales Netzwerk'. Schäfers, B. (Hrsg.): *Grundbegriffe der Soiologie.* Leske & Budrich, Opladen: 225-228.

Wellman, B., Carrington, P.J., and Hall; A. (1988) 'Networks as Personal Communities' in Wellman et al. (Eds.): Social Structures. A Network Approach. Cambridge: 130-184.

Wirth, L. (1938) 'Urbanism as a Way of Life'. *American Journal of Sociology,* (44): 1-24.

World Bank (Ed.) (1995): *World Development Report 1995,* Oxford University Press, Washington, D.C.

16 Two Decades of Urban Poverty Reduction through Income Generation: What have we learnt?

Pushpa Pathak

16.I Introduction

Until very recently, addressing urban poverty was not very high on the list of priorities of the government or NGOs in most developing countries. Poverty alleviation programmes and plan investments were generally directed toward tackling rural poverty. According to one school of thought, investment in urban poverty alleviation may have little durable impact on general poverty alleviation, divert resources from more urgent rural poverty needs, and could be self-destructive by attracting more migrants from rural areas (Lipton, 1996). Some others view transfer of surplus rural labour to urban areas as a long-term desirable solution for rural poverty (Dasgupta, 1995). But the opinion which is gaining strength is that due to urban growth in most developing countries, the urban poor will soon out-number rural poor, and therefore, meeting the shelter and employment needs of the urban poor should also be given due attention (Mathur, 1995: UNCHS, 1995; and ILO, 1996). For India the projected trends of rural-urban migration and urbanisation imply that over half of the country's population will be identified as urban by the year 2021 (Pathak and Mehta, 1995; and Mehta, 1996a). If the current rural-urban poverty ratios do not change drastically, about half of India's poor are also expected to be living in urban areas by around the same time.

Within the context of the future magnitude of urban poverty in India, this paper focuses on employment and income generation as the most effective strategy for urban poverty reduction. The paper examines the incidence and determinants of rural and urban poverty, presents a brief overview of the major urban poverty reduction programmes of the government as well as initiatives of NGOs and international agencies, and identifies the key constraints faced in the successful implementation of these programmes in India.

16.2 The Incidence and Determinants of Poverty

There has been a long controversy arising out of the significant difference between the 'official' and 'unofficial' estimates of poverty. Since 1962, the official estimate of the incidence of poverty has been based on the per capita monthly income required for purchasing average daily food intake per person of 2100 calories in urban areas and 2400 calories in rural . Unofficial estimates of poverty have been higher, defining the poverty line using the same caloric norm but state specific cost of living indices for rural and urban areas (Hashim, 1996). In March 1997 the Planning Commission used a variation on the recommendations of the Expert Group on Estimation of Proportion and Number of Poor to adopt the 'consumer price index for industrial workers' for estimating and updating the urban poverty line (Government of India, 1997).

Using this approach with data for the year 1993-94, the urban poverty line varied between Rs. 212.42 per capita per month in the case of Assam to Rs. 328.66 per capita per month in Maharashtra (Table 16.1). The lowest rural poverty line of Rs. 163.01 was estimated for Andhra Pradesh while the highest rural poverty line of Rs. 243.84 was identified for Kerala.

According to the newly adopted poverty estimates, 32.36 per cent of the country's urban population was below the poverty line in 1993-94 (Table 16.2). The rural poverty ratio in the same year was 37.27 per cent. The national rural poverty ratios have been higher than the urban poverty ratios at all points of time during the period under consideration. In absolute terms the number of urban poor was 76.34 million and rural poor amounted to about 244 million.

There is considerable variation across India. Bihar has the highest proportion of population below the poverty line, 54%, while Punjab, 12%, has the lowest proportion of poor. Madhya Pradesh has the highest incidence of urban poverty at 48%. Andhra Pradesh, Goa, Haryana, Karnataka, Madhya Pradesh, Rajasthan and Tamil Nadu have a higher incidence of urban than rural poverty – which is against the general trend. This may in part be explained by declining rural poverty – in the case of Andhra Pradesh see Parthasarathy (1995). Another plausible explanation for declining rural poverty in Andhra Pradesh is the increasing transfer of rural unemployed to urban areas in the state as well as to other parts of the country.

Ravallion and Dutt (1996) have made an analysis of the determinants of poverty in India for the period 1951-55 to 1991-92. They have found that: (i) economic growth has a beneficial impact on the incidence of national poverty; (ii) redistribution has helped in reducing the depth and severity of poverty; (iii) while rural economic growth has had an impact on national poverty reduction urban economic growth has helped in reducing only urban poverty; (iv) rural-urban migration contributed very little to general poverty reduction; and (v) while growth in the primary and tertiary sector had a positive impact on rural and urban poverty reduction, growth in the secondary sector

Table 16.1 State Specific Rural and Urban Poverty Lines, 1993-94 (Modified Expert Group Method)

States/UT's	Rs. per capita per month 1993-94	
	Urban	Rural
Andhra Pradesh	278.14	163.01
Arunachal Pradesh*	212.42	232.05
Assam	212.42	232.05
Bihar	238.49	212.16
Goa*	328.56	194.94
Gujarat	297.22	202.11
Haryana	258.23	233.79
Himachal Pradesh	253.61	233.79
Jammu & Kashmir	248.45	213.83
Karnataka	302.89	186.63
Kerala	280.54	243.84
Madhya Pradesh	317.16	193.10
Maharashtra	328.56	194.94
Manipur*	212.42	232.05
Megahalaya*	212.42	232.05
Mizoram*	212.42	232.05
Nagaland*	212.42	232.05
Orissa	298.22	194.03
Punjab	253.61	233.79
Rajasthan	280.85	215.89
Sikkim*	212.42	232.05
Tamil Nadu	296.63	196.53
Tripura*	212.42	232.05
Uttar Pradesh	258.65	213.01
West Bengal	247.53	220.74
Delhi	309.48	233.79
A & N Island	296.63	196.53
Chandigarh	253.61	242.05
D & N Haveli	328.56	194.94
Lakshadweep	280.54	243.84
Pondicherry	296.63	196.53

Source: Rajeev Malhotra, "Incidence of Poverty in India: Towards a Consensus on Estimating the Poor", Indian Journal of Labour Economics, March 1997.

Note: * Poverty line of Assam is assumed for Sikkim and North Eastern States. Poverty line of Maharashtra for Goa and D & N Haveli, Poverty line of Urban Punjab for Chandigarh, Poverty line of Tamil Nadu for A & N Islands and Pondicherry and Kerala for Lakshadweep.

Table 16.2 Number and Percentage of Population Below the Poverty Line in India, 1973-74 to 1993-94

Category	1973-74	1977-78	1983	1987-88	1993-94
Number (in million)					
Rural	261.29	264.25	251.96	231.88	244.03
Urban	60.05	64.65	70.94	75.17	76.34
Combined	321.34	328.90	322.90	307.05	320.37
Percentage					
Rural	56.44	53.07	45.65	39.09	37.27
Urban	49.01	45.24	40.79	38.20	32.36
Combined	54.88	51.32	44.48	38.86	35.97

Source: Government of India: Estimate of Poverty, Press Information Bureau, 11 March 1997, New Delhi.

Table 16.3 India: Worker Population Ratios by Rural-Urban Residence and Sex, 1972-73 and 1993-94

Year	India			Rural areas			Urban areas		
	Person	Male	Female	Person	Male	Female	Person	Male	Female
1972-73	40.7	52.7	27.8	42.8	53.6	31.4	32.6	49.4	13.2
1993-94	42.0	54.5	28.6	44.4	55.3	32.8	34.7	52.0	15.4

Source. Sarvekshana - Journal of the National Sample Survey Organisation, Vol. XI, No. 4, Issue No. 35, April 1988.

growth did not contribute in poverty reduction, either in urban or rural. Tendulkar, Sundaram and Jain (1996) have concluded that the incidence of urban poverty is twice as sensitive to food prices as the incidence of rural poverty ; and that rural poverty is more sensitive to changes in real incomes than urban poverty (Tendualkar, Sundaram and Jain, 1996).

Since 1991 when the Indian Government adopted liberalisation and structural adjustment policies, a considerable amount of work has also been done on assessing the likely impact of these policy measures on employment and poverty. It is widely believed that there will be an increase in under-employment and poverty levels in India in the short-run as has been experienced in many developing countries which have adopted similar structural adjustment policies (e.g. Cornia, Jolly and Stewart, 1987; Horton, Kanbur and Mazumdar, 1991; Desai, 1992; Ghosh, 1992; Kundu, 1993; and Gupta, 1996). It is however predicted that the work participation rate of women may

Table 16.4   India: Employment Status of Workers (Usual Status) by Sex and Rural-Urban Residence, 1972-73 to 1993-94

Sex	Year	Self-employed	Regular employees	Casual labour
RURAL INDIA				
Persons	1972-73	65.3	9.3	25.4
	1977-78	62.6	7.7	29.7
	1983	61.0	7.5	31.5
	1987-88	59.4	7.7	32.9
	1993-94	58.0	6.4	35.6
Males	1972-73	65.9	12.1	22.0
	1977-78	62.8	10.6	26.6
	1983	60.5	10.3	29.2
	1987-88	58.6	10.0	31.4
	1993-94	57.9	8.3	33.8
Females	1972-73	64.5	4.1	31.4
	1977-78	62.1	2.8	35.1
	1983	61.9	2.8	35.3
	1987-88	60.8	3.7	35.5
	1993-94	58.5	2.8	38.7
URBAN INDIA				
Persons	1972-73	41.2	46.3	12.5
	1977-78	42.4	41.8	15.8
	1983	41.8	40.0	18.2
	1987-88	42.8	40.3	16.9
	1993-94	42.3	39.4	18.3
Males	1972-73	39.2	50.7	10.1
	1977-78	40.4	46.4	13.2
	1983	40.9	43.7	15.4
	1987-88	41.7	43.7	14.6
	1993-94	41.7	42.1	16.2
Females	1972-73	48.4	27.9	23.7
	1977-78	49.5	24.9	25.6
	1983	45.8	25.8	28.4
	1987-88	47.1	27.5	25.4
	1993-94	45.4	28.6	26.0

Sources: Sarvekshana - Journal of the National Sample Survey Organisation, Vol. XI, No. 4, Issue No. 35, April 1988 and Sarvekshana, Special Number, Sept. 1990, Results of the Fourth Quinquennial Survey on Employment and Unemployment (All India) and National Sample Survey Organisation. Report No. 406. Key Results on Employment and Unemployment: Fifth Quinquennial Survey. NSS Fiftieth Round. July 1993-June 1994, New Delhi, 1996.

improve in response to the macro-economic policies, but they will be concentrated mostly in the low productivity urban informal sector work as self-employed persons and casual wage labour with very little or no social protection and their real income could decline (e.g. Deshpande and Deshpande, 1992; Moser, Herbert and Makonnen, 1993; Papola, 1993; and Pathak, 1993a). There is evidence that since 1991 the casualisation of the workforce both in rural and urban areas has continued to increase, or is again increasing after a short period of decline. This is an indication of increasing irregularity and insecurity of employment and decreasing average wages.

16.3   Urban Poverty Policies and Government Programmes

In the early 1980s, when urban poverty caught the attention of Indian planners, it was perceived as a shelter and services related problem of slums in urban areas. The result was formulation of the Environmental Improvement of Slums Scheme, aimed solely at improvement in the physical environment of authorised urban slums. Since the Eighth Plan (1992-97), a sociological-economist approach was adopted and income generating programmes for urban poverty alleviation through vocational training, provision of wage employment, and subsidised credit for acquiring productive assets were initiated (Amis, 1995; and Mehta, 1996a). Attempts have been made to incorporate women's perspective in employment and income generating programmes only in the past ten years. Quotas for women have been fixed in some of these programmes. Formulating women-specific programmes for enhancing their employment and income generation is still not very common (Pathak, 1993b).

The current government programmes for enhancing employment opportunities and increasing incomes of the urban poor in India are concerned with the provision of vocational training, institutional subsidised credit and wage employment. The major government programmes are briefly described in this section of the chapter.

16.3.1 Vocational Training

The vocational training programme was initiated by the Ministry of Labour in 1977 with assistance from the International Labour Organisation and Swedish International Development Authority. A large number of national and regional vocational training institutes as well as state government supported industrial training institutes/centres were set up, both for men and women. Programmes of the Central Social Welfare Board and the Ministry of Urban Affairs and Employment also have provisions for vocational training for poor men and women residing in low-income urban neighbourhoods. The Ministry of Education has also initiated Shramik Vidyapeeth, a national scheme to aid the educational and vocational development of workers and their families. The scheme has special provisions for women in low-income households for training in skills such as tailoring, embroidery, knitting, food processing, typing and nursing (National Institute of Urban Affairs, 1991).

16.3.2 Differential Rate of Interest Scheme

The Differential Rate of Interest Scheme (DRI) is one of the major poverty alleviation strategies which was initiated by the Government of India in 1971 to generate employment and increase productivity by providing institutional credit on easy terms. Small loans can be availed to meet the fixed and working capital requirements for economic activities of the self-employed men and women in urban as well as in rural areas. The households having an annual income of less than Rs.7,200 in urban areas and Rs.6,400 in rural areas are eligible for borrowing under this scheme. All the nationalised banks are expected to lend 1 per cent of the previous year's advances to the poor at the concessionary interest rate of 4 per cent, against the prevailing interest rate of 12.5 to 18 per cent (Reserve Bank of India, 1993-94).

16.3.3 Nehru Rozgar Yojana (NRY)

The NRY consists of the following three schemes: The Scheme of Urban-Micro Enterprises (SUME); The Scheme of Urban Wage Employment (SUWE); and The Scheme of Housing and Shelter Upgradation (SHASU). The SUME is designed to encourage unemployed and under-employed youth to take-up self-employment ventures in urban settlements of all sizes. The scheme has loan-cum-subsidy component as well as training and infrastructure support. The scheme has 30 per cent quota for women in the loan programme. The SUWE is designed to provide employment to the urban poor through the creation of socially and economically useful assets in the low income neighbourhoods in towns with below 100,000 population size. The SHASU aims at providing employment for persons involved in housing and building activities. The scheme is applicable to urban settlements having a population between 100,000 and 2,000,000 with relaxation in the population criteria for hill states, Union Territories and new industrial townships. The Housing and Urban Development Corporation monitors this component of NRY and also provides the requisite institutional finance (Government of India, 1992).

16.3.4 Rashtriya Mahila Kosh

The Government of India has set up a national credit fund for women called Rashtriya Mahila Kosh in 1994. The fund is an autonomous government body which lends to NGOs and parastatal agencies for women's development projects, both in rural and urban areas. Urban women with a family income of less than Rs. 11,800 per annum are eligible for taking 75 per cent of the short-term loans of up to Rs. 2,500 and medium term loans of up to Rs. 5,000. NGOs with a minimum registration of three years qualify for taking a loan from the Fund. The Fund gives credit to NGOs at the interest rate of 8 per cent per annum and loans are given to poor women at a maximum interest rate of 12 per cent per annum. The surplus generated in this manner is expected to be given as grants to the NGOs concerned for institutional capacity building. The government has earmarked an initial sum of Rs. 310 million for the Fund (National Institute of Urban Affairs, 1996a). Up to March 1997, 170 organisations have been linked with the Fund and loans worth Rs. 205 million have been disbursed (Rashtriya Mahila Kosh, 1997).

16.3.5 Urban Basic Services for the Poor (UBSP)

The Urban Basic Services Scheme (UBSS) was initiated in India on a pilot basis in 1986 during the Seventh Plan with the involvement of UNICEF and state governments. In the Eighth Plan, this scheme was modified and it was called The Urban Basic Services for the Poor (UBSP). The primary objective of the programme is to promote people's participation and the co-ordination of resources of various concerned agencies. The services meant to be delivered under the programme include environmental sanitation, primary health care, pre-school learning, vocational training and convergence of other social services at the slum level. The scheme also enables formation of registered societies/cooperatives of slum dwellers at the community level and creation of an organisation for providing marketing assistance, monitoring and evaluation. The financial responsibilities are supposed to be shared on matching basis between the Centre and the states and it is to be implemented in slums of selected cities through Neighbourhood Development Committees. The target coverage of UBSP during the Eighth Plan period (1992-97) is 500 towns and cities of various sizes. By the end of 1995, UBSP was being implemented in 283 towns and cities with a volunteer force of over 100,000 women from low income communities and was reaching about 10 million urban poor (National Institute of Urban Affairs, 1996a).

16.4 NGO Initiatives

Inadequate government allocation for urban poverty reduction through increasing incomes of the poor and operational limitations of these programmes in reaching the poorest have been the main cause of the emergence of NGOs and CBOs in urban areas. The numerous NGOs and CBOs concerned with increasing employment and incomes of the urban poor can be put in three broad categories.

First, a large number of urban-based NGOs are particularly concerned with women's development. In addition to the relatively low priority given to women's economic needs in government programmes, the availability of financial support from international agencies and neglect of the interests of poor women workers in the informal sector by the organised trade unions has led to setting up of exclusively women's NGOs in the recent past in most developing countries (Kalpagam, 1986). These NGOs address a wide range of issues pertaining to poor women's most immediate needs, such as adult literacy and vocational training, health and family planning, credit, procurement of raw materials and marketing of the finished goods. SEWA bank was identified as one of the 12 best global practices at the Habitat II conference held at Istanbul in June 1996.

Second, there are NGOs which focus on one of the key inputs required by the poor for starting and improving their economic activity. Quite often this input is credit made available as per the need of the poor, that is small and frequent loans on low interest rates given against group collateral. For instance, the Crisis Credit Scheme of Mahila Milan in Bombay is a savings and credit programme which offers loans for a variety of emergencies, including those related with economic activities. Mahila Milan also acts an intermediary to facilitate poor women obtain subsidised credit available under government programmes, such as DRI and NRY (Patel and D'Cruz, 1993). Operating at a much larger scale, there are seven Regional Associations of Thrift Cooperatives (RATC) based in Andhra Pradesh, Karnataka and Goa. All the seven cooperatives are members of the Federation of Thrift and Credit Association of India. Each RATC has several Employees Thrift Cooperatives, Neighbourhood Thrift Cooperatives and Women's Thrift Cooperatives (National Institute of Urban Affairs, 1996b). The organisation and operations of these savings and credit cooperatives is very similar to the extensive network of Thrift and Credit Cooperative Societies in Sri Lanka (Albee and Reid, 1991; and Perera and Mudalige, 1993).

Third, there are a very large number of smaller NGOs and CBOs operating in one or in a few low income localities in various cities in India. These agencies often follow area-based approach and work toward reducing all the disadvantages faced by residents of the selected communities. This includes community health, hygiene, education, shelter upgradation and support for income generating activities. Some of these agencies focus only on economic betterment of the poor and provide a comprehensive range of services required for this purpose. Many of these lesser known NGOs and CBOs are making significant contribution in urban poverty reduction, albeit at a much smaller scale.

16.5   International Agencies' Interventions

The direct involvement of international agencies in urban poverty issues is more recent. Some of the multi-lateral international agencies have adopted a combination of strategies for macro-level change and micro-level direct intervention for urban poverty reduction. For example, United Nations Development Programme (UNDP), Delhi, has recently formulated a comprehensive strategy of intervention based on the principle of growth with equity. The emphasis of the proposed programme is on technology upgradation, poverty eradication, rapid expansion of employment opportunities, provision of basic social services, consolidation of economic reforms, and environmental protection (UNDP, 1997). The International Labour Organisation (ILO) has a much broader agenda for supporting poverty alleviation and income generation for the poor, that is increasing productive employment, organisation and participation of people and deliberate and positive action to reduce gender-based poverty. Recently, ILO has also constituted an Inter-Agency Working Group on Employment and Poverty. The main objective of the Group is to facilitate interaction between multi-lateral and bi-lateral agencies, minimise duplication of efforts, and identify areas for future action irrespective of which agency undertakes the work.

Of late, international agencies are getting increasingly involved in urban poverty reduction through project based direct interventions in India. For instance, the Dutch Government's Bangalore Urban Poverty Project initiated in 1993 involves setting up of an institutional structure as well as implementing a number of comprehensive poverty alleviation projects in selected slums. The Self-Help-Fund Project of the German Development Cooperation (GTZ) initiated in 1994 has recently been extended to the urban sector as well. The first urban project is based in four resettlement colonies of Delhi. The objective of the project is to support identification and implementation of need based income generating activities. The programme also provides legal aid and helps in setting up savings and credit mechanisms for the poor women, particularly single woman. The USAID's Delhi office has a programme for supporting informal credit delivery for the urban informal sector and also has an explicit objective of supporting women's economic activities. At present USAID is providing funds for SEWA bank and Housing Services Trust in Ahmedabad, Friends of World Women's Banking in Ahmedabad and also support for micro financing routed through The Reserve Bank of India. The Ford Foundation's Delhi office at present has one programme for increasing the incomes of rural and urban poor entitled "Women's Livelihoods and Empowerment" (The Ford Foundation, 1996-97). The Department for International Development (DFID – formerly ODA), U.K., has recently started a multi-dimensional project in Cochin aimed at slum development and increasing income earning opportunities of the poor (Pathak, 1997). These are a few illustrations of the increasing interest of international agencies in urban poverty reduction and the range of initiatives supported by these agencies for increasing employment and income earning opportunities of the urban poor in India.

16.6   Major Constraints

The poor are faced with several constraints: lack of capital, lack of space, inadequate information about employment opportunities, and too much competition in most activities in which urban poor are likely to be engaged. The most significant personal constraint is lack of suitable skills and educational qualification which acts as a barrier for the poor in gaining access to many economic opportunities. In the case of poor women, household related constraints are also important, such as, division of labour within the household, attitude of the family members towards their economic participation, child bearing and rearing responsibilities, and lack of labour saving devices and necessary basic services in the household and in the community. However, the constraints faced by the poor during their active participation vary a great deal depending on their employment status and the nature of economic activity (National Institute of Urban Affairs, 1991).

16.6.1 Inadequate Scale of Intervention

Although government programmes have provisions for reaching large numbers of poor men and women they are not adequate to solve the problems urban poverty and deprivation in India. The limited scale of government's intervention largely stems from the national policy perspective which assigns a lower priority to addressing urban poverty. There are a number of barriers to upscaling and expansion of NGO activities including inadequate financial support, lack of dedicated personnel and management problems.

The small scale of government intervention for women is of particular relevance in this context as provisions for poor women do not take into consideration the actual extent of poor women in the labour force who work or are seeking work and who may require support for their income generating activities (Banerjee, 1992; and Pathak, 1993b). This is because the Census and the National Sample Survey significantly underestimate the female work participation rate. A study of women in the urban informal sector in six cities in India shows that female work participation rates for all age groups was double the official estimate provided by National Sample Survey and three times more than the Census estimate, and also, male-female work participation rates were almost the same in the 15 years and above age group in poor households (National Institute of Urban Affairs, 1991).

16.6.2 Underutilisation of Government Funds

It is a paradoxical situation where on the one hand it is felt that provisions for urban poverty reduction are far less than the reality demands and on the other we find that there is underutilisation of government funds available for employment and income generation in urban areas..

The reasons for underutilisation of government funds for poverty alleviation and income generation projects such as DRI, SEPUP and NRY needs further probing. It is difficult to ascertain on the basis of the available empirical evidence whether it is because of the criteria laid down in the programme which make identification of poor and needy difficult, or a relatively low motivation on part of the implementing agencies, or inefficient implementation of the programmes leading to lapsing of annual allocation of funds, or a combination of all these factors.

Table 16.5 Eighth Plan Allocations for Nehru Rozgar Yojana (NRY) (1992-97) and Expenditure (in million Rs)

Scheme	Allocations			Expenditure up to Feb. 1996 (%)
	Centre	State	Total	
SUME	1238	822	2060	63
SUWE	1197	794	1991	80
SHASU	693	458	1151	35
Total	3580	2360	5940	61

Source: Compiled on the basis of data available in the Annual Reports of the Ministry of Urban Affairs and Employment, New Delhi.

Table 16.6   Achievements under Nehru Rozgar Yojana (figures in millions)

Scheme	1991-92		1992-93		1993-94		1994-95	
	Target	*Achievement*	*Target*	*Achievement*	*Target*	*Achievement*	*Target*	*Achievement*
Families assisted under SUME	0.19	0.16	0.09	0.12	0.12	0.15	0.12	0.13
Employment generated under SUWE and SHASU	16.50	12.95	15.82	13.39	14.30	12.37	10.07	6.40
Persons trained under SUME and SHASU	0.05	0.01	0.05	0.03	0.06	0.05	0.06	0.04

Source: Economic Survey, 1991-92, 1992-93, 1993-94, 1994-95, Government of India, Ministry of Finance, Economic Division.

It has also been observed that grant funds allocated for NGOs and voluntary organisations have not been fully disbursed in many states. The plausible explanations for this are stated to be lack of identification of suitable NGOs as well as inadequate confidence on part of the concerned government agencies in the capacity of NGOs to undertake serious implementation of urban poverty projects (Working Group on Urban Poverty, 1996).

16.6.3 Lack of Inter-agency Coordination

Each government programme is designed to provide one of the inputs, be it vocational training, wage employment or credit, and is implemented by specific department, agency or institution. Often even a comprehensive programme like NRY providing all the three inputs is implemented by three key agencies, that is, the urban local bodies, Housing and Urban Development Corporation and commercial banks. Lack of inter-agency co-ordination leads to inefficient implementation of the programme (Jain, Gupta and Kumat, 1994; Operations Research Group, 1995; Thamarajakshi, 1996; and Kruse, 1997). Also, often the people who receive vocational training under one programme do not relevant wage employment or credit under another programme to make them economically viable.

16.6.4 Inexperience of Urban Local Governments

Two recent policy initiatives of the government have direct implications for the poverty reduction efforts to be made by urban local governments. First, the 74th Constitutional Amendment Act was passed in 1992 aimed at democratic decentralisation of urban governance. This Act empowers local governments with greater responsibilities and fiscal autonomy. The devolution of discretionary functional responsibilities according to the Act includes promoting local economic development and poverty alleviation. These are entirely new operational areas for most urban local bodies in India.

Second, the government's pronounced in 1995 the integration of all urban poverty attempts through the institutional structure created for UBSP. Although UBSP is supposed to be implemented predominantly through community based organisations, the entire institutional network of the project involves national and state governments, District Urban Development Agency and local governments. It also includes setting up of Urban Poverty Eradication (UPE) cells within each urban local government, which will function as a co-ordinating and implementing agency. This is a new area for local governments and they do not have the prerequisite skills or experience for effectively implementing these programmes.

16.6.5 Difficulty in Identification of the Poor

Government programmes meant to provide institutional subsidised credit for the development of micro-enterprises on the basis of the average yearly household income have not revised the income limits in line with inflation. A case study of SEPUP in Bombay shows that as a result of the low household income limit of Rs. 600 per month only one-third of the target number of loans could be disbursed during 1988-91 (Reddy, 1994).

The government programme such as NRY in India and Million Houses Programme in Sri Lanka generally follow area-focused strategy for their wage employment and shelter and community facilities construction schemes. These schemes are implemented in selected low-income neighbourhoods, predominantly those which have officially authorised status. Poor persons living in a number of slum settlements, some authorised and all the unauthorised ones are thus left out of the reach of such employment programmes.

16.6.6 Delivery Mechanism Based on Meeting the Targeted Numbers

In the implementation of government programmes there is more concern with meeting the target numbers rather than making the intervention a real success (Nagaraj, 1993). For instance, in the provision of institutional credit, little effort is made to follow-up on the most effective utilisation of the loan amount and to provide support services, such as, materials and markets to ensure the success of credit made available through government programmes.

16.6.7 NGOs' Ambition for Good Performance and Expansion

The development assistance, both provided by the governments and NGOs on the one hand challenges the existing forms of patronage and dependence on money-lenders and traders, and on the other, creates new forms of clientalism and dependence on functionaries of the state and local bodies as well as on other intermediaries (Feldman, 1990). Two kinds of intermediaries have emerged, namely, (i) brokers known by the banks as social workers, including politicians, slum lords, materials suppliers and officials of various government welfare agencies, and (ii) women's organisations, such as, SEWA in Ahmedabad, WWF in Madras and Bangalore and AMM in Bombay (Everette and Savara, 1986).

There is the potential for conflict between the 'voluntary' spirit and 'enterpreneurism' that some of the NGO initiatives, such as SEWA and Grameen Bank, begin to face once they become successful and their operations expand like any other business enterprises (Mehta, 1996b). While upscaling of NGO operations is desirable considering the current scale of urban poverty reduction efforts, important lessons have to learned from the increasing trend of ambitious expansion of NGO activities which negatively affects the very purpose of empowerment of the people and of other smaller NGOs and CBOs (Ebdon, 1995).

16.6.8 Legal Constraints

The poor have some legal disadvantages that arise from their residential and work status in urban areas. First, a large number of poor live in slums and squatter settlements under the constant threat of being evicted. Second, strict land-use zoning may prohibit undertaking commercial and industrial activities in residential areas. Informal sector trade and other businesses operating from the streets and pavements in the commercial areas and in the open spaces in other parts of the cities attract both eviction and harassment by the police, local government tax collectors as well as by the rightful owners of the shops and residential buildings in that area (Pathak, 1995; and ILO, 1996). Constant struggle by the informal sector workers and negotiations with the local governments have brought about some changes in a few cities. Third, environmental policies aimed at checking industrial pollution which result in shifting of industrial units out of the cities, rather than enforcing pollution checking technologies of production, also have an adverse impact on employment of the poor (Banerjee, 1997).

16.6.9 Leakages

It is a common knowledge that leakage of allocated funds is one of the major constraints in reducing the positive impact of poverty reduction programmes. There are three ways in which leakages occur: (i) diversions of poverty funds to other uses by the agency concerned; (ii) identification of ineligible, often not poor, beneficiaries; and (iii) substantial amounts taken as a commission by the middle persons or brokers who facilitate the poor in getting access to subsidised credit. The known categories of such middle persons are local politicians, slumlords, materials suppliers, piece-rate work contractors and officials of the banks and government agencies administering the programme.

16.6.10 Predominance of Micro-Enterprises and Lack of Occupational Diversification

The income generation and poverty alleviation programmes implemented so far have also not been particularly concerned with diversification of economic activities and facilitating upward occupational mobility of the poor men and women, which may offer them better monetary returns. Most of the government and NGO interventions have generally provided necessary inputs and services for improvement of their existing economic activities, especially in low skill, low technology and low productivity informal sector activities (Papola, 1993).

With reference to women, these interventions have assisted mainly home-based economic activities of self-employed women rather than increasing their access to wage employment or independent income earning opportunities outside the home (The World Bank, 1990). Although assisting home-based work of women is undoubtedly a significant measure for meeting the most immediate need of improving the income levels of large numbers of women home-based workers, it does not challenge the division of labour prevailing in the household and in the society nor does it offer an opportunity for occupational diversification and upward mobility (Jain, 1980; and Feldman, 1990).

16.6.11 *Problems in Vocational Training*

It is generally believed that skill acquisition will eliminate the supply side constraints and enhance the human capital of labour. However, there are several problems associated with the effectiveness of most vocational training programmes designed for the poor. The most important amongst these are: (i) the training is imparted in traditional skills which are not necessarily marketable; (ii) the training enables very superficial level of skill acquisition which is not sufficient for increasing the access of poor men and women to income earning opportunities; (iii) no attempt is made to link the provision for training in specified skills and demand in the labour market; and (iv) often provision of a stipend for the trainees becomes an end in itself, particularly in the case of very poor who perceive training as a means of enhancing their current income, however meagre it may be (for instance Bardhan, 1987, the World Bank, 1989; National Institute of Urban Affairs, 1990 and Banerjee, 1992).

16.6.12 *Limitations in the Access to Institutional Credit*

Although government supported credit schemes are designed to reach large numbers of poor, the poorest among the poor have limited access to institutional subsidised credit. There are several constraints faced by the poor in accessing these funds, such as: (i) lack of adequate and reliable information about the programmes and procedures involved in getting the credit, (ii) requirement of a ration card as a proof of residence in the city for a minimum of three years implying that new migrants in the city as well as those who have not been able to get a ration card for any reason do not qualify for these loans, (iii) lengthy and complicated procedures, (iv) the illiterate urban poor not having the capacity to prepare a project proposal which will be accepted by the banks, (v) not having the capacity to deal with banks themselves needing some kind of reliable intermediary support, and (vi) banks reluctance to grant many loans to the poor as they do not consider many of the proposals commercially viable and also it involves high administrative cost for extending these subsidised small loans.

16.6.13 *Gender Specific Constraints Faced by Women*

Gender-specific constraints faced by women have negatively affected their access to the available provisions as follows. First, the poverty alleviation programmes aimed at providing credit and wage employment address the needs of poor households, and hence, the male heads of households. Second, government programmes for women are more oriented towards providing vocational training in women specific skills while general poverty alleviation programmes are formulated to extend credit and wage employment, predominantly to the males in the poor households. So, more men have had access to subsidised institutional credit while women have been able to get vocational training, which may or may not lead to income generation (NIUA, 1990). Third, gender bias is institutionalised. A simple example of such prejudice is when a male bank official ignores a loan application made by women because of her sex (NIUA, 1990). Fourth, female illiteracy is much higher than male illiteracy.

16.7 Main Lessons

16.7.1 Government-NGO Cooperation

One of the major lessons which can be drawn from this analysis of government programs and NGO initiatives in India is that co-operation between governments and NGOs appears to be a necessary and effective strategy for economic empowerment of urban poor men and women. The government programmes are designed to meet the needs of large numbers of the urban poor and have the potential for making significant impact on enhancing employment and income generation opportunities for them. The governments also have more financial resources and a broader administrative network while NGOs have greater capacity to reach the poorest men and women down to the community and household level. Therefore, co-operation between the two kinds of agencies is expected to be an effective strategy for urban poverty reduction. The governments should involve leading NGOs both in designing and implementation of the programmes. The NGOs can facilitate implementation of the government programmes by helping in identification of the target groups, dissemination of information regarding plan provisions, motivation, establishing links between the poor and government and commercial institutions, and in monitoring the utilisation of the resources made available through government programmes.

16.7.2 Capacity Building of Urban Local Governments

The financial, technical, managerial and staff capacities of urban local bodies need to be strengthened. Sensitising the urban local government officials to various poverty issues and building their capacity to implement poverty programmes more effectively will also be necessary in this regard.

16.7.3 Linking Skill Formation with Labour Market Demand

Linking skill formation with labour market demand, as against designing ad hoc training programmes, is absolutely essential for making it effective. The local governments of Pune and Sholapur cities in Maharashtra have set the trend in this respect. They hired professionals to asses the labour market conditions and to identify the marketable skills for designing their training package under the NRY programme. It is too early to assess the success of this initiative in terms of the extent of skilled labour absorption. But the initiative itself is worth making a note of.

16.7.4 Emphasis on Wage Employment

Wage employment is generally associated with stability, regularity, security and at times higher income. This is also a more cost effective means of providing an income earning opportunity to the predominantly assetless poor. Nirmala Niketan, a relatively small Delhi-based NGO, acts as a recruitment and placement agency for migrant women who have very low educational and skill levels and are most suited to work as domestic maids. These women stay in the NGOs hostel free of cost up to a fortnight after arriving in the city. Some training in domestic chores is provided during this period. They are then placed in suitable middle class homes after negotiating the terms of their employment with the employers. Part-time classes for typing and shorthand are also organised for the enterprising women to facilitate their upward occupational mobility. These maids are the most sought after domestic help in the city and often employers have to wait up to six months for getting a maid. In response to the prevailing demand, Nirmala Niketan tries to recruit more women from the tribal areas of Bihar and Orissa through churches located in these areas as well as through the network of women already working in the city (National Institute of Urban Affairs, 1992).

16.7.5 Targeting of Women

Many of the successful NGOs cited in this paper had a more focussed goal of assisting poor urban women, rather than poor households, and in increasing their incomes as also enhancing their organisation, awareness, visibility, general empowerment and collective bargaining power. Their success was also due to the fact that many of these organisations were led by dynamic middle class women who had links with the political, administrative and financial institutions, and also had some experience of working as a trade union or political party activist. In addition they were able to disseminate information regarding the available schemes and procedures; they could motivate and organise women into groups which substituted the conventional collateral requirement; and they were familiar with the functioning of the government and banking.

16.7.6 From Minimalist to Comprehensive Sector-Focused Strategy

Minimalist credit provision was used as an entry point by the most successful NGOs which gradually developed into a comprehensive sector-focused strategy, including training for specific skills, supply of materials, markets, health services and legal support. The strength of the incremental approach generally adopted by NGOs lies in avoiding over ambitious beginning, and hence, reducing the risk of failure in the incipient stages. It involves identifying a critical constraint faced by the poor in a given sector, finding low-cost ways of eliminating it, building the organisational capacity for dealing with more complex and a wider range of issues, and then broadening the scope as well as the coverage of the programme. In the case of Women's Work Centres initiated within the broader Orangi Pilot Project in Karachi, the initial intervention was better sanitation in the neighbourhood, then came supporting women's home-based piece-rate work, followed by an integrated programme for supporting improvement in economic activities of poor men and women and their neighbourhoods (The World Bank, 1989; and Hasan, 1996).

The comprehensive sector focused strategy of intervention was followed by the NGOs to assist self-employed and piece-rate workers engaged in individual level vertically integrated production processes. For instance, SEWA provided all types of inputs, required for ready-made garments production by self-employed women in Ahmedabad. SEWA has also provided varied assistance to piece-rate women workers in Lucknow who are engaged in doing embroidery in a multi-stage production process of garment making, where all stages of production are being undertaken by different sets of individual piece-rate workers. The garments made by women in Ahmedabad are sold locally to low income buyers whereas garments made in Lucknow have a nation wide market. However, it is hard to find examples of NGOs providing comprehensive support for setting up cooperatives or small workshops for undertaking sub-contracted work as a part of a larger decentralised production process.

The above stated experiences suggest that a package approach for providing more than one necessary input needs to be evolved for making poverty reduction initiatives more viable. For instance, training and placement, training with credit, or credit with access to materials and markets will significantly improve the income earning opportunities for the poor (Haruo, 1996).

16.8　Conclusions

The recent evidence on urban poverty in India suggests that in spite of a discernible declining trend in the incidence of urban poverty, the number of urban poor is increasing and the number of urban poor is likely to become double in the foreseeable future of about 20-30 years. Therefore, more concerted efforts have to be made for dealing with urban poverty. The literature on determinants of poverty also shows that high rate of national economic growth and direct poverty reduction interventions together have helped in employment generation, increase in incomes and also in urban poverty reduction. Therefore, future urban poverty reduction efforts should address both macro-policy issues for supporting national and regional economic growth and micro-level direct interventions for increasing employment and income levels of the poor.

A minimum policy condition for making a change at the micro-level already exists, what is needed is effective implementation of various poverty reduction initiatives. Finally, it is imperative to move away from the dichotomy between government versus NGO interventions to co- operation between government and NGOs. Of course, there are important lessons to be learnt from the successes and failures of the poverty reduction efforts made by both kinds of agencies. But, what is needed is the pooling of all the available resources for dealing with the impending magnitude of urban poverty in India.

References

Albee, A. and K.D. Reid (1991): "Women in Urban Credit in Sri Lanka", in Centre for Women's Research, Women Poverty and Family Survival, CENWOR, Colombo: 1-11.

Amis, Philip (1997): "Indian Urban Poverty : Where are the Levers for its Effective Alleviation?" IDS Bulletin, Vol.28, No. 2: 94-105.

Amis, Philip (1995): "Employment Creation or Environmental Improvements: A Literature review of Urban Poverty and Policy in India," Habitat International, 19(4): 485-498.

Bamberger, M. and A. Aziz (1993): Poverty and Strategies for Poverty Alleviation, EDI Seminar Series, The Design and Management of Sustainable Projects to Alleviate Poverty in South Asia, collected papers of the EDI seminar held in Bangalore in July-Aug., 1991, The World Bank, Washington D.C.

Banerjee, N. (1997): "A Note on the Informal Sector in the Indian Economy", paper presented at the Workshop on 'Contribution of the Unorganised Sector', NCAER and SEWA, March 31 - April 2, New Delhi.

Banerjee, Nirmala (1992): Poverty, Work and Gender in Urban India, Occasional Paper Number 133, Centre for Studies in Social Sciences, Calcutta.

Bardhan, Kalpana (1987): Women Workers in South Asia: Employment Problems and Policies in the Context of the Poverty Target Groups Approach, ILO/ARTEP Working Paper, New Delhi.

Bennett, L. and M. Goldberg (1993): Providing Enterprise Development and Financial Services to Women: A Decade of Bank Experience in Asia, The World Bank Technical Paper No. 236, Washington D.C.

Cornia, A. Giovanni, Richard Jolly and Frances Stewart (eds.) (1987): Adjustment with a Human Face, Vol. I, Protecting the Vulnerable and Promoting Growth, Clarendon Press, Oxford.

Dasgupta, Biplab (1995): Institutional Reforms and Poverty Alleviation in West Bengal, Economic and Political Weekly, XXX (41 and 42), 14-21 October: 2691-2702.

Delhi Development Authority (1990): Master Plan for Delhi 2001, New Delhi.

Desai, V. Ashok (1992): "Output and Employment Effects of Recent Changes in Policy", in ILO/ARTEP, Social Dimension of Structural Adjustment in India, Geneva: 41-83.

Deshpande, Sudha and L.K. Deshpande (1992): "New Economic Policy and Female Employment", Economic and Political Weekly, Vol. 27, No. 41: 2248-52.

Ebdon, Rosamund (1995): NGO Expansion and the Fight to Reach to Poor: Gender Implications of NGO Scaling up in Bangladesh, IDS Bulletin, 26(3), July: 49-55.

Everett, Jana and Mira Savara (1986): "Bank Loans to the Poor in Bombay: Do Women Benefit?", in Gelpi, Barbara C. et al. (eds.), Women and Poverty, The University of Chicago Press, Chicago: 83-101.

Feldman, Shelley (1990): "Formalising the Informal Sector: New Forms of Domestic Exploitation for Bangladeshi Women", Paper presented at the 42nd Annual Meeting of the Association for Asian Studies, 5-8 April, Chicago.

Getubig, I.Jr. (1993): "The Role of Credit in Poverty Alleviation", in Bamberger, M. and A. Aziz (ed.), Poverty and Strategies for Poverty Alleviation, EDI Seminar Series, The Design and Management of Sustainable Projects to Alleviate Poverty in South Asia, collected papers of the EDI seminar held in Bangalore in July-Aug., 1991, The World Bank, Washington D.C.

Ghosh, Ajit (1992): "Structural Adjustment, Labour Market and Employment: What Can India Learn from Latin America?" Paper presented at the National Seminar on Manpower and Employment Implications of Economic Restructuring, Institute of Applied Manpower Research, December 3-4, New Delhi.

Government of India (1997): Estimate of Poverty, Press Information Bureau, New Delhi.

Government of India (1996): The Approach Paper to the Ninth Five Year Plan (1997-2002), Planning Commission, New Delhi.

Government of India (1995): A Compendium of Central Schemes for Urban Employment Poverty Alleviation and Housing, Ministry of Urban Affairs and Employment, Department of Urban Employment and Poverty Alleviation, New Delhi.

Government of India (1992): The Eighth Five Year Plan, 1992-97, Vol. II, Planning Commission, New Delhi.

Gupta, S.P. (1996): "Deepening Inequalities", in the Financial Express, 12 June, New Delhi.

Haruo, N. (1996): "Planning for Employment in the Urban Informal Sector", Regional Development Dialogue, Vol. 17, No. 1, Spring.

Hasan, A. (1996): "A Case Study of the Urban Basic Services Programme in Sukkur, Sindh Province, Pakistan", in Shubert, C. (ed.), Building Partnerships for Urban Poverty Alleviation Approach; Community Based Programmes in Asia, UMP/UNCHS, Kuala Lumpur.

Hashim, S.R. (1996): "Dimensions of Poverty and Approach to Poverty Alleviation", IASSI Quarterly, Vol. 15, No. 1.

Horton, Susan, Ravi Kanbur and Dipak Mazumdar (1991): "Labour Markets in an Era of Adjustment: Evidence from 12 Developing Countries", International Labour Review, Vol.

130, No. 5-6: 531-58.

ILO (1996): The Future of Urban Employment, prepared for the Habitat II Dialogue for the 21st Century, held at Istanbul, Geneva.

ILO (1995): Gender, Poverty and Employment: Turning Capabilities into Entitlement, Geneva.

ILO (1993): India : Employment, Poverty and Economic Policies, ARTEP/ILO, New Delhi.

Islam, N. and A. Khan (1996): "Community-Based Programmes for Urban Poverty Alleviation in Bangladesh: The Role of City Governments and Local Authorities", in Shubert, C. (ed.), Building Partnerships for Urban Poverty Alleviation Approach; Community Based Programmes in Asia, UMP/UNCHS, Kuala Lumpur.

Jain S.C., Gupta M.L. and M.S. Kumat (1994): Urban Poverty Alleviation: Citizen Management as an Alternative, Nagarlok, XXVI (3), July-Sept.: 44-56.

Jain, Devaki (1980): Women's Quest for Power, Vikas Publishing House, Delhi.

Jhabvala, Renana (1986): "Claiming What is Theirs : Struggle of Vegetable Vendors in Ahmedabad," Manushi, Vol. 6, No. 2: 34-40.

Kalpagam, U. (1986): Organising Women in Informal Sector: Politics and Practice, Offprint No. 14, Madras Institute of Development Studies, Madras.

Kalpagam, U. (1985): Working Women's Forum: A Concept and an Experiment in Mobilization in the Third World, Offprint No. 6, Madras Institute of Development Studies, Madras.

Kruse, Beate (1997): "Employment Generating Programmes in the Urban Context : The Nehru Rozgar Yojana," IDS Bulletin, Vo.28, No. 2: 86-93.

Kundu, A. (1993): Employment Growth, Changing Workforce Structure and Poverty Employment Linkages in Urban Areas: An Analysis with Special Reference to Industrial Economy, ILO/ARTEP Working Paper, New Delhi.

Lipton (1996): Successes in Anti-Poverty, Issues in Development, Discussion Paper No. 8, ILO, Geneva.

Malhotra (1997): "Incidence of Poverty in India: Towards a Consensus on Estimating the Poor", Indian Journal of Labour Economics, March.

Mathur, O.P (1995): Governing Cities: Facing up to the Challenges of Poverty and Globalisation, Report prepared for the Global Urban Research Initiative, University of Toronto, Toronto.

Mehta, D. (1996a): "Community-Based Programmes of Urban Poverty Alleviation in India", in Shubert, C. (ed.), Building Partnerships for Urban Poverty Alleviation Approach; Community Based Programmes in Asia, UMP/UNCHS, Kuala Lumpur.

Mehta, M. (1996b): GO-NGO Partnerships in the Field of Human Settlements: A Global Review of Case Studies from Five Regions, Paper presented at the Meeting of the Habitat International Coalition - Action Research Group, 31 October, Mexico.

Moser, Caroline O. (1989): "Gender Planning in the Third World: Meeting Practical and Strategic Gender Needs", World Development, Vol. 17, No. 11, 1799-1825.

Moser, Caroline O., A.J. Herbert and R.E. Makonnen (1993): Urban Poverty in the Context of Structural Adjustment: Recent Evidence and Policy Responses, Discussion Paper, The World Bank, Washington D.C.

NABARD (1997): Informal Bank of the Poor: Fighting Poverty Through Community Action, circulated at Social Development Fair, 12-20 April, New Delhi.

Nagaraj, K. (1993): "Labour Market Characteristics and Employment Generation Programmes in India", Paper presented at the seminar on 'Poverty, Basic Services, and Environment in Urban Areas: The Asian Experience', 24-26 March, New Delhi.

National Institute of Urban Affairs (1996a): Urban Poverty, January-March.

National Institute of Urban Affairs (1996b): Papers presented at the National Workshop on 'Mobilising Urban Poor: Approach and Issues', 12-13 December, Aurangabad.

National Institute of Urban Affairs (1997): Single Women Migrant Workers in Asian Metropolis: A Case of Delhi, Report prepared for UNESCO, New Delhi.

National Institute of Urban Affairs (1991): Women in the Urban Informal Sector, Research Study Series Number 49, New Delhi.
National Institute of Urban Affairs (1990): Women, Urban Poverty and Economic Development, Research Study Series Number 43, New Delhi.
Noponen, Helzi (1990): Loans to the Working Poor: A Longitudinal Study of Credit, Gender and the Household Economy, Working Paper No. 6, Centre for Urban Policy Research, Rutgers University, Piscataway, New Jersey.
Operations Research Group (1995): Study on Management and Organisation Aspects of Nehru Rozgar Yojana, summary report submitted to the Planning Commission, New Delhi (cited in Tamarajakshi, 1996).
Papola, T.S. (1993): "Employment of Women in South Asian Countries", The Indian Journal of Labour Economics, Vol.36, No.1: 48-56.
Parthasarthy, G. (1995): Employment and Unemployment in Andhra Pradesh: Trends and Dimensions, Economic and Political Weekly, XXX(15): 811-827.
Patel, Sheela and Celine D' Cruz (1993): "The Mahila Milan Crisis Credit Scheme: From Seed to a Tree", Environment and Urbanisation, Vol.5, No.1: 9-17.
Pathak, P. (1997): Review of Income Earning Opportunities for the Urban Poor in Indian Cities, Prepared for ODA, New Delhi.
Pathak, P. (1995): Identification of Appropriate Locations for Informal Sector Activities in Dar es Salam, Report prepared for the ILO Area Office, Dar es Salam.
Pathak, P. (1993a): "The Impact on Economic Reforms on Urban Informal Work of Women in India?" Proceedings of the National Workshop on Employment Equality and Impact of Ec16.6.3 Lack of Inter-agency Coordination.
Pathak, P. (1993b): "Thematic Review of Poverty, Alleviation and Income Generation Strategies for Women in Urban Informal Sector in South Asia", Paper prepared for the Employment and Development Department, ILO, Geneva.
Pathak, P. and D. Mehta (1995): "Recent Trends in Urbanisation and Rural-Urban Migration in India: Some Explanations and Projections", *Urban India*, Vol. 15, No. 2.
Pathirana, V. and Y.K. Sheng (1992): "The Community Contract System in Sri Lanka: An Innovative Approach for the Delivery of Basic Services to the Urban Poor", *Habitat International,* Vol.16, No.4: 3-14.
Perera, M. and R. Mudalige (1993) : *Self-Employment Schemes for Women in Sri Lanka: The Macro-Economic Context,* International Labour Organisation, Colombo.
Prasad, D.R. (1992): *Small Loans for the Urban Poor: A Study of the Small Loan Scheme for Women for Income Generation Activities Under UBSP in Andhra Pradesh*, Regional Centre for Urban and Environmental Studies, Osmania University, Hyderabad.
Punjab National Bank (1988): *Concurrent Evaluation Studies of SEPUP in Ambala, Ahmedabad and Saharanpur*, New Delhi.
Rashtriya Mahila Kosh (1997): A Brief Introduction, New Delhi.
Reddy, I.U.B. (1994): Poverty Alleviation Programmes: A Case of Self-Employment Programmes for Urban Poor in Bombay, *Nagarlok*, XXVI (2), April-June: 40-52.
Reserve Bank of India (1993-94): *Report on Currency and Finance, Vol. I: Economic Review*, New Delhi.
Reserve Bank of India (1991-92): *Report on Currency and Finance, Vol. I: Economic Review*, New Delhi.
Ravallion, Martin and G. Datt (1996): India's Checkered History in Fight Against Poverty: Are There Lessons for the Future? Economic and Political Weekly, XXXI (35-37), September: 2479-2486).
Rodgers, G. (1989): "Trends in Urban Poverty and Labour Market Access", in G. Rodgers (ed.), *Urban Poverty and the Labour Market: Access to Jobs and Incomes in Asian and Latin American Cities*, ILO, Geneva.

Tendler, J. (1989): "Whatever Happened to Poverty Alleviation?" *World Development,* Vol.17, No.7: 1033-1044.

Tendulkar, S.D., K. Sundaram and L.R. Jain (1996): *Macro-Economic Policies and Poverty in India*, Report prepared for the SAMAT/ILO, New Delhi.

Thamarajakshi (1996): *Micro Interventions for Poverty Alleviation, Country Study: India*, prepared for the South Asia Multidisciplinary Advisory Team, ILO, New Delhi.

The Ford Foundation (1996-97): *Statement of Current Interests in India and Nepal*, New Delhi.

The World Bank (1997): *India, Andhra Pradesh: Agenda for Economic Reforms*, Washington D.C.

The World Bank (1996): *Poverty Reduction and the World Bank: Progress and Challenges in the 1990s,* Washington D.C.

The World Bank (1994): *Enhancing Women's Participation in Economic Development*, Policy Paper, Washington D.C.

The World Bank (1991): *Gender and Poverty in India,* Washington D.C.

The World Bank (1990): *Bangladesh: Strategy Paper on Women in Development,* Washington D.C.

The World Bank (1989): *Women in Pakistan: An Economic and Social Strategy*, Washington D.C.

UNCHS (1995): *Shelter, Employment and the Urban Poor,* prepared for the World Summit for Social Development held at Copenhagen.

UNDP (1997): *First Country Cooperation Framework for India*, 1997-2001, New Delhi.

United Nations (1995): *The Job Crisis*, Backgrounder No. 1, prepared for the World Summit for Social Development at Copenhagen, New York.

Vaidya, Chetan (1995): Role of Community Savings and Loan Association, Baroda, in Meeting Credit Needs of Urban Poor, *Nagarlok* XXVII(1), January-March: 33-37.

Visaria, P. and B.S. Minhas (1991): "Evolving an Employment Policy for the 1990s: What do the Data Tell Us?" *Economic and Political Weekly*, April 13.

Working Group on Urban Poverty (1996): *Report of the Working Group on Urban Poverty Alleviation in the Ninth Five Year Plan,* submitted to the Planning Commission, New Delhi.

Wignaraja, Ponna (1990): *Women, Poverty and Resources*, Sage Publications, New Delhi.

17 Waste Disposal Problems in Metro Manila and the Response of the Urban Poor

Therese Gladys Hingco

17.1 Introduction

As with many other cities in developing countries, the majority of the urban population in Metro Manila live below established poverty lines. While the Philippine government claims the country is currently undergoing "rapid growth and development", nearly half of Metro Manila's population remain impoverished and live in very poor and occasionally life-threatening conditions. The urban poor have limited access to and control over resources and employment opportunities. Often they live as squatters in dangerous, unhealthy and sometimes extremely polluted areas. These living conditions are further aggravated by lack of utilities and sanitary facilities. In most cases they have inadequate and unsafe water supply, with little or no provision for the safe disposal of solid or liquid waste. The poor are defined as those who live below the poverty threshold, defined as "the minimum amount a family of six needs to satisfy all its nutritional requirements and other basic needs e.g. shelter, clothing, education, utilities etc." For those living in Metro Manila, this figure has been set by National Economic Development Authority at P5,821 (£145.50) per month while the food threshold is set at P2,283 (£57.00). More than 55% of the urban poor population in the Metropolis earn no more than P2,000, an income which is even less than the food threshold figures.

The urban poor are those who are most vulnerable to suffer from the impacts of pollution and waste disposal. This paper will review the extent of waste disposal problems in Metro Manila and will look into the government's current initiatives in response to the waste disposal problems in the Metropolis. Many studies have shown how the initiatives of the urban poor and their economy have contributed to resolving the waste disposal problems in Third world cities (Furedy, 1989 & 1992; Mehrah, R. et.al. 1996). This paper will therefore also examine how the urban poor have responded to the worsening waste disposal problems.

17.2 Pollution in the Metropolis

17.2.1 Solid Waste

The solid waste problems in Metro Manila are similar to those encountered in most cities in developing countries (Schertenleib, 1993). Lack of garbage collection, and disease laden open dump sites, continue to be the main problems. The amount of solid waste generated in has increased over the years (ANAWIM, 1989, Presidential Task Force on Waste Management, 1993 in IBON, 1994). Nearly a decade ago it was estimated that the total volume of solid waste produced daily was around 3,000 tons per day (ANAWIM, 1989). Currently, it is estimated that Metro Manila generates a total of 5,440 tons of solid waste per day (Presidential Task Force on Waste Management as cited in IBON, 1994), which translates to 0.69 kg/capita per/day.

Table 17.1 Total Domestic Waste Produced, 1993 (in tons per day)

Type of waste	Volume	Percent
Residential	2,655	48.81
Market	702	12.90
Commercial	299	5.50
Industrial	316	5.81
Construction and demolition	60	1.10
Street waste	1,000	18.38
Institutional	283	5.20
Other wastes	125	2.30
Total	5,440	100.00

Source: Presidential Task Force on Waste Management, Integrated National Solid Waste
    Management System Framework, 1993, in IBON, 1994).

Figures reported on the volume of waste collected per day are conflicting. ANAWIM (1989) cited a De la Sale University study which states that 70% of the total volume of waste generated daily is collected and the remaining 30% is either recycled, burned or disposed of in open sewers and creeks in Metro Manila. Douglass (1992) reports that less than half of the solid waste generated is collected and hauled to dump sites. Lastly, IBON (1994) reports that as much as 4,624 tons or 85% of the total solid waste is collected by both government and private sector. If the most current figures cited are true, then it may be assumed that there must have been some radical improvement in the garbage collection service in Metro Manila in recent years. Past trends in garbage collection however show that the efficiency of this service has been declining from the mid 1980s (ANAWIM, 1989). For instance it was cited in the same report that the volume of garbage collection in 1988 was down by two percent from 1987 figures.

The main government body responsible for solid waste management is the Metro Manila Authority (MMA). MMA is a manager-council type organisation with jurisdiction over the delivery of basic services requiring coordination and direction, including solid waste management (Passe, 1993). Solid waste is collected by garbage collection trucks maintained and operated by the MMA or by private hauliers contracted by the MMA (IBON, 1994, Passe, 1993). A significant proportion of waste collection is consigned to private contractors. There are 43 contractors who operate a total number of 432 dump trucks, while the MMA operates 139 garbage collection vehicles (IBON 1994).

Collection is generally carried out by workers who pick up refuse containers from the houses, street curbs, or at designated collection points (Passe, 1993). Street cleaners or sweepers are also hired by the MMA to collect garbage from public areas such as markets for pick up by garbage collection trucks (Passe, 1993). Not all of Metro Manila's population are able to benefit from this service. As seen from figures reported by the World bank (1995), not all of households in Metro Manila are served by the garbage collection system run by the MMA. Figures on Table 17.2, show access to waste disposal by various income groups in Metro Manila.

Table 17.2   Percentage of Population with Access to Solid Waste Disposal

	National Capital Region		
Income Bracket	*Lowest 30%*	*31-50%*	*>50%*
Regular collection	9	68	74
No service	91	32	26

Source: Staff calculations from NEDA and Herrin and Racelis (1994) as cited in World Bank Report No. 14933 - Philippines.

Problems Associated with Solid Waste Management

Garbage collection is supposed to be conducted daily. Areas served by garbage collection services cover most residential areas, commercial or industrial establishments and institutions in Metro Manila (Passe, 1993). This service is generally inadequate or absent in peripheral and depressed areas (Passe, 1993; ANAWIM, 1989; Personal communication). Passe (1993) attributes the absence of waste collection service in slum areas to the inaccessibility of these areas because of narrow streets, and to the fewer recyclable components of waste, which means it is of less value.

For lower income households garbage collection is a matter of "now you see it now you don't". Garbage collection service becomes more regular towards the Christmas season, when the garbage collection crew can ask for a tip. Uncollected garbage generally accumulates and decomposes in vacant lots, road sides or gets dumped in rivers and canals. In 1989, the Metro Manila Commission governor estimated that more than 47 truck loads of garbage are thrown into these waterways daily (ANAWIM, 1989). It has contributed greatly to the high levels of pollution in these waterways (South, 1997; Florentino-Hofilena, 1994; ANAWIM, 1989; Ilog ko Irog KO, 1989).

Key obstacles to the final resolution of the garbage problem cited in ANAWIM's reports are: financial, administrative and technical constraints. There is inadequate budgetary allocation for garbage collection (Passe, 1993; ANAWIM 1989). In 1986, contractors threatened to stop their garbage collection operations unless the MMA paid its P74 - M debt to them (ANAWIM). For a number of years the MMA has aired the difficulty of paying the garbage collectors in full. There is inadequate budgetary for the maintenance of collection vehicles: most are old or obsolete while the newer ones lack the necessary spare parts.

Efficiency of garbage collection is further hampered by the low wages of the collection crew and corruption. To augment low wages, collection crews sort recyclables from garbage collected and then sell these to waste dealers (Pers. communication). Sorting of recyclables increases the official collection time and affects the collection efficiency. Since garbage collection trucks and the collection crew of private contractors are paid on a per trip basis, some of them demand payment for garbage collection trips which they have not conducted. This is because so much time is consumed in sorting recyclables that they are unable to finish their collection rota.

MMA's funds come from contributions of seventeen local government units within its boundaries. Many of these local government units are unwilling to pay their mandatory contributions and consequently place strains on the MMA's ability to deliver the much needed basic services. This problem is aggravated by the enactment of the Local Government Code of 1991. This Code provides that the management and collection of solid waste are devolved to Local Government Units (LGUs). Most of the LGUs have signed a Memorandum of Agreement with the regional authority wherein the collection and disposal of solid waste will be handled by local government units

(Passe, 1993). This is expected to create more problems for the MMA.

17.2.2 Role of the Informal Sector

Collection of garbage is not solely administered by the formal sector. Government authorities however, fail to recognise and give credit to the role and contributions of the informal sector in solid waste collection and disposal. Although there are no available statistical figures as to the extent of the contribution of the informal sector to solid waste collection and disposal in the Metropolis, it is well known that there are thousands of scavengers who rely on collection of solid waste and in the recovery of recyclable materials as their means of livelihood.

Most low income families recycle some of their household wastes. These households use organic wastes such as leftover food and some kitchen waste as feed for their domesticated animals (Pers. communication). Other households operate composting pits and use resulting compost for gardening purposes.

17.2.3 Disposal of Solid Waste

At present there are 5 open dump sites, one transfer point and two sanitary landfills which serve the population in Metro Manila. Most of these dump sites are already filled to capacity or overflowing (IBON, 1994; ANAWIM 1989). Since the 1950s, most solid waste collected was disposed of in open dump sites. Open dumpsites are regarded as eyesores and are also considered unsanitary and hazardous to health. Because of these dangers the government has long drawn out in the Integrated Solid Waste Management Plan (ISWMP) the plan to close the open dump sites and to eventually replace them with the more modern sanitary land fills. Of the remaining open dump sites, those located in Paranaque and Muntinlupa are already scheduled for closure (IBON, 1994).

After several attempts, the government has recently succeeded in eventually closing down and levelling off the infamous Smokey Mountain[1] . The closure of the Smokey mountain was speeded in conjunction with the present government's clean-up and beautification efforts in time for the Asia-Pacific Economic Conference hosted by the Philippine government. All of the resident scavengers and junk shop owners who used to live on the Smokey Mountain have either been moved to government showcase housing or relocated to other areas. (KMU Correspondence, 1996) Following the closure of the

---

1 *A vast tip of waste that was continually smouldering with deep fires. Despite noxious smoke and gases, scavengers continued to work the tip.*

Smokey Mountain, waste collection trucks have been using the Payatas dumpsite as the alternative dumping ground. Payatas is fast becoming known as the Smokey Valley (ANAWIM, 1989). Like the former Smokey Mountain, thousands of scavengers eke out a living there. Local residents who live in subdivisions surrounding the Payatas dump site have been demanding for its closure due to health hazards associated with open dump sites (IBON, 1994). The residents claim that waste dumped in the Smokey Valley consists of toxic and industrial waste such as sewage sludge, toxic chemical wastes and expired medicinal wastes. They also raised its potential for contaminating the nearby La Mesa Dam which provides drinking water for the population of the Metropolis (IBON, 1994; ANAWIM 1989).

17.2.4 Hazardous Waste

Another growing concern at present is the disposal of hazardous waste, specifically the infectious wastes generated by hospitals and clinics in the Metropolis. There are existing ordinances and regulations for disposal of these types of wastes, but they are not properly enforced (Health Alert, 1997). Most hospitals in Metro Manila use the open dump sites mainly to dispose of dispose their general waste (domestic, non infectious and packaging). However there are some hospitals which dispose of their pathological wastes though the same methods (IBON, 1994). Recently, the Metro Manila Development Authority operations chief has been quoted in saying that "hospital waste are either discharged in public land fills in San Mateo (Rizal) and Carmona (Cavite) or are burned in open pits inside hospital compounds. Such practice may contaminate surface and ground water with infectious waste" (HAIN, 1997). Some hospitals have already been prosecuted for violating existing regulations (HAIN, 1997). It is necessary therefore that more effective monitoring and enforcement procedures are put into place so that these forms of hazardous wastes and any other forms of toxic wastes for that matter do not find their way into the open dump sites.

17.3 River and Coastal Water Pollution

The pollution of the rivers and coastal waters of Manila Bay has become an increasing concern for both government authorities and residents of the Metropolis. The importance of Manila Bay's waters lie in the fact that it is one of the major fishing grounds and the major aquaculture site for mussels, oysters and prawns. It is also the site of the biggest domestic and international shipping ports in the country. Pollution of these waters come from two main sources: domestic waste and industrial wastes. Most untreated domestic sewage are discharged directly or indirectly into Manila Bay's waters. No less than 85% of the establishments and houses flush untreated domestic sewage and waste waters into open canals and waterways, while only 15 % are served by sewers or have their own septic tanks (Environmental Management Bureau, 1989; Robles, 1988 cited in Jimenez and Velasquez, 1989).

In addition to untreated sewage, other pollutants are also dumped into the rivers and eventually drained into Manila Bay. The deficiency in the solid waste collection service means that most uncollected waste find its way into these waterways. Agricultural run-off and chemicals used in inland aquaculture also contribute to polluting these waters. Likewise, untreated industrial effluents are generally directly discharged into rivers by industries lining the stretch of the river banks.

The major rivers in Metro Manila are already biologically dead. The Pasig River for instance is regarded as "an open sewer, a stinking dumpsite and as waste depository not only of 820 industrial factories along its bank but also of the 70,000 urban poor dwellers whose houses line its length" (Florentino-Hofilena, 1994). The Navotas-Tullajan-Tenejeros river system also receives waste from 111 big industrial firms and 200 smaller industrial and commercial firms (Upstream, 1989 as cited in Hingco, 1989).

Other sources of pollutants come from domestic and international shipping ports and the large fishing port in Manila Bay. Pollutants are discharged from ships docking in the North and South Harbours and from commercial

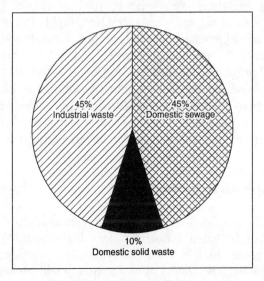

Figure 17.1 Sources of Pollution in Pasig River

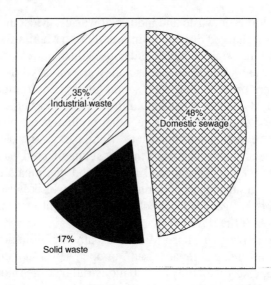

**Figure 17.2 Sources of Pollution in Navotas Tullajan Tenejeros River
System**

and medium-scale fishing vessels during routine operations or during dry
docking.

Oil spills have also occurred in Manila Bay's waters in recent years.

Dredging operations are another source of pollution. Dredging spoils
are mainly made up of silt and when taken from highly industrialised estuar-
ies, usually contain appreciable amounts of heavy metals and other accumulated contaminants. A section of the Navotas channel was dredged as part of
the river revival programme —Ilog ko, Irog ko—. Some 80,000 cubic metres
of silt was removed and the were reportedly dumped in Manila Bay (Upstream 1989 as cited in Hingco, 1989). The dredging of Pasig River in March
1990 removed 71,849 cubic metres of silt, which was also dumped some
five to seven kilometres offshore in Manila Bay (Bulletin Today, 1989 in
Hingco, 1989).

17.3.1 Trace Elements or Heavy Metals

These pollutants find their way into the rivers and coastal waters through
direct discharge of untreated industrial wastes. Jimenez and Velasquez (1989)
reported that there are high levels of heavy metals in the major river systems
in the Metro Manila. The results of an Environmental Management Bureau
(EMB) survey for the presence of heavy metals in coastal waters have shown

that the concentrations of heavy metals in parts of the Manila Bay are greater than the safe level limits set by the government authorities.

Table 17.3 Trace Metals in Manila Bay's Waters, 1989

	Cu *Copper*	*Pb* *Lead*	*Zn* *Zinc*	*Mn* *Manganese*	*Fe* *Iron*	*Ag* *Silver*	*Co* *Cobalt*	*Cd* *Cadmium*
1 metre depth level	0.2	0.8	0.43	0.6	1.7	0.05	24	0.1
Safe levels for marine waters	0.02	0.05	-	-	-	0.05	-	0.01

EMB Admin. Order No. 34[2]
Source of data: Environmental Management Bureau, 1989

Fish samples taken from the Bay reveal also that these contain significant concentrations of heavy metals such as Mercury, Cadmium Zinc and Copper in their liver and muscle tissues. This EMB survey have shown that the Hg concentration in fish liver and muscle tissues for various fish species, exceeds the FAO limits set for Hg concentrations in marine organisms. The concentration of Hg in various fish samples range from 2.5X to 8X greater the safe limits set.

Table 17.4   Selected Metal Concentrations in Fish Liver and Muscle Tissues (in ppm), 1983

Species	*Hg*	*Cd*	*Zn*	*Cu*
Epinephelus tauvina	0.11	0.72	15.95	21.93
Eleutheromena tetradactylum	0.16	0.59	92.00	46.60
Lutjanus lutjanus	0.10	0.30	85.15	39.81
Epinephelus fasciatus	0.05	0.12	75.89	3.91

FAO limits for Hg in marine organism = 0.02 - 0.05 ppm
Source of data: Environmental Management Bureau, 1983

Up to the present, there has been no reported incident of heavy metal poisoning from the ingestion of contaminated fish and shellfish taken from

---

2 *Based on this document, the values safe level limits set for heavy metals are the maximum concentrations of these elements in marine and coastal waters for it to be safe for the propagation and harvesting of shellfish, commercial and sustenance fishing and for bathing and recreational purposes.*

Manila Bay. It is important however to note that most marine organisms like algae, molluscs, seaweed and fish are able to accumulate significant concentrations of heavy metals present in the waters before exhibiting any signs of toxicity to these elements (UNEP, 1985). Molluscs are able to accumulate high concentrations of these heavy metals in their bodies. In fish these accumulate in the liver, gills and fin tissues, spleen and gut and sometimes in muscle tissues. Shrimp and crustaceans do not appear to bio-accumulate these trace metals. The bio-accumulation of these heavy metals in most marine organisms, can therefore pose serious health risks in the long term for those who consume contaminated fish.

Studies have also shown that heavy metals are present in surface and core sediments in Manila Bay and in surface sediments from inflowing rivers (EMB, 1983). Prudente et. al (1993) report highly fluctuating concentrations of Pb, Cd, Zn and Cu in surface sediments, with generally higher concentrations of these elements in riverine sediments as compared with marine sediments. Data from the same study also revealed elevated values for Pb and Cd in comparison to metal concentration levels in sediments obtained from other areas in the world.

17.3.2 Pesticides

Pollution due to extensive use of pesticides in surrounding farming communities add to the pollution of coastal water of the rivers. Jimenez and Velasquez (1989) have shown in their report that there is varying concentrations of levels pesticides in waters of three selected river systems in Metro Manila. Results of sampling surveys conducted by the EMB in 1983, have also revealed that pesticides were found in the livers of various fish species (common names: grouper, hairtail, whiting and mackerel) samples taken from the Bay. Pesticides found in fish samples are benzene hexachloride (BHC), Dieldrin and Aldrin. The use of these substances is banned in many first world countries (Clark, 1997)

17.3.3 Coliform Bacteria

The level of sewage contamination is reflected in the number of Coliform bacteria found in waters. In the absence of adequate sewage treatment facilities, it is not surprising that water samples taken from the Bay have shown high levels of sewage contamination.

These very high levels of Coliform bacteria present in coastal waters is a great cause for concern in terms of recreational use of the waters and for those who rely on the extraction and harvesting of marine products.

Table 17.5   Coliform Bacteria Counts in Three Sampling Stations in Manila Bay, 1989

Stations	Coliform count MPN/100 ml	
	Total	*Faecal*
Navotas	17,000,000	17,000,000
Bacoor	920,000	240,000
Luneta	460,000	330,000

Limits for safe bathing: 1000 MPN/100 ml
Source of data: Environmental Management Bureau

17.3.4 Red Tide

The input of large quantities of decaying organic matter, nitrates and phosphates in sewage serve to enhance conditions for development of red tides (Clark, 1997). Red tide is the red discoloration of the sea due to a bloom or proliferation of a dinoflagellate called *Pyridinium bahamensis var compresa*. Red tide has detrimental effects as it produces toxins that can result in illness or death otherwise known as Paralytic Shellfish Poisoning (PSP) to those who ingest shellfish or filterfeeders taken from areas where such blooms occur.

In the Philippines, red tide blooms has first reached public awareness in 1983, and since then there have been almost 2000 cases of PSP and over 80 deaths from the illness all over the country (PCHRD Health Advisory, 1997). Interviews with fishermen reveal that red tides in Manila Bay are regular occurrences. Actual figures and the records for frequency of red tide blooms are recorded by the Red Tide Task Force an inter-agency body headed by the Department of Agriculture.

In the first half of 1997 alone, there were at least two reported incidents of red tide blooms in Manila Bay. In January 22, 1997, a ban on harvesting of all types of shellfish from Manila Bay was imposed by the Red Tide Task Force when routine monitoring of the waters in the Bay showed that there were very high levels of micro-organisms causing PSP. Tests conducted on waters off Cavite showed levels between 129 - 56,404 cells/ltr of sea water (Health Alert, 1997). The tolerable level is 5 cells/ltr of sea water. Further tests showed that the red tide bloom spread to other parts of Manila Bay i.e. waters in Navotas and Bulacan. Information on the total number of individuals who suffered from PSP in Metro Manila over the years is currently not available. During the most recent red tide bloom in Manila Bay in

June this year, as many as 90 people have fallen ill and 10 others have died from PSP (Health Alert, 1997).

17.4   Government's Response to the Waste Disposal Problem

17.4.1 Integrated Solid Waste Management Plan (ISWMP)

Addressing the solid waste management problem from the time of the Marcos government up to the present, has remained a challenge for local government authorities who aim to improve the situation in the Metropolis. It was only during the Aquino administration when the garbage problem was included in the government's top agenda. In an attempt to address this prob-lem, the former President Aquino created the Presidential Task Force on Waste Management through the Memorandum Circular No. 30 dated No-vember 2, 1987 (ANAWIM, 1989). This body was tasked with formulating an Integrated Solid Waste Management Plan (ISWMP) for Metro Manila with the Metro Manila Commission (MMC)as the lead agency. A technical com-mittee on solid waste management was organised and another committee was mandated to formulate a viable programme for the scavengers who will be affected by the ISWMP was also formed (ANAWIM, 1989).

The ISWMP intended to achieve 100% efficiency in solid waste man-agement within four years of its implementation. The programme also aimed to level the open dump sites serving Metro Manila, and put into place an alternative solid waste collection and disposal system (ANAWIM, 1989). The existing mountains of decomposing garbage will be replaced by a more modern land fill system which will be located outside of the Metropolis. With this plan, the MMC also intended to set up five transfer stations where gar-bage will be collected for delivery to land fill sites. Open dump trucks were to be replaced with the more modern compactor trucks to complement the intended new disposal system.

The efforts and programmes of the of the previous government to ad-dress the solid waste management problem in Metro Manila appears to have had limited success. Garbage collection remains a major problem with ma-jority of the lower income communities not having access to formally es-tablished waste collection service (pers. communication; World Bank, 1995). The government is also faced with more problems in its search for appropri-ate areas for the disposal of solid waste as a consequence of the "not in my backyard" attitude. Due to the image associated with existing open dump sites— odours, smoke , dust etc.— government authorities are faced with the difficulty of finding new landfill sites which are acceptable to the public and which are located at a reasonable distance from the collection area (Passe, 1993; Schertenleib, 1993). The present land fill sites are 20-40km. from the central collection area. This results in high transfer and transportation costs as well as the need for additional investments in infrastructure (Schertenleib, 1993).

As intended in the ISWMP, the present government has eventually succeeded in finally closing down and levelling off the Smokey Mountain despite protests of thousands of scavengers who depended on garbage dumped there for income. Three thousand families who used to live in the Smokey mountain have been relocated. Some were provided temporary housing near the former dumpsite with the promise that they will eventually be awarded permanent housing once the redevelopment of the area and housing construction are completed. Others were relocated to nearby provinces. The government had also promised that these scavengers will be trained for new skills and provided with alternative sources of livelihood. The scavengers however have no faith in what they believe to be empty promises of the government.

17.4.2 Pasig River Rehabilitation Project (PRRP)

The present government is responsible for the much publicised Pasig River Rehabilitation Project This project aims mainly to improve the river's water quality the environmental conditions along the banks of the river (Florentino-Hofilena, 1994). Through this project the government hopes to redevelop the river bank area for commercial and residential purposes and to also revive tourism in the area (South, 1997). This initiative was started in 1992, and is a jointly financed project of the Philippine government and the government of Denmark and by the private sector (Florentino-Hofilena, 1994).

Through this project the government hopes to relocate the squatter communities lining the banks of the river (South, 1997) The proposal has been severely criticised by Non Governmental Organisations (NGOs) working with urban poor communities in the Pasig River area, as the intended relocation sites for these squatters are regarded as unfit for human habitation and as too far from the city to be a reasonable alternative residential area for the squatters (South, 1997).

The NGO CO-TRAIN has been working towards keeping the squatters from being evicted by organising communities to protect the Pasig River through alternative environmental programmes, but say that the government has not acknowledged these programmes and has not kept its promise to relocate communities to areas nearby their original homes (South, 1997).

17.5 Response of the Informal Sector to Waste Disposal Problem

17.5.1 Scavenging for Precious Waste

In 1994, it was estimated that as many as 50,000 individuals earn a living from scavenging in these open dumpsites. (IBON, 1994). And prior the closure of the Smokey Mountain, no less than 3,000 families lived on that huge mound of garbage and relied mainly on scavenging as their primary source of income.

Various groups of individuals are involved in this complex waste economy. Scavengers are classified into various groups: the itinerant scavengers, collection crew scavengers and the dump site scavengers (IBON, 1994). Itinerant scavengers are those roam the streets and retrieve recyclable materials with resale value from garbage cans or vacant lots dumped with thrash (IBON, 1994). In areas where waste collection service is deficient or absent, itinerant scavengers have provided this service to residents (Personal communication). Some household owners have actually to pay them a fee for their garbage to be collected. These scavengers sort the recyclable materials from the "waste" and sell the former to waste dealers or junk shop owners. There are also those scavengers who sift through household garbage before it is eventually collected by waste collection trucks.

In one of the Barangays in Tondo, there is a group of scavengers who specialise in collecting the garbage produced by various fast food chains in the Metropolis. They sort the recyclable materials- i.e. disposable or plastic cups, paper plates, spoons and forks separate these from leftover food portions. The former are sold to junk shops while the scrap food is generally used to make up the daily meals of the scavengers and their families. Sometimes these are repacked and then sold in markets, again for consumption of very low income households.

The collection crew scavengers— are those who are part of the formal waste collection service. They separate recyclable materials while collecting garbage from residential areas and later sell these to junk shop owners. And lastly, the dump site scavengers, are those who retrieve materials of value from dump sites.

Out of the total 5440 tons of waste generated daily in Metro Manila, 10% of these waste are either reused or recycled (IBON, 1994). It is not known however which type/s of solid waste fall into this category and who are those responsible for or involved in recycling of these wastes. There is also no available information on the contribution of the various types of scavengers to recovery of recyclable materials. The work of scavengers complements the deficient waste collection service while at the same time it provides a source of income for one of the poorest sectors in urban areas. Despite this fact many scavengers end up being prosecuted and fined by local government authorities for collecting recyclables from household garbage.

17.5.2 The "Non-Conventional" Approach

Furedy (1992) defines the non-conventional approach to solid waste management as those small scale, community-level initiatives that go beyond clean-ups and community efforts designed to improve conventional system. These projects have some general and ecological goals, and the potential to change the simple collect-transport -dump view of waste services.

One project which falls under this category is the San Juan Linis Ganda project in Metro Manila, as described by Furedy (1992). This is a community-based source separation project, started and initiated by the Metro Manila Council of Women Balikatan Movement (MMWBM) in 1983. This project developed as a result of a growing concern about the increasing quantities of wastes, and the deterioration of collection and cleaning services (Furedy, 1993). This project aimed to improve the collection of recylables as part of a solid waste reduction strategy. The collection and trading of these recyclable materials is conducted through existing waste dealers. By 1992, as many as 60% of the 18,000 household in the area supported the project by separating their waste and by selling these to the collectors. It was estimated then through this project that as much as 50 tons of recyclables were recovered per month for most of the year.

This project has eventually gained the support of local government authorities and is currently being replicated in many other areas in Metro Manila. So far 17 co-operatives organised with a total of 890 waste dealers or junk shop owners as members who employ more than 1500 waste collectors or eco-aids (Camacho, 1997).

17.5.3 The Urban Social Movement Vis-à-Vis the People's Response to Waste Disposal Problems

The organised urban poor communities in Metro Manila have a long history of fighting for the improvement of their quality of life and living conditions, and in bringing issues which affect their lives to the attention of a broader audience. However, the deterioration of the local urban environment due to problems in waste disposal has not been part of the recent agenda of the urban social movement.

Community organising work among the urban poor of Metro Manila began in the late 1960's. Tondo, the largest slum area in Metro Manila and possibly in Southeast Asia was the birthplace of the first and possibly one of the largest and most militant urban poor organisations in the country. Until early 1970s, the goals of urban poor organisations focused mainly on improving the quality of life and general environmental conditions in the local area through self-help and self-organisation and in gaining tenure to land they have occupied (see Ruland, 1984). Priority was given to immediate community issues, through negotiations and confrontations with authorities (Van Naerssen, 1989). The focus on the immediate improvement of the environment has gained urban poor groups the broad support in their communities (Van Naerssen, 1989). In its early days the urban poor organisations had no clear ideology. They were however closely linked with and supported by socially conscious church groups and social workers (Ruland, 1984).

Eight years of Martial law and oppression of the urban poor organisations had transformed the nature of the urban social movement in Metro Manila. Repression of community organisations had a profound influence on the character and ideology of urban poor groups (Van Naerssen, 1989). It was during this period that their initial goal of improving living conditions through self help projects was abandoned, and their activities were limited to political struggle (Ruland, 1984; Van Naerssen, 1989). This change was brought about by the realisation that the demands would only be fulfilled when the authoritarian Marcos regime was overthrown. Consequently, the demands of the urban poor expanded to include the political demands of the broader Philippine left .e.g. nationalisation of basic industries, genuine agrarian reform. Squatters not only confronted the national government but also challenged international power structures which maintains the Philippines' dependency and causes widespread poverty (Van Naerssen, 1989).

The change in government during the time of President Aquino did not lead to any substantial change in urban policy nor to the quality of life of the urban poor (Van Naerssen, 1989). This fact plus the continued demolition of squatter colonies disillusioned the urban poor organisations which expected that a change in government would lead to a substantial change in urban policy. These circumstances have consequently reinforced the need for urban poor organisations to pursue the political nature of their struggle. The struggle to achieve structural reforms based on an analysis that the problems of the urban poor are firmly rooted in the structure of an underdeveloped nation within a world capitalist system (Van Naerssen, 1989). Based on this analysis the struggle of the urban poor organisations is not distinct from the wider political movement in the country.

17.6 Conclusions: Political Ecology and Ecological Politics

Thus the examination of the problems of waste disposal in the Philippines has widened out to concern about good governance. Without good governance and proper representation the urban poor can see little alternative to their current predicament. But even if the agenda of the urban social movements has drifted away from environmental issues, the significance of attaining local sustainable development will not go away. The degree to which the squalor of waste accumulation and pollution directly impact on the poor and the rich may vary in the short term, but in the long term all sectors of the economy may suffer from the destruction of renewable resources and increased health hazards. Ecology will re-insert itself in politics.

References

Azanza-Corrales, R. and Martin M.C. (—) *Red Tide and Paralytic Shellfish Poisonings in the Philippines*. Newstep.

Camacho, L. (1997). Resource Recovery Programme in Metro Manila Philippines. In: http://www.hds.ait.ac.th/bestprac/metmanil.htm

Clark, R.B. (1997). *Marine Pollution*. Fourth edition. Clarendon Press.

Dirty cities, deadly cities (1994) In: http://web.unfpa.org/dirtbx96.html

Douglass, M. (1992). 'The political economy of urban poverty and environmental management in Asia: access empowerment and community based alternatives'. *Environment and Urbanization*, Vol.4, No.2, October 1992: 11-32.

Florentino-Hofilena, C. (1994) 'Reviving the Pasig River'. *Philippine Political Update*: 6-7.

Furedy, C. (1992). 'Garbage: exploring non-conventional options in Asian cities'. *Environment and Urbanization*, Vol. 4, No.2, October, 1992.

Furedy, C. (1989). 'Social considerations in solid waste management in Asian cities'. *Regional Development Dialogue*, Vol. 10, No. 3, pp 13-41, Autumn, 1989.

IBON (1994). 'Litter in the metropolis'. *IBON Facts and Figures*, Vol. 17, No. 3: 2-3

IBON (1994). 'Wealth from waste'. *IBON Facts and Figures*, Vol. 17, No.3, p. 5.

Health Advisory, Hazard Watch (1997). Heavy metal pollutants (cadmium, arsenic) in Apalit Pampanga. In:http://www.pcrd.dost.gov.ph/h-issues/hazard-watch/pollutant.html

Health Advisory, Hazard Watch (1997). Red Tide and Paralytic Shellfish Poisoning: What can the public do? In: http://www.pchrd.dost.gov.ph/h-issues/hazard-watch/bayanrt.html

Health Advisory, Hazard Watch (1997). Red Tide. In:http://www.pchrd.dost..gov.ph/h-issues/hazard-watch/redtide.html

Health Alert Online-February 22, 1997 (1997). Hospital waste. In: http://www.hain.org/healthalert/ha022297.html

Health Alert Online-February 7, 1997 (1997). Manila Bay shellfish ban lifted. In: http://www.hain.org/healthalert/ha020797.html

Health Alert On Line-January 31, 1997(1997). Poisoned fish:then and now. In: http://www.hain.org/healthalert/ha013197.html

Health Alert On Line-January 24, 1997 (1997). Ban on Manila Bay shellfish. In: http://www.hain.org/healthalert/ha012497.html

Health Alert Online-September 12, 1996 (1996). Cholera, Dengue Fever, Red Tide in Manila.

In: http://www.hain.org/health alert/sept12.html

Health Alert Online-October 18, 1996 (1996). Fish kill in Manila Bay. In: http://www.hain.org/healthalert/ha1018.html

Hingco, T.G. (1989). *Pollution in Manila Bay.* Tambuyog Research Series.

Jimenez, R.D. and Velasquez, A. (1989). 'Metropolitan Manila: a framework for its sustained development'. *Environment and Urbanization*, Vol.1, No.1, April 1989: 51-58.

KMU Correspondence January-February 1996 (1996) Smokey Mountain: A bloody demolition. In: http://www. pactok.net.au/docs/paul/Bsmokey.html

Passe, S. (1993).' Metropolitan Manila: Issues and future prospects of solid waste disposal'. *Regional Development Dialogue*, Vol. 14, No.3, Autumn, 1993: 177-187.

PCHRD Bulletin (1997). Red Tide. In: http://www.pchrd.dost.gov.ph/publications/bulletin/2qr-96/page07.html

Prudente, M.S., Hideki Ichihashi and Ryo Tatsukawa (1994). 'Heavy metal concentrations in sediments from Manila Bay, Philippines and inflowing rivers'. *Environmental Pollution*, 86, pp. 83-88.

South (1997). Face lift for Manila's river. p. 57, May, 1997.

Schuurman, F. and Van Naerssen, T. (1989). *Urban social movements in the Third World.* Routledge, London.

World Bank (1995). Philippines a strategy to fight poverty. Report No. 14933-PH.

18 Urban-Rural Health Differentials in Developing Regions

B.R.K. Sinha

18.1 Introduction

According to Kamble (1984) the standard of living of a nation is affected by the health of its people. Health, according to him, is not only an output of a society, and worthwhile in its own terms, it is also an asset for a community, a resource in the form of the energy, ability, talents and other mental and physical capabilities of normal functioning in a given environment.

We know that in many developing regions there are many health problems, related variously to poor nutrition and calorie intake, poor access to health and educational institutions, poor housing, lack of potable water, and poor sanitation. In addition high fertility rates put extra pressure on women, and on the economics of poor households. The results are high general morbidity and mortality rates, high infant mortality, a low life expectancy, and quite often the incapacity to work effectively. Previous researchers have also been able to show that there are major urban-rural health differentials (Clarke (1987), Akhtar and Learmonth (1986), Desai (1988)) and that usually the health of urban people is far better than that of rural people, despite the overcrowded and insanitary living conditions of many urban people. In most cases their income is higher than rural counterparts, and their diet is in consequence better.

18.2 Survey in West Bengal

This study is an empirical investigation within West Bengal to discover the kinds of urban-rural health inequalities that exist there, disaggregated by gender, class and age, and to assess the implications for health improvement strategies. The study is exclusively based on the primary survey data relating to quantitative and qualitative health indicators collected through questionnaire in 1995 from 100 households in Durgapur Industrial Township and from 310 households in Rampurhat rural Block selected on the basis of stratified random sampling technique.

An extensive set of variables was used, all directly or indirectly related to human health. These covered the incidence and type of disease(s) and ailments, blood pressure, dizziness; capacity to work a full 6 or 8 hour day, food intake – quantity, variety and frequency – housing quality, access to health facilities, and personal harmful habits (e.g. smoking, drinking), as well as education and income. All the health indicator variables were included in a single weighted index, with scores running 1 (Low) to 4 (High). The frequency distribution over these classes is used to calculate the average weighted health scores of different cross-tabulated groups. The original frequency data are shown in Tables 18.1 and 18.2. The weighted average scores are shown in Table 18.3. The pattern of results is very persuasive – but due note should be taken that in some categories the sample number is very small – for example there are only 3 urban male children under 4 years old in the survey. The sex ratios also indicate that there should be some degree of caution in interpreting some of the figures. For the urban sample (386 persons) the sex ratio is 1032 females per 1000 males, while for the rural sample (1404) the ratio is 798. Now the survey has been undertaken in North India, which is known for an overall deficiency of females – even so this is an exceptional value. The sex ratio is normally more balanced (but still adverse) in towns in North India – the favourable ratio here is noteworthy.

At the highest aggregate level, there is a difference in scores between the urban and rural populations – 3.58 as opposed to 3.13 (Table 18.3). These figures can be kept in mind as the respective bench marks around which the disaggregated figures will vary. Both populations are young – in keeping with India's population pyramid, the average ages for these populations are about 35 in the urban areas and about 27 in the rural areas. The difference

Table 18.1   Health Status of Surveyed Individuals, by Urban/Rural, Age and Sex, West Bengal Sample

age	0-4		5-14		15-34		35-59		>60		Total	
	Urban	Rural	Urban	Rural	Urban	Rural	Urban	Rural	Urban	Rural	Urban	Rural
Males												
VeryHigh		11	13	79	57	169	42	41	2	0	114	300
High	3	43	2	101	21	123	44	81	6	15	76	363
Medium		5		5		8		59		20		97
Low						1		14		6		21
Total	3	59	15	185	78	301	86	195	8	41	190	781
Females												
VeryHigh	4	14	10	46	55	108	39	12	1		109	180
High		42	5	87	26	134	55	54	1	1	87	318
Medium		3		3		7		68		14		95
Low				1		1		19		9		30
Total	4	59	15	137	81	250	94	153	2	24	196	623

Table 18.2   Health Status of Surveyed Individuals, by Urban/Rural, Caste Status and Sex, West Bengal Sample

age	0-4 Urban	0-4 Rural	5-14 Urban	5-14 Rural	15-34 Urban	15-34 Rural	35-59 Urban	35-59 Rural	>60 Urban	>60 Rural	Total Urban	Total Rural
Males	sc		st		obc		hc		others		total	
VeryHigh	12	104	2	6	2	79	97	36	1	75	114	300
High	4	130	3	79	3	89	63	20	3	45	76	363
Medium		28		23		28		5		13		97
Low		10		8		2				1		21
	16	272	5	116	5	198	160	61	4	134	190	781
Females	sc		st		obc		hc		others		total	
VeryHigh	2	62	2	6		42	104	20	1	50	109	180
High	5	111		67	2	77	74	20	6	43	87	318
Medium		33		18		20		8		16		95
Low		13		4		6				7		30
	7	219	2	95	2	145	178	48	7	116	196	623

Sc= Scheduled Caste, st=Scheduled Tribe, obc= Other Backward Castes, hc=High Caste

Table 18.3   Summary Weighted Average Health Scores by Urban/Rural, Age, Sex and Caste

	Total urban	rural	*Total* male	female	*Male* urban	rural	*Female* urban	rural
0-4	3.57	3.14	3.10	3.24	3.00	3.10	4.00	3.19
5-14	3.77	3.36	3.44	3.34	3.87	3.40	3.67	3.30
15-34	3.70	3.47	3.57	3.47	3.73	3.53	3.68	3.40
35-59	3.45	2.60	2.99	2.78	3.49	2.76	3.41	2.39
>60	3.30	2.02	2.39	1.81	3.25	2.22	3.50	1.67
total	3.58	3.13	3.28	3.16	3.60	3.21	3.56	3.04
scheduled caste	3.61	3.12	3.24	3.02	3.75	3.21	3.29	3.01
scheduled tribe	3.57	2.75	2.74	2.81	3.40	2.72	4.00	2.79
other backward castes	3.29	3.17	3.24	3.07	3.40	3.24	3.00	3.07
high castes	3.59	3.39	3.58	3.51	3.61	3.51	3.58	3.25
others (e.g. Muslim)	3.18	3.32	3.44	3.17	3.25	3.45	3.14	3.17
Total	3.58	3.13	3.28	3.16	3.60	3.21	3.56	3.04

may in part be explained by differences in mortality rates in the two sectors, but a greater factor must be the smaller average family size in urban areas – the urban pyramid does not have quite as wide a base. There is no significant difference between the average age of the female and male samples.

The overall urban-rural difference can be seen in the simple total scores - 3.58 and 3.13. This contrasts with the difference between males and females in aggregate – 3.28 versus 3.16. These figures show that though sex is a determinant of health (through a multiple of reasons from nurture to nature), the urban rural difference is greater.

At every age-level there is a disparity between urban and rural health values, though the disparity widens drastically in the two higher age groups (35-59 and > 60). In the youngest group there seems to be a disparity in favour of females – but after that there is a widening of the sex disparity with age in favour of males. This provokes speculation about the inherent toughness of females, but their long-term disadvantage in terms of nutrition etc.

The distinctions by social background show some interesting trends. In general there is a bias towards better health in urban areas, but not for Others (which includes many Muslims). The health of the male and female scheduled tribes in rural areas seems to be equal, but in urban areas the females seem healthier. (But note some samples are very small in some categories).

The composite picture suggests that the worst health will be suffered by elderly rural females – and so it is – 1.67 being the lowest figure in the table. The highest figure is for the youngest urban girls: but thereafter the best figures are for youthful urban males, followed by youthful urban females.

In sum, though sex, class and age have much to do with health, the greatest divide is between urban and rural areas.

18.3 Conclusion

The differences in health status of urban and rural people in West Bengal are accounted for in many ways. The most important contributory factors are that incomes are higher on average in urban areas, and access to food better. In addition, urban access to medical services and general education is much better.

This leaves the government with some difficult policy decisions. First, access to good jobs and good income has an obvious health impact. This means maximising the delivery of reasonably paid jobs – and these are to be created most easily in urban areas with services, transport and local demand.

Another advantage of urban population clusters is that it is cheaper and easier to deliver to them such services as health clinics and education. Everything suggests therefore that if the government is to maximise the marginal return on its social infrastructure investments, it should do so in urban areas. But the differences we have just highlighted in the health of people is one of the reason stimulating rural-urban migration. To stem this flow, the government should invest more in rural areas, to reduce the disparities, even if the marginal rate of return on capital might be a little lower.

References

Akhtar, Raise and Learmonth A.T.A. (1986) Geographical Aspect of Health and Disease in India, Concept Publishing House, New Delhi.

Desai,V. (1988) Rural Development: Issues and Problems, Vol. I, Himalayan Publishing House, Delhi.

Eyles, John (1987) The Geography of the National Health, Groom Helm, London.

Jayachandran, S. (1988) in Vidyanath, V. and Rao, R.R.M.(eds) Development of India's Resource Base, Pattern, Problems and Prospects, Gain Publishing House, Delhi.

Clarke, John. I. (1987) Population Geography, Pergamon Press, New York.

Kamble, N.D. (1984) Rural Health, Ashish Publishing House, New Delhi.

Mukherjee, B.M. (1986) 'Aging Members and Their Health in Changing Techno-Economic Condition', in Chaudhury, B.(ed.) Tribal Health: Socio-Cultural Dimensions, Inter-India Publications, New Delhi.

Pacione, M. (1988) The Geography of the Third World: Progress and Prospects, Routledge, London & New York.

Park, J.E. & Park, K. (1991) Preventive and Social Medicine, Banarsidas Bhanot Publishers, Jabalpur, India.

Raza, Moonis (1990) Education, Development and Society, Vikas Publishing House Pvt. Ltd., New Delhi.

Sinha, B.R.K. (1977) 'Human Resources Utilization in Dhanarua Block, Patna Dist., Bihar' (Unpublished Ph.D. thesis).

Smith, D.M. (1977) Human Geography: A welfare Approach, Edward Arnold Pub. Ltd.

Trewartha,G.T.; Robinson, A.H. and Hamond, R.H. (1967) Elements of Geography, Physical and Cultural, Mac Graw Hill Book Company, New York.

19 Spatial Patterns of Crime in Indian Cities

George Pomeroy, Ashok K. Dutt and Vandana Wadhwa

19.1 Introduction

In a seminal work, Louis Wirth (1938) pointed out that urbanism was not only characterised by the size, density, and diversity of cities, but also by anomie, moral degradation and deviance. In India, a study by Bhatnagar (1990) attributed increases in crime to the increase in urbanisation and industrialisation, which may cause family and cultural disorganisation.

Of the various studies conducted on the incidence of crime, only a small portion of them focus on spatial patterns (Pyle, 1974, Georges, 1978, Georges-Abeyie and Harries, 1980, Evans et al, 1992). Dutt et al (1979) conducted a district level analysis of crimes in India, which was a refinement of Nayer's (1975) state level analysis. The 1979 study confirmed the spread of violent crimes in North-Central India; which included parts of Punjab, Haryana, Madhaya Pradesh, all of Bihar, and all of Uttar Pradesh[1]. This north central area of India was designated by Dutt et al (1979) as an area of subculture of violence. Another study consisted of a city level analysis of crimes by Dutt and Venugopal (1983), which is the basis on which the present study identifies changes in the national crime pattern. The 1983 study used 1971 census and crime data to present a spatial pattern of crime among Indian cities. The study identified two distinctly separate areas of violent crimes in North Central India. Both of them lie in the area of the subculture of violence of the earlier study (Dutt et al, 1979), although one of them extended southwest into Rajasthan and Madhya Pradesh. The purpose of the present study is to provide a comparative scenario of the earlier 1983 study, using data averaged for the years 1988, 1989, and 1990. It also provides the shifts of change over the nineteen year period spanning these two points in time, i.e., 1971 to 1990.

19.2 Data Evaluation

The data set chosen for analysis consists of city-wise incident of cognizable crimes for 1988, 1989, and 1990. Collected by the Ministry of Home Affairs' National Crime Records Bureau, the particular variables used represent an assortment of both violent and non-violent serious crimes (Table

---

1 *West Bengal, Assam and Manipur were excluded from the violent crime region.*

19.1). There are sixteen total variables. Seventy-three cities are considered in the analysis (Map 19.1). Crime rates used in the analysis are based on 100,000 population for each crime type. Most of these cities have an estimated population greater than 500,000. The terminology of the variables is generally self-explanatory (i.e., theft is the act of stealing). However, dacoity is a term derived from Hindi word "dakoiti" and is defined as robbery committed with violence by a gang of five or more persons (Dutt and Venugopal, 1983).

The technique chosen for analysis is factor analysis, accompanied by several sets of maps illustrating the patterns of standardized descriptive scores

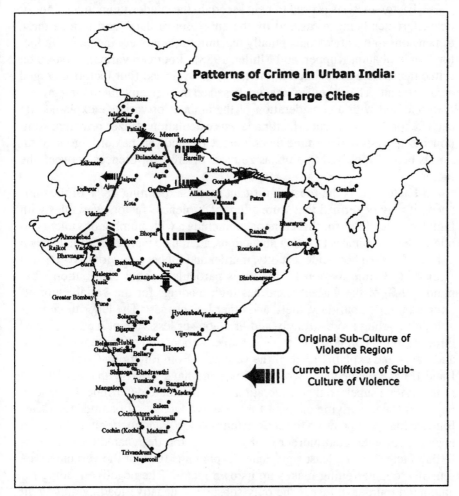

Map 19.1 Patterns of Crime in Urban India

("z" scores) and standardized factor scores. Factor analysis is used to help capture the underlying elements of criminal activity as indicated by the variables and to regionalize different sets of crime. Furthermore, and in addition to the stand-alone merits of these technique, the use of it allows us to meaningfully compare our results to previous work of Dutt and Venugopal (1983) and Dutt, et al, (1979) and assess any temporal changes.

19.3 Analysis

Factor analysis is used to help ascertain the "underlying dimensions or characteristics being measured by the entire set of data" and reduce these dimensions into "a few conceptually meaningful, relatively independent factors" (Kleinbaum, Kupper, and Muller, 1988). Fourteen variables, based on crime rates, were considered in the factor analysis and four factors emerged as significant. Their significance was based on their eigenvalues being greater than one and with a consideration of the amount of variance explained by each factor. This particular factor analysis calculation utilizes principal components analysis to determine the initial factors and varimax orthogonal rotation is being employed to emphasize more discrete differences between the factors.

Factor one is the most significant factor, explaining 28 % of the variance. It may be termed the "Subculture of Violence" factor. Variables with high factor loadings for this component include a wide number of violent and non-violent criminal acts - other abductions, attempted murder, criminal breach of trust, criminal homicide, dacoity, murder and robbery. Factor two - termed "Emerging Crime Region I" due to its particular spatial distribution - explains 19 % of the variance and has high loadings for the variables of attempted murder, burglary, theft, and other IPC crimes. The latter three variables all loading more strongly and of a non- or less violent nature. Factor three is largely composed of three variables - abduction of females, cheating, and riots - and explains 17 % of the variance. Both Emerging Crime Region I and II have elements of violent crimes and have specific spatial distributions. With a superficial consideration it is difficult to determine the general nature of the underlying element for these two factors. Loadings for factor four are high and positive for counterfeiting (+.90) and moderately high and negative for attempted murder (-.48). This factor, designated the "counterfeiting factor", is the least significant, explaining 10 % of the variance. Essentially, counterfeiting makes up its own factor. The negative loading for attempted murder in fact is the only substantial negative loading among all four factors.

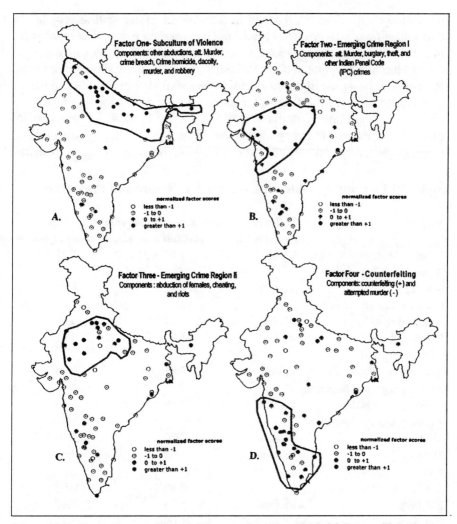

Map 19.2 Four Factor-Based Maps using the 1988-90 Data, Showing Distinct Regional Concentrations

When mapped, factor scores for each of the four factors reveal very striking patterns (Map 19.2). Factor one (Map 19.2.a), which explains the greatest amount of variation in the data and therefore is the most substantial component, shows very high factor scores in the region. This "subculture of violence" area corresponds, in part, to the findings obtained by Dutt and Venugopal (1983) in their examination of crime in Indian urban centres for 1971. The one notable difference is that this region of violence has become more widespread, now occupying the whole of the north Indian plain from the frontier with Pakistan through to the state of Assam with a very heavy concentration in western Uttar Pradesh, Haryana, and Bihar. The reasons for this diffusion of violence are discussed later in this paper. Factor two (Map 19.2.b) has a very regional concentration, with cities in Madhya Pradesh and Rajasthan scoring the highest. Factor three (Map 19.2.c) straddles the areas of concentration for the first two factors. Factor scores for this factor are highest in Rajasthan, Haryana and Western Uttar Pradesh. These two regions, may be termed "emerging crime regions I and II", for factors two and three, respectively. Factor four (Map 19.2.d) is the most unique in its distri-

Table 19.1 Crime Variables in Urban India, Nature and Prevalence

Variable	Violent / Non-Violent	Avg. Rate per 100,000	Percentage of Total Cognizable Crimes
Murder	Violent	4.47	1.21
Attempt to Commit Murder	Violent	4.42	1.22
Criminal Homicide not Amounting to Murder	Violent	0.57	0.16
Rape	Violent	1.50	0.42
Kidnapping and Abduction - Total	Violent	3.81	1.05
Kidnapping and Abduction of Women and Girls	Violent	3.09	0.85
Kidnapping and Abduction of Others	Violent	0.70	0.19
Dacoity	Violent	1.09	0.30
Preparation and Assembly for Dacoity		0.19	0.05
Robbery	Violent	5.36	1.47
Burglary		36.04	9.91
Theft		100.23	27.55
Riots	Violent	19.90	5.47
Criminal Breach of Trust		4.87	1.34
Cheating		9.00	2.48
Counterfeiting		1.06	0.29
Other Indian Penal Code Crimes		177.56	48.82
Total Cognizable Crimes	- - -	363.74	100.00

Source: National Crime Records Bureau, *Crime in India*, 1988-1990.

bution. The highest scores for this factor are for those larger cities south of the two urban giants of Bombay (now Mumbai) and Hyderabad. In the 1983 study of Dutt and Venugopal, counterfeiting was also a discrete factor, with concentrations in some south Indian cities, but the present study finds an enlarged areal spread of this factor. Now it is primarily concentrated in a large area of south India, where the rate of murder is considerably lower.

19.4   The Subculture of Violence: An Expanding Phenomena?

Previous research established that a subculture of violence exists through a large portion of north India and speculated about several possible explanations for this. These explanations include 1) the 'lack of long-continued and intrinsically ingrained civic institutions'; 2) a historical - traditional culture of dacoity and thuggery; 3) a 'vacuum of cultural and religious leadership'

Table 19.2   Crimes in Urban India: Factor Analysis: Variables Used, Rotated Component Matrix and Significance

Variable	*Factor*			
	1	*2*	*3*	*4*
Abduction of Others	0.77	0.05	0.19	0.08
Criminal Homicide	0.80	-0.26	-0.03	-0.19
Breach of Trust	0.58	0.02	0.46	0.05
Dacoity	0.79	0.15	0.24	-0.06
Robbery	0.76	0.39	0.07	-0.14
Murder	0.84	0.26	0.01	0.02
Attempted Murder	0.43	0.43	0.13	-0.48
Burglary	0.20	0.85	0.24	0.11
Other Indian Penal Code Crimes	-0.06	0.90	0.02	0.09
Theft	0.21	0.72	0.40	-0.05
Abduction of Females	0.44	0.16	0.72	-0.29
Cheating	0.12	0.22	0.82	0.32
Riots	-0.01	0.16	0.82	-0.15
Counterfeiting	0.03	0.16	-0.07	0.90
Eigenvalue	5.41	2.33	1.42	1.20
Variance Explained % (after extraction)	28.24	19.15	17.09	9.58

* based on rates per 100,000 persons.
Source: National Crime Records Bureau, *Crime in India*, 1988-1990.

because of the lack of a stable presence of Hindu élites who had been crushed by Moslem rule in previous centuries; 4) a disaffection with Hindu élites who had been co-opted by the British colonial administration, with a resultant turn toward charismatic "rustic" leaders of questionable moral fibre; and 5) absence of a well defined "sequence of castes" resulting in defective patterns of social interaction (Dutt and Venugopal, 1983:223-224).

Examining the areas where factors one, two, and three of the present study are prevalent (Map 19.1, 19.2), we find that the subculture of violence may be expanding geographically. The first expansion leading to the coalescence of the two sub-culture of violence regions of the Ganges Valley found in previous studies. The second expansion is to the west and southwest; diffusing into central and southern Madhya Pradesh, portions of Rajasthan and Gujarat, and as far south as parts of Maharashtra. Perhaps elements of social order and stability in this expanded and contiguous region are deteriorating. Certainly, several trends and notable events over the last several years illustrate or point to such a deterioration of the social order.

19.5 Conclusion

As mentioned earlier in the chapter, this study reveals that the north-central subculture of violence area has not only intensified, but also spread southwestwards, embracing parts of Rajasthan, Gujarat, Maharashtra, and Madhya Pradesh. Dutt and Venugopal's (1983) study revealed existence of violent crimes in two separate sub-areas of the north-central violent subculture region. However, this study found that these areas have coalesced. During 1971-1990, the time span between these studies, the cause for the intensification and spread of violent crime in this area can be primarily attributed to political factors. They include both protection of criminal elements and extensive use of criminals by politicians. Secondary factors such as terrorist activities, and communal conflicts involving religion and caste, operate under the umbrella of political manoeuvring and unrest. It will be interesting when a future researcher uses 2001 census data and crime data to find out the spatial characteristics and changes in the crime pattern.

References

Bhatnagar, R.R. (1990) *Crimes in India: Problems and Policy*. New Delhi: Ashish Publishing House.

Dutt, A.K., Noble, A.G., and Singh, H. (1979) "Is There a North-Central Subculture of Violence in India?" *The National Geographical Journal of India*. 25(2):101-111.

Dutt, A.K., and Venugopal, G. (1983) "Spatial Patterns of Crime Among Indian Cities" *Geoforum.* 14(2):223-233.

Evans, D.J., Fyfe, N.R., and Herbert, D.T. (eds.) (1992) *Crime, Policing, and Place: Essays in Environmental Criminology.* New York: Routledge.

Georges, D.E. (1978) *The Geography of Crime and Violence: A Spatial and Ecological Perspective.* Washington, D.C.: American Association of Geographers.

Georges-Abeyie, D.E., and Harries, K.D. (1980) *Crime: A Spatial Perspective.* New York: Columbia University Press.

Kleinbaum, David G., Lawrence L. Kupper, and Keith E. Muller (1988) *Applied Regression Analysis and Other Multivariable Methods.* 2nd ed. Belmont, California: Druxbury Press.

Ministry of Home Affairs (1988) *Crime in India, 1988.* New Delhi: Bureau of Police Research and Development.

Ministry of Home Affairs. (1989) *Crime in India, 1989.* New Delhi: Bureau of Police Research and Development.

Ministry of Home Affairs. (1990) *Crime in India, 1990.* New Delhi: Bureau of Police Research and Development.

Nayer, B.R. (1975) *Violence and crime in India: A Quantitative Study.* Delhi: MacMillan Company of India.

Pyle, G.F. (1974) *The Spatial Dynamics of Crime.* Chicago: The University of Chicago, Department of Geography, Research Paper 159.

Sukla, D. (1977) *Crime and Punishment in Ancient India: AD 300 to AD 1100.* New Delhi: Abhinav Publishing.

Wirth, L. (1938) "Urbanism as a Way of Life". *American Journal of Sociology.* 44(1):3-24.

PART III
MIGRATION

Editors' Notes to Part III
For no reason other than chance, this is the shortest Part of Volume II.
These two chapters nevertheless are very strong contributions on a
very important topic. The first by Cindy Fan and Youqin Huang shows
how migration in China is both controlled by the state – through its
system of urban passes – and not controlled – in that migration flows
from poor rural areas to wealthier rural areas in urban hinterlands. It
is also an important statement on women's opportunities and roles in
China. Pannell and Ma deal with the important topic of the role of
urbanisation and migration in affecting the ethnic composition of ter-
ritories. In any age in any country urbanisation has changed ethnic
distributions, and set off complex migration patterns. The state has
therefore always had the opportunity to steer these changes to alter the
political circumstances of different areas – with results that may be
either stabilising or destabilising.

20 Female Marriage Migration in China

C. Cindy Fan and Youqin Huang

20.1 Female Marriage Migration in China

Research on women's mobility has proliferated recently, as more attention is given to the role of gender in the migration process (Chant and Radcliffe 1992; Pedraza 1991; Ellis et al. 1996). The neoclassical perspective emphasizes the economic rationality of migrants, and argues that women, just like men, move in response to regional differentials in economic opportunities (e.g. Thadani and Todaro 1979). The structural approach, on the other hand, explains female migration in relation to transformations of regional and national economies and gendered segmentation of the labour market (e.g. Bennholdt-Thompson 1984; Sassen-Koob 1983). In addition to the above competing approaches, and from a more behavioural perspective, alternative studies examine not only the economic factors but also cultural constraints that shape female migration (e.g. Bourque and Warren 1981; Caplan 1985; Moser 1981). The household strategies approach emphasizes that migration can be used as a means of human resources allocation and risk diversification, mediated by gendered division of labour and power relations within the household (e.g. Wood 1981).

This structural approach facilitates the incorporation of historical, social and cultural perspectives for understanding the interlinkages between migration and gender, for examining the constraints and opportunities which influence the freedom and choices of prospective migrants, and for evaluating the role of agents in explaining migration (Ellis et al. 1996; Lim 1993; Ortiz 1996; Riley and Gardner 1993). But there are relatively few empirical studies that articulate how constraints, opportunities and agents interact to produce and shape female migration. This chapter aims at using a case study to highlight the importance of these factors and their interlinkages in female migration.

Studies on migration in China mostly lump men and women together, or treat gender as just one of many independent variables that explain migration differentials (e.g. Shen and Tong 1992; Zhang 1990). Yet structural forces differentially affect men and women and their migration experiences. Although the state has relaxed migration control since the mid-1980s, and many Chinese (women and men) have found their way to new employment opportunities in urban industrial areas, the bulk of peasant women from poorer areas remain disadvantaged in their mobility because of the household registration system (*hukou*) (Chan 1994; Cheng and Selden 1994), the underdeveloped labour market which affords fewer opportunities for non-hukou migrants (Knight and Song 1995), and the historically and generally low social status of women which undermines their access to education and chances for waged work. On the other hand, the economic reforms have widened the regional gap in development, intensified the push and pull forces of migration, motivated women to participate in long-distance migrations to desirable locations, and enabled various agents that play important roles in the formation of chain migration and a marriage market. Indeed, we argue that marriage is a means for achieving mobility, especially for women who lack access to other means of migration.

20.2 Marriage and Female Migration

Marriage is one of the most important events in the life cycle, and it is also an institution which imposes economic and social-cultural constraints on both women and men. In most societies, women are subject to a more demanding set of gendered expectations and responsibilities associated with marriage, and with their roles as wives and mothers. As tied movers, women's careers are often given a lower priority in household decision making, and marriage may provide "the mechanisms through which women become domestic labourers" (Fincher 1983). The notion of tied movers has dominated most studies on marriage migration, including studies of the relationship between marital status and propensity of migration (e.g. Ellis et al. 1996; Ortiz 1996).

There are two aspects to the relationship between marriage and migration - migration as a consequence of marriage; and marriage as a strategy for achieving migration or migration-related goals. Much of the existing research focuses on the former, and assumes a unidirectional relationship between marriage and migration, that is, migration is the result of marriage. Marriage as a strategy for women to achieving migration is rarely studied. One reason is the assumption that marriage is a social contract based on affection and mutual commitment, which downplays the pragmatic (e.g. economic) aspect of such an institution. In reality, the social-romantic and pragmatic facets of marriage are often intricately intertwined and difficult to be observed independently. Another reason is that the decisions for marriage and migration are also intertwined, so that it is very difficult to determine if marriage motivates migration or if the desire for migration induces marriage. This chapter highlights marriage as a strategy enabling women to achieve migration, in relation to structural factors which constrain and provide opportunities for women's mobility.

20.3   Women, Marriage and Migration in China

In China, marriage is a social institution that connotes directly pragmatic and economic values, such as continuation of the family line (Wolf 1972), increase of family labour (Croll 1984), formation of networks (Ebrey 1991), provision of old age security (Potter and Potter 1990) and transfer of resources (Croll 1984).   Before the 20th century, the labour, fertility and person of Chinese women were considered a property exchangeable in trans-actions, most notably during marriages (Croll 1984).   Under the patrilocal tradition, daughters will eventually move out and join the husbands' family, adding to the latter's labour resources.   Parents of sons are eager to recruit the labour of daughters-in-law, hence the motivation for early marriages (Croll 1987).   On the other hand, there is little incentive for the natal family to invest in daughters (Li 1994), since they will eventually leave the household, and since sons, rather than daughters, are expected to take care of the parents during their old age.   The belief that "daughters married out are like water spilled out" has led to persistent lower education among Chinese women.

Although "arranged marriages" have been outlawed by the Chinese Communist Party (1950 Marriage Law), proposals initiated by a third party (e.g. parents, go-betweeners), with the consent of the prospective bride and groom, remain the most popular form of marriages in rural China (Croll 1984; Shen 1996).   Underlying the persistence of the older generation's interven-tion is the deep-rooted notion and practice that marriage is a contract negoti-ated between two families, which involves monetary and material transfers but above all the transfer of rights over women and their labour. Marriage is a unique, perhaps the only, opportunity for the natal family to be compensated for raising a daughter.   The most direct compensation is in the form of brideprice, which is often negotiated between the older generations, and which may offer a   handsome return from the prospective groom's family.   This, combined with rising income in the countryside, has led to a revival of hefty brideprices and extravagant wedding celebrations (Honig and Hershatter 1988; Min and Eades 1995).

Plenty of evidence shows that gender inequality has not declined, de-spite Maoist policies which aimed at "liberating" women by increasing their labour force participation (Maurer-Fazio et al. 1997; Park 1992).   The Chi-nese Communist Party's articulation of inequalities exclusively through class, while viewing gender as peripheral to the proletarian struggle, has been suggested as one of the reasons why a large gender gap persists (Gilmartin et al. 1994; Park 1992). While peasant men may improve their social and economic mobilities by joining the military, going to school and becoming cadres, many Chinese women in the countryside, poor and uneducated, must resort to marriage to achieve upward social mobility and as a compensation for their lack of other opportunities (Bossen 1984; Honig and Hershatter 1988; Wang and Hu 1996, 287).

Traditionally, Chinese brides move over a short distance to join the husbands' family (Wang and Hu 1996, 283; Yang 1991; Zhuang and Zhang 1996). Typical marriages in rural areas involve a go-betweener or matchmaker who, when notified or observing that a woman or man is reaching "marriage-age," approaches the family about suitable candidates for a prospective spouse in the same village or in a village not too far away. A survey in the late 1980s found that most rural marriages did not exceed a 25 km radius (Renmin ribao 1989), and underscored the prominence of same-locality (same town or village) marriages.

Given the impetus to stay close to the natal family, and observations that rural households are motivated to find marriage partners locally, the large number of interprovincial female marriage migrants since the 1980s may seem an anomaly to the norm. According to the 1990 Census, marriage accounted for respectively 28.2% and 28.9% of intraprovincial and interprovincial female migrations between 1985 and 1990 (Table 20.1). While the magnitude of interprovincial female migration (1.4 million) was smaller than that of intraprovincial moves (3.1 million), as in the case of all types of migration,[1] marriage was indeed the leading reason for both interprovincial and intraprovincial female migrations, which suggests that distance is not as constraining in marriage migration as one might expect. The concentration of the origins and destinations of interprovincial female marriage migrants, and the distance between them, as will be shown in the empirical analysis, further underscore the prevalence of long-distance marriage migration to selected regions in China. Studies have shown that in some parts of China, female marriage migrants, many from distant provinces thousands of miles away, accounted for the bulk of in-migrants, and that their numbers have increased over time (Xu and Ye 1992; Wang 1992). This type of long-distance migration is a relatively new phenomenon (Shen 1996; Wang 1992; Yang 1991), which cannot be fully explained by the patrilocal tradition. We argue that it reflects macro structural forces which define unique sets of constraints and opportunities for the migrants and their spouses, and that at the same time various agents actively interact with these forces to produce large waves of

---

1 *The total numbers of interprovincial and intraprovincial female migrants were respectively 4.9 million and 11.2 million (Table 20.1).*

interprovincial female marriage migration.

Table 20.1 China: Reasons for Female Migration

	Intra-provinical		Inter-provincial	
	All	*Aged 15-29*	*All*	*Aged 15-29*
Total Number	11153000	7570000	4892700	3065600
		Percent		
Job Transfer	8.0	4.8	8.4	4.1
Job assignment	5.0	7.2	2.6	4.0
Industry/busines	15.1	17.8	16.6	21.2
Study,Training	11.6	16.9	6.5	10.2
Seek help from friends/relatives	11.7	6.2	14.7	8.9
Retirement	0.5	0.0	0.9	0.0
Joining family	14.5	6.8	16.3	8.4
Marriage	28.2	36.8	28.9	40.0
Other	5.4	3.5	5.1	3.2

20.4 Constraints, Opportunities and Agents

With special reference to female marriage migration, the following describes the structural factors in China and their changes since the reforms, which impose constraints on, while also opening up, new opportunities for women's mobility and various agents in the migration process.

20.4.1 Household Registration System (hukou)

The hukou system is a key institution for defining an individual's opportunities and socioeconomic position in China (Christiansen 1990; Cheng and Selden 1994). Hukou may refer to one's registration type or registration location. In terms of registration type, it bifurcates the nation into the non-agricultural (mostly urban) population that are heavily subsidized by the state (e.g. grain rationing, housing, medical care, pension, etc.), and the agricultural (mostly rural) population who have rights to farm but receive little state welfare or benefits. In terms of registration location, the hukou system resembles an "internal passport system" (Chan 1996), analogous to the green card for immigrants to the United States. Until the mid-1980s it tied Chinese peasants to their birth place - without a hukou in the destination place, a migrant is shut out from many desirable jobs (especially in the formal sector) and subsidised welfare benefits (e.g. housing, education) that are necessary for their survival. In the mind of most Chinese, hukou location and hukou classification not only define their general well being but also their status - non-agricultural hukou is superior to agricultural hukou; cities (shi) are superior to towns (zheng), and towns superior to villages (xiang).[2]

It is extremely difficult to upgrade one's hukou. Behind the government's strict control on hukou are the practical purposes of limiting rural-urban migration and of protecting the state from bankruptcy (if state subsidies were extended to all citizens).

Responding to the burgeoning agricultural labour surplus since the rural reforms, the state has relaxed its control over temporary migration, by allowing peasants to get "temporary residence permits" (zhanzhuzheng) in towns and cities, provided that they are responsible for their own grain and housing (zili kouliang hu) (Renmin ribao 1984). Under this directive, many temporary migrants (also loosely referred to as the floating population) have taken to the road, but permanent migration which entails the transfer of hukou classification and/or hukou location continues to be strictly controlled. Marriage migration is usually considered permanent migration, since the 1950 Marriage Law stipulates that a woman's hukou location can be transferred to the husband's locality after marriage, and her land, food and housing quota are also transferable to the husband's household.[3] On the other hand, recent waves of marriage migration also included some women who did not transfer their hukou locations to the destinations, mostly for the purpose of evading fertility control (Ma et al. 1995).

Permanent migration to urban areas continues to be strictly controlled. The larger the city, the tighter is the control on residence (Shen 1996), which explains why most female marriage migrants choose rural areas as their destinations, as will be illustrated in the empirical analysis.

20.4.2 Labour Market

The Chinese labour market is underdeveloped and highly segmented (Knight and Song 1995). The segmentation reflects the hukou system, as the urban labour market, especially the formal sector, is largely closed to individuals with agricultural hukou. Enterprises who assume that women are less productive because of maternity reasons and child care are reluctant to hire

---

2 *Both cities and towns are urban entities, and villages are rural. Another set of administrative units, cities (shi) and counties (xian) are often employed, such as in the 1990 Census as types of destination for migrants. Counties may consist of towns and villages but for all practical purposes are considered primarily rural areas.*

3 *But a woman cannot change her agricultural hukou into a nonagricultural hukou even if she marries a man who has nonagricultural hukou.*

them (Park 1992). A woman without local hukou is therefore a double jeopardy in the labour market (Leeds 1976). Marriage, which offers an opportunity to obtain local hukou, provides a means for overcoming some of the disadvantages that a peasant woman faces during her search for economic opportunities.

20.4.3 Status of Women

Despite Mao's attempt to raise the status of Chinese women, they continue to be constrained by traditional views of women's role in the family. The Chinese woman is defined in relation to others, first to her father, then to her husband, and in her old age to her children. Peasant women who have agricultural hukou, have low education and are unskilled, are at a particular disadvantage in non-agricultural work and in the urban labour market. To them, there are very few means to achieve social and economic mobilities other than marriage, which may be the only chance for them to exert some control over their future. Since the daughter "married out" is not expected to have full responsibility for her natal family, she may be motivated to seek marriage even if it entails long-distance migration, and especially if it promises to bring about significant improvement in economic well being.

Many men in rural areas near cities and in coastal provinces, have temporarily left the farm for work in township-village enterprises in nearby small towns, while continuing to keep an agricultural hukou classification. This is the "leaving the land but not the village" (litu bu lixiang) model, which has been publicized since the reforms as a means to alleviate agricultural labour surplus. Peasant women who are married to men who return only during peak periods of the agricultural season or who seldom participate in farm work, have become the key labourers in the farm. By "marrying to the farmland," female marriage migrants anticipate that their farm labour will legitimize their use of and right to the land while their husbands' labour is utilized somewhere else (Bossen 1994). The gendered division of labour within the peasant household is therefore also an occupational division of labour - women are the farm labourers and men work in urban industrial sectors. This is a model conducive to raising household income, but is more probable in rural areas near towns, cities and rapidly growing regions.

20.4.4 Economic and Spatial Restructuring

Despite the socialist ideology of promoting equality, including spatial equality, in development, policies during the Maoist regime have not been successful in reducing uneven regional development (Cole 1987; Paine 1981).

Regional policy since the economic reform has further widened the gap between inland and coastal areas (e.g. Fan 1995; Wei and Ma 1996), and intensified the push and pull forces of migration. Market reforms in rural and urban areas, and increases in foreign investment, have opened up new economic and employment opportunities especially in coastal provinces. The relaxation of migration control, as mentioned earlier, has significantly increased migration propensity (Liang and White 1997), and has made it possible for millions of Chinese to migrate. Their dominant direction is from inland areas toward the coast, and from the west toward the east.

Uneven regional development is also the basis for the "spatial hypergamy" in mate selection (Lavely 1991). If marriage is a precious opportunity for a woman to achieve social and economic mobilities, and if she follows the patrilocal tradition to join the husband where he lives, then the prospective husband's location becomes an important factor in marriage decision-making (Li and Lavely 1995). Place-based characteristics, especially the local economy, create opportunities or set constraints for men's success in the marriage market. In the case of China, rural men in coastal provinces that are experiencing rapid economic growth are considered more desirable mates than men in inland, remote or mountainous locales.

Men who marry *wailainu* are typically older and poorer, and some are mentally or physically handicapped, which impose constraints on their finding marriage partners (Ma et al. 1995; Xu and Ye 1992). The larger number of single and older men[5] than their female counterparts may be attributable to male infants' better chance of survival in difficult times (Min and Eades 1995), such as during the famine in the late 1950s and early 1960s. This not only reflects the low social status of women in general, but also more specifically female infanticide and strong preference for sons (Bullough and Ruan 1994). In addition, in the midst of rising brideprice and marriage expenses, marrying wailainu seems like a good bargain since they usually request less brideprice, do not expect extravagant ceremonies and are known to be diligent (Liu 1990; Xu and Ye 1992). To the wailainu, the favourable location of these men and the promise of a "better life" compensate for what may be perceived as unfavourable personal attributes (Ma et al. 1995). A popular saying in rural Zhejing, one of the major destinations of female marriage migrants, describes the current prevalence of long-distance marriage migrants: "In the 1960s, wives were from Subei (poorer parts of Jiangsu, a province adjacent to Zhejiang); in the 1970s, they were from rustication;[6] and in the 1990s, they come from afar"

---

5 *Men who are over 30 or 35 years old and remain single are considered dailing weihun or "above marriage age" in China.*
6 *Rustication refers to a Maoist policy to send youths and intellectuals from cities to the countryside in order to "learn from the peasants."*

(liushi niandai kao Subei; qishi niandai kao chadui; bashi niandai yuanfang lai) (Xu and Ye 1992). It suggests that marriage migrations from another nearby province are not a new phenomenon in China, but those that take place across provinces and over thousands of miles are a product of the reform period.

Among the main channels for the prospective husband and wife to meet are kinship and social networks, and marriage brokers and media. Some of these channels have existed historically, but recent market reforms, improvement in information flows, and increased population mobility, have provided increased opportunities for agents in the marriage market. Pioneer female marriage migrants inform their sisters, relatives, friends and people from the same village (tongxiang) about marriage opportunities (that is, prospective husbands), and may in fact bring them along to the destination when returning from a visit to home villages (Wang and Hu 1996; Xu and Ye 1992; Yang 1991; Yang 1994). These "chain" or "snowballing" migrations are well documented (Min and Eades 1995; Wang 1992), and are not unlike the effect of kinship and social networks on other types of migrations, which explain streams of population movement from specific origins to specific destinations, and which are reflected by migrant enclaves and communities such as the "Zhejing Village" in Beijing (Xiang 1993). Rise in entrepreneurship and materialism, permitted and directly or indirectly encouraged by the economic reforms, are conducive to the work of marriage brokers, who collect a fee or commission by arranging prospective husbands to meet potential marriage partners (Shen 1996; Yang 1991). Some men who have difficulties finding a wife locally welcome the brokers' service, although incidents of abduction and fraud have led to a perception that such channel is "cheap but risky" (Min and Eades 1995). Marriage media, such as advertisements and agencies, are also used (Shen 1996), again reflecting better information flows and rise in entrepreneurship in China during the reform period.

The following empirical analysis seeks to illustrate further the constraints, opportunities and agents which explain the prevalence of marriage migration in China.

20.5 Empirical analysis

Recent census and population surveys in China have inquired the (primary) "reason of migration". Both the 1987 1% Sample Survey and the 1990 Census offered nine options for reason of migration: "job transfer", "job assignment", "industry/business", "seek help from friends/relatives", "retirement", "joining family", "marriage", "study/training" and "other".[7] They have been interpreted and categorized in different ways, most commonly as one or more of the following types: plan (institutional), economic, life cycle, family and social (Chan 1994, 115; Li and Siu 1994; Rowland 1994; Shen and Tong 1992, 202; Tang 1993; Zhai and Ma 1994). Marriage is typically considered a life cycle or family reason of migration, but is also linked to economic considerations (Ding 1994).

The empirical analysis employs a 1% village-level sample of the 1990 Census[8] (SSB 1994). It contains information about every individual in all households of the sampled village-level units (and their urban equivalents in cities and towns). The 1990 Census defines a migrant as an individual five years or older whose usual place of residence on July 1, 1985 was in a different city, town or county than that on July 1, 1990. Although this definition underestimates the actual volume of migration by excluding multiple moves, return migrants, migrants younger than five years old and moves within the same city, town or county, the 1990 Census remains by far the most comprehensive source of migration data in China.

20.5.1 Female Migration

Census data show that in China, men's propensity to move continues to be higher than that of women. Between 1985 and 1990, a total of 20.4 million men (13.4 million intraprovincial and 6.96 million interprovincial) and 16.0 million women (11.2 million intraprovincial and 4.89 million interprovincial) migrated, reflecting mobility rates (ratio of migrants to the total population in 1990) of 3.3% and 2.8% respectively.

---

7 *Definitions of reasons of migration are (SSB 1993, 513-514, 558): job transfer — migration due to job change, including demobilization from the military; job assignment — migration due to assignment of jobs by the government after graduation and recruitment of graduates from different schools; industry/business — migration to seek work as laborers or in commercial or trade sectors; study/training — migration to attend schools or to enter training or apprentice programs organized by local work units; seek help from friends/relatives — migration to seek the support of relatives or friends; retirement — cadres or workers leaving work due to retirement or resignation, including retired peasants in rural areas with retirement benefits; joining family — family members following the job transfer of cadres and workers; marriage — migration to live with spouse after marriage; other — all other reasons.*
8. *The 1% sample data set takes villages/towns/neighborhoods as the sampling unit, and includes all households within the sampled units. It contains a total of 11.8 million records (individuals) from 8,438 villages/towns/neighborhoods. All population figures extracted from the sample and reported in this paper have been multiplied by 100, except the number of cases in the logistic regression (Table 4).*

The reasons for migration of Chinese women were (in percentage) :-

marriage	28.4
industry/business	15.6
joining family	15.0
seek help from friends/relatives	12.6
study/training	10.1
job transfer	8.1
other	5.3
job assignment	4.2
retirement	0.6

Although industry/business, primarily economic in nature, was the second most important reason, family-related motives (marriage, joining family, friends/relatives) seemed to dominate female migration. On the contrary, employment-related reasons (particularly industry/business and job transfer) accounted for the majority of male migrants. These statistics appear to suggest that women are primarily dependants in the process of migration, that is, they migrate after marriage to join the spouses and their families, follow their spouses as tied movers, and move to seek the support of friends and family

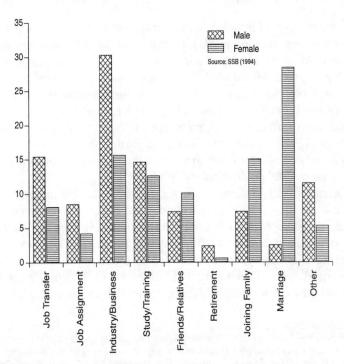

Figure 20.1 Reasons for Migration: Male and Female

members. But a closer scrutiny of the data will reveal more complex mechanisms underlying female marriage migration in China.

20.5.2 Female Marriage Migration

Marriage is the leading reason of female migration in China. It accounted for 28.2% (3.1 million) of all intraprovincial, and 28.9% (1.4 million) of all interprovincial female migrants between 1985 and 1990 (Table
20.1). The relative importance of marriage was even more marked for the 15-
29 age group,[9] accounting for respectively 36.8% and 40.0% of intraprovincial
and interprovincial female migrants. Given the traditional prevalence of short-
distance marriages, the magnitude and relative importance of interprovincial
marriage migration are quite exceptional. Interprovincial marriage migration
is more revealing of the complexity of migration considerations because it
generally involves longer distance, greater institutional hindrance and more
permanent moves.

20.5.3 Demographic and Locational Characteristics of Female Migrants

A comparison of female marriage migrants with female industry/busi-
ness migrants, female migrants as a whole and female non-migrants, may
shed some light on the characteristics of female marriage migrants and their
migration process (Table 20.2). Migrants as a whole were younger than non-
migrants; and both marriage migrants and industry/business migrants were
younger than migrants as a whole. The proportions of female marriage migrants and industry/business migrants from villages (>84%) were also substantially higher than that of female migrants as a whole (66.9% for
intraprovincial and 64.9% for interprovincial migrants), suggesting that both
types of migrants had predominantly rural origins.

In terms of destinations, however, female marriage migrants and female industry/business migrants differed. The bulk of intraprovincial and
almost half of interprovincial female industry/business migrants chose to go
to cities, twice the rate of female marriage migrants. Not only were female
marriage migrants largely from rural areas, the majority of them also chose to
migrate to rural areas. This is particularly the case for interprovincial female
marriage migrants, with 88.2% coming from villages and 81.8% going to
counties.

9 *Although the 1980 Marriage Law stipulates that the minimum age of marriage for women is
20, the practice of early (younger than 20) marriages continue to exist in China, especially in
rural areas (Yang 1991). The age group 15-29 represented 88.1% of all female marriage
migrants recorded in the 1990 Census.*

Table 20.2 Demographic and Locational Characteristics of Female Migrants and Non-Migrants

	Intraprovincial Migrants			Interprovincial Migrants			Non-migrants
	Industry/ business	Marriage	All	Industry/ business	Marriage	All	
Total number	1,686,900	3,141,000	11,153,000	812,400	1,415,300	4,892,700	500,311,100
(%)	15.1	28.2		16.6	28.9		
Age (mean)	25.3	25.7	26.5	25	25.4	27.2	32.2
Agricultural hukou (%)	90.8	91	57.4	91.9	92.6	60.6	81.3
Origin (1985) (%)							
City (shi)	3.5	2.8	12.5	5.3	3.5	21.4	-
Town (zhen)	12.1	11.8	20.6	8.6	8.3	13.8	-
Village (xiang)	84.4	85.4	66.9	86.2	88.2	64.9	-
Destination (1990) (%)							
City (shi)	69.6	36.6	59.2	47.1	18	45	24.6
County (xian)	30.4	63.4	40.8	52.9	82	55	75.4
Education (15-29) (%)							
Illiterate	3	9.1	4.8	4.4	13.4	7.6	9.7
Primary	25.4	38.3	21.9	32.6	44.1	28.9	37.6
Junior high or above	71.6	52.6	73.3	63	42.5	63.5	52.7
Labor force participation (15+) (%)	98.3	8.5	64	97.8	81.8	68.1	72.8
Occupation (15+) (%)							
Agriculture	10.1	83.1	38.2	8	89.2	42.1	75.6
Industry	53.4	8.6	30	56.5	6.5	28.4	11.9
Services	36.5	8.3	31.8	35.5	4.2	29.5	12.6

Source: SSB (1994).

Female marriage migrants also had the lowest levels of education, compared with female industry/business migrants, female migrants as a whole, and female non-migrants. Among the 15-29 year olds,[10] only 52.6% of intraprovincial and 42.5% of interprovincial marriage migrants had education at the junior high or above level, significantly lower than other groups that they are compared with. The majority of female industry/business migrants, on the other hand, had at least high-school level education. Marriage

---

10 *Comparison of education levels is valid if it is made for a well-defined age group, such as 15-29, since the age range for certain migrants (e.g. retirement) differs significantly from marriage migrants, and since the age range of non-migrants is large. An older average age is likely related to lower levels of education and a younger average age to higher levels of education, since many currently older Chinese women were not encouraged to pursue education or gain access to schooling when they were young. The 15-29 age group accounted for respectively 67.9% and 62.7% of interprovincial and interprovincial female marriage migrants (Table 1).*

migrants also had the highest illiteracy[11] rates (9.1% and 13.4% respectively for intraprovincial and interprovincial migrants).

Despite female marriage migrants' low education, their labour force participation rates after migration (at the destination) were high. Although their rates were not as high as that of female industry/business migrants, 80.5% (intraprovincial) and 81.8% (interprovincial) were substantially larger than that of female migrants as a whole and that of female non-migrants. These statistics suggest that female marriage migrants were active participants in the economy, contradicting the view that marriage migrations are primarily social or family-related moves and involve passive or tied movers.

The occupation structure of female marriage migrants also stands out. The bulk of them engaged in agriculture (83.1% for intraprovincial and 89.2% for interprovincial migrants), and the proportions were significantly higher than that of female industry/business migrants (who were primarily in industry and services), female migrants as a whole, and even female non-migrants.

It is clear from the above comparisons that female marriage migrants were a distinct group of women. They were young, relatively uneducated, came from rural areas, settled in rural areas, were economically active in the labour force, and mostly engaged in agriculture. They did not fit the typical profile of family-oriented, passive and tied movers. These peasant women sought to migrate to the destination *and* join the agricultural labour force there.

Interprovincial female marriage migrants were even more inferior to their intraprovincial counterparts — the former were younger, had lower education, and higher proportions of them had agricultural *hukou* classification and rural origin. Their willingness to move long distance and be away from affinal and familiar environments can be interpreted as a price to pay in order to overcome their constraints.

Nonetheless, the statistics on destination and occupation are quite puzzling, because it seems that female marriage migrants did not accomplish significant improvements in social or economic status, since they moved from one rural area to another, and from agricultural work to agricultural work. But not all rural areas are the same. Those near big cities or in more developed provinces are more desirable, particularly because the household responsibility system has brought about commercialisation of agriculture, hence giving farmers near markets and in well-endowed locations more profit opportunities. Therefore, moving to another rural area, which affords better opportunities, may still enhance a peasant woman's economic status (see

---

11 The formal definition in the census is "illiterate and semi-illiterate," referring to individuals who recognize less than 1,500 Chinese characters, cannot read popular literature nor write a simple letter (SSB 199, 514).

analysis on spatial pattern). Finally, as mentioned earlier, some peasant women stay in the farm in order to enable their right to use the land while their husbands work in non-agricultural sectors.

20.5.4 Who did Female Marriage Migrants Marry?

The 1990 Census data do not allow perfect matching of household members into husbands and wives, except when one of the husband or wife is also the household head. Since the bulk of household heads in China are men, we have selected male household heads who were married to marriage migrants, other migrants and non-migrants in 1990 in the 25-39 age group (Table 20.3).

While the majority of marriage migrants' husbands had junior-high or above education, they were as a whole less educated than husbands of non-marriage migrants. In particular, husbands of interprovincial marriage migrants had the lowest level of education, with only 57.5% receiving junior-high or above education, the lowest level among all groups, and the highest illiteracy rate (5.9%). As expected, large percentages of husbands of marriage migrants were engaged in agriculture, since the bulk of female

Table 20.3 Education and Occupation of Migrants and Non-Migrants' Husbands*

	Intraprovincial Migrants		Interprovincial Migrants		Non-migrants
	Marriage	Non-marriage	Marriage	Non-marriage	
Total number	1,499,900	1,159,300	637,400	520,700	92,993,000
Education (%)					
Illiterate	2.6	2.8	5.9	3.7	4.3
Primary	27.9	15.8	36.6	19.7	29.7
Junior high or above	69.5	81.4	57.5	76.6	66.1
Occupation (%)					
Agriculture	67.2	15.0	75.7	17.2	67.6
Industry	22.2	41.8	17.5	43.3	18.6
Services	10.6	43.2	6.7	39.5	13.8

Source: SSB (1994)
*Husbands who were household heads and between 25 and 39 years old in 1990.

marriage migrants chose rural destinations. This contrasts with husbands of non-marriage migrants, who were highly represented in industrial and services sectors. Husbands of interprovincial marriage migrants again stand out as the group with the highest proportion engaged in agriculture (75.7%). These statistics support a prevailing argument in the literature, primarily based on case study surveys, that husbands of *wailainu* have relatively lower social and economic status, which lowers their competitiveness in the marriage market and motivates them to seek brides from other provinces.

20.5.5 Spatial Pattern of Interprovincial Female Marriage Migration

Interprovincial female marriage migration has very distinct spatial patterns. Marriage was the most important reason for female out-migration in 12 provinces,[12] with the highest proportions in the southwestern and poorer provinces of Yunnan (72.7%), Guizhou (71.2%), Sichuan (48.6%) and Guangxi (42.0%). Although the volume of out-migration varied among these four sending provinces, they together accounted for more than half (50.5%) of total interprovincial female marriage migrants, forming a "cradle of brides" in China. For 14 provinces,[13] marriage was the most important reason for female in-migration. The eastern coastal provinces of Hebei (63.0%), Jiangsu (54.5%), Fujian (50.6%) and Zhejiang (47.2%), and Anhui (59.1%) in central China, had the highest proportions of female marriage in-migrants. Most of these receiving provinces are economically more developed, which is a major factor of marriage-migration destination. The three municipal cities of Beijing (11.2%), Tianjin (10.5%) and Shanghai (5.1), on the other hand, had the lowest proportions of female marriage in-migrants (except Tibet). Despite large numbers of temporary in-migrants (primarily for industry/ business), Beijing, Tianjin and Shanghai exert stricter control over permanent migration, and provide few opportunities for peasant women to migrate there through marriage.

Census data indicate that 84.8% of all interprovincial female marriage migrants were from the central and western regions, and 60.0% migrated to the eastern region.[14] Map 20.1, which illustrates the largest 15 net flows[15]

12 They are: Gansu, Shaanxi, Yunnan, Guizhou, Sichuan, Guangxi, Hebei, Jiangxi, Jilin, Liaoning, Inner Mongolia and Tianjin.
13 They are: Hebei, Shanxi, Inner Mongolia, Shandong, Jiangsu, Zhejiang, Anhui, Fujian, Jiangxi, Hunan, Guangxi, Sichuan, Guizhou and Ningxia.
14 These regional delineations are according to the regional scheme developed in the Seventh Five-Year Plan (1986-1990).
15 The spatial pattern of gross flows is similar to that of net flows, except that the former also denotes large flows between adjacent provinces of Anhui and Jiangsu, and of Sichuan, Yunnan and Guizhou.

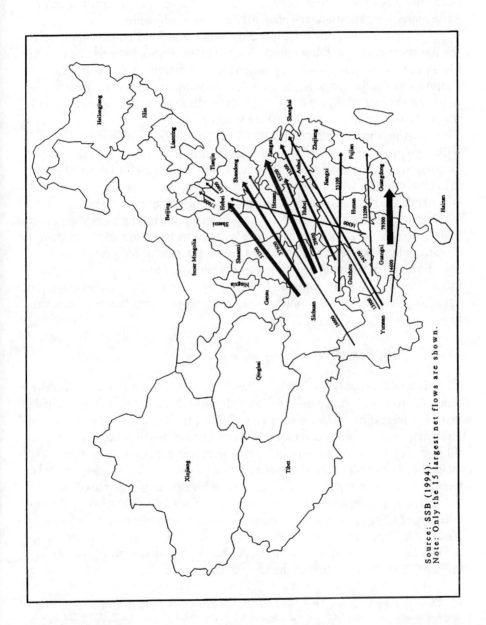

Map 20.1   Largest Interprovincial Migration Flows

between pairs of provinces, confirms the observation that interprovincial female marriage migration was primarily an eastward phenomenon.

Although marriage migrants did not account for a large proportion of female in-migrants in Guangdong, Map 20.1 shows that the net flow from Guangxi to Guangdong was the largest in the nation. Like in the case of Beijing and Tianjin, large numbers of female industry/business migrants also migrated to Guangdong, and as a result the relative proportion of marriage in-migrants was smaller even though its volume was large.

Within the major receiving provinces, pockets of "marriage clusters," with high proportions of female marriage in-migrants, exist.[16] In the case of Guangdong, marriage accounted for more than 80% of all female in-migrants in six counties,[17] which are primarily rural and poorer counties in the western periphery of the province, adjacent to neighbouring poorer sending provinces. And in Jiangsu, seven[18] of the ten counties whose proportions of female marriage migration exceeded 75% were in the north of the province (Subei), where per capita income was only a fraction of the provincial average. Even if female marriage migrants chose to go to more developed provinces, they were mostly confined to relatively poorer locations, although the latter may already be economically more developed than the migrants' origins.

20.5.6 Logistic Regression

The above analyses provide general support to the importance of institutional, structural, economic, social and cultural factors that shape female marriage migration. They also give weight to the argument that women in disadvantaged positions are more likely to pursue marriage as a strategy to achieve migration and to improve their social and economic mobilities. We would like to further quantify the effect of the above factors on interprovincial female marriage migration, by conducting a logistic regression analysis.

The dependent variable has value 1 for marriage migration; and 0 for other types of migration. There are four sets of independent variables (Table 20.4). The first set addresses the effect of the *hukou* system and the segmented labour market, and includes (1) *hukou* classification of the female migrant; (2) *hukou* location of the female migrant; (3) destination 1 (urban or

16 *The 1% sample data of the 1990 Census do not allow comprehensive mapping of subprovincial units. Instead, we use the 100% volumes (GDPPCO 1992; JSPPCO 1992), which provide county-level data for female marriage in-migrants, but do not differentiate between intraprovincial and interprovincial moves.*

17 *They are: Wuchuan, Gaozhou, Xinyi, Dianbai, Huazhou and Luoding.*

18 *They are: Feng, Tongshan, Suning, Pi, Shuyang, Siyang and Lianshui.*

rural); and (4) destination 2 (municipal cities or other provinces). We expect women with agricultural *hukou* classification and rural *hukou* location, and those who chose rural and non-municipal cities destinations, more likely to be marriage migrants. The second set of independent variables deals with the status of female migrants. Among demographic variables reported in the census, education is the most appropriate indicator of women's status. We use three education variables to examine possible non-linear effects of education on migration (Ortiz 1996): (5) education 1 (primary and junior high); (6) education 2 (senior high); and (7) college or above. We expect women with lower education to be more likely marriage migrants. The third set of independent variables represents economic factors: (8) income of origin is measured by agricultural household income per capita[19] of migrants' province (before migration), and is evaluated for the year 1988, near the mid-point of the period 1985-1990; and (9) destination 3 (coastal provinces versus inland provinces). We expect income of the origin provinces to be negatively related, and coastal destination to be positively related, to the likelihood of marriage migration (versus other types of migration). Finally, the sex ratio variable (10), which compares the number of single men over 30 years old with their female counterparts, aims at testing the effect of demographics on marriage migration. We expect high sex-ratio provinces to be related to high propensities of female marriage in-migration.

Estimates of the model are reported in Table 20.4. The goodness of fit measure is 0.28, suggesting that the model is a relatively good fit for the data (Hensher and Johnson 1981, 51). The results are generally consistent with our expectations. Female migrants with agricultural *hukou* classification were 5.0 (odds ratio) times more likely than those with non-agricultural *hukou*, and female migrants with rural *hukou* location were 1.7 times more likely than those with urban *hukou* location, to be marriage migrants. In terms of destination, female migrants to rural destinations were 3.0 times more likely than those to urban destinations, and female migrants to non-municipality provinces were 1.2 times more likely than those to the three municipal cities (Beijing, Tianjin, Shanghai), to be marriage migrants. The parameter estimates and odds ratios confirm the importance of institutional and structural factors. Peasant women are constrained by their *hukou* status and location, and are likely to migrate through marriage into other rural areas, but they

---

19 *Agricultural household income per capita is deemed a more appropriate indicator of regional development than wage or employment measures, because the latter were not designed to reflect well being in rural areas, and because the bulk of female marriage migrants were rural to rural migrants. The value 500 yuan, median of agricultural household income per capita and an appropriate divider of poorer provinces from more developed provinces, was selected as the cut point of the dummy variable (1: 500 yuan or above; 0: otherwise).*

Table 20.4   China: Logistic Regression of Interprovincial Female Marriage Migration*

Independent variable		Parameter estimate	Odds ratio[a]
Institutional and structural factors			
(1) *Hukou* classification	(1: agricultural; 0: nonagricultural)	1.62**	5.03
(2) *Hukou* location	(1: rural; 0: urban)	0.51**	1.66
(3) Destination 1	(1: rural; 0: urban)	1.10**	3.00
(4) Destination 2	(1: non-municipal provinces; 0: municipal cities)	0.19**	1.20
Status of women			
(5) Education 1	(1: primary and junior high; 0: otherwise)	0.36**	1.44
(6) Education 2	(1: senior high; 0: otherwise)	0.45**	1.57
(7) Education 3	(1: college or above; 0: otherwise)	-1.48**	0.23
Economic factors			
(8) Income of origin	(1: 500 yuan or above; 0: otherwise)	-0.88**	0.41
(9) Destination 3	(1: coastal provinces; 0: otherwise)	0.22**	1.24
Demographics			
(10) Sex ratio	(single men and women 30 years or older)	0.00**	1.00

Intercept	-6.56**
Number of classes[b]	48927
Degree of freedom	10
Model schi-square	16375**
-2 log likelihood with intercept only	58859
-2 log likelihood with intercept and covariates	42484
Goodness of fit[c] (r^2)	0.28

Source: SSB (1994).
* dependent variable in interprovincial female migration (1: marriage, 0: other reasons)
** significant at 0.0001 level
[a] odds ration = e (parameter estimate)
[b] The number of cases refers to actual cases from the 1% sample of the 1990 Census used in the logistic regression, and has not been mulitplied by 100.
[c] r^2 = 1-(log likelihood with intercept and covariates/log likelihood with intercept only)

continue to be shut out from urban areas and large cities that have stricter control over permanent migration.

Odds ratios for the education variables suggest that generally women with higher education are less likely than those with lower education to engage in marriage migration. Specifically, female migrants with college or above level of education were 77.3% (1 - odds ratio = 1 - 0.227) less likely than those without to be marriage migrants. But the effect of education seems to be curvilinear. Female migrants with primary and junior high education were 1.6 times, and those with senior high education 1.4 times, more likely than those with either lower or higher education to be marriage migrants. What these estimates suggest is that some degree of education facilitates the gathering of resources and information (Ortiz 1996), and motivates women to pursue marriage migration. Interprovincial marriage migration is not traditional, and the long distance and many intervening obstacles involved demand a certain spirit of adventure and creativity that women with very little or no education may not possess. On the other hand, those with the highest education were more likely to pursue other types of migration, including migrating to urban areas where they may be more competitive in the labour market.

20.6 Conclusion

The main objective of this chapter has been to explain the prevalence of female marriage migration and of the relatively new phenomenon of long-distance marriage migration in China. We have argued that interpretation of these population movements must be made in relation to underlying structural forces, including institutional, economic, social and cultural factors. They as a whole define the constraints on and possible opportunities for the mobility of women. Our analyses support the argument that peasant women in disadvantaged institutional, economic and social positions are severely constrained in their mobility and in their choices of possible destinations. They are shut out from cities because of their agricultural *hukou* classification and rural *hukou* location, and from the urban labour market because of their low education and skills. Their positions reflect not only centuries-old traditions that limit women's access to knowledge, resources and power, but also the unique socialist institution of China which denies its rural residents access to benefits and opportunities in urban areas.

We have found that interprovincial female marriage migrants had some degree of education, probably at a level conducive to gathering information and resources regarding long-distance marriage migration, but not sufficient for competing in urban industrial sectors. This, in conjunction with the notion that marriage is an economic strategy, and the focused destinations of interprovincial female migrants in China, suggest that these women are active agents negotiating their options and engineering population movements, and challenge the conventional view that female marriage migrants are passive actors whose mobility is simply a response to marriage.

Not only were the destinations of interprovincial female marriage migrants focused, but their origins were also spatially concentrated, as the majority of them were from the "cradle of bride" (Yunnan, Guizhou, Sichuan, Guangxi) in southwestern China. These spatially defined streams of female marriage migrants support the observation made in previous case studies, that social and kinship networks are an important agent in facilitating the waves of rural brides finding mates in desirable locations. They also suggest that agents such as marriage brokers, whose role is facilitated by rise in entrepreneurship, have contributed to such movements. As for the men who married female migrants, our analyses suggest that they were also socially and economically disadvantaged. But their favourable position in the spatial hierarchy seemed to have compensated for what may be considered less desirable personal attributes, and allowed them to draw peasant women from poorer regions, perhaps with the aid of social and kinship networks or other agents.

Although parental intervention has gradually receded, the traditional Chinese notion that marriage is a pragmatic transaction between two parties (husband and wife), arranged with the aid of a third party, seems to have revived in the reform period, in a form that is accompanied by substantial population movements. Although there is a neoclassical economic flavour to this phenomenon, this study has shown that the structural approach, which entails more attention to historical, social and cultural complexities underlying migration, and which enables discourses around the constraints, opportunities and agents of migration, must be included for an adequate explanation of women's mobility.

References

Bauer, John, Feng Wang, Nancy E. Riley, and Xiaohua Zhao. 1992. Gender inequality in urban China. *Modern China* 18 (3): 333-370.

Bennholdt-Thompson, Veronika. 1984. A theory of the sexual division of labour. in *Households and the World Economy*. ed. J. Smith, I. Wallerstein, and H. Deiter-Evers, 201-231. Beverly Hills, California: Sage.

Bonney, Norman, and John Love. Gender and migration: Geographical mobility and the wife's sacrifice. *Sociological Review* 39 (2): 335-348.

Bossen, Laurel. 1994. Zhongguo nongcun funu: shime yuanyin shi tamen liuzai nongtianli? (Chinese peasant women: What caused them to stay in the field?). in *Xingbie yu Zhongguo*

(Gender and China). ed. X. Li, H. Zhu, and X. Dong, 128-154. Beijing: Sanlian Shudian.

Bourque, Susan, and Warren Key. 1981. *Women of the Andes: Patriarchy and Social Change in Two Peruvian Towns*. Ann Arbor, Michigan: Michigan University Press.

Bullough, Vern, and Fang Fu Ruan. 1994. Marriage, divorce and sexual relations in contemporary China. *Journal of Comparative Family Studies* 25 (3): 383-393.

Caplan, Patricia. 1985. *Class and Gender in India*. London: Tavistock.

Chan, Kam Wing. 1994. *Cities with Invisible Walls: Reinterpreting Urbanization in post-1949 China*. Hong Kong: Oxford University Press.

—. 1996. Post-Mao China: a two-class urban society in the making. *International Journal of Urban and Regional Research* 20 (1): 134-150.

Chant, Sylvia, and Sarah Radcliffe. 1992. Migration and development: The importance of gender. in *Gender and Migration in Developing Countries*. ed. S. Chant. New York: Belhaven Press.

Cheng, Teijun, and Mark Selden. 1994. The origins and social consequences of China's hukou system. *The China Quarterly* 139: 644-668.

Christiansen, Flemming. 1990. Social division and peasant mobility in Mainland China: the implications of huk'ou system. *Issues and Studies* 26 (4): 78-91.

Cole, J. P. 1987. Regional inequalities in the People's Republic of China. *Tijdschrift voor Economische en Sociale Geografie* 78 (3): 201-213.

Croll, Elisabeth. 1984. The exchange of women and property: Marriage in post-revolutionary China. in *Women and Property - Women as Property*. ed. R. Hirschon, 44-61. London: Croom Helm.

—. 1987. New peasant family forms in rural China. *The Journal of Peasant Studies* 14 (4): 469-499.

Ding, Jinhong. 1994. Zhongguo renkou shengji qianyi bieliuchang tezheng tan (Characteristics of cause-specific rates of inter-provincial migration in China). *Renkou yanjiu (Population Research)* 1994 (1): 14-21.

Ebrey, P. 1991. Introduction. in *Marriage and Inequality in Chinese Society*. ed. R. Watson, and P. Ebrey, marriage, inequality, China. Berkeley: University of California Press.

Ellis, Mark, Dennis Conway, and Adrian Bailey. 1996. The circular migration of Puerto Rican women: Towards a gendered explanation. *International Migration* 34 (1): 31-64.

Fan, C. Cindy. 1995. Of belts and ladders: state policy and uneven regional development in post-Mao China. *Annals of the Association of American Geographers* 85 (3): 421-449.

Fincher, Ruth. 1993. Gender relation and the geography of migration (commentary). *Environment and Planning A* 25: 1703-1705.

Gao, Xiaoxian. 1994. China's modernization and changes in the social status of rural women. in *Engendering China: Women, Culture, and the State*. ed. C. K. Gilmartin, G. Hershatter, L. Rofel, and T. White, 80-97. Cambridge, Massachusetts: Harvard University Press.

Gilmartin, Christina, Gail Hershatter, Lisa Rofel, and Tyrene White. 1994. Introduction. in *Engendering China: Women, Culture, and the State*. ed. C. K. Gilmartin, G. Hershatter, L. Rofel, and T. White, 3-23. Cambridge, Massachusetts: Harvard University Press.

Guangdong sheng renkou pucha bangongshi (Guangdong Province Population Census Office) (GDPPCO). 1992. *Guangdong sheng 1990 nian renkou pucha ziliao (Tabulations on the 1990 Population Census of Guangdong Province), Vol. I*. Taishan: Zhongguo Tongji Chubanshe.

Hensher, D A, and L W Johnson. 1981. *Applied Discrete Choice Modelling*. London: Croom Helm.

Honig, Emily, and Gail Hershatter. 1988. Marriage. in *Personal Voices: Chinese Women in the 1980s*. ed. E. Honig, and G. Hershatter, 137-166. Stanford, California: Stanford University Press.

Houstourn, M. F., R. G. Kramer, and J. M. Barrett. 1984. Female predominance of immigration to the United States since 1930: A first look. *International Migration Review* 18: 908-963.

Humbeck, Eva. 1996. The politics of cultural identity: Thai women in Germany. in *Women of the European Union: The Politics of Work and Daily Life*. ed. M. D. Garcia-Ramon, and J. Monk, 186-201. London: Routledge.

Ji, Ping, Kaiti Zhang, and Dawei Liu. 1985. Beijing jiaoqu nongcun renkou hunyin qianyi qianxi. *Zhongguo shehui kexue (Social Sciences in China)* 3: 201-213.

Jiangsu sheng renkou pucha bangongshi (Jiangsu Province Population Census Office) (GDPPCO). 1992. *Jiangsu sheng 1990 nian renkou pucha ziliao (Tabulations on the 1990 Population Census of Jiangsu Province), Vol. I*. Beijing: Zhongguo Tongji Chubanshe.

Knight, John, and Lina Song. 1995. Towards a labour market in China. *Oxford Review of Economic Policy* 11 (4): 97-117.

Lavely, William. 1991. Marriage and mobility under rural collectivization. in *Marriage and Inequality in Chinese Society*. ed. R. S. Watson, and P. B. Ebrey, 286-312. Berkeley: University of California Press.

Leeds, A. 1976. Women in the migratory process: A reductionist outlook. *Anthropological Quarterly* 49: 69-76.

Li, Jiang Hong, and William Lavely. 1995. Rural economy and male marriage in China: Jurong, Jiangsu 1933. *Journal of Family History* 20 (3): 289-306.

Li, Ling. 1994. *Gender and Development: Innercity and Suburban Women in China*. Working Paper No. 11, Centre for Urban and Regional Studies, Zhongshan University, Guangzhou, China.

Li, Si Ming, and Yat Ming Siu. 1994. Population mobility. in *Guangdong: survey of a province undergoing rapid changes*. ed. Y. M. Yeung, and D. K. Y. Chu, 373-400. Hong Kong: The Chinese University Press.

Liang, Zai, and Michael J. White. 1997. Internal migration in China, 1950-1988. *Demography* 33 (3): 375-384.

Lim, Lin Lean. 1993. The structural determinants of female migration. in *Internal Migration of Women in Developing Countries*. ed. United Nations Department for Economic and Social Information and Policy Analysis, 207-222. Proceedings of the United Nations Expert Meeting on the Feminisation of Internal Migration. Aguascalientes, Mexico, 22-25 October 1991. New York: United Nations.

Liu, Xiankang. 1990. Guanyui Xiaoshanshi "wailainu" zhuangkuang ji qi guan li wenti (The conditions and management problems of "women from outside" in Xiaoshan city). *Renkou yanjiu (Population Research)* 6: 31-36.

Ma, Lanmei, Zhongmin Chen, and Guizhen Du. 1995. Dui "wailaimei" hunyu guanli qingkuang de diaocha yu sikao (Investigation and contemplation of the fertility management of female inmigrants). *Renkou yanjiu (Population Research)* 10 (1): 56-58.

Maurer-Fazio, Margaret, Thomas G. Rawski, and Wei Zhang. 1997. Gender wage gaps in China's labour market: Size, structure, trends. Manuscript.

Min, Han, and J. S. Eades. 1995. Brides, bachelors and brokers: The marriage market in rural Anhui in an era of economic reform. *Modern Asian Studies* 29 (4): 841-869.

Moser, Caroline. 1981. Surviving in the suburbios. *IDS Bulletin* (Institute of Development Studies) 12 (3): 19-29.

Oberai, A S, and Manmohan Singh. 1983. *Causes and Consequences of Internal Migration: A Study of the Indian Punjab*. New Delhi: Oxford University Press.

Ortiz, Vilma. 1996. Migration and marriage among Puerto Rican women. *International Migration Review* 30 (2): 460-484.

Paine, Suzanne. 1981. Spatial aspects of Chinese development: issues, outcomes, and policies 1949-1979. *Journal of Development Studies* 17: 132-195.

Park, Kyung Ae. 1992. *Women and Revolution in China: The Sources of Constraints on Women's Emancipation*. Michigan University, Franklin and Marshall College, Working Paper

No. 230.

Pedraza, Silvia. 1991. Women and migration: The social consequences of gender. *Annual Review of Sociology* 17: 303-325.

Potter, S, and J Potter. 1990. *China's Peasants: The Anthropology of a Revolution.* Cambridge: Cambridge University Press.

Renmin ribao (People's Daily). 1984. Guowuyuan dui nongmin banli jizhen hukou zuochu guiding (State Council regulations for peasants seeking permission to live in towns). *Renmin ribao* December 22: 1-2.

—. 1989. Duoshu nongmin tonghunchuan bu chaoguo 25 gongli (Most rural people's marriage boundaries are less than 25 km). August 11: 4.

Riley, Nancy E., and Robert W. Gardner. 1993. Migration decisions: The role of gender. in *Internal Migration of Women in Developing Countries.* ed. United Nations Department for Economic and Social Information and Policy Analysis, 195-206. Proceedings of the United Nations Expert Meeting on the Feminization of Internal Migration. Aguascalientes, Mexico, 22-25 October 1991. New York: United Nations.

Rosenzweig, Mark R., and Oded Stark. 1989. Consumption smoothing, migration, and marriage: Evidence from rural India. *Journal of Political Economy* 97 (4): 905-926.

Rowland, D. T. 1994. Family characteristics of the migrants. in *Migration and Urbanization in China.* ed. L. H. Day, and X. Ma, 129-154. Armonk, New York: M.E. Sharpe.

Sassen-Koob, S. 1983. Labour migration and the new international division of labours. in *Women, Men and the International Division of Labour.* ed. J. Nash, and M. Fernandez-Kelly. New York: SUNY.

Shen, Tan. 1996. The process and achievements of the study on marriage and family in China. *Marriage and Family Review* 22 (1-2): 19-53.

Shen, Yimin, and Chengzhu Tong. 1992. *Zhongguo renkou qianyi (China's population migration).* Beijing: Zhongguo Tongji Chubanshe.

State Statistical Bureau (SSB). 1993. *Zhongguo 1990 nian renkou pucha ziliao (Tabulation on the 1990 Population Census of the People's Republic of China), Vol. VI.* Beijing: Zhongguo Tongji Chubanshe.

—. 1994. *The 1990 Population Census of China (1% Sampling).* Beijing: Zhongguo Tongji Chubanshe.

Tang, Xuemei. 1993. Beijing shi renkou qianyi he renkou liudong (Population migration and mobility in Beijing). *Renkou yanjiu (Population Research)* 1993 (4): 52-55.

Thadani, Veena N., and Michael P. Todaro. 1979. Female migration in developing countries: A framework for analysis. *Centre for Policy Working Paper* 47, Population Council, New York.

—. 1984. Female migration: A conceptual framework. in *Women in the Cities of Asia: Migration and Urban Adaption.* ed. J. T. Fawcett, S. Khoo, and P. C. Smith. Boulder, Colorado: Westview Press.

Wang, Jianmin, and Qi Hu. 1996. *Zhongguo liudong renkou (China's Floating Population).* Shanghai, China: Shanghai Caijing Daxue Chubanshe.

Wang, Jin Ling. 1992. Zhejiang nongmin yidi lianyin xin tedian (The new characteristics of peasant's marriage - Husband and wife from two different regions - in Zhejiang Province). *Shehuixue yanjiu (Sociological Research)* 40 (4): 92-95.

Watts, Susan J. 1983. Marriage migration, a neglected form of long-term mobility: A case study from Ilorin, Nigeria. *International Migration Review* 17 (4): 682-698.

Wei, Ye Hua, and Laurence J. C. Ma. 1996. Changing patterns of spatial inequality in China, 1952-1990. *Third World Planning Review* 18 (2): 177-191.

Wolf, Magery. 1972. *Women and the Family in Rural Taiwan.* Stanford, California:: Stanford University Press.

—. 1985. *Revolution Postponed: Women in Contemporary China.* Stanford, California: Stanford

University Press.

Wood, Charles. 1981. Structural changes and household strategies: A conceptual framework for the study of rural migration. *Human Organization* 40 (4): 338-344.

Xiang, Biao. 1993. Beijing youge "Zhejiang cun" (Beijing has a "Zhejiang Village"). *Shehuixue yu shehui diaocha (Sociology and Sociological Survey)* 3: 68-74; 4: 48-54; 5: 51-54 and 48.

Xu, Tianqi, and Zhendong Ye. 1992. Zhejiang wailai nuxing renkou tanxi (Analysis of female inmigrants in Zhejiang). *Renkou xuekan (Population Journal)* 2: 45-48.

Yang, Qifan. 1991. Nannu beijia xianxiang ji qi libi qianxi (The phenomenon of southern women marrying to the north and its advantages and disadvantages). *Renkou xuekan (Population Journal)* 5: 51-55.

Yang, Yunyang. 1994. *Zhongguo renkou qianyi yu fanzhan di changi zhanlue (Long Term Strategies of Population Migration and Development in China)*. Wuhan, China: Wuhan Chubanshe.

Zhai, Jinyun, and Jian Ma. 1994. Woguo guangdong sheng renkou qianyi wenti tantao (Migration in Guangdong Province). *Renkou yanjiu (Population Research)* 1994 (2): 18-24.

Zhang, Shanyu. 1990. Dangdai zhongguo renkou qianyi di dili tezheng (Geographical characteristics of contemporary Chinese population migration). *Renkou xuekan (Population Journal)* 1990 (2): 17-21.

Zhuang, Shanyu, and Zhang Maolin. 1996. Chabie renkou qianyi yu xingbie goucheng diqu chayi de kuodahua (Migration between different regions and the enlargement of regional sex composition). *Renkou xuekan (Population Journal)* 1: 3-10.

21 Urbanisation and Migration in Xinjiang Uygur Autonomous Region, China

Clifton W. Pannell and Laurence J.C. Ma

21.1 Introduction

The Xinjiang Uygur Autonomous Region, hereinafter Xinjiang Uygur A. R. or simply Xinjiang, is China's largest administrative region and is located in the far western interior of the country (Map 21.1). This region historically has been a rugged and isolated frontier traditionally viewed as China's gateway to central Asia. Culturally it has been a meeting and mixing ground for people of Turkic and Persian origin, Mongols, Manchus, Tibetans, Chinese, and even Russians. Its relationship with China has waxed and waned historically depending on political, economic and military conditions of China and its neighbours (Gladney, 1990). Chinese military outposts here go back to Han times. Direct political control of the region was established in the late Qing period. During the recent period of Chinese communist control after 1949, Xinjiang has witnessed substantial Han Chinese in-migration and colonisation. This has had a far-reaching effect on urbanisation and cities, the topic of this chapter.

The goals of this chapter are to describe and explain the process of urbanisation and urban transition in Xinjiang with emphasis on the past half century, the period of most rapid population growth, inmigration, economic development and concomitant urbanisation and city growth. In doing this, we seek to offer explanations of causal processes involved such as migration that determine political and economic changes that have shaped Xinjiang historically and more recently. Specifically, we shall describe in detail the recent urban transition in Xinjiang and the numerical increases in urbanisation and city growth. In explaining the processes we shall offer five main factors that we consider crucial in understanding the urban transition. These are population growth, urban policy and its effects on urbanisation in Xinjiang, largely Han Chinese in-migration, structural shift in the economy, and the role of trade. All of these must be seen in the context of the new socialist China and the political and security imperative of seizing control of and settling crucial and sensitive frontier areas of which Xinjiang is one of the most vital.

It is this latter overarching notion that provides a conceptual framework on which we may proceed to our analysis of urbanisation and the urban

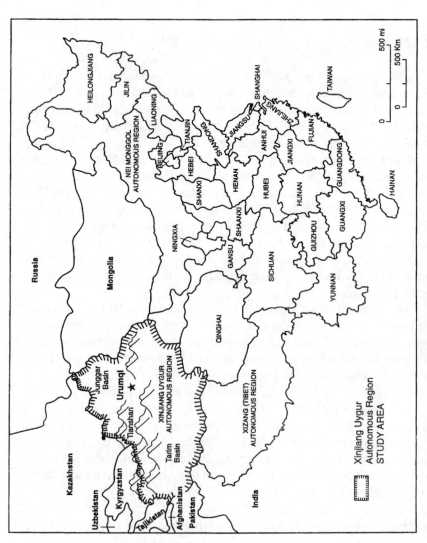

Map 21.1   Xinjiang Uygur Autonomous Region

transition in Xinjiang. This framework has many supporting parts. One is the broad and substantial literature that offer theories and ideas on how frontiers in general operate and more specifically how frontiers have functioned in Chinese history (Lattimore, 1940; Kristof, 1959; and Von Glahn, 1987). China from its very beginning has steadily and continually accreted frontier regions to its ever-enlarging core area. While this process has been more successful in some regions and with certain neighbouring peoples than others and there has been an ebb and flow of the success of control and integration, the Chinese long used garrisons and cities as essential elements in expanding their empire in frontier regions. As Gaubatz (1995) has noted, the Chinese historically have employed techniques of settlement and control to exercise dominion over frontier areas. Both methods have relied on the construction of cities, although as she notes, historically, the great northwest of China was controlled through the use of garrisons and urban settlements rather than agricultural settlements.

We postulate the communist era has brought the use of both techniques, as large numbers of Han Chinese were transmigrated to Xinjiang in the 1950s to serve as agricultural colonists on large military farms. They belonged to the organisation known as the Production and Construction Corps, a modern adaptation of the traditional Chinese military garrisons established as an initial wave of colonisation in frontier territories. These Corps-operated military farms, first established informally in 1952, have served both as garrisons and as rural settlements. While the exact number of resettled Han military migrants is not known, by 1993 their number had been estimated at 2.2 million, obviously an important contributor to the overall Han increase in Xinjiang (Bureau of Statistics, 1994; see also Yuan, 1990 and Allen, 1996). Some of these corps-operated farms over time evolved new functions and activities such as manufacturing, for example. In some cases the rural character and functions of such places was transformed into modem industrial cities, of which Shihezi, with a 1994 population of 543,100, is the most notable.

At the same time many if not most of the cities of Xinjiang during the last half century of rapid growth and urbanisation are made up largely of Han Chinese who dominate the civil affairs, the commerce and the industrial labour forces of these cities and especially the larger cities. Thus, we see contemporary behaviour in regards to the settlement, economic development and urbanisation of Xinjiang as building on long established traditions of Chinese national expansion and territorial integration, albeit with intensified force and speed. To begin our explanation of urbanisation and city development, we focus on population and demographic issues and the transition occurring there as it provides the basic human material out of which the urban process and form grow and develop.

21.2   Demographic Considerations and Urban Growth

Population growth in Xinjiang in this century has been remarkably rapid with the greatest increases occurring during the last half century of the socialist period. At the beginning of the 20th century, Xinjiang was estimated to have had a population of 2.1 million in 1902 (Zhou, 1990, as reported in Mackerras, 1994). By 1949 this had grown to 4.3 million. The census of 1953 reported a figure of 4.9 million (see Table 21.1) (Banister, 1987). In 1996, the population was estimated at 16.8 million. Obviously this has provided a substantial population base and growth on which urbanisation and city development could take place (Tables 21.1 & 21.2).

Table 21.1 Xinjiang Uygur A.R. Population Growth 1953-96

Year	Total population	Males	Females	Male'Female ratio
1953	4,873,608	2,597,769	2,275,839	.53
1964	7,270,067	3,894,740	3,375,327	.54
1982	13,081,538	6,732,231	6,349,307	.51
1990	15,156,883	7,832,195	7,333,688	.52
1993	16,052,648	8,244,822	7,807,826	.51
1995	16,610,000	8,471,100	8,138,900	.51(est)
1996(est.)	16,817,000	8,574,500	8,242,500	.51

Source: China Statistical Yearbook, 1992, pp 67 and 68; 1996, p.70.

Table 21.2 Comparative Demographic Patterns, 1982-96 in Xinjiang UygurAutonomous Region and China

	Total Population	Crude Birth Rate	Crude Death Rate	Rate of Increase
XINJIANG UYGUR AUTONOMOUS REGION				
1982	13,081.538	29.08	8.41	20.67
1996 (est.)	16,817,000	18.00	6.00	12.00
CHINA				
1982	1,016,540,000	22.28	6.60	15.68
1996	1,217,600,000	17.00	7.00	10.00

Source: State Statistical Bureau, China Statistical Yearbook 1996 p.70; 1995 p.59; 1994 p.59; 1992 pp.63 & 64.
*Population Reference Bureau, 1996 (midyear estimate); Banister, p.252;
State Statistical Burear, Xinjiang Statistical Yearbook, 1994, p.39.

Yuan (1990) has described in detail the chronology of population growth in Xinjiang during the socialist period. As he noted, Xinjiang grew very rapidly during the 1950s, and much of this growth was the result of the migration of Han Chinese to the region and the role of the Production and Construction Corps in setting up military farms and resettling soldiers and their families. Thus, the Han share of the population grew especially rapidly during this period.

Xinjiang did not suffer the serious famine of the Great Leap forward in 1958, and it witnessed explosive growth as refugees flooded the region from other parts of China in search of food. As conditions improved, many of these refugees returned to their homes thus leaving an absolute reduction in population in 1962. For the next decade, birth rates were extremely high and led to renewed rapid population growth. This growth only subsided in the mid-1970s following the implementation of a serious family planning program especially among the Han Chinese. Since then the rate of population growth has declined based on reduced migration and birth rates. The great influx of Han Chinese largely abated after the early 1960s and has stabilized at about 40% of Xinjiang's total population (Yuan, p..52).

Crude birthrates in Xinjiang in recent years have been slightly higher than the average for China, for example in 1995 - 18.90/1,000 in Xinjiang versus 17.12/1,000 for China. Presumably this results from the more flexible rules that apply to minority nationalities that allow a larger number of children for each minority family because of the much smaller total population of ethnic minorities relative to the Han. At the same time the crude death rate remains higher than China's national average which resulted in a 1995 annual rate of increase of 1.245%. Based on a 1995 total population 16.61 million, this yielded a net natural increase of 206,800 new souls. It is clear from Xinjiang's recent population growth that while natural increase is the largest factor, it is only one facet of the process of population increase and its concomitant process of urbanization in Xinjiang.

An interesting aspect of this population growth is the extremely rapid increase in the Han Chinese share of the total population, increasing from an estimated 5-6% in the early 1940s to approximately 38% in 1993. Since Han are strongly although not exclusively concentrated in urban places, their increase has paralleled the rapid growth in urbanisation during the socialist period of the last 45 years (Table 21.3). For example, in Urumqi, Xinjiang's largest city, almost 3/4s of the population are of Han nationality. All of the cities north of the Tien Shan range have at least half of their population as Han. Yuan (1990) has noted that Han are especially concentrated along an axis east-west through Urumqi and its adjacent cities and towns. The in-migration and rapid growth of the Han population, we postulate, accounts in large part for the rapid urbanisation and city growth in Xinjiang since 1949.

Table 21.3 Population of Major Nationality Groups in Xinjiang, 1990-95

Nationality Group	1990	1993	1995 (EST.)	1995 % share of Provincial Population
Uighur	7,207,024	7,589,468	7,849,532	47
Han	5,695,626	6,036,700	6,243,217	38
Kazak	1,110,758	1,196,416	1,237,059	07
Hui	681,527	732,416	757,129	05
Kyrgyz	139,781	154,282	159,287	01
Mongol	137,740	149,198	154,115	01
Tadjik	33,223			
Uzbek	14,763			
Russian	8,802			
Tatar	4,821			

Sources: Xinjiang Statistical Yearbook, 1994: 50-51.
China Statistical Yearbook, 1996, p. 56.

21.3   Urban Policy and Urban Development

As Zhou (1993, p.9) noted recently in an essay on China's urban growth policy, the central government has had a formally established urban policy in place for 10 years that seeks, "to control the size of large cities, with populations greater than 500,000, properly develop medium sized cities (200,000 - 500,000) and actively promote small cities, less than 200,000." Zhou makes the point that such a policy had in fact been in use for 30 years despite its formal articulation only recently. It is useful to review what has happened to the urban system and network of cities in Xinjiang in the context of this urban policy and to evaluate the extent to which this policy has been used or ignored in terms of actual developments in Xinjiang. As shall be noted below, there has indeed been an expansion and articulation of smaller cities and towns in the provincial hierarchy during the last four decades. At the same time, Urumqi has also experienced remarkable growth as the great regional administrative, transportation, industrial and commercial centre. Urbanisation and the urban population have grown dramatically in the period of socialist development of Xinjiang (Figure 21.1). As the graphs demonstrate, the urban population, defined generally as the share of the population in cities and towns, has increased from about 560,000 in 1950, which was approximately 13% of the population, to almost five million and an urban share of roughly 34% in 1996 (State Statistical Bureau, a, 1995) which was greater than China's reported national average figure (28%) for urbanisation. At the same time, we note, the non-agricultural share of the urbanised population in Xinjiang was also higher than the national average. This suggests to us a structural difference in the economic and functional role of urban populations in Xinjiang. Xinjiang's urban population has grown steadily during the last half century in step with and more rapidly than the overall growth in the region's total population (Table 21.4) The population growth indicated periods of especially rapid increase such as from 1965-1975 with an increase of almost four million amounting to 68%, a remarkable rise. This occurred during a period of political turmoil in China that witnessed forced migration which almost certainly had an impact. At the same time there was very little increase in the urban population.

There sometimes appear to be inconsistencies in Chinese official data that relate to cities and urban populations. Often these may be attributed to various definitions used either in the location of residents and administrative boundaries of cities or in the employment of the urban and suburban residents. Ma and Cui (1987) have investigated and explained the varying definitions in full detail. Here we seek to employ consistent figures based on common definition such as location of urban residents, although this is not always

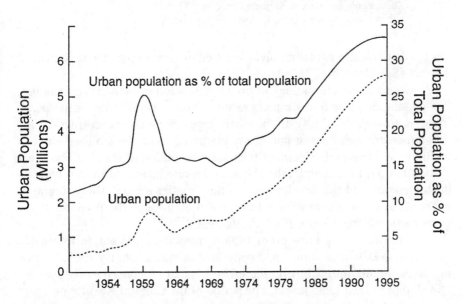

Figure 21.1 Growth of Xinjiang Urban Population

Table 21.4 Xinjiang Uygur A.R. Level of Urbanisation

	Urban %	Urban Population
1949	12.21	529,300
1954	15.02	751,100
1957	16.86	940,700
1960	26.00	1,800,400
1963	16.98	1,210,900
1967	16.50	1,438,700
1970	15.37	1,501,400
1973	16.80	1,829,300
1975	19.04	2,198,400
1978	20.09	2,476,900
1985	27.16	3,696,500
1993	31.77	5,099,100
1995 (est.)	33.31	5,532,800
1996 (est.)	34.08	5,731,300

1993 and 1994 figures are based on city and suburban districts. Earlier figures are based on Shizhen totals (city and township) and include some agricultural populations. These measures while not comparable, both include commercial agriculturalists in suburban areas.
Sources: China, Forty Years of Urban Development:. pp188-189.
  Zhou, Zhongguo renkou Xinjiang Fence. pp 187, 188.
  Urban Statistical Yearbook of China, 1994, p. 51; 1995, p. 51.

easy to do or clearly explained and identified in some of the official statistical sources (See also Chan, 1994).

Consider the chronology of urban population growth in Xinjiang. Urban population growth in Xinjiang resulted from several forces seen operating over time (Table 21.4). In the early stages of socialist construction, the urban increase was modest but steady involving some demobilised soldiers and migrants from other parts of China. In the period of the first Five Year Plan, 1953-57, for example, the urbanisation rate increased in step with industrialisation and the development of this frontier region. Many migrants, however, as noted above were soldiers resettled through the Production and Construction Corps (Yuan, 1990; Zhou, 1990).

The Great Leap Forward of 1958 witnessed a rapid but unsustainable growth in industries accompanied with rapid urbanization. By 1963, following an economic retrenchment, the urban population consequently also declined to pre-Great Leap levels. The period of the Cultural Revolution again brought erratic policies on migration and economic growth. Defence considerations were also involved, as the perceived threats from the USSR and the

United States led to industrial development and construction in isolated areas. Overall, the level of urbanisation increased modestly to about 17% by the mid-1970s (Zhou, 1990).

The period following the end of the Cultural Revolution in 1977 witnessed a rapid surge in migration to cities. Policies on farm labourers were relaxed to allow these people to move to cities to supply needed labour services. At the same time, previously rusticated youths who had been sent down to the countryside during the aftermath of the Great Leap and The Cultural Revolution were allowed to return to the cities. This led to renewed migration to cities and quickened rates of growth. At the same time criteria defining the designation of cities and towns were modified which led to expansion of the number of such places thereby further inflating the legally defined number of urban residents (Zhou, 1990).

This growth in population and urbanisation has paralleled a sharp increase in the number of cities and towns especially since the beginning of the economic reforms in the late 1970's. For example, in 1978 there were only seven officially designated cities of which only Urumqi was a prefectural level city. Today there are seventeen official cities, and three have been designated as prefectural cities. (Table 21.5). A similar trend has followed in the designation of towns, and many urban places in fact had their origins as the administrative and service centres of military farms. Such places over time simply grew, accreted new economic and administrative functions and transformed themselves into functioning urban places. It is in such transformations that the Han Chinese have played a particularly significant role in Xinjiang's recent urbanization.

City population data are provided in Table 21.5. It is clear that Urumqi is in fact a primate city having a population almost three times the population of the next city, Akesu, in the hierarchy (city proper population only). If we look at the non-agricultural population only in the city proper, Urumqi's primacy is even more prominent at almost five times the size of the next city, Kelemayi. Certainly a visit to Urumqi discloses its multi-functional role as commercial, transportation, administrative, and industrial centre for the Junggar Basin and all of Xinjiang.

Of the seventeen cities in Xinjiang, only five of them are located in the large Tarim Basin south of the Tian Shan Range (Maps 21.1 and 21.2), and these are smaller cities. Despite the historical significance of the ancient Silk Road and the traditional routes into Central Asia through the Tarim, it is clear that the most dynamic recent growth and urbanization has occurred north of the Tian Shan in the Junggar Basin. Transportation development has followed and enhanced this pattern of urban settlement which is also reflective of the industrialisation of the region (Map 21.3). Urunqi serves as an urban magnet,

Table 21.5 Xinjiang Uygur A.R., 1993 Urban Populations of Major Nationalities

	Total pop.	Uygur	Han	Kazakh	Hui	Kirghiz	Mongol
Xinjiang Total	16,052,548	7,589,468	6,036,700	1,196,416	732,416	154,282	149,198
City							
Urumqi	1,379,327	173,788	1,007,478	39,889	135,177	760	4,680
Kelemayi	220,088	33,939	166,356	8,744	5,652	94	1,613
Shihizi	536,071	5,587	511,576	2,895	11,977	40	491
Tulufan	230,291	165,252	47,238	29	17,359	-	15
Hami	306,173	78,574	203,567	9,305	12,213	3	492
Changji	293,053	8,304	222,731	15,760	42,377	49	665
Fukang	132,535	6,745	97,809	10,965	15,795	14	251
Bole	176,214	31,890	110,987	15,192	6,513	31	10,554
Kuerle	290,202	88,329	191,830	44	6,216	6	2,453
Akesu	425,856	188,764	231,095	26	4,284	94	265
Atushi	176,449	144,844	9,805	17	74	21,616	12
Kashi	236,019	176,057	56,997	40	1,159	143	60
Hetian	140,233	117,438	22,308	18	390	15	10
Kuitun	231,585	646	22,858	3,149	5,261	23	574
Yining	204,258	140,825	96,314	12,886	24,219	266	594
Tacheng	136,677	4,675	87,844	20,951	9,417	1,595	1,327
Aletai	187,918	4,818	112,507	61,425	5,621	9	2,128

Sources: Bureau of Statistics, Xinjiang Uygur, A.R. 1994
        Xinjiang Statistical Yearbook, 1994: 50-51
Note: Columns and rows will not balance as totals because some population groups are omitted.

and metropolitan growth may be seen in the clustering effect of smaller cities around Urumqi. In addition, this is where the greatest concentration of Han Chinese are, and this is clearly where the fastest growth and recent urbanisation are occurring.

21.4   Growth and Development of Towns

In the early years of socialist development, prior to 1960, Xinjiang had only a few cities, and the town population accounted for the preponderance of the urban population (Table 21.6). In the 1950s, more of these towns were upgraded to cities, and the town share of the urban population fell, although during the politically turbulent periods of the 1960s and early 1970s there

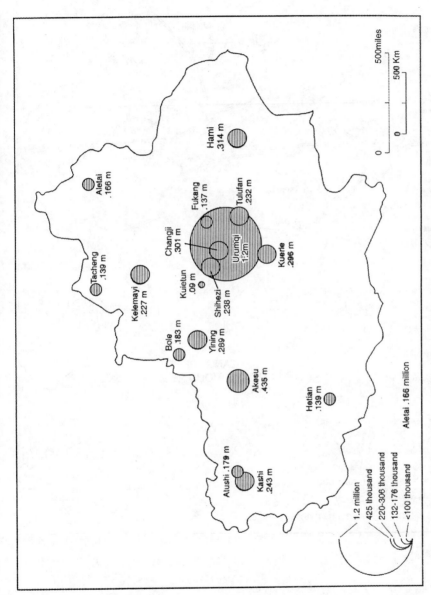

Map 21.2 Xinjiang Uygur: Cities 1994 (Population of City Proper)

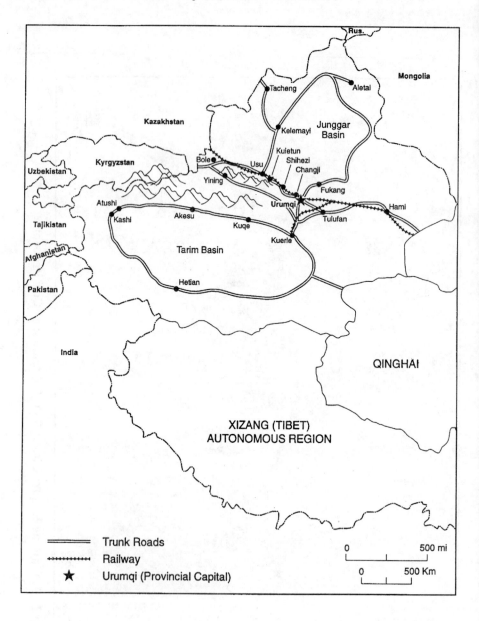

**Map 21.3 Xinjiang Uygur Autonomous Region: Cities and Main
Transport Links**

were erratic increases and declines in town populations (Zhou, 1990, p.205).

In the reforms that followed 1977, many new cities and towns have been designated and the number of towns has increased greatly. At the same time, however, the share of urban population in designated towns has continued to decline. By 1990, the number of towns had increased to 131, and the non-agricultural populations in these towns had reached 978,192, figure that climbed to 1,274,831 by 1993 (Bureau of Statistics, Xinjiang, 1994) (State Statistical Bureau, 1995 b).

These towns and their growth are clearly important in the overall process of urban growth and evolution in Xinjiang. Examination of their functional role disclosed in 1982 more than 25% of their employment was on average in industrial activities with another 16% in commerce and 11% in governmental activities, 10% in agriculture, 9% each in construction and transportation, and 8% in education. Based on recent discussions with town officials, we postulate the continued importance of industrial and commercial activities with growing needs in both the construction and transportation sectors.

Table 21.6 Xinjiang, Town Population

Year	Population	% Oof Xinjiang uban population
1949	441,300	83
1952	499,000	81
1954	455,100	61
1959	868,300	54
1963	538,700	44
1969	647,400	41
1972	763,300	45
1975	1,089,100	49

Source: Bureau of Statistics, Xinjiang, 1994.

Based on our recent field visits in 1995, it seems clear the towns have a crucial role to play in providing a subordinate framework on which the urban hierarchy of Xinjiang continues to unfold and elaborate itself. Agricultural activities continue to be important, but the towns provide a transitional mechanism including industrial as well as service and commercial employment opportunities for local people to transform their activities and lifestyles from rural to urban. Town development is also typically seen as subordinate to but closely related to city growth both functionally and locationally given the special circumstances on which both agriculture and society depend and thrive.

21.5 Migration

In recent years (1985-1990) net inter-provincial migration to and from Xinjiang, according to official statistics, is modest and accounted for a total gain of only 13,586 people. Yet migration has been a very significant factor in Xinjiang's earlier population and urban growth under socialism (Li, 1989; Barnett, 1993). The first 14 years (1949-1962) was the period of greatest migration and growth, although subsequently urban growth has mainly depended on natural increase of the population (Zhou, 1990: 194-197).

The major migration of Han Chinese as noted, occurred during the 1950s with the resettlement of many soldiers and peasants from eastern China. This settlement and migration continued during the 1960s with workers sent to Third Line and other critical extractive industries that were being developed especially in the politically sensitive Junggar Basin adjacent to the former Soviet border (Li, 1989). The 1960s were a period of political turmoil with substantial numbers of refugee migrants and transferred city dwellers and youth looking for better conditions. Many of these "drifters" wound up in Xinjiang. Once politics stabilized in the late 1970s, migration to Xinjiang slowed (Yuan, 1990).

More recent migration data (Table 21.7) from the last half of the decade of the 1980s are instructive in what they show of the destination of inter-provincial migrants to Xinjiang. More than two-thirds of the almost 350,000 in-migrants settled in cities and towns. Since the origin places of most of these migrants were the densely populated provinces of eastern China, especially Sichuan and Henan, we assume they are preponderantly of Han nationality. Thus, on the one hand it seems safe to assert this facet of Xinjiang's population growth and urbanisation will likely continue although at a diminished rate.

On the other hand, it is clear from Table 21.8 that there is also a substantial out-migration to other areas of China, and there are no published data to tell us the nationality of these people. During the five year period, 1985-1990, the net urban migration was only 13,586 people which seems a comparatively modest, almost insignificant, and less than 10% of the overall urban growth in Xinjiang during that period.

The reasons for migrating are consistent with our conceptual understanding of the motives and reasons for migrations in other developing and developed countries (Todaro, 1989; Skeldon, 1990; and Chan, 1994, p. 115). Work, job transfers and job assignments accounted for almost half of all migrants (see Table 21.9). Another third of all migrants listed the move as related to their need to be with family or friends, and some of these likely were in search of employment opportunities. At this point, it seems clear that the

**Table 21.7 Inter-Provincial Migration to Xinjiang, 1985-90
(Number of Migrants)**

Province Of Origin	Total Immigration, (A)	% Rural in Origin, (B)	To Cities, (C)	To Towns, (D)	To Villages, (E)	Columns (C+D) as % of (A), (F)
Beijing	1,027	7.7	948	42	37	96.4
Tianjin	480	21.0	401	21	58	87.9
Hebei	5,150	69.1	3,554	604	992	80.7
Shanxi	2,215	76.9	1,239	560	416	81.2
Nei Monggol	1,292	44.7	905	295	92	92.9
Liaoning	1,188	34.9	938	74	176	85.2
Jilin	920	36.7	684	85	151	83.6
Heilongjiang	1,195	51.2	772	181	242	79.7
Shanghai	1,319	9.3	1,172	59	88	93.3
Jiangsu	20,794	87.3	12,064	3,291	5,439	73.9
Zhejiang	11,137	87.1	6,912	2,169	2,056	81.5
Anhui	12,929	92.2	6,549	1,946	4,434	65.7
Fujian	821	77.6	592	76	153	81.4
Jiangxi	1,212	65.4	575	158	479	60.5
Shandong	16,048	88.3	8,300	2,270	5,478	65.9
Henan	58,130	92.8	29,115	8,474	20,541	64.7
Hubei	6,843	79.0	4,397	702	1,744	74.5
Hunan	7,329	80.5	4,350	1,131	1,848	74.8
Guangdong	1,907	65.9	494	87	1,326	30.5
Guangxi	1,289	86.4	441	173	675	47.6
Hainan	290	81.7	14	11	265	8.6
Sichuan	118,233	94.0	59,159	18,090	40,984	65.3
Guizhou	532	71.6	307	60	165	69.0
Yunnan	350	43.4	210	41	99	71.7
Xizang	145	22.1	105	13	27	81.4
Shaanxi	20,660	76.1	12,784	3,160	4,716	77.2
Gansu	38,743	91.0	18,055	4,896	15,792	59.2
Quinghai	2,722	67.5	1,398	442	882	67.6
Ningxia	6,818	90.6	2,130	712	3,976	41.7
Total	341,759	88.2	178,596	49,826	113,337	66.8

Source: Calculated from 1990 Census: 156-331.

Table 21.8 Inter-Provincial Migration to and from the Cities and Towns of Xinjiang, 1985-90 (Number of Migrants)

Province	In-migration to the cities and towns of Xinjiang from:* (A)	Out-migration from the cities and towns of Xinjiang to:* (B)	Net migration to the cities and towns of Xinjiang from:*
Sichuan	77,249	28,759	48,490
Henan	37,589	26,143	11,446
Gansu	22,951	15,159	7,792
Jiangsu	15,355	22,525	-7,170
Shaanxi	15,944	21,328	-5,384
Shandong	10,570	16,804	-6,234
Zhejiang	9,081	6,123	2,958
Anhui	8,495	6,560	1,935
Hunan	5,481	7,287	-1,806
Hubei	5,099	8,997	-3,898
Hebei	4,158	10,364	-6,206
Ningxia	2,842	1,040	1,802
Qinghai	1,840	1,123	717
Shanxi	1,799	3,531	-1,732
Shanghai	1,231	14,222	-12,991
Nei Monggol	1,200	1,651	-451
Liaoning	1,012	2,508	-1,496
Beijing	990	5,633	-4,643
Heilongjiang	953	490	463
Jilin	769	1,112	-343
Jiangxi	733	1,232	-499
Fujian	668	1,098	-430
Guangxi	614	1,364	-750
Guangdong	581	3,926	-3,345
Tianjin	422	4,119	-3,697
Hainan	25	268	-243
Guizhou	367	593	-226
Yunnan	251	724	-473
TOTAL	228,269	214,683	13,586

*All places (cities, towns and villages) in the provinces of origin/destination.
Source: Calculated from the 1990 census, Vol. 4: 156-331.

periods of great migration, especially of Han Chinese, to Xinjiang are over. While there is likely to be some inter-provincial migration, its effect on urbanisation and city growth will be modest unless there is a radical change in policy or circumstance.

Of equal interest is the matter of internal migration in Xinjiang. Here it is clear that recent trends have witnessed a substantial flow of ruralites and small town folk from the villages and towns of Xinjiang to the cities. This is a process (see Table 21.10) one would expect as the region modernises its economic structure and accelerates its shift from a traditional oasis farming and herding economy to a modem industrial and service economy, the kind of process that has been especially prominent in the Junggar Basin of northern Xinjiang. The net migration to cities in the intercensal period was 140,000 with only a very small flow from cities to towns and villages. One intriguing trend worth noting is the continuation of village to village movement of more than 22,000 during the same period. Such a movement of people suggests continuation of traditional movement of indigenous people within well established social and perhaps related commercial networks of a traditional society.

21.6 Economic Shift and Development

Urbanisation in Xinjiang, offers a somewhat different pattern in terms of structural change in the economy of cities. Data for only two were available, but they offer two remarkably different examples of the structural patterns of urban economies in Xinjiang (Table 21.11). In this way they also provide insights into the economic roles of different ethnic groups in the region. Urumqi, as early as 1978, had more than half its labour force classified as industrial, obviously in keeping with the Maoist dictum to serve as a "producer" city.

At this time it had more than one-third of its labour force in tertiary or service activities. This had grown to 40% by 1988, while the industrial share had declined slightly. At the same time paradoxically, the share of city's labour force in agriculture had actually increased which seems illogical in a situation of rapid economic growth and development. Yet the pressure to produce enough food to satisfy local needs is great, and the city commands water resources from adjacent mountains to support its oasis agriculture.

Kashi, by contrast, has only data for 1988, but it indicates an urban labour force heavily engaged in primary activities (73%) with a substantial share (23.4%) in tertiary activities, and very few workers in industrial jobs. Kashi is located at the western end of the Tarim Basin and has a largely Uygur

Table 21.9 Reasons for Inter-Provincial Migration to Xinjiang 1985-90

Reason	Number	Percent	Cities	Towns	Villages
			Places of Origin		
Job transfer	11,425	3.4	4,055	2,699	4,671
Job assignment after college	9,653	2.8	7,462	953	1,238
Work in factory or enter business	136,494	40.0	2,657	4,365	129,472
Study or job training	2,306	0.7	834	511	961
To live with relatives or friends	99,229	29.0	2,684	3,757	92,788
Retirement	411	0.1	160	103	148
Family dependent	28,133	8.2	1,587	2,210	24,336
Marriage	26,711	7.8	555	953	25,203
Others	27,356	8.0	3,155	1,584	22,617
Total	341,718	100.0	23,149	17,135	301,434

%Columns many not total 100% due to rounding.
Source: State Statistical Bureau, 4th National Census, 1990.

Table 21.10 Intra-Provincial Migration in Xinjiang, 1985-90

(Number of persons)

From cities to cities:	81,345
From cities to towns:	9,798
From cities to villages:	14,077
Subtotal:	105,220
From towns to cities:	68,036
From towns to towns:	17,509
From towns to villages:	15,067
Subtotal	100,612
From villages to cities:	98,827
From villages to towns:	13,994
From villages to villages	22,765
Subtotal:	80,672

Source: PRC 1990 census, Vol. 4: 330-331.

Table 21.11   Xinjiang, Urban Economics Indicators and Shift, 1978-88

URUMQI URBAN LABOUR FORCE ALLOCATION, 1978-1988

	1978	(%)	1980	(%)	1985	(%)	1988	(%)
Primary	2.68	8.3	2.75	7.5	3.11	5.4	7.92	11
Secondary	17.63	54.6	20.05	54.9	30.15	52.3	33.69	49
Tertiary	11.97	37.1	13.69	37.5	24.41	42.3	22.77	40

Units = 10,000 persons

KASHI URBAN LABOUR FORCE ALLOCATION, 1978-1988

	1978	1980	1985	1988	(%)
Primary	nd	nd	nd	3.94	73.0
Secondary	nd	nd	nd	0.19	3.5
Tertiary	nd	nd	nd	1.26	23.4

Units = 10,000 persons

GNP PER-CAPITAL

	1980	1985	1988
Urumqi	945	nd	3,894
Kashi	458	1,000	1,162

Units: RMB Yuan

Source: China: *Forty Years of Urban Development: 138-145; 158; 159.*

population. Its economy is traditional and depends on trading and activities related to the primary sector. It has no railroad and must rely on highway traffic traversing extremely high mountains to trade with Central Asia or a long haul across the northern or southern margins of the Taklamakan to link to other regions of Xinjiang and China. If we look at growth in per-capita gross national product, Kashi's rate has more than doubled in the decade of the 1980s, but the increase in per-capita GNP in Urumqi more than quadrupled.

Such data illustrate a substantial discrepancy between the key urban centres in what might be described as two regional networks of cities in Xinjiang, the dynamic, industrial, and well integrated northern network located mainly in the Junggar Basin north of the Tien Shan and the more traditional, rural-associated, largely indigenous peopled urban network of the south, the Tarim Basin. This is not a perfect characterization as transport expansion occurs in the extension of the rail line to Kuerle in the eastern zone of the Tarim. This line will eventually be extended to Kuqe, Akesu and on to Kashi. Kuerle is an industrial city with good transport links and has a much larger

Han share of its population. Such a pattern may be a portent of industrial growth and city development in other places in the Tarim. At the same time expansion and development of new industries are becoming more important in all of these cities and many towns. Greater availability of manufactured products provides more goods for the growing cross-national trade, on important and complementary aspect of economic development in the Xinjiang region.

21.7 Trade and Urban Development

Trade is an essential element of economic activity and growth that has a substantial if non-quantifiable impact on urban growth and development within Xinjiang at this time. It affects both the Han population and the indigenous peoples, although in different ways. The role of international trade, especially that focused on the neighbouring former Soviet republics, is profound for the indigenous peoples as they trade with those of common cultural background (Toops, 1994).

The border towns and cities such as Kashi, Tacheng, and Ining are the loci for much of this trade and exchange, but the effects extend into the centres for the manufacture of a variety of goods in demand across the border. Thus, Urumqi is much affected and benefits in a number of ways as the commercial, transportation and industrial centre of Xinjiang from such increased trade. Trade has been crucial in the ebb and flow of people and caravans across this vast region, and its benefits once again are reflected in intensified trading activities and linkages across this region.

The improved political climate and reduced tensions along the borders with the former Soviet republics coupled with the effect of Chinese economic reforms have led to rapid growth in cross border trade with improved transport linkages and expanded movement of commodities and traders. As Toops (1994) noted, the most profound effects have been on people and families cut off from one another for 30 years who have been able to re-establish their connections and ties. China's continued economic growth and expanding foreign policy initiatives argue for increased trade and cross-border linkages in Xinjiang. Such activity will have a positive and constructive effect on urban development and city growth in the region.

21.8 Conclusions

Urbanisation after a slow beginning in previous centuries associated with a small trans-Asian trade flow increased in the 20th century. The real growth in cities, however, has paralleled the growth in population and Han Chinese in-migration to Xinjiang. This is associated with a Chinese communist policy of military and agricultural colonisation consistent with traditional Chinese approaches to deal with frontier territories. The process was simply intensified in scale and pace as a result of the sensitivity of Xinjiang's border with the former Soviet Union, the rapid growth of China's population and the search for new agricultural land and resources to exploit. All of the factors have led to expansion and improvement of the transportation system, the growth of cities and towns, the rapid expansion of industries especially those associated with extractive industries and local products such as wool and an overall provincial rate of urbanisation greater than the national average.

The migration processes offer an interesting parallel to the forces of urbanisation. During the 1950s and 1960s there was substantial in-migration of Han Chinese. While there continues to be a perceptible stream of in-migration from other provinces, it is almost offset by a substantial out-migration as well. So the net effect of into-provincial migration today on population and urbanisation is slight. At the same time there is clearly a substantial flow of rural people from the villages and towns of Xinjiang into its cities, and this likely will continue as a significant force in the urban transformation of the region.

There are in Xinjiang today clear regional variations in the urban systems perhaps most easily associated with a Junggar or northern hierarchy focused on Urumqi and a series of smaller industrial centres and trading centres located near the border with central Asia states. The Tarim Basin south of the Tian Shan Range supports a smaller and less dynamic network of cities that reflects the less hospitable regional environment, the poorly developed transportation network and a poorly developed industrial sector. The hierarchy of subordinate towns is also much smaller and less dynamic. In addition, this southern region has only a small number of Han Chinese in its ethnic mix.

Cities in Xinjiang in part play the traditional role of frontier centres of trade and administrative and military control. However, many now play a vital role as industrial centres with the rapid growth of extractive industries or industries that serve the needs and demands of local, regional and cross-national populations. Improved transport links have thrust Xinjiang increasingly into a role as bustling frontier tying greater China to its outlying parts as well as intensifying the connections it has with its central Asian neighbours.

References

Allen, Thomas B. (1996), 'Zinging,' *National Geographic*, Vol. 189, No. 3: 2-43.

Banister, Judith (1987) *China's Changing Population*, Stanford, CA: Stanford University Press.

Barnett, A. Doak (1993) 'Chinese Turkestan: Zinging' in *China's Far West*. Boulder CO: Westview Press: 341-409.

Bureau of Statistics, Zinging Uygur A.R., (1994) *Zinging Statistical Yearbook*, 1994, Urumqi: Zinging Bureau of Statistics.

Chan, Kam Wing (1994) *Cities with Invisible Walls*, Hong Kong: Oxford University Press.

Gaubatz, Piper (1995) *Beyond the Great Wall, Urban Form and Transformation on the Chinese Frontiers*, Stanford, CA: Stanford University Press.

Gladney, Dru (1990) 'Ethnogenesis of the Uighur', *Central Asian Survey*, Vol 9, No. 1: 1-28.

Kristof, Ladis (1959) 'The nature of Frontiers and Boundaries,' *Annals of the Association of American Geographers*, Vol. 49, No. 3: 269-282.

Lattimore, Owen (1940) *Inner Asian Frontiers of China*, London: Oxford University Press.

Li, *Rose Maria, (1989) 'Migration to China's Northern Frontier,' Population* and Development Review, Vol. 15, No. 3: 503-538.

Ma, L. J. C. and Cui, G. H. (1987) 'Administrative Changes and Urban population in China,' *Annals Association of American Geographers* Vol. 77: 373-395.

Mackerras, Colin (1994) *China's Minorities*, Hong Kong: Oxford University Press.

Population Census Office, State Council and Department of Population Statistics State Statistical Bureau (1991) *1990 Population Census of the PRC*, Beijing: China Statistical Publishing House, Vol. 4.

Skeldon, Ronald (1990) *Population Mobility in Developing Countries*. London: Belhaven press.

State Statistical Bureau (1990) *Forty Years of Urban Development* Beijing: China Statistical Publisher.

State Statistical Bureau (1995a) *China Statistical Yearbook*, 1994, Beijing: China Statistical Publisher.

State Statistical Bureau (1995b) *Urban Statistical Yearbook of China* 1993-94, Beijing: China Statistical Publishers.

Todaro, Michael (1989) *Economic Development in the Third World*, New York: London.

Toops, Stanley (1994) 'Trade between Zinging and Central Asia,' in L. Benson, J. Rudelson and S. Toops, *Zinging in the Twentieth Century*, Washington, D. C.: the Woodrow Wilson Centre Occasional Paper No. 65.

Von Glahn, Richard (1987) *The Country of Streams and Grottoes: Expansion, Settlement and the Civilizing of the Sichuan Frontier in Song Times*. Cambridge, MA: Council on East Asian Studies, Harvard University.

Yuan, Qingli (1990) 'Population Changes in Zinging Uighur Autonomous Region (1949-1984) *Modern Asian Survey*, Vol. 9: 49-73. Zhou, Chongjing, (1990, Zhongguo renkou: Zinging Fence (*China's Population*: Zinging Volume) Beijing: China Finance and Economics Press.

Zhou, Yixing (1993) 'China's National Urban Growth Policy,' in Kok Chiang Tan, Wolfgang Taubmann and Ye, Shunzan, eds. *Urban Development in China and South-East Asia*, Bremen, Germany: University of Bremen: 9-27.

PART IV
GOVERNMENT AND INSTITUTIONS

Editors' notes to Part IV

*In one sense cities can be seen as anarchic spontaneous growths re-
flecting the new spatial configurations which changing production
technologies make desirable. But by definition they also have to represent social co-ordination – in pure anarchy there could, for example,
be no pattern of major and minor roads, and no provision for the
wayleave of services. There is no rule which says whether this co-
ordination relies or should rely on the public sector, or on NGOs or
other CBOs. Who undertakes the functions of social co-ordination –
and in what spheres over what issues – varies from society to society ,
and period to period. In this Part, Hung-Kai Wang and Chun-Ju Li
show how changes in Shanghai's administration of land represent a
hand-over from public to a mixture of privatised and semi-privatised
public bodies, and some private investors, with intriguing side effects
and substantial changes in wealth patterns. Vandana Desai looks very
specifically at the relations between local government and NGO's in
Mumbai – a relationship advocated as a partnership, but which always falls short of that goal for identifiable reasons. Hamish Main
tackles very similar structural issues, though specifically on the topic
of environmental quality in Calcutta. Jan Veenstra takes a more meta-
level approach. Who needs what sort of data to aid their decision-
making? How can we co-ordinate information held in different agencies, but which would be more valuable if brought together? His answers overlap with the chapters in the next Part. Finally Okuno Shii
considers the extent to which major cities – in this case port cities –
can mould their own future.*

22 Shanghai's Land Development: A View from the Transformation of Mainland China's Administrative Systems since 1978

Hung-Kai Wang and Chun-Ju Li

22.1 Introduction

Changes in the institutions related to land development are among the central elements of the economic reforms in mainland China that started in 1978. They also generated some of the most critical issues faced by the nation which has been under the transition from a basically orthodox socialist economy to a "socialist market economy with Chinese characteristics". The purpose of this paper is to clarify the relationship between urban land development and the institutional changes as they are carried out by the administrative systems at local levels. Because of its phenomenal growth since early 1990s, the city of Shanghai is used as an example in the analysis.

The chapter is composed of three major parts. First, we briefly review the development and changes that have taken place in the institutions related to land and its usage, emphasizing the differences that existed among institutions before/after the 1949 "liberation", and before/after the on-going economic reform's commencement in 1978. Then, based on some findings from our empirical studies on the post-1978 Shanghai, we try to show how land has been treated as a means to help achieve the all-important economic development. Finally, the interactions among institutions of land use, city planning, enterprise reforms, and delegation of administrative powers between local governments, that determine the geographic pattern of spatial development, are to be clarified. Hopefully this type of empirical research will shed light on the way to a fuller understanding of the spatial structure of China's transforming socialism.

22.2 A Brief Description of the Development of Land Policies and Related Institutions in Mainland China

There are two types of land ownership in mainland China: national ownership and collective ownership. The former applies to towns and cities, and the latter to rural areas.[1] No individual or establishment can occupy, trade, lease, or transfer rights on land by means not allowed by law. This socialist public land ownership was of course based on communist doctrines.[2] A land revolution was deemed the only solution to old China's land problem and thus determined the land policies of the early-stage Chinese Communist Party.[3] However, there were some technical variations among different time periods and geographic regions.

22.2.1 Before the "Liberation" (1927-48)

Communist forces were basically contained in the rural areas of the nation, land policies being therefore focused on those territories, and the central issue was how the old "feudal" land ownership system could be abolished and mass impoverished peasants could have their own land ("land to the tiller", as an element of agricultural production). Policies fluctuated between outright confiscation of land from the landowners (and the head-count-based even distribution to poor peasants), and more moderate means of reducing the land rents or interests, depending on national political situations and local conditions.

22.2.2 Between the "Liberation" and the Economic Reforms (1949-77)

With the formal establishment of the socialist government, necessities rose for policies and administrative systems to be modified to cover urban land and non-agricultural land user entities. The "Land Reform Act of P.R.C." was enabled in 1950 to liberate agricultural productivity. In 1951, the "Land Reform Regulations for Cities and Suburbs" was enacted, so local governments could confiscate or commandeer suburban land owned by individuals or organizations. By 1952-53, basic tasks of land reform were considered accomplished under the system wherein land was controlled by the state while

1 See article 10 of the Constitution of the People's Republic of China and article 2 of the Land Management Act. But the state retains the right to commandeer collectively owned land when it is needed for urban expansion or public interests.
2 See, for example, the Communist Manifesto among numerous other communist statements and conference resolutions.
3 See a resolution adopted by the 6th plenary meeting of the Chinese Communist Party, 1928.

peasants could own their land. An important decision was made by the central government in 1954 to relinquish the land-use charges and rents on state-owned enterprises as well as educational, military and other types of establishments.[4] After the mid- and late-1950s when the peasant private land ownership was circumscribed and transformed by a number of regulations and policies (including the development of agricultural cooperatives and finally the effectuating of the communes), the co-existence of the dual national as well as collective land ownership was secured until the commencement of the current economic reforms in 1978.[5]

The notion then held by the Chinese Communists was the utopian assumption that once the private land ownership was done away with, so would be the land rent. But curiously, the usage of land, one of the most basic elements of production, was not subject to the strict central planning control as was almost any other resource in those hey days of the socialist economy. Possible reasons include the fact that: a) due to the rent-less notion of land and the vast land area of the nation, of which the Chinese have long been boasting, land as a form of resource might have failed to assert its fundamental significance in national development; b) agricultural land supplies were not subject to apparent competition pressures from the slow urbanisation process of land, because of the insufficient investment in non-agricultural infrastructure; and, probably most importantly, c) the power of land management was split among so many functional branches of the government (e.g., agriculture, forestry, water resources, transportation, energy, and urban development), there was no one unitary local administrative authority powerful enough to carry out effective planning and control (Chou,1993). A myriad of problems had thus resulted, such as lack of land-use efficiency, illegal occupancy and construction, shortage of funds for construction of urban infrastructure (partially due to the inability to recapture adequate portions of profits from urban land development), chaotic land-use patterns, and the impossibility of economic implementation of the state ownership of land (the effectual paring of the rights to benefit from and handle the land on the part of the state).[6]

22.2.3 Since the Economic Reforms (1978 to Present)

There have been drastic changes in the conception of land held by the Chinese Communists since the economic reforms went under way. Among

---

4 *As long as the land area is commensurate to the land user agent's actual needs and future development; see Chou Cheng, 1989. P.263.*

5 *See Hsiao Tze-yueh,1991; Wang Shung-san,1990; and Gue Chiang-fang,1994.*

6 *Numerous authors have pointed out land-use problems associated with the non-market land development system, e.g., Ma Keh-wei, 1992 and Chou Cheng, 1993.*

the most influential and fundamental is the switch from the assumption that land was an unredeemed social resource to be allocated by the state according to its all-embracing planning apparatus, to the conception of land basically as an element of production (and profit-making) and as a commodity to be priced and appropriated by the market. From this change of heart, starting in 1979, came a series of new legislations, amendments, and administrative adjustments, including the decision by the central government in 1983 to levy new land-use charges, the enabling of the Land Management Act and the establishment of the National Bureau of Land Management in 1986, the all important amendments to the Constitution and Land Management Act in 1988 to allow the lawful transfer of the right to use land,[7] and the Temporary Regulations on Land Value Increment Tax in 1993. In addition to the chronic financial difficulties on the part of local governments, judging from the fact that the first cities designated by the central government to try out the new system of land-use-right transfer are all in the coastal areas along the Pacific Ocean where international investment has been thriving, the involvement of foreign capital in the real estate industry seems to be another critical catalytic factor in the design and adoption of the system of transferring land-use rights for fees and various compensatory charges related to land development (e.g., expanses induced by relocation of previous occupants and provision of urban services). The six designated cities were Shenzheng, Shanghai, Xiamen, Guangzhou, Fuzhou, and Tianjin. (see Map 22.1).

For the purpose of stimulating the economic growth through development of real estate industry, numerous relevant new laws and regulations and changes to old ones have been put into effect. Besides those mentioned above, many real estate-related laws, regulations and organisational modifications have also been made, e.g., the 1989 Urban Planning Act, the Regulations for Demolishing and Relocating Urban Buildings in 1991, and a series of management regulations for urban real estate development, rental, and rights transfer in 1995. In addition, up to late 1992, the following measures, among others, have been put into effect: a) creation of profit-oriented real estate companies, mostly financed with public sector equities, with a mandate to develop commercial estate or properties, and sell these at prices that include locational premiums; b) promotion of economic development zones, often far from the city center, to attract foreign investments; c) introduction of land use development fees, taxes, and other exactions; d) promotion of spot redevelopment of inner-city areas, with occasional recourse to "value added" strategies linked to a change in land

---

7 *In 1988, article 10 of the Constitution and the Land Management Act were amended to this effect.*

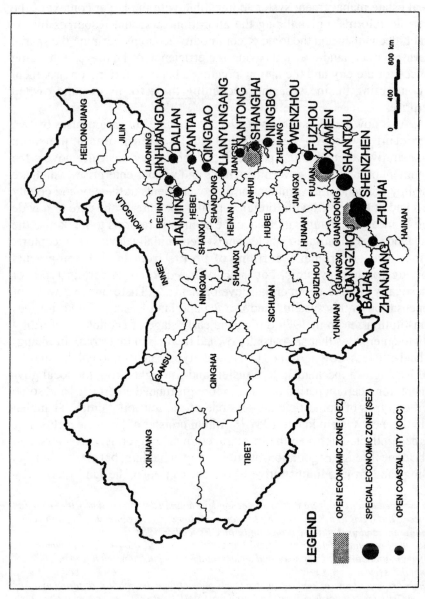

Map 22.1 Special Economic Zones in China

use; e) reintroduction of land and building registration (World Bank,1994:xii-xiii). All these are for the multiple purposes of making the whole apparatus of real estate management system compatible with the larger context of the economic reforms, rationalizing the allocation of spatial resources by the market mechanism and the logic of commodity economy, refining the spatial pattern of urban land-use, improving the efficiency of land-use, enhancing finances for the city and the nation, creating a better and fairer environment for conducting businesses, and deepening the reforms of state-owned enterprises.

As it now stands, state-owned land is allocated to various uses by two co-existing systems (the so-called dual system): uncompensated administrative allotment and paid usage. The former basically covers the assignment of land to all government units and various enterprises which are owned by the central government or by governments at the city and county levels and not involved with foreign capital;[8] the latter is the core of a wide range of measures inaugurated since the economic reforms to marketise the urban land. It is a land-use-right leasing system initially devised to recapture, for the local government, portions of profits from land developments involving foreign investors, but later extended to cover certain types of domestically funded commercial developments.[9] There are two ways of compensation in this system: land-use fee and land leasing. Land-use fees (an institution set up in 1979 during the early stage of economic reforms) apply to enterprises that are partially owned by foreign investors. In Shanghai, land-use fees are determined by land-use types and location of the land.[10] Land leasing is a mechanism to transfer land-use rights from the local government, for a certain period of time, to foreign-funded enterprises and some specified types of domestic ones. As one of the four pilot cities, Shanghai began this new system in late 1987.[11] Initial transfer of land-use rights may only be conducted between the local government and foreign investors, and can be done through negotiation, auction, or open bidding; but establishments holding land from administrative allotment can enter the land market by

---

8 *The expected land-user agent gets to use the land for unlimited period of time without paying any price. But it has to pay costs of related compensations (e.g., commandeering, relocation of the present land user) if there is any, and ,since November, 1988, the landuse tax.*

9 *Since the beginning of 1995, land used for domestically-funded businesses in commerce, travel, recreation, finances, services, and commercial housing in Shanghai has to be obtained through this system.*

10 *There are seven types of landuse and ten levels of locational desirability, resulting in a 7 by 10 matrix with fee standards currently ranging from RMB 0.5 to 170 per sq. meter per year.*

11 *The policy of paid landuse rights transfer was proposed by the central government in early 1987, and Tianjin, Shanghai, Guangzhou, and Shenzheng were assigned the task of trying out the new policy.*

re-compensating the local government with appropriate land price (bu-di-jia).[12]

22.3 A Brief Description of Recent Reforms of Administration and Enterprises in Shanghai

In addition to these land-related institutional reforms, Shanghai has launched other also influential amendments in its administrative and enterprise fronts. In this section we will briefly touch upon two with the most far-reaching effects.[13]

One of the basic post-reform attempts of the leadership of the country has been eradicating bureaucratic inefficiency. The strategy has been clarifying the relationship between the central and local governments, between the state and the enterprises, and among the party, the state and the masses (Ju,1991:145).

Regarding the delineation of administrative powers between the city and the lower level government, one of the relevant important events is the so called "two-tiered management" in planning. It was implemented in a staged fashion and has proved highly effective in stimulating the administrative enthusiasm and resourcefulness on the part of the local government. (Zheng, 1996:35) In 1986, the upper limits of site area a district government was allowed to be autonomous in cases of land-use rights leasing were raised. In 1987, after the central government's approval of a contracted tax package with Shanghai (which was a part of central government's delegation of financial autonomy to the city), the city government in turn entrusted district and county governments[14] with financial sovereignty as well as a whole array of

---

12 *Shanghai's first case of landuse rights transfer happened in 1988. This market has been booming since 1992. Until the end of 1995, the total number of cases was 1303 with a total land area of 103,920,000 sq. meters. See issues of* The Shanghai Real Estate Market, China Statistics Publishing Co., *and* The Land of Shanghai, *The Land of Shanghai Publishing Co., 1990-1996. The system of land price re-compensation (which excludes land related to industrial relocation and housing policies) is important in that it further revitalize the market by allowing the administratively distributed land, which is still the absolute bulk of the land stock (the percentage figure varies between 95% and 99% according to sources), to enter the market. It thus also greatly enhance the financial benefit of the local government.*

13 *There have also been organisational and administrative adjustments in the areas of urban planning and land as well as real-estate management. We will only consider administrative changes deemed most obviously influential in terms of urban land development.*

14 *Currently there are fourteen 'districts' (or 'chu', for more urbanized areas) and six 'counties' (or 'hsian', for less urbanized outlying areas) under the jurisdiction of the city of Shanghai. Each chu or hsian has its own administration with an appointed head and a council of elected representatives.*

360 Urban Growth and Development in Asia: Volume II

administrative powers, including planning and related management authorities.[15] Thus districts and counties were spurred to adopt development strategies centred on economic growth and infrastructure building. Planning and land-use regulating powers were further granted to the district and county governments in 1992 and 93, allowing them to draft "detailed plans" and grant permits to land development projects virtually of all types and in all areas (except major cases in important areas or along major streets, which have to be controlled by the city).[16]

Based on the interviews that we conducted in November, 1996 and March, 1997,[17] and surveys by Zheng Shi-ling and Tsao Jia-ming (1996:36-38) and by urban planning students of Tong-ji University (Urban Planning Department, Tong-ji University, 1996), we summarise the problems attributed to administrative amendments as follows.

(1)   The conflict between the city as a whole and the districts as independent entities: This is the first and most obvious difficulty involved. It is indisputable that Shanghai needs a well conceived, relatively comprehensive "master plan" (or at least a set of widely accepted, workable guidelines) for its overall development as a metropolitan region. This overall plan or set of guidelines will hopefully lead to an orderly manner of regional development on the long run, and thus escaping a myriad of urban and regional problems, many of which have proved to be extremely costly to correct in social as well as financial terms. With districts and counties acting basically as independent (and thus localistic) decision-making authorities, the coherence of overall development inevitably suffers.[18] Liberating the local energies and resourcefulness is a necessary and plausible policy, but the accompanying question of maintaining a balance between the wholeness and oneness of overall growth, and the vitality of local administration has to be tackled seriously and promptly.

(2)   The developmentalist localism: developmentalist mentality is

---

15 In addition to urban planning and related functions, the delegation included powers in the areas of financial/fiscal management, public works, labor affairs, personnel, pricing of staple commodities, foreign trade, industrial and commercial management., etc.
16 Worried by the omnipresent over-development induced by the relatively high autonomy of lower levels of governments, there had been an attempt to retake some of the powers in granting land leases by district and county governments, but was eventually thwarted by strong opposition from the districts.
17 The interviews were carried out in Shanghai. Interviewees included local planning professionals, relevant officials in various city and district governments, academics in related fields, and investors from Taiwan.
18 The development of hierarchy of city-level and district-level commercial centers is a case in point: e.g., the emergence of Hsu-jia-hui as a city-wide commercial attraction, Kung-jiang Street as a Yung-pu District's commercial core, and many other similar example are basically results of local efforts instead of being planned and promoted by the city; while the city-designated centers of Zhen-ru and Hua-mu have so far failed to grow.

common among political and bureaucratic decision-makers in developing countries, and present Shanghai has more than its share. This "the bigger the more the merrier" and "the economy is everything" attitude, which permeates through all levels of decision-making, has combined with the competition among localities and the incentives generated by differences in tax revenue sharing to make local governments greatly interested in luring high-intensity commercial and service sector growth.[19]   The local interest is so high that, it is reported many times during our interviews, the district and county governments would rather grant unauthorised variances in land-use type and increase in building floor area ratio to satisfy pressures from the land developer than uphold city-imposed plans and regulations. Because planning is usually idealistic and restrictive owing to considerations on behave of city-wide reasons, disagreements and tension may evolve between planning and development forces. This is nothing new in capitalist societies all over the world. What is really academically intriguing is that, according to our interviews, strong distrust or even animosity exists between local governments and city-level planning, i.e., the division of attitude between levels of administration instead of between public and private sectors. As will be touched upon later in the paper, this has to do with the particular roles played by the local governments in China's present transitional process toward a "socialist market economy" and the awkward position of planning in such a process.

(3)   The dragging of urban planning behind urban development: The recent speed of economic and physical growth of Shanghai has been astonishing and unprecedented. But preparing and ratification of city plans is time consuming. There has been an unavoidable time lag between planning (and the ability to control and regulate) and the need of guidance in the real world of development (one conspicuous example is that the prolonged failure on the part of the central government to ratify the badly needed new Master Plan has let Shanghai's recent rampant growth run on an uncharted path and thus

---

19 Since 1994 a new system of taxes has been in effect, causing basic changes in tax categories, rates and sharing of tax revenues between the central and local governments. In the system, there are centrally collected taxes (e.g., excess tax, import tax), locally collected taxes (e.g., personal income tax, land value increment tax), and taxes that are shared by the central and local governments (e.g., tax on securities trading, sales tax, and value-added tax). The implementation of these taxes has resulted in various fascinating phenomena (one of them that closely relates to our subject is the fact that many localities, reasoning that land value increment tax being a local tax, lowered or waived the tax on their own in order to attract more real estate development). Because the value-added tax (25%) and business income tax (varies with the capital structure and ownership level) has become the main revenues for the city and district governments, the tertiary industries which generate these tax moneys have thus been vigorously courted by local governments.

worsening the situation). The magnitude and the fact that there are fourteen districts and six counties under the city that are fiercely competing for growth only made the present condition more confusing and urgent.

(4)   The disparity between high-intensity development and low standards of urban infrastructure and services: Ever since its early stages of development, Shanghai has been a high density urban settlement.[20]   The almost forty years of orthodox Communist rule before the economic reforms had done little in providing basic urban infrastructure.[21]   With the rapid growth in recent years, the hardly-controlled inter-district vying, and the rising expectations on the part of the residents, the shortage of urban infrastructure and services has become a critical problem to be seriously faced by the city and local governments.

On the front of reforms of enterprises, the basic strategies have been the separation of administration and enterprises (or the separation of the ownership and management of state-owned enterprises) and decentralisation of power.   Under these strategies, many reform measures have been put into effect.   Among the most significant are: capitalization of properties owned by

---

20 *At the time of liberation (1949), the average population density was around 60,000 persons/km² and per capita living space was only 3.9m². As the city's jurisdiction has extended over the years, especially when the Bao-shan and Pu-dong new districts were annexed in 1989 and 1992 respectively, overall density reduced. However, the densities remain very high in the old central areas, such as districts of Huang-pu, Nan-shi and Lu-wan. In some extreme areas, the figure can be as high as 160,000 persons/km², and the per capita living space has merely increased by 0.4 since the reforms started. The problem of housing quality has been very serious. The recent increase of investment in and construction of housing has caused the rise of housing standards. See the table below for density changes:*

Year	1952	1957	1962	1965	1970	1975	1978	1980	1982	1984	1986	1988	1990	1992	1994
Density	61.38	52.32	45.14	45.65	41.18	39.54	35.15	37.92	27.32	19.72	18.92	19.51	10.46	10.00	4.63

(unit: 1,000 persons/sq. km²)

Source: Shanghai Municipal Statistics Bureau, Statistical Yearbook of Shanghai, *China Statistical Publishing House.*

21 *Before the reforms, investments in industrial capital improvement had out paced those for urban construction and improvement. Quantities and qualities of urban public services, including housing, transportation, and utilities could not keep up with demands generated by urban growth. From 1949 to 78, the total investment in urban infrastructure was 5.38 billion RMB, averaging merely 0.185 billion per year. Investment figures for other periods are: 4.84 billion RMB for 1979-84 (0.807 billion per year, or more than four times the previous period); 15.38 billion RMB for 1985-89 (3.08 billion per year, or 3.8 times the previous period); 19.3 billion for 1990-92 (6.43 billion yearly, or more than 2 times the previous period); 68.45 billion for 1993-95 (22.82 billion yearly, or about 3.5 times the period before). Thus the total investment between 1978 and 1995 was 47 times the amount before 1978.*

Year	1949-78	1980	1982	1984	1986	1988	1990	1992	1994	1995
	53.78	9.6	7.22	9.77	24.78	37.08	47.22	84.35	238.16	273.78

(unit: 100 million RMB)

Source: Shanghai Municipal Statistics Bureau, Statistical Yearbook of Shanghai, *China Statistical Publishing House.*

the state, and delegating managerial powers, responsibilities, and interests to the enterprises per se (instead of governmental regulatory or supervisory offices which used to assert direct control of the enterprises' daily operations). Therefore governments at various levels are hoped to relate to business only through financial and fiscal policies and regulations, while enterprises are left alone with enough incentive and decision-making powers to respond to and compete in the market on behave of the state ownership. Since these policies are not yet fully implemented, it's difficult to speculate on their final outcomes. But because land, especially urban land, is the major element of state properties, these reforms, through their effects on behaviour of the management, have tremendous consequences on urban land development in China. Basically speaking, so far the management has behaved just like landowners in any capitalist society- profit-motivated, development-oriented. However, there is a crucial difference between the capitalist landowner (or developer) and the land-user agent in China: the latter lacks a consciousness of the risk associated with investment. The main reason, we speculate, must be that, unlike the real landowner or real estate investor, the manager for state-owned (or collectively owned, for that matter) properties does not have to shoulder the loss that may result in risky investment decisions—the state or the collective will absorb it. This difference makes them that much more adventurous. Because this type of mentality can be widespread, we suspect, it must have had very significant effect on the supply of urban space (both in terms of quantities and location) in Shanghai where land is highly valuable and public landuser agents abound.

There have also been problems stemming from the reforms aimed at state-owned enterprises. One type of problem is due to the self-perpetuating nature of the bureaucracy. According to Wu Guo-guang, the delegating of management power toward the lower-tier enterprises has great impact on local governments. Because of the fear of losing the benefits and influences associated with directly controlling or running government-owned enterprises, the local government may "intercept" the management power meant by the central government for individual enterprises. (Wu, 1995:27-28) As a result and also owing to the possibility of wielding the enormous government-owned properties in the emerging markets, the local government may now enjoy more influences on the local economy through policy or non-policy measures.[22] Another type of problems generated by the great trend of marketisation is the confusion and negative effects caused by the double-roles played by the

---

22 *Judging from the fact that bureaucratic decision-makers are prone to expansion of power through inflated budget, and engaging in real estate development is a good way to do just that, we believe the general tendency is for the local government to undertake more development projects rather than less.*

local government. The local authorities in China are now simultaneously playing two roles which, in capitalist eyes, are conflicting: on the one hand, it performs all the functions which are expected from a local government as provider of public services and promoter of public interests, usually by restricting the market rationality and supplementing services that are not likely to be rendered by profit-motivated investors in the market; on the other hand, it joins the profit-seeking market through the government-owned businesses either by directly running their operations by way of functional branches in the administration, or by high-ranking officials' serving in the management of the enterprises. So we see in Shanghai a remarkable phenomenon that can only be called "marketisation of the state". The problems are twofold: unfair market competition with privately-owned businesses, and the possible sacrificing of public interests which must be provided for and protected by the government against market rationales.

22.4 Effects of Administrative Reforms on Land Development in Shanghai

The first effect of all the reforms which enable the acquiring and transfer of urban land-use rights (thus urban space) as a "commodity" is of course the great increase of the marginal productivity of urban land (and space). Urban land being the major property of the local government, this increase of land productivity greatly enhanced the fiscal situation of the local government (and to a large extend, of all the units in the government or in government-controlled businesses which posses land or urban space). Thus, through the urban land market, part of the profits generated in China's current economic growth is being recouped for a large portion of the masses. The possibilities of keeping the basic system of public land ownership (this is the socialist ideological part) while taking the advantages of the market mechanism (this is the Chinese pragmatism part) seem to exist, though imperfections in the newly designed reform measures abound.

In addition to the conflicts between city government and district government, as well as among different branches of government, there are other discernible difficulties resulting from the reforms. Since the economic reforms taken as a whole is a wholesale substitution of an economy based on market principles for a centrally planned one. The decline of the stature of urban planning institution which used to be an integral part of the state economic planning system is all but destined, as its wisdom is continuously called into question by land developers and even local government officials. The problem of the discord between plans and real-world land-use practice is only

a reflection of this larger revolutionary contextual change. The task now is to
develop a mechanism which is reasonable, flexible, and sensitive to market
needs, but at the same time capable of maintaining acceptable environmental
qualities by minimizing externalities of urban development and providing
adequate urban services. However, there also seems to be conflicts and
disaccordances among levels and sectors of governmental planning itself.[23]
One of the most obvious effects that are directly related to our interests here
is of course the oversupply of urban space[24] resulting from the unwary or
even reckless investments made by the management of state-owned enterprises and other public land user entities, due to their lack of risk consciousness. Doubtlessly, this should be stressed as one very essential flaw in the
present assortment of reforms. It not only endangers public properties, wastes
the resources that go into the construction of urban space, but also de-stabi-
lizes the real estate market and contribute to chaotic land-use patterns which
in turn generate a wide range of environmental problems. The answer to this
flaw lies in the combination of a fair merit-based salary system, and (in the
case of capitalised establishments) an effective supervision mechanism on
behave of the shareholders or (in the case of non-capitalised ones) political
pressure from the public. At the present time none of these conditions exists
in China. We believe that one of the goals of real reforms must be to create
these elements.

---

23 *For example, there are obvious conflicts among the so-called 'four plannings': National
Land Development Planning, City Planning, Comprehensive Agricultural Development Planning, and Master Landuse Planning. The object of the first planning was natural, social and
economical resources, and its duty focuses on the overall allocation of population and man
power for national economic development. City planning tries to develop orderly town and
city systems and provide the environment for economic as well as social development by planning and control of landuse in cities and towns, and by construction of various types of public
works in the planned areas. The aim of comprehensive agriculture development planning is
the expansion and improvement of agricultural land and the related infrastructure. The landuse
master planning covers the total land body of the country. It is supposed to consider the
natural characteristics of the land, and the landuse requirements for national economic and
social developments in order to set goals, strategies, and patterns for national landuse. It also
should establish control guidelines for important landuse sectors. In real practice, however,
since the involvement of a great number of administrative units, causing serious overlaps,
inconsistencies, and bureaucratic conflicts and buck passing.*
24 *From this perspective, what we now observe in Shanghai's real estate growth is not a true
expression of its economic strength but an exaggerated statement of over optimism, and the
slowdown since 1994 must be deemed inevitable.*

22.5 Conclusions

1) The new system of paid transfer of land-use rights and the de-centralisation of decision-making powers (both between levels of government and within the managerial system of state-owned enterprises) are the double-power propeller of the astonishing post-reform urban development, because they provided the basic incentives which stimulate the aggressiveness and resourcefulness of the front-line decision-makers involved in the land development process.

2) To put it simply, the total and final effect on urban land development of all the related reforms is the increase of land-use efficiency and oversupply of urban space, the latter being due to the lack of risk consciousness and the almost congenital bureaucratic over-supply of "services" on the part of the local government and other public land managers.

3) The whole assemblage of reforms has been conflict-prone. There is the conflict of roles played by the local government: the government as implementer of national policies and protector of public interests vis-a-vis the new role of aggressive, profit-oriented land developer; there is the conflict between the central and the local governments as well as between the city and district/county governments; overall interests and direction vis-a-vis partial and local autonomy; there is the conflict between public interests and commercial profits; the contradiction of planning and economic growth; and there is the conflict among different functional branches of the government. Conflicts and contradictions teem in other countries, too. What makes these types of inconsistency particularly significant is the fact that social conflicts have to be checked or supervised in order to avoid severe adversary consequences, but there is no mechanism in present mainland China to perform this function (because these contradictions involve the local government which enjoys many powers and privileges not subject to market competition, and neither are there any meaningful checks and balances in the political arena). This is one of the most serious and fundamental dilemmas in the process of economic reform which must be faced squarely, if the great reform is to be really successful.

4) What is now happening in mainland China is an endeavour of marketisation without (or with limited) privatisation. This is a daring (if not clever) attempt of historical proportions. How likely is this to be successfully accomplished? Going one step beyond what is pointed out by Peter Marcuse that ownership is a bundle of rights to be divided between government and individuals (Marcuse, 1996: 119-122), we can say that land ownership in present mainland China is to be divided between government, bureaucrats, and, to a far lesser degree, individuals. These rights are being re-divided

among these actors during the economic reform process. How the partitioning is devised and carried out will largely determine the outcome of the reform. With luck and prudence, the possibility of success appears to be there.

5)   Switching the basic system of a society is a complex and time consuming process. Establishment and amendment of legal and administrative systems are necessary but not sufficient conditions. Social, cultural, and bureaucratic factors always play significant roles in shaping a country (and a society). For the reform to be successful much more attention has to be paid to these fronts.

References

(All references are in Chinese except those indicated otherwise.)
Chou Cheng (1989) *Land Economics*, Beijing: Agriculture Publishers.
_____ (1993) "Macro-Tuning the Land-use in Mainland China", *A Collection of Essays for Cross-Taiwan-Strait Academic Exchange*. Taipei: Dept. of Land Economic, National Chengchi University Press.
Gue Chiang-fang (1994) *How Foreigners Can Invest in Real Estate in China*, Taipei: Yung-ran Publishers.
Hsiao Tze-yueh (1991) *Real Estate-related Institutions in Mainland China*, Taipei: Wan Guo Wei Li Publishers.
Ju Shin-min (1991) *A Study on Chinese Communists' Reforms in Political Institutions, 1978-1990*, Taipei: Yung Ran Publishers.
Ma Keh-wei (1992) *A Comprehensive Book on Chinese Reforms: 1978-1991*, Dai-ren: Dai-ren Publishers.
Marcuse, Peter (1996) "Privatization and Its Discontents: Property Rights in Land and Housing in the Transition in Eastern Europe", in Andrusz, G., Harloe, M. and Szelenyi, I. (eds.), *Cities after Socialism: Urban and Regional Change and Conflict in Post-Socialist Societies*, Oxford, UK: Blackwell. (in English)
Urban Planning Department, Tong-ji University (1996) *The Implementation of City Planning in Shanghai: a Report of Surveys Shanghai*: Tong-ji University Press.
Wang Shung-san (1990) *A Study on Land Problems in China*, Taipei: Ching-yu Publishers.
World Bank (1994) *China: Urban Land Management in an Emerging Market Economy*. Washington, D.C.: World Bank Publishers. (in English)
Wu Guo-guang & Jeng Yeong-nian (1995) *On the Central/Local Relationship: the Pivotal Issue in Institutional Transformation in China*. Hong Kong: Oxford University Press.
Zheng Shi-ling and Cao Jia-ming (1996) "Planning and Administration of Shanghai as an International Metropolis" in Zheng Shi-ling, *The Renewal and Redevelopment of Shanghai*, 31-42. Shanghai: Tong-ji University.

23 Urban NGO - Government Relationship: Experiences from Bombay

Vandana Desai

23.1 Introduction

This chapter is about identifying what is feasible and effective in terms of inter-organisational arrangements. In this case the setting is NGO and Government interaction in Bombay, and the question then becomes one of examining the types of relationships that are possible under particular circumstances and their implications for the urban poor. The chapter is based on my experience through on-going research into the urban NGO sector in Bombay.[1] I use the term NGO as a shorthand for all non-governmental, non-profit development organisation who are working in slums and providing different services, who support grassroots work through funding, technical advice and advocacy. The data used here is of 67 grassroots NGOs working with the urban poor[2], which was collected during six months of fieldwork in 1994 studying the grassroots NGO sector working in the slum communities of Bombay.

Figure 23.1 shows the frequency of contact between NGOs and official agencies and Table 23.1 shows the identity of the agencies with the most contacts. (Agencies in contact with fewer than three NGOs are not listed). Most NGOs have linkages with Municipal departments. These are mainly NGOs which are related to welfare activities. Interaction with the state and central government departments seems less common.

Here I assimilate comments and criticisms that various NGOs and government officials have made on the basis of their on-going experience, using

---

1 *The author is conducting research on urban NGOs in Bombay, which is funded by an ESCOR grant of the British Department for International Development DFID (formerly Overseas Development Administration). The main objectives of this research are - (i) to analyse the ways in which NGOs fill the gap between partial public sector service delivery and the needs of the urban poor; (ii) to analyse how effective urban NGOs are in this role; (iii) to develop a set of indicators to monitor the effectiveness of NGOs in urban areas. The views expressed in this paper are of none others than the authors.*
2 *A paper entitled "Anatomy of the Bombay NGO Sector" (available from the author on request) analyses the ways in which NGOs fill the gap between partial public service delivery and the needs of the urban poor in Bombay. It describes data on activities, target groups, funding, linkages and evaluation of a sample of 67 grassroot NGOs working with the urban poor*

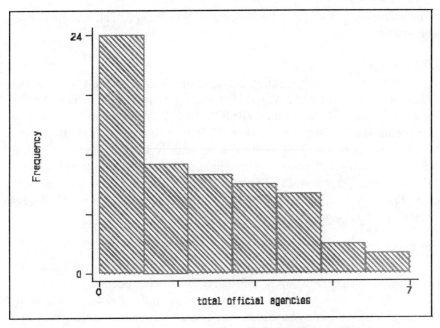

Figure 23.1 Number of Agencies with which NGO is in Contact

Table 23.1 NGO Links with Official Agencies

Official Agencies	*Total Number of NGOs*	*% of NGOs*
Bombay Municipal Corporation	16	24
State Govt Ministry of Welfare	13	19
BMC Hospitals	11	16
BMC Dept of Health	10	15
Maharashtra Housing Area Development Authority (MHADA)	8	12
DHSM, Bombay Police	7	10
Law Courts	6	9
BMC Dept of Education, Railway Authority, Housing Development Finance Corporation (HDFC)	4	6
Central Govt Ministry of Welfare, Prime Minister's Grant Project, BMC Nehru Rojgar Yogana (NRY), SULU, Tahasildars	3	4

four main programmes, as a background to the chapter. The four main programmes are:

(I) HEALTH:

An innovative approach to Urban Health Management, funded by the World Bank entitled India Population Project V was implemented by the Bombay Municipal Corporation (BMC). In 1991 there were fifteen health post (centres) in collaboration with the NGOs[3]. Another collaboration in the health sector is of the BMC collaborating with NGOs for Leprosy Control and Eradication - The present programme in the city, is run on the Survey, Education and Treatment (SET) pattern. The highlight of this multi-agency effort has been geographical division of various municipal wards to different NGOs[4] for total leprosy control.[5]

(II) SHELTER

Slum Upgradation Programme (SUP) funded by the World Bank entitled Bombay Urban Development Project (BUDP), has been implemented by Maharashtra Housing and Area Development Authority, Government of Maharashtra. The main objectives were to regularise existing slum sites and to create new serviced plots, by granting occupants security of tenure. Greater emphasis was laid on shifting of private capital into the production of legal affordable shelter to stimulate an increase in land and infrastructure servicing by the private sector. SUP initiated a pioneering step of creating a Community Development Cell as an intrinsic part of project structure[6].

(III) CHILDREN - Coordination Committee for Vulnerable Children (CCVC)

A UNICEF aided effort for street children. The NGO experiences have pointed to the need for a judicious mix of an institutional plus a non-

---

3 *NGOs involved in this programme are Nagapada Neighbourhood House, Mobile Creches (an exception as this NGO does not work within any one specific geographical area, but scattered at many construction sites), Streethitkarini, Apanalya.*
4 *Some of the NGOs involved and who were interviewed are Alert India, Maharashtra Lok Hit Seva Mandal, Lok Seva Sangam and Committed Communities Development. At present there are 14 organisations working in Bombay for leprosy control and 156 centers are established where free clinical examination and free treatment is available (Source: Alert India Report July 1993).*
5 *Traditionally the field of leprosy control and eradication, was seen as one where the voluntary sector could have much greater impact, because of the highly sensitive nature of the ailment and the social stigma still attached to its detection and subsequent treatment.*
6 *The Community Development Cell has now been dismantled as the World Bank funding has ceased in September 1994.*

institutional approach. The Social Welfare Department of the Government of Maharashtra initiated a novel strategy in 1988 to enable Government to serve the function of planning, coordinating, monitoring and reviewing the "Institutional - Plus Programme" whereas the actual function of implementing the programme was to be left to the NGOs[7]. The Coordination Committee for Vulnerable Children (CCVC) was an outcome of this.

(IV) ERADICATION OF ILLITERACY

In 1986, the National Literacy Mission was set up by the Government of India to provide the framework of Adult Education and Functional Literacy Programmes all over the country (particularly in the 15-35 age group)[8]. "Environment building" has been the main objective of the National Literacy Mission (this means the supportive social environment). This work is mainly entrusted to the NGOs. The government's role is minimal and basically supportive and as a resource provider. It is expected that mobilisation would ensure speedier action and sustain participation in this venture.

Many NGOs have participated in collaborative programmes related to health, children and literacy. It is worth noting that these sectors seem to have had better success than collaboration relating to shelter and housing in Bombay, which is far more complicated.

23.2 Why study NGO-GO Relationships

Currently urban NGOs have two main functions: service delivery and policy advocacy.[9] As service delivery agents NGOs provide welfare, techni-

---

7 *Some of the NGOs and their programmes involving the street children in Bombay were - Doorstep School (functional literacy through pre-school), Pavement Club (provision of bathing, toilet facilities and recreation), Sneha Sadan (residential institution with formal schooling, vocational training), Support (drug-addicted children), Parishar Asha (development of a curriculum for street children), SPARC 9identification and enumeration of vulnerable children in Bombay).*

8 *In the 1981 Census, Bombay had a total literacy percentage of 68.1 per cent, 73.91 male and 60.75 female (Source: Census Handbook on Bombay, 1981). According to the 1991 provisional census figures, among the present male population, 77 per cent have been termed literate. The literacy rate among men has gone up from 74 per cent in 1981. The literacy rate among the female population stands at 65 per cent, this has gone up from 60 per cent in 1981 (Report in Times of India, March 13, 1991).*

9 *It must also be noted that many urban NGOs started operating on welfare models (service delivery) rather than being dynamic grassroots organisations with these two new objectives, namely advocacy in policy changes and empowerment of the poor through participatory projects. Besides they are now operating in increasingly more turbulent political environments than before.*

cal, legal and financial services to slumdwellers or work with community organisations in basic service and infrastructure provision. Policy advocacy seeks social change by influencing attitudes, policy and practice, seeking to reform state services on the basis of NGO experiences and to lobby directly for the policy changes. NGOs are engaging more and more in macro-policy reform: a level of action that is often institutional in its nature.

NGOs function as a representative/intermediate body of the slumdwellers, they relate to the community organisations and their leaders within slum settlements (assisting community based organisations and individuals to access other institutions eg. municipalities, banks, technical training etc.). NGOs develop their own meaning of and approach to people's participation and their own way to build effective participation of the poor, to make the official system more open, flexible and responsive especially when infrastructure and service delivery are limited in the context of the whole city.

There are three stages that can be distinguished in the growth or development of an NGO: formation and development, consolidation and institutionalisation, and a further feature can be added and that is the ability to make a strategic impact (by greatly increasing the scale of operation, or by influencing policy and governmental institutions). This could possibly be achieved through either supportive and complementary or critical relations with government.[10]

NGOs' successes[11] in the important role of mobilizing the poor in community participatory projects has led to acceptance and then encouragement by government of NGO participation in slum development within cities. NGOs may seek to fill "gaps", often in the hope of eventually attracting government services into the area. As NGOs move to fill the gap left by the public sector, there has been a rapid growth of expectations, leading to a complex set of objectives.

Over the past twenty years or so, there has been a clear trend among development NGOs away from direct involvement in service provision, towards a concern for the broader processes of development - a concern for

---

10 *It is important to remember that there are also different age groups of NGOs, some have been long established, while others are a few years old, and some started very recently for service to particular marginalised groups.*

11 *NGOs are regarded as being appropriate institutions because they are better at targeting the poor; participatory in their approach; flexible; working conventionally with existing community organisations/structures; and involved in advocacy of policy reform. But relatively little is known about this sector, about how they are going about their work, or how effectively they are performing. Or perhaps NGOs are best not at being innovative but at providing services in the traditional and known way to populations not yet served. It would be important to understand which kinds of NGOs are more innovative, participatory, or cost effective than others - rather than to talk about NGOs as a group as being innovative, etc.*

people rather than projects, and therefore for training, awareness-raising, social organisation, capacity-building and institutional development. The main characteristics of this transition are:

(1) a move away from pure reliance on organisational or programme growth as a strategy to increase NGO impact, towards a catalytic role, "multiplicative and diffusive" strategies whereby NGOs aim to influence others through working together, sharing ideas, training and so on (Edwards and Hulme 1992).

(2) the increasing importance of information in NGO work as they begin to utilise the power of ideas and information to promote positive change in the wider structures of government and the official aid community (Clark 1991).

(3) a widespread move into advocacy - using experience from the grassroots to influence others at local, national and international levels, reshape resource allocation and promote policy change.

(4) a heightened concern for institution building and consequently a shift in focus among NGOs away from operational work towards support for local organisational development.

The aim of the government departments in collaborating with NGOs has been to (i) strength service delivery capacity; (ii) development of effective out-reach (iii) involvement of community in government programmes and strengthening of infrastructural facilities such as water supply, sanitation and roads; and subsequently helping to ensure that these were properly maintained.

23.3 Types of Relations

Diversity of NGOs and their Interactions

NGOs' actions and their relations with the state are determined to a large extent by the political, economic and cultural context in which they operate. Differences between cities are particularly important in this respect. The particular political conditions and bureaucratic procedures of government authorities experienced by the NGO control many of the opportunities of NGO activity, and set very specific parameters to the extent to which NGOs participate in different provisions.

Few development interventions undertaken by NGOs are politically neutral. It is possible to conceive of a continuum of NGO activities in terms of their increasing political sensitivity, with "non radical" NGOs at one end and radical NGOs at the other[12]. Non-radical NGOs have for obvious reasons found more favour with government in partnerships. But as Clark points out, development does not take place on the basis of projects which will "remain irrelevant to the majority of the needy unless used as beacons to light up pathways for others - notably the state - to pursue. Popular participation on a significant scale will only come about through reforms in official structures, not through multiplying NGO projects" (Clark 1991:75). Hulme and Edwards (1992) distinguish between strategies in which an NGO can increase its size in order to expand its operations, and those in which it can transfer strategies to or have a "catalytic" effect on other agencies.

Experiences with the NGO sector in Bombay reveal that the great majority of interactions have been initiated by NGOs in the last ten years and still evolving. These have sought to draw government resources into their own (NGO) programmes, to influence government at project level (i.e. implementational issues), or policy levels to relieve constraints faced by themselves and the urban poor. NGOs tend to initiate links with government agencies[13] when they come up against particular problems (such as input delivery, legal rights, etc.) or when they identify a "gap" in government services, either in terms of inefficient provision of services and infrastructure (eg. India Population Project V) or the exclusion of particular sections of the population (eg. poor urban women within slums). If a government agency is prepared to admit its weakness in an area identified by an NGO, then there are possible grounds for interaction on a complementary basis. Virtually all NGO innovations originate from direct experience in working with local groups. It is therefore tailored to meet specific needs and requirements. Linkages with government agencies/department, whenever achieved, are still very much at the formative stages and are highly diverse.

Urban NGOs are now involved in a broad spectrum of activities, but beyond this, they exhibit potentially illuminating contrasts in emphasis and packaging of activities, as well as in client group and organisational style. Individual organisations have evolved their own strategies and modus operandi

---

12 *A potentially useful distinction is that between radical and non-radical NGOs (Clark 1991), a distinction which often cuts across the traditional divisions between left and right. "Radical NGOs" regard all development efforts to be in some sense political, since they must involve the transfer of power to those previously denied access to it. "Non-radical NGOs" are content to attempt to work in what they regard as an apolitical context.*
13 *External funding agencies have played an important role in many of the NGO initiatives. This has been part of a wider and explicit objective to facilitate productive NGO-GO partnerships. On the other occasions, donor funding for NGOs has been stimulated by a sense of frustration with public sector organisations and by a view that NGOs provide an "alternative". The problems and prospects of the roles that external funding agencies might play is, however, a focus of the policy discussion.*

from within this spectrum of options (Tandon 1987). Some, like SPARC[14] in Bombay, have given greater emphasis to social welfare and community mobilization (Daswani and D'Cruz 1990); others like People's Participation Programme (PPP)[15] in Bombay have concentrated more on the provision of technical advice. Some are relatively large and professionally organised, like Youth for Unity and Voluntary Action (YUVA) in Bombay, whilst others are smaller and more informal in their mode of operation. Some enjoy a high level of international funding, whilst others are much more dependent upon domestic resources. Some work relatively effectively with each other, while others adopt a more isolated posture. Some enjoy a much closer relationship with government than others. Some aim to work with specific groups such as women, pavement dwellers and street children, whilst others do not have any particular targeting strategy.

All this has involved NGOs in a series of trade-offs. They can focus on certain groups at the expense of others, perhaps with quite strong implications for the overall degree of apparent success achieved. They can engage intensively with a small number of communities, or more superficially with larger numbers. They can seek to build the capacities of slum institutions (like the National Slum Dwellers Federation) to deal with official bodies, or can choose to perform this function by themselves. They can approach government on an individual basis to have certain decisions implemented, or work in a more consolidated fashion with others to achieve more fundamental change in the way in which the system as a whole operates.

The number of initiatives taken by government is much smaller, reflecting perhaps some uncertainty over how relations with NGOs might best be taken forward, especially in Bombay where government departments in the past have been faced with demands by NGOs which challenge policy or strategy decisions, or even their legitimacy.

A much wider range of government initiatives is found in the last few years, where consultation with NGOs in matters of economic and social development is enshrined in the Sixth Five Year Plan, which declared that the state shall encourage NGOs that promote the welfare of the nation. In response to this macro-political initiative, several government departments be-

---

14 SPARC (Society for Promotion of Area Resource Committees) is a well-known innovative housing NGO formed in 1984. It has been working with various groups among the urban poor (women, slum and pavement dwellers, street children and drug addicts). SPARC has worked first to create an information base about each group and then hs worked with local community organisations in order to support the struggle for a just allocation of resources and free access to resources for the poor.
15 This organisation is dedicated to the cause of slum dwellers in Bombay. PPP has motivated this sector to work for its own upliftment and has also provided technical, managerial and organisational support and taken up their problems at all levels of authorities.

gan to prepare procedures for informing NGOs of their proposed activities, obtaining their views, and responding to their requirements. Overall, government agencies/departments appear to have initiated interaction less frequently, and usually when they require a more efficient channel for service delivery.[16]

Networking of NGOs

The other type of interaction NGOs have with Governments is through networking. NGOs establish fora in which ideas are exchanged among themselves and/or between NGOs and government agencies.[17] These generally have a mandate to represent NGO interests to government or about their activities. On a wider scale, NGOs have much to learn from each other. As the densities of NGOs operational at field level increase, the need for institutionalized means of communication (and, where appropriate, co-ordination) among NGOs and between NGOs and government has become all the more urgent.

However, experiences from Bombay show that these high levels of interaction among NGOs appear exceptional. By contrast, the high density of NGOs in Bombay, for instance, has led to overlapping activities, and few successful efforts to liaise among NGOs on specific issues. Lack of co-ordination among NGOs, and inadequate liaison between "service" NGOs and community grassroots organizations is a conflictual and wasteful use of resources (Bebbington and Thiele 1993). NGO networking is more geographically localized and thematically focused than are efforts put by national-level NGOs. More city based attempts at liaison are found and, perhaps for that reason, appear to have been more successful (eg. Coordination Committee for Vulnerable Children - CCVC). For some NGOs (eg. SPARC), generally operating at international level, advocacy is a central, and sometimes their only, function. With others, (eg. YUVA) operating at both national and international levels, the distinction between objective investigation and advocacy tends to become blurred.

Three different types of NGO-GO relationships have emerged within Bombay:

(i) a dependent-client relationship with the government, in which NGOs

---

16 *The drawback here is that they may not recognize the wider NGO programme, which may become "distorted" by this type of contact (see discussion in the later sections).*
17 *The term "networking" is open to a wide range of interpretations. Useful definitions of research networks are provided by Plucknett et al. (1990). Networking here is defined loosely as interaction among a group of institutions in order to realize anticipated benefits for themselves or for their clients.*

implement state-prepared programs and/or receive funding through the state eg. the health projects mentioned above eg. Alert India, Committed Communities Development, Population Service International.

(ii) NGOs which do not see any common grounds of collaboration and have no wish to agree upon or reach out areas of agreement eg shelter project mentioned above. NGOs that are vocal in their advocacy of urban reform (such as access to land, low-income housing) see little prospect of functional collaboration with government eg. Niwara Hak Sureksha Samiti.[18]

(iii) A healthier relationship exists where NGOs want a genuine partnership to tackle various issues, collaborate at times but also have a constructive on-going debate on areas of disagreement (see Tandon 1991 and Clarke 1995). Very few NGOs fall in this category eg. NARC, SPARC, SRS, Apanalaya.

23.4 Advantages from the Relationship (Benefits)

Individual NGOs clearly need to assess the advantages and disadvantages of varying modes of interaction with Government in terms of their individual development philosophies. From this relationship, government stands to gain access to a better network of distribution and a higher quality of contact with sections of the population that it is generally poor at reaching and so greater cost effectiveness.[19] The NGO stands to benefit from access to policy-making, to skills and facilities of government agencies/departments and above all the greater resources available through government (especially if the government has priority access to scarce resources).

NGOs may perform better, learn, and be more accountable precisely because their shoulders are being looked over. "Roles" evolve over time. Many

---

18 *Niwara Hakk Sureksha Samiti has been working on housing issues of slumdwellers and has actively advocated access to housing for the urban poor in various situations.*

19 *The issue of cost and cost effectiveness, and the claims by NGOs of cost advantages over the public sector, should be transformed into a set of research questions - regardless of claims one way or the other. For example, it would be useful to NGOs to know the circumstances under which they actually do deliver services at reasonable costs, which types of NGOs are better at it, and how they are able to do so. All this suggests that an accumulating body of individual case studies on NGOs delivering services at "low" cost (or being participatory or innovative) is really not sufficient to establish that NGOs in general deliver at costs lower than the public sector. More importantly, by assuming that the determinant of costs has to do with inherent traits of the NGO vs. the public sector, one runs the risk of missing what actually is the determinant of low costs. This is an important research question because it could provide findings of considerable use to NGOs.*

begin by performing a "substituting" role in the expectation that government may learn from the approaches that they are adopting and eventually take over. NGOs' evolving relationship with community grassroots organizations provides an important additional dynamic: many aim to strengthen local organizations so that, when NGOs withdraw, these can take over many of the functions previously performed by the NGO, and can generate a "demand-pull" on government to ensure adequate continuing provision of the services required.

23.5 Disadvantages from the Relationship (Problems)

Some bureaucrats in Bombay do not see NGOs as "effective policy actors". There is limited commitment to the relationship by government staff, so that the burden of making the relationship work falls disproportionately heavily on the NGO. Besides, lack of senior staff continuity in government departments not only contributes to co-ordination problems among departments, but also costs NGOs' time and effort to re-establish their credentials and familiarize new staff with key issues.   The example of CCVC is very relevant in this context . CCVC was formed from local, spontaneous action and from higher-level contacts achieved around the efforts of key personalities. A very conscious effort was made by one bureaucrat in this collaborative effort to ensure equal status of government and NGOs. Though the original proponent of the idea was a senior government official, visibility of the bureaucracy diminished in the later stages and was available only on specific request from the NGO partners, when policy issues had to be sorted out with relevant government departments. Since this senior government official has now moved to another department, the CCVC has suffered and lacked momentum.

While the relationship with government gives NGOs the opportunity to use resources provided by them to complement their own programmes, its emphasis is on the formation of community groups around particular functions defined in the government programme/schemes. This may detract from, or even be in conflict with NGOs' efforts towards awareness creation and social organization formation in the wider context of that particular geographical area. Similarly, if NGOs become heavily involved in input delivery in support of functional groups for the government programmes, the resources NGOs have available for other wider activities are likely to be reduced or become unavailable. It can also be used by governments and donors as a cost cutting exercise to fit in with wider agendas of privatization. While some of the more opportunistic NGOs (a large number of which have emerged in order to take advantage of increased funding[20]) may welcome service delivery contracts resulting from privatization, others may resist being pushed into this role for fear of diluting their capacity for awareness creation, loss of independence and innovativeness or compromising its principles with the government (i.e co-optation leading to loss of credibility among NGOs beneficiaries). Some may find that service delivery contracts may reduce an NGOs own space for reflection and action (see experiences from South America in Aguirre and Namdar-Irani 1992). Korten (1990) rightly points out that a wholesale conceptualisation of NGOs as service deliverers may serve to compromise the integrity of the wide-ranging programmes followed by many of the better NGOs: "the distinctive role of the voluntary sector is not to serve as a cheap contractor to implement government-defined programmes" (Korten 1990: 207).

Those pressing for social reform in a highly conflictive mode such as issues of access to land, security of tenure, low-income housing, may find it difficult to engage with government at any other level or see little prospects of functional collaboration (as they may see the governments interest remain linked to those of the local elites). This is very much seen in the NGO sector in Bombay. Very few NGOs take up housing issues, and those who take initiative in collaborating with the government agencies haven't had much success in providing housing to their beneficiaries on a wide scale. SPARC, for instance, has faced this issue with regard to its work with pavement dwellers, and Niwara Hakk Sureksha Samiti with regard to the issues of rehabilitation of slumdwellers who were evicted from south Bombay to north Bombay.

After the initial positive response from the field and the support of most of the communities the SUP project itself seems to be shying away from responding adequately to these demands because of the middle class functionaries who did not have the perceptions nor the commitment and appreciation of the impact of the scheme on the beneficiary population. The project had been assiduously build up by the front line staff, in active collaboration with the local groups, to convince and motivate eligible communities to join the scheme, but its credibility was then damaged. The chaos created at the community level because of indecision and its further exploitation by unscrupulous local level bureaucracy and local leaders further damaged the credibility of governments intentions to seek partnership efforts with local community groups in the execution of the SUP. This experience and the closure of the community development cell lead to a continuation of existing "top-down" strategies which run counter to the participatory approaches of most

---

20 *Some donors have already channelled substantial funds through government to create projects in which NGOs have mutually agreed roles.*

NGOs and fail to address the need for improving the responsiveness of governments to people.

Similarly with respect to the issue of contracting and charging for services, and the objection to the neo-liberal transformation of the beneficiary into "consumer", I have often run across cases in the field in which it was clear that NGOs were afraid to charge for services because they couldn't "compete" with either government or other zero or low-cost providers in the same area. Even though they couched their objection to charging in terms of "sympathy" for the poor, they were clearly fearful that their "beneficiaries" would prefer other providers. Charging for services, in other words, can also be a way to introduce "beneficiary" needs and judgements quite powerfully into a program that is not that participatory or in other ways accountable. This may seem strange, but, given that some NGOs are really not "participatory", charging may be a second-best approach to introducing a proxy for "participation" and pressures for accountability under some circumstances.

Most of the large NGOs or internationally reputed NGOs get called for government funding and programmes, while small and medium size NGOs get excluded. Instead of open and formal interaction or opposition and confrontation (which is what is expected in the value system and ethos of NGO voluntarism) their modus operandi in dealing with the government is to use personal contacts and influence, favouritism and nepotism, all the traits that the activists have otherwise so severely criticised among the public systems.

Although there are exceptions, NGOs take little interest in identifying from their work what might be generalisable beyond the confines of their immediate target group. NGOs rarely address the wider structural and policy factors which ultimately influence the environment in which they operate. NGOs' capacity for documenting and disseminating the results of their work tends to be severely constrained, thus depriving others of potentially useful results. Further, they have a poor record of setting up the types of co-ordinating mechanisms that might help to overcome shortcomings of this kind.

A major drawback in advocating the use of NGOs in community participation is the inability of the NGO sector to redistribute resources between groups on a sizeable scale. The experiences expose the difficulties of implementing a process meant to close the gap between those who "think" and those who "execute"; between those responsible for the technical and social advance of development projects and the participants themselves. One of the problems here is that NGOs find themselves in the middle of a dynamic debate in which the relationships between theory and practice are often weak and the relationships between actions and outcome are uncertain. The fear at least among NGOs, is that it is the official donors who make policy, the

NGOs who implement it whilst the governments of the South are mere onlookers.

23.6 Implications of NGO-GO Relationship

The enhancement of certain NGOs in delivering services to the poor has prompted many governments and donors to take a simplistic view of the potential that NGOs offer for delivering services to the urban poor. Donor pressures towards structural reform and privatization in India underlie the increased interest in NGOs as "service deliverers".[21] Some donors see the promotion of better contracts between NGOs and GOs as a way of increasing the efficiency of the latter (Bebbington 1991). Is this strengthening civic society or is it an attempt to shape civil society in ways that external actors believe is desirable?[22] What is not clear is what impact this is having on NGO programming, performance, legitimacy and accountability.[23] The "inherent" advantage of the NGOs themselves are gradually worn away by increased funding, professionalisation, bureaucracy and the shifting of objectives away from social "mobilization" towards service delivery. This may lead NGOs towards a role as contractors following the agendas of outsiders.

At a deeper level, there are worries about the long-term impact of NGO service-provision on the sustainability of national health and education systems (rather than programmes) and access to quality services for all. Robinson (1991 & 93) points out that large, influential and well funded NGOs may be able to "concentrate resources in regions and sectors that might not be most important for national development", with a "patchwork quilt" of services of varying quality emerging without any overview of overall needs. There are echoes here of debates about public/private mix in social services in countries such as the UK and USA. The evidence from these debates suggests that such fears are well founded, with unequal access and spiralling costs already

---

21 *There is great reliance placed on markets and private sector initiative as the most efficient mechanisms for providing most services to most people, even if they do this imperfectly. "Imperfect markets are better than imperfect states" (Colclough 1991:7) NGOs are viewed as market-based actors which are more efficient and cost effective than governments, and give better value for money.*

22 *At this point it is worth registering a note of concern about the extent of external influence on NGO activity. Bebbington and Thiele (1993:182) describes the clear politicisation of NGOs in Central America during the 1980s when USAID funded a range of right-wing groups, and Northern NGOs supported a range of left-wing groups.*

23 *It would be interesting to do research on NGOs not funded by international donors as vs. those that are, with respect to several of the questions that have been raised. It would be worth looking at both the positive and negative side of this issue.*

a reality.

An obvious question raised by "successful" NGO-based activities is whether they can be replicated on a larger scale by government or other NGOs. In Bombay, for example, even if the combined efforts of all the NGOs working in the city are taken together, it is unlikely that more than 20% of the urban poor will be reached. This would assume that these efforts are in some way compatible or co-ordinated, which of course most are not. Hence some kind of relationship between government and NGOs is needed if poverty issues are to be addressed on a comprehensive, country-wide basis. The relationship between them cannot be viewed on a purely functional basis.

The new approach is to focus on external pressures to perform. The argument is that organisations will tend to solve their own problems about means; the point is to ensure that they have the right pressures and incentives to achieve the right result. This could all sound very neo-liberal or New Public Management-ish. There are indeed those variants; but there is nothing intrinsically neo-liberal about the approach. The "external pressures to perform" need not be those of quasi-competition between alternative providers or tight budgetary scrutiny; they can include various kinds of exposure to pressures from users, other organisations, local politicians, etc. One important implication of the "new" approach is that "institutional performance" may be neither a stable nor a generic attribute of particular organisations: an organisation may be temporarily good at getting a particular thing done because of a conjunction of "environmental" pressures, and then collapse into apparent uselessness.

Pfeffer and Salancik (1978:7) make an important point that because of the normal human bias in favour of attributing causality to observable human action, both participants in organisations and observers of organisations have a bias in favour of explaining organisational performance in terms of what they can directly and easily observe, which is basically intra-organisational behaviour. The influence of "environmental" variables is far less evident.

23.7 Challenges for the Future

NGOs have traditionally defined themselves in relation to the state. As the state is transformed by the wider agendas of political change, democratisation and a reduction in resource flows to governments, NGOs are required to rethink their role (Bebbington and Farrington 1993). Some will be content to become sub-contractors for services, receiving a greater share of public resources, while others will take on new roles influencing policy. Political circumstances are changing rapidly, but it would be a mistake to conceive of this change as a linear movement towards greater freedom.

The role of the NGO begins with the learning capacity of the agency: how well it copes with mistakes and contingencies, how it uses its experience to strengthen institutional capacity and to what extent it shares the knowledge gained with the community. The way an NGO approaches and works with the community at the planning and subsequent stages is crucial. Governments/Donors probably will be unable or unwilling to support the long time horizons, slow careful work, and gradual (and often non-quantifiable) results which characterise successful local institutional development. Current donor claims about a commitment to institutional development are inconsistent with the short term, output oriented project methodologies they utilise.

As NGOs diversify in their activities and operations (in comparatively small, but rapidly expanding, area) it appears that organisations must often engage, from a much earlier stage in their development, in such wider "relational" work, where even comparatively routine service delivery frequently has to be combined with aspects of management of the wider environment (Yap 1982 & 1983). How can NGO's engage in the political process in order to achieve fundamental changes in the distribution of power and resources *without* becoming embroiled in partisan politics and thereby losing their independence? It is necessary to be creative and adapt in setting up appropriate mechanisms that will enable NGOs to engage directly in partisan politics with minimum risk to their credibility, independence and survival. This seems a very tall order indeed.

A few recommendations can also be put forward from the experiences in Bombay:

(i) Institutionalised Means of Communication

Agencies with proven track record of community work and specially institutional capacity building, seem to feel stifled by the highly structured, target oriented time bound agenda for action as was laid out in the programme definition of IPP- V. The potential sources of tension can be mitigated by careful planning and open and free communication both ways between NGOs and Government.

(ii) Community Groups

Apart from the formalised collaborative process with the NGOs sector, a vast relatively untapped potential for collaboration lies within the local community organisations or groups in the communities. None of the programmes mentioned above try and use this to its maximum level. Most of us are aware of the role of the community organisations and its potential to bring about change and the process of learning by involvement in the service delivery activities themselves. Some NGOs in IPP-V are already involving community groups in organising exhibitions for campaigns related to health and social issues on major festivals within the communities. Also members from within the community are trained to become community health workers to work within the targeted area, which also helps the community worker to establish its credentials in government departments when liaising with them on a particular issue or case. Popular participation by beneficiaries on a significant scale will only come about through reforms in official structures, not through multiplying of NGO projects.

(iii) Training

To the majority of local authorities, the community-based approach to urban management is something new. It entails making important policy and programmatic choices for the government and significant organisational and decision -making structure adjustments for the communities. From the perspective of the government , the implementation of the community based approach on a large scale will require not only new techniques but an array of community professionals trained and committed to implement them.

Training should be given to government officials to improve their skills to work with local groups, understand methodologies and techniques of community participation, and communication and interpersonal skills[24]. It is important to recognise that not only institutional restructuring but organisational climate building are both crucial to sustain an on-going commitment to collaboration with NGO-GO and people's involvement in programmes, otherwise most of the schemes will only exist on paper (Panwalkar 1991).

Induction of young and dynamic bureaucrats, rigorous input of in-service training and conscious exposures to the 'voluntary-spirit' has rendered administrators more amenable to people. The corollary to this has also been the conscious induction of 'trained social workers' in the staff of government projects to evolve strategies for service delivery systems with greater responsiveness to people's need. The professional social workers in India have been quick to respond to this need, as they see in it not only (i) new scope for enhancement of job opportunities; (ii) but also opportunities to operate in large systems, where systematic feed back from the field, can effect policy

---

24 *In the year 1989-90 all the Health Post Staff of about 600, had undergone a one week intensive training input in 'Community Work' organised by Department of Urban and Rural Community Department, Tata Institute of Social Sciences, Bombay.*

changes and ensure better services to target population. For professional social workers who cherish their image of 'advocacy and change oriented role', there is a major challenge in this new field. While they are keen to operate from within the government structure, the constant danger of being sucked in to the vortex of bureaucratic sloth, indifference and red-tapism is very real. In the case described, the project funding from the World Bank for the IPP-V and BUDP has prompted the appointment of trained social workers in these projects. The Bombay experience shows that this team has been able to work effectively, within the existing policy and institutional constraints of the project, towards enhancing programme efficiency and effectiveness. It can also perform the task of improving efficiency of both government and NGOs, as well as in increasing its accountability to a wider section of the population.

23.8 Conclusion

NGOs innovate - whether in technical, procedural, institutional or methodological ways - in the expectation that government will "scale up". It is worth reiterating that these innovations are rooted in a "problem" - or "issue" - oriented approach to urban change. By contrast with traditional, and still widely found, adherence in the public sector or discipline-based approaches, NGOs' prime concern in the present context is to respond to opportunities and constraints identified by the urban poor. In practice, most NGOs have shown reluctance to become involved in long-term programmes of trials: their interest is in what will work within their chosen geographical areas, not in the wider conditions under which schemes will work, which must necessarily be the concern of government agencies that have a national mandate.

The chapter highlights how divergent expectations of the roles to be played by each side is generated. Analysis of their respective roles supports a view that relations between NGOs and Government agencies/departments is both multifaceted and dynamic. Some relations are clearly collaborative, a successful outcome depending on adequate fulfilment of prearranged obligations by the respective partners; other types have been termed "incorporative" (as coined by Farrington and Lewis 1993) where NGOs offer lessons from innovative experience for incorporation, and so scaling up by government programmes, although Government agencies, may, choose simply to disregard what is on offer. At another level, NGOs simply establish fora for information exchange on activities both among themselves and between themselves and GOs to generate complementarity, or simply to avoid duplication of effort.

The Indian government will continue to experience financial stringency which will limit their capacity to deliver a full range of services to the urban poor. This capacity is further limited by corruption and inefficiency. The trend for donors to look to NGOs as democratizing influences on the state as a whole, and on its institutions, appears set to continue as, therefore, will funds for NGO-GO collaborative projects.

NGOs are a means whereby the efficiency of service delivery systems might be enhanced, and in this context are little more than a tool of management. This understanding of NGOs is necessarily static, passive and ultimately about control by management. Different management styles need to be developed to allow for greater strategic NGO participation. These must recognise the importance of indigenous knowledge and local decision-making activity networks.

The focus is on building institutions which are flexible and sustainable on the part of both government and local organisations. In many cases this requires a renegotiation of the relationship between those who control resources, whether they are public or private interests, and the recipients of those resources. It requires not only a more responsive public bureaucracy but also a more realistic recognition by local communities that their objectives for radical structural change and the objectives of implementing agencies intending to maintain the status quo do not always coincide.

Development policy in the 1990s is moving increasingly towards an emphasis on securing political rights and representation for all sections of the community, and opening governments to increased accountability to the poor in service provision, legal rights and policy formulation. The facilitation of such changes requires creative thinking among all the actors involved (NGOs, government agencies, donors and community organizations) to find ways of ensuring that the interests of disadvantaged groups are represented in and addressed by governments.

References

Aguirre, F. & Namdar-Irani, M. (1992) 'Complementaries and tensions in NGO-State relations in agricultural development: the trajectory of AGRARIA (Chile)', *Agricultural Research and Extension Network, Network Paper no: 32, ODI* London.
Bebbington, A.J. (1991) 'Sharecropping agricultural development: the potential of GSO-government cooperation' *Grassroots Development* 15(2):20-30.
Bebbington, A.J. & Farrington, J. (1992) 'The scope for NGO-government interactions in agricultural technology development: an international overview' *Agricultural Research and Extension Network, Network Paper no.33, ODI*, London.
Bebbington A. & Farrington J. (1993) 'Governments, NGOs and Agricultural Development' in *The Journal of Development Studies*, Vol.29 no.2, January.
Bebbington, A.J. & Thiele, G. (1993) *Non-Governmental Organizations and the State in Latin*

America: Rethinking Roles in Sustainable Agricultural Development, Routledge, London.

Clark, J. (1991) *Democratising Development: The Role of Voluntary Organisations*, Earthscan, London.

Colclough, C and Manor, J (1991) *States or Markets? Neo-liberalism and the development policy debate*, Clarendon Press, Oxford.

Daswani Mona & D'Cruz Celine (1990) 'The Right Track: A case study of Resettlement Initiatives by women in Bombay' in *Community Development Journal* Vol.25, No.1.

Edwards, M.D. & Hulme, D. (eds) (1992) *Making a Difference? NGOs and Development in a Changing World*, Earthscan, London.

Farrington John & Lewis David J. (ed) (1993) *Non-Governmental Organisations and The State In Asia: Rethinking Roles In Sustainable Agricultural Development* Routledge, London.

Korten, D.C. (1990) *Getting to the 21st Century: Voluntary Action and the Global Agenda*, Kumarian, West Hartford, Conn.

Marsden, D. (1991) 'What is Community Participation?' in Richard C. Crook and Alf Morten Jerve (eds.) *'Government and Participation: Institutional Development, Decentralisation and Democracy in the Third World*, Chr. Michelsen Institute, Department of Social Science and Development, Bergen.

Moser, Caroline (1989) Community Participation in Urban Projects in the Third World, *Progress in Planning*, Vol. 32, No.2.

Panwalkar, V.G., Sharma, J.C. and Panwalkar, Pratima, (1991b), *Training Need Assessment*, Studies conducted for Training Cell, IPP-V, Public Health Department, Municipal Corporation of Greater Bombay.

Paul, S. & Israel, A. (eds) (1991) 'Non-governmental organisations and World Bank: an overview', in *Non-Governmental Organisations and the World Bank: Cooperation for Development*, World Bank, Washington, D.C.

Pfeffer, J. and G.R. Salancik (1978) *The External Control Of Organisations: Resource Dependence Perspective*, Harper and Row, New York.

Plucknett, D.L; Smith, N.J.H. & Ozgediz, S.(1990) *Networking in International Agricultural Research*, Cornell University Press, Ithaca, New York and London.

Robinson M. (1991) *Evaluating the impact of NGOs in Rural Poverty Alleviation: India Country Study*, Working Paper No.49 Overseas Development Institute, London.

Robinson M. (1993) *Governance, Democracy and Conditionality: NGOs and the New Policy Agenda.*

Sevilla, M. (1987) 'The Private NGOs in Institutional Change: Lessons from El Salvador', presented at the World Bank's meeting 'Lessons from the Past and Directions for the Future', Hot Springs, Virginia, (mimeo), El Salvador.

Stein Alfredo (1990) 'Critical Issues in Community Participation in Self-help housing Programmes: The experience of FUNDASAL' in *Community Development Journal* Vol.25 No.1. Jan.

Tandon, Rajesh (1987) *'The Relationship between Non-Governmental Organisations and Government'* Society for Participatory Research in Asia, New Delhi, August.

Yap, K.S. (1982) 'Leases, Land and Local leaders, and analysis of a squatter settlement upgrading Programme in Karachi, Free University, Amsterdam.

Yap, K.S. (1983) 'Access to Resources as a form of participation' in *UNCHS Community Participation for Improving Human Settlements*: 54-59, Nairobi.

24 Environmental Improvement in Calcutta: Non-Governmental Organisations and Community-Based Organisations

Hamish Main

24.1 Introduction

The past decade has seen the beginnings of a major shift in urban govern-ance emphasis in much of the Third World, with the withdrawal to some ex-tent of the state from direct provision of infrastructure and services, and the increasing involvement of non-governmental organisations (NGOs), the pri-vate sector, communities and householders themselves. This shift is an out-come of several processes which became more apparent from the early 1980s: reductions in government budgets arising from both macro-economic prob-lems and a desire in some quarters to reduce the role of government, the failure of existing urban governance to cope with the needs of cities and their residents, the increasing involvement of NGOs in the organisation of the ur-ban poor, and encouragement from the World Bank and other transnational agencies (UNCHS 1996, ch5). The need for municipal and national govern-ments to pursue policies designed to enable NGOs and others to provide ur-ban infrastructure and services was first formally outlined by the UNCHS in 1988, followed soon afterwards by other major global agencies (UNCHS, 1988; UNDP, 1991; World Bank, 1991).

Government now supposedly should seek to facilitate action by its citizens, private firms or non-government organizations, to provide for themselves such serv-ices and at such standards as people themselves might choose. The capital project now became replaced by the programme of technical assistance and "enabling". (Harris 1992: xix)

In low-income communities, the participation of community groups and the NGOs that support them is a powerful instrument for bringing about necessary politi-cal commitment and implementing affordable solutions. (UNDP et al 1994: 3)

Low-income communities' greater involvement in the improvement of their environmental infrastructural provision might be frustrated by a number of obstacles: the prohibitive cost of such provision, the feeling among the urban poor that such services should be provided by government, their lack of technical capacity, and their lack of connections with relevant decision-makers (Cheema, 1992). If these obstacles are to be surmounted, NGOs are most likely to possess the means to help low-income communities to do so. Once some success has been achieved in this direction, community-based organisations (CBOs) will become more confident in their dealings with government personnel, and motivated to go on to other elements in what can become a programme of progressive infrastructural improvement (Choguill 1994:940-41).

On the face of it, Calcutta is not a city where the reduction of state provision and its replacement by non-state organisations might be expected to have advanced very far. Despite the more positive view of economic globalisation in India as a whole during the 1990s, the left-front Government of West Bengal led by the Communist Party of India (Marxist) has resisted the 'opening up' of the economy and governance in this part of the country. Considerable investment in programmes designed to improve Calcutta's environment has been made since the 1970s, financed by the World Bank and more recently by the UK's DFID (formerly ODA) as well as by central government, and administered by Calcutta Metropolitan Development Authority and implemented by various branches of local government. This has achieved a great deal especially through the Bustee Improvement Programme, which had provided a range of improvements by 1986 for nearly two-thirds of the population in Calcutta's approximately 3,000 bustees (Roy, 1994). A high proportion of Calcutta's residents are poor even by Indian standards, many of them having migrated to the city following environmental disasters or political ructions (many from East Pakistan/Bangladesh); this has meant a low ability to pay for local environmental improvement. Combined with the municipal authorities' high-profile provision of urban infrastructure and services, both in projects like the Bustee Improvement Programme and in ongoing service provision, this seems to have fostered a strong culture of dependence on 'government as provider' — a dependence which has discouraged potential movement towards 'government as enabler' on the demand as well as the supply side.

Devolution from government control of environmental improvement planning and implementation in low-income neighbourhoods potentially means a growing role for NGOs. But the prospects for Calcutta NGOs in this endeavour are problematic, and not only because of the scale of physical and organisational problems associated with environmental improvement here as in large cities throughout the region. NGOs in general have been more successful at one-off projects than in continuing environmental improvement work (Choguill & Choguill 1996: 90). Recognising the need for progressive improvements that can be sustained in a given community and replicated elsewhere, many NGOs now acknowledge the desirability of an empowerment approach in their interactions with low-income communities. This contrasts with the paternalism of much previous interaction when charitable organisations both designed and implemented ad hoc projects (Lee 1994 : 167). Rather than an imposition of priorities not shared by low-income 'recipients', the replicability and sustainability of which is likely to be diminished accordingly, empowerment means that needs perceived by members of the community should form the basis of NGO-CBO partnerships through which a dependent relationship can be avoided. But environmental improvement is a low priority for very poor people in Calcutta, who understandably tend to be more concerned with income generation, access to shelter, and education for their children, and who feel quite strongly that local infrastructure and services should be provided by the municipal authorities. An empowering approach by NGOs is also liable to create friction with the Government of West Bengal, which sees the urban poor as one of its natural constituencies and distrusts NGO attempts to raise political consciousness and organise low-income communities around local issues.

This is not a promising milieu for NGOs seeking to pursue environmental issues. The paper illustrates these problems, and NGOs' responses to them, by outlining the cases of four Calcutta NGOs, examining the importance of environmental issues for each of them among the totality of their activities, and indicating how they have dealt with the awkward circumstances in which they operate.

24.2 Environmental Improvement

Environmental improvement may refer to human endeavour in rather different urban arenas, each of which tends to be the concern of identifiable urban social groups. The construction of infrastructure for the supply of water, sewerage and drainage, paths and lighting, and the provision of associated services such as the removal of solid waste or carrying of water, tend to be concerns of poorer people for their own residential areas. These are traditional environmental health issues, alongside the lack of land or housing access for the poor. Local infrastructural needs like these are more likely to have been partly or fully satisfied for better-off people, or those who have been established in the city for some time, and they might then seek to satisfy other infrastructural needs such as electricity or telephone supply. Pollution of air (including noise), water or land is less likely to be restricted to a particular urban group, though pollution in the vicinity of home or workplace might well crystallise concerns about pollution in the city in general. Needs for pollution controls on growing industrial and transport activity are voiced by better-off people as well as by the urban poor, though the latter are usually worst affected. Management of the urban fabric, including the use of open spaces and conservation of green areas (and perhaps of buildings), tends to be a concern of wealthier people and often refers to the wider urban environment away from their homes or workplaces.

The first two of these three principal types of urban environmental issue — local infrastructure and servicing, and pollution — are closely associated with poverty, and together comprise the 'Brown Agenda'. Although in this context they are in an urban setting, space management and conservation may be considered part of the 'Green Agenda' (UNDP et al 1994:1). The broad associations indicated above between these three types of urban environmental issue, and people and areas within a given city, hold for urban development in general and have been demonstrated in Calcutta (CEMSAP 1995; Main, 1995).

24.3 Community-Based Organisations

Most low-income communities in Calcutta house one or more community-based organisations apart from the most local level of municipal administration. These local clubs or associations, which as a rule are dominated by the communities' men in some cases to the exclusion of women, often operate within networks of political patronage. Indeed some CBOs receive small regular funds from political parties. The CPI(M) is widely supported here, especially in neighbourhoods that have benefited from upgrading under the Bustee Improvement Programme or similar municipal action.

Urban environmental improvement appears to be a low priority among Calcutta's CBOs, not because the residents of these communities do not see a need for such improvement but because more immediate and pressing needs must take precedence. Many of the poorest residents in these neighbourhoods, who work long hours and some of whom have little commitment to a future for their families in the city, tend to be unresponsive to community organisation unless it is for cultural satisfaction or immediate economic benefit. Most of Calcutta's CBOs are organised around sport or preparations for religious festivals, for example by constructing *puja pandals*. Stronger support for CBOs is likely to be found in better-off neighbourhoods with more stable populations, where environmental improvements are also more likely to be a focus of organisation.

A survey in sixteen of south-east Calcutta's bustees and squatter settlements in October 1994, which examined the activities of a total of nineteen CBOs, found that social work (resolving disputes, counteracting the effects of alcohol, providing financial help for the destitute), education (for the children) and health (blood donation, family planning and immunisation as well as medical care) also appeared to be more important than environmental improvement. Specifically environmental improvement activities — garbage disposal, general cleaning of the local area, the installation of tubewells and latrines, and tree-planting along the road —were a major element in the activities of only four of these CBOs. None of these four CBOs was in a squatter settlement; they were all in more consolidated bustees that had benefited from the Bustee Improvement Programme and were trying to maintain their improved environments. In most of the improved bustees, maintenance of these improvements seemed to be organised at a household rather than a community level: some of these neighbourhoods were relatively clean and well-provided with drainage, water-supply, paving and/or street lighting. Elsewhere the gains from the Bustee Improvement Programme in the 1970s and '80s seemed to have been overtaken to some extent, perhaps partly by population growth; and many of these neighbourhoods' residents expressed criticism of Calcutta Municipal Corporation for not having adequately maintained infrastructure or continued servicing.

24.4 Non-Governmental Organisations

NGOs have been active historically in Calcutta in a range of spheres, especially in culture and education and poor relief (Larsen 1984:136); and many of them have operated in bustees and squatter settlements, the city's lowest-income neighbourhoods (Nair 1981:184). Environmental issues have become a relatively high priority for Calcutta's NGOs only in recent years: the roots of this date from the 1960s and 1970s, when it was particularly apparent that government could not cope alone with the diverse problems of the city's slums. But this produced tensions between NGOs and the Communist Party of India (Marxist)-led government of West Bengal, which was deeply suspicious of NGOs' political motivations and/or effects. These tensions were to some extent reflected elsewhere in India, and a series of national legislative changes during the 1970s and '80s were designed to control or limit NGO activity in the country. The past decade has seen a loosening of these controls, however, as Delhi has come to recognise the potential contribution of NGOs in various spheres of development, including the provision of urban infrastructure and services (Sen 1991:34-35). Even the Government of West Bengal has begun to show a more positive attitude towards NGOs during the

1990s.

Health and education are the principal issues around which Calcutta's NGOs organise today. Crosscutting with these are the particular concerns shown by many such organisations for women and children. The poverty of families who came to Calcutta as refugees, and of pavement dwellers, also occupy large numbers of NGOs. After these, much smaller numbers organise principally around civil liberty and environmental issues, many of the latter focusing on rural issues such as forestry and agriculture and nature conservation (Unnayan, 1994). Although urban environmental improvement is not a major concern for Calcutta's NGOs, environmental knock-on effects are implicit in a host of other NGO endeavours. Community healthcare might include not only personal health (drugs, AIDS, nutrition) but also questions of environmental health such as water supply and waste disposal; environmental education is becoming part of the wider educational curriculum, in non-formal as well as formal schools; improvements in the lives of pavement dwellers might help them to move into residential environments where they are less vulnerable to problems like traffic pollution encountered on streets around the city centre; and so on.

Much of the activity of Calcutta's NGOs with a bearing on urban environmental improvement, then, is not in organisations devoted to urban environmental improvement but in those for which this is one of several considerations, perhaps even a minor or incidental consideration. The first and second of the following four illustrations of Calcutta NGOs come into this latter category, while the other two NGOs portrayed here both have specifically environmental concerns but operate in contrasting arenas.

(i) Kalyani Karlekar

Kalyani Karlekar funds the Calcutta Social Project, which works mainly in the overlapping fields of education and healthcare, with an emphasis on the needs of women and children: nursery and primary schools, creches, girls' and boys' craft centres, women's cooperatives and a mother-and-child health programme. CSP has been active in Monoharpukur since the early 1970s. From 1983, as its experience and support grew, CSP expanded into an open-air school for rag-picking children at the city's major rubbish dump at Dhapa; this was supplemented by more permanent schools, a creche and a primary healthcare programme in the same area. But local politicians wanted greater control over CSP's activities in Dhapa, and CSP's unwillingness to allow this resulted in its Dhapa involvement ending in 1991. CSP then devoted more attention to another community on the eastern periphery of the city at Choubaga, where the village club had invited the NGO to set up a non-formal school like the one at Dhapa. Recently CSP has begun to operate among pavement dwellers both near its headquarters in Monoharpukur and in the centre of Calcutta at Madan Street: in the latter, contacts were established with women and children, a pavement school was begun for the children where nourishment and inoculations were provided as well as a range of basic education and cultural activities.

(ii) Church's Auxiliary for Social Action

CASA began in 1947 as a charity wing of the National Council of Churches in India, the umbrella organisation of protestant and orthodox churches in the country, and is now one of several NGOs with church connections active in Calcutta's bustees. Less evangelistic than previously, the organisation has become more holistically mission-orientated for poor and marginalised people irrespective of religion or other background. In the 1960s and '70s it devoted much of its attention to disaster relief, organising food-for-work projects after floods and distributing USAID wheat and oil. An internal re-evaluation in 1979 identified the need to encourage greater self-reliance among its recipients, which directed the NGO's attention towards building community organisations. CASA was also finding that poor people lose out all too often from project approaches which provide goods that are appropriated by the wealthier members of the community. Another re-evaluation in the late '80s laid greater emphasis on sustainability, environmental as well as organisational, and more recently additional resources have gone into raising recipients' awareness of their own needs and rights and potentials. CASA has proved to be more progressive than some of its funding sources in Europe, which still prefer a project approach because it can produce more visible results.

The NGO now has projects in regions throughout India, all of which are rural except the Calcutta Slum Development Project now operating in thirteen city neighbourhoods. CASA's Calcutta work began in the 1960s with food distribution and medical care, before being transformed in 1981 into the integrated development project of the CSDP. An awareness campaign focuses on education and skill development, forming or improving CBOs, networking, enhancing women's participation in health and socio-economic activities, and raising awareness on alcohol and drug abuse. The CSDP has always aimed to involve community members in identifying issues, needs and plans of action, though a hardened cynicism has often been encountered in the attitudes of poor people to the idea of participation.

The women's groups with which CASA works have been among the more successful of their initiatives. Among the principal issues of concern to the women of these communities are healthcare (eg birth control, malaria control, nutrition and blood donation), income generation (eg embroidery and tailoring), "eve-teasing" (i.e. sexual harassment) and coping with the men's abuse of alcohol and drugs (eg through detoxification programmes). Again, little of this appears to be directly relevant to environmental improvement, but sometimes an issue is raised by one of the neighbourhoods where the CSDP operates which has a clear bearing on environmental issues. One such was in the Etalghata neighbourhood in 1996, when it was becoming apparent that drinking water supplies in some parts of Calcutta were contaminated with arsenic. This has been a problem in some parts of rural West Bengal since about 1981, but it had not been recognised in the city until 1994; millions of people are already affected by arsenic poisoning in the Ganga Delta of both India and Bangladesh[1], and some have already died as a result (Pearce, 1995; Chakraborti, 1997). CASA contacted a renowned expert on arsenic contamination in one of the Calcutta universities who addressed a public meeting in the area and demonstrated how contaminated water could be treated for human consumption. Soon afterwards, responding to approaches from CASA and other organisations, Calcutta Municipal Corporation provided tap water to the area and the tubewells drawing on contaminated supplies were capped.

(iii) PUBLIC (People United for Better Living In Calcutta)

PUBLIC is a small but very influential organisation that was formally launched on Earth Day 1990. Its specifically environmental concerns are those of middle-class Calcuttans — vehicle pollution, greening the city, protecting the wetlands among which the city is growing. Its successes derive especially from effective use of the media, with frequent appearances in print and television, and attractively-presented materials like newsletters and calendars and booklets distributed quite widely to influential people. Most unusually, PUBLIC has made good use of legal advocacy.

In an early campaign PUBLIC tackled the problem of noise generated by Calcutta's traffic, in particular by the electronic airhorns of large commercial vehicles. Based on noise level data from several thousand vehicles monitored by PUBLIC, and following street demonstrations by schoolchildren coordinated by the NGO, silence zones have been created around some of Calcutta's hospitals and schools. PUBLIC has also worked in conjunction

---

1 *The arsenic poisening has not been caused by anthropogenic pollution. High levels of contamination occur in some of the aquifers in the delta, which were reached by deep tube wells in the 1980s, ironically in a programme to bring clean drinking water to the people. The water looks clear and has no biological contamination. It was not tested at the time for heavy metals.*

with Calcutta Traffic Police to enforce pollution control requirements, setting up autopollution testing camps to check exhaust emissions and to provide education in vehicle maintenance.

In 1993 PUBLIC organised a mass tree planting campaign to mark Calcutta's 300th anniversary, in conjunction with the State Forestry Department and involving large numbers of schoolchildren; 300 trees were planted along the Eastern Metropolitan Bypass and many more in other parts of the city. In a campaign against companies damaging trees by nailing their metal advertisements to tree trunks, PUBLIC succeeded in getting Calcutta Municipal Corporation to issue warning notifications. Encouraged by PUBLIC, Calcutta's 'bhadralok' middle-class even took to the streets to demonstrate against incessant power cuts. Neither of these two campaigns achieved a great deal directly, but their high-profile conduct brought more support for the organisation and raised long-term awareness of green issues and campaigning in general. When the Indian Museum in the city centre planned to fill in a nearby pond in order to construct an annexe, PUBLIC went to court along with three other NGOs and obtained a stay order in the public interest, arguing that the pond should be protected both for fire-fighting and for ecological reasons. A survey of the city's parks was used by PUBLIC for an exhibition in St Paul's Cathedral to impress on Calcuttans how much park space had been lost.

Probably the most famous campaign in PUBLIC's short history was to protect the ecologically valuable East Calcutta Wetlands from urban encroachment. These seasonally-flooded depressions produce much needed vegetables and fish. When the Government of West Bengal planned to reclaim a sizeable area of wetland for construction of a World Trade Centre and associated developments on a 187-acre site on the edge of the wetlands, the NGO took a public interest petition to the High Court and, against the odds, won their case. This was the first time a green issue had appeared before Calcutta's High Court, and it gave permanent protection to this portion of wetland from development planning (though the World Trade Centre is going ahead on existing land nearby).

(iv) Unnayan

Unnayan ("development" in Bengali) was formed by a group of housing professionals and students in 1977 with the aim of supporting very poor people in their attempts to secure housing. At first, much of its work was in rural West Bengal, in the construction of housing for flood victims, and of schools and community centres. From about 1980, however, Unnayan concentrated more on Calcutta and less on actual construction.

Those active at the heart of Unnayan have always been consciously reflective on their actions and their effects, actual and potential; they see "housing" in the broad sense of the term, not just as physical shelter but also as security, as a base, as the source of access to related infrastructure and the range of neighbourhood activities and services integral to improving the lives of the urban poor: craft organisations, self-managed schools and health centres, the development of appropriate technologies, and so on. Unnayan has also been active in researching and documenting the lives and labour circumstances of the people with whom it has worked, and this has helped to generate a well-stocked library in the Unnayan office at Baliganj.

An early decision was taken by Unnayan to concentrate not on Calcutta's bustees, where the governing Communist Party of India (Marxist) and many other institutions were involved, but on squatter settlements where government-provided improvement had not been forthcoming and was unlikely in the future. Work in some of the squatter settlements of East Calcutta evolved from income-generating activities to the organisation of squatters' campaigns to fight evictions and to pressurise government. But squatter settlements in this part of Calcutta are small in size (compared with those of the industrial districts, and certainly compared with some of those in Mumbai or Delhi), and divided politically; and getting their inhabitants to organise or take part in protests was found by Unnayan to be a losing battle. Government intransigence to the squatters' plight through the 1980s culminated in a spate of evictions about the end of the decade.

Unnayan began to move about that time into activities supporting squatter settlements that were designed to bring them less into conflict with government. A civic rights campaign sought to obtain rights for squatters to register to vote and to receive ration cards. Environmental improvement became a higher priority: the provision of water supply (through tubewells) and of sanitation (latrines), and the planting of trees. The environmental work has been focused on squatter settlements that are seen by Unnayan as slightly more secure — less threatened by demolition than some of the others where it is not so involved. Squatters tend to be less responsive to Unnayan's environmental improvement initiatives than to its help with education and food and income-generating activity. Unnayan sees a need for environmental improvement not only as a worthwhile end in itself, however, but also in the strategic consideration that an improved physical environment can give a squatter settlement better prospects for future consolidation and greater security.

Unnayan has also networked with NGOs from other parts of India, most effectively in the National Campaign for Housing Rights which began in Calcutta in 1986 as a result of organisation by Unnayan. The campaign's success in terms of improved housing rights for poor people is as yet unclear, although the National Housing Policy did incorporate some of its demands (Kumar, 1989). But a network of like-minded NGOs was established, and experience was gained in strategic actions for social progress. The association set up by Unnayan in 1984 as an umbrella group for community organisations based in squatter settlements (the Organisation for the Rights of the Uprooted Toiling People) has been active in defending the rights of Calcutta's poorest residents. But some of those in Unnayan feel that much of what they set out to do has been frustrated, and that even a supposedly leftist government like that of West Bengal has not effectively represented the interests of society's poorest people.

24.5 Interpretation of Case Study NGOs' Environmental Contributions

Neither Kalyani Karlekar nor CASA is oriented towards environmental improvement activities in their dealings with Calcutta's bustee and pavement communities. Each of these NGOs is primarily involved in issues identified as higher priorities by those with whom they are working — income generation, job training, education, community healthcare, childcare and (in the case of CASA) family planning. CASA in particular has moved away from implementing projects of their own creation towards strategies designed to empower their community partners, and this seems to have grown during the past twenty years chiefly from the NGO's own experiences and evaluations, rather than in response to ideas in the wider development field. CASA's emphasis on sustainable improvement has been supported since 1992 by its awareness campaign as well as by its focus on local economic development needs identified by community members. Notwithstanding the narrow success in responding to one neighbourhood's fears regarding arsenic contamination of water supply, CASA feels that environmental improvement is more likely to be a focal issue in future years as the thirteen low-income communities where it is involved in Calcutta develop economically and consolidate socially. But its existing projects also relate to environmental improvement in a broader sense, though perhaps tenuously, as do those of Kalyani Karlekar. Through its varied support for rag-pickers at the city's main rubbish dump, the CSP has enabled more efficient recycling of Calcutta's waste as well perhaps as less precarious livelihoods for those who benefited directly from the initiative. Pavement schools are a long-term investment in pavement dwellers' lives that might result in their finding more secure shelter and avoiding the detrimental health impacts of their present situation.

PUBLIC is an NGO with aims, methods and support distinctive from most organisations active in improving India's urban environments. Its concerns for pollution and green issues, in which it has achieved considerable publicity as well as success, are middle-class advocacy concerns. They have less to do with the lives of Calcutta's poorest residents; PUBLIC does not aim specifically to improve the environmental circumstances of low-income communities, nor does it seek to empower their residents except in a broad sense along with other Calcuttans. Part of the explanation of this NGO's successes lies in the fact that the issues taken up by PUBLIC also exercise many people in government as well as in large companies and the media. But those farmers, fishermen and others who earn their living from the East Calcutta Wetlands now protected from urban expansion as a result of PUBLIC's court victory over the government might feel that they have benefited from the NGO's actions. And the court victory also made a great impact in the consciousness of many Calcutta people, firmly establishing NGOs as a potential element in urban development decision-making.

Of the four NGOs illustrated here, Unnayan is clearly the most directly involved in improving the environmental circumstances of Calcutta's low-income communities. It has contributed directly to the construction of environmental infrastructure in squatter settlements, and has also been active in a range of wider issues including income generation, education and community healthcare that have potential knock-on effects to environmental improvement. For much of its twenty-year history, Unnayan has focused on activities designed to empower poor people in Calcutta — encouraging squatters to organise in defence of their own needs, lobbying on their behalf in government, and explaining their housing-related needs to politicians and others. In all of these endeavours, Unnayan has consciously and self-critically sought to serve the needs of some of the city's poorest communities.

There is no doubt that Unnayan has achieved much during the past two decades both in its activities designed to empower low-income communities, despite the difficulties of assessing success in this endeavour, and in the projects implemented by the NGO itself. In seeking to serve the local environmental and other needs of some of Calcutta's poorest communities, Unnayan has had to tussle with the difficulties associated with this sort of endeavour that were indicated in the paper's introduction above. The NGO's pragmatism towards the state in recent years has evolved from the hard experience of its involvement in the 1980s with squatter settlements that were eventually bulldozed. Environmental improvement is perceived by Unnayan to be less of a direct threat to government policy on squatter settlements than was their 1980s campaign to organise squatter resistance.

24.6 CBOs and NGOs

The distinction indicated in this paper between the poorest of Calcutta's neighbourhoods, especially where these are squatter settlements, and bustees that are not quite so poor and feel some security in their accommodation, corresponds to a salient distinction between the cities' poorest and slightly less poor residents throughout the region. With this sense of security comes a reordering of priorities in which improvements in shelter are less prominent and other felt needs can be given more room; after education, environmental improvement is one of these. At the same time, rising commitment to the community encourages the formation and support of local organisations based on needs felt within the community and expressed in terms of local initiatives.

But such changing priorities occur unevenly, and are apparent in some infrastructural elements while not in others. A new attitude seems to be emerging in some of Calcutta's bustees, for example, to manage the solid waste generated in the neighbourhood more carefully: instead of garbage being dumped on the road, it is now more likely to be deposited in polythene bags at the community dump; some CBOs arrange for one of their members to go around, perhaps with a whistle early in the morning, to collect the bags from houses and take them to the dump. Grassroots changes like this have occurred in some communities autonomously, without direct influence from NGOs or government or other external agencies. However, changes of this nature are not so apparent in squatter settlements. Widespread resentment has been apparent in Calcutta, and not just in the poorest communities, at the idea of having to pay for water supply. Some of those in arsenic-affected areas of south-east Calcutta have continued to draw their drinking water from contaminated local sources unless and until these tubewells have been capped by the Corporation; the distance from (or the cost of access to) alternative water sources and the long-term nature of health effects related to arsenic poisoning combine against residents' moves towards alternative water-access arrangements (The Telegraph, 1996). Few communities have benefited from new tap water supplies as quickly as the Etalghata neighbourhood on whose behalf CASA was able to lobby the municipal authorities in 1996. When a community organisation in a Taliganj bustee recently decided that its members could afford between them to pay for legal electricity house connections, Unnayan helped them to organise the collection of money within the community and to deal with the municipal electricity supply department. Instances like this provide encouragement for the view that NGOs and CBOs can work effectively in partnership with local government for the improvement of environmental conditions in low-income communities.

Although sporadic environmental improvement has been achieved by such partnerships in squatter settlements, a dependence on government provision remains. Unnayan continues to lobby the Government of West Bengal on behalf of squatter communities, and to mediate where the opportunity arises between the latter and external organisations: Water Aid, a British NGO, has recently been providing tubewells for some of the slightly more secure squatter settlements. But NGOs can do more when squatter settlements' tenure is regularised by the authorities. When a Kamarhati squatter settlement was legalised a year or two ago, Unnayan negotiated house-building loans from the Housing Development Finance Corporation and is now monitoring their repayment. The NGO is optimistic that this exercise will continue successfully, and that environmental improvement will follow both at a household level and through community organisation. But squatter settlements constructed close beside railway tracks and canals, or blocking roads, are unlikely to be regularised; and although some NGOs continue to lobby government on behalf of these communities, the authorities feel that the provision of housing or environmental improvements here would make its clear aim of an end to residential development in such precarious sites the more difficult to implement. Given its more pragmatic attitude to government during the 1990s, Unnayan limits its involvement in these most marginal of urban communities to the provision of food and education along with the organisation of income-generating activities.

Distinctions are apparent in Unnayan's work between squatter settlements that remain insecure, under threat of eviction and demolition, and squatter settlements with grounds for optimism that consolidation will be permitted and regularisation might result. Crosscutting this dimension is the question of political patronage: Unnayan has found that the CBOs which approach it for help are usually those where the ruling party's political patronage is not so strong. Thus Unnayan's environmental improvement activity has been concentrated recently in slightly more secure squatter settlements where political patronage is weak. Here, besides the sinking of tubewells, Unnayan has given assistance to communities in the provision of latrines and the planting of trees. In marginal squatter settlements where there is least interest in environmental improvement, Unnayan might support the local club with its sporting and cultural activities — while for example helping to put on an evening *puja* entertainment with a message relating to local environmental improvement, with the aim of influencing community leaders' and residents' attitudes in this direction.

24.7 Conclusion

Government achievements in environmental improvement for Calcutta's bustees have been impressive. But these improvements have not reached all bustee communities, and squatter settlements have hardly benefited at all from infrastructural or service provision by government. Environmental improvement activity by the formal private sector has been very limited as yet even in middle-class neighbourhoods, and prospects for low-income communities benefiting from input by this sector seem minimal.

Although it is not possible to obtain any sort of overview from the research reported in this paper, the impression is that NGO achievements in the field of environmental improvement are somewhat limited. This is not for lack of NGOs; large numbers are active in Calcutta's low-income communities, but few of them focus on environmental improvement activity. Neither does it stem from a lack of understanding of the need for action on environmental issues. The constraints with which Unnayan has struggled offer perhaps the most salient explanation of the limited environmental improvement achieved by NGOs in Calcutta's low-income communities: the low priority afforded to environmental improvement by the city's poorest communities, and the unwillingness of the Government of West Bengal to involve NGOs in the management of these neighbourhoods.

Government in West Bengal sees itself as a grassroots organisation, in touch with the poor people of Calcutta as elsewhere in the state; it doesn't see a need for intermediaries in its dealings with low-income communities. Although a few NGOs do seem to be taken into government confidence more than Unnayan, for example, direct NGO input to policy decisions does not follow.

The sidelining of NGOs like Unnayan appears to be confirmed by the present Calcutta Environmental Management Strategy and Action Plan (CEMSAP), which has involved a number of CBOs in assessing priorities and the feasibility of various management options, but which does not seem to envisage much government-NGO participation in Calcutta's future environmental management: "The responsibilities of the NGOs will be enhanced with time to come. They would act as major catalysts for public awareness, and the strengthening of this additional level of competence is badly needed within [Calcutta]" (CEMSAP 1995, p9.8).

Note

Principal sources for information on the four case study NGOs were interviews with their representatives, as follows:

Kalyani Karlekar Interview with Mr Sirkar (Secretary) and Captain Basu (President), Kalyani Karlekar office, Calcutta, 31st January 1996. See also Calcutta Social Project (n.d.).

CASA Interviews with Mr S Agrawal (CASA Chief Zonal Officer, East India), CASA office, Calcutta, 24th September 1996; and with Mrs S Banerjee (Project Director, CSDP), CASA office, Calcutta, 25th September 1996. See also Church's Auxiliary for Social Action (1984)

PUBLIC Interview with Mrs B Kakkar (President), Calcutta, 23rd September 1996.

Unnayan Interviews with Mr A Deb (Secretary), Unnayan office, Calcutta, 20th January 1996; 17th September 1996. On Unnayan, see also Sen, J (1996); Sen, S (1991), pp105-17.

References

Calcutta Environmental Management Strategy and Action Plan (CEMSAP) (1995) Working Paper 1 (Revised Version).

Calcutta Social Project n.d. The endangered family. Information leaflet produced by CSP

Chakraborti, D. (1997) personal communication.

Cheema, S. (1992) 'The challenge of urbanization'. In N. Harris (ed.), *Cities in the 1990s: the challenge for developing countries*. London: UCL Press.

Choguill, C.L. (1994) Crisis, chaos, crunch? Planning for urban growth in the developing world. *Urban Studies* 31 (6), pp935-45.

Choguill, C.L. & Choguill, M.B.G. (1996) Towards sustainable infrastructure for low-income communities. Chapter 3 in C. Pugh (ed.), *Sustainability, the environment and urbanisation*. London: Earthscan.

Church's Auxiliary for Social Action (1984) *Calcutta slums: problems and challenges*. Calcutta: CASA.

Harris, N. (ed.) (1992) *Cities in the 1990s: the challenge for developing countries*. London: UCL Press.

Kumar, A. (1989) National Housing Policy: the implications. *Economic & Political Weekly* XXIV (23), pp1285-94.

Larsen, A. (1984) Calcutta who cares. In Section IV of CASA, *Calcutta slums: problems and challenges*. Calcutta: CASA.

Lee, Y.-S.F. (1994) Community-based urban environmental management: local NGOs as catalysts. *Regional Development Dialogue* 15 (2), pp158-76.

Main, H.A.C. (1995) Attitudes to environmental improvement in the bustees and squatter settlements of south-eastern Calcutta. Report of Phase One of the Environmental Improvement in Calcutta Project, Staffordshire University.

Nair, P.T. (1981) Bustee service. Chapter Eight in Calcutta Municipal Corporation, *Calcutta Municipal Corporation — at a glance*. Calcutta: CMC.

Pearce, F. (1995) Death and the devil's water. *New Scientist* (16.9.95), pp14-15.

Roy, M.B. (1994) *Calcutta slums: public policy in retrospect*. Calcutta: Minerva.

Sen, J. (1996) Foundations of our lives. *New Internationalist* 276, pp20-22.

Sen, S. (1991) Role of Indian NGOs in housing and development: a critical appraisal. Unpublished PhD thesis, University of Illinois at Urbana-Champaign.

The Telegraph (1996) daily newspaper, Calcutta (16.9.96).

United Nations Centre for Human Settlements (Habitat) (1988) *Global strategy for shelter to the year 2000*. Oxford & New York: Oxford University Press.

United Nations Centre for Human Settlements (Habitat) (1996) *An urbanizing world: global report on human settlements 1996*. Oxford & New York: Oxford University Press.

United Nations Development Programme (1991) *Cities, people and poverty: urban development co-operation for the 1990s*. Oxford: Oxford University Press.

United Nations Development Programme / United Nations Centre for Human Settlements / World Bank (1994) *Towards environmental strategies for cities; policy considerations for urban environmental management in developing countries*. Urban Management Programme. Washington: World Bank.

Unnayan (1994) *Directory on social and development documentation units in Calcutta*. Calcutta: Unnayan.

World Bank (1991) *Urban policy and economic development: an agenda for the 1990s*. Washington: The World Bank.

25 Think Big, Start Small: Towards Sequential Capacity Improvement in Urban Planning and Management

Jan Veenstra and Jan Turkstra

25.1 Changing Context of Municipal Government and Theory-Driven Shifts in Information Requirements

The urgent need for Third World countries to improve the material, as well as social living and bargaining conditions for a growing population makes the planned development of collectively available resources unavoidable. Therefore, adoption of an efficient and effective, problem- and action-oriented approach to public-cum-private development planning is of utmost importance, particularly at sub-national levels of regions, provinces, municipalities and (peri-)urban neighbourhoods. Here, municipal administrations have been (over)burdened during the last decades by increasingly integrative, problem- and location-specific resource development tasks. These latter have been grafted on to traditional responsibilities such as enforcing law and order, raising public revenues (often on behalf of the central treasury), land-use registration and controls, regulatory taxation, tariff and pricing systems. Local government often has to provide and maintain physical and social infrastructure such as roads and public transport, water and electricity supply, public markets, schools and hospitals, sanitation and garbage disposal, low-cost housing, etc. This makes a wide span of responsibilities.

It is to be emphasised that recent drives towards decentralisation in government administration not only increase quantitatively the workloads of local bureaucracies, but also diversify qualitatively the statutory functions and multi-level authority structures, day-to-day control, budgeting and planning capabilities needed at the municipal tier of governance. In accordance with a threefold distinction made between urban planning theories (McConnell, 1981: 14-17; Low, 1991: 2, 257-280) this changing context is selectively perceived and overtly accentuated by:

- antagonistic resource development views of UPM (Urban Planning and Management) stakeholders, shifting during past decades in substance from staged economic growth towards distributive/basic-human-needs concepts, but also towards environmental protection on behalf of future generations;

• local institutional development, bureaucratic re-orientation and "bot-tom-up" community participation being induced from the outside in public control and planning procedures; but simultaneously by

• a growing "top-down" squeeze on local public expenditures: the cen-tral power of the purse pressing hard for reductions in state interven-tion and regulation in favour of local financial self-sufficiency, (semi) private enterprise and free-market forces, -thus changing the rules of political power games between public and private interest groups, in-cluding the roles of socio-spatial planners.

All in all, these opposing trends of development thought and practice result in an increasing demand for area-specific and community-based, urban action planning and resource mobilisation, its inter-sectoral coordination, budg-eting, monitoring and evaluation between and within local government ma-chinery itself. Here, internal shortcomings result from out-of-date adminis-trative capabilities and attitudes. In addition, to cope with externally induced transformations currently taking place in Third World countries at large, gov-ernments have defensively hived-off the legal competencies and functional responsibilities to lower-level bureaucracies, to handle problems such as: population growth and rural-urban migration, agricultural intensification, deforestation, land degradation and illegal encroachment by the vulnerable, rural and urban poor having unequal access to inadequate public services, jobs, shelter and lending capital, and being threatened by air, water and soil pollution.

A crucial aspect of local (non-)governmental organisations is their in-formation processing capacity, i.e. generating and managing area-specific (geo) information for small-scale urban interventions such as neighbourhood (drink-ing) water supply, mother and child care, (house) building control and related tariff and tax collection. Of prime interest, here, is the matching point be-tween local administrations and their eventually computerized geo-informa-tion bases, for instance addressing so-called urban poverty pockets to be iden-tified and diagnosed on their specific problems, and subsequently upgraded and monitored in accordance with inter-sectoral goal-directed indicators (Hall and Conning, 1992: 87-102.) Lower-level institutions "dictate" their own decentralised requirements for spatially-bound information, while in turn these organisations themselves are influenced by supporting, inter-departmental and interpersonal information leading towards single- and double-loop organisa-tional learning, and eventually towards gradual administrative capacity im-provement (Argyris and Schÿn, 1978: 18-29, 268-276 and 319-331). These trial-and-error interactions are indeed not static and one-off: during sequen-tial learning rounds, local development institutions may build up increasingly integrated, multi-sectoral and multi-disciplinary packages of (geo-)information, supporting a wide range of controversial functions from law-and-order, revenue collection, utility operation, maintenance and cost recovery, to problem-solving and strategic urban planning tasks. Thus, through information exchange, institutional weaknesses derived from inward-looking departments are to some extent mitigated.

25.2 From Theory-Driven Problem Identification Towards Pragmatic Test Criteria: Emergence of Threefold Knowledge Base

In what follows, three basic themes are seen to underlie the problems of UPM. These are associated with three bodies of practical knowledge, i.e.
   a) theories-in-use (Bolan, 1980: 261-274), e.g. the socio-spatial expression of land-use development processes;
   b) the contestable rationality of public decision-making procedures, and
   c) pluralist, neo-liberal and (neo-) Marxist perspectives on the contextual rules of political power games.

a) Theories-in-Use

Ideally , in dealing with urban management practices a sequence of deductive steps are taken by the multi-disciplinary mixture of civil engineers, natural resource scientists, urban geographers and economists, public administration and management, social and political scientists (McConnell, 1981: 43-54):
   • Partial conceptualisation of "really-felt" problems initially informing the academic scholars and planners alike on their different methods and techniques of inquiry; but also resulting in
   • explanatory cause-effect and incentive-response generalizations which generate predictions (what, if?); leading up to
   • normative goal-effect prescriptions for problem solutions as differently viewed by various UPM stakeholders; and
   • pre-established policy-test criteria regarding impacts of socio-spatial strategies, policy instruments and action projects to be implemented; and, ultimately
   • re-appraisal of resource-use assumptions made, and theory-driven impact evaluation through verifiable policy-test indicators (Chen, 1990: 39-76).

a) Contestable Truths

However, UPM practitioners are confronted every day with the bewildering scene of conflicting urban policies, and consequently with an uneasy awareness of partially contestable truths about a problematic urban reality. As a consequence, too, adherents of rival development views embodied in urban management practices "normally" deny opposing policy options; because they claim that there exists an incontestable underlying real-life structure by which things are as they are: "the hard facts". When espoused and over-simplified theories thus inform urban development practitioners, they function as ideologies (MacIntyre 1979: 42-57; Low, 1991: 39-50) which:

- express a partial truth produced by methodological canons which establish one- dimensional cause-effect relationships;
- obscure from view other arguments and conflicts, i.e., contestability and unpredictability as real-life phenomena; and thus
- justify the bureaucratic routines and polity rules by which private and (semi) public authority controls urban resources.

a) Contextual Power

In promoting genuine urban development in Third World countries, city planners and managers have to reconcile conflicting sets of short- versus long-range policy options held up by different stakeholder groups (Moris, 1981: 89-97):

- on the one hand, there are the paternalistic interests of central government and large-scale private enterprise favouring politico-administrative stability and (sometimes jigged) market forces "from above"; and
- on the other hand, there are the demands of poverty-stricken urban masses favouring redistribution, and an increase in bargaining power, citizen participation and resource mobilisation "from below"

25.3 What Kind of Settlement Hierarchy?

Socio-spatial planners are to be mindful of the ideological hotch-potch of academic disciplines operating with different concepts and conflicting policy criteria - such as, economic efficiency and individual gratification, social equity and distributive justice, as well as environmental sustainability and biological diversity in (natural) resource development (Devas and Rakodi, 1993: 48-61).

Paying specific attention to the hierarchy of urban centres, it has been a fashionable western belief, too, that with increasing city size, diseconomies (such as rising land values, rents, costs of physical and social infrastructure, noise and pollution, crime, poverty and political unrest) outweigh economies of an enlarged urban scale. However, against the conventional policy option of curbing primate city growth, it is argued nowadays that in Third World situations where capital, institutional capacities and technical skills are scarce, cities of eight million people or more should be allowed to grow.

First, mega-cities generate faster macro-economic growth rates. Second, whereas per capita incomes rise in direct proportion to city size, and even where high urban unemployment exists, the survival chances of the poor are greater because of increased participation in the informal sector and access to social support systems. Third, the costs of social overhead capital tend to fall with increased city size. That is to say, where these costs of (overloaded) urban facilities actually rise, macro-economic productivity is rising still faster because of external economies of scale: big cities yield a greater net return per worker or inhabitant than smaller towns. Finally, it is argued that while problems of rapid mega-urbanisation do exist, these are less a consequence of the inefficiency and distributive injustice inherent in large cities, than of intervening factors such as the physical form and structure of cities, uncontrolled land speculation and pollution, weak municipal management, poor utility cost recovery and taxation policies, and so on.

So, whereas it may well be possible for urban planners to formulate increasingly integrative, strategic development frameworks for coping with big-city problems, it may not be possible to implement them in Third World countries where public land-use controls are highly influenced by power games of interest groups, and where local revenue sources are scarce. By inference, though, the conventional wisdom to curb primate city growth may in practice be an obvious socio-spatial strategy (Dewar, Todes and Watson, 1986: 127-161).

A pragmatic compromise position is often found in the promotion of secondary growth centres. Here, restrictive measures aimed at diverting economic growth may actually result in a national loss of jobs if alternative locations are not genuinely viable and competitive. Except where heavy industrial complexes have been built, the policy instruments for activating growth poles are generally too weak or inadequate to divert manufacturing activities from core regions. Particularly in relatively small and poor (e.g. South-Saharan) countries, trickling of innovations down the hierarchy has not taken place, nor has horizontal diffusion fared better. On the contrary, from lower-ranking central places economic growth "normally" filters upward in response to agricultural developments in their direct surroundings. Here, other structural factors are to be taken seriously, particularly in (rural and urban) reciprocal exchange "economies of clan affection", as related to land tenure, access to credit, storage and transport facilities, national price and wage policies, etc. (Hyden, 1983, ch. 1; Harriss in Booth, 1994: 172 - 194).

In conclusion, it appears that regional growth centre policies have their greatest prospects of success in Third World contexts in which a system of significantly sized, intermediate cities already exists, like in South-East Asian and Latin American countries, and where mutually complementary instruments are directed towards changing newly designated core areas from being exploitative to distributive: towards increasing their positive impact on their hinterlands and towards tackling urban and rural poverty directly, instead of being policy instruments solely for maintaining spatial domination (Veenstra, 1970: 66-82; Hilhorst, 1990: 259-297).

25.4 How do Medium-Sized City Plans Work and Perform?

There is an irony in the delivery performance of big cities: despite the relatively high incomes of urban populations, the quality of services inside major cities is poor. These internal service failures have adverse effects on economic growth, forcing enterprises to seek higher-cost production alternatives – such as the installation of generators to provide alternate power supplies. They also have distributive impacts too: poor urban households must increasingly resort to consumption alternatives that imply not only lower quality but higher cost as well (Dillinger, 1994: 2 - 40). Available evidence suggests that the constraint on improved service delivery is not merely one of private and public resources per se, but of municipal mis-management of those resources. Aspects of inter-departmental public management thus receiving considerable attention at present are those of professionalisation (:training) and socialisation, bureaucratic reorientation and administrative decentralisation (Israel, 1990: 146-165 and 193-201; Uphoff, 1986: 192 – 231).

These new approaches can be reconciled with the older tradition of rationalist, organisational learning and behaviouristic planning theory (from Friedmann and Hudson, 1974: 2-14; until and up to Devas and Rakodi, 1993: 41-46). As shown in Figure 1, the processes A-E are required at three territorial levels of municipal management III-I, resulting in short-range action projects at street and building-block level, middle-range strategic programmes at neighbourhood level and long-range policy options at urban district level. , - thus corresponding with different (computerized) geo-information bases, as presented below (Veenstra, 1971: 106-118; ESCAP/UN, 1976: 61-80; Kok,

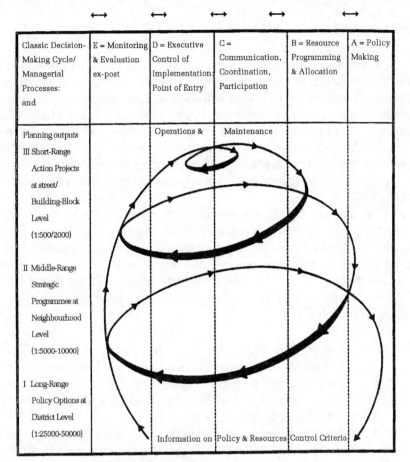

Classic Decision-Making Cycle/ Managerial Processes: and	E = Monitoring & Evaluation ex-post	D = Executive Control of Implementation: Point of Entry	C = Communication, Coordination, Participation	B = Resource Programming & Allocation	A = Policy Making
Planning outputs III Short-Range Action Projects at street/ Building-Block Level (1:500/2000)		Operations &	Maintenance		
II Middle-Range Strategic Programmes at Neighbourhood Level (1:5000-10000)					
I Long-Range Policy Options at District Level (1:25000-50000)		Information on	Policy & Resources	Control Criteria	

Figure 25.1 Urban Management Processes (A-E) and Multi-Level Planning Outputs (III-I)

A =**Policy making** on contested problems, development objectives and alternative courses of action such as rural/urban employment generation, income distribution, supply of public services and physical infrastructure, environmental protection, etc.

B =**Area Programme and Action Project Planning** for allocating, among other things, renewable natural resources (land/water, forest/vegetation, fishery and livestock/wildlife resources) in combination with capital/infrastructures, human/institutional resources, equipment and managerial skills.

C =**Communication**, inter-departmental coordination and community participation for channeling policy making and resource allocation outcomes (A + B) into and between organizations, both vertically and horizontally, thus pressing for local organizational change.

D =**Control** of policy and programme/project implementation (among others) through land use zoning, water rating, wage structures, credit schemes and legal statutes of urban development authorities, including enforcement of regulatory norms and standards collectively agreed upon.

E =**Internal monitoring and impact evaluation** of management functions A-D regarding such policy-test criteria as economic efficiency, distributive effectiveness, political acceptability and ecological sustainability.

1981: 68-69; Veenstra, 1982: 29-31; 1994: 147-167).

Planning requires all five decision-making processes A-E, although any one of these elements may be overemphasised by a particular planning professional. Therefore the following definition of public planning emerges: it is a multi-annual process of successive rounds to explicitly select a multi-disciplinary range of policy and control criteria, to appraise alternative development options and means, to identify available human, capital, natural and institutional resources, and to implement, monitor and evaluate future policies, programmes and projects collectively decided upon (Conyers and Hills, 1990: 3-20).

For rationalising this consensus building process, but particularly for stimulating integrative (versus bureaucratically fragmented) urban control and planning in medium-sized cities, a staggered three-pronged approach is proposed to training municipal departmental officers in the use of (geo-) information technology. So, the inter-departmental integration of data from a multi-disciplinary range of surveys, climbing the territorial planning stairway, principally "from below":

III	From the detailed information type at a mapping scale of about 1:500/2,000 supporting the small-scale and location-specific
↑	project feasibility, implementation, operation and maintenance planning directed at street/building- block level, in anticipation of higher-order plans II + I;
II	Towards the semi-detailed information type at a mapping scale of about 1:5,000, supporting mid-level strategic pre-feasibility
↑	programming of inter-sectoral interventions directed at neighbourhood level; thus ultimately reaching out towards
I	The reconnaissance type of information at a mapping scale of 1:25,000, supporting the (economic growth versus distributive and environmental) policy options at municipal (district) level including the relevant multi-sectoral and multi-disciplinary, urban policy indicators.

However, to introduce this capacity improvement successfully into UPM practice, it would be necessary to consider a decentralisation exercise of 5-6 years. This would be in conformity with a politically sustained, innovative period within which central guidelines for lower-level policy making, plan formulation, coordination, popular participation, control and evaluation were to be conceived, distributed and administratively completed. This is in conformity as well with on-the-job training programmes aimed at gradually increasing the application of geo-information and remote sensing technology to development planning procedures and methods, from macro- to micro-levels by (non-) governmental organizations.

25.5 The Political and Moral Imperatives: What are we Ultimately Planning For?

Only through political manoeuvring can planning practitioners take into account the value-laden and conflicting policy criteria governing municipal management. Neglecting political sustenance during plan formulation is the same as designing a car, but overlooking its fuel system! In other words, in introducing professional capacity improvements in internal urban management, planners have to deal simultaneously with political and institutional issues pertaining to the legitimate "rules of the game" governing the production, distribution, but above all financing of public functions and services by the different tiers of governance.

Political knowledge provides criteria both for social inquiry and action, i.e. describing and prescribing roles for political actors who happen to be planners as well. The state supplies legitimacy for the bureaucrat planner, and the latter stability and continuity for the state. This proposed connection suggests a rather rigid form of blueprint planning, usually centring on engineering problems which are assigned a consistent and clearly defined set of development objectives. Assuming complete access to information and technical know-how, physical planners rely on the idealised model of economically rational (wo)man fully capable of collecting and processing all necessary data, dealing with all alternative planning options, and apparently surrounded by a stable and predictable physical, economic and socio-political environment. This technocratic planning practice relies indeed on a "natural" scientific rationality. Along this reductionist route, scientists verify or falsify any proposition by assuming that the tangible natural and social reality involved is an objective entity "out there" (Guba and Lincoln, in Denzin and Lincoln (eds.), 1994).

In opposition to this positivist style of research and blueprint planning, both pluralists and neo-liberalists, but critical theorists above all, contend that our UPM drama is as a struggle between (corporate) interest groups. Here, considering an increasingly complex and turbulent environment, and recognising that human behaviour is never fully understandable, predictable and controllable, planners are to limit the wide range of socio-structural problems and goals, to restrict the number of appraised alternatives and interventions in accordance with a few well understood, collective policy criteria. Socio-spatial planners are thus bound to merely strive for public consensus with incremental changes, i.e. by improving existing UPM practices in successive rounds of trial and a lot of error. So, planning becomes the science of muddling through and disjointed incrementalism, a transactive process of learning-by-doing, grasping for development targets which are constantly on the move and in need of progress monitoring and impact evaluation through policy indicators - to prepare for novel policies becoming increasingly more efficient and effective, i.e. socio-politically more legitimate and responsive. As a consequence and by way of examples, in the pluralist view, urban land-use planners are seen as mediators of (corporate) interest group adjustment. What role can information technology play in this post-positivist, reflexive and engaged process?

25.6 An Emancipatory Three-Pronged Approach to UPM Data Handling in Figure 25.2

By considering the rule-laden decision-making structures employed, planned interventions undertaken and inherently restricted roles of planners acted out at the various territorial levels of municipal government, the three-fold knowledge base of preceding sections 2.1-3 conjures up an increasingly broad range of socio-spatial and moral policy criteria for evaluating UPM performances. This methodical material is not to be reviewed but merely ordered here, as shown below in Fig. 25.2 , neither in a technocratic "top-down", nor radical "bottom-up" UPM perspective.

III.   During the phase of executive action attention is restricted to the short run (what, where, when, for whom?):
- for solving urgent and visible problems on a small scale, and trying out priority-area project packages;
- guided by such targets as economic efficiency, income and employment creation in (agro-) industrial production, including fair distribution of social and physical infrastructure; and
- using/improving central bureaucratic leadership including (trained) planners and administrators in standardised project-feasibility planning, implementation control, performance monitoring and impact evaluation, - for instance, through rigid
logical-framework procedures (Rosenberg and Hagebroeck, 1972: 1-32; Callewaert, 1988, pp 1-15).

II.   During the phase of programme diversification emphasis is laid in the medium run (how, for and with whom?):
- on second-round, re-defined selection of inter-sectoral, albeit area-specific problem approaches district and province-wide;
- on working towards a full-fledged area development profile, or pre-feasible framework including large-scale infrastructural investments, thus incorporating multiple policy-test criteria for ecological, financial and local administrative sustainability, accountability, operation and maintenance; and
- on stimulating the outward- and future-directed, umpire or mediating role of local government, - for instance, through (training in) strategic-choice procedures including inter-connected decision areas and management of uncertainty (Steenbergen, 1990: 301-304; Friend and Hickling, 1987: 1-26).

I.   During the policy formulation phase attention is yet to be focused in the long run (what for?):
- on a limited number of controversial and complex policy issues like land/water degradation and pollution; like unequal access to land/shelter and inadequate provision of public services, credit, etc.; like the over-controlled public sector, bureaucratic red-tape; like community participation and self-help.
- on building local consensus and professional integrity in interpreting and counteracting central (sectoral) policy objectives through (training for) action-oriented policy evaluation responsive to multiple stakeholder expectations, values and needs (Majchrzak, 1984; Kelly 1987: 270-295); and
- on stimulating the divergent role, both in public and private spheres, of the local statesman/general manager assisted by mediating and advocacy planners, and confronted with ever changing, external and internal (phycho-) milieux.
Note, finally, that along this emancipatory path, collective meaning and iteratively grounded knowledge is sought, rather than a single universal truth.

25.7 Phased Introduction of (Geo-)Information Technology into Municipal Administrations

Municipal administrations are responsible for a wide variety of tasks. Decentralisation, as argued before, expands the functions of local government with increasing complexity through a combination of day-to-day administration and middle-range strategic development and investment decisions. These functions are corresponding to routine and structured work processes for recurrent, operation and maintenance (O/M) activities, on one hand, and (although not strictly separated) more strategic and non-structured work processes for policy decisions, on the other hand (Lewis, 1994: 87-151).

Currently many municipal departments are developing digital databases to support data storage and retrieval. The structure of these databases is very similar to the previous (non-digital) method of data storage. In this way information technology supports mainly the O/M level, and hardly the strategic and policy levels.

Mushrooming of databases occurs within municipal organisations and even within a single department, a mass of data is stored many times by many individuals. People and physical structures are recorded differently many times, adversely affecting the cost of data collection and data quality.

Take as an example of the first stage of computerisation the use of census databases. Census data are characterized by simple data structures but with many records. Information technology has here clear advantages allowing fast data processing to describe population, housing and other characteristics. Census data are not only used to present aggregated municipal data for national policy purposes, but census data at detailed spatial level (neighbourhood) are also employed by information users (town planners) themselves for the analysis phase of spatial planning. But temporal analyses using two or more census dates are usually flawed because of changing spatial boundaries and changing definitions of variables. The increasing understanding of the importance of data consistencies is positively affecting the way databases are currently designed and adapted.

Automated mapping is also considered part of this first round. This process observed in (advanced) developing countries like Chile, Colombia, India and China. In the latter a rapid expansion of digital map production (national, provincial and local level) is noted (Sliuzas and Turkstra, 1995, pp 762-770). Applications of these maps can be found, besides in mapping agencies, also in the industry, utility companies and architectural/engineering bureaus.

Summarising, we can conclude that the analog-to-digital transformation of data without changes in the data structures itself is improving the efficiency of O/M projects and day-to-day monitoring and control tasks, but the digital products are operating in isolation: "stand-alone" databases.

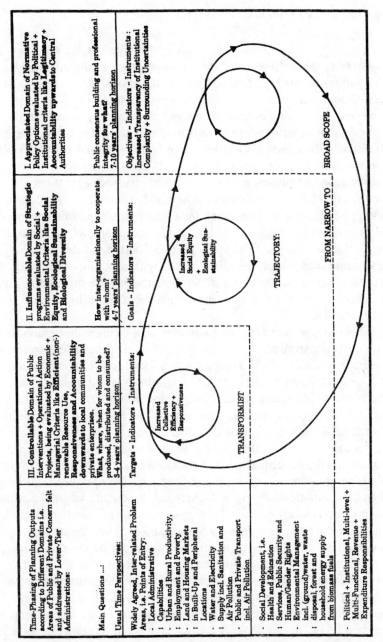

Figure 25.2 Sequential Learning Rounds/Loops III-I in Introducing UPM Policy Indicators into Medium-Sized City Administrations

Second Phase: Intra-Sectoral Data Integration

The support information technology provided to the O/M level has proven to be cost-effective. Here, the 'computer tool' is implemented without major changes in working procedures, organisational structure or positions of the different staff members. Investments (computers, software, staff training) are transparent and output (increased productivity) is measurable. The policy level in a department soon starts to question itself how all these different automated databases at O/M level can be transformed into useful information to support action and strategic planning tasks and policy decisions. The introduction of automatization at the O/M level should in theory improve communication (quality and cost of information) from the O/M to the strategic and policy level in a department, thus optimizing departmental coordination. Information at the policy level is, besides external information, based on aggregated data from the O/M level. Data on building characteristics (size, quality, value) can simply be summarized with descriptive statistics. Data from the section on building control combined with those on building characteristics could allow the city managers to analyse relationships between these different variables.

This requires however the adaptation to the (internal) organisation of data within a department. A clear analysis of information needs from all the data users (e.g. staff on O/M, strategic and policy level) is needed to successfully design databases can be used for combining and summarising data. This second round of intra-sectoral data integration is characterised by standardisation of the different databases used at the O/M level to make possible the combination of variables from different database.

An example of this phase is the linking of a census database with the corresponding digital census maps. This allows the (large-scale) mapping of variables or combination of variables. Summarising spatially relevant phenomena by thematic mapping will increase the quality of information for programme and policy makers. Further improvement can be realised when databases of different years are made compatible. This second round of automatisation is characterised by improved intra-departmental communication and understanding of relationships between variables. It is also in this phase that it is realised that the restricted room for introducing information technology, and especially of geoinformation technology (GIT) and systems (GIS) in municipalities, is more related to the organisation of the urban administration and far less to the technology itself. There is a need for a clearly defined information management strategy, personal commitment of individuals at all levels in the organisation, and organisational and environmental stability (Masser and Campbell, 1991: 55-67).

Third Phase: Inter-Sectoral Data Integration, Networking

This phase is reached when organisations begin to consider their information needs and management systems in a corporate sense. The information needs at policy level can only partly be fulfilled by the data collected and maintained by a department on its own, and should be supplemented by information derived from databases maintained by other departments. So far the analytical phase of town planning in Third World countries has tended to be poor due to limited access to data from the different departments. When the amount and quality of data improve in the sectors (automatisation phases 1 and 2) and access to these databases is possible by the planning department, the incentives for town planners to make more and better analysis are increased (relevant questions can be answered by the planners themselves by processing and combining sectoral databases). This also activates the debate on how improved knowledge can help to develop urban models to support the planning process (Batty, 1991: 42/43).

A geo-information system is seen as a tool to support this integrative planning process. Although the tool is from a technical point of view well developed, to implement GIS successfully a municipal organisation has to allow the sharing of data and thematic knowledge - if not GIS will keep too long the label 'promising'. Adaptation of organisations, however, can only successfully take place through trial-and-error from data duplication mistakes, information technology and GIS developed by municipal staff members themselves; a continuous learning process, in which increased efficiency at O/M level should expand into improved effectiveness of the other municipal UPM levels (action planning, strategic programmes and policy formulation); from single- to double-loop learning (Morgan, 1986: 81-93).

An example of this third automatisation round is the integration of databases from different departments. The linking of census data with databases on social subsidies in Chile makes a much more profound analysis possible which is of special importance for multi-faceted tasks inherent in the integrative character of spatial planning. For example urban poverty is defined as a combination of physical (dwelling and infrastructure) and socio-economic (income) characteristics. Mapping the concentration of low-income households with poor living conditions requires access to databases which are under the responsibilities of different departments.

Summarising we can conclude that GISs introduced into local government can be grouped into three categories: automation of O/M through Geoinformation technology, problem solving GIS and multi-purpose GIS (Somers, 1991: 25-31). The last option requires integration of data from various departments as well as clearly defined tasks and responsibilities, and is commensurate with a mature system of this third phase. The analog-to-digital transformation of data without changes in the systems themselves is improving the efficiency of short- and medium- term O/M projects for implementation and monitoring tasks. In the longer term there is considerable potential for GIS to be linked more closely with the planning process of a city through the development and application of relevant methods and models. For the moment though the main role of GIS is likely to be: an integral part of an organisation's information system in a decentralised computing environment, thematic mapping and simple spatial analysis through map overlay.

25.8   Concluding Remarks: Strategies to Introduce GIS Technology

With the rapid expansion of the GIS industry it is useful to examine what org-ware and soft/hardware strategies may be appropriate for introducing GIS in an organisation and what pitfalls may be anticipated.

The introduction and adoption of information technology typically goes through a number of development phases in any organisation (Nolan, 1979) similar to the three phases described above: initiation and take-off; control and integration; data administration and maturity.

Attempts to prematurely introduce corporate solutions to GIS in organisations with little or no experience with IT (phases 1 and 2) will not have a high chance of success. However, the message reaching municipalities today is that the future is digital. 'All registers will gradually be stored in digital form. Both the public and institutions of various kinds will have access to these databases' (Jones, 1989: 21-31). For a municipal administrator computer technology is an attractive proposition; he is seen as a modern manager and, according to computer system vendors, financially the investment is recovered with the savings and improvements made in the organisation. If computerisation is inevitable, then the real problem is how to implement it in the most efficient and effective manner and more particularly how to introduce a GIS in a municipal organisation.

Experience by the United Nations Centre for Human Settlements shows that a top-down centralised, non-participatory approach to the introduction of computer technology should be avoided. It also shows that systems should be able to learn by doing and expand over time. Many arguments and experiences are in favour of gradually implementing automatisation in municipal administrations. In practice this means that 'one step at a time' (Masser and Campbell, 1991, page 65) is seen as a necessary approach in the development of a comprehensive multi-purpose information system. It avoids the risk of over-investment in an orgware situation where it cannot properly be implemented.

Important strategic choices have to be made in the process of introducing information technology; such a strategy should make clear:
- which O/M and UPM tasks will receive priority.
- how should the organisation and personnel be shaped for the use of the new technology.
- data: what should be collected and in what manner will it be captured, stored and maintained (information resources).
- which hardware/software should be chosen (information technology).

Research in the development both of general purpose information systems and GIS suggests that a learning-by-doing framework is essential. 'There is a need for a guiding philosophy supported by policy and management guidelines and an organizational structure to implement and monitor the policy and

Outputs in Time Perspective ? Elements ?	Phase 1 "stand-alone"	Phase 2 "integration"	Phase 3 "networking"
IT acquisition (databases, Computer Aided Drafting software)	learning by doing; increased O/M **efficiency**	increased information quality, reduced cost	inter-sectoral communication; data (information) exchange
Awareness seminars at senior level	guide use of **IT** avoid over-investment	adapt internal organisation/ work processes	define sectoral work and data responsibilities
Technical workshops	adapt structure of single databases	adapt departmental databases	search for data duplication/redundancy
GIS taskforce	develop potential simple GIS applications	information system design	develop corporate vision with effective data structure
IT acquisition (GIS)	combine graphic with attribute data	(graphic) data exchange	inter-sectoral system design
Training	technical training	project management "team spirit"	communication training: "common view"
Pilot project	end-user involvement	information needs analysis	measure results
Implementation	complex GIS applications	overall datasharing	increased **effectiveness**
Maintenance/Adaptation	incorporate new GIT developments	adapt datastructure and organisation to new technology	develop (decision support) models (Batty, 1991)

Figure 25.3   Elements of a Prototype Showing GIS Implementation Phases in Municipalities

guidelines...' (Huxhold and Levinsohn, 1995, page 31). Figure 5 illustrates the effects of a series of activities related to the three GIS implementation phases. It is now commonly accepted (Masser and Campbell, 1991; Huxhold and Levinsohn, 1995) that GIS implementation is complex because it concerns a technology which can function only through the integration of data. This makes a GIS project an orgware problem, rather then a mere hard/software problem. Organisational changes (people, data, processes) ask for a step-by-step approach, bottom-up but with a clear strategic vision about the path to follow: about how GIS can support an organisation; how to reach its objectives better; from increased efficiency to better effectiveness.

Urban planning is inter-sectoral, it needs data from other sectors, data should be accessible and compatible. If data cannot be integrated the possibility of duplication of data collection exists and, very likely, the poor quality of the data will reduce the quality of information based on these data. Consequently uncertainties can reach such dimensions that analysis will be of limited practical value.

In conclusion the O/M levels of the different sectors in municipal organisations will need to develop experience with information technology to improve the efficiency and effectiveness of their work. With this experience it is possible to show that methods of data storage should be changed to improve the functioning of the municipality as a whole. Many sectors in a municipal organisation operate isolated from each other; due to the integrative character of town planning this department cannot operate without data from other departments. Digital databases and working procedures can improve the functioning of an individual sector and will gradually evolve to encompass a truly effective corporate information system GIS.

References

Amer, S. (1993) 'Spatial Decision Support Systems for Urban Planning and Management' *Fourth European Conference and Exhibition on GIS.*
Arbeit, D. (1993) 'Resolving the data problem: a spatial information infostructure for planning support', in *Proceedings Third International Conference on Computers in Urban Planning and Management*, Atlanta, Georgia, USA, July 1993.
Anker, D.W.L. (1973) 'Rural development problems and strategies', *Intern. Labour Review*, Vol. 108: 461-484.
Argyris, C. and Schÿn, D.A. (1978) *Organizational learning: a theory of action perspective*, Reading, Addison-Wesley Publ. Cy. Mass, USA.
Batty, M. (1991) 'GIS in urban planning and policy analysis' in UNCRD *Proceedings of the Study Group Meeting on Regional and Global Economic Integration, Development Planning and Information Technology*, Nagoya: 27-60.
Bolan, R.S. (1980) 'The practitioner as theorist: the phenomenology of the professional epi-

sode', *Journal of the American Institute of Planners*, July: 261-274.

Bouman, Z. (1993) *Postmodern Ethics*, Oxford, Blackwell Publ., UK.

Callewaert, L. (1988) *Objective oriented planning of development projects*, Brussels, Belgian Administration for Development Cooperation. Bureau for Organisation and Auditing, Marseveldplein 5.

Chen, H-T. (1990) *Theory-driven evaluations*, London, Sage Publications.

Conyers, D. and Hills, P. (1990) *Introduction to development planning in the Third World*, Chicester, Wiley, U.K.

Crook, s.; Pakulsky, j. and Waters M. (1992) *Postmodernization. Change in advanced society*, London, Sage Publ.

Guba, E.G. and Lincoln, Y.S. (1994) 'Competing paradigms in qualitative research' in Denzin, N.K. and Lincoln, Y.S. (eds) *Handbook of qualitative research*, London, Sage Publications: 105-117.

Devas, N. and Rakodi, C. (1993) *Managing fast growing cities. New approaches to urban planning and management in the developing world*, New York, Longman Group.

Dewar, D.; Todes, A. and Watson, V. (1986) *Regional development and settlement policy. Premises and prospects*, London, Allan and Unwin.

Dillinger, D. (1994) *Decentralization and its implications for urban service delivery*, Washington, D.C. World Bank Urban Management Programme, USA.

Economic and Social Commission for Asia and the Pacific (1976) *Proceedings of the symposium on social and non-economic factors in water resources development*, New York, Water Resources Series, no. 47, United Nations.

Economic and Social Commission for Asia and the Pacific (1979) *Guidelines for rural centre planning*, New York, United Nations.

Etzioni, A. (1988) *The moral dimension. Toward a new economics*, London, Collier Macmillan Publ.

Friedmann, J. (1969) 'Notes on societal action', *Journal of the American Institute of Planners*, Sept.: 311-318.

Friedmann, J. (1973) *Retracking America. A theory of transactive planning*, New York, Anchor Press/Doubleday.

Friedmann, J. and Hudson, B, (1974) 'Knowledge and action: a guide to planning theory', *Journal of the American Institute of Planners*, Jan. pp. 3-15.

Friedmann, J. (1992) Empowerment. The politics of alternative development, Oxford, Blackwell, UK.

Friend, J. and Hickling, A. (1987) *Planning under pressure. The strategic choice approach*, Oxford, Pergamon Press, UK.

Hall, G.B. and Conning, A. (1992) 'Integrating demographic and socio-economic data with PC-based GIS in Latin America' in Teeffelen, P. van; Grunsven, L. van and Verkoren, O. (eds.) *Possibilities and constraints of GIS applications in developing countries*, Utrecht, Ned. Geogr. Studies 152. Utrecht Univ., The Netherlands.

Harriss, J. (1994) 'Between economism and post-modernism: reflections on agrarian change in India' in Booth, D. (ed.) *Rethinking social development. Theory, research and practice*, Essex, Longman Group Ltd., England.

Hilhorst, J.G.M. (1990) *Regional studies and rural development*, Brookfield, Avebury/Aldershot, USA.

Huxhold, W.E. (1991). *An Introduction to Urban Geographic Information Systems*, New York, Oxford University Press.

Huxhold, W.E. and Levinsohn, A.G. (1995) *Managing Geographic Information System Projects*. Oxford University Press, New York.

Hyden, G. (1983) *No shortcuts to progress. African development management in perspective*, Berkeley, University of California Press, USA.

Israel, A. (1990) *Institutional development*, Baltimore, J. Hopkins Univ. Press.

Jantsch, E. (1975) *Design for evolution. Self-organization and planning in the life of human systems*, New York, George Braziller, USA.

Jones, K.J. (1989) 'Strategic choices when introducing GIT in small municipalities' *Proceedings Urban Data Management*, Lisbon, Portugal.

Kelly, R.M. (1987) 'The politics of meaning and policy inquiry' in Palumbo, D.J. (eds.) *The politics of program evaluation*, London, Sage Publ.

Kok, R. (1981) *Nogmaals: de Urbanistiek*, The Hague, Stedebouw en Volkshuisvesting, February, The Netherlands.

Lele, U. (1975) *The design of rural development: lessons from Africa*, Baltimore, Johns Hopkins Univ. Press.

Lewis, P.J. (1994) *Information-systems development*, London, Pitman Publ., Chapters 5, 6 and 7.

Low, N. (1991) *Planning, politics and the state. Political foundations of planning thought*, London, Unwin Hyman.

Macintyre, A. (1979) 'Social science methodology as the ideology of bureaucratic authority' in Falco M.J. (ed) *Through the looking-glass: epistemology and the conduct of inquiry. An anthology*, Washington, University Press of America, U.S.A.

Macintyre, A. (1992) *After virtue. A study in moral theory*, London, G. Duckworth.

Majchrzak, A. (1984) *Methods for policy research*, London, Sage Publ.

Man, W.H.E. de, (1988) 'Establishing a geographical information system in relation to its use: a process of strategic choices', *Int. J. Geographical Information Systems* 2, 3: 245-261.

Masser, I. and Campbell, H. (1991) 'Conditions for the effective utilisation of computers in urban planning in developing countries', *Comput, Environment and Urban Systems*, Vol. 15.

McConnel, S. (1981) *Theories for planning. An introduction*, London, Heinemann.

Moris, J. (1981) *Managing induced rural development*, Bloomington, International Development Institute, Indiana University, U.S.A.

Morgan, G. (1985) *Images of Organization*, Sage Publications London.

Nolan, R. (1979) *Managing the crisis in data processing*, Harvard Business Review, March-April.

Peursen, C.A. van (1974) *The strategy of culture. A view of the changes taking place in our ways of thinking and living today*, Amsterdam/Oxford, North-Holland Publ. Cy.

Rosenberg, L.J. and Hageboeck, M. (1972) *Management technology and the developing world*, Washington D.C., Practical Concepts Inc.

Sliuzas, R. and Turkstra, J. (1995) 'Geoinformation support for cities in transformation; the example of Wuhan, P.R. China, in *Proceedings Geoinformatics '95*. The Chinese University of Hong Kong.

Smith, D.M. (1979) *Where the grass is greener. Living in an unequal world*, Middlesex, Pelican Books.

Smith, W.E. et al. (1980) *The design of organisations for rural development projects*, World Bank, Staff Working Paper no. 375, Washington D.C.

Smith, B.C. (1985) *Decentralization. The territorial dimension of the state*, London, G. Allan and Unwin.

Somers, P. (1991) 'GIS in local US Government' in *Cities*, February.

Steenbergen, van F. (1990) 'The strategic choice approach in regional planning. A professional note; *Third World Planning Review* 12 (3): 301-304.

United Nations Centre for Human Settlements and the World Bank (1995) *Urban Indicators Programme*, Nairobi, Vol. 1-3., Kenya.

UNESCO/UNEP (1977). *Human settlement managers' training programme*, Paris, France.

Uphoff, N. (1986) *Local institutional development: an analytical sourcebook with (rural de-*

velopment) cases, Connecticut, Kumarian Press, USA.

Veenstra, J. (1970) 'Historical notes on an eventual regionalisation of national development efforts in Sierra Leone, West-Africa', Civilisations XX-1: 66-82 and *Netherlands Journal of Agricultural Science*, 18: 12-25.

Veenstra, J. (1971) 'Naar een prototype voor sociaal-ruimtelijke management-systemen', The Hague, *Stedebouw en Volkshuisvesting*, 53, 3: 102-119, The Netherlands.

Veenstra, J. (1982) 'Towards a classic sociological conceptual framework for socio-spatial planning', Eindhoven, *Open House International*, 7-1/2: 25-45, The Netherlands.

Veenstra, J. (1989) 'Theory and practice of foreign assistance to regional development planning: the case of peripheral rural areas in Aceh, Indonesia' Public *Administration and Development*, Vol. 9: 523-542.

Veenstra, J. (1994) 'A sequential approach to decentralised area development planning: the case of a peripheral water catchment basin in Cameroon, West Africa', Nagoya, *Regional Development Dialogue*, UNCRD, Japan, 15-1: 145-170.

Wit, J.W. de (1993) *Poverty, policy and politics in Madras slums. Dynamics of survival, gender and leadership*, Amsterdam, Vrije Universiteit.

Zoja, L. (1995) *Growth and guilt. Psychology and the limits of development*, London, Routledge, UK.

26 Urban Policies of some Port-Cities in the Asia-Pacific Region

Shii Okuno

26.1 Introduction

Geographers, sociologists, economists, planners or engineers who study urban development are often driven to formulate new models to match the reality of what they observe. In the context of studies of Third World cities, for example, Santos (1977) propounded the model of the two circuits of capital in the urban economy (in the formal and informal sectors); McGee and Yeung (1977) developed similar ideas on rural-urban migration and informal economy ; McGee (1997) wrote on the process of proletarianisation ; Armstrong and McGee (1985) saw Third World cities as both centres of production and at the same time "theatres of accumulation" ; and Rimmer (1986) demonstrated the varieties of urban transportation modes and incorporation process in Southeast Asian cities. Recent contributions include the comprehensive review by Lin (1994) on major features such as the role of cites in regional development, dualism, transnational capital, socialism, and extended metropolitan regions; and the conception of *desakota* (McGee 1985) for new regions of urban functions in rural contexts. Gilbert (1993) reviews the changing national settlement system of the Third World, and the emergence of polycentric forms of metropolitan development, and then he comments that regional policy has not been as effective as expected. Richardson (1989) concludes in his study on mega-city growth that perhaps there are now declining productivity advantages, and that negative externalities may be increasing, more than the official statistics show.

The many different ways in which development is occurring raise specific issues which urban and national governments have to face. The responses may include policies for the promotion or containment of growth, or its diffusion to satellite areas. However, Rondenelli (1991) criticises the ineffectiveness of urban containment in the past three decades, and observes changes in urban development policies in the 1990s as follows: "(1) mobilising financial resources for investments in services and infrastructure, (2) improving the efficiency of metropolitan areas as economic units, (3) investing in secondary cities and towns with growth potential and integrating urban and rural markets, (4) seeking greater participation of the private sector in urban development, and (5) decentralising more administrative and financial responsibilities to local governments in urban areas."

This chapter is concerned with an empirical investigation into government responses to developments in port cities in the Pacific Rim. This region embraces both developing and developed nations, and has seen some very high growth rates in recent decades, based on increasing levels of international trade. Rimmer (1993), modifying concepts from Batten (1990) and Andersson (1990), forecasts that the transport and communications in the Pacific Economic Zone during the early 21st century will be denser with new infrastructure based on multi-layered links. This pattern will replace the former focus on central place hierarchies of conventional cities and mega-regions with networks of development corridors where infrastructure endowment is closely related with knowledge, culture and accessibility. He then outlines six macro-economic development corridors in the Pacific Economic Region.

Specifically with regard to port cities and their port-city interface Hoyle (1988) observes five stages of development:- i) the primitive city-port in the ancient-medieval to 19th century; ii) the expanding city-port of the 19th-early 20th century; iii) the modern industrial city-port in the mid-20th century; iv) the post World War II retreat from the waterfront due to changes in maritime technology in the 1960s-80s and the development of containerisation; v) the redevelopment of the waterfront in 1970s-90s. The last stage suggests that the large-scale modern port consumes large areas of land- and water-space, and that the renewal of original core takes place. The phenomenon of locational and functional separation of port and city system is not only experienced by city-ports in industrially advanced nations, but also by city-ports of the less developed world.

The same pattern has also been reported by Yang (1990) with respect to Chinese port cities. Yeung ranks and classifies different Chinese port cities according to their economic importance, and he shows that redevelopment of the old city core is crucial in improving the spatial functioning of coastal cities. Other development issues include improvement in transport, industrial restructuring and the transfer of polluting industries, decentralisation of population, environmental improvement and historical preservation. Yeung and Hu (1992) also stress particularly the importance of Chinese coastal cities as catalysts for modernisation, and they note with caution the possible contradictions between economic development and political reform or administrative inefficiency in the process.

Japanese studies have placed importance on the rationale for and techniques of revitalising the waterfront (Ishizawa, 198 and Nippon Hoso Kuokai, 1992) An integrated study of Japanese port-cities (Kitami 1993) covered the evolution of the interface between the components of urban fabric (the castle-town-port), the culture of the port-cities, and their economic revitalisation and development policy. Urban planning departments sometimes initiate comparative studies on urban development or policies, for example, the Asian Urban Information Centre of Kobe (Ness and Tanigawa 1992) compiled a report on the population dynamics and urban problems in ten Asian port-cities. Cheung has studied both the urban development strategies of cities in the Asia-Pacific (1991) and Europe (1992).

26.2 A Survey of 12 Port-Cities of the Pacific Rim

This study is empirically based, and concentrates on the perception by Mayors/Senior Planners of developments in their own cities. It has been carried out by mailing a structured questionnaire to mayoral offices or economic/physical planning in 1994 and 1995. Forty-six cities were addressed, out of which twelve responded fully, and a further five gave incomplete answers. The twelve full respondents were:- metropolitan Manila (Philippines), Fukuoka and Osaka (Japan); Honolulu and Oakland (USA); Vancouver (Canada) ; Sydney (Australia), and Dalian, Ningbo, Shanghai, Weihai, Hong Kong (China). (Map. 26.1). In Figure 26.1 these cities are plotted on a graph which shows the annual national growth rate of per capita GDP 1965-1990

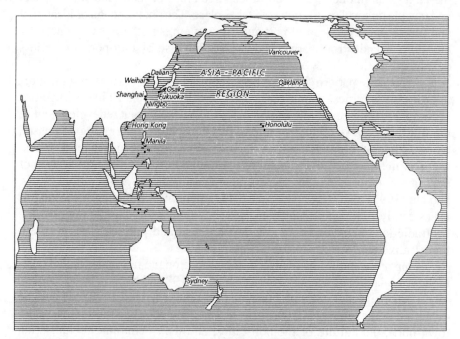

Map 26.1 Surveyed Port Cities of the Pacific Rim

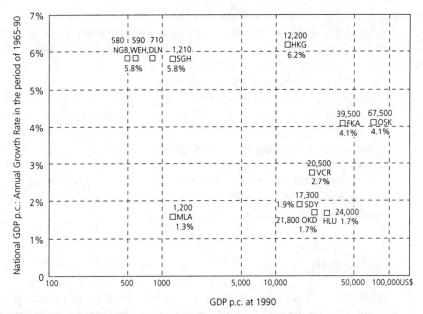

Figure 26.1 Growth Rates and Income Levels of the Surveyed Port Cities

against the 1990 level of per capita GDP. In addition the growth rate of the city per capita GDP over the same period is recorded alongside each city – and in every case it is higher than the national figure , showing the extent to which these cities are leading economic motors in their national economies.

The cities clearly fall into five groups. The three Chinese cities and Manila are separated from the others by virtue of belonging to low income countries – but Manila is also distinguished by its low GDP p.c. growth rate, compared with the high growth rates for the per capita wealth of the Chinese cities. Hong Kong is on its own – with a wealth growth rate slightly higher than the three Chinese cities, but a much higher per capita income. It is the outstanding performer on this graph. Next comes the two Japanese cities, with high incomes per capita and also the second best levels of economic growth. The four non-Asian American-Pacific cities are distinguished by their low rates of growth (but none as low as Manila's) yet having a higher standard of living.

Table 26.1 shows the population size and population growth rates of the metropolitan areas. The significant feature of this table is that three of the four Chinese cities actually have low population growth rates – not perhaps quite conforming with the popular image. But the fourth - Ningbo – has a staggeringly high population growth rate – and next highest comes Manila, poor and underperforming economically, but growing very fast.

The other five who responded to part of the questionnaire were Xiamen, Guangzhou, Qingdao, Shenzhen and Yantai from China, who omitted some of the material on their attitudes and priorities.

The survey concentrated on the following:-

i) the population and employment status of port-cities in the Asian-Pacific region and the direction of changes in the last two decades with forecast for the future;

ii) the urban development strategies of the port-cities looking towards the next century;

iii) opportunities for greater economic regional co-operation of cities and countries in the Asia-Pacific region. (This study aims to identify priority areas for exchange programmes.)

26.3   City Growth

Table 26.1 shows the population sizes of the twelve cities (metropolitan area statistics) in the early nineties, plus their growth rate from the earlier given date (1970 or mid 80's). Two of the cities are true mega-cities on the world scale, and five others are also above the 5 million threshold. This clearly suggests that these are much more than port cities: metropolitan areas this size acquire their own raison d'être – or, to put it in other words, the economic basic/non-basic industrial employment ratio decreases, as more of the city economy is serving itself, and less is involved in exchange with other regions. The average annual growth rate of Manila is high, that of Ningbo in China exceptionally high – in contrast to the low or moderate growth of the other Chinese cities. In terms of age structures, one variable in particular stands out – the percentage under 15 years old. Here the youth of Manila stands out, but equally the lack of youth in Sydney and Shanghai – the former presumably because of the end stages of the demographic transition in Western societies, the latter presumably because of the one-child policy and the strict policies on urban migration.

26.4   Strategic Development Emphases of City Respondents

The questionnaire responses are tabulated in Table 26.2. A '1' in a column simply means that the respondent selected to stress this item as a policy goal. First those policies are mentioned here which received strong support (9 or 10 'votes') or obviously weak support (1 or 0 votes). Not sur-

Table 26.1 Metropolitan Area Population Statistics

	Date	Population	Date	Population	Annual % growth rate	Age structure 1990	% 0-14	% 15-64	% >65
Hong Kong*	1970	3,959,000	1993	5,878,100	1.0173	1.7	21.4	70.1	8.5
Manila	1970	3,900,000	1990	8,500,000	1.0397	4.0	33.5	64.1	2.4
Fukuoka	1970	1,280,000	1994	2,076,000	1.0204	2.0	18.9	72.0	9.1
Osaka	1970	13,640,000	1985	15,891,000	1.0102	1.0	18.1	71.5	10.4
Vancouver	1980	1,243,900	1993	1,719,393	1.0252	2.5	18.6	69.2	12.2
Oakland	1970	4,754,000	1992	6,332,000	1.0131	1.3	23.9	64.0	12.1
Honolulu	1970	630,258	1992	836,100	1.0129	1.3	20.8	68.2	11.0
Sydney	1986	3,364,858	1991	3,538,448	1.0101	1.0	8.0	80.5	11.5
Dalian	1985	4,852,600	1990	5,178,000	1.0131	1.3	n/a	n/a	n/a
Nignbo	1970	373,138	1992	5,167,020	1.1269	12.7	21.0	72.2	6.8
Shanghai	1970	10,720,550	1992	12,890,370	1.0084	0.8	9.4	81.2	9.4
Weihai	1970	2,100,000	1992	2,393,000	1.006	0.6	21.1	71.4	7.5

* Hong Kong city

prisingly, since the sample is of port cities, the development of better deep water and container facilities both rank highly. It is the other high priorities which are more revealing. Nothing shows strongly under Housing Policy. Under Economic Activity ten cities stress Hi-tech industry, but it is not clear whether this is because of perceived high employment, perceived high value added, or simply the 'route to the future'. Only one, Ningbo, stresses heavy industry – the chemical industry which has underlain its meteoric growth. In general, it is this group, Economic Activity, which has attracted the most attention, suggesting that the general concerns of metropolitan economic centres are more important than the specific concerns relating to port cities. Under Urban transport, only one city, Sydney, is interested in light rail: mass transit subways are higher priority – also better planning of the relationship between home and work, to minimise commuting distances. Under Employment nine cities stress the development of human capital. In terms of Landscapes, nine cities wish to preserve historic buildings, none are interested in low rise development. Prevention of pollution and the provision of open space both score well. In the Information Sector nothing scores well. This prima-facie is surprising, given the hype about communications – but detailed consideration shows that all the low income cities except Ningbo do want enhanced communications – presumably the others are already supported by telecom companies which maintain adequate services. Interestingly, the ex-

Table 26.2 Questionnaire Responses

	Hong Kong	Manila	Fukuoka	Osaka	Vancouver	Oakland	Honolulu	Sydney	Dalian	Nignbo	Shanghai	Weiha	
Housing Sector	**1**	**1**	**1**	**1**	**1**	**1**	**1**	**1**	**1**	**1**	**1**	**1**	**131**
number of housing units	1				1	1	1			1	1		6
improvement of housing quality		1	1	1				1	1		1	1	7
new town development in new environment	1	1	1				1		1	1	1	1	8
city redevelopment	1			1		1		1	1	1			6
others			1	1	1			1					4
Economic Activity													**33**
development in agriculture										1			1
basic industry										1			1
processing industry		1				1						1	3
hi-tech industry	1	1	1	1		1	1		1	1	1	1	10
services	1	1	1	1				1	1		1		7
financial and real estate	1	1	1					1	1		1	1	7
others				1	1	1	1						4
Employment													**23**
employment strategy		1					1				1		3
investment in human capital and skills	1	1		1			1	1	1	1	1	1	9
training in internationalcorporate management		1								1		1	3
admission of foreign guest workers	1											1	2
avoiding brain and skill drain	1		1	1				1	1				5
others					1								1
Transportation Sector													**23**
developing mass transit/subway	1	1	1	1				1		1	1		7
public bus network							1	1	1			1	4
developing light railway								1					1
joint planning of work/home locations	1		1	1	1	1	1	1				1	8
others		1				1				1			3
Urban Landscape													**25**
high-rise development	1	1					1			1	1		5
low rise development													0
human scale environment			1		1	1		1	1	1	1		7
efficient scale environment	1							1	1				3
historical preservation		1	1			1	1	1	1	1	1	1	9
others					1								1
Ecological													**33**
recycling of resources		1	1	1	1	1	1						6
prevention of industrial pollution	1	1		1	1	1			1	1	1	1	9
abundant provision planning of green space	1	1		1	1		1	1	1	1	1	1	10
monitoring and conservation of coastal and port environments	1	1	1				1		1	1		1	7
others											1		1
Information and Communication													**18**
improve telephone network		1					1		1	1		1	5
develop Local Area Network		1	1						1	1			4
direct satellite communication services		1								1	1	1	4
advanced cargo handling systems									1			1	2
others					1	1	1						3

	Hong Kong	Manila	Fukuoka	Osaka	Vancouver	Oakland	Honolulu	Sydney	Dalian	Nignbo	Shanghai	Weiha	Total
Airports													**24**
expansion of international capacity	1	1	1	1	1		1		1		1	1	9
expansion of domestic capacity		1				1	1		1	1	1		6
aviation town			1										1
international hub-status	1	1		1	1				1		1		6
others							1	1					2
Seaport													**29**
deeper and additional berths	1	1	1	1	1	1			1	1	1	1	10
container port development	1	1	1		1		1	1	1	1	1	1	10
separation of new port from city	1		1				1					1	4
reduction and rationalisation		1											1
others			1				1	1	1				4
Waterfront													**32**
import/export facility development	1	1	1				1	1	1		1		7
heavy and chemical industry									1				1
marine-sports recreation etc	1	1		1			1				1	1	6
tourism and shopping		1			1				1			1	4
housing				1	1							1	3
artificial island development		1	1	1									3
land reclamation	1	1	1				1		1		1		6
others						1				1			2
Legislation													**17**
export processing tariff exemption		1					1				1		3
import commercial zone		1		1					1			1	4
industrial estate - incentive		1							1		1	1	4
enterprise zone		1											1
coastal zone legislation	1	1		1					1				4
others					1								1
International Centre													**34**
international financial centre	1	1		1	1			1	1		1		7
key entrepot	1	1				1	1		1	1	1	1	8
cultural centre		1	1	1				1	1				5
research and innovation centre		1										1	2
convention centre		1	1	1			1	1					5
tourist resort		1					1	1	1			1	5
others						1					1		2
Social Welfare													**22**
strategy for ageing			1	1	1		1	1			1	1	7
strategy for single parents					1	1							2
strategy for handicapped		1	1	1	1			1	1			1	7
social insurance									1		1	1	3
others								1		1	1		3
	27	42	26	30	26	21	24	22	35	23	33	35	

pansion of international airport capacity also scores highly – as indispensable a part of growth as the seaports themselves. High status in the one seems to require also high status in the other. (Six cities aspire to international hub status: whether it is possible for so many to attain that status is open to question). Waterfront development does not get much stress. Presumably it is important, but not a central concern. Reflecting on the experience of cities elsewhere, one can recollect that London left its docklands empty for decades before starting the concerted redevelopment of this vast land-and-water-scape.

Looking at the table the other way round, by columns rather than rows, the poorest city with a low per capita income growth rate – Manila – has 'voted' for the greatest number of policies – 42 out of 75. This may perhaps suggest the greatest range of perceived needs, rather than the capacity to tax and deliver. The smallest number is for Oakland – 21 votes – perhaps because it is most 'satisfied'?

26.5 Priorities for Exchange of Expertise in Urban Management

One of the main points of this chapter is explore the idea of knowledge exchange between the cities. Knowledge, and the exchange of knowledge, is seen as crucial to all development and the subject of the 1998 World Bank Development report entitled *Knowledge for Development*. Respondents in the cities were asked to tick those subjects in which they had expertise that they were prepared to share with others, and those subjects where they wished to receive opinions and expertise from elsewhere. The results are shown in Table 26.3. This Table shows that there is a greater desire or perceived need to receive knowledge, than to offer it (is this undue modesty?). The topics on which knowledge is sought are fairly well spread – although Industrial and Economic Growth are highest – consistent with the statement about policy emphasis noted in the section above. Port Management comes low – perhaps because there is a sense of established competence in this area. (In the previous section Port Management was not an issue: it was improving the physical infrastructure that scored highly.) A curious feature is that Manila, which emphasised the greatest range of policies in Table 26.2, here seems to need help on so few.

Overall there is a mismatch between what is offered and what is wanted. In particular there is little offered on Economic and Industrial Development. This perhaps points to the very difficult distinction between responsibility and authority. Many city managers may feel themselves in some sense at least in part responsible for the economic health of their city, but often the authority for economic well-being lies elsewhere, either at the national or

Table 26.3 Exchange of Urban Management Know-how

To Offer

	Hong Kong	Manila	Fukuoka	Osaka	Vancouver	Oakland	Honolulu	Sydney	Dalian	Nignbo	Shanghai	Weiha	
Mass Railway													
Road Transport								1					1
Port Management						1	1	1					3
Physical Planning	1							1	1		1		4
Housing Development									1	1			2
Industrial Development									1				1
Economic Vitalisation									1				1
Convention and Tourist Development							1						1
Historical Preservation								1		1			2
Park and Green Space								1	1				2
Financial Management									1	1			2
	1					1	2	5	6	3	1		19

To Receive

	Hong Kong	Manila	Fukuoka	Osaka	Vancouver	Oakland	Honolulu	Sydney	Dalian	Nignbo	Shanghai	Weiha	
Mass Railway							1	1	1		1		4
Road Transport					1		1	1	1		1		5
Port Management							1			1	1		3
Physical Planning	1							1	1			1	4
Housing Development		1					1	1				1	4
Industrial Development		1				1	1	1			1	1	6
Economic Vitalisation		1				1	1	1			1	1	6
Convention and Tourist Development						1	1	1	1				4
Historical Preservation					1		1					1	3
Park and Green Space								1	1			1	3
Financial Management							1		1			1	3
	1	3			2	3	9	8	6	1	5	7	45

even the international scale.

Other interesting features are that Honolulu and Sydney both want to receive and offer information on lots of topics – one might typify them as open-minded. By contrast, the Japanese cities have offered nothing and wish to receive nothing, and Hong Kong wants to send and receive knowledge on one topic only – physical planning. Does this mean that these cities believe that either they have no problems, or that they are already self-sufficient in the knowledge base needed to confront their problems?

26.6 Current Trends of Urban Development Strategy in Cities in the Asia-Pacific Region

The significance of this study is limited by the number of respondent cities and the results have to be verified in further surveys, but yet it does reveal differing priorities amongst these cities. The priority given to economic activities reflect the planning and development needs of cities (Honolulu and Oakland) in the USA for more better-paid jobs and a strategy for the emerging group of urban poor, some unemployed or homeless. They have to enable the economy to grasp opportunities from the expanding flows of trade, capital and people between other places. For Hong Kong, the results reflect its planning needs for its continual development into a regional world city even after the handover of 1997. For Osaka, it means directing development as a regional world city based on finance, culture, high-tech and bio-industries. For Fukuoka, it also means its intention to play a bigger role in the international arena, and especially more exchange and flows with neighbouring Asian nations and cities. For Manila, which is seeking 'development', it means taking a more important role in the Southeast Asian region in most aspects - economic, financial, export, technological and tourism – and this requires a raft of supporting policies. For Sydney, which like Oakland 'has development', it means placing emphases first on the quality of life - on urban landscape, environment and ecology and strengthening its international role in finance, culture, conventions and tourism.

To Dalian, it means further development in its service economy and high-tech industries, environment and ecology and intra-urban transportation. To Ningbo, which stands out as being in an earlier phase of development with respect to its region, it means expansion and transformation of its seaport and further development in its economic sector, both in high-tech and raw-material oriented industry, or agriculture. To Shanghai, as an established metropolis, it means pushing further in the service economy, financial and real estate, and high-tech industries, along with building up its infrastructure like intraurban transportation, information and communication sector. To Weihai, it then means development in processing, high-tech and real estate industries, and attention to its environment and promoting development in information and communication sector.

26.7 "Port" Functions, "World City", and Hinterland Relationship

Many local authorities see that infrastructure developed to advanced level and operated at reasonable costs is vital for the development of what Friedmann (1982,1986,1995) has called a 'world city.' Infrastructure now encompasses container port with berths over fourteen meters in depth, good and efficient intermodal access, and software programs to speed up the import-export customs. It also means having a hub-airport with many direct connections to overseas and domestic airports, and with low operating costs. It furthermore means a strengthened "teleport" for serving telecommunications from satellites and optic fibre network to establish a broader wide-area-network for the metropolitan region. World city competition among major city-ports in the Asia-Pacific region will require establishing national priorities, to strengthen selected ports situated at strategic locations, not an equitable upgrading for any and all ports. The concepts of "localised economic zones", "development corridors", "growth triangles", or "metroplex" extend over national borders and indicate that single or multiple nodal formations are taking place within a networked region.

26.8 Conclusion: Networking among Local Authorities and Information Exchange

International agencies such as United Nations Centre for Regional Development and United Nations Development Programme organise workshops or symposiums at various times to promote transfer of know-how in building housing, transport, industrial development, urban and regional development, and disaster prevention. Now major cities are also engaged in exchange programs, setting-up overseas representative offices, co-operating in technical workshops, and exchanging urban data for comparative research. Results of this survey suggest many topics for such workshops, but they also suggest that most are more anxious to hear other people's ideas than to reveal their own. It is hoped that cities of developed and emerging nations can be more supportive for such exchange or transfer activities to promote a better and liveable world for all.

Acknowledgements

Cities who have been helpful in providing data and answering the questionnaire are gratefully acknowledged, namely, Hong Kong, Manila, Fukuoka, Osaka, Vancouver, Oakland, Honolulu, Sydney, Dalian, Ningbo, Shanghai and Weihai. Thanks are also due to Xiamen, Guangzhou, Qingdao, Shenzhen and Yantai for their cooperation. Needless to say, viewpoints expressed in the study remain to be the sole responsibility of the author. This paper is based on a former draft presented to the 2nd ICIS, Dalian, in October 1995, and with additional data inputs from the China's port-cites. For that thanks are due to Professor Liu Ze-yuan, Dalian Institute of Technology and his assistant Cui Shan, and Mr Tang Yong-Qiang, Economic Planning & Research Office, Dalian Municipal Government, and Professor Zhang Xing-Kai, Dalian Institute of Light Industries.

References

Andersson, A.E. (1990) 'The Emerging Global Network of C-regions,' pp.57-64 *Cosmo Creative Regional Consequences in Osaka - Towards a Cosmo Creative City*, Osaka.

Armstrong , W. & T.G. McGee (1985): *Theatres of Accumulation: Studies in Asian and Latin American Urbanization*, Methuen, London.

Batten,D.F. (1990)' Network Cities versus Central Place Cities: Building a Cosmo-creative Constellation,' pp.83-85,. in *Cosmo Creative Regional Consequences in Osaka - Towards a Cosmo Creative City*, Osaka.

Cheung, Chiwai, (1991) 'Urban Development Strategies for the 1990s: a survey of 16 Cities in the Asia-Pacific Region,' pp 25-44 in *Memoirs of the Institute of Economics Research*, Tokuyama University.

Friedmann, John (1982) & G. Wolff, 'World City Formation, An Agenda for Research and Action,' *International Journal of Urban and Regional Research, No* 3 pp 309-44.

Friedmann, John (1986) 'The World City Hypothesis', *Development and Change*, No 1 pp 69-84.

Friedmann, John (1995) 'Where We Stand: a Decade of World City Research,' pp.21-47 in P. L. Knox and P. J. Taylor, eds., *World Cities in a World-System* Cambridge University Press.

Gilbert, Alan (1993) 'Third World Cities: The Changing National Settlement System,' *Urban Studies*, Nos 4-5 pp 721-740.

Hamada, Takaakai and Chiwai Cheung (1985), 'Urbanisation, Urban Problems and Policy Responses: Some Frameworks for International Comparison,' pp 127-164 in *Memoirs of the Faculty of Engineering* Osaka City University.

Hoyle, B.S. (1988) 'Development Dynamics at the Port-City Interface,' pp.3-19 in B.S. Hoyle ,et al., eds., *Revitalising the Waterfront*, Belhaven.

Ishizawa, Takashi (1987) *Uotafronto no Saisei (Revitalization of Waterfronts)*, Toyokeizai Shimposha.

Lin, G. C-s (1994) 'Changing Theoretical Perspectives on Urbanization in Asian Developing Countries,' *Third World Planning Review*, No 1 pp1-24.

McGee, T.G. (1977) 'The Persistence of the Proto-proletariat: Occupational Structures and Planning of the Future of Third World Cities,' pp.257-270. in J. Abu-Lughod and R. Hay,

Jr., eds., *Third World Urbanization* Methuen, London.

McGee, T.G. (1989) 'Urbanisasi or Kotadesasi? Evolving Patterns of Urbanisation in Asia', Ch 6 pp 93 – 108 in *Urbanization in Asia: Spatial Dimensions and Policy Issues*, Eds Costa, F.J., Dutt, A.K., Ma, Laurence J.C. and Noble, Allen G. Hawaii University Press, Honolulu.

McGee, T.G. and Y. M. Yeung (1977) *Hawkers in Southeast Asian Cities* International Development Research Centre, Ottawa.

Ness, G.D. & K. Tanigawa, eds. (1992) *Population Dynamics and Port City Development: Comparative Analysis of Ten Asian Port Cities*, Asian Urban Information Centre, Kobe.

Nijkamp, Peter & N. Vermond (1994) 'Scenarios on Opportunities and Impediments in the Asian Pacific Rim, ' *Studies in Regional Science*, No 2, 1-46.

Richardson, H.W. (1986) 'The Big, Bad City: Mega-City Myth?' *Third World Planning Review*, No 4 pp: 355-372.

Rimmer, P.J. (1993) 'Transport and Communications in the Pacific Economic Zone during the early 21st Century,' pp.195-232 in Y.M. Yeung, ed., *Pacific Asia in the 21st Century: Geographical and Developmental Perspectives* Hong Kong: The Chinese University Press.

Rimmer, P.J. (1986) *Rikisha to Rapid Transit, Urban Public Transport Systems and Policy in Southeast Asia*, Pergamon, Oxford.

Rondenelli, D.A. (1991) 'Asian Urban Development Policies in the 1990s: from Growth Control to Urban Diffusion,' *World Development*, No 7 pp 791-803.

Santos, Milton (1977) *The Shared Space: Two Circuits of Urban Economy in Developing Countries*, Methuen, London.

Toshiro Kitami, Toshiro (1993) Kowan Toshi (Port-Cities), Seisando.

Waterfront 2001 Project (1992) Yomikaeru Toshi Uotafronto (The Urban Waterfronts under Revitalization), Nippon Hoso Kyokai.

Yang, Guangshiung, (1990) 'Zhongguo Yanhai Gangkou Chengshi Leising yu Jiekou Tedian Fenxi (Analysis on Types and Structural Characteristics of Chinese Coastal Cities)' ,pp 1-13 in Xuwei Hu and G.Yang, eds., *Zhongguo Yanhai Gangkou Chengshi (The Chinese Coastal Cities*: Kexue Chupanxie, Beijing.

Yeung, Yue-man and Xuwi Hu, eds., (1992) *China's Coastal Cities: Catalysts for Modernization* Hawaii University Press, Honolulu.

PART V
OBSERVING THE CITY

Editors' notes to Part V

What, objectively, can we say about cities – where things are, where growth is occurring, what they look like, how land-uses are confounded in high-rise districts? This Part looks at some examples of technical approaches to providing some answers. Geographical Information Systems and Remote sensing are the techniques looked at in the first chapters. They illustrate how information can be brought together – in Satish Davgun's case to look at areas of Ludhiana which are badly serviced, in the case of Bentinck et al to look at the growth of Delhi's periphery – which is happening at a speed defying conventional terrestrial mapping's capacity to keep up.

Kyunghee Kim and colleagues' chapter and Seiji Sato and colleagues' chapter are very different and very original. Kim Kyunghee asks if it is possible to show objectively what we all sense – that there are different kinds of townscapes and that our visual experiences of them change. They show how it is possible to map the different visual experiences of Pusan in Korea. The next chapter shows how we have to think of land use in three dimensional terms. This is a point which is obvious in one sense, but at another level challenges any simple two-dimensional mapping, upon which most planning is based.

27 Application of GIS in Evaluating the Availability of Services in Ludhiana, India

Satish K. Davgun

27.1 Introduction

The rapid urbanisation of developing countries has resulted in the haphazard growth of most of their cities. In some cities in India, the urban landscape has spilled over the city limits. This 'leap and bound' expansion of urban centres has caused a plethora of problems. In spite of the efforts by different agencies, a majority of the population in the urban areas does not find easy access to basic facilities. Many cities face practical administrative difficulties in planning the various public services in the face of unplanned changes in the population of users (Preston, 1988). The improvements in the provision of basic services are nullified by the influx of immigrants and the spatial changes in the city population. This chapter looks at the availability of some of the transportation and recreational facilities to the residents of Ludhiana, a rapidly growing city in northwest India. The analysis of the spatial patterns and interaction among different variables are performed by Geographic Information Systems (GIS).

27.2 Geographic Information Systems

The application of GIS makes it easier to analyse the spatial patterns of the urban facilities and the distribution of population. There has been a rapid increase in the application of this technology in evaluating the spatial patterns of urban landscape. GIS improves the operational and decision-making effectiveness (Budi, 1994). The location and the spatial interaction among various variables in different investigations strongly suggests the use of GIS for analysis. This technology has moved forward to make it easy to perform multi-dimensional data integration, the application of spatial analysis, and mapping of the output information (Marks, et al. 1992; Johnson, 1997). This technology is applied to investigate the presence of these facilities in different parts of the metropolitan area. The attempt is to highlight the under-

and un-served areas, to suggest the optimum sites and locations for these services.

27.3 The Model

In the Developing World the availability of basic urban facilities has not expanded in parallel with the rate of expansion of the cities. The major postulate of this study says that although the city of Ludhiana has expanded rapidly, basic services are available mainly in the central part. The peripheral sections are still devoid of most of the urban services.

The investigation is confined to the availability of some selected urban services. It looks at the availability of long-route bus stops, police stations, hospitals, and the movie theatres in this rapidly expanding metropolitan area. The multi-layered transportation facilities have been the answer to the urban transportation demands. Although there are different modes of transportation available to the residents for daily commuting, the presence of different types of bus routes and bus stops is very important for different aspects of urban mobility in this city. The availability and frequency of long-distance bus routes in the metropolitan area is particularly important. Among the health care facilities, hospital services are very important. Although a number of diverse medical practitioners are located in different parts of this urban centre, hospitals provide most of the medical services. The location of police stations, and the movie theatres are also included in this study.

The data for this research were gathered from census publications, the maps and publications from the Town Planning Agency, and the transportation offices located in Ludhiana.

27.4 Ludhiana: The Millionaire City

Ludhiana has emerged as a millionaire city in Punjab state. It is a major industrial, commercial, educational, and administrative centre. The city emerged during the Lodhi (Afghan Sultanate of Delhi) dynastic rule. Later it was important to the Mughals and Sikhs, and then it was embraced within the British Indian empire, when it was a military base and administrative headquarters for the district of Ludhiana.

During the later part of 19th century many small-scale hosiery plants were located in this city. Since then Ludhiana has been considered as the hosiery centre of India. Other small scale industries were also attracted to this rapidly growing city. At Partition and Independence in 1947, a rapid

Table 27.1 Population Growth of Ludhiana

Year	Persons	Percent Growth
1901	48,649	-
1911	44,170	- 9.2
1921	51,880	+17.5
1931	68,586	+32.2
1941	111,639	+62.8
1951	153,795	+37.8
1961	244,032	+58.7
1971	401,476	+64.4
1981	607,052	+51.3
1991	1,042,740	+74.8

Source: Census of India, 1991: Final Population Tables, 1992.

increase in population was triggered by the influx of Hindu and Sikh refugees from Pakistan. The 1951-61 census decade shows the highest increase in the population. The population increased from 153,795 in 1951 to 244,072 in 1961.

With growing agricultural prosperity in Punjab, urbanisation also increased, and many towns developed engineering industries. In Ludhiana small iron and steel rolling mills, machine tool plants, agricultural implements, bicycles, mopeds, motorcycles, sewing machines, and various other consumer goods' industries all grew in importance. In addition, the town boasted the main campus of Punjab Agricultural University, Guru Nanak Engineering College, two medical colleges, and other technical and undergraduate institutes. By the 1991 Census of India, this metropolitan area had about 1.2 million people. (i.e., the Punjab Agricultural University and an engineering college. The expanding rail and road transportation systems linked it with other parts of India. Ludhiana has very busy passenger and freight railway terminals, while the bus terminal is also one of the busiest in the region.

Many commercial activities are concentrated in the main bazaars and along the major arteries. The land use map shows the central part of the city, and the major roads and streets radiating from the core cluttered with shopping and commercial strips. The high density residential areas (Map 27.1) are located in the inner old part of the city. The planned industrial sectors are located in the eastern part of the metropolitan area. The large and medium size industrial plants are located in the zone between Chandigarh Highway and the G.T. Road. The railway tracks radiating from the railway station, located at the centre of the city, divide this metropolitan area into different parts. This exaggerates the traffic congestion and the difficulty of movement

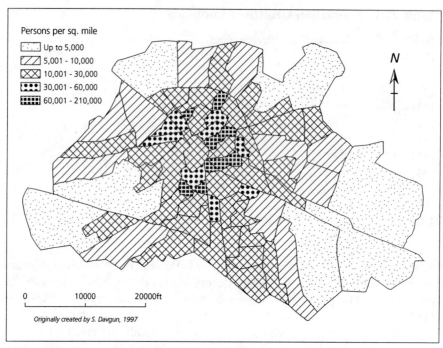

Map 27.1   Ludhiana: Population Density

within the city.

The unabated growth has resulted in unplanned encroachment of urban landscape on the surrounding agricultural land, and brought some villages within the metropolitan area. Much of the expansion of this metropolitan area has been towards south, west, and east. The Budda Nallah (an abandoned old bed of the Sutlej River) restricted the spread of the built up area towards the north. The expansion of the city focused upon the radiating highways to Chandigarh, Ambala, Jagraon, and Malerkotala.

This growth has been accompanied by the eruptions of slums and shanty towns (*jhuggies* and *jhompris*) within this city. About 40 percent of Ludhiana's population live in these deteriorated and undesirable neighbourhoods (Krishan, nd). The quality and coverage of urban services tends to be the worst in these poor neighbourhoods. These shanty towns and slums dot various sectors of the metropolitan areas. The problems of crowding, slums and shanty towns, mobility, and the mal-distribution of recreational, educational, health, and other basic amenities plague this millionaire city.

27.5 Spatial Patterns of Some Facilities

Most of the recreational facilities are located in the interior of the city. The common source of recreation available to the residents is cinema, and some parks. A majority of the movie theatres are located in and around the inner city. The stretch of old G.T. Road through the city, is dotted by six theatres. The major parks are also located at the periphery of the inner city. The major police stations are also located in the core area of the city. Two major hospitals associated with the medical colleges are also located in the inner city. The Christian Medical College and Hospital complex, and the Civil Hospital are in the thickly populated part of the city, whereas the Dayanand Medical College and Hospital is in the Civil Lines. The concentration of hospitals in the central city magnifies the problems of congestion, lack of space to expand, and extra travel time for most of the patients. The railway station and the bus terminal are also in the inner city.

The map showing the long route bus-stops reveals an interesting pattern (Map 27.2). The movements within the city is mainly by state-run local bus service, and private vehicles, i.e. automobiles, scooters, motorcycles, and

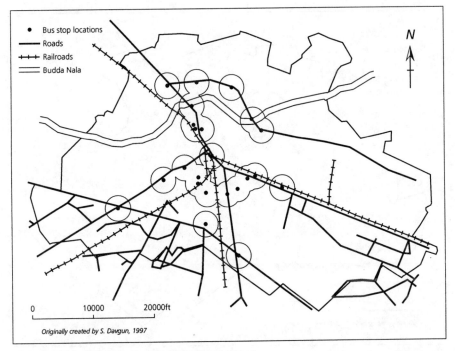

Map 27.2   **Ludhiana: Public Transport**

bicycles. But a considerable size of the workers who are engaged in commuting and reverse-commuting depend on the long-route bus service. Many commuters come to Ludhiana from the surrounding settlements to utilize the economic, administrative, and recreational facilities and services. Also, a considerable number of individuals who commute from Ludhiana to the nearby settlements or lateral commuting use the bus services. These bus services are available to the individuals residing close to the major roads. There appears to be an absence of lateral commuting services.

The volume of reverse commuting is quite substantial. A number of workers living in this metropolitan area commute to the nearby villages and towns daily. There are number of bus stops along the main radiating roads to pick up the passengers. The thickly populated part of the inner city is quite well served , while the peripheral sections have larger tracks of under-served areas.

The distribution of police stations and the movies theatres show interesting patterns (Map 27.3). An empty zone of 1.5 kms around these locations shows that much of the population in the outer parts of the city have no easy access to these services. Although the mobile police groups serve different

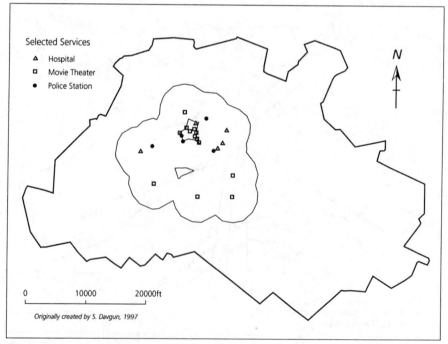

Map 27.3   Ludhiana: Location of Selected Public Services

parts of the city, fixed police stations are absent in the peripheral part of the city. Movies are the affordable and common source of entertainment for most of the people. Although the older movie theatres are located within a half-mile distance from the main chauk (Ghanta Ghar), the new cinema halls are dispersed in the central zones. Some new cinema halls are on Gill Road, Jagraon Road, and Dholewal Chauk.

The locational patterns of these facilities indicate that these facilities are located to serve the people living in the inner city (Map 27.4). The older part of the city has most of these facilities available to the residents. However, the horizontal growth of the city necessitates the decentralization of these and other basic facilities. As new residential localities emerge and the surrounding rural settlements are engulfed by the extensions of the urban boundaries. The residents in these peripheral sectors need to have easy provision of the facilities.

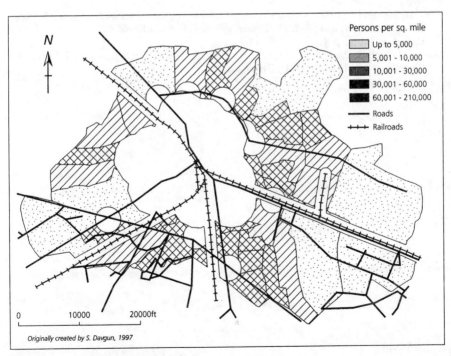

Map 27.4   Ludhiana: Public Access to Services

27.6 Conclusions

The examination of some basic facilities in Ludhiana indicate the central clustering of these services. Locations of many of these facilities were decided prior to the rapid expansion phase of this metropolitan area. As the population of these peripheral sectors has increased, the need for the provision of services has also increased – but the demand has not been satisfied. The gaps have been identified by use of GIS mapping.

References

Budic, Zorica D. (1994) 'Effectiveness of Geographic Information Systems in Local Planning'. *Journal of American Planning Association,* vol 60, pp 244-263.

Johnson, William F. (1997) 'From Road to Rail; Agencywide Deployment Brings GIS to Diverse Use' *Geo Info Systems*, vol 7, no. 5, pp 24-32.

Krishan, Gopal, and Saini, L. D. (nd) *Ludhiana: The Hosiery Metropolis*, unpublished report.

Marks, Allen P., Thrall, Grant I., and Arno, Michael (1992) 'Siting Hospitals to Provide Cost-Effective Health Care' *Geo Info Systems*, vol 2, no.8 pp 58-66.

Nandy, Pritish (1989) "The Homeless: 25 Million Indians Nave Nowhere to Go" *Illustrated Weekly of India*, July 2, pp 10-19.

Preston, Samuel H. (1988) 'Urban Growth in Developing Countries: A Demographic Reappraisal' in Gugler, Josef (ed) *The Urbanization of the Third World*, New York: Oxford University Press, p. 11.

Saini, L.D. (1992) *Slums in an Industrial City: A Case Study of Ludhiana.* Panjab University, Chandigarh (unpublished Ph.D. Dissertation).

28 The Degradation of Rural Land in the Rural-Urban Fringe of Delhi: Integration of GIS and Remote Sensing

J.V. Bentinck, J. Skornsek and A.C. de Vries

28.1 Introduction

The pressure on the land of the rural-urban fringe of fast-growing cities such as Delhi is tremendous. The mechanisms are explained by the increasing demand for land in terms of expansion of residence, industry or other urban functions but are also related with the food and resource demand of the city. The purpose of this paper is to combine the analysis of the land and its uses through remote sensing with the available data on the occupational structure of the population and agricultural land use, and to validate these through field work. The selected research area is Alipur Development Block, north of the city within the National Capital Territory. The current research attempts to map the land of the rural-urban fringe through the application of remote sensing.

This analysis of land use is part of the research project 'Environmental degradation and its socio-economic implications in the rural-urban fringe of Delhi' (Singh and Druijven 1994). The meaning of environmental degradation, in terms of land degradation is, however, very arbitrary. Purely physical indicators of soil quality (fertility) have little relevance in a rural-urban fringe. Land in the rural-urban fringe fulfils many different uses besides agricultural or other natural resource uses. This leads to the conclusion that the analysis of land degradation must start with the study of land use and its changes. Whether the different types of land use changes can be seen as the degradation of land as a 'satisfier of a particular use' (Blaikie and Brookfield, 1988) can be concluded only after an in-depth socio-economic study of the local population and its dependence on land has taken place. Consequently, the application of remote sensing and GIS is relevant for studying land degradation because the land use changes are the first objects of analysis. Although it is not included in the current paper, the results will further be used for socio-economic research about the impact of the degradation of rural land on the livelihoods of the local population.

The results of the classification of land use through remote sensing (de Vries et al., 1997) provides the basic information for this paper, which will focus on the integration with other data in a GIS. The overlay with the census

451

areas of villages enables us to calculate the area of each land use category for every village. With this information, a claim by Ramachandran (1988) could be tested: the occupational structure of the population in the villages changes from agricultural to non-agricultural employment before urban land use becomes dominant in the villages. The determining variables of urban expansion were thought to be 'accessibility to roads' and 'proximity to Delhi'. Spatial analysis in GIS was applied to relate these variables with the extension of urban area versus the (remaining) rural land.

28.2   The Interpretation of the Remote Sensing Classification

The main types of land use changes that are directly the consequence of urban expansion and occur at the expense of rural land (agricultural land, common land and forest) are of three types. First, expansion of the villages, settlement of industries and warehouses, and the expansion of infrastructure occupy rural land. Second, many plots are being prepared or are even vacant for more than a necessary period (land speculation). Third, an indirect land use effect of the city is exercised through the requirement of construction materials. The most important types are sand and clay for bricks which both require quarries. A counter process comprises changes in agriculture; especially because the profitability of cultivation of vegetables, fruits and flowers increases with the city markets coming nearer and more accessible.

28.2.1 A Priori: The Theoretically Desired Classification

Rural land can be defined as agricultural land, common land and forest; the main resource bases for an agriculturally oriented society. The purpose is to detect the extension of urban land use to this rural land. These considerations led us to desire a priori the use of the following classification:

I. '*Urban*' land:
1. Village areas, industry and other built-up area. The expansion of the already existing village built-up area and the settlements of new colonies, and industries/warehouses.
2. Infrastructure and urban facilities. This includes roads, dams, garbage dumps, sewage treatment areas, broadcasting stations and parks.
3. Brick kilns. These are almost exclusively located on former agricultural land.
4. Clay and sand quarries. Quarrying takes place almost exclusively on agricultural land.

5. *Speculative land.* This is the consequence of the anticipation on the change in the form of abandoning the rural function of the land. This often leads to land speculation and under use of land.

6. *Farm houses* (or luxury mansions). These are often owned by rich city dwellers, are another aspect of land speculation. Although the name suggests differently, within these fenced and walled areas there is little or no agriculture going on.

II. 'Rural' land:

7. *Forests and common land.*

8. *Agriculture* . Many cash-crops are very profitable due to the easy access to the city's markets. On many plots there is also an intensification going on of the 'ordinary' agriculture. With the increased availability of inputs and expertise, wheat, paddy and fodder harvests are increasing.

9. *Horticulture.* This is an indicator of (intensification of) agriculture highly concentrated on urban markets in the nearby city.

28.2.2 A Posteriori: Results of the Analysis of Land Use with Remote Sensing

The application of remote sensing could not classify all of the above main classes on the land with equal detail and reliability. We had therefore a posteriori to revise our classification:

A. Built-up land, barren land, and quarries. These three categories could not be separated to adequately. Still, the new aggregate class can serve as an indicator for urban expansion and conversion of agricultural land. All built-up land is included, except when the area is very small (e.g. one house). Also non-cultivated agricultural land is included, as well as land which is prepared for housing. Of the quarries, only the recent ones are part of this category. When a quarry is old and is left unused, vegetation grows on it and sometimes the land is flooded as well.

B. Brick kilns. The brick kilns can be distinguished very well, except for some very small ones.

C. Natural vegetation. Land with vegetation excluding agriculture, woodland, wetland, horticulture. Much of this land is alongside roads and canals where there are small trees and bushes. It is often land which is left unused for a specific time (speculative land). This is a reason why it is concentrated alongside infrastructure. Also, it is seen in parts of (urban) infrastructure such as radio transmission centres, parks, etc. Farmhouses also consist of 'natural vegetation'.

D. *Agriculture.* The agricultural category includes all land that was used for agriculture for the winter crop (rabi) in the year 1995 and 1996. This is mostly wheat, but also other crops such as fodder are included. Agricultural land which does not fulfil this criteria will fall in C or E. Theoretically this land can also include areas on which (substantial) vegetation has developed between May 1995 and March 1996 (possibly a new park or a former quarry), but a validation confirmed that this bias is very limited.

E. *Horticulture.* This includes flowers and vegetables. It is somewhat under classified because in the season analysed horticulture does not dominate. Besides, horticulture has very irregular harvest dates and this makes it difficult to analyse with the available images.

F. *Woodland.* This is forested area, usually a forest, or (part of) common land. It is also there in or along infrastructure because trees grow there. It can also be a plantation.

G. *Wetland.* This small category includes some flooded land with vegetation. This can be natural but can also be the consequence of clay or sand mining.

The resultant land use map, with an overlay of census areas (villages), is shown in figure 1.

Table 28.1   Match of the Theory of Rural to Urban Change and the Results of the Remote Sensing Application

From RS Classification perspective		*From theoretical perspective*	
RS classification	*Match with theory*	*Theoretical classification*	*Match with RS results*
A	1. (4, 2, 5)	1	A
B	3	2	C (a)
C	6 (5, 4)	3	B
D	8	4	C (g, c)
E	9	5	C (a)
F	7 (2,6)	6	C
G	(4, 2)	7	F (c)
H		8	D
		9	E

( ) = not exclusively in this category
bold = categories with complete match

( ) = not exclusively in this category
Capital letters = Contains majority of this category
Small letters = small part included
bold = categories with complete match

28.2.3 Matching theoretical requirements with the remote sensing classification

Table 28.1 shows how the categories of 3.1 and 3.2 correspond. From that it becomes clear that there are inconsistencies as well as matches.

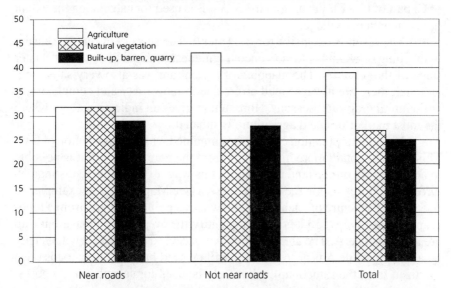

Figure 28.1 Land Use and Accessibility

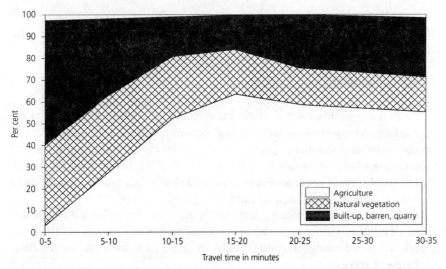

Figure 28.2 Land Use and Proximity

28.3 Interpreting the Results

It can be concluded that the following sum of classes from the remote sensing analysis provides an indication of 'urban land': A +B (+ part of C + part of G). The next sum provides an indication of 'rural land': D + E (+ part of C, part of G + F). In paragraph 3.3, A + B is used for calculating the extent of urban area per village.

The result is exclusive for B, D and E. The success of remote sensing in mapping brick kilns is a very encouraging result; this will be used in a later stage of the research. The mapping of agriculture was also very satisfying, although there are always small errors due to the variety and complexity of agricultural crops and seasons. Horticulture gives an indication about where the most market-oriented agriculture is situated.

Visual interpretation can also be combined with the application of GIS. This helps to obtain more information from the map. With GIS it is possible to add overlays on the land use map. In this way it is possible to distinguish different features within the defined classes (see Map 28.2). For example, an overlay of the centre of each village shown as a point (digitized from a topo-graphic map) helps to identify and quantify the area of the village built-up area within class A. The areas of class A adjacent to a brick kiln will usually be a quarry, while A near to the river will be sand banks. C near roads (also digitized from the same map) will mainly be used for speculation purposes; the same will be flood prone area if located near the river.

28.4 The Rural to Urban Transformation: Integrating Census Data in GIS

28.4.1 Theoretical Considerations

It is a complex issue to study the effects of the land use change on the population. Many sources suggest that before the rural land disappears in favour of urban land, many people already have changed their employment to non-agricultural occupations (Ginsburg et. al. 1991, Ramachandran 1989). Urban employment becomes better accessible for villagers since travelling to the city is enhanced through a better transportation network. Besides, some commercial and service components settle in or near the village itself, which requires relatively little from the agricultural land. Ramachandran (1989) in-tegrated this in a categorization of villages in the rural to urban 'continuum' in different stages:

    1. Rural

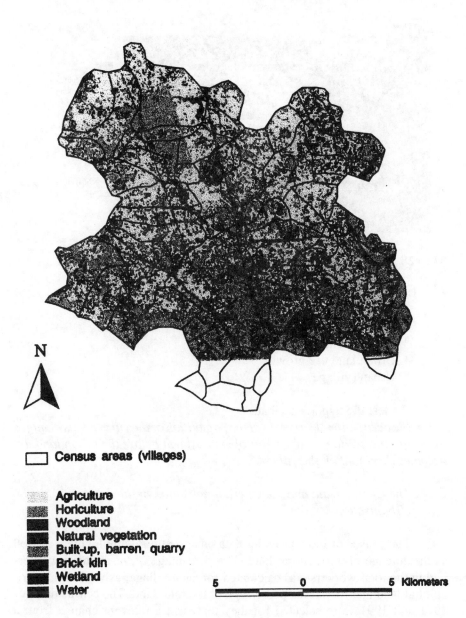

N

☐ Census areas (villages)

Agriculture
Horiculture
Woodland
Natural vegetation
Built-up, barren, quarry
Brick kiln
Wetland
Water

5   0   5 Kilometers

Map 28.1   Census Areas and Land Use, Alipur Block, Delhi, 1996
Note: The editors regret the original colour map has been reproduced monotone.

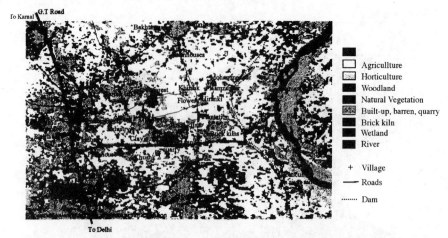

To Delhi

**Map 28.2   Interpretation of Remote Sensing Classification of a
Subarea in Alipur Block, Delhi**

Note: The editors regret the original colour map has been reproduced monotone.

2. Agricultural land use change
3. Occupational change
4. Urban land use growth
5. Urban (village)

We test the hypothesis that:
*the occupational structure of the population of the villages has changed
from agricultural to non-agricultural employment before the urban land use
becomes dominant on the village.*

*28.4.2 The Census Data and the Operationalisation of the Stages of
Urbanisation*

The census of India provides data on agricultural employment as well
as the acreage of agricultural land. The percentage of agricultural workers
within the total workers was calculated for each village, as well as the agricultural land and forest as a percentage of the total land. The census dates of
1971 and 1991 were selected for they represent a relevant change from a
predominantly rural situation to the recent situation of mixed rural and urban
features. The stage of agricultural land use change (subsistence crops to market-oriented agriculture) was omitted because no data is available on crops
for both dates. Besides, it was considered less relevant because the villages in

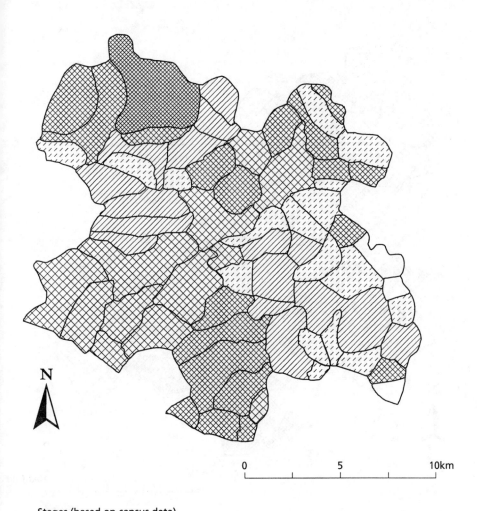

N

| 0 | 5 | 10km |

Stages (based on census data)
- Rural
- Pre-occupational change
- Occupational change
- Urban land use growth
- Urban (village)
- No data

Map 28.3   Stages of Urbanisation 1971, Alipur Block, Delhi

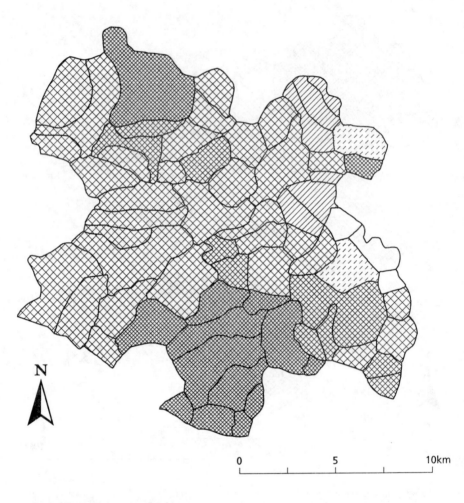

N

Stages (based on census data)
Rural
Pre-occupational change
Occupational change
Urban land use growth
Urban (village)
No data

Map 28.4   Stages of Urbanisation 1991, Alipur Block, Delhi

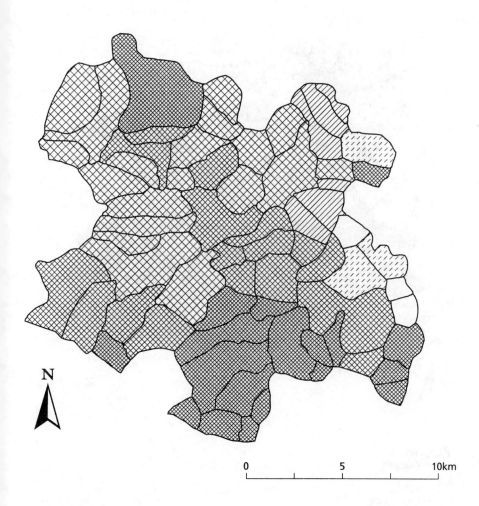

N

0   5   10km

Stages (based on census data)
- Rural
- Pre-occupational change
- Occupational change
- Urban land use growth
- Urban (village)
- No data

Map 28.5   Stages of Urbanisation 1991-96, Alipur Block, Delhi

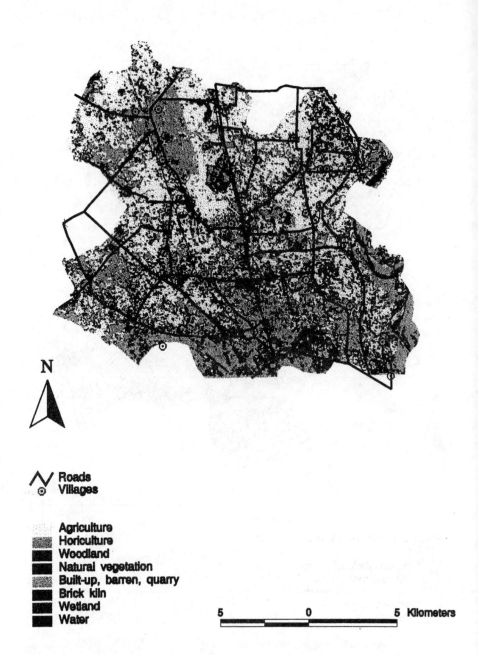

Map 28.6   Infrastructure and Land Use, Alipur Block, Delhi, 1996
Note: The editors regret the original colour map has been reproduced monotone.

Alipur Block cannot even in 1971 be considered remote villages with only subsistence agriculture. For this reason, the first two stages were joined into one category of (relatively) rural villages. Within the stage of occupational change two stages were distinguished. The following is the result of the re-categorization of the stages and the Operationalisation of the census figures:

1. Rural: > 70 per cent of the working population is working in agriculture.

2. Pre-occupational change: ≥ 50 and £ 70 per cent of the population employed in agriculture.

3. Occupational change: < 50 per cent of the working population is employed in agriculture.

4. Urban land use growth: ≥ 20 and £ 50 per cent of the land used for agriculture and forest.

5. Urban (village): < 20 per cent of the land used for agriculture and forest.

To make the stages internally consistent, all villages in stage 4 and 5 should have less than 50 per cent of the work force working in agriculture. This assumption proved correct after a check of the data. This was also essential for the hypothesis. The results could also be biased by a relative decline of employment in general, but that was not true. In fact employment participation rose from 25 to 30 per cent (1971-1991). However, the population of the Alipur Block rose from 78,069 to 297,123. This is mainly due to migration to the villages. The villages which officially belong to urban Delhi in 1991 are not counted in this, neither is the town of Narela (the black area in the north of the block). The results can be seen in Maps 28.3 and 28.4.

28.4.3 The Integration of the Remote Sensing Classification

The land use data in the Census of India cannot always be considered very exact. Besides, ideally we want to have data right up to date. In a final assessment of the stages of urbanisation (Map 28.6) we replaced the land use data of the census for a calculation of the urban categories of A and B > 50 per cent. The occupational data are still derived from the census of 1991. The map confirms the expected extension of more villages in stage 4. This is partly because the census figures generally give an overestimation of rural land and partly because in the five years between 1991 and 1996 additional land has been occupied by urban land uses.

28.4.4 Additional Spatial Analysis in GIS: Proximity and Accessibility

Two factors are expected to determine the extension of urban land into rural land: the existence of a nearby road (accessibility) and the closeness of the urban area of Delhi (proximity). The accessibility of the land was calculated by classifying all land within 300 metres of a road (Map 28.6). The road map of the 1970s was used. The results for the main land uses (Fig. 28.1) clearly show that agriculture within the buffer is less than that of the remaining land while class A is relatively well represented. Other classes are less convincing. Natural vegetation is slightly higher because of peculative land and vegetation along the roads. The results are biased by a few factors, e.g. class A and C near the river and class A as brick fields, which are also located on cheaper land and therefore not so near to the main infrastructure.

For proximity, the distance to the centre of the villages was calculated through a network analysis. The same road map was used with a few recent additions. This was again recalculated in terms of travelling time from the centre of the village to the node on the Outer Ring Road (most southern road on Map 28.6). The travel times were used to construct a map of interpolations to make categories of proximity of land. The result (Fig. 28.2) shows that the agricultural land is less and the built-up land is more up to about 15 minutes from a node, but other conclusions could not be drawn from this analysis.

28.5 Conclusions

Remote sensing can provide very useful information on land in a rural-urban fringe environment although its reliability should always be checked. In this case the study area shows a highly heterogeneous pattern and the patches of a particular land use can be very small. Therefore, some generalization was necessary for making clear and useful maps. The classification was a success for mapping agricultural land, brick kilns, and distinguishing between land with and without vegetation. It came short in distinguishing village built-up land, other built-up land, sand and clay quarries. Visual interpretation with the resulting map, however, can further be useful in determining different land uses within our classification. For that purpose the overlay of a GIS based coverage of infrastructure provides clear objects of reference.

The integration of the remote sensing classification into a GIS also enables us to make an overlay with the village boundaries. Each land use class can be calculated for every individual village. The theory of Ramachandran has been applied on the rural-urban fringe to classify the villages according to land use and occupational structure of the population. Both census and remote sensing data were integrated. Sufficient evidence was found to confirm that occupational change precedes land use change. Spatial analysis of the relation between accessibility and proximity of land shows that there is a pattern of urbanization along the better accessible routes, closest to the urban area of Delhi.

References

Blaikie, P. and Brookfield H. (eds.) (1987), *Land Degradation and Society*, Methuen, London.
Census of India (1971/91) *Delhi Village and Town Primary*, New Delhi.
Census of India (1971/91) *Village Directory Amenities and Land Use Directory*, New Delhi.
Ginsburg, N., Koppel B. and. McGee, T.G (eds.) (1991) *The Extended Metropolis, Settlement Transition in Asia*, University of Hawaii Press, Honolulu.
Nagpaul, H. (1996) *Modernisation and urbanisation in India; problems and issues*, Rawat Publications, Jaipur.
Ramachandran, R. (1989) *Urbanization and Urban Systems in India*, Oxford University Press, Delhi.
Singh, R.B., and Druijven, P.C.J.) (1994) *Environmental degradation and its socio-economic implications in the rural-urban fringe of Delhi*, project outline IDPAD 4.1.1, Delhi/ Groningen.
Survey of India (1977) Toposheet map 1:50,000 sheet 53 h/1 first edition.

29 Land Use Mapping of Delhi's Rural-Urban Fringe using Remote Sensing

A.C. de Vries, J. Skornsek and J.V. Bentinck

29.1 Introduction

The influences of urban expansion are increasingly dispersing far into the rural area around large Asian cities. Especially agricultural land and other rural land uses (forest, common land) are vulnerable to such conversion, which can result in land degradation if seen from a rural perspective (Blaikie and Brookfield, 1987). There is little information available on the extent and location of land under such pressure and its effects on the population in the villages. The current study is part of the research project 'Environmental degradation and its socioeconomic consequences in the rural-urban fringe of Delhi' (Singh and Druijven, 1994). It attempts to map the conversion of land in the rural-urban fringe, north of Delhi, using remote sensing.

Delhi is one of the largest metropolitan cities of India with a population of almost 10 million and a growth rate of more than 4 percent per year (Nagpaul, 1996). Major land use changes which take place need to be studied and quantified. Remote sensing is a powerful tool for studying such land use changes as it can provide land use inventories, but also allows the monitoring of changes. In the urban area of Delhi, remote sensing has been utilized by Gupta et al. (1985). They studied urban change in the period 1959-1980 using maps and Landsat TM images. Mishra et al (1994) found, through the analysis of SPOT and IRS-1B images a decline in vegetation cover over the Delhi urban area. Fung (1992) illustrated the use of remote sensing in mapping urban expansion of Hong Kong. He found that major land development can be detected and mapped using different remote sensors.

The study concentrates on the Alipur Block, an area just north of Delhi. The study area is classified as a rural area consisting of 53 villages and 4 towns. Due to expansion of urban Delhi, the southern edges of the area are constantly changing. The objective of the current paper is to generate a land use classification for Alipur Block using two IRS-1B (Indian Remote Sensing Satellite) images from May 1995 and March 1996.

29.2 Methodology

29.2.1 Data

The study includes two IRS-1B images acquired on May 28, 1995 and March 31, 1996. The sensors operate in a multi spectral four band mode with a spatial resolution of 25m. The March 1996 image was acquired prior to the winter harvest (Rabi) while the May 1995 image was acquired in a period after that harvest. A sub-area covering the rural urban fringe, north of urban Delhi was extracted. This study area encompasses the rural area of Alipur Block lying in the National Capital Territory of Delhi.

29.2.2 Pre-Processing

Both images were geo-referenced and atmospherically corrected. Geo-referencing was based on 6 control points with coordinates derived from GPS field measurements at intersections of roads and/or canals, and map co-ordinates. Co-registration displayed a total RMS error of approximately 0.5 pixel. In order to facilitate comparisons between images of different dates, raw reflection values were converted into calibrated radiances by subtracting the offset value. The offset was taken equal to the minimum grey value. For classification purposes two false colour images were compiled based on the near-infrared band 4 (0.77-0.88 μm), the red band 3 (0.62-0.68 μm) and the green band 2 (0.52-0.59 μm) with a 0.5% saturation.

A vegetation change cover map was prepared using the NDVI (normalized difference vegetation index). The NDVI is the result of rationing the near-infrared spectral band and the red spectral band. It enhances the variation in vegetation cover and can therefore be an ideal tool for land cover classifications.

29.2.3 Classification

An unsupervised clustering did not give satisfactory results. This is mainly due to the high level of heterogeneity of the study area, resulting in a large number of mixed pixels and small classes. A supervised classification approach was therefore necessary. This classification was carried out using the maximum likelihood classifier which is based on the probability density function associated with a particular training site signature. Pixels of unknown class are assigned to the most likely class based on a comparison of its signature with the signatures of the training sites that were considered.

Fourteen different classes were selected using the false colour of the

March 1996 image and field data. An inspection of the signatures of the train-ing sites through a scatter diagram of spectral band 4 versus spectral band 3 showed a large overlap in reflectance of the agriculture, woodland and other "green" objects. Furthermore the plot indicated that sufficient classes were selected explaining most of the variance in reflectance.

To overcome the problem of overlapping classes, the image of May 1995 was classified through a supervised classifier with special reference to the "green" objects. As this image was taken after the harvest, implying an almost absence of crops, a more accurate identification and classification of woodland could be generated. This woodland class was used as an overlay for the March 1996 classification.

To further improve the classification results, a comparison was made between both NDVI images. The May 1995 NDVI image was subtracted from the March 1996 NDVI image. This image was reclassed into three classes, a negative change, a positive change and little change in vegetation. A nega-tive change in NDVI indicates a decrease in areas with vegetation. No change in NDVI is an indicator for vegetated areas not consisting of agricultural crop harvested in April. A positive change in NDVI implies the existence of agri-cultural areas, harvested in April and areas with an increase in vegetation form 1995 to 1996. This layer was used as an overlay for the March 1996 classification, representing the agriculture.

The land use map consisting of fourteen classes was finally re-grouped to seven general classes. Post-classification comparison of the final result and GPS points, with detailed site descriptions, was used for validation.

29.3 Results

Maps 29.1 and 29.2 show the false colour images of May 1995 and March 1996. The difference in vegetation due to the main harvest in April can be observed. Also the high level of heterogeneity of the rural-urban fringe can clearly be seen. This vegetation may consist of agricultural crops, wood-land, grassland or natural vegetation. Map 29.3 shows the classification of the Alipur Block, consisting of seven different land use classes. The seven land use types that were identified are:

- agriculture
- horticulture
- forest, common lands
- natural vegetation
- built up, quarry, barren
- brick kilns

**Map 29.1   False Colour (Band 432) Image of Alipur Block, North of
Urban Delhi, May 1995**

Note: The editors regret the original colour map has been reproduced monotone.

**Map 29.2   False Colour (Band 432) Image of Alipur Block, North of
Urban Delhi, March 1996**
Note: The editors regret the original colour map has been reproduced monotone.

N

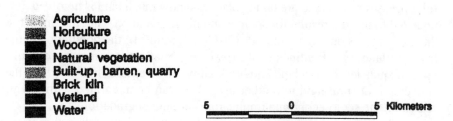

Agriculture
Horiculture
Woodland
Natural vegetation
Built-up, barren, quarry
Brick kiln
Wetland
Water

5   0   5 Kilometers

Map 29.3   Land Use Map of Alipur Block, North of Urban Delhi
Note: The editors regret the original colour map has been reproduced monotone.

- wetlands
- water

For a detailed description of the different classes see Bentinck et al. (1997).

29.4 Discussion and Conclusions

The application of remote sensing in the study of land degradation has great potential. The current paper has shown that for a very heterogeneous area as the rural-urban fringe of Delhi it is feasible to compute a relatively accurate land use map.

Errors might be introduced in the selection of land use classes. As unsupervised classification did not give any useful results, the selection of training areas is fully based on field data and patterns visible in the false colour images. Differences in the field do not automatically result in spectral separation. This might result in a misinterpretation of the classes. This problem might be resolved by applying fuzzy classification methods.

A second error might be introduced with the definition of agricultural areas. The method of subtracting NDVI images only works if we assume that no substantial increase in "green" area has taken place from 1995 to 1996. However, in the present study area, with major urbanisation, this increase can probably be neglected. It is probably more accurate to use two images from the same year.

The integration of RS images with infrastructure and village boundaries in a GIS allows for integration with socioeconomic data from secondary data sources and household surveys.

Analysis in a GIS can also provide insight about where the most harmful processes on the land are taking place and how much land is involved. It is intended to use the results for socioeconomic research on what the impact of these changes is on the livelihoods (different groups) of the population in the fringe villages (see Bentinck et al., 1997). Especially, the expansion of built-up area, quarries, barren land and brick kilns can be used as indicators for the conversion of rural land into other uses. This can be integrated with the research on the socio-economic implications of land degradation.

Classification at different dates will allow for change detection in order to determine the extent and nature of land use and land cover change. Future analysis will concentrate on generating a land use map for the period 1988/89 with similar data set and hence on the detection of land use change of the rural urban fringe of Delhi from 1988 to 1996.

References

Fung, T., 1992, Land use and land cover change detection within Landsat MSS and SPOT HRV data in Hong Kong, *Geocarto International*, 3:33-40.

Gupta, D.M. and Munshi, M.K., 1985, Urban change detection and land-use mapping of Delhi, *International Journal of Remote Sensing*, 6 (3/4): 529-534.

Mishra, J.K., Aarathi, R. and Joshi, M.D., 1994, Remote sensing quantification and change detection of natural resources over Delhi, *Atmospheric Environment*, 28 (19): 3131-3137.

Nagpaul, H., 1996, Modernisation and urbanisation in India; problems and issues, Rawat Publications, Jaipur.

Singh, R.B. and Druijven, P.C.J., 1994, Environmental degradation and its socioeconomic implications in the rural-urban fringe of Delhi, *project outline IDPAD 4.1.1*, Delhi/Groningen.

30 Landscape Evaluation by Multivariate Analysis: Characteristics of the Landscape in Pusan, Korea, using a Picture Database

Kyunghee Kim, Seiji Sato, Takafumi Arima, Naishen Hsiao, Satoshi Hagishima and Sungkon Kim

30.1 Introduction

Pusan, the biggest international port city in Korea, lies on the southeast coast of the Korean peninsula. It has achieved rapid growth over the last 50 years, with its population increasing from 280,000 to 4 million. As a port city, Pusan has many water-side landscapes, and an urban landscape with many sloping areas on the flanks of the surrounding hills and mountains.

In the last few years, the management problems of urban landscapes have become an important factor in urban planning policy in Korea. Due to rapid urbanisation and zoning restrictions on development in some districts, a dense and high-rising urban space has been produced in Korean cities. The above situation has resulted in many undesirable phenomena, such as congestion and the destruction of natural landscape.

There is increasing interest in the preservation of the quality of the urban landscape, and a new landscape control policy that is suitable to the circumstances of Korea is to be tried. In order to make effective landscape control regulations which maintain the original landscape, at first it is important to grasp the present state of the urban landscape. This study examines the characteristics of the landscape composition elements in Pusan city using a landscape picture database.

30.2 Building a Picture Database for Landscape Evaluation

30.2.1 Setting the View Point

When preparing a picture database, first we selected 35 view-points that represented a balanced range of various visual scenes, using a background information on urban planning zones and the constituent elements of their landscapes. Then, approximately 1,100 photographs were taken at the view-points in a field survey. Finally, 300 of the photographs were chosen to make up the representative database.

30.2.2 Organisation of the Landscape Picture Database

Each of the 300 photographs is classified according to the following five characteristics:
1) view-point attribute,
2) view-object attribute,
3) classification by objective point,
4) landscape composition elements by near-distance, medium-distance and far-distance in view area, and
5) landscape obstacles obscuring possible sights

The way these variables are coded is clear from Fig. 30.1, showing a record for one photograph.

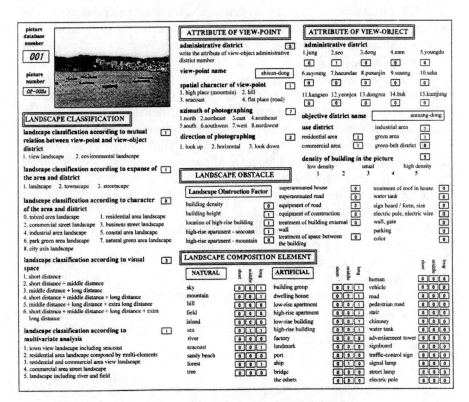

Figure 30.1 One Record in the Urban Picture Database

30.3 Classification of Urban Landscape in Pusan City

By using the following data, the urban landscape in Pusan city was classified according to the landscape composition elements and by distance. We established landscape distances as follows: near-distance landscape is 0-200 meters, mid-distance landscape is 200-1,000 meters, and far-distance landscape is beyond 1,000 meters. Landscape composition elements consist of 11 natural composition elements and 25 artificial composition elements, divided into 3 distance categories.

The data for all 300 records was analysed using a factor-analytic approach to find the basic dimensions of the set of variables. This produced two factors, as shown in Table 30.1.

For factor 1, there are high scores for variables 'advertisement tower in near-distance', 'sign board in near-distance and mid-distance' and 'signal lamp in near-distance'; and there are strong negative scores for 'river in far-distance', 'factory in far-distance' and 'sea coast in far-distance'. This suggests that this axis is associated with denser and more commercial street. The landscape is positively associated with many small-scale elements – and negatively with large-scale elements. We name it the 'element scale axis' for Pusan's landscapes.

For factor 2, there are high positive scores for 'river in near-distance and far-distance' and 'field in mid-distance and far-distance', and negative scores for variables such as 'mountain in near-distance', 'seacoast in near-distance and far-distance', 'port in far-distance', 'advertisement tower in mid-distance' and 'high-rise building in far-distance'. The positive values for factor 2 show the topographical character of the west suburban area in Pusan city, which is surrounded by designated green-belt districts. A negative value for factor 2 shows the topographical character of the downtown area and describes the town landscape. And so, factor 2 is called "the high density town - low density suburb" axis, and it reflects the unique land use system of Pusan city. (i.e. designated green-belt districts)

These two axes are used to plot the 300 photographs, as in Fig. 30.2. The clustering suggests to us that there are five distinct visual landscape types – although there is some arbitrariness about the edges between the lower arc of types 1 to 4.

Examples of picture records and their factor scores for these landscape types are shown in Fig. 30.3.

Table 30.1 Factor Analysis of Visual Urban Attributes

Item		Factor 1	Factor 2
Sky	L	0.1184	0.1102
Mountain	S	-0.9055	-2.6048
	M	-0.3054	0.3684
	L	-1.0398	0.4280
Hill	S	-0.0253	-0.7716
	M	-0.8611	-0.2688
Field	S	-0.0430	3.3323
	M	-0.3659	5.7483
	L	-1.0784	5.6081
Island	S	-1.8896	0.9829
	M	-1.4371	-1.4393
	L	-1.4999	-1.3448
Sea	S	-1.0173	-0.9273
	M	-1.4530	-1.2125
	L	-1.7554	-1.7414
River	S	-1.1889	5.1498
	M	-1.3597	4.9225
	L	-2.0604	5.7908
Seacoast	S	-1.7644	-1.8878
	M	-1.6361	-1.2351
	L	-1.9532	-1.9276
Sandy beach	S	-0.7145	-0.5085
	M	-0.9621	0.2531
	L	-1.0388	-1.2229
Forest	S	-0.1668	-1.1533
	M	-0.1569	0.5539
	L	-1.1328	0.5116
Tree	S	0.3675	0.2925
	M	0.1109	0.5790
Building group	M	-0.5644	0.3189
	L	-1.2536	-0.1758
Dwelling house	S	0.1133	0.0216
	M	-0.4100	0.3218
	L	-1.4721	-0.3758
Low-rise apartment building	S	0.1372	-0.2898
	M	-0.3570	0.3893
	L	-1.6745	-0.9351
High-rise apartment building	S	1.0718	0.5087
	M	-0.0548	0.7613
	L	-1.5056	-0.1881

Item		Factor 1	Factor 2
Low-rise building	S	1.0818	-0.3669
	M	-0.1203	-0.0518
	L	-1.7659	-0.3989
High-rise building	S	1.2973	-0.9978
	M	-0.4284	-0.4131
	L	-1.8459	-1.4305
Factory	S	-0.5701	1.8797
	M	-1.0447	0.9676
	L	-1.9958	1.0002
Landmark	S	1.4387	-0.9046
	M	0.2595	-0.8344
	L	-1.7660	-1.2214
Port	M	-1.6573	-1.2621
	L	-2.0442	-1.9061
Ship	S	-0.9424	2.3428
	M	-1.6521	-1.2366
	L	-1.9735	-1.8453
Bridge	S	-0.2680	0.0631
	M	-1.5490	-1.5927
The others	S	0.6479	-1.5927
Human	S	1.1042	-0.6822
	M	0.6785	-0.6249
Vehicle	S	1.2429	-0.2748
	M	0.6814	0.3199
Road	S	1.1153	0.0027
	M	0.5522	0.4664
Pedestrian road	S	1.0296	-0.5596
	M	0.5109	0.4693
Stair	S	0.5657	-0.8063
	M	-1.6689	-0.9188
Chimney	S	-0.0321	0.0220
	M	-0.6245	1.6124
	L	-1.1724	3.0189
Water tank	S	-0.6693	-0.2485
	M	-0.7793	0.2750
Advertisement tower	S	2.0260	-1.5685
	M	0.7497	-1.8682
Signboard	S	1.6875	-0.8726
	M	1.6504	-0.9835
Traffic control sign	S	1.5019	-0.6267
	M	1.5565	-0.2488

Item		Factor 1	Factor 2
Signal lamp	S	0.7161	-1.1401
Street lamp	S	1.0637	-0.2986
	M	0.6367	0.4569
Eletric pole	S	0.6434	-0.0204
	M	0.6472	0.9650
Range		4.0864	8.3956
Coefficient of correlation		0.716	0.521

S   short-distance
M middle-distance
L   long-distance
High positive score   High negative score minus

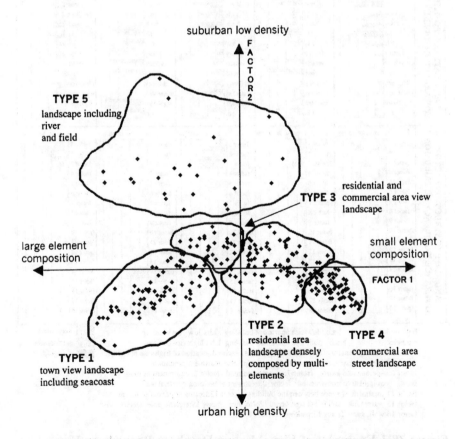

Figure 30.2 Five Landscape Types Produced by Two Factor Scores

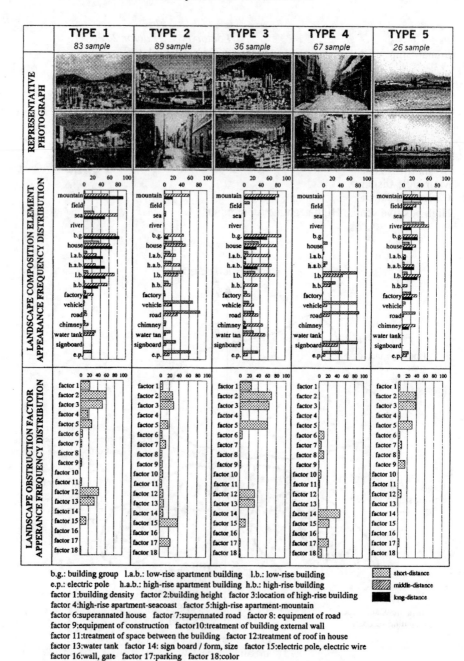

b.g.: building group l.a.b.: low-rise apartment building l.b.: low-rise building
e.p.: electric pole h.a.b.: high-rise apartment building h.b.: high-rise building
factor 1:building density factor 2:building height factor 3:location of high-rise building
factor 4:high-rise apartment-seacoast factor 5:high-rise apartment-mountain
factor 6:superannated house factor 7:supernnated road factor 8: equipment of road
factor 9:equipment of construction factor10:treatment of building external wall
factor 11:treatment of space between the building factor 12:treatment of roof in house
factor 13:water tank factor 14: sign board / form, size factor 15:electric pole, electric wire
factor 16:wall, gate factor 17:parking factor 18:color

short-distance
middle-distance
long-distance

Figure 30.3 Examples of Visual Urban Database Records by Five Landscape Types

Type 1; Town view landscape including seacoast

These are panoramas – and obviously therefore involving large scale elements of Pusan's landscape. The elements of sea, mountain and building group in the far-distance are common. There is a high expectation of views of the sea. There are two major types of landscape with mountainous in the background. One is a view of the city across water, and the other is the view from the edge of the sea coast. Building height and location of high-rise buildings are the main landscape obstruction factors blocking parts of the panoramas.

Type 2; Residential area landscape densely composed of multiple-elements

In near-distance landscapes, the elements of vehicle, road and electric pole are common. In the mid-distance landscape, houses, apartment buildings, and low-rise buildings are common. Views in this kind of residential area range from narrow street level views to wider perspectives on an area from higher up on a slope. Concerning landscape obstructions, the commonest are electric poles and parked vehicles.

Type 3; Residential and commercial area view landscape

The elements of mountain in mid-distance and far-distance, and building in far-distance are common. Representative photographs show panoramas overlooking the combined residential and commercial areas. These views are different from Type 1 not only by lacking the connection with the sea, but also because of the high level of obstruction - from high-rise buildings located on slopes.

Type 4; Commercial area street landscape

The elements of road, sign board, electric pole, vehicle and low-rise building are common to these derived landscapes. Representative photographs are of streets in commercial areas. The Composition of this type of landscape is the street landscape perspective. The landscapes are obstructed by sign boards, electric poles and parking.

Type 5; Landscape including river and field

The elements of field, river and mountain are common with this derived landscape. Far-distance elements include building groups (e.g. high-rise apartment building and factories). But the view is otherwise open.

30.4 Distribution of Landscape Types

In order to grasp the characteristics of Pusan's urban landscape we plot (Figs. 30.4 – 30.7) view points and types on maps, showing the direction of the view point and the view object area for each landscape type. Therefore, we clarify the relationship between landscape types and conventional land use and topographical maps.

Landscape types 1 and 5 are shown at the whole city scale. Distribution of landscape type 2, landscape type 3 and landscape type 4 is concentrated in the urban district, and so these types are shown on more detailed urban district maps.

As Figure 30.2 indicates, the distribution of landscape types 1 and 5 are disjoint. The view object area of landscape type 1 is located in urban areas around the seacoast, and the view objective area in landscape type 5 overlaps part of the green-belt district surrounding Pusan city. The western part of Pusan city has a natural environment with large rivers and open fields. Therefore, we can recognize from this result that there is a close relation between the distribution of both types and the character of land use. Residential districts are widely distributed in hilly districts, since more than 70% of Pusan

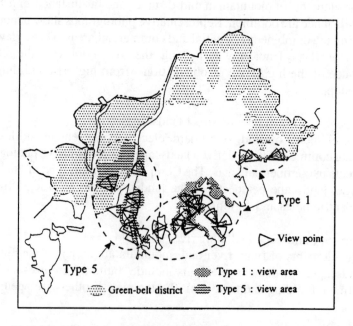

Figure 30.4 Distribution of Landscape Types 1 and 5 in Pusan

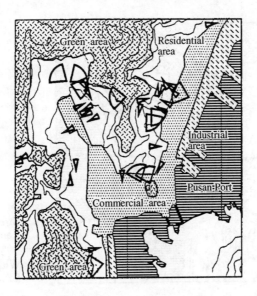

Figure 30.5 Distribution of Landscape Type 2 in Pusan

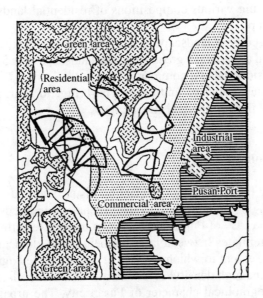

Figure 30.6 Distribution of Landscape Type 3 in Pusan

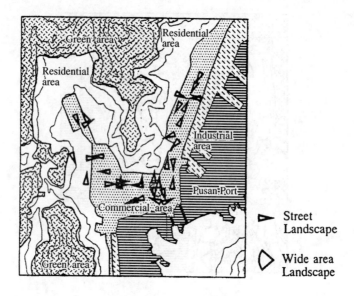

Street
Landscape

Wide area
Landscape

Figure 30.7 Distribution of Landscape Type 4 in Pusan

city area is mountainous.

Many view points of landscape type 2 (Fig. 30.5) are situated in residential areas, being various compositions of residential landscapes looking both down and up.

The view point of landscape type 3 (Fig. 30.6) is located in green areas and in residential areas near a green area. The landscape type 3 is overlooking landscape on residential and commercial area.

Most of view points of landscapes type 4 (Fig. 30.7) are narrow – laterally confined by the commercial streetscapes.

30.5 Conclusion

It is clear that the idea of subjecting visual landscape clues as seen from specific angles to multi-variate analysis has provided us with interesting results. In the case of Pusan there are two major axes grouping the variables: one differentiates between large element-small element composition, which shows the extent to which the viewer is compressed against the view, and the other is the high density- low density axis which reflects the land use system and topographical character of Pusan city. The urban landscape is classified by these factors into 5 types. Mapping these shows distinct spatial variation and clustering with Pusan. This extends our appreciation of the visual characteristics of places from mapping simply what is in a place, to mapping the extent of 'knowing' or seeing beyond that immediate place.

References

Hagishima, S. and Ohgai, A. (1990) 'A study of the urban landscape in the 19C European landscape paintings', *Journal of Archit. Plann. Environ. Engng*, ALJ, No 413.

Kawasaki, K. and Hirao, K.H. (1994), 'Settlement of the view-points and classification of the mountain-views in Kyoto', *Journal of Archit. Plann. Environ. Engng*, ALJ, No 462.

Pusan Metropolitan City, (1996), *Municipal white paper*, Pusan Metropolitan government

Seoul Development Institute, (1994), *Proposed Master Plan for the Urban Landscape Management for Seoul*, 94-R-2 .

31 Analysis of Change of Three Dimensional Land Use in a High Density and Mixed District

Takafumi Arima, Seiji Sato, Satoshi Hagishima and Naishen Hsiao

31.1 Introduction

In Japan, the appearance of high-rise buildings in the central districts of cities has created a complicated land use pattern. The fact that land is used as three dimensional space suggests that land resources are utilized effectively. However, the excessive accumulation of different uses on single sites is a major factor behind problems such as traffic jams and noise. Mixed land-use can also adversely affect residential environments.

The government is implementing a system of land-use zoning and floor area restrictions in order to regulate the accumulation and mixture of land use. A use zoning system is a measure to create a good environment in each district by designating it as commercial, industrial or residential. However, because there has been so much construction of high-rise and high-density buildings in the central districts, it is difficult to say that these regulations function effectively.

Here we propose a method to grasp the mixture and accumulation of land use by three dimensional analysis, and to clarify the current state of land use change quantitatively. The term "land use" in this paper is meant to describe how each floor of a building is used. The word "land use" has been generally used to show the use of urban space. For that reason, we also defined use of each floor as land use in this research.

Over the past few years, although a large number of studies of land use have been made, most have analysed the use of land in two dimensions only. We investigated all floor uses of buildings in 1987 and 1992, built three dimensional data sets of detailed land use, and clarified the relationship between the use zoning system and the change of land use mixture.

31.2 Building the Three Dimensional Land Use Data

The study area of this research is the approximately 2km by 2km central district of Oita City which is composed of Category I exclusive residential districts, Category II exclusive residential districts, Residential districts,

Neighbourhood commercial districts, Commercial districts and Light industrial districts (Map 31.1). We furthermore classify the Neighbourhood commercial districts and Commercial districts into five districts by the value of floor area restriction, and analysed the relation of these districts and land use.

Firstly, land use in the study area was investigated. The criteria of land use classification were the 104 land use codes which are presented in Table 31.1. Next, co-ordinates of building shapes in this area were input, and the number of land use code for every floor. Flow charts of the data collection method are shown in Figure 31.1.

Detailed explanations of the data collection method are given here.

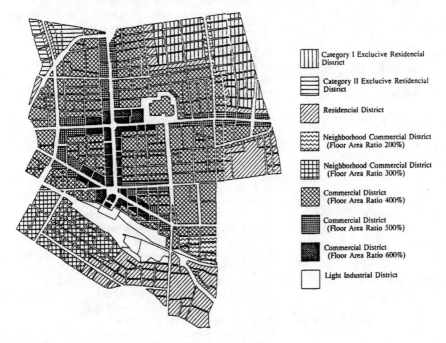

Map 31.1   Oita City, Central Land Zoning

1. The map which was used for data input is a map of a scale 1:1000 which was enlarged from a map of scale of 1:2500 issued by Geographical Survey Institute. We divided this map into block units.

2. Co-ordinates of the temporary origin of the block map and building shapes were input using a digitiser. When there are multiple uses of one floor of a building, dividing lines were also input.

3. An integrated building data map was completed by integrating the

Table 31.1 Land Use Codes: Oita City Study

	Type	*Land Use Code*
1	Dwelling I	1. Detached house
2	Dwelling II	2. Row house, 3. Dormitory, 4. Lodging house,
		5. Apartment house (rental house), 6.Apartment house,
		7. Apartment combined with other use
3	Dwelling with other use	8. Dwelling with shop, 9. Dwelling with office,
		10. Dwelling with workshop
4	Education I	11. University, 12. College, 13. Special school, 14. Museum,
		15. Public hall, 16. Public assembly hall, 17. Gym, 18. Pool,
		19. Practical factory, 20. Laboratory, 21. Training institute,
		22. Meeting hall
5	Education II	22. Primary school, 24. Junior high school, 25. High school,
		26. Kinder garten, 27. Library, 28. Shrine, 29. Gym, 30. Temple,
		31. Church, 32. Pool, 33. Practical factory, 34. Laboratory,
		35. Others.
6	Welfare I	36. Hospital
7	Welfare II	37. Clinic, 38. Doctor's office, 39. Dwelling with clinic,
		40. Dwelling with Doctor's office, 41. Laboratory
8	Welfare III	42. Old people's home, 43. Day nursery, 44. Day school,
		45. Public bath-house
9	Welfare IV	46. Welfare facilities for the aged, 47. Welfare facilities for
		children, 48. Welfare facilities and the like
10	Business	49. Bank, 50. Company, 51. Office
11	Commerce	52. Department store, 53. Market, 54. Speciality store,
		55. Wholesale store, 56. Restaurant, 57. Coffee shop,
		58. Commercial facilities and the like,
12	Lodging	59. Hotel, 60. Japanese style hotel, 61. Motel
13	Amusement I	62. Theatre, 63. Cinema theatre, 64. Entertainment hall,
		65. Exhibition hall, 66. Japanese restaurant, 67. Cabaret,
		68. Bar, 69. Dancehall, 70. Others
14	Amusement II	71. Bowling alley, 72. Skating rink, 73. Po0l, 74. Mah-jong house,
		75. Pinball house, 76. Driving school, 77. Others
15	Public and Communication	78. Public office, 79. Police station, 80. Fire station,
		81. Post office, 82. Communication facilities,
		83. Telephone office, 84. Broadcasting facilities
16	Transportation and Warehouse	85. Station, 86. Tram dept, 87. Garage,
		88. Warehouse for business, 89. Warehouse
17	Heavy chemical industry	90. Heavy chemical industry
18	Light chemical industry	91. Light chemical industry
19	Service industry	92. Service industry
20	Home Industry	93. Home industry
21	Supply	94. Filtration plant, 95. Transformer substation,
		96. Sewage treatment plant, 97. Garbage burning place,
		98. Crematorium, 99. Slaughter house, 100. Wholesale market,
		101. Supply facilities and the like
22	Cattle shed	102. Cattle shed
23	Parking lot	103. Parking lot
24	Communal lavatory	104. Communal lavatory

building data sets with the temporary original coordinates of each block map.

4. The 104 kinds of land use codes were input by mouse operation on a computer as colour data. The area of each land use is calculated by counting the number of pixels in an area of a given colour.

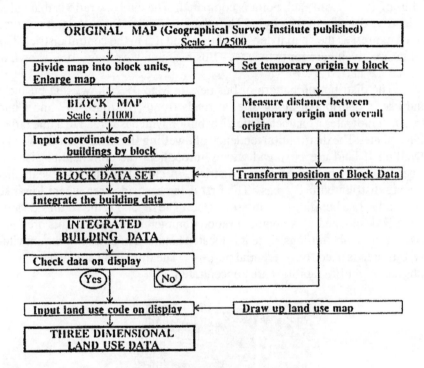

Figure 31.1 Flowchart of Methodology

31.3 Analysis

We conduct four analyses using the three dimensional land use data. The first analysis grasped the horizontal distribution of each land use situation, and clarified its relationships with the use zones. The second analysis compared the ratio of land use area by floor in order to grasp the vertical land use situation in the city space. The third analysis clarified the mixture situation of each land use using Simpson's Index. The fourth analysed city changes in the city space by comparing the mixtures of land use in 1987 and 1992.

31.3.1 The Horizontal Distribution of Land Use

We use an index of a land as follows.

Points are set on intersections of a 100 meter grid on the map. The total area of the buildings of a given land use which are contained within a radius of 100m from each point is computed. The land use ratio is that value divided by the area of the circle. Thus there is a value for each land-use type which expresses the spatial density of that land use in the central district. The results are given here for two codes - Business and Dwelling - II as shown in Maps 31.2 and 31.3 .

The distribution pattern of business in Map 31.2 shows that business land use is distributed along arterial roads (route 10, route 197 and Chuo street). It indicates a characteristic distribution which is spread in a line rather than a plane. The distribution tendency of dwelling II in Map 31.3 shows that Dwelling II land use is spread widely throughout the commercial districts rather than only in the residential districts. A close look at this reveals that they are distributed in 3 areas. The first is the east side area where low-rise and middle-rise buildings are intermingled. The second is the south side area which is designated as a neighbourhood commercial district. This area has few commercial buildings since it is located behind a railway station. Inevitably, this area is used for residential purpose. The third is an area where many pubs and night life facilities are concentrated.

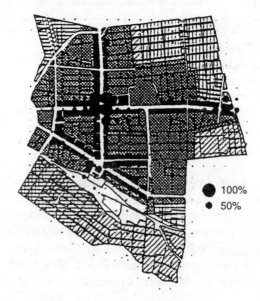

● 100%
• 50%

Map 31.2   Spatial Density of Businesses

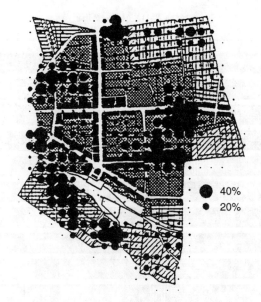

Map 31.3   Spatial Density of Dwellings

31.3.2 Land Use Area Ratio by Floor Level

The land use area ratio by floor level is the index which calculates an area percentage for all land use types by each floor level in the central district. In short, this index expresses the vertical situation of land use.

Figure 31.2 The 3-Dimensional Cityscape

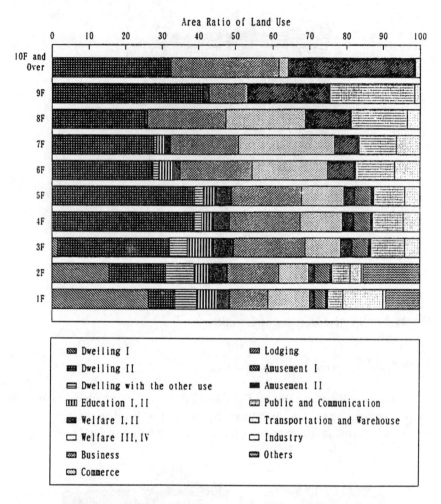

Figure 31.3 Vertical Land-Use

Figure 31.3 shows this index. The characteristics of each land use type are as follows.

The use of Dwelling I (detached house) and Other (parking lot) appear in low floors only. Dwelling with other use, Education I.II, Welfare I,II (hospital, laboratory) and Commerce (department store, speciality store, restaurant, coffee shop) decrease with an increase of floor level. Dwelling II (apartment), Business, Lodging, Public and Transportation are shown in all floor levels.

31.3.3 Index of Degree of Land-Use Mixture

We calculated two versions of Simpson's index to investigate the mixtures of land-use. The Area Simpson Index and the Number Simpson Index, both use the same formula. But in the former ASI we use data for the area of each land use type, and for the NSI we use the number of codes present in the area. The formula of this index is as follows.

$$SI_i = 1 - \sum_{j=1}^{k} \{n_{ij}(n_{ij}-1)/100(100-1)\}$$

In the formula, n_{ij} is in the range 0 to 100 per cent and is the ratio of land use j against the total land use in area i.

This index takes a value from 0 to 1. When the value is large, the mixture of land use is high. The results of the distribution of ASI and NSI appear in Maps 33.4 and 33.5. Lastly we derive a new value, NASI which is NSI − ASI. Moreover, the relationship of the mixture degree index and the use zoning is made clear in Table 31.2.

If we look at common characteristics of ASI and NSI in Maps 33.4 and 33.5, we will see that the degree of mixture in commercial areas is higher than in residential areas. On the other hand, a glance at NASI in Map 33.6 will reveal that the difference between NSI and ASI is large and negative in residential areas, and large and positive along arterial roads. Put simply, it means that although the number of land use codes is less mixed in residential areas, the area of land use is more highly mixed. This is mostly a function of the small size of the buildings. In the latter positive case it means that although the number of land use codes is highly mixed, the area of land use is less mixed, because a few of the uses dominate. This is influenced by large-

Table 31.2 Degree of Land-Use Mixture by Zone

	Category I Exclusive residential	Category II Exclusive residential	Residential	Neighbourhood Commercial (200%)	Neighbourhood Commercial (300%)	Neighbourhood Commercial (400%)	Neighbourhood Commercial (500%)	Neighbourhood Commercial (600%)	Light Industrial
ASI	.68	.75	.66	.79	.74	.76	.73	.70	.67
NSI	.59	.69	.60	.67	.76	.80	.80	.80	.72
NASI	-.10	-.08	-.06	-.12	.02	.03	.07	.13	.06

Table 31.3 Changes of Land-Use Area

	Category 1 exclusive residential district		Category II exclusive residential district		Residential district		Neighbourhood commercial district (200%)	
	Change Ratio	Area	Change Ratio	Area	Change Ratio	Area	Change Ratio	Area
Dwelling I	-1.8	1408	-1.5	193	3.5	3773	-4.5	834
Dwelling II	12.8	4758	18.9	1438	17.5	12907	8.4	1217
Dwelling with the other use	30.7	1070	5.1	177	-0.6	76	3.4	168
Education I	12.9	9	0.0		0.0		0.0	
Education II	0.0		0.0		-0.1	17		810
Welfare I	0.0		0.0		0.0		0.0	
Welfare II	0.0		0.0		-3.9	110	14.2	242
Welfare III	0.0		0.0		0.0		0.0	
Welfare IV	0.0		0.0		0.0		0.0	
Business	4.8	376	44.2	1509	9.8	1192	-8.0	540
Commercial	19.3	1171	3.7	41	6.0	312	-0.6	31
Lodging	0.0		0.0		0.6	60	0.0	
Amusement I		-130	0.0		0.0		0.0	
Amusement II		-136	0.0		-71.3	87	0.0	
Public and Communication	0.0		0.0		0.0		0.0	
Transportation & Warehouse	-14.2	725	-76.6	3292	23.0	1789	20.3	362
Heavy industry	0.0		0.0		0.0		0.0	
Light industry	0.0		0.0		-68.1	358	0.0	
Service industry	0.0		0.0		-2.9	62	-8.6	132
Home industry	0.0		0.0		0.0		0.0	
Supply	0.0		0.0		0.0		0.0	
Cattle shed	0.0		0.0		0.0		0.0	
Parking lot	30.9	7225	52.0	4061	51.4	10737	41.7	2614
Communal lavatory	0.0		0.0		0.0		0.0	
TOTAL	7.5	12220	8.8	3741	10.6	30060	6.2	3876

Neighbourhood commercial district (300%)		Neighbourhood commercial district (400%)		Neighbourhood commercial district (500%)		Neighbourhood commercial district (600%)		Light industrial district		Total	
Change Ratio	Area	Change Ratio	Area	Change Ratio	Area	Change Ratio	Area	Change Ratio	Area	Change Ratio	Area
-7.3	2297	-7.8	10221	21.8	785	-16.2	595	0.0		-2.8	10990
20.2	12642	39.9	105955	25.1	7625	-7.3	1040	354.3	1828	29.1	147312
-6.4	804	-9.2	6734	-10.1	1133	-20.1	1351	-13.7	90	-6.8	8773
-17.5	1217	3.5	1107	2.0	337	165.1	2499	0.0	32	4.8	2735
12.0	1146	4.5	2035	3.0	130		117			4.8	3993
-76.5	3623	-13.3	6114	160.0	4076	0.0		0.0		-8.8	5661
3.9	88	8.0	2142	-24.5	1131	21.1	851	0.0		4.9	2127
	-109	-5.2	101	0.0			308	0.0		2.4	98
0.0		0.0		0.0		0.0		0.0		0.0	
57.2	5428	22.4	26273	4.7	4671	26.0	27335	-8.4	1295	17.2	64949
-4.4	502	9.8	18783	-4.9	897	-4.0	2989	9.2	142	5.1	16030
-13.3	258	18.4	6489	57.6	7670	-3.6	766	0.0		16.0	13195
4.3	9	11.2	8376	33.1	1278	30.5	1187	0.0		130	10730
199.8	1307	-1.9	165	0.7	18	78.9	3147	0.0		24.3	4084
-44.1	184	0.6	680	9.4	1816	23.9	8683	-30.5	762	6.2	10233
3.5	569	7.2	6355		3408	2.8	473	-5.0	543	4.6	8396
0.0		0.0				0.0		0.0		0.0	
0.0		-17.8	460			0.0		0.0		-21.0	818
4.3	42	-10.2	173		83	0.0		96.8	276	-1.8	132
0.0		13.2	74			0.0		0.0		10.6	74
6.5	7	0.0				0.0		0.0		3.0	7
0.0		0.0				0.0		0.0		0.0	
175.1	12248	43.8	45766		12175	4.6	515	15.6	1461	44.5	96802
0.0		0.0				0.0		0.0		0.0	
13.7	24474	14.8	200067		40485	12.3	38419	2.5	1049	13.0	354391

scale buildings such as a department stores, hospitals, city hall or hotels along an arterial road.

Table 31.2 shows the relationship between the mixture degree index and use zoning. We would like to focus attention on a characteristic point. Referring to the ASI values, a Neighbourhood commercial district is highest with 0.79. This means that land use is mixed. The reason why ASI of this district has a high value is that this district has few large-scale buildings. Next, the ASI of Category II exclusive residential district is highest in the residential group. It is a problem worthy of note that in spite of the district being zoned as an exclusive residential area, the mixture of land use is high. Referring to the NSI values of commercial group, Commercial districts (floor area ratio 400- 600%) are highest and Neighbourhood commercial district (floor area ratio 200%) is lowest in its group. According to the trend of NSI values in the commercial group, it is likely that this index is related to the floor area ratio. Next, the NSI values of the residential group Category II (exclusive residential) district is the highest, showing that this zone is still mixed.

31.3.4　Changes of Land-Use Area from 1987 to 1992

Table 31.3 shows change of area for each land use type from 1987 to 1992 by each use zone. The total of land use area (remember this counts all floors) in the central district increased by 13% in an already very dense city space. The land use zone which has the highest increase is the Commercial district (floor area ratio 400) at 14.8%. Referring to the residence group, we see that the category Dwelling I, which is a detached houses, is decreasing in many districts. It decreased 2.8%. It follows from this that we may say that suburbanisation of residence is proceeding. On the other hand, Dwelling II, such as middle-rise apartments shows a rise of 29.1% in total. Construction of middle-rise buildings for residences is extensive. In the commercial group, the values of Dwelling with other use are decreasing. It shows a tendency of separation between work and residence. The values of business are increasing in all use zones except Neighbourhood commercial district (floor area ratio 200%) and Light industrial district. Especially, the important point to note is that the Category II exclusive residential district shows a large rise of 44.2%. Since the values of commerce are decreasing in Neighbourhood commercial district (floor area ratio 200%, 300%) and Commercial district (floor area ratio 500%, 600%), we can infer that the suburbanisation of commerce is proceeding. The increase in Parking lots in all districts shows the progress of motorisation.

31.3.5 *Change of Degree of Mixture Index*

There is a change of the degree of mixture (ASI and NSI) from 1987 to 1992 in every use zone (Fig. 31.4). The mixture degree index indicates a rise in most of the use zones. The use zones which have a large rise in both ASI and NSI are Category I exclusive residential district and Light industrial district. Category I exclusive residential district increases Dwelling with other use and Parking lot and Light industry district increased due to the Dwelling II (apartment) and Service industry. The districts which shows decreases are Commercial district (floor aria ratio 400%) and Category II exclusive residential district. Since NSI of these districts increased, we can suppose that small-scale buildings were replaced by large-scale buildings.

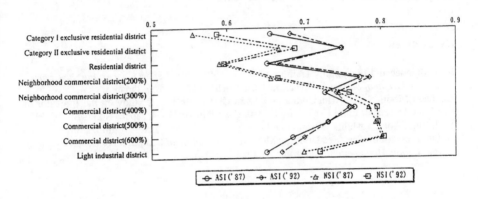

Figure 31.4 Change of Degree of Mixture over Time

31.4 Conclusion

Business land use is distributed along arterial roads. Dwelling II land use is spread widely throughout the commercial districts rather than only in the residential districts.

As for the mixture of land use, the mixture degree in commercial areas is higher than in residential areas. A close look at this, in areas along arterial roads, shows the number of land use codes is highly mixed. Regarding the change of the area of land use, the total of land use area in the central district increased 13% , as it changes to a denser city space. The land-use zone which has the highest rate of increase is the Commercial district (floor area ratio 400%). By checking each land use categories, we see that Dwelling I, which is a detached house, is decreasing in many districts. On the other hand, Dwelling II shows a rise of 29.1% in total. Construction of middle-rise buildings for residences is extensive. In the commercial group, the values of Dwelling with other use are decreasing. It shows a tendency of separation between work and residence.

The mixture degree index indicates a rise in most of the use zones. The use zones which have a large rise in both ASI and NSI are Category I exclusive residential district and Light industrial district.

This works suggests that ideas of controlling city growth and form by simple area zoning cannot and will not work. More sophisticated legislation might work, but would become very complex and cumbersome. Interestingly, even in this modern age of high-rise buildings, this Asian city remains a model of the mixed-use high density settlement.

References

Japan Science and Technology Training Institute (1976), *The Report Concerning the Characteristic Grasp of an Urban Structure Pattern with a Mesh Data*, Japan.

Tae-heon Moon, Satoshi Hagishima and Akira Ohgai (1991) 'A Study on the Indicator of Mixed Degree of Land Use', *City Planning Institute of Japan*, Japan, No.26-B, 505-510.

Yoshitsugu Aoki, Toshihiko Osaragi and Akiko Nagai (1995), 'Error Minimization of Land-Use Forecast by The Area Dividing Method', *Proceeding of Computers in Urban Planning and Urban Management, Australia*, Volume 2, 341-352.

Editors' Epilogue

Graham P. Chapman, Ashok K. Dutt and Robert W. Bradnock

The first urban revolution occurred in several ancient civilisations – indeed in a sense the very idea of civilisation was predicated on the development of new urban centres and cities, in which the élites accumulated knowledge and culture in a more sustained way than previous more tribal societies had been able to do. The first urban revolution probably occurred spontaneously in separate civilisations, sometimes simultaneously as in ancient Egypt and the Indus Valley, sometimes at distant time periods – witnessed by the later occurrence of urban centres in the New World. In the Old World nearly all of the important early urban advances took place in Asia – from modern Turkey to China, and of course including greater India. Even the Egyptian kingdoms were in sufficient proximity to the developments in West Asia that they can be conceived as having an Asiatic connection. In both the Old and the New World the precondition for this urbanisation was the development of sedentary agriculture – quite often connected as well with the development of large scale irrigation systems. Surplus production from agriculture formed the economic basis of urban formation.

Europe was an oceanic peninsula, marginal to the major developments taking place in the great civilisations of the East. But as its inhabitants acquired greater mastery of first their skirting seas, and then of the oceans, increasing trade began a rapid expansion of major ports and cities. Spain and Portugal emerged to use their military supremacy to gain control of much of the New World. Then, in the 17th century, to this expansion was added the full impact of the second urban revolution, based on the harnessing of inanimate power and the productivity of the new industrial revolution. In a short period of perhaps no more than 200 years Northwest Europe emerged as the dominant world core, in economic wealth, in military power, and in the quest for overseas empire. Most of Asia became subordinate directly or indirectly to this new power. This new power imposed colonial economic regimes of different depths and intensities. New colonial cities developed and new colonial appendages formed alongside many existing indigenous cities.

Much has been written about the extent to which European power also either de-urbanised and de-industrialised Asia, or at least suppressed its economic and urban take-off. It is however a fact that most of Asia (outside of Japan) remained overwhelmingly rural and agricultural at the end of the 2nd

World War. But over the last two decades in particular, the process of urbanisation in Asia has been accelerating, and the projections for the future are that
we will see the emergence of new urban and industrial societies, which individually (e.g. China) will be some of the world's biggest economies, or even
the biggest, and collectively will constitute the global centre of production
and consumption. Some Asian societies (Taiwan, South Korea and Singapore) have effectively made the transition in just a few decades. Effectively,
Asia may be bidding to establish in the 2nd urban revolution the dominance it
had millennia ago in the first.

That there is a major swing from agricultural to 'modern' economies in
Asia is without doubt, but exactly what forms this shift is taking and why is
the subject of controversy. To what extent is this change, this modernisation,
entangled with globalisation and westernisation? Are these terms synony-
mous? Is it possible for modernisation to occur without westernisation? How
does urbanisation in Asia occur in conditions of autarkic economic development, or open trading economies? Is Asian urbanisation different from Western urbanisation, but yet still dependent on it through the international system?

As Asian urbanisation has got into its stride, these questions have been
answered many times over, but often with different and often with contradictory answers. In asserting Asian pride and independence, many commenta-
tors have stressed that the economic-miracle has rested on 'Asian values'.
And yet others have commented on the effectiveness of the 'bamboo network' (the social cohesion of the overseas Chinese). But other writers have
observed that the first gains in productivity from a shift from agriculture to
urban occupations can indeed result in rapid growth rates, but that sustaining
such growth rates becomes much harder in the new world of global competition after the first easy gains have been made. Then it is possible to point to
the economic bubble bursting in 1998, and non-Asians reporting with grim
satisfaction not positively on Asian-values but negatively on Asian-cronyism,
and the stagnation of Japan (which, much to the consternation of Western
economists, defies all western economic medicine, and seems to have an economics peculiar to itself). Most observers believe the bubble to be a temporary period of adjustment, and that East and Southeast Asia will be catching
up again very soon.

The urbanisation and industrialisation of the West created a new proletariat – the lowly paid worker's (many children and women) working in the
appalling conditions of 19th Century London that Charles Dickens portrayed
in his novels (reacting to the social injustice of it) , or, in other terms, the
alienated working class that Marx, writing in the same city at much the same
time, foresaw as the natural incubators of revolution. In this world of unequal

wealth and environmental squalor there was though no informal sector on the scale of many modern Asian cities. In Asia a large number of the modern equivalent of this proletariat is engaged in the informal sector. In India and China and the Philippines and elsewhere, the new cities are no longer under-written by the transplanted labour intensive industries of the old west – that phase has gone not just for the West but for much of the rest too. The service economies are much bigger, but as important is the growth of both of micro-enterprises – often based on crude and simple technologies - and the adoption of sophisticated information technologies (whether in an informal sector or not.) Urbanisation creates far more opportunities for the diversification of employment, but does not of itself dictate what forms of enterprise will be possible or successful.

The inter-digitated micro-enterprise metropoli are saddled with health-threatening environmental problems. These do not afflict all countries equally – Japan is comparatively 'clean', whereas the big cities of India are facing ever-deteriorating air quality, to the point where several Bhopal's worth of premature deaths occur on a year-on-year basis. But it is worth remembering that it is not just C.19th century or C.mid-20th London that went through appalling conditions of hopeless sanitation and air pollution – Japan has had its share of these too (dramatised by the Minimata experience). The message is that no society has yet managed to urbanise and industrialise without going through some sort of environmental crises, but that in nearly all cases condi-tions improve with greater wealth. This is not just because it is financially possible to indulge in clean-ups, it is also because the wealthier societies generally have better, fairer and more systematic tax collection for urban au-thorities. The governance of the great cities is also something that can follow as much as it precedes or it guides the explosive phases of growth.

Arthur Lewis pointed out that in the mid C.19th Germany's population was growing at about 1.2% per annum, that it was about 50% urban too, and that therefore to accommodate all the natural increase in its populations ur-ban areas should increase by about 2.4% per year – which is what they man-aged to do. Lewis also noted that the difference between the borrowing and the lending countries in the later C.19th depended on the rate of growth of their urban populations – which of course demanded so much capital for new housing and new infrastructure and services. "Those whose populations grew by less than 3 per cent per annum (France 1.0, England 1.8 and Germany 2.5) loaned, and those whose urban populations were growing by more than 3 per cent per annum (Australia 3.5, United States 3.7, Canada 3.9, Argentina 5.3) borrowed." (Lewis,1978: 39). We do not know where such a current line would fall, but it is clear that many of the developing and urbanising societies of Asia do require substantial financial investment. Indeed it is this need which has forced liberalisation on India, even if it is still working out how, for example, private finance can share in the India public service sector. (The first American-owned power plant has just opened outside Mumbai). We can also point to the fact that for many of these countries population growth rates at or even above 2 per cent are common, and that the U.N. estimates for Asia's level of urbanisation in 1995 was 38%. This would imply that urban areas had to grow at nearly 6 per cent per year to accommodate the natural increase – something which has happened in a few societies, but not many. Indeed in India's case in the decade 1981-1991 rural populations grew annually by 1.8%, urban populations by 3.2 %, and the share of increase in urban areas by natural increase (58%) far exceeded the share due to in-migration (21.7%). (The remainder is through areas newly classified as urban). Nevertheless the U.N. estimates that by 2010 the urban share of the population in Asia will have reached 50%.

What we have seen in these pages is the breadth of experience which different countries and indeed individual cities in Asia face, as the relationships between the national demography and economy interface with the international system of finance - something made starkly explicit in the reviews of Honk Kong and Shanghai by Felicity Rose and Hung-Kai Wang and others.

One justification for publishing two volumes specifically on urbanisation in Asia was included in our opening remarks to both – that we are witnessing the greatest migration in absolute numbers ever seen on this planet. (Although we readily agree that there are definitional problems over what constitutes 'a migration', and in relative terms other periods may loom larger). A second justification that simply falls out of these pages is that this urbanisation is not just in Asia, it is Asian in its characteristics: indeed perhaps more than that, it is marked by the cultural traits of the different civilisations of Asia. In the terms of Huntington's (1998) World Civilisations, five of the nine are predominantly Asian. These are Islamic, Buddhist, Sinic, Japanese, and Hindu. (The other four are Western, Latin American, African and Eastern Orthodox – the latter of course being represented to some extent in Asiatic Russia). Some of the chapters have been explicitly cultural – for example those by Weiss on women's lives within the Islamic culture of urban Lahore or Mubarak Faisal's chapter on urbanisation in Saudi Arabia, or Tomoyoshi Hori's chapter on the characteristics of Asian urbanisation, in which he draws attention to the degree to which land-uses in East Asian cities are often very mixed – something referred to by Coton Mather and P.P. Karan as interdigitation (in Japan). But in other chapters, on general themes, like new towns, or poverty alleviation, the individual chapters implicitly evoke cultural understanding at virtually every turn – for example in Alain Jaquemain's analysis of new Bombay, or Amitabh's chapter on Lucknow's land market, the social structures allied to Hinduism are explicitly revealed, and in Shue Tuck Wong's chapter on Chinese urbanisation policies, the modes of explanation are not just of a communist society, but of a Confucian one as well. To understand the workings of these cities requires the understanding of experts who are well immersed in local cultures and politics.

Given this as a first major contribution from these volumes, it is not surprising that the second major contribution is to reveal the diversity of experience in many other ways as well. The technopoles of Japan that Natalie Cavasin writes about could be models of the future of any advanced urban society, but are in fact also distinctly Japanese. It is already evident that India's urban technological frontier city (Bangalore) is both international (Gale Sommers Gordon) and distinctively Indian (Sampas Srinavas). Jakarta's transmogrification into Jabotabek (Sanders and Winarso) is *sui generis* – it cannot be compared with anything else, and can in some senses only be explained in its own terms.

The chapters have spoken for themselves and we wish to add little more here – but we will indulge in one closing thought. The Asian cities display all the hope for the future which Nigel Harris noted in his opening remarks in Volume I. But we have also noted in these two volumes the levels of poverty and despair, and the levels of environmental squalor that also exist in many of these cities. Whether these cities are seen to offer the alchemy of hope, wealth and justice, or whether they are feared to reduce their citizens to be denizens of pits of despair, crime and squalor, in part depends upon your chosen viewpoint. But which ever way we or you, the reader, currently see them, these cities are the future of Asia, and it is incumbent on all those involved in guiding their development to whatever limited degree is possible, to take those smallest of decisions at every stage which cumulatively increase the chances of a better future. If these two volumes can in their smallest way help share knowledge and experience to that end, then we are satisfied.

References

Huntington, S.P. (1998) *Clash of Civilisations and the Re-making of World Order*. Touchstone Books London and New York.

Lewis, A.E. (1978) *The Evolution of the International Economic Order*. Princeton, N.J. Princeton University Press.